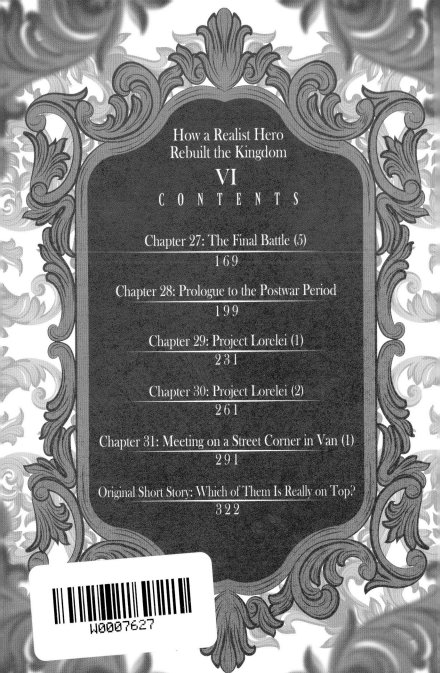

How a Realist Hero
Rebuilt the Kingdom

VI

CONTENTS

V

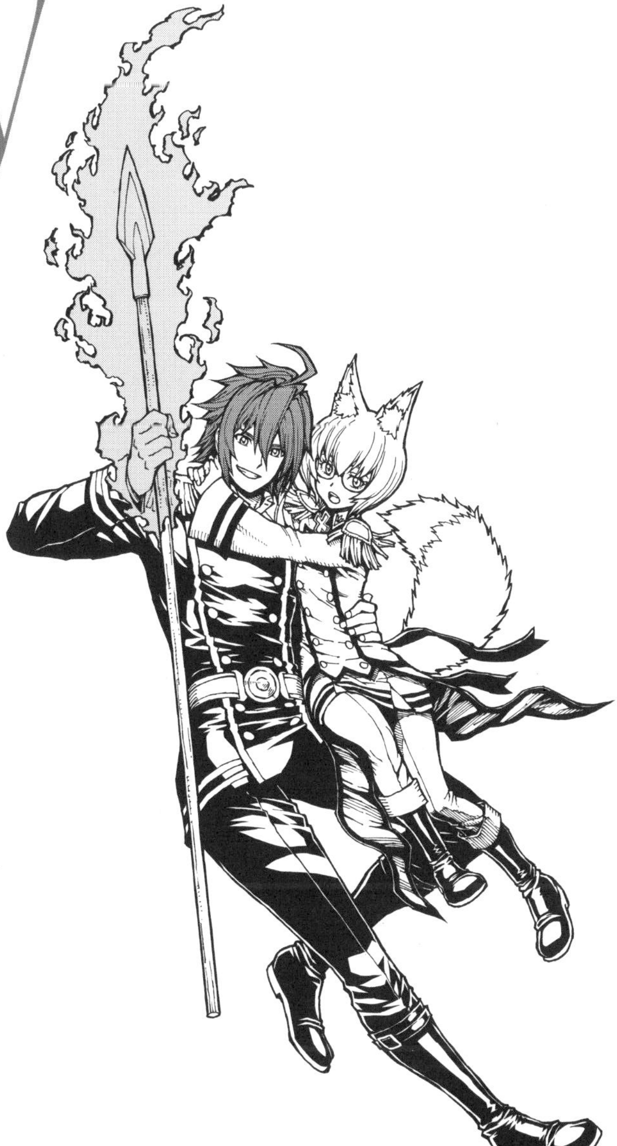

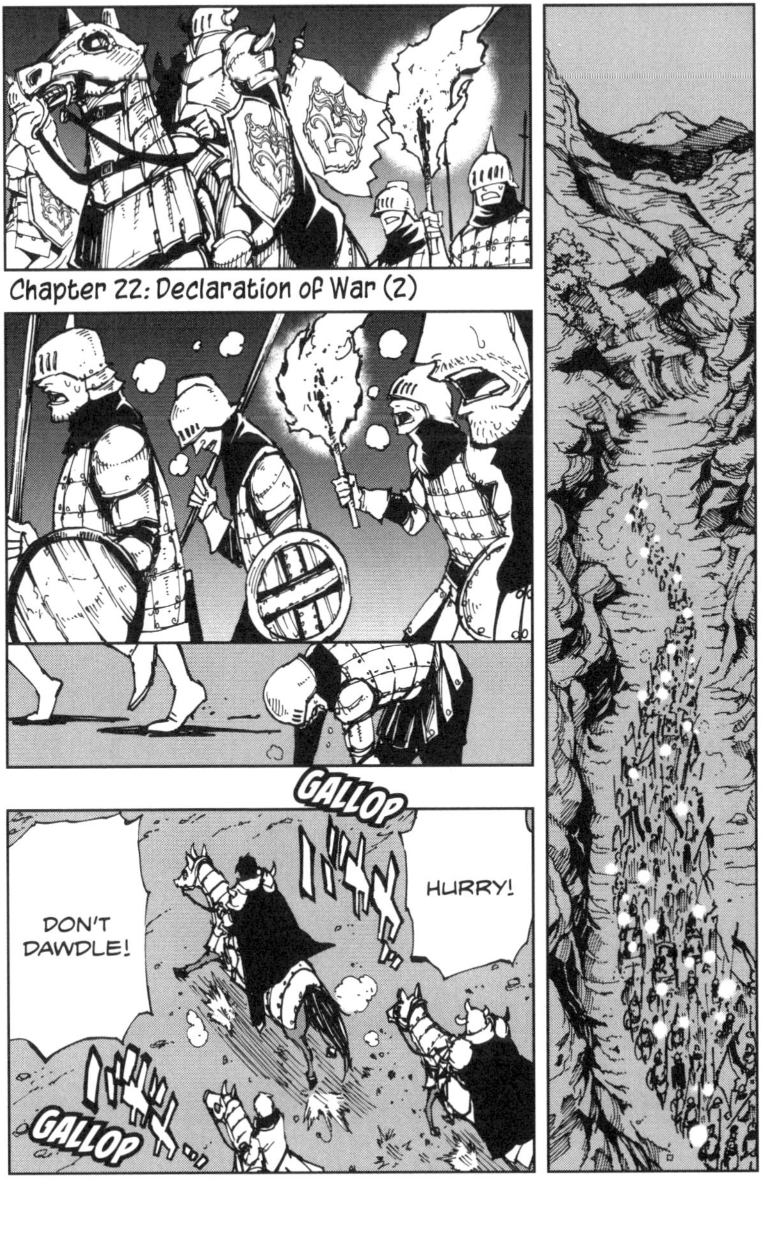
Chapter 22: Declaration of War (2)
GALLOP
HURRY!
DON'T DAWDLE!
GALLOP

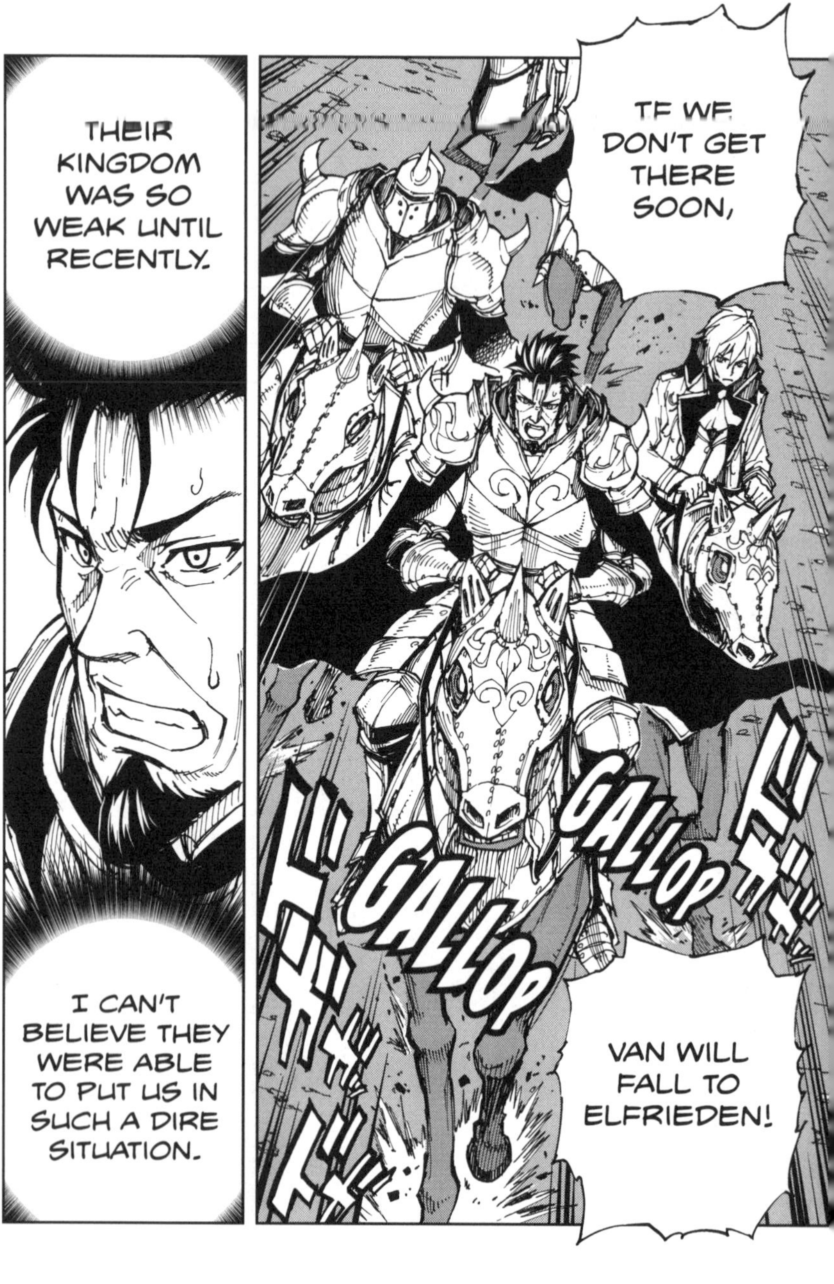
IF WE DON'T GET THERE SOON,
GALLOP
GALLOP
VAN WILL FALL TO ELFRIEDEN!
THEIR KINGDOM WAS SO WEAK UNTIL RECENTLY.
I CAN'T BELIEVE THEY WERE ABLE TO PUT US IN SUCH A DIRE SITUATION.

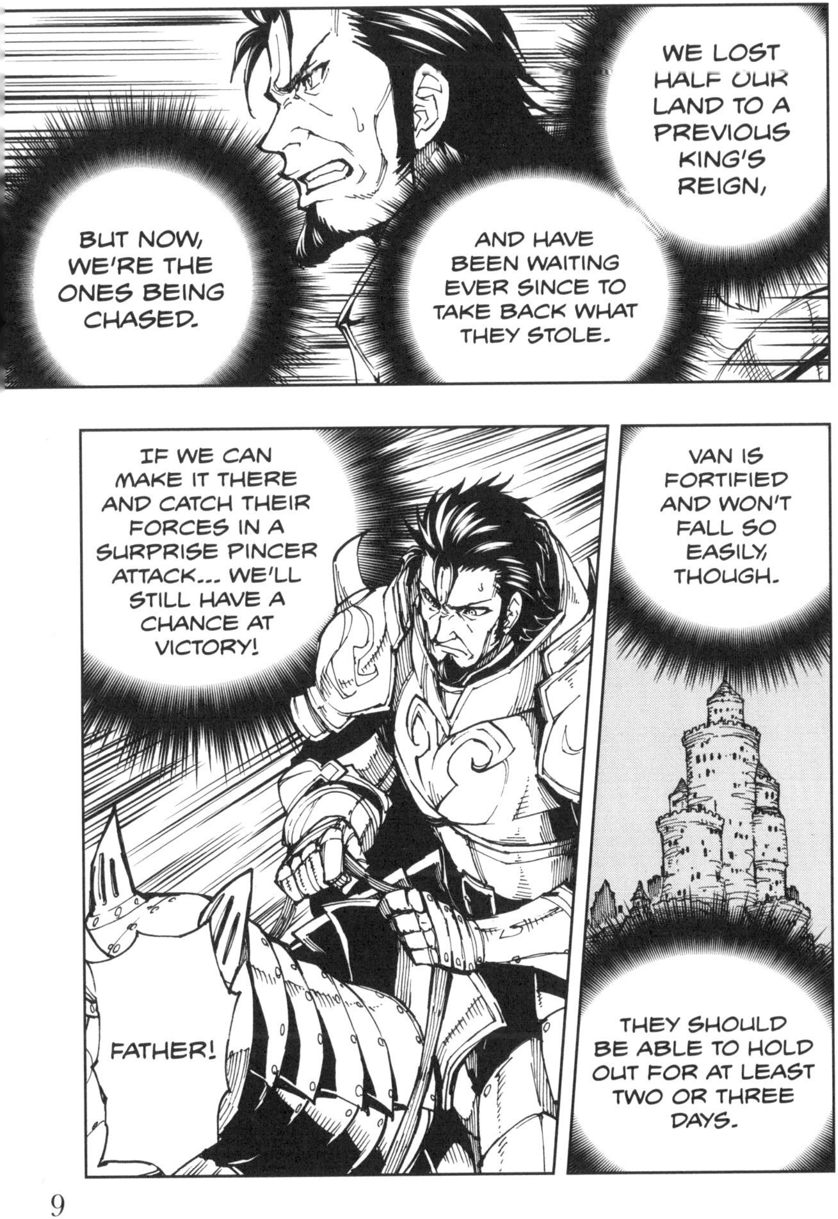
WE LOST HALF OUR LAND TO A PREVIOUS KING'S REIGN,
AND HAVE BEEN WAITING EVER SINCE TO TAKE BACK WHAT THEY STOLE.
BUT NOW, WE'RE THE ONES BEING CHASED.
VAN IS FORTIFIED AND WON'T FALL SO EASILY, THOUGH.
THEY SHOULD BE ABLE TO HOLD OUT FOR AT LEAST TWO OR THREE DAYS.
IF WE CAN MAKE IT THERE AND CATCH THEIR FORCES IN A SURPRISE PINCER ATTACK... WE'LL STILL HAVE A CHANCE AT VICTORY!
FATHER!

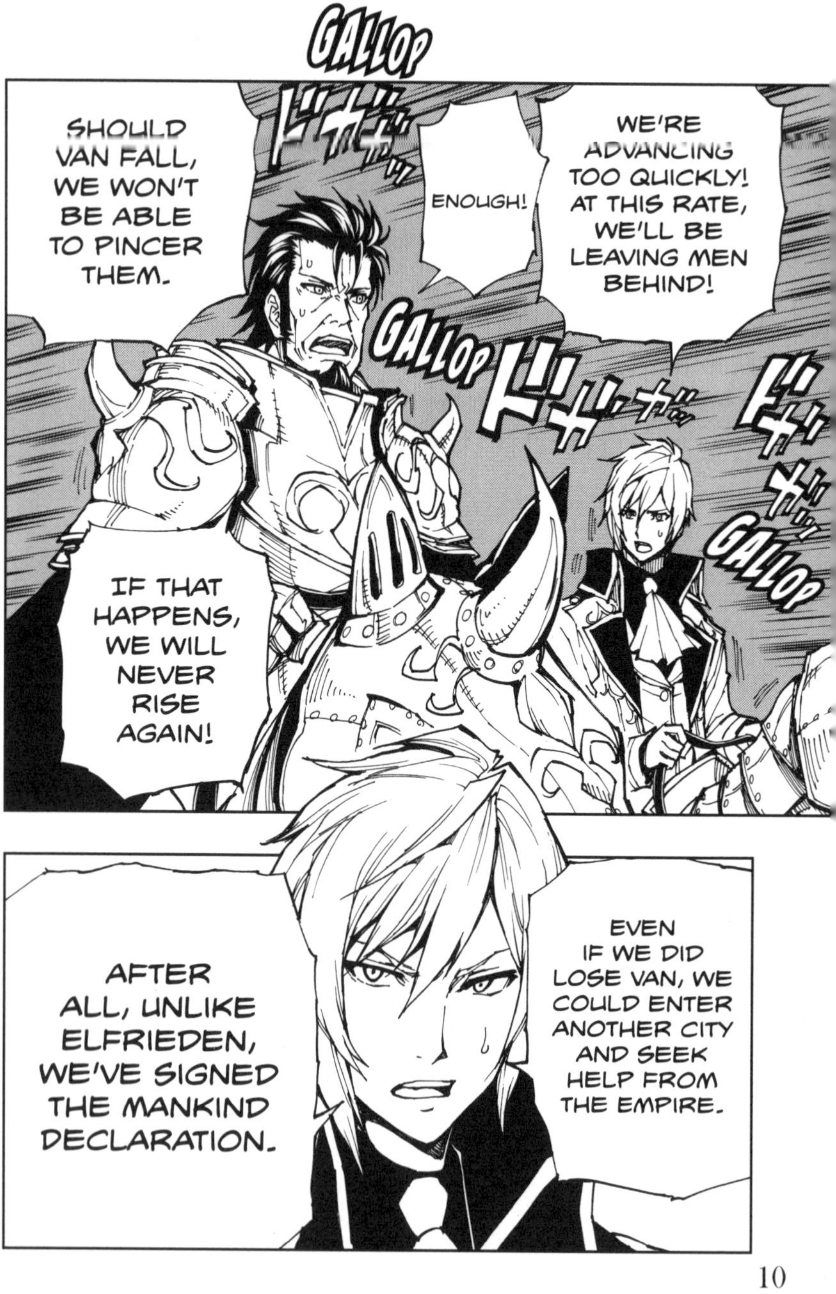
GALLOP
WE'RE ADVANCING TOO QUICKLY! AT THIS RATE, WE'LL BE LEAVING MEN BEHIND!
ENOUGH!
SHOULD VAN FALL, WE WON'T BE ABLE TO PINCER THEM.
GALLOP
GALLOP
IF THAT HAPPENS, WE WILL NEVER RISE AGAIN!
EVEN IF WE DID LOSE VAN, WE COULD ENTER ANOTHER CITY AND SEEK HELP FROM THE EMPIRE.
AFTER ALL, UNLIKE ELFRIEDEN, WE'VE SIGNED THE MANKIND DECLARATION.

Declaration of Mankind's Common Front Against the Demon Race

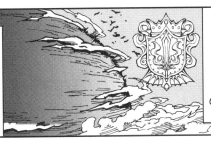

The largest, most powerful state on the continent, the Gran Chaos Empire,
proposed a policy to counter the Demons' advances.

First: The acquisition of territory by force between the nations of mankind is deemed inadmissible.

Second: The right of all peoples to equality and self-determination is to be respected.

Third: Countries that are distant from the Demon Lord's Domain will provide support to nations neighboring it in order to support them as they provide a defensive wall.

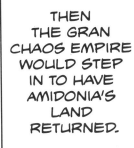

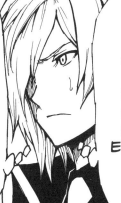

IF OUR CAPITAL IS SEIZED BY A NON-SIGNATORY STATE LIKE ELFRIEDEN...
THEN THE GRAN CHAOS EMPIRE WOULD STEP IN TO HAVE AMIDONIA'S LAND RETURNED.

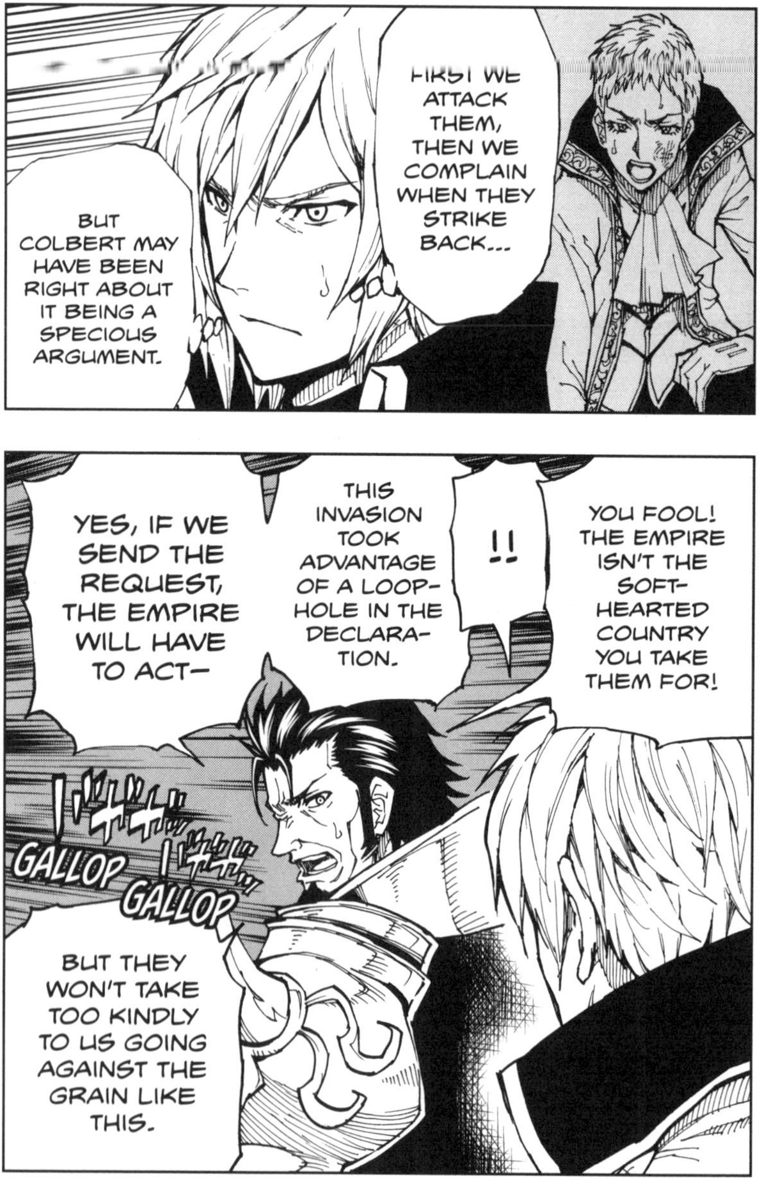
FIRST WE ATTACK THEM, THEN WE COMPLAIN WHEN THEY STRIKE BACK...
BUT COLBERT MAY HAVE BEEN RIGHT ABOUT IT BEING A SPECIOUS ARGUMENT.
YOU FOOL! THE EMPIRE ISN'T THE SOFT-HEARTED COUNTRY YOU TAKE THEM FOR!
!!
THIS INVASION TOOK ADVANTAGE OF A LOOP-HOLE IN THE DECLARA-TION.
YES, IF WE SEND THE REQUEST, THE EMPIRE WILL HAVE TO ACT—
GALLOP
GALLOP
BUT THEY WON'T TAKE TOO KINDLY TO US GOING AGAINST THE GRAIN LIKE THIS.

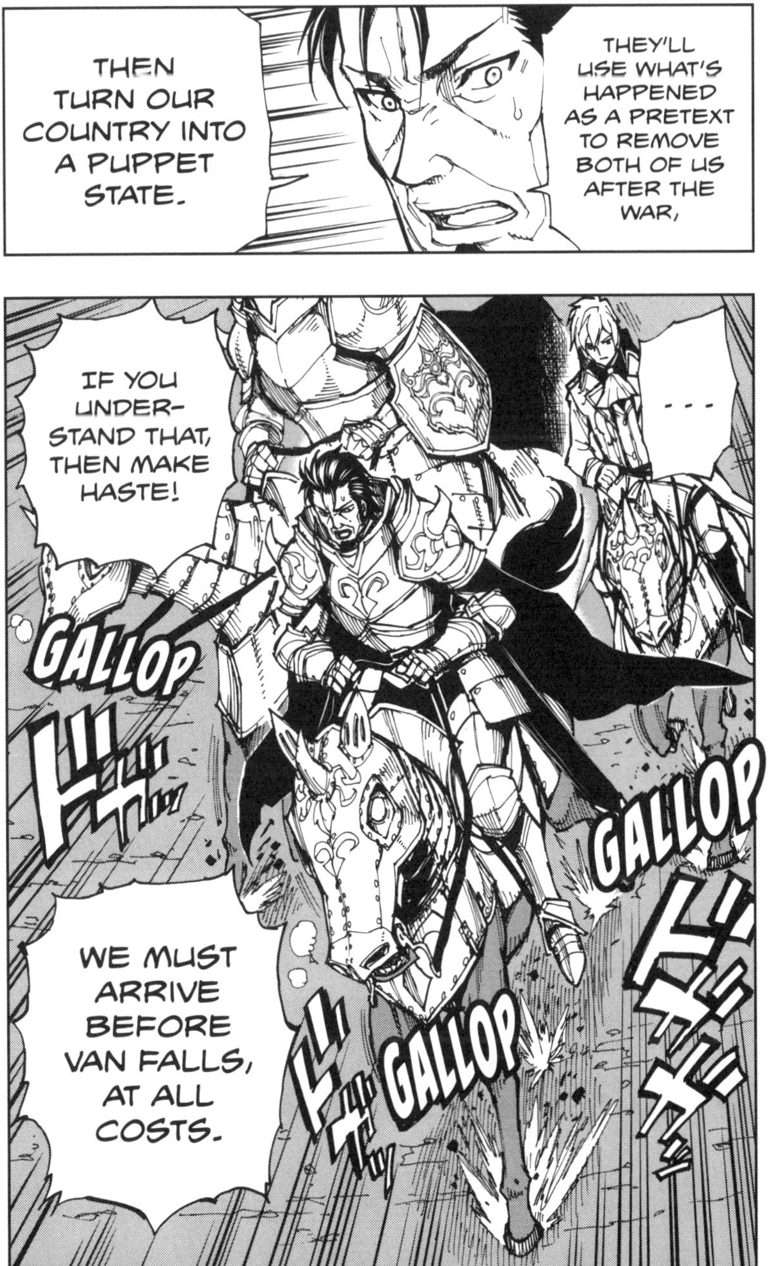
THEY'LL USE WHAT'S HAPPENED AS A PRETEXT TO REMOVE BOTH OF US AFTER THE WAR,
THEN TURN OUR COUNTRY INTO A PUPPET STATE.
...
IF YOU UNDER-STAND THAT, THEN MAKE HASTE!
GALLOP
GALLOP
GALLOP
WE MUST ARRIVE BEFORE VAN FALLS, AT ALL COSTS.

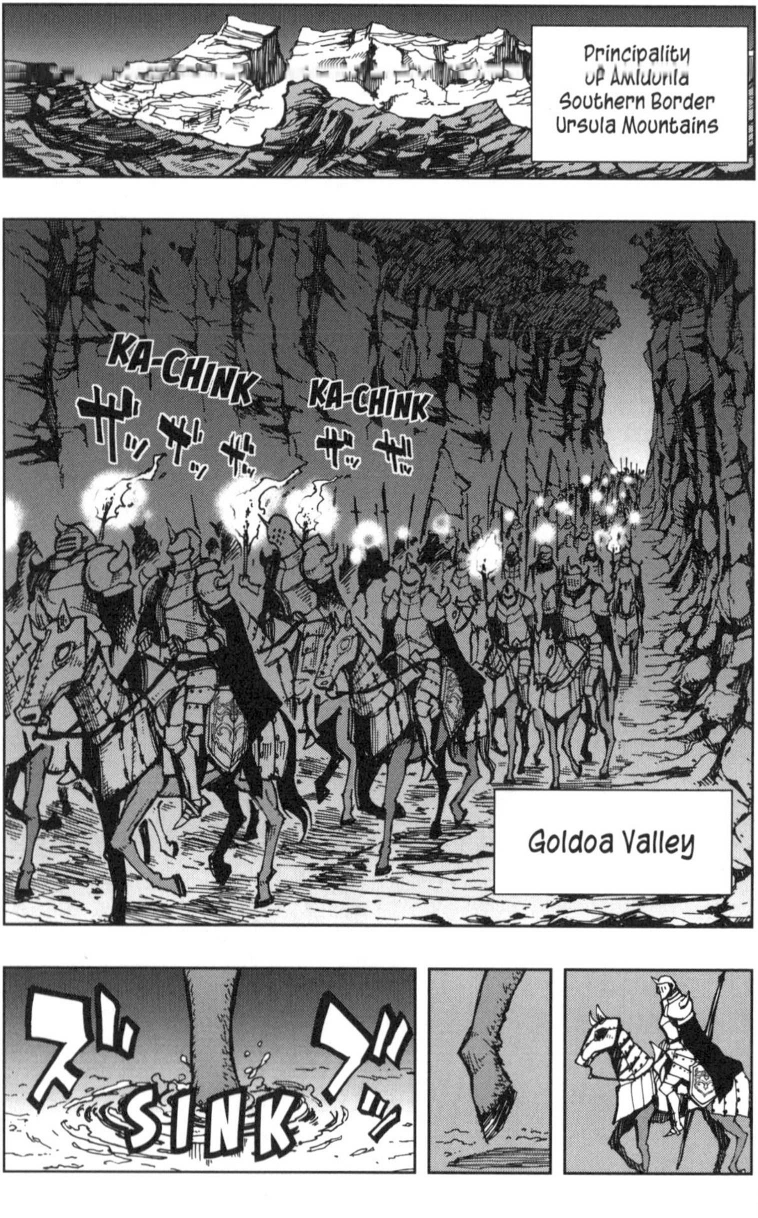
Principality
of Amidonia
Southern Border
Ursula Mountains
KA-CHINK
KA-CHINK
Goldoa Valley
SINK

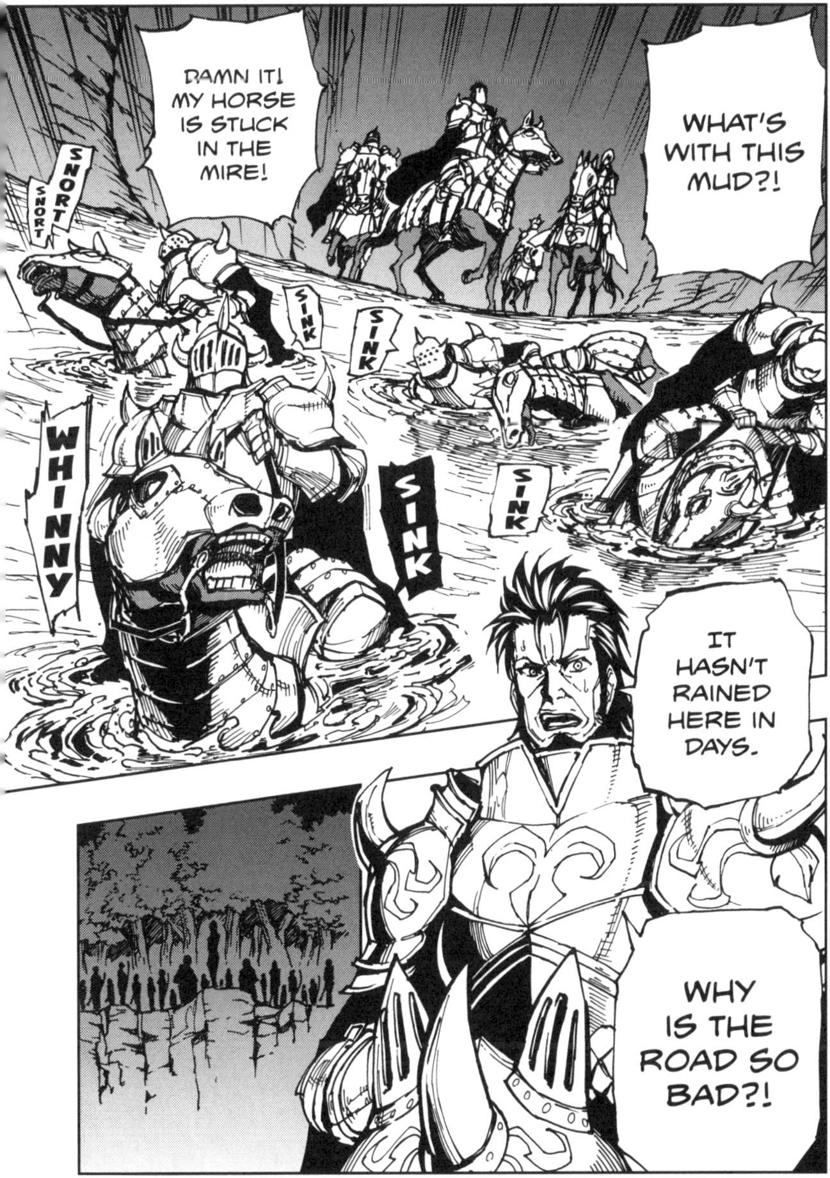
WHAT'S WITH THIS MUD?!
DAMN IT! MY HORSE IS STUCK IN THE MIRE!
SNORT
SNORT
SINK
SINK
SINK
SINK
WHINNY
IT HASN'T RAINED HERE IN DAYS.
WHY IS THE ROAD SO BAD?!

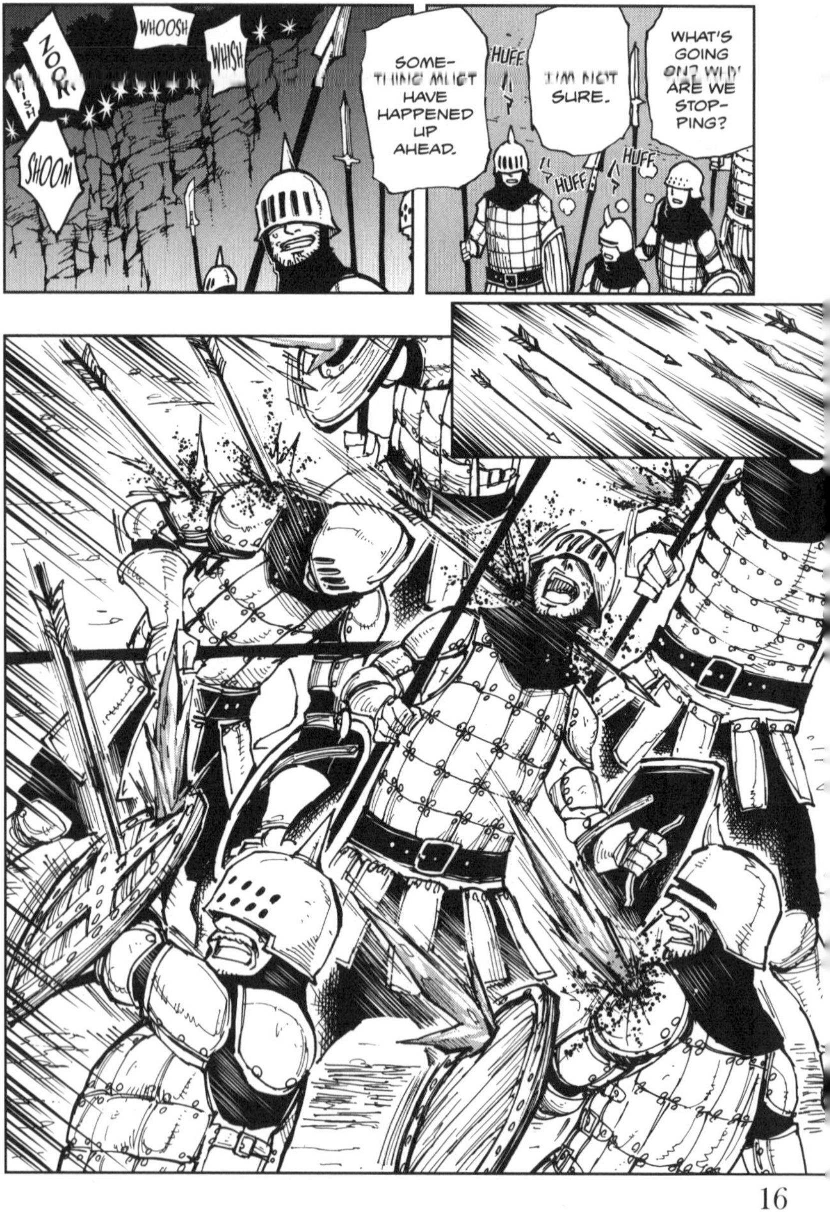
WHAT'S GOING ON? WHY ARE WE STOPPING?
I'M NOT SURE.
HUFF
HUFF
HUFF
SOMETHING MUST HAVE HAPPENED UP AHEAD.
WHISH
WHOOSH
ZOOK
WHISH
SHOOM

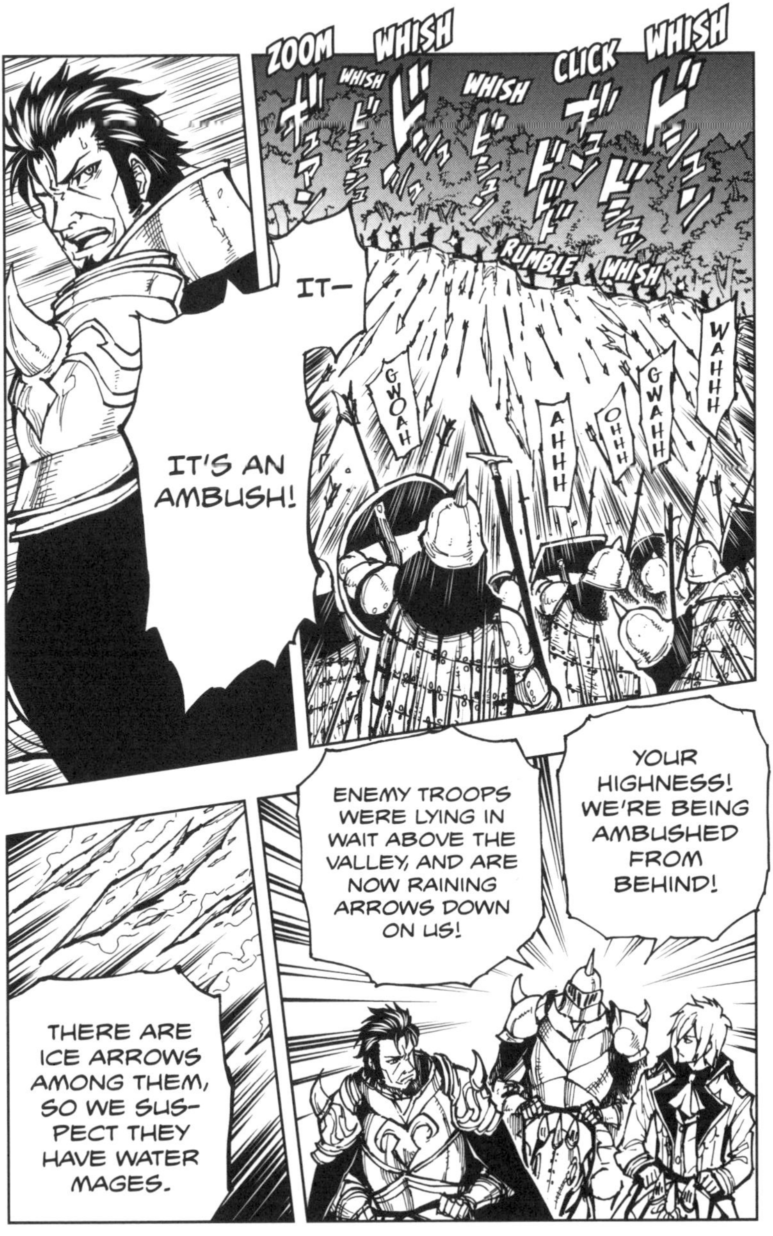
ZOOM
WHISH
WHISH
WHISH
CLICK
WHISH
RUMBLE
WHISH
WAHHH
GWAHH
OHHH
AHHH
GWOAH
IT—
IT'S AN AMBUSH!
YOUR HIGHNESS! WE'RE BEING AMBUSHED FROM BEHIND!
ENEMY TROOPS WERE LYING IN WAIT ABOVE THE VALLEY, AND ARE NOW RAINING ARROWS DOWN ON US!
THERE ARE ICE ARROWS AMONG THEM, SO WE SUSPECT THEY HAVE WATER MAGES.

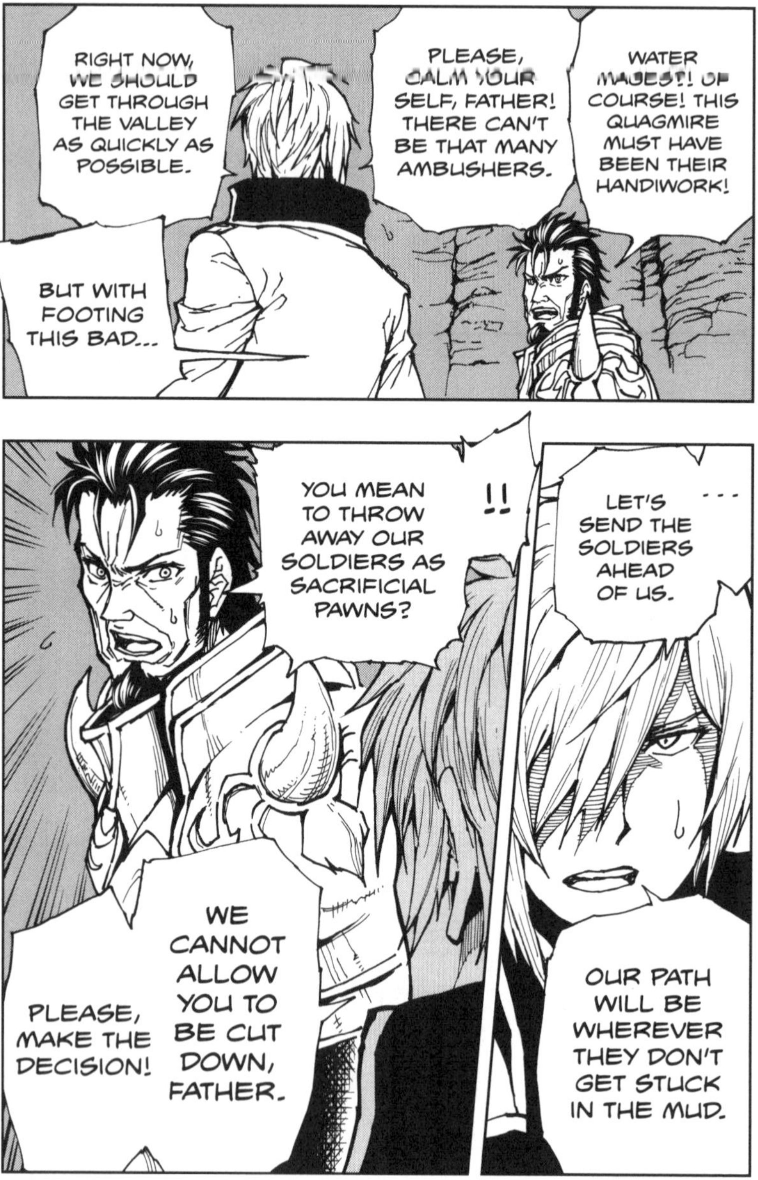
WATER MAGES!! OF COURSE! THIS QUAGMIRE MUST HAVE BEEN THEIR HANDIWORK!
PLEASE, CALM YOURSELF, FATHER! THERE CAN'T BE THAT MANY AMBUSHERS.
RIGHT NOW, WE SHOULD GET THROUGH THE VALLEY AS QUICKLY AS POSSIBLE.
BUT WITH FOOTING THIS BAD...
LET'S SEND THE SOLDIERS AHEAD OF US.
...
OUR PATH WILL BE WHEREVER THEY DON'T GET STUCK IN THE MUD.
!!
YOU MEAN TO THROW AWAY OUR SOLDIERS AS SACRIFICIAL PAWNS?
WE CANNOT ALLOW YOU TO BE CUT DOWN, FATHER.
PLEASE, MAKE THE DECISION!

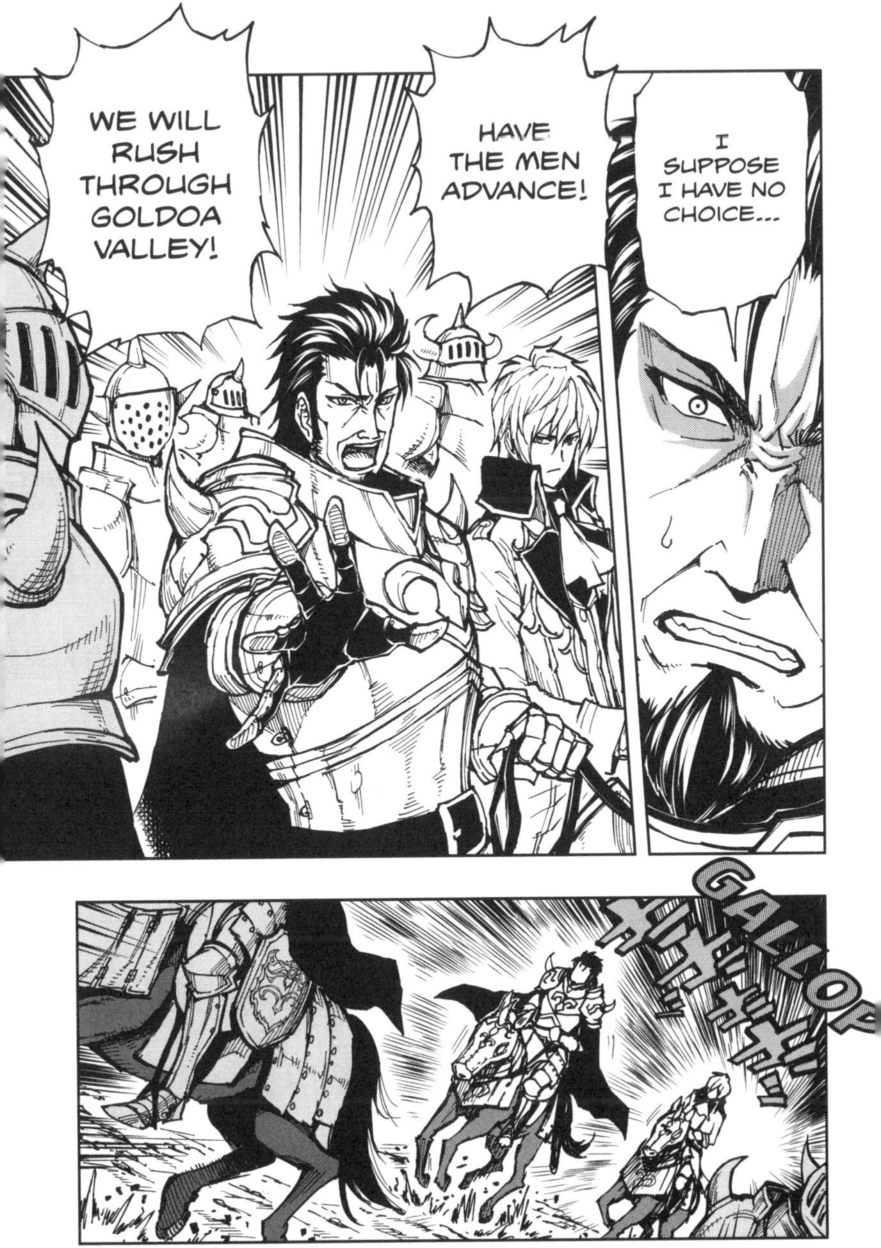
I SUPPOSE I HAVE NO CHOICE...
HAVE THE MEN ADVANCE!
WE WILL RUSH THROUGH GOLDOA VALLEY!
GALLOP

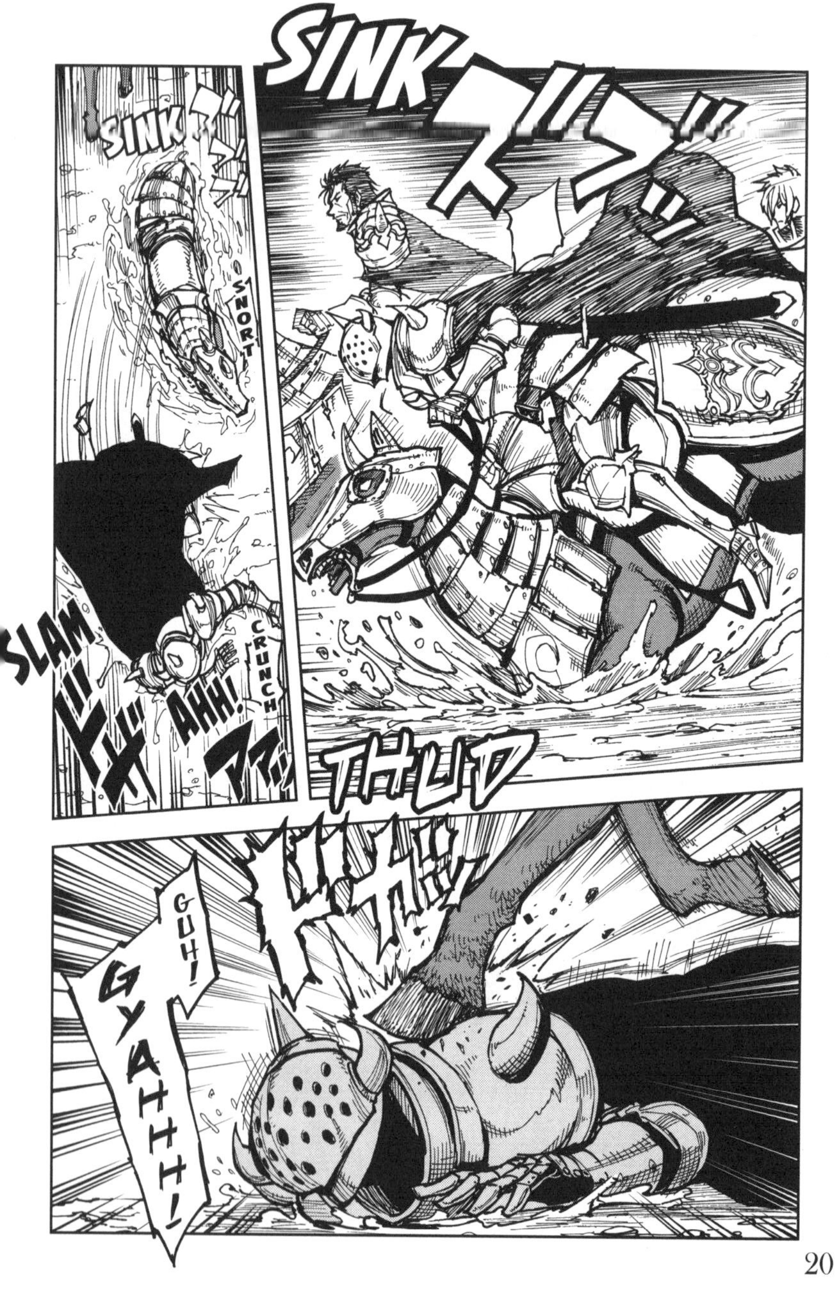
SINK
SINK
SNORT
SLAM
CRUNCH
AHH!
THUD
GUH!
GYAHHH!

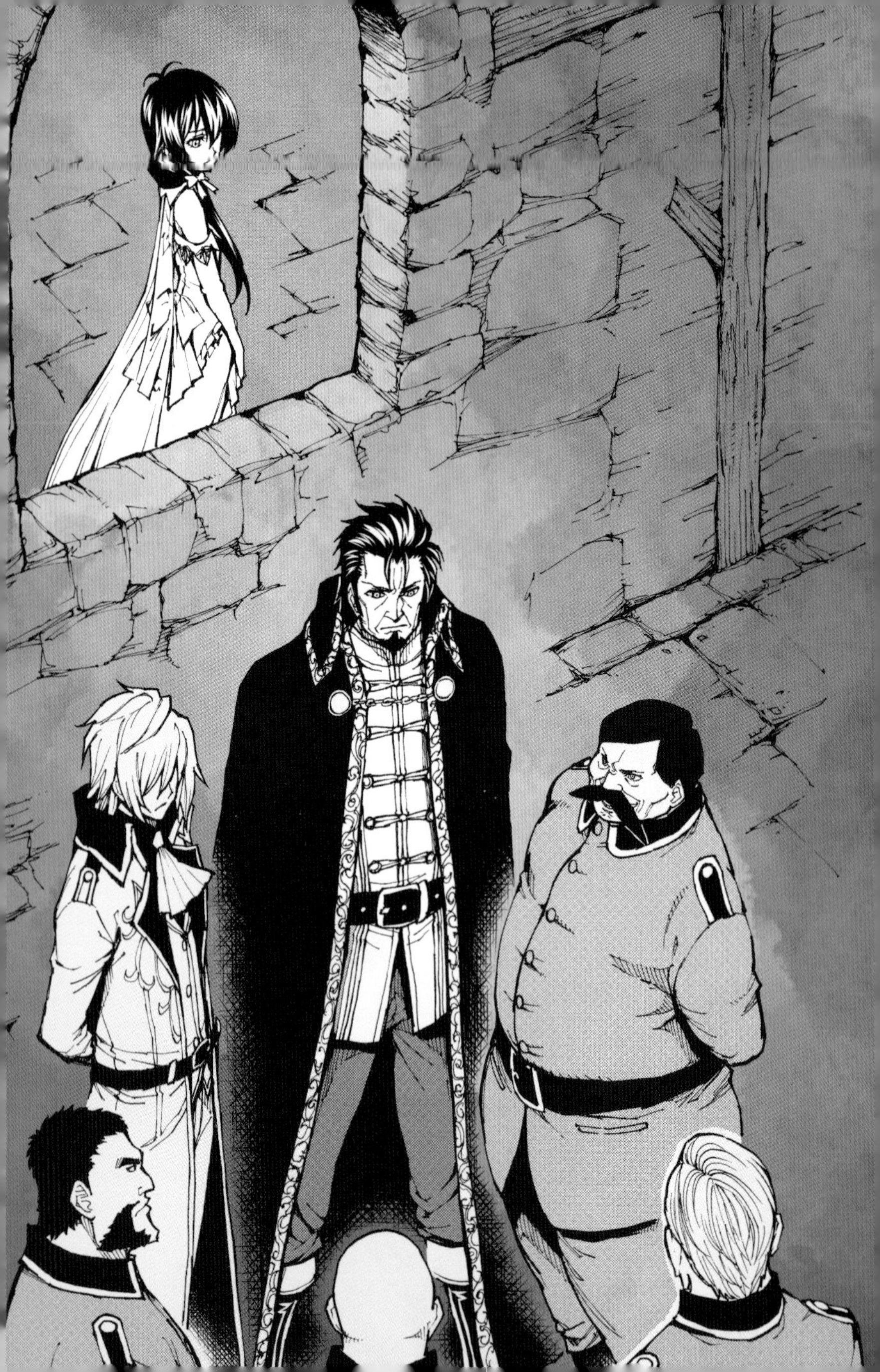

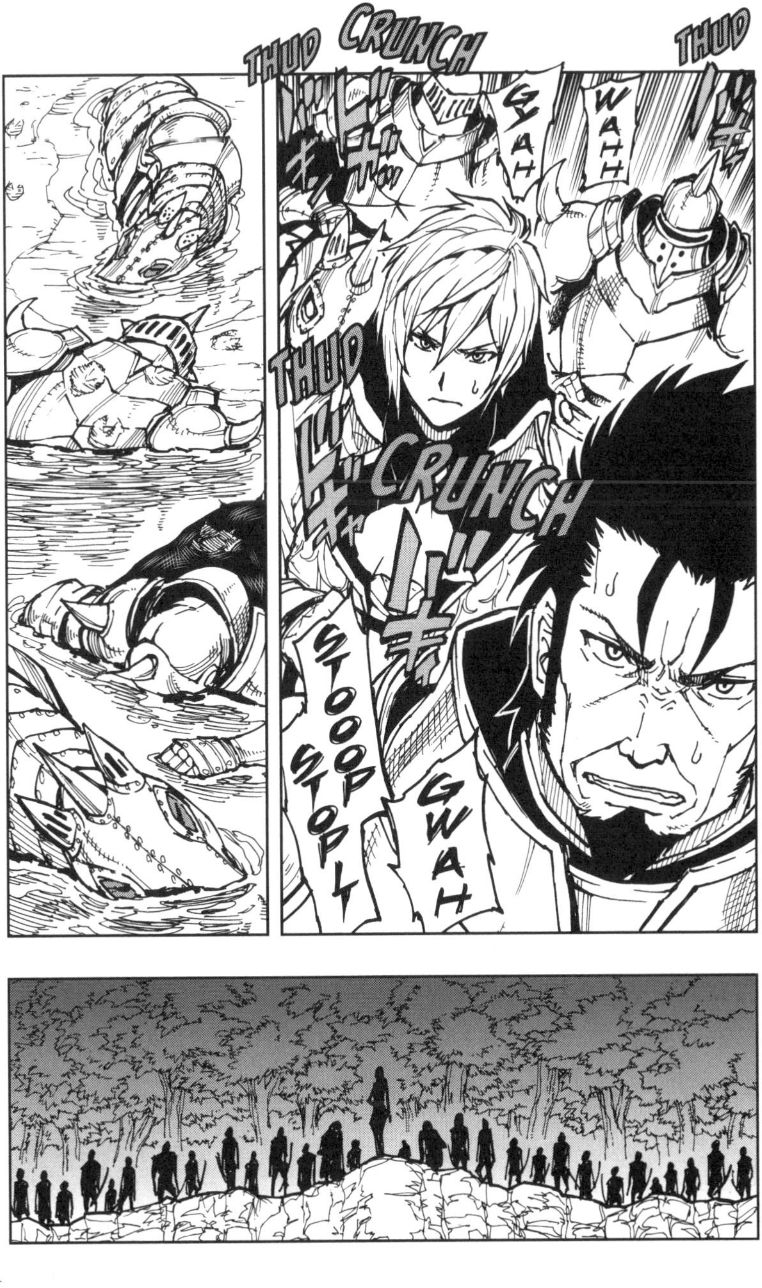
THUD
WAHH
GYAH
CRUNCH
THUD
THUD
CRUNCH
GWAH
STOOOOP STOP STOP

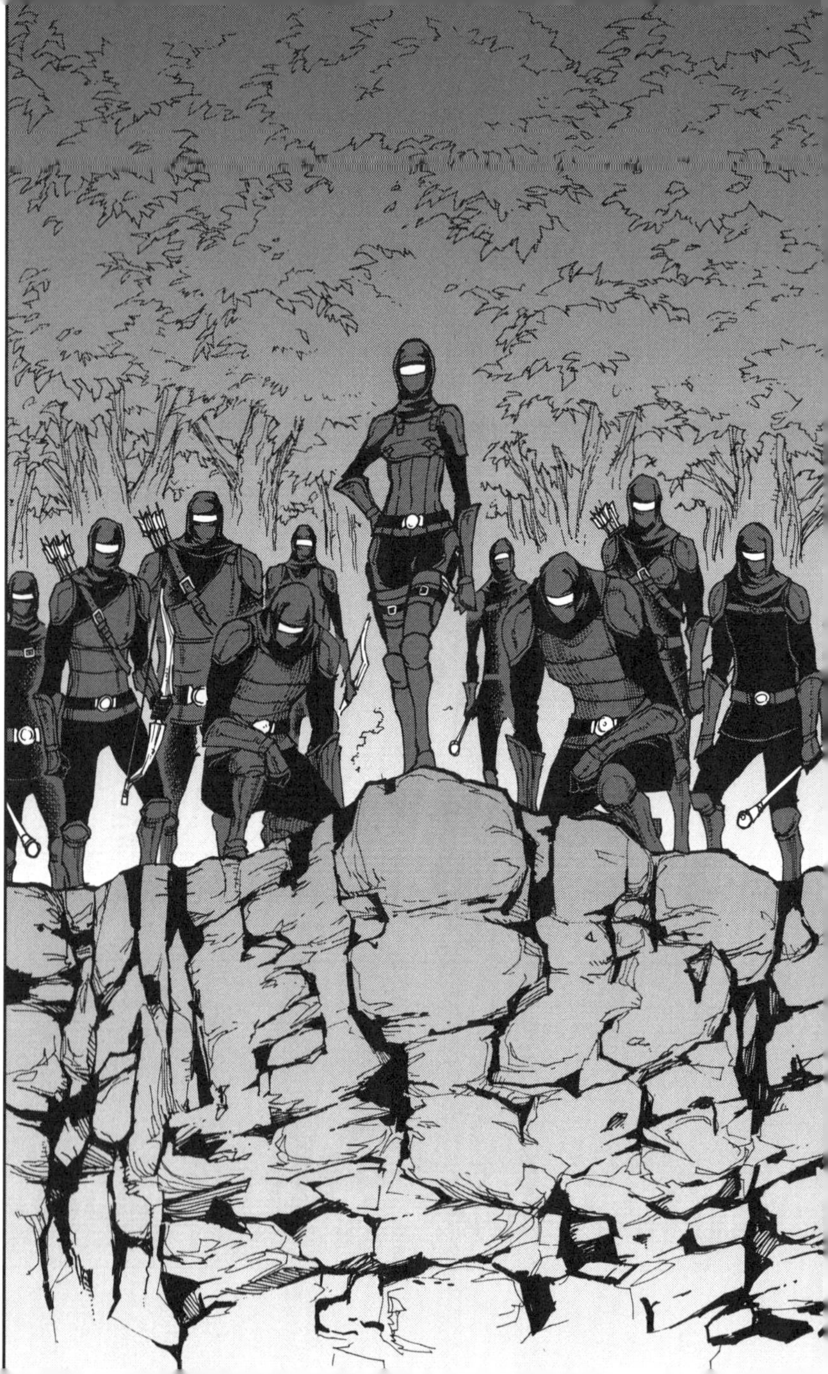

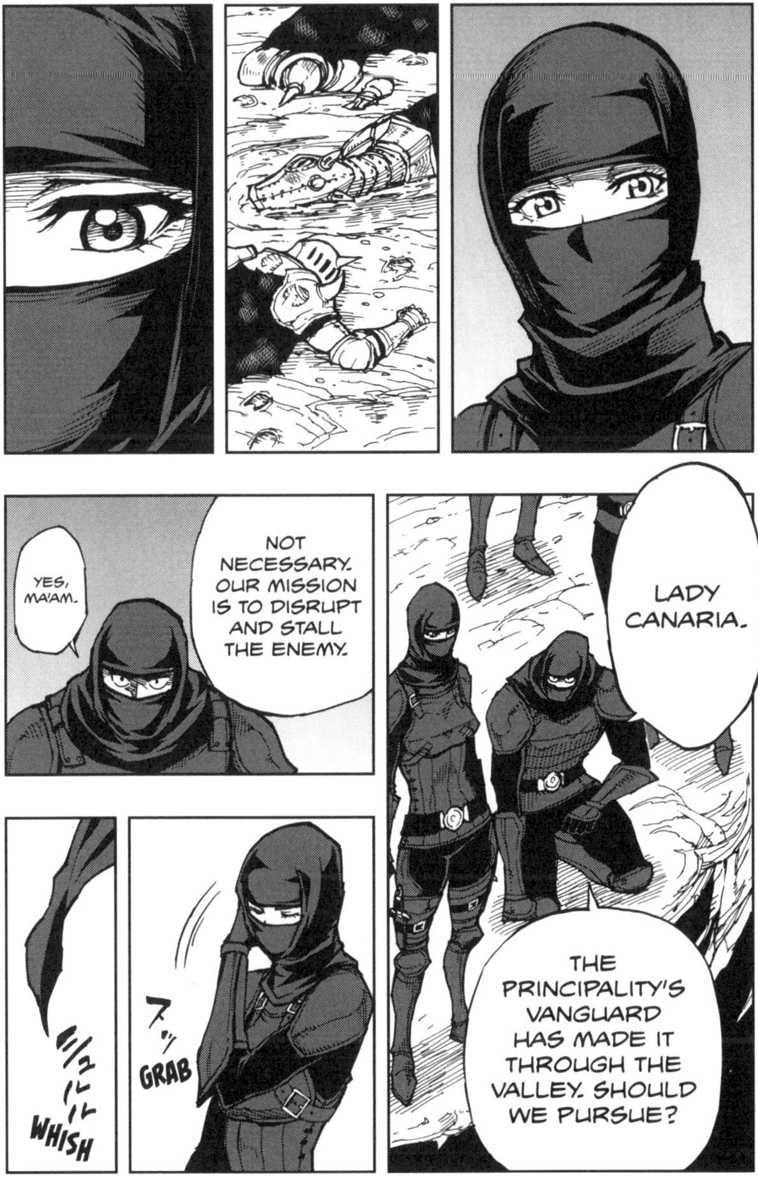
LADY CANARIA.
THE PRINCIPALITY'S VANGUARD HAS MADE IT THROUGH THE VALLEY. SHOULD WE PURSUE?
NOT NECESSARY. OUR MISSION IS TO DISRUPT AND STALL THE ENEMY.
YES, MA'AM.
GRAB
WHISH

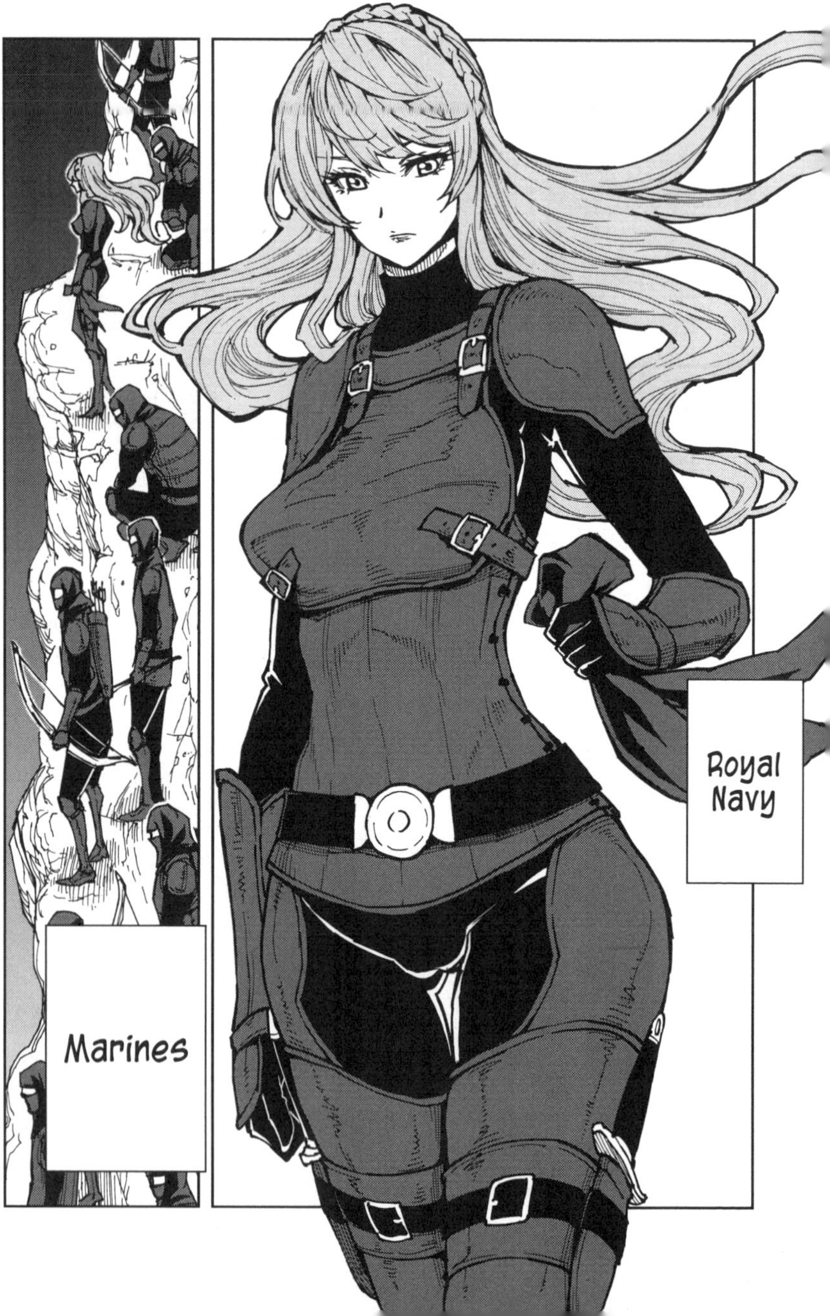
Royal Navy
Marines

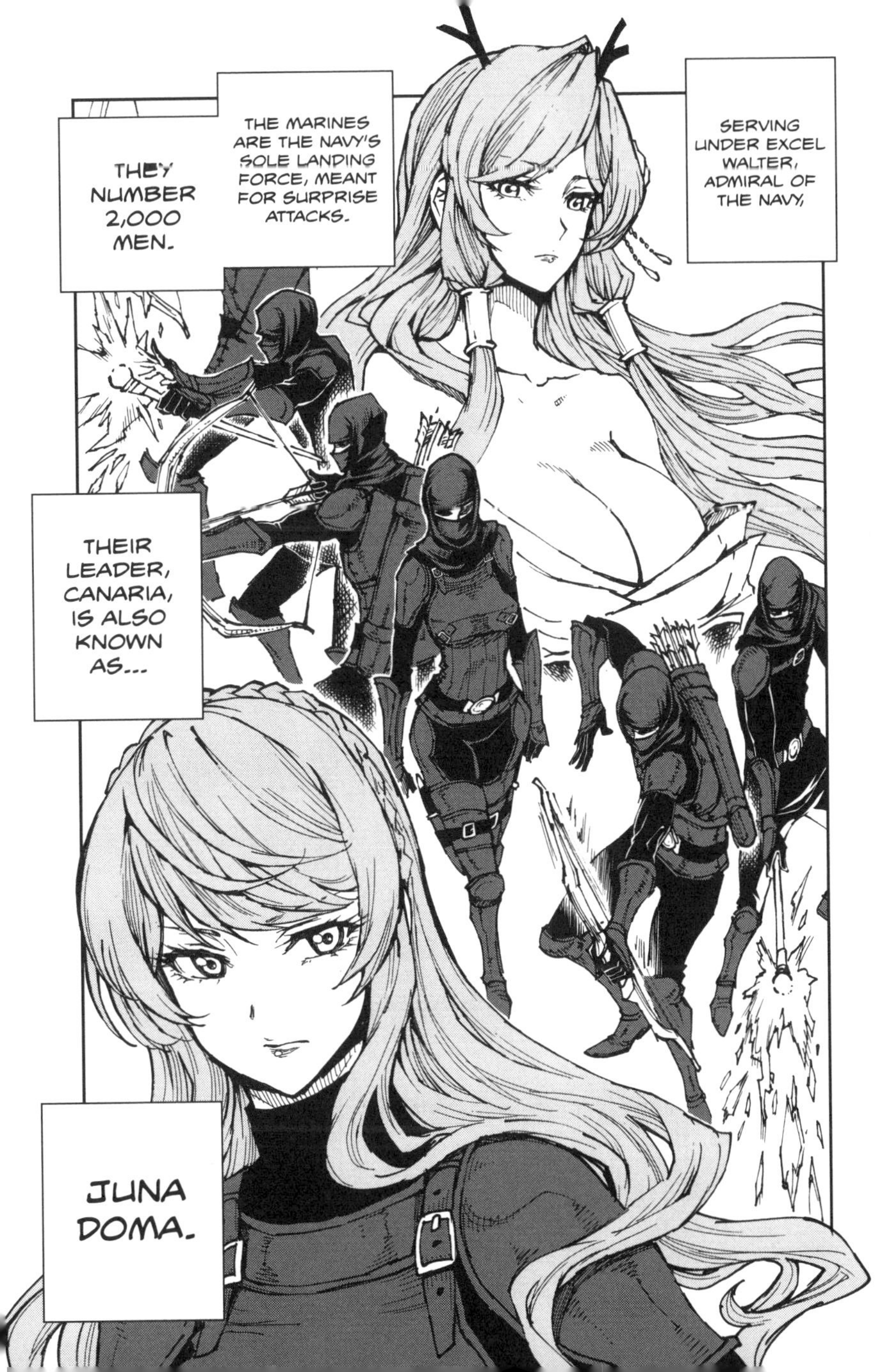
SERVING UNDER EXCEL WALTER, ADMIRAL OF THE NAVY,
THE MARINES ARE THE NAVY'S SOLE LANDING FORCE, MEANT FOR SURPRISE ATTACKS.
THEY NUMBER 2,000 MEN.
THEIR LEADER, CANARIA, IS ALSO KNOWN AS...
JUNA DOMA.

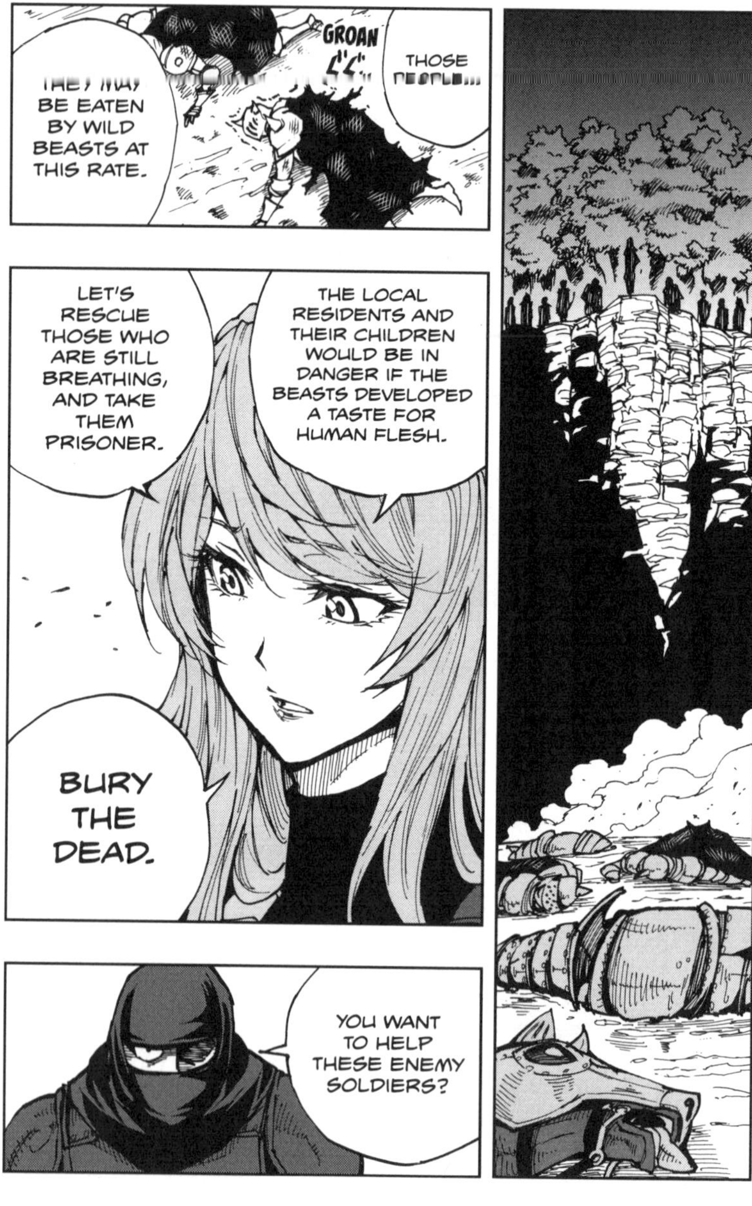

THOSE PEOPLE...
GROAN
THEY MAY BE EATEN BY WILD BEASTS AT THIS RATE.
THE LOCAL RESIDENTS AND THEIR CHILDREN WOULD BE IN DANGER IF THE BEASTS DEVELOPED A TASTE FOR HUMAN FLESH.
LET'S RESCUE THOSE WHO ARE STILL BREATHING, AND TAKE THEM PRISONER.
BURY THE DEAD.
YOU WANT TO HELP THESE ENEMY SOLDIERS?

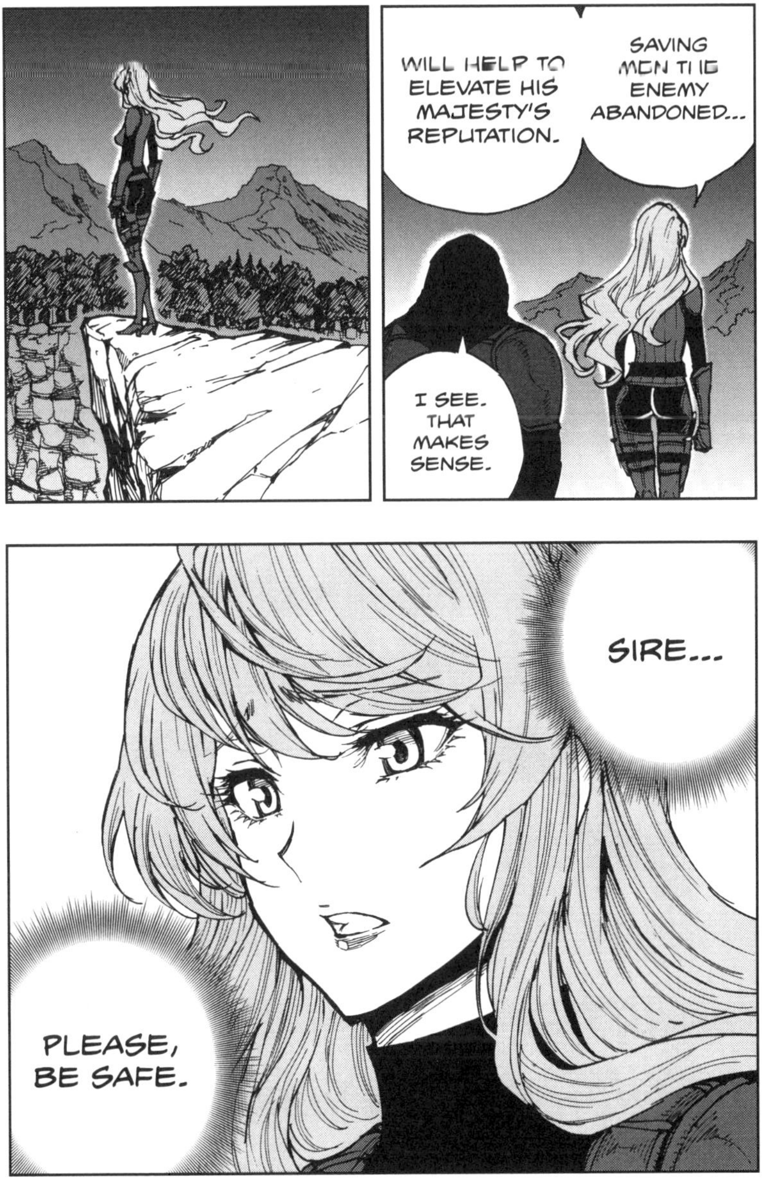
SAVING MEN THE ENEMY ABANDONED...
WILL HELP TO ELEVATE HIS MAJESTY'S REPUTATION.
I SEE. THAT MAKES SENSE.
SIRE...
PLEASE, BE SAFE.

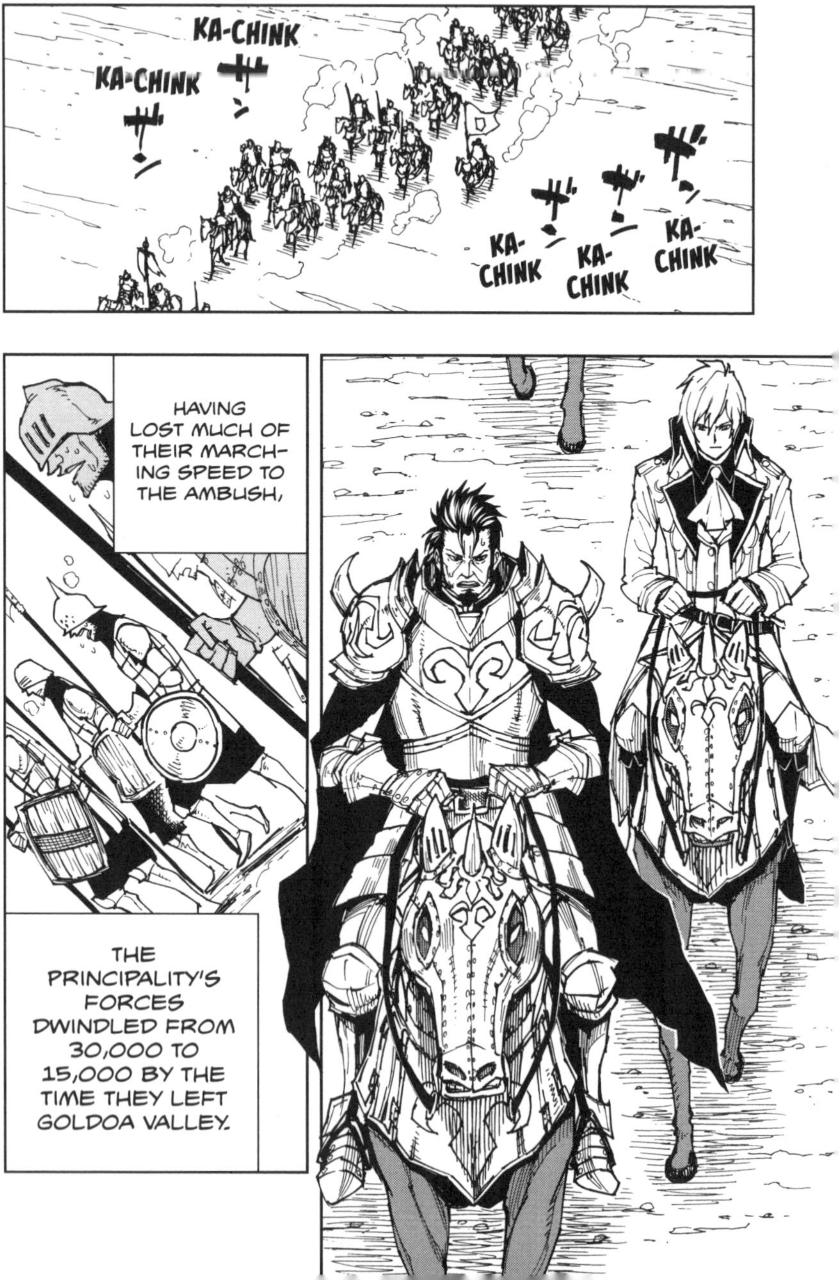
KA-CHINK
KA-CHINK
KA-CHINK
KA-CHINK
KA-CHINK
HAVING LOST MUCH OF THEIR MARCHING SPEED TO THE AMBUSH,
THE PRINCIPALITY'S FORCES DWINDLED FROM 30,000 TO 15,000 BY THE TIME THEY LEFT GOLDOA VALLEY.

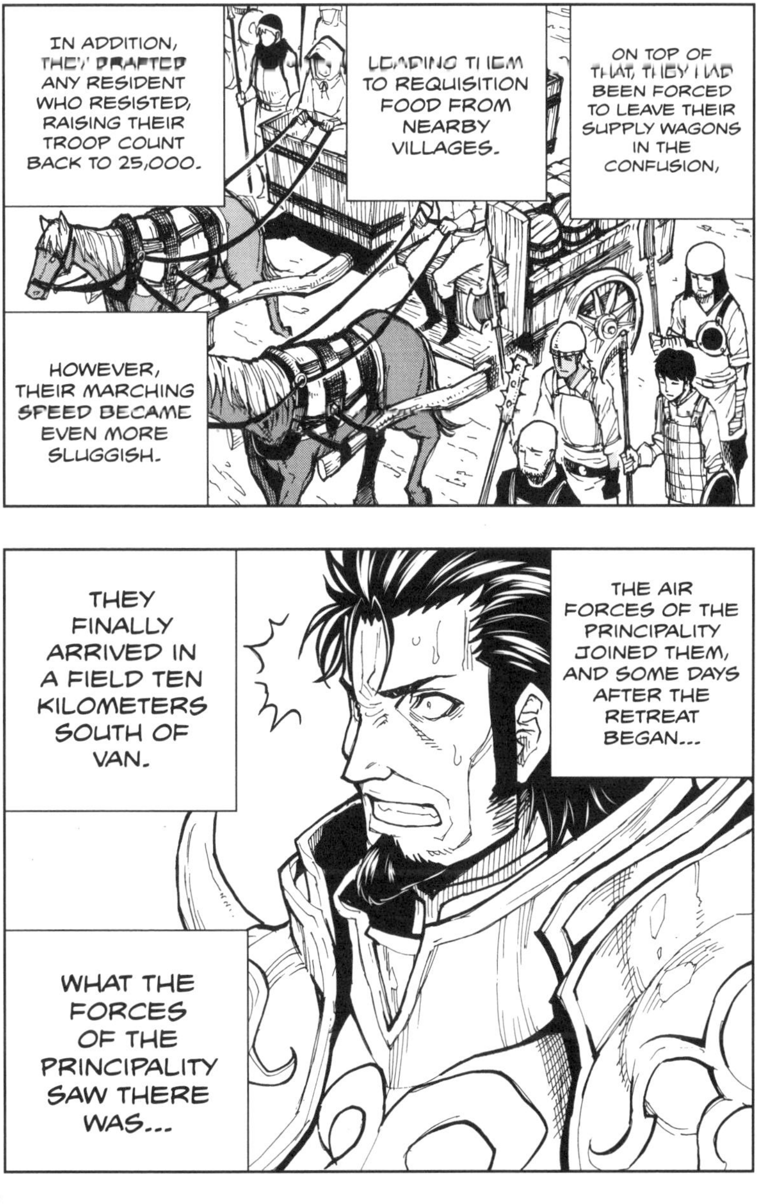
ON TOP OF THAT, THEY HAD BEEN FORCED TO LEAVE THEIR SUPPLY WAGONS IN THE CONFUSION,
LEADING THEM TO REQUISITION FOOD FROM NEARBY VILLAGES.
IN ADDITION, THEY DRAFTED ANY RESIDENT WHO RESISTED, RAISING THEIR TROOP COUNT BACK TO 25,000.
HOWEVER, THEIR MARCHING SPEED BECAME EVEN MORE SLUGGISH.
THE AIR FORCES OF THE PRINCIPALITY JOINED THEM, AND SOME DAYS AFTER THE RETREAT BEGAN...
THEY FINALLY ARRIVED IN A FIELD TEN KILOMETERS SOUTH OF VAN.
WHAT THE FORCES OF THE PRINCIPALITY SAW THERE WAS...

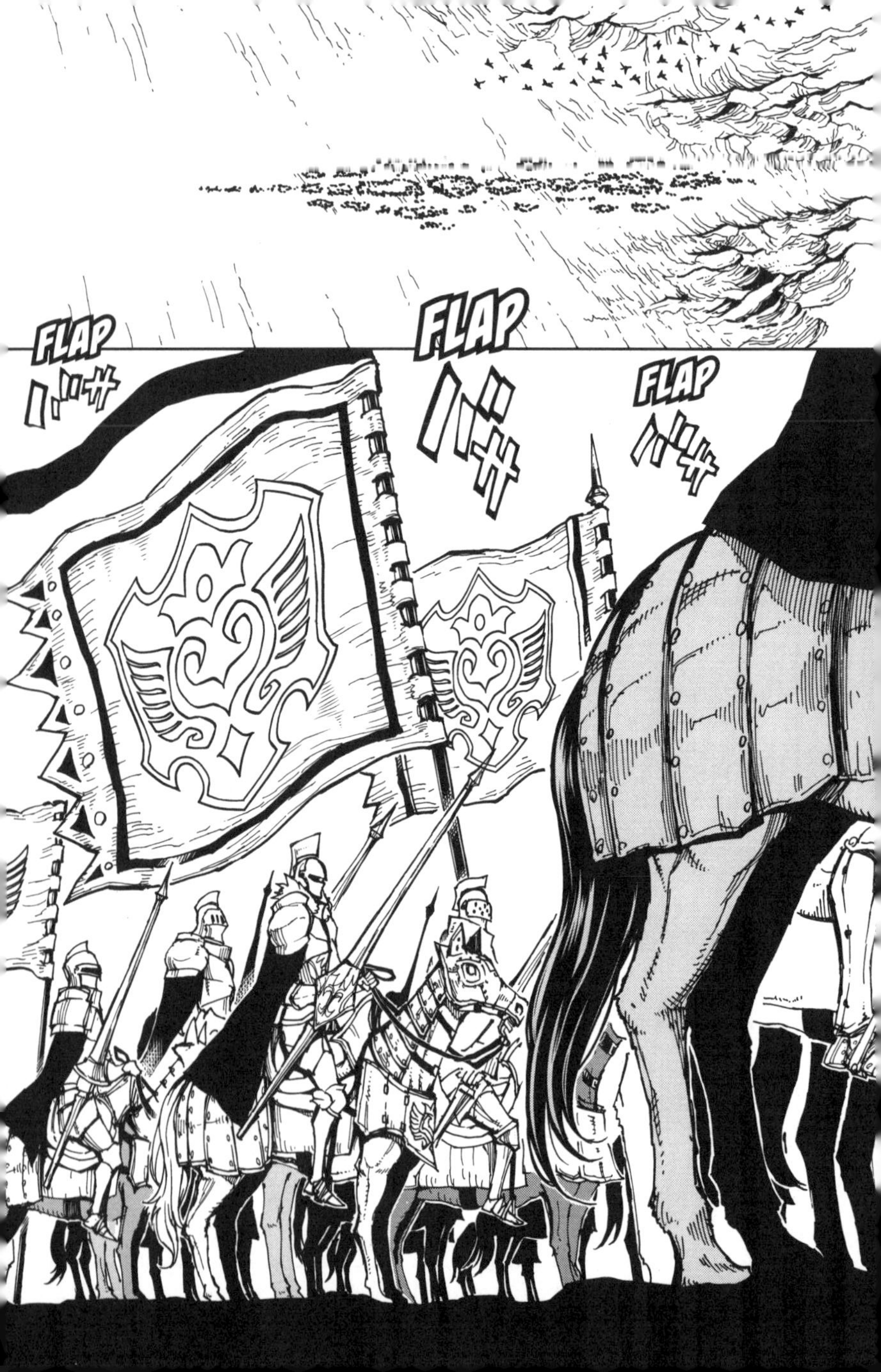

FLAP
バサ
FLAP
バサ
FLAP
バサ

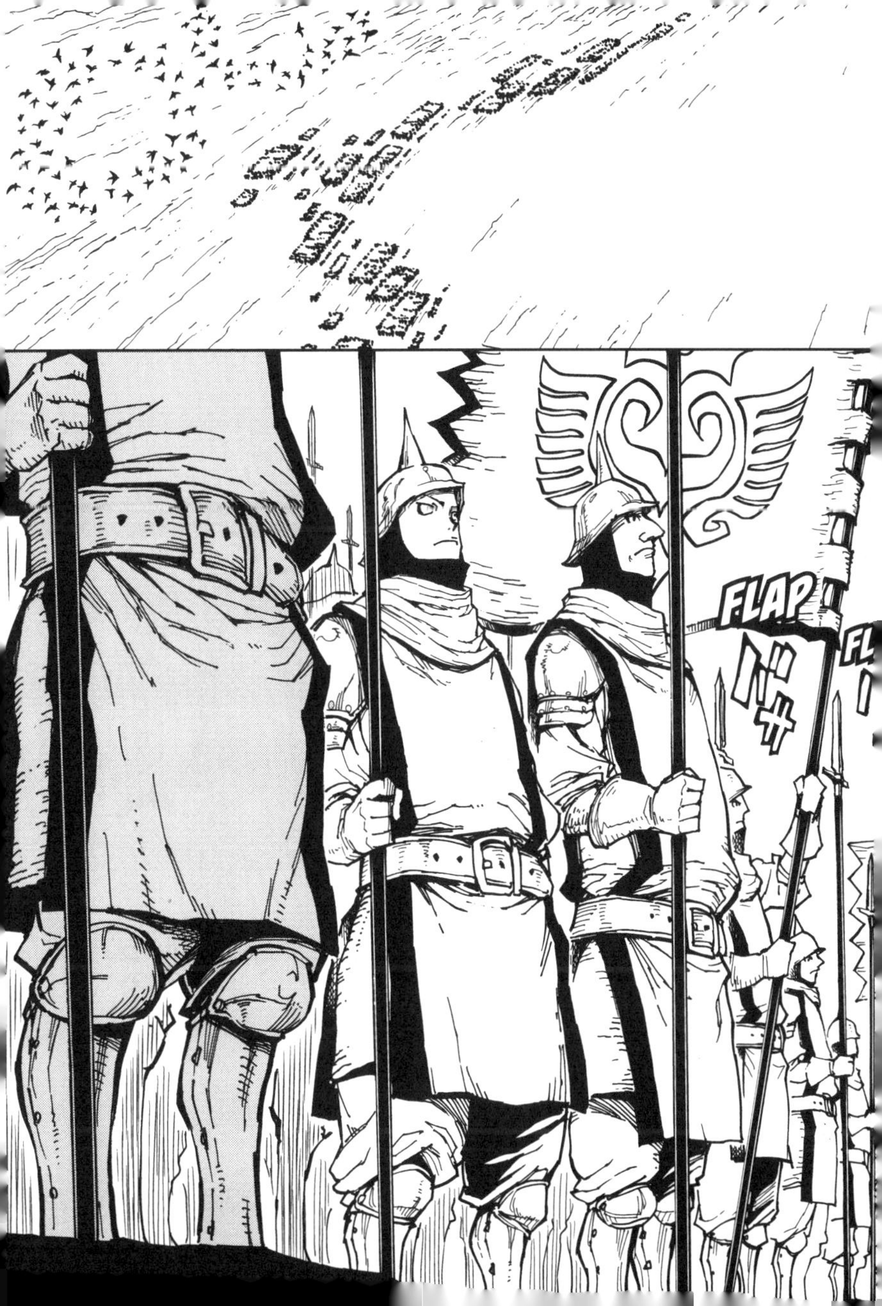
FLAP

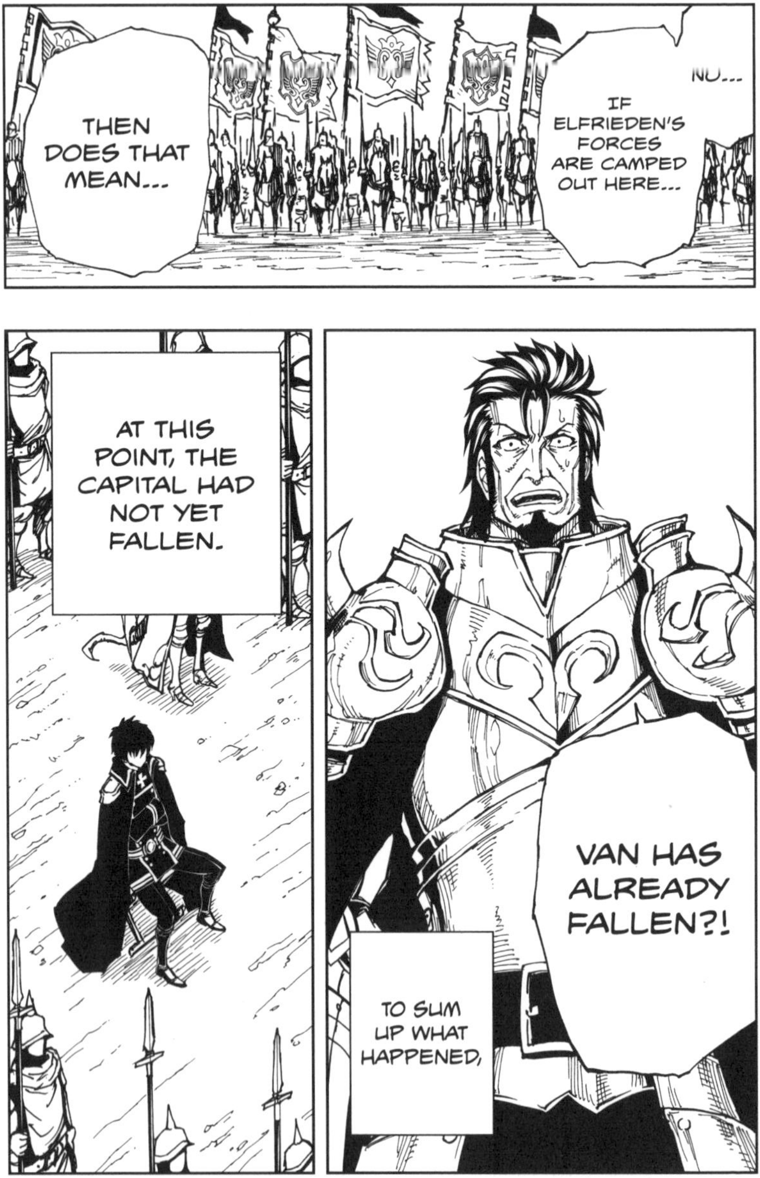
NU...
IF ELFRIEDEN'S FORCES ARE CAMPED OUT HERE...
THEN DOES THAT MEAN...
VAN HAS ALREADY FALLEN?!
TO SUM UP WHAT HAPPENED,
AT THIS POINT, THE CAPITAL HAD NOT YET FALLEN.

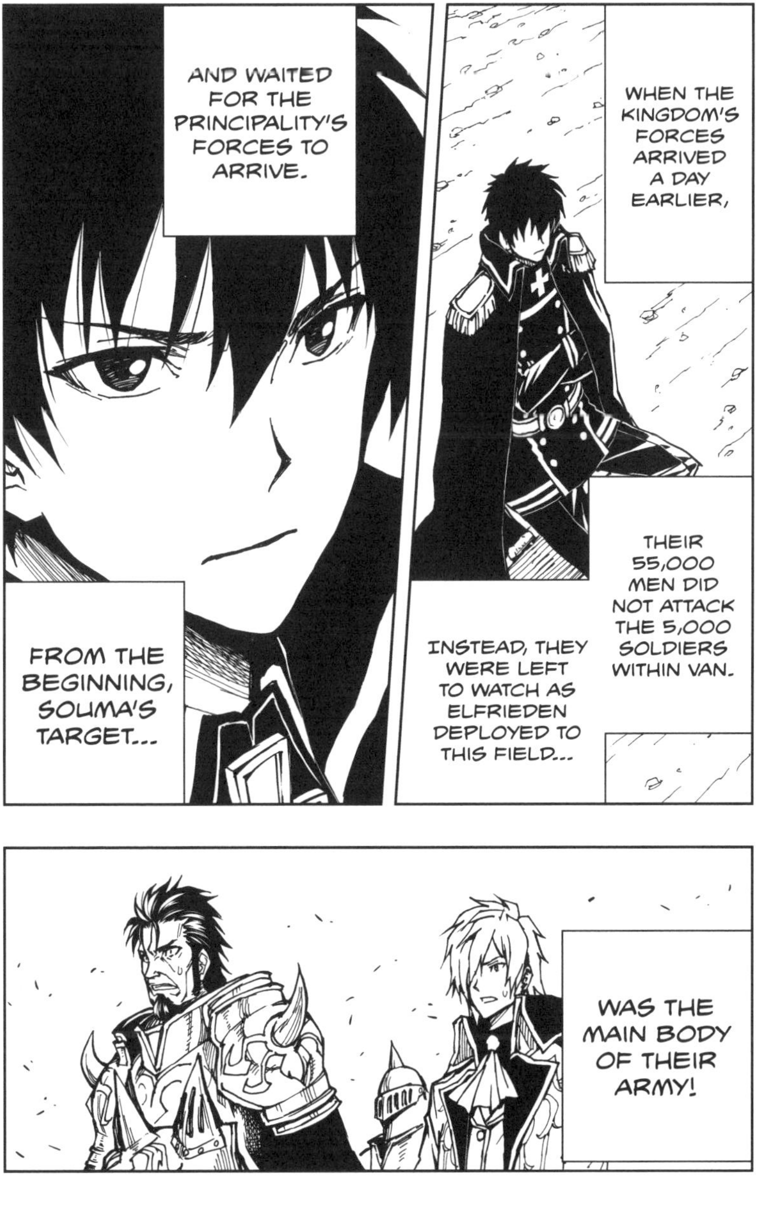
WHEN THE KINGDOM'S FORCES ARRIVED A DAY EARLIER,
THEIR 55,000 MEN DID NOT ATTACK THE 5,000 SOLDIERS WITHIN VAN.
INSTEAD, THEY WERE LEFT TO WATCH AS ELFRIEDEN DEPLOYED TO THIS FIELD...
AND WAITED FOR THE PRINCIPALITY'S FORCES TO ARRIVE.
FROM THE BEGINNING, SOUMA'S TARGET...
WAS THE MAIN BODY OF THEIR ARMY!

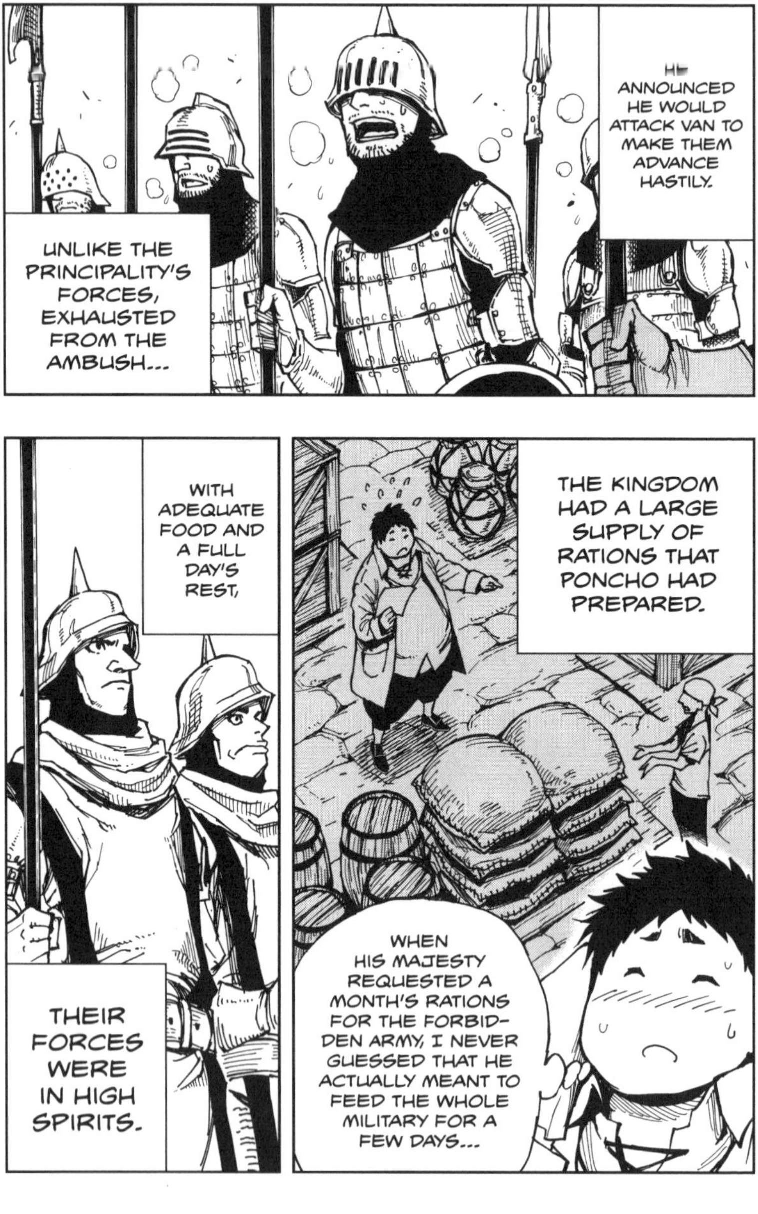
HE ANNOUNCED HE WOULD ATTACK VAN TO MAKE THEM ADVANCE HASTILY.
UNLIKE THE PRINCIPALITY'S FORCES, EXHAUSTED FROM THE AMBUSH...
THE KINGDOM HAD A LARGE SUPPLY OF RATIONS THAT PONCHO HAD PREPARED.
WHEN HIS MAJESTY REQUESTED A MONTH'S RATIONS FOR THE FORBID-DEN ARMY, I NEVER GUESSED THAT HE ACTUALLY MEANT TO FEED THE WHOLE MILITARY FOR A FEW DAYS...
WITH ADEQUATE FOOD AND A FULL DAY'S REST,
THEIR FORCES WERE IN HIGH SPIRITS.

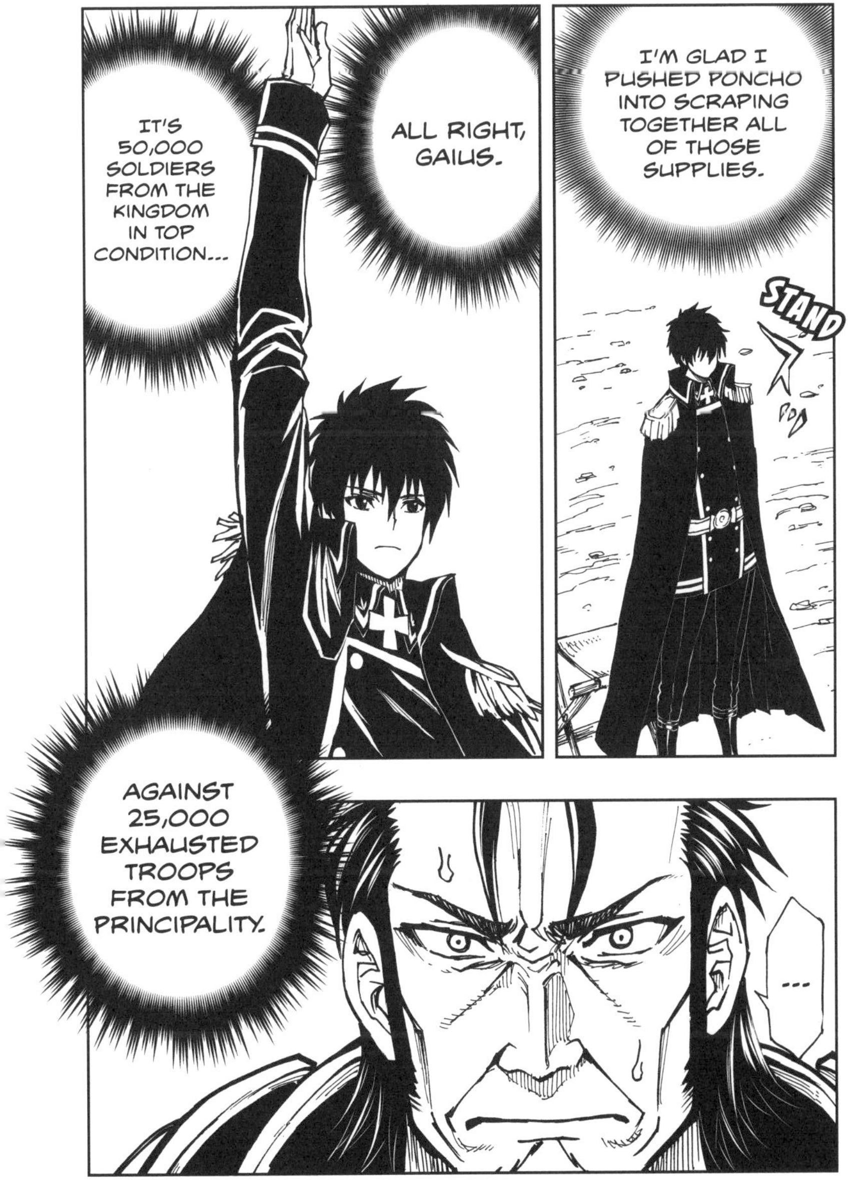
I'M GLAD I PUSHED PONCHO INTO SCRAPING TOGETHER ALL OF THOSE SUPPLIES.
STAND
ALL RIGHT, GAIUS.
IT'S 50,000 SOLDIERS FROM THE KINGDOM IN TOP CONDITION...
AGAINST 25,000 EXHAUSTED TROOPS FROM THE PRINCIPALITY.
...

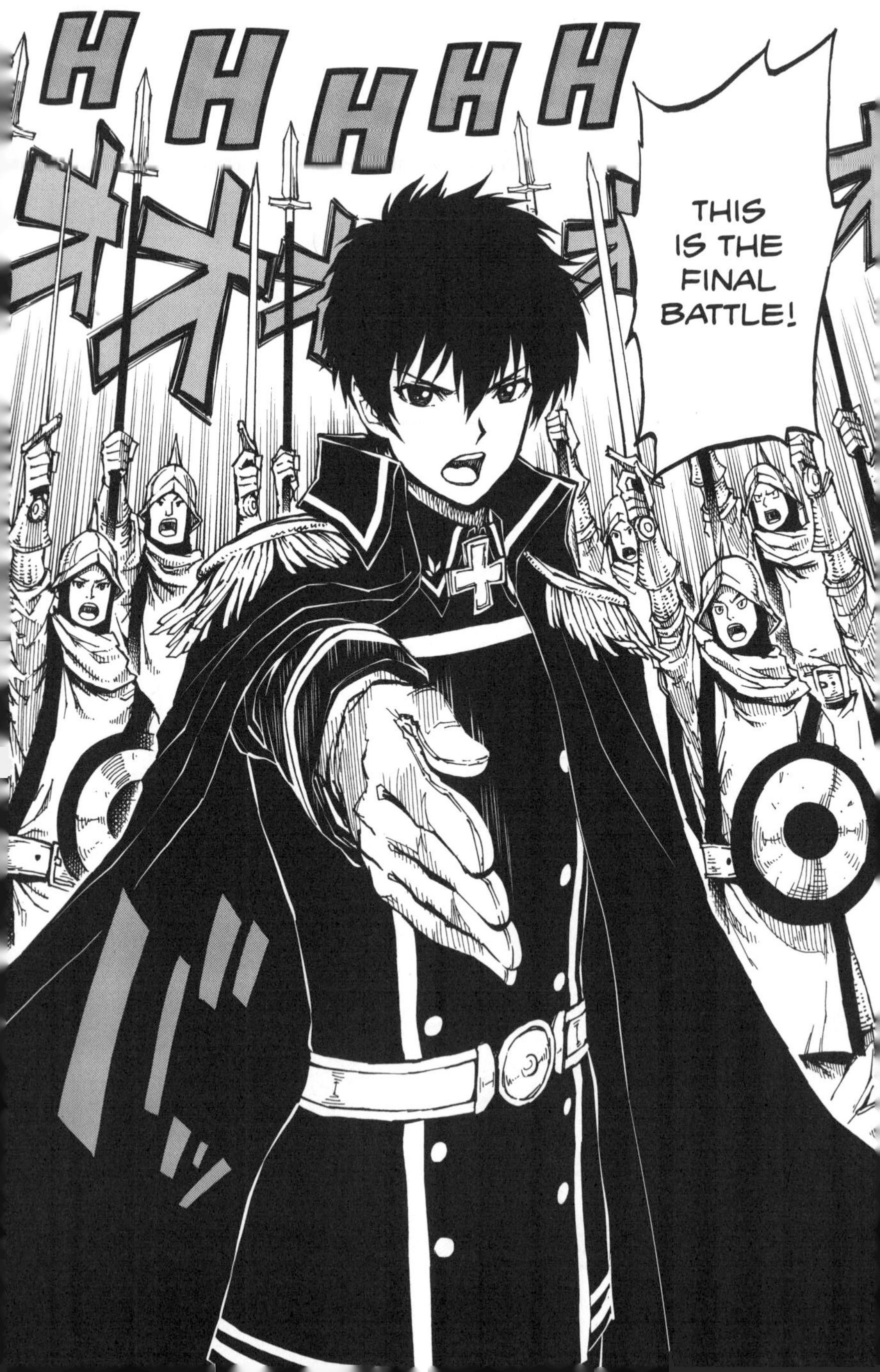
HHHHHH
THIS IS THE FINAL BATTLE!

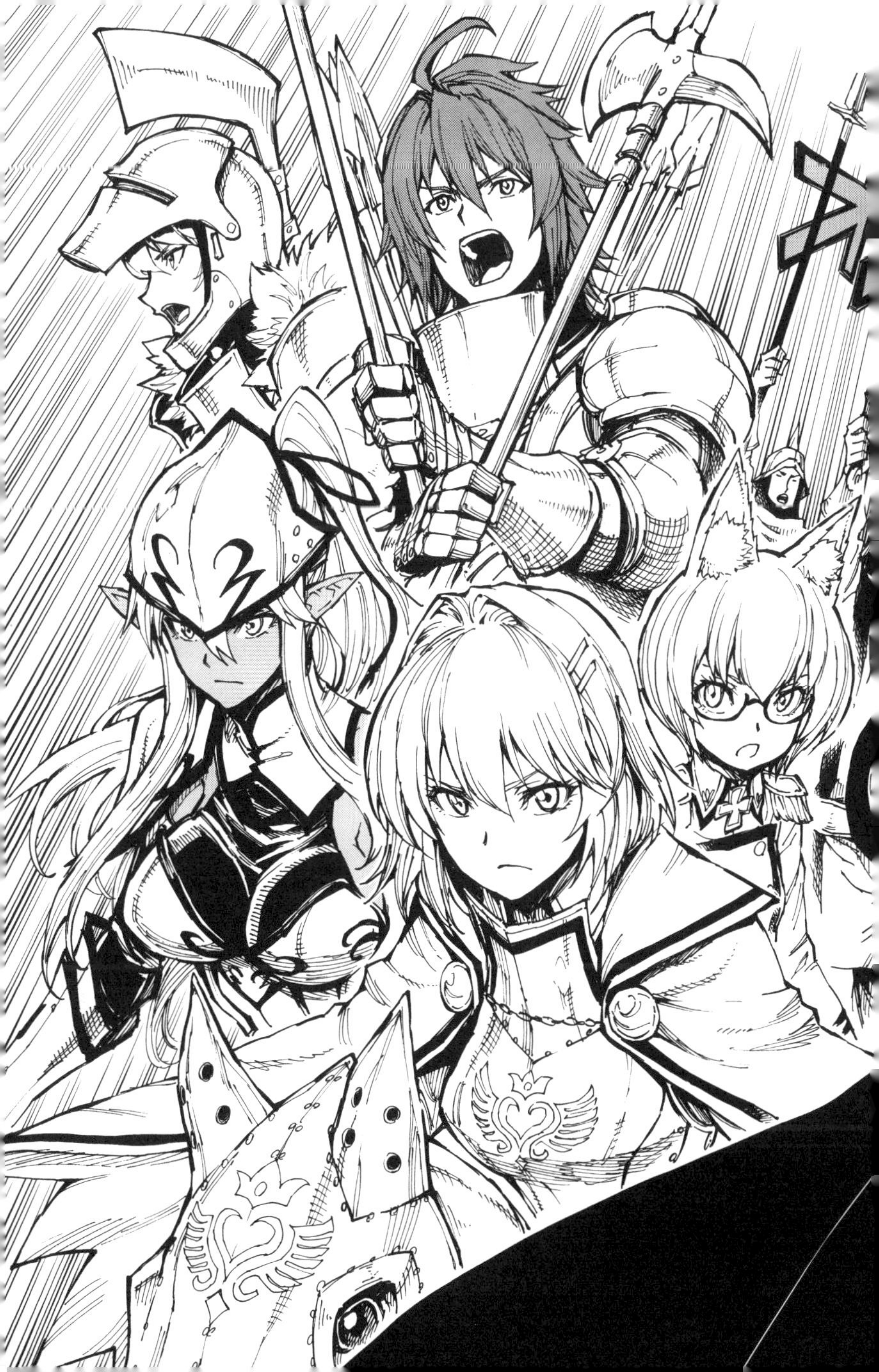

How a Realist Hero
Rebuilt the Kingdom

Chapter 23: The Final Battle (1)

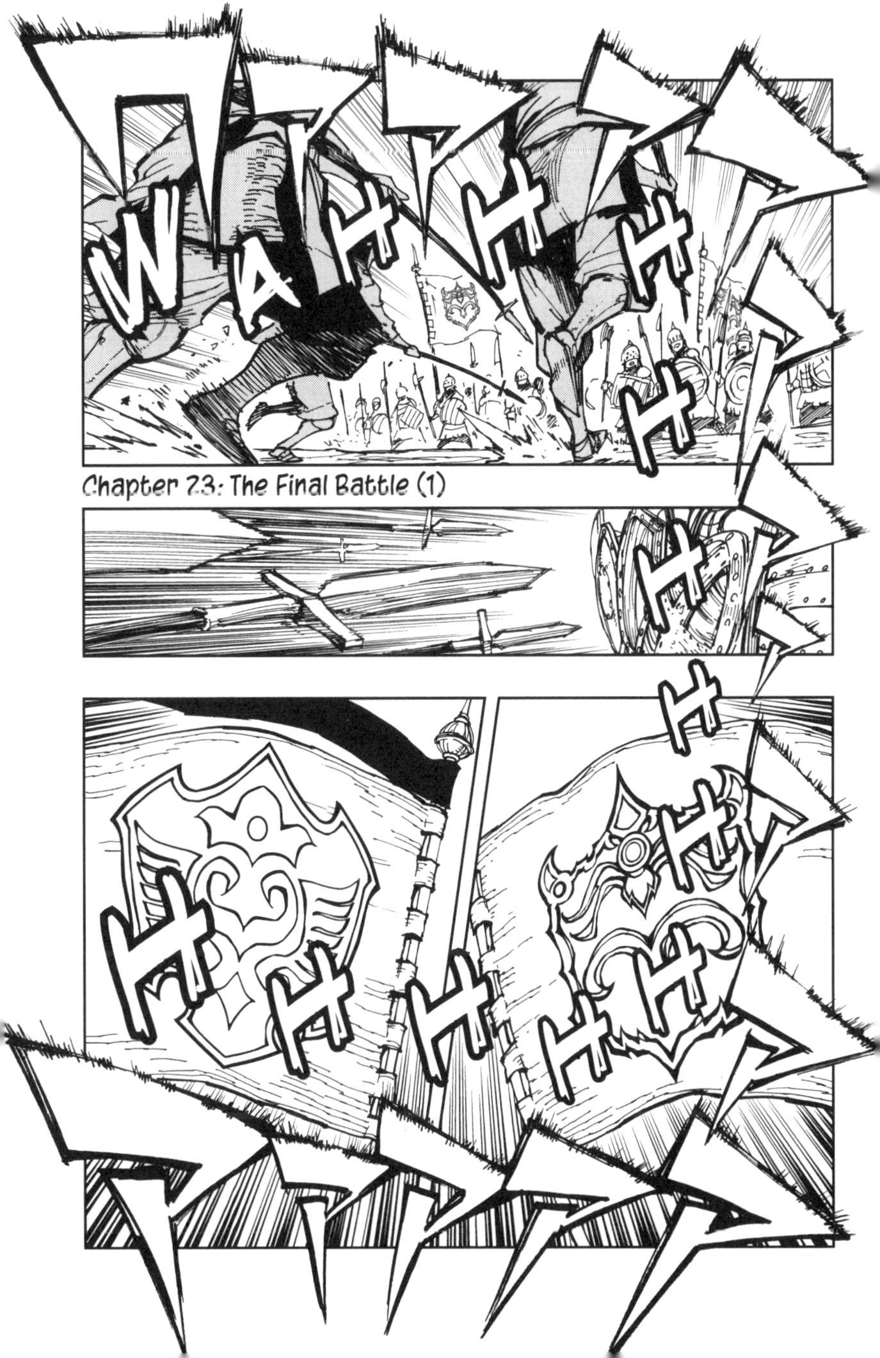
WAHHHHHHHHHHHHHHHH

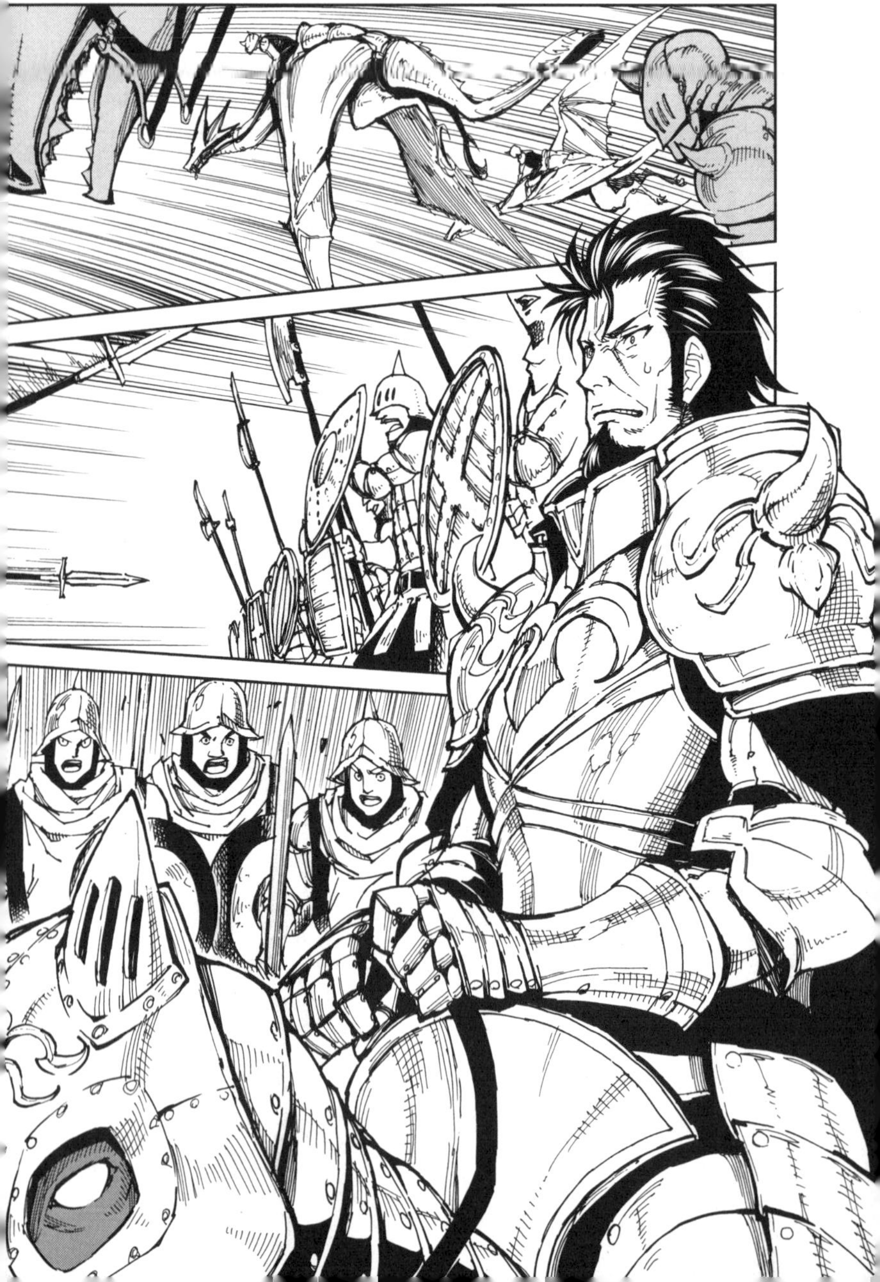

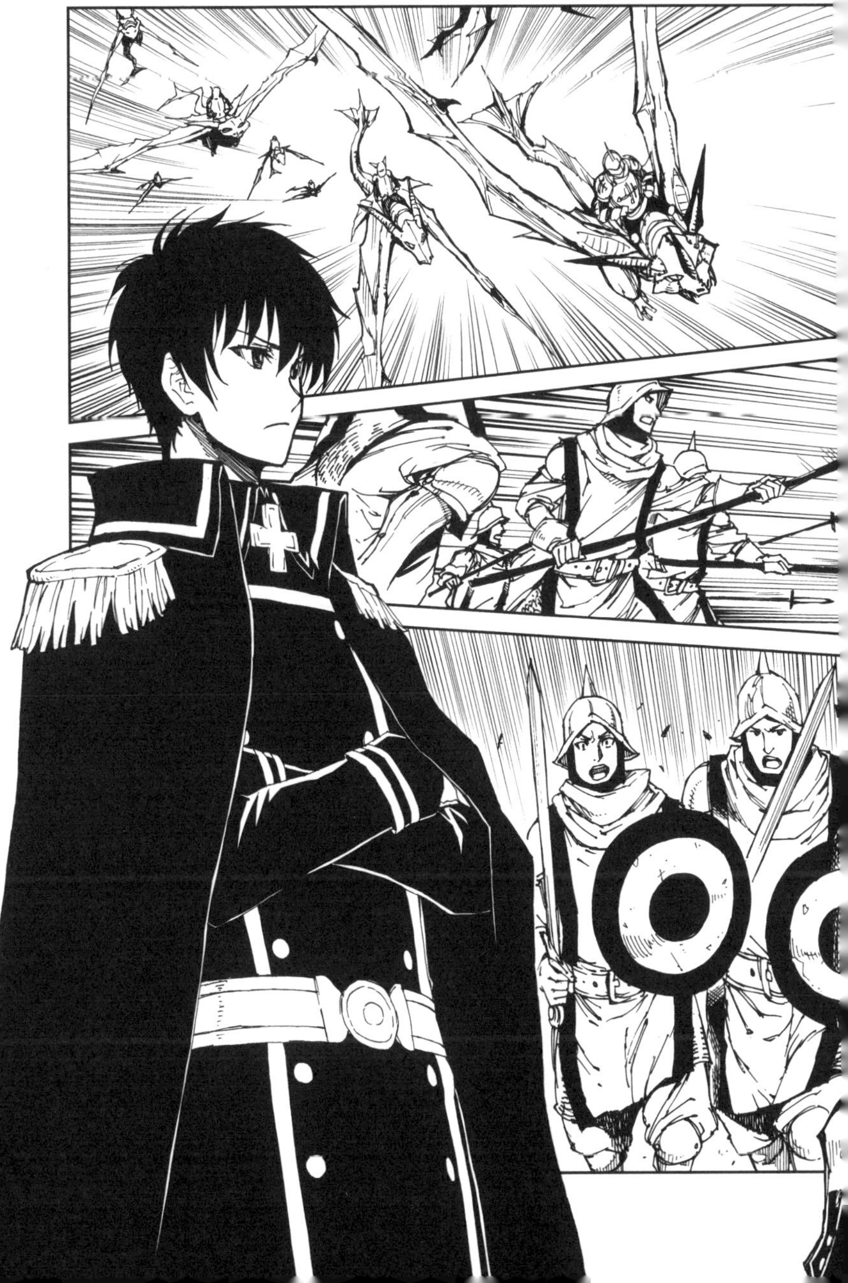

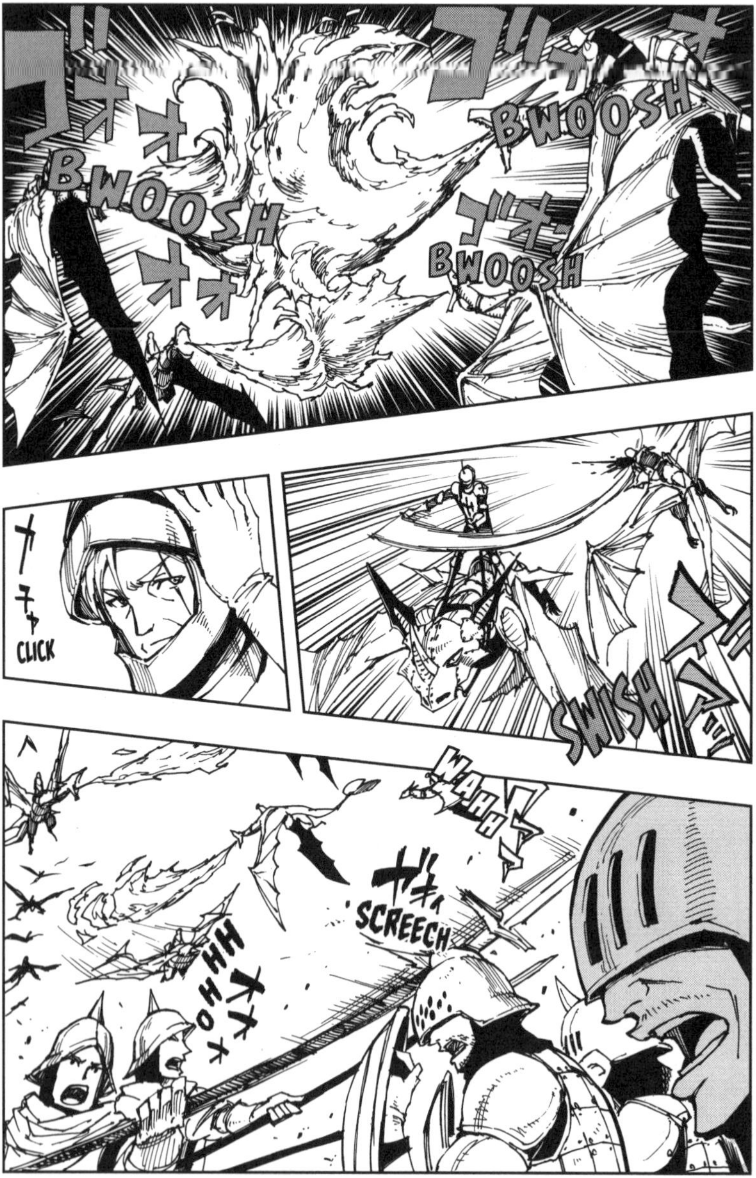
BWOOSH
BWOOSH
BWOOSH
SWISH
CLICK
WAHH
SCREECH
HHHO

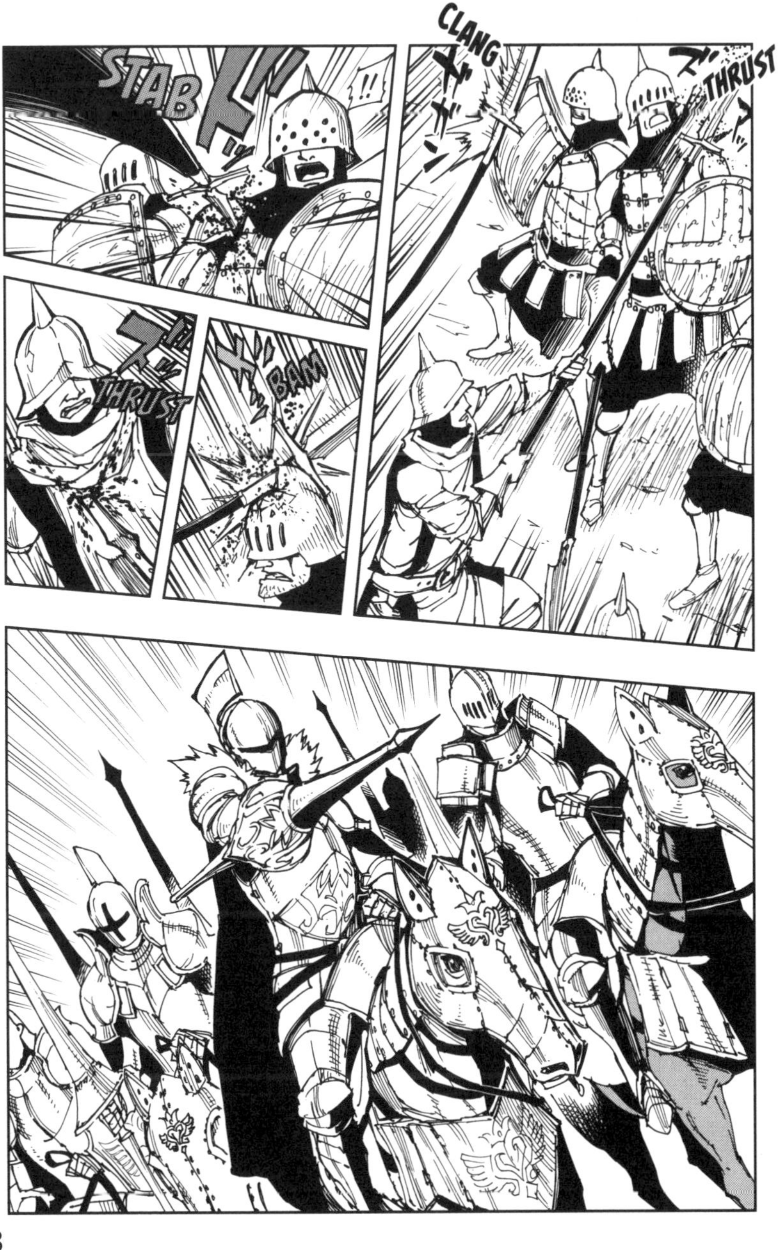
THRUST
CLANG
STAB
!!
BAM
THRUST

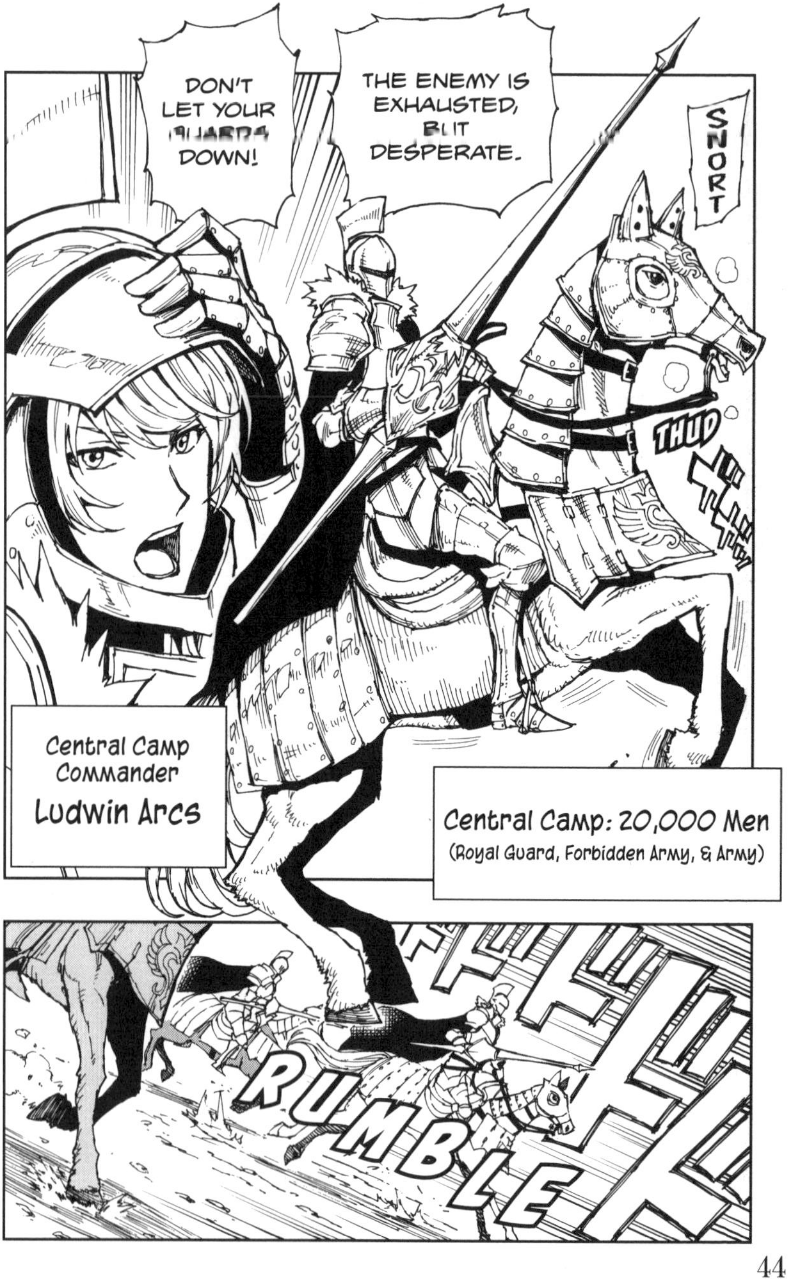
SNORT
THE ENEMY IS EXHAUSTED, BUT DESPERATE.
DON'T LET YOUR GUARDS DOWN!
THUD
Central Camp: 20,000 Men
(Royal Guard, Forbidden Army, & Army)
Central Camp Commander
Ludwin Arcs
RUMBLE

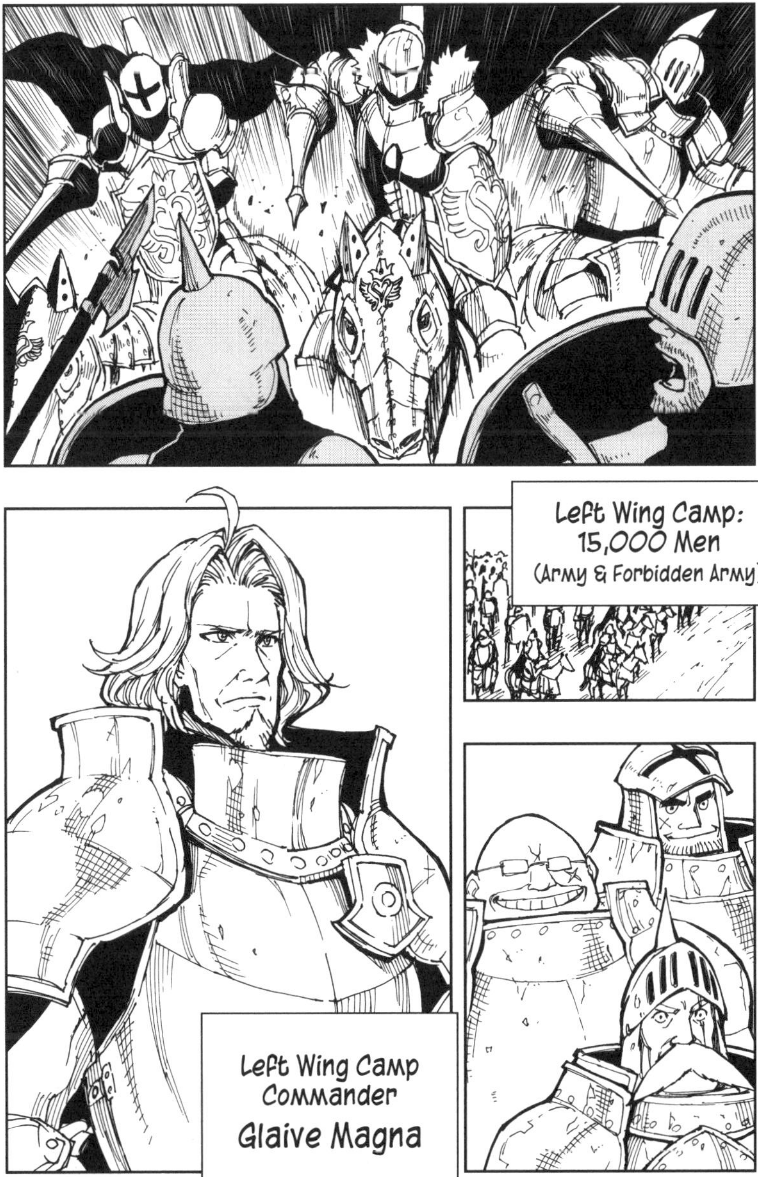
Left Wing Camp: 15,000 Men
(Army & Forbidden Army)
Left Wing Camp Commander
Glaive Magna

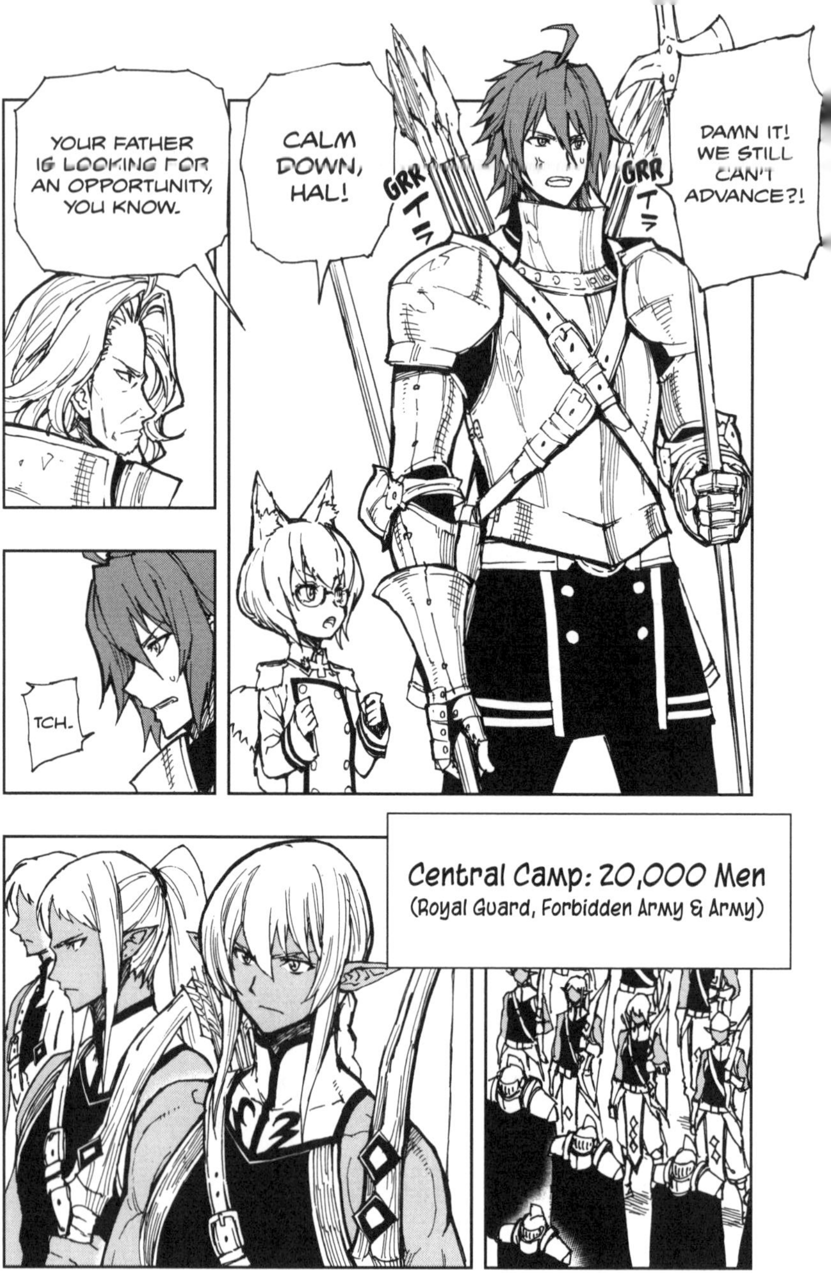
DAMN IT! WE STILL CAN'T ADVANCE?!
GRR
GRR
CALM DOWN, HAL!
YOUR FATHER IS LOOKING FOR AN OPPORTUNITY, YOU KNOW.
TCH.
Central Camp: 20,000 Men
(Royal Guard, Forbidden Army & Army)

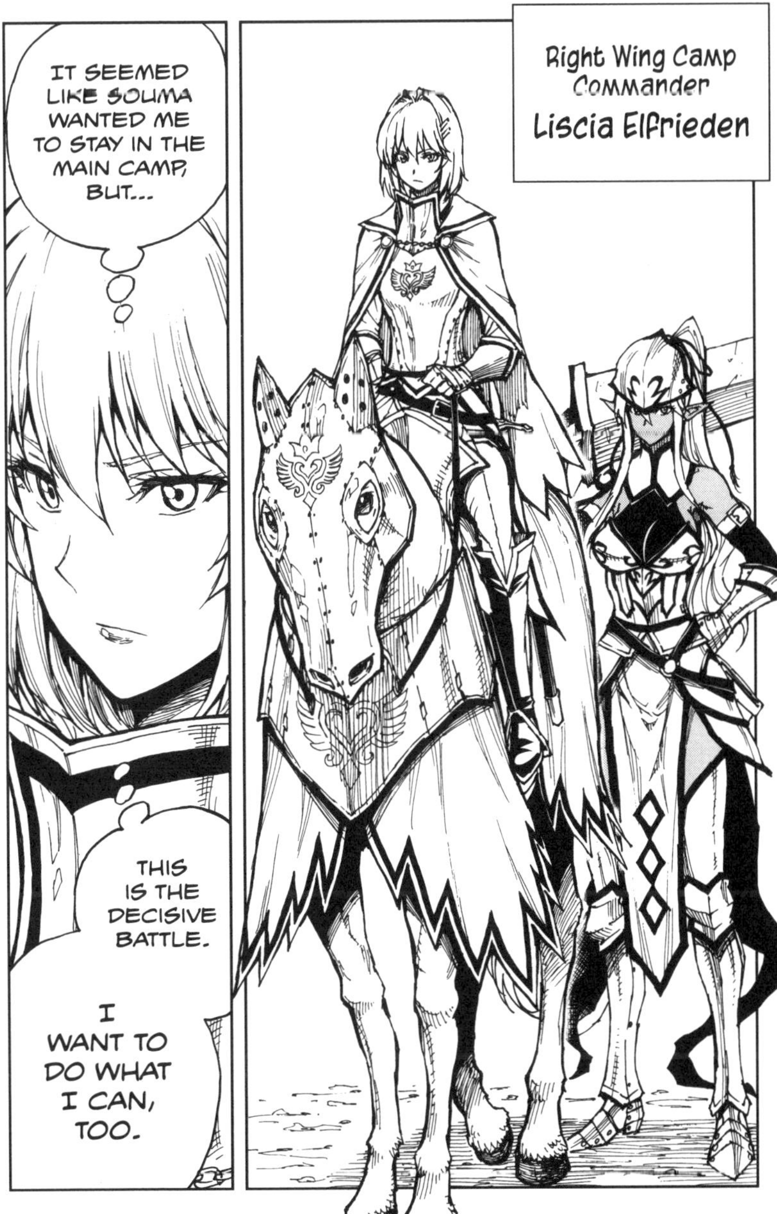
Right Wing Camp Commander
Liscia Elfrieden
IT SEEMED LIKE SOUMA WANTED ME TO STAY IN THE MAIN CAMP, BUT...
THIS IS THE DECISIVE BATTLE.
I WANT TO DO WHAT I CAN, TOO.

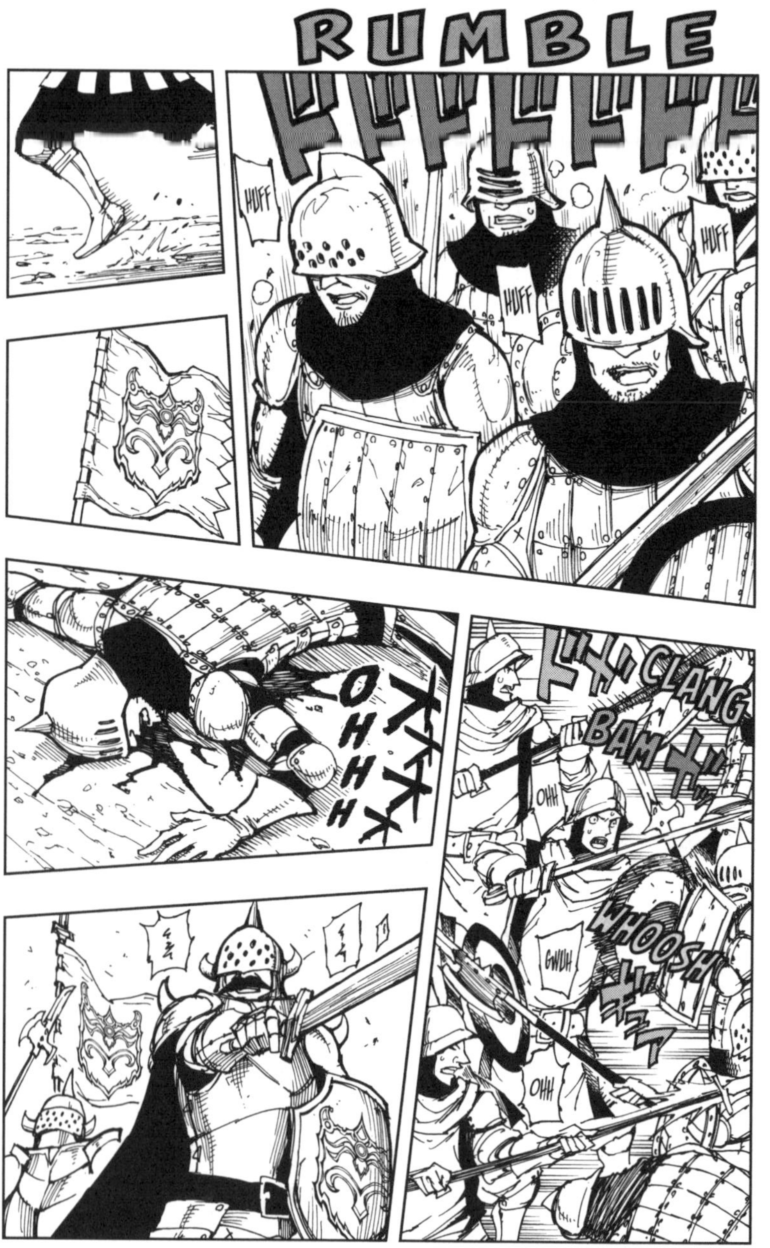
RUMBLE
HUFF
HUFF
HUFF
HUFF
CLANG
BAM
OHH
GWUH
WHOOSH
OHH
OHHHH

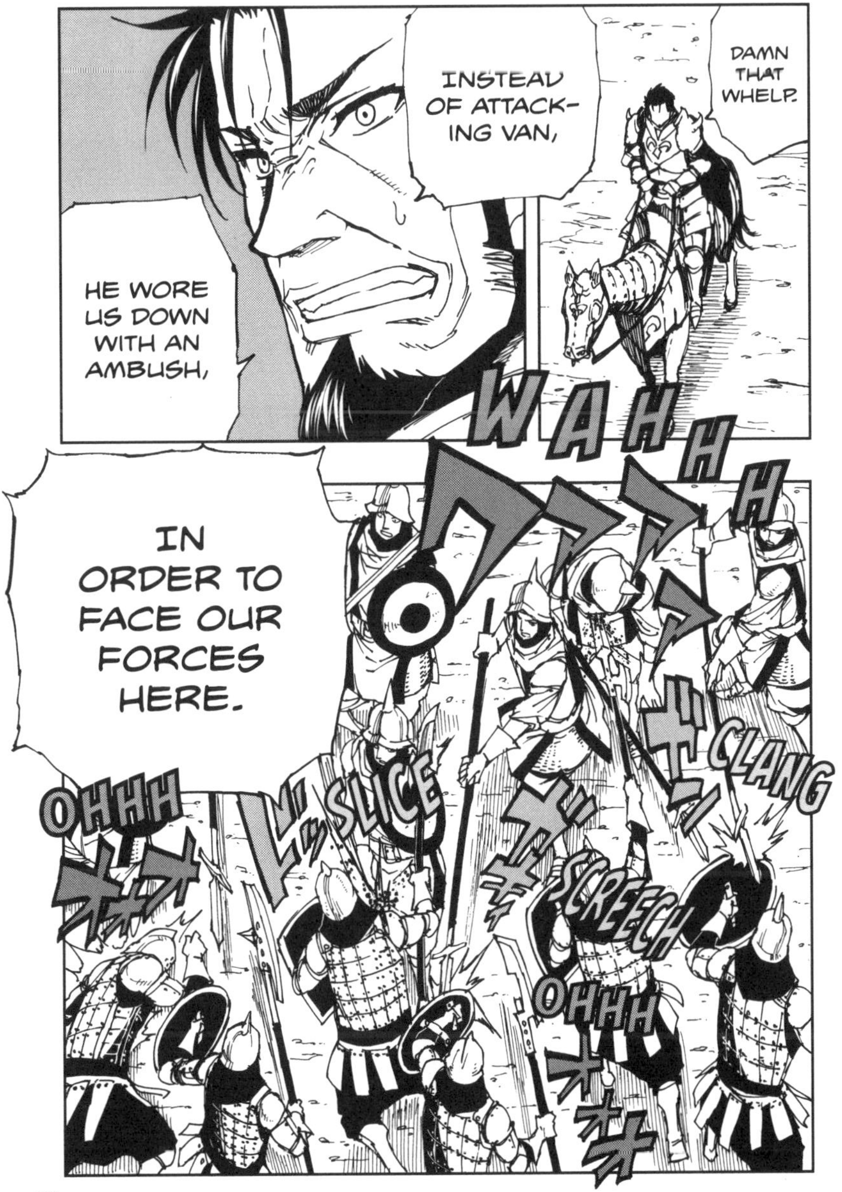
DAMN THAT WHELP.
INSTEAD OF ATTACK-ING VAN,
HE WORE US DOWN WITH AN AMBUSH,
WAHHHH
IN ORDER TO FACE OUR FORCES HERE.
CLANG
SCREECH
OHHH
SLICE
OHHH

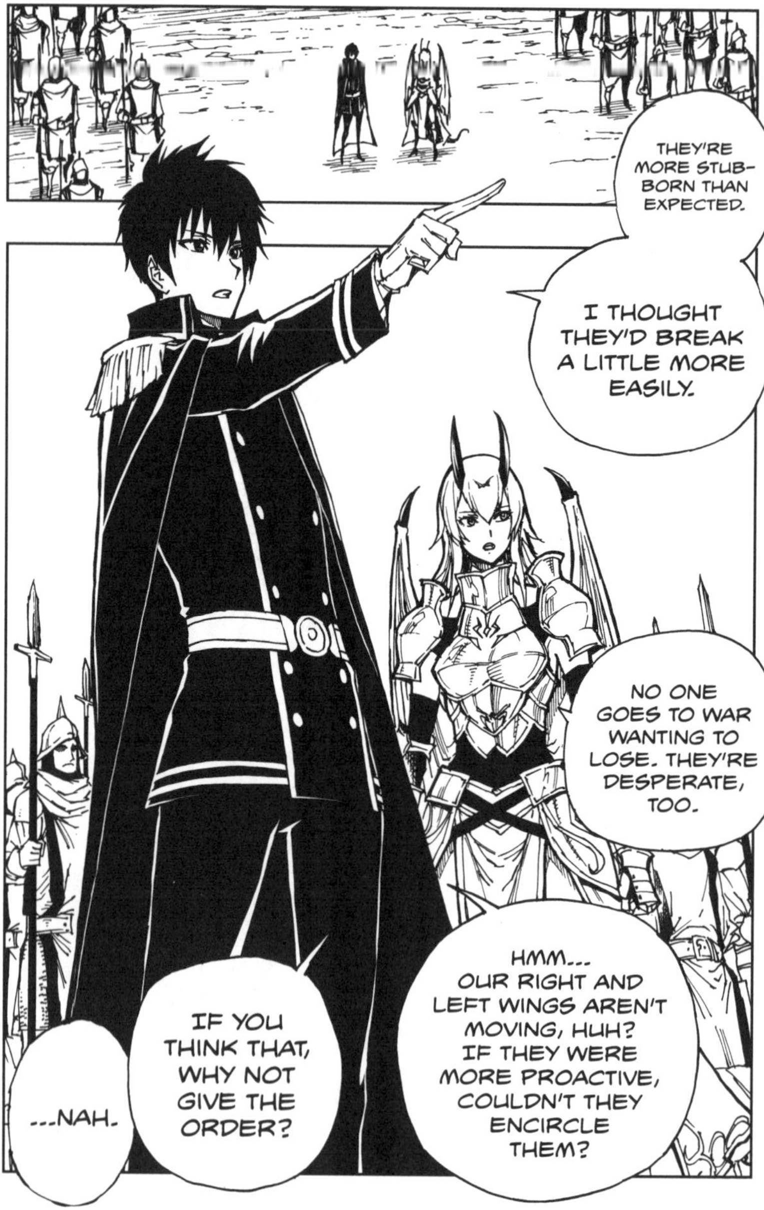
THEY'RE MORE STUBBORN THAN EXPECTED.
I THOUGHT THEY'D BREAK A LITTLE MORE EASILY.
NO ONE GOES TO WAR WANTING TO LOSE. THEY'RE DESPERATE, TOO.
HMM... OUR RIGHT AND LEFT WINGS AREN'T MOVING, HUH? IF THEY WERE MORE PROACTIVE, COULDN'T THEY ENCIRCLE THEM?
IF YOU THINK THAT, WHY NOT GIVE THE ORDER?
...NAH.

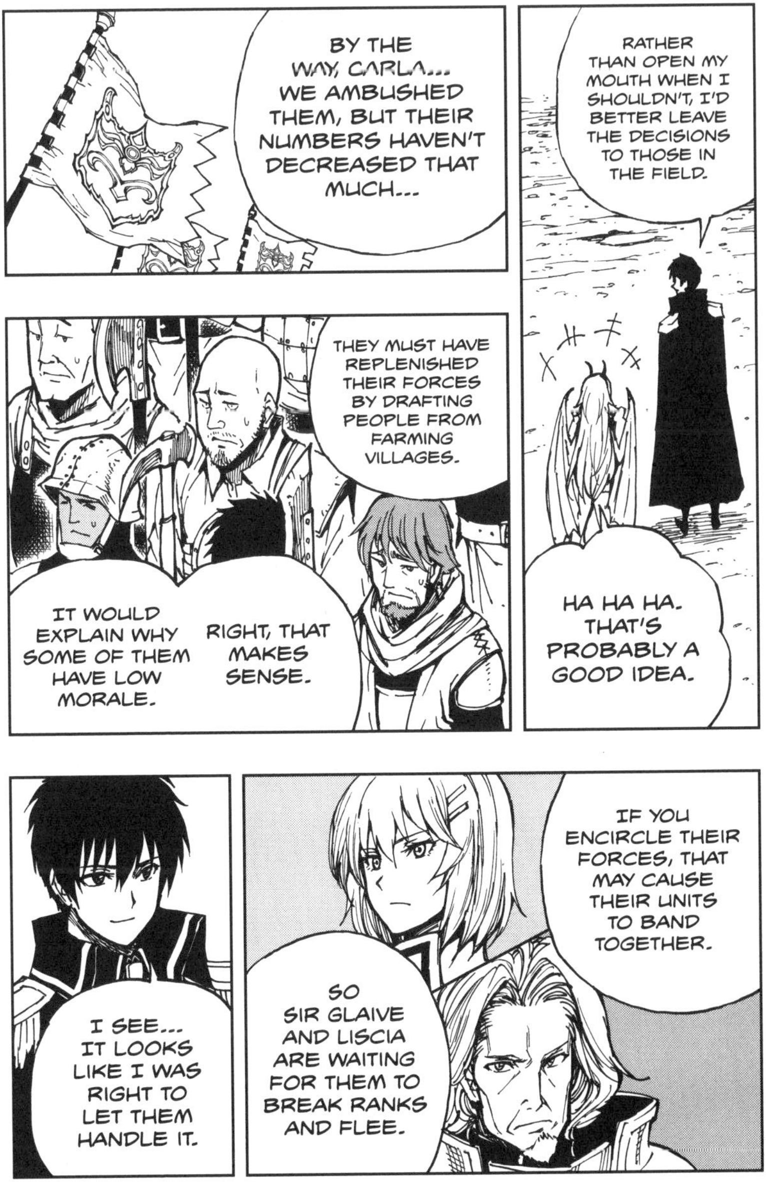
RATHER THAN OPEN MY MOUTH WHEN I SHOULDN'T, I'D BETTER LEAVE THE DECISIONS TO THOSE IN THE FIELD.
HA HA HA. THAT'S PROBABLY A GOOD IDEA.
BY THE WAY, CARLA... WE AMBUSHED THEM, BUT THEIR NUMBERS HAVEN'T DECREASED THAT MUCH...
THEY MUST HAVE REPLENISHED THEIR FORCES BY DRAFTING PEOPLE FROM FARMING VILLAGES.
IT WOULD EXPLAIN WHY SOME OF THEM HAVE LOW MORALE.
RIGHT, THAT MAKES SENSE.
IF YOU ENCIRCLE THEIR FORCES, THAT MAY CAUSE THEIR UNITS TO BAND TOGETHER.
SO SIR GLAIVE AND LISCIA ARE WAITING FOR THEM TO BREAK RANKS AND FLEE.
I SEE... IT LOOKS LIKE I WAS RIGHT TO LET THEM HANDLE IT.

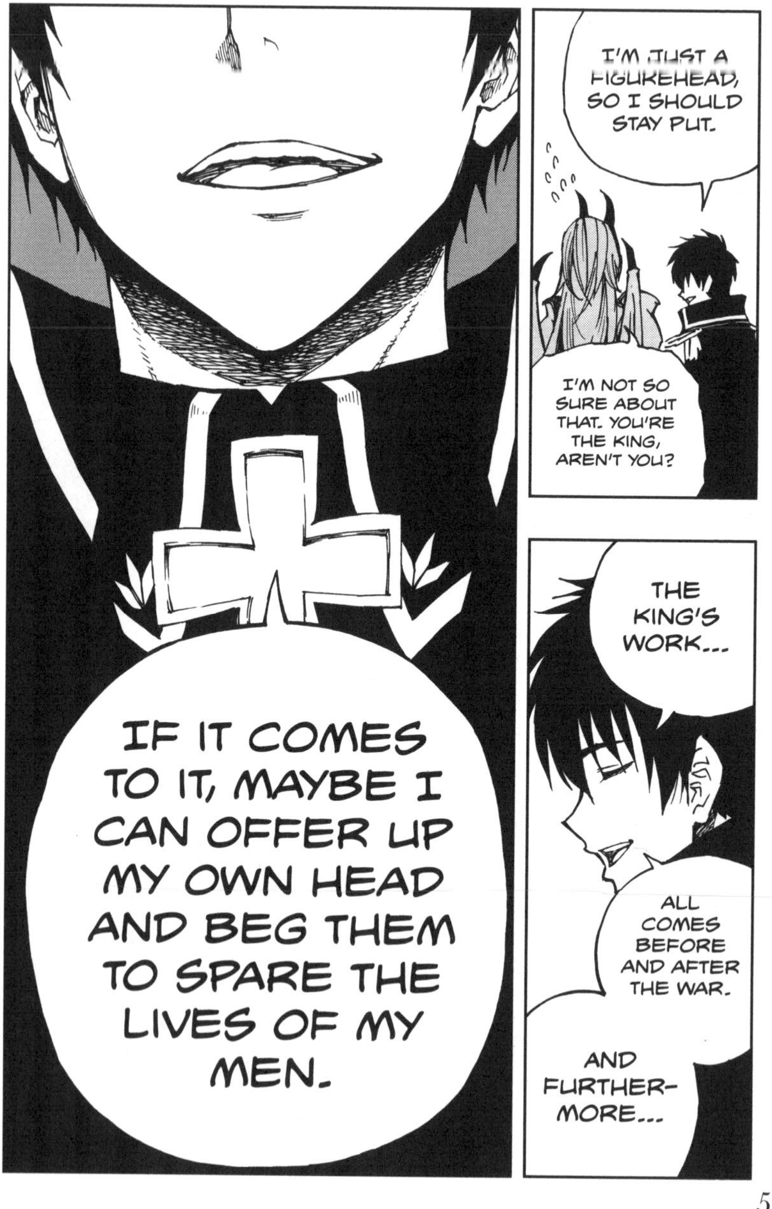
I'M JUST A FIGUREHEAD, SO I SHOULD STAY PUT.
I'M NOT SO SURE ABOUT THAT. YOU'RE THE KING, AREN'T YOU?
THE KING'S WORK...
ALL COMES BEFORE AND AFTER THE WAR.
AND FURTHERMORE...
IF IT COMES TO IT, MAYBE I CAN OFFER UP MY OWN HEAD AND BEG THEM TO SPARE THE LIVES OF MY MEN.

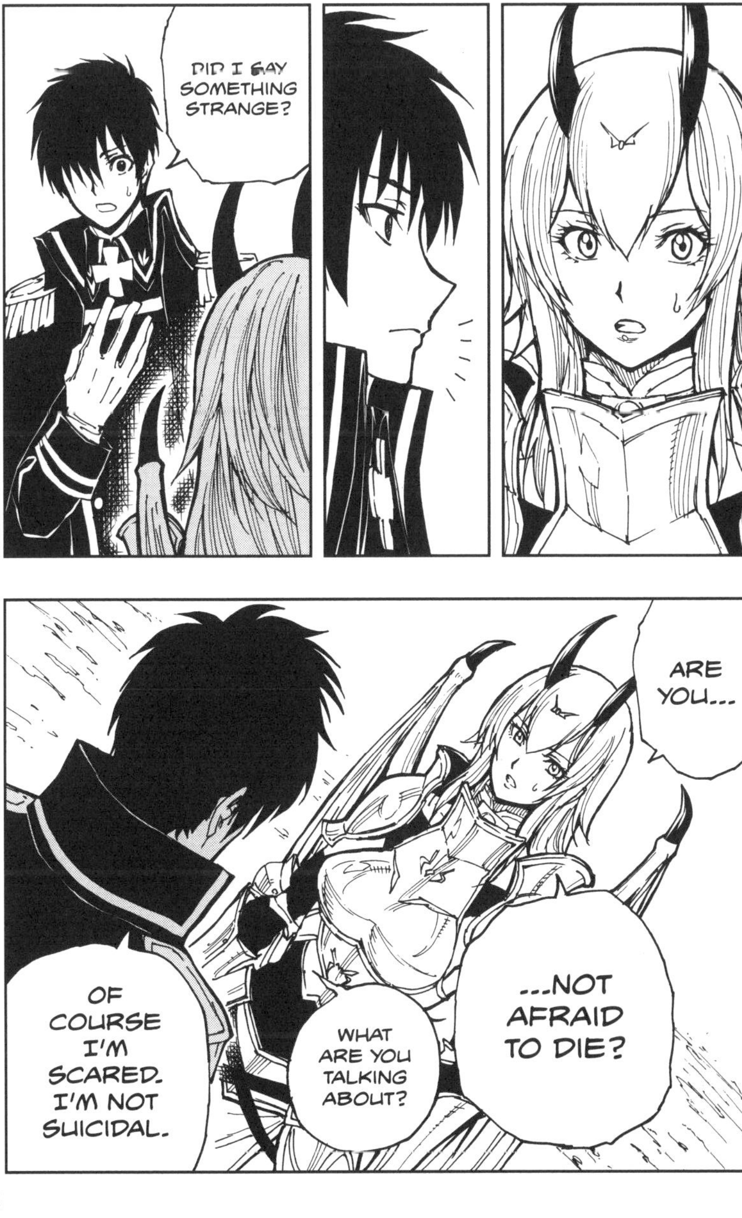
DID I SAY SOMETHING STRANGE?
ARE YOU...
...NOT AFRAID TO DIE?
WHAT ARE YOU TALKING ABOUT?
OF COURSE I'M SCARED. I'M NOT SUICIDAL.

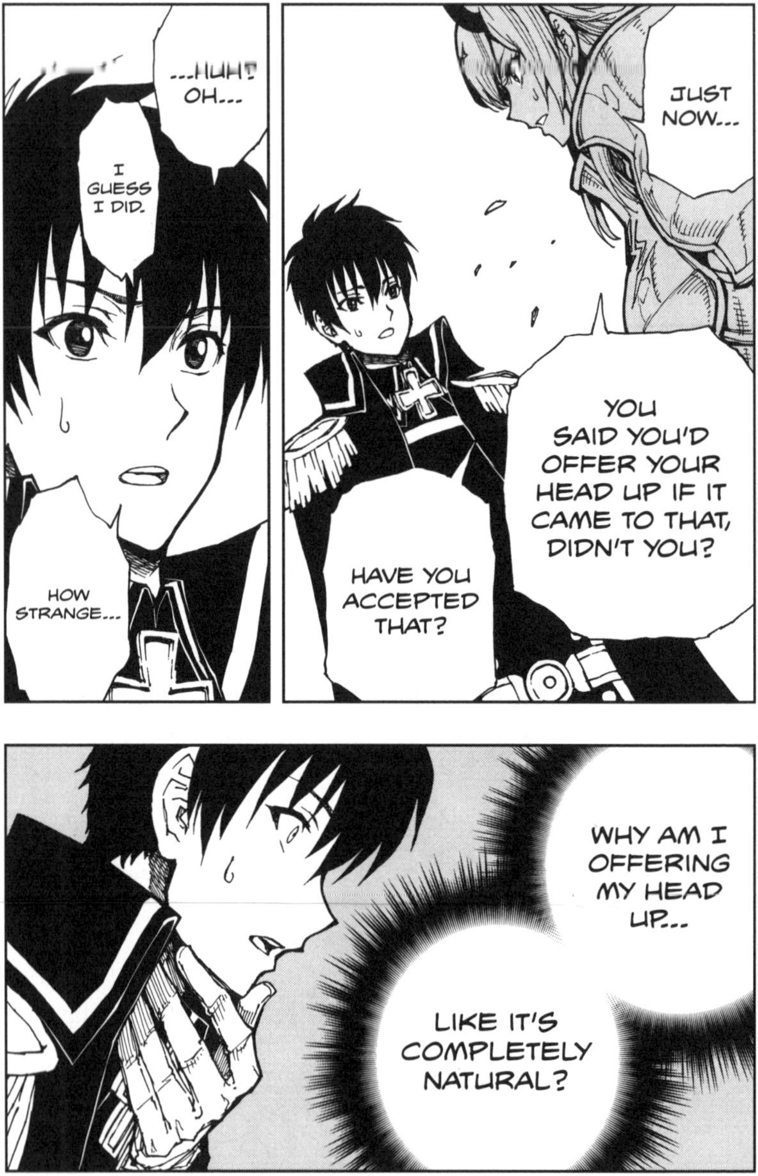
JUST NOW...
YOU SAID YOU'D OFFER YOUR HEAD UP IF IT CAME TO THAT, DIDN'T YOU?
HAVE YOU ACCEPTED THAT?
...HUH? OH...
I GUESS I DID.
HOW STRANGE...
WHY AM I OFFERING MY HEAD UP...
LIKE IT'S COMPLETELY NATURAL?

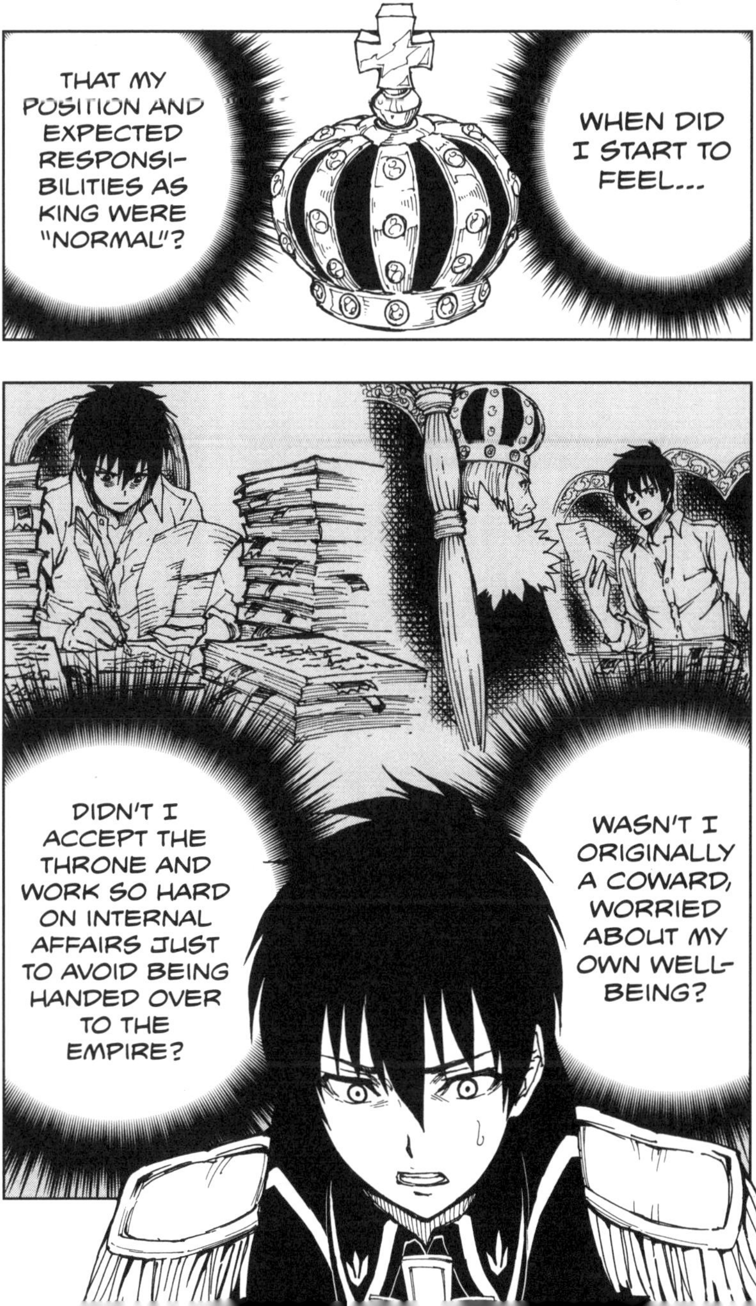
WHEN DID I START TO FEEL...
THAT MY POSITION AND EXPECTED RESPONSI-BILITIES AS KING WERE "NORMAL"?
WASN'T I ORIGINALLY A COWARD, WORRIED ABOUT MY OWN WELL-BEING?
DIDN'T I ACCEPT THE THRONE AND WORK SO HARD ON INTERNAL AFFAIRS JUST TO AVOID BEING HANDED OVER TO THE EMPIRE?

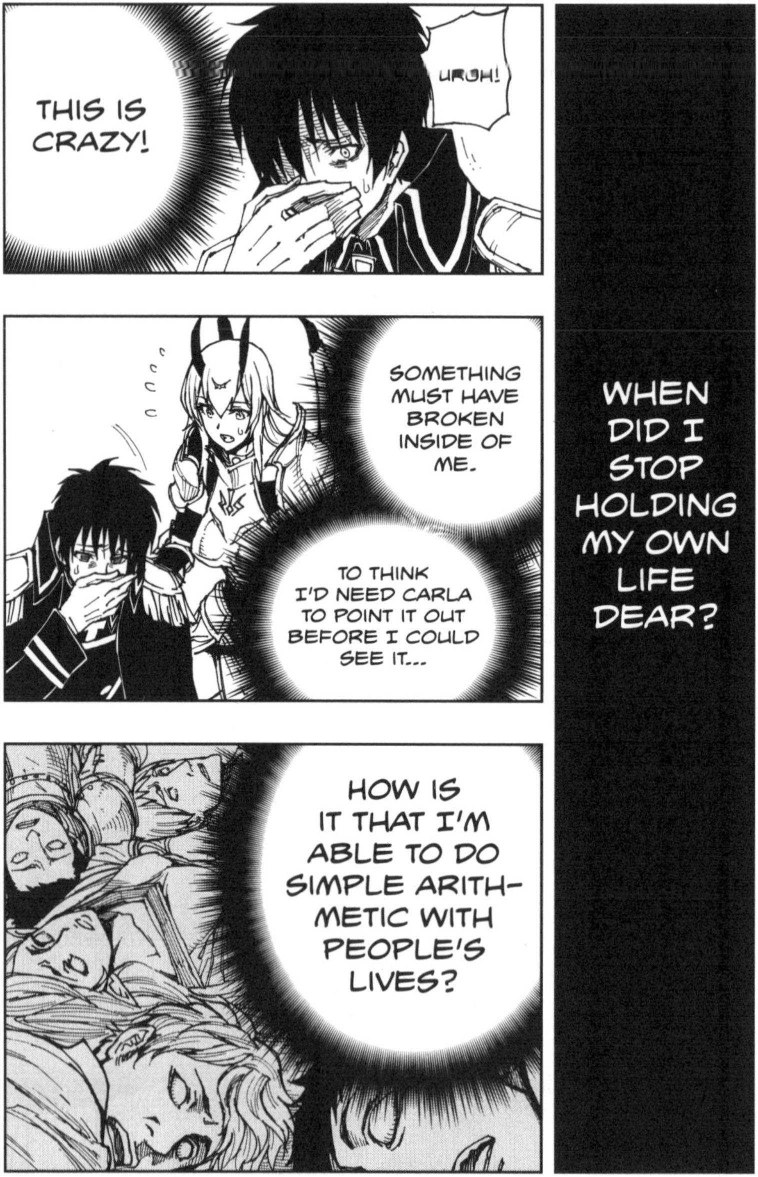
WHEN DID I STOP HOLDING MY OWN LIFE DEAR?
URGH!
THIS IS CRAZY!
SOMETHING MUST HAVE BROKEN INSIDE OF ME.
TO THINK I'D NEED CARLA TO POINT IT OUT BEFORE I COULD SEE IT...
HOW IS IT THAT I'M ABLE TO DO SIMPLE ARITH-METIC WITH PEOPLE'S LIVES?

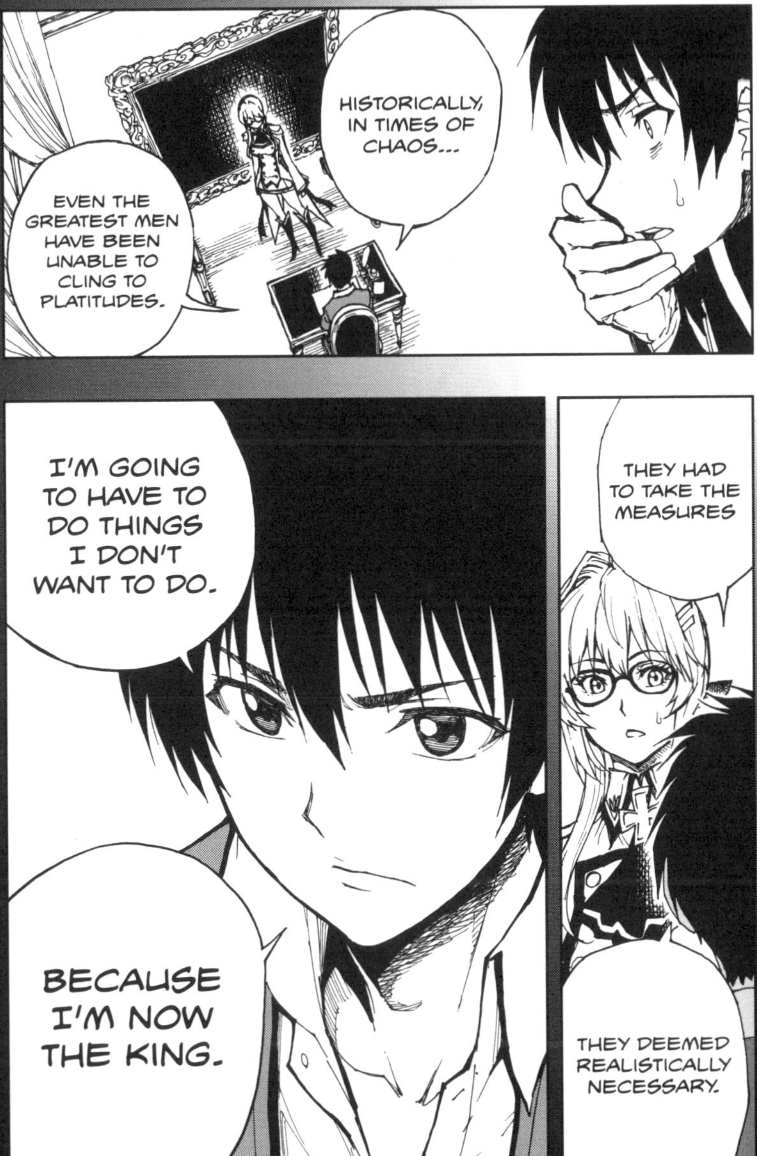
HISTORICALLY, IN TIMES OF CHAOS...
EVEN THE GREATEST MEN HAVE BEEN UNABLE TO CLING TO PLATITUDES.
THEY HAD TO TAKE THE MEASURES
THEY DEEMED REALISTICALLY NECESSARY.
I'M GOING TO HAVE TO DO THINGS I DON'T WANT TO DO.
BECAUSE I'M NOW THE KING.

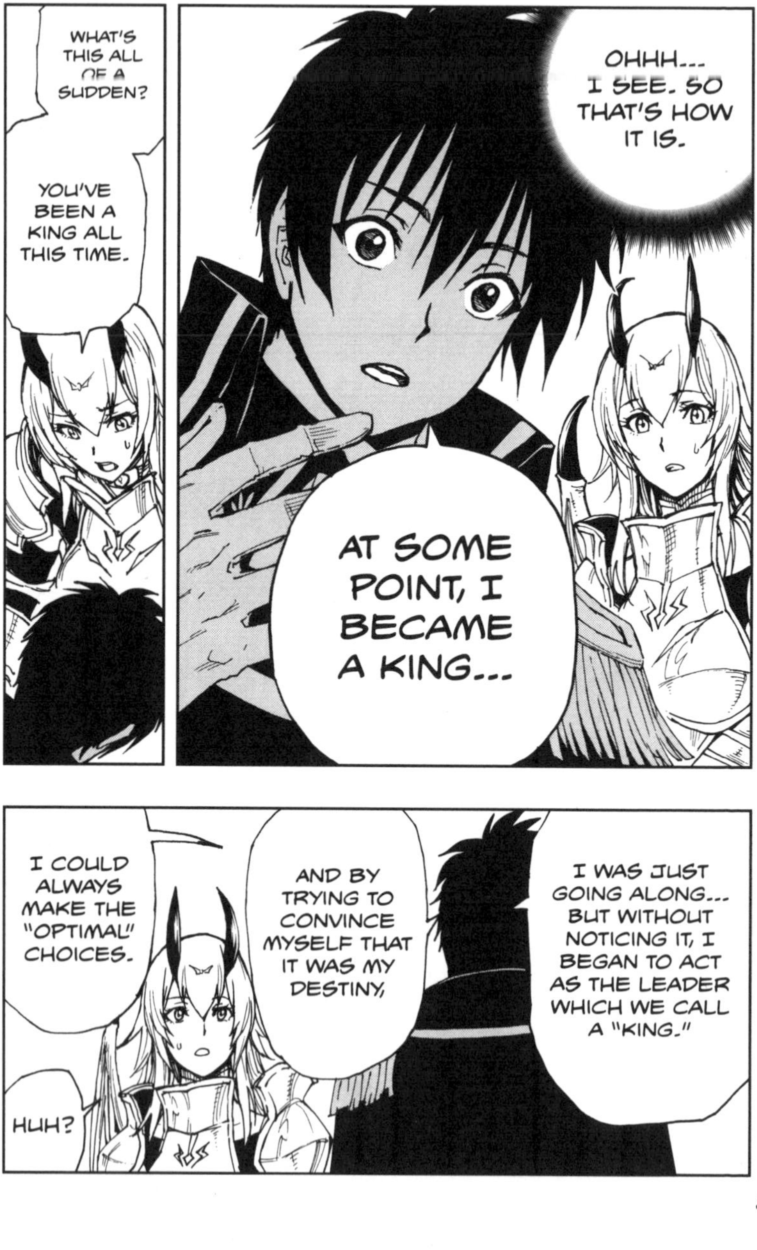
OHHH... I SEE. SO THAT'S HOW IT IS.
AT SOME POINT, I BECAME A KING...
WHAT'S THIS ALL OF A SUDDEN?
YOU'VE BEEN A KING ALL THIS TIME.
I WAS JUST GOING ALONG... BUT WITHOUT NOTICING IT, I BEGAN TO ACT AS THE LEADER WHICH WE CALL A "KING."
AND BY TRYING TO CONVINCE MYSELF THAT IT WAS MY DESTINY,
I COULD ALWAYS MAKE THE "OPTIMAL" CHOICES.
HUH?

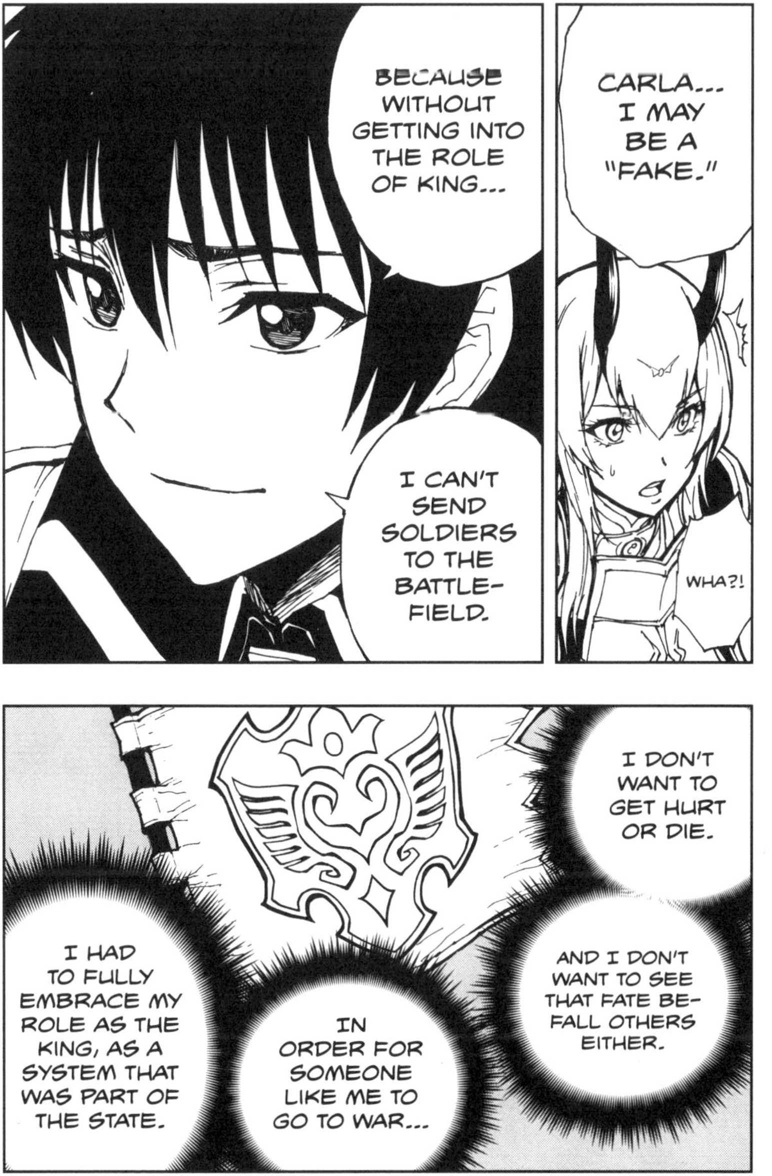
CARLA... I MAY BE A "FAKE."
WHA?!
BECAUSE WITHOUT GETTING INTO THE ROLE OF KING...
I CAN'T SEND SOLDIERS TO THE BATTLE-FIELD.
I DON'T WANT TO GET HURT OR DIE.
AND I DON'T WANT TO SEE THAT FATE BE-FALL OTHERS EITHER.
IN ORDER FOR SOMEONE LIKE ME TO GO TO WAR...
I HAD TO FULLY EMBRACE MY ROLE AS THE KING, AS A SYSTEM THAT WAS PART OF THE STATE.

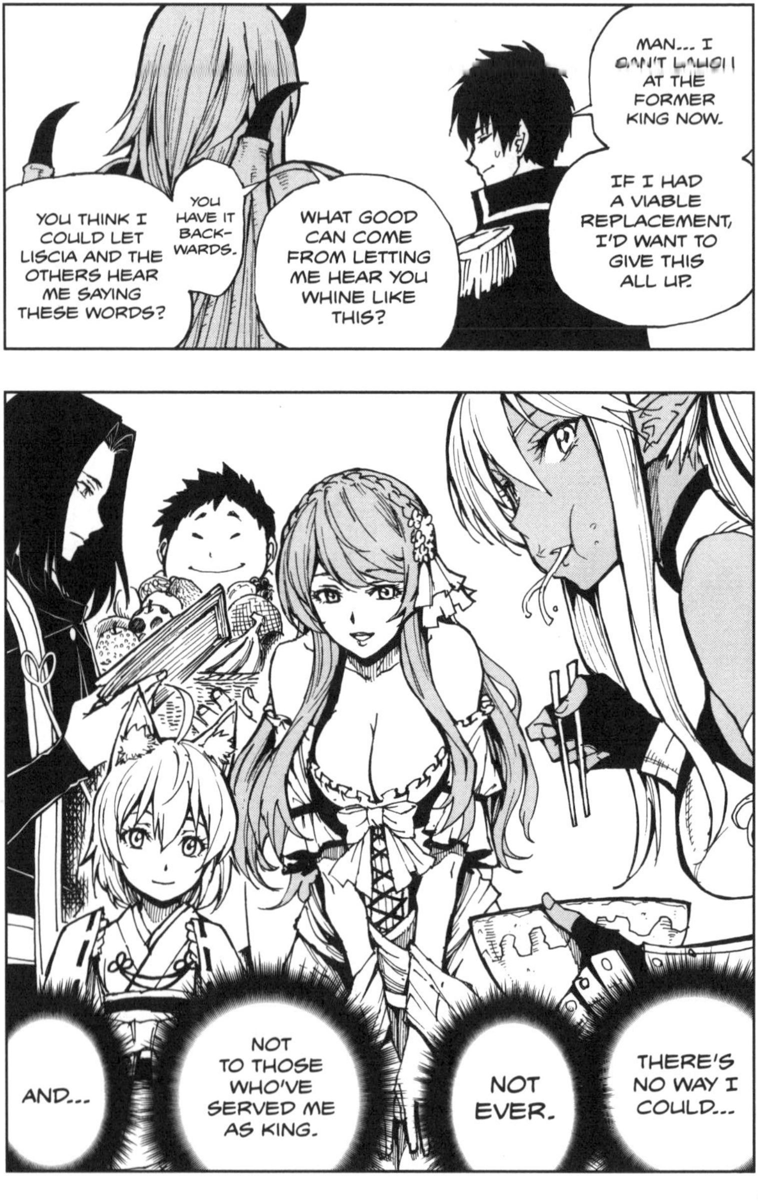
MAN... I CAN'T LAUGH AT THE FORMER KING NOW.
IF I HAD A VIABLE REPLACEMENT, I'D WANT TO GIVE THIS ALL UP.
WHAT GOOD CAN COME FROM LETTING ME HEAR YOU WHINE LIKE THIS?
YOU HAVE IT BACKWARDS.
YOU THINK I COULD LET LISCIA AND THE OTHERS HEAR ME SAYING THESE WORDS?
THERE'S NO WAY I COULD...
NOT EVER.
NOT TO THOSE WHO'VE SERVED ME AS KING.
AND...

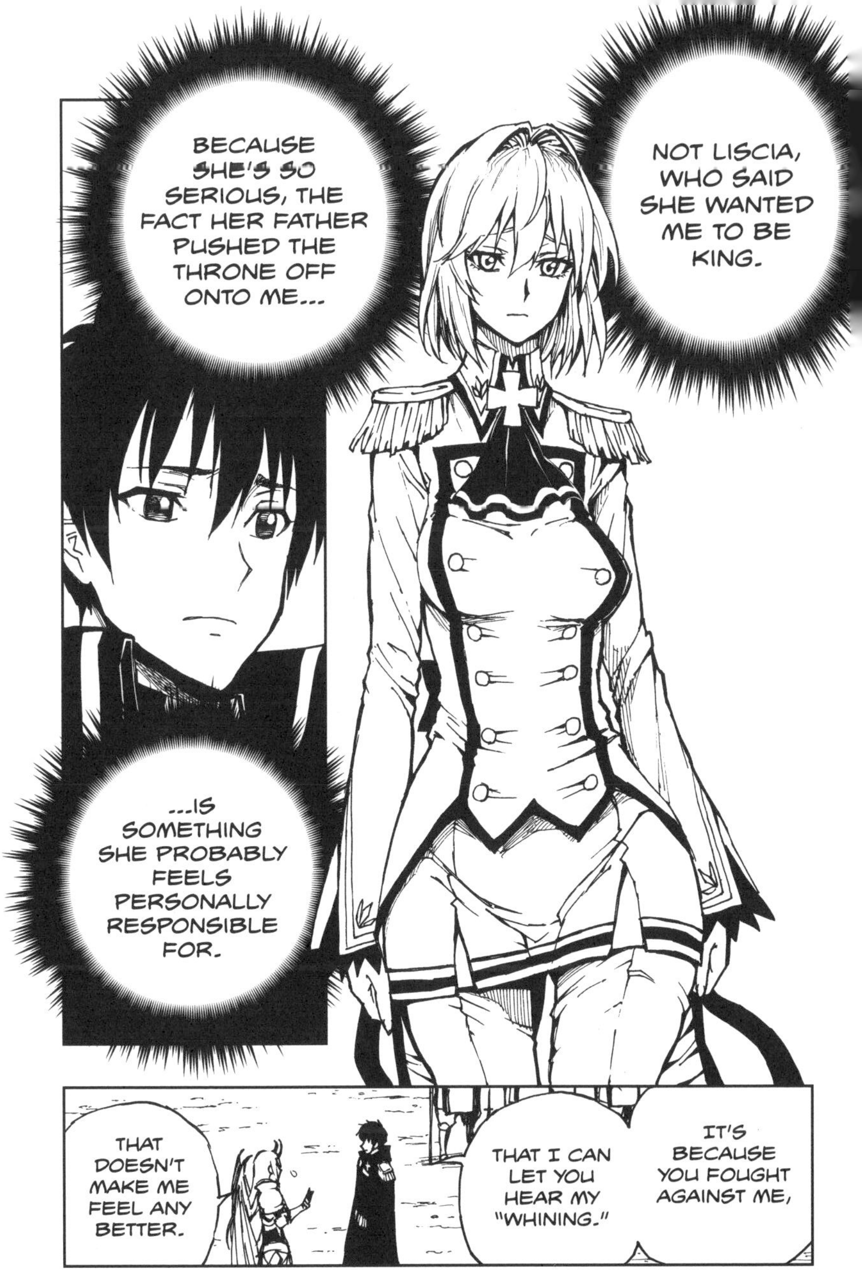
NOT LISCIA, WHO SAID SHE WANTED ME TO BE KING.
BECAUSE SHE'S SO SERIOUS, THE FACT HER FATHER PUSHED THE THRONE OFF ONTO ME...
...IS SOMETHING SHE PROBABLY FEELS PERSONALLY RESPONSIBLE FOR.
IT'S BECAUSE YOU FOUGHT AGAINST ME,
THAT I CAN LET YOU HEAR MY "WHINING."
THAT DOESN'T MAKE ME FEEL ANY BETTER.

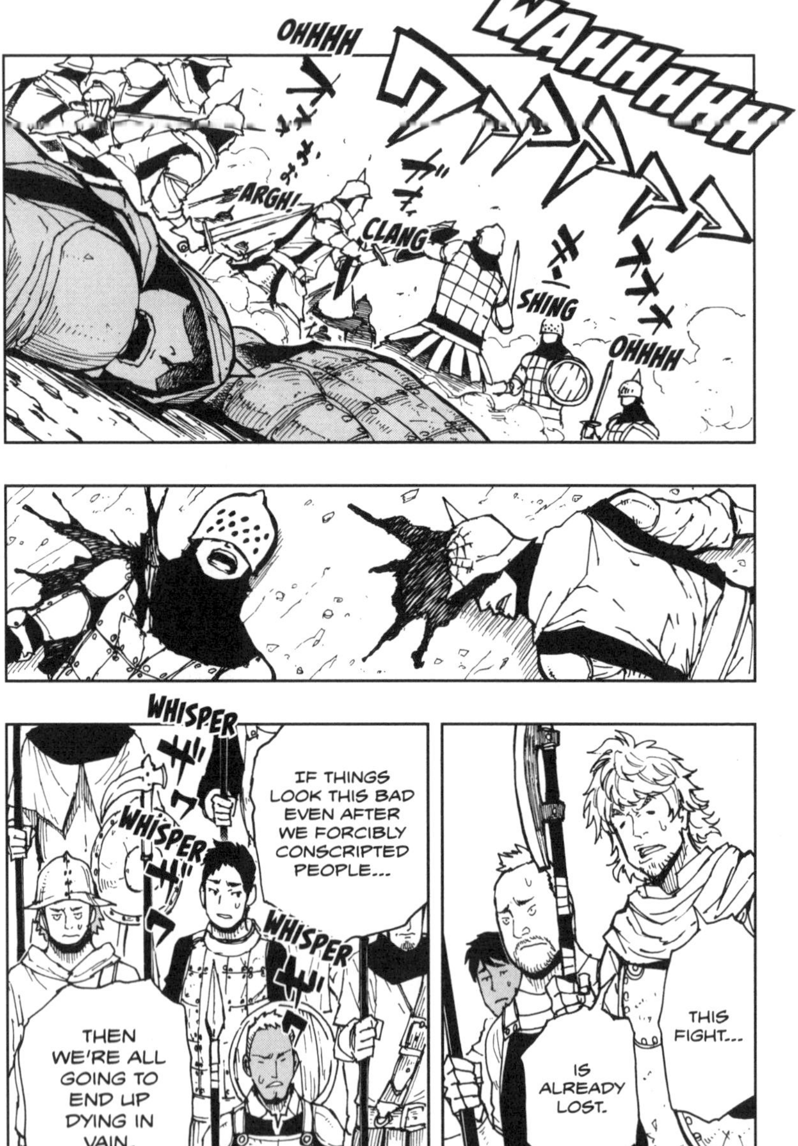
WAHHHHHH
OHHHH
ARGH!
CLANG
SHING
OHHHH
THIS FIGHT...
IS ALREADY LOST.
IF THINGS LOOK THIS BAD EVEN AFTER WE FORCIBLY CONSCRIPTED PEOPLE...
WHISPER
WHISPER
WHISPER
THEN WE'RE ALL GOING TO END UP DYING IN VAIN.

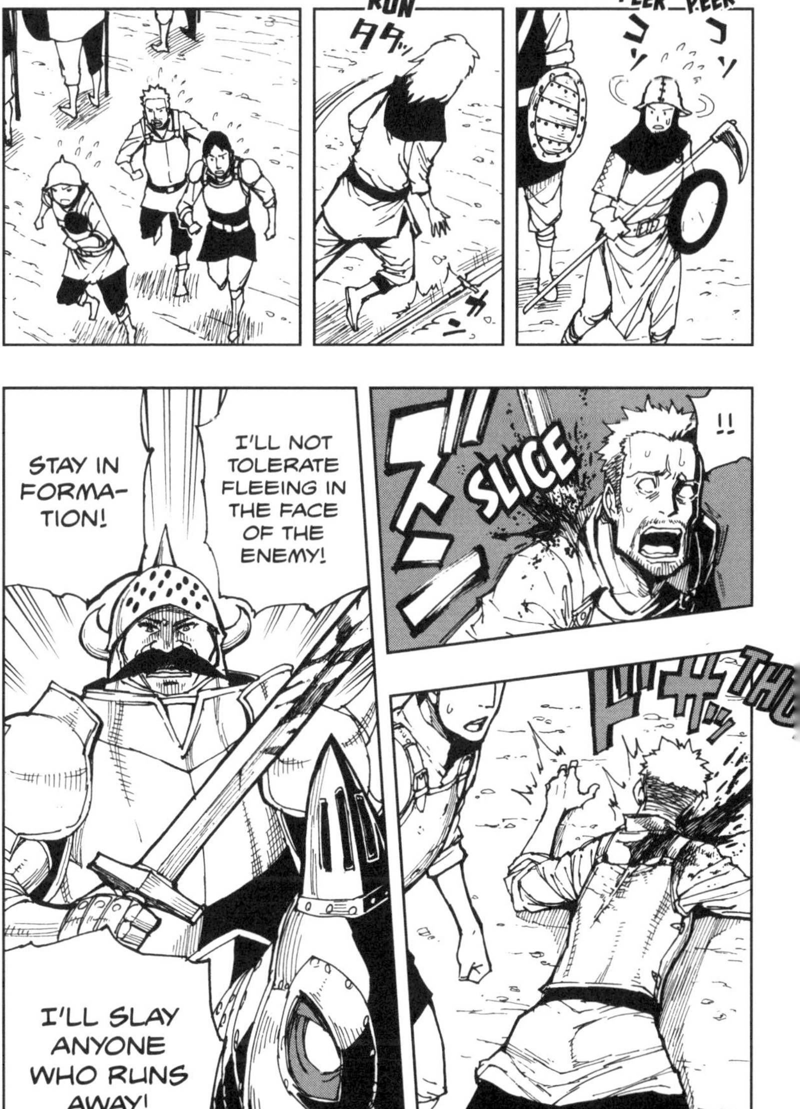
PEEK PEEK
コソ コソ
RUN
タタッ
!!
SLICE
THU
STAY IN FORMATION!
I'LL NOT TOLERATE FLEEING IN THE FACE OF THE ENEMY!
I'LL SLAY ANYONE WHO RUNS AWAY!

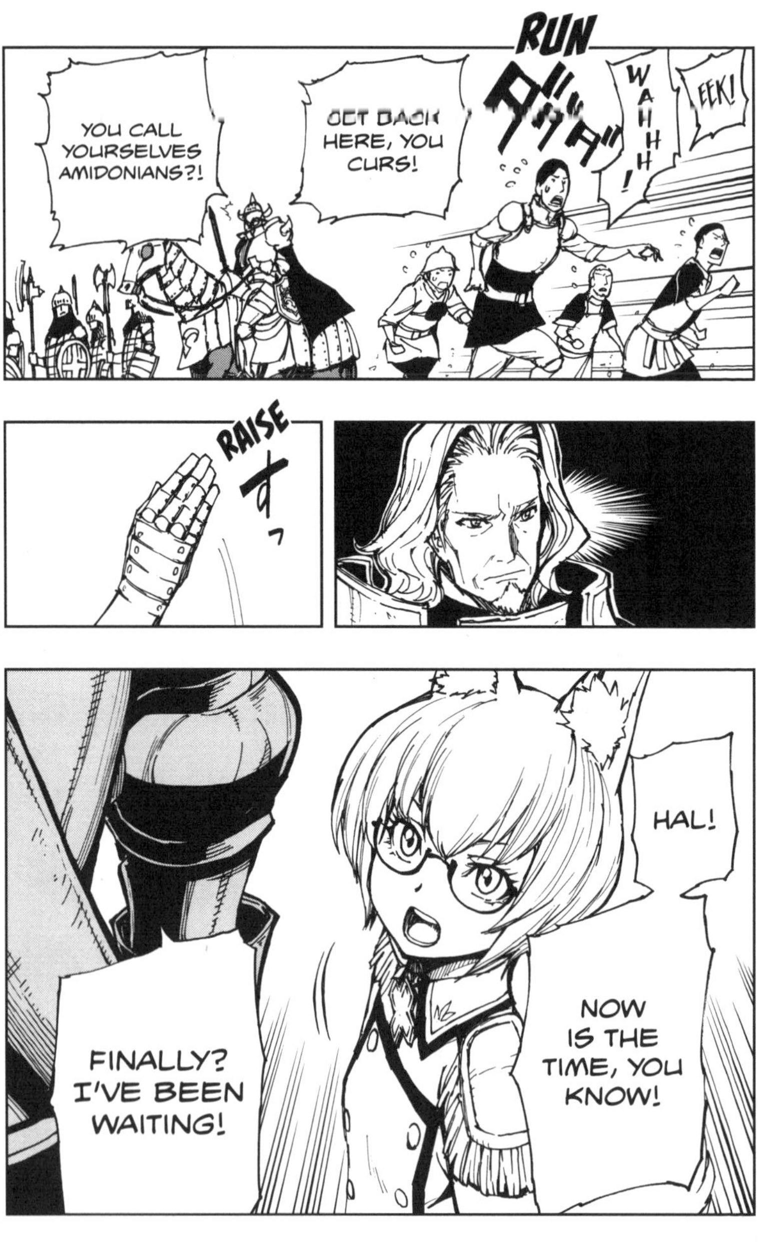
EEK!
WAHHH!
RUN
GET BACK HERE, YOU CURS!
YOU CALL YOURSELVES AMIDONIANS?!
RAISE
すっ
HAL!
NOW IS THE TIME, YOU KNOW!
FINALLY? I'VE BEEN WAITING!

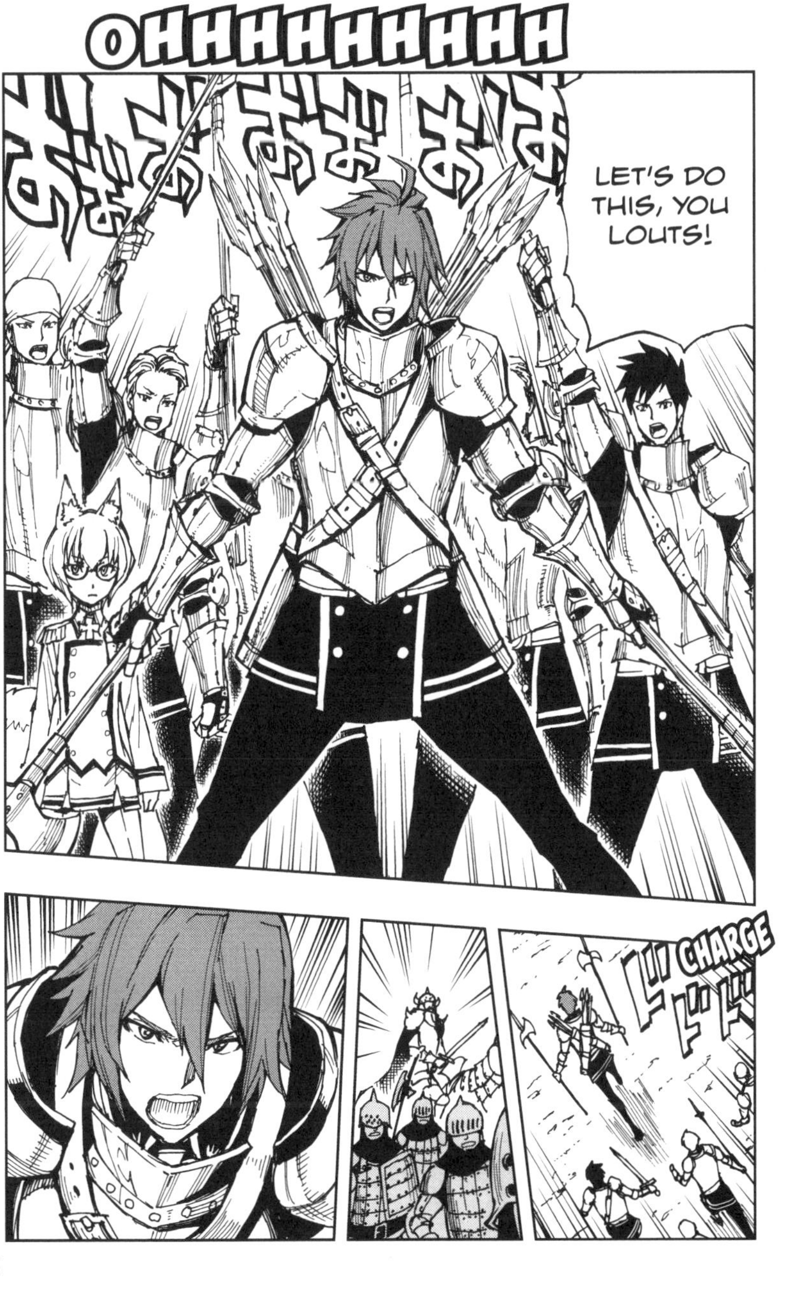
OHHHHHHHHHH
LET'S DO THIS, YOU LOUTS!
CHARGE

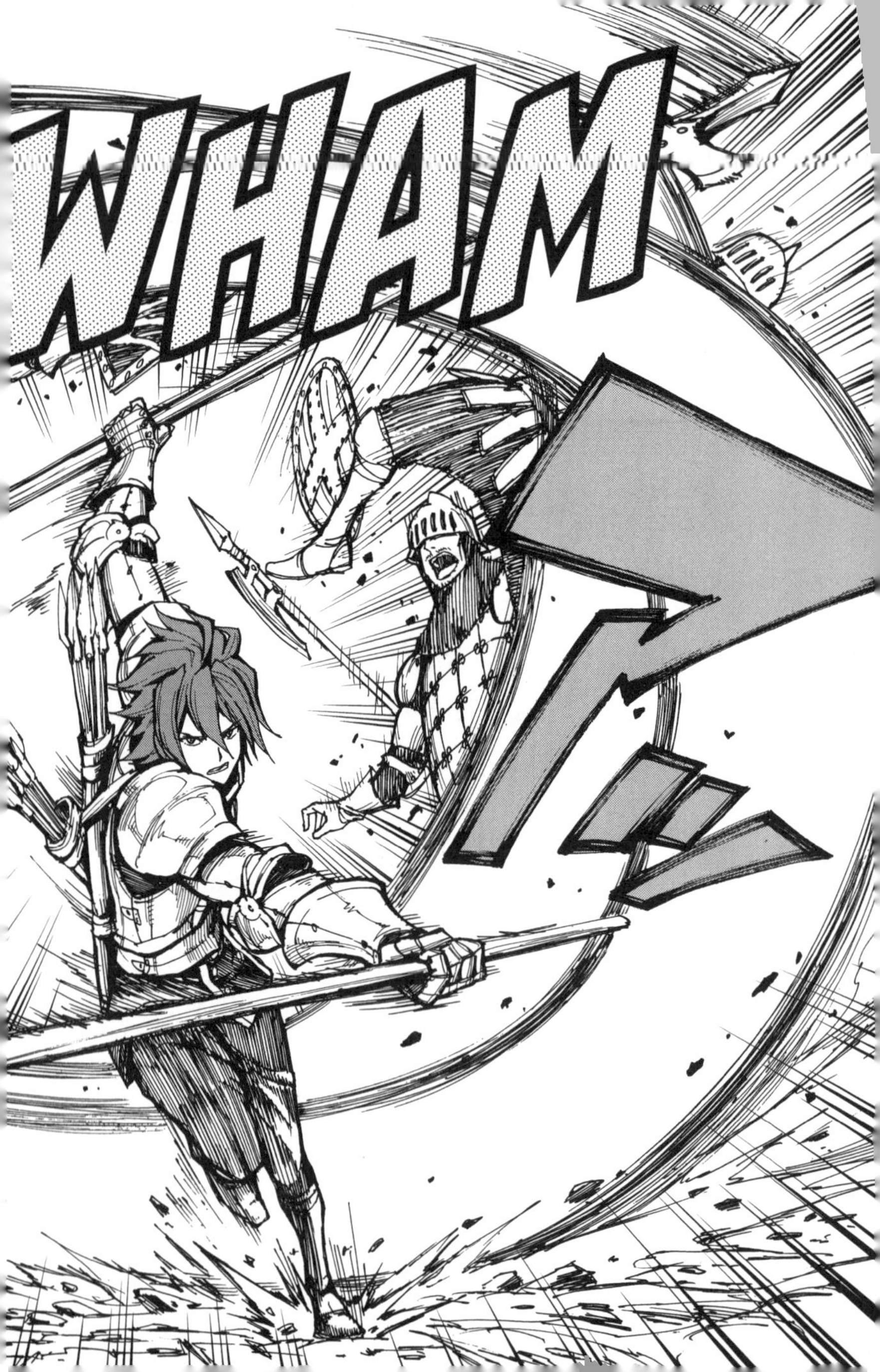
WHAM

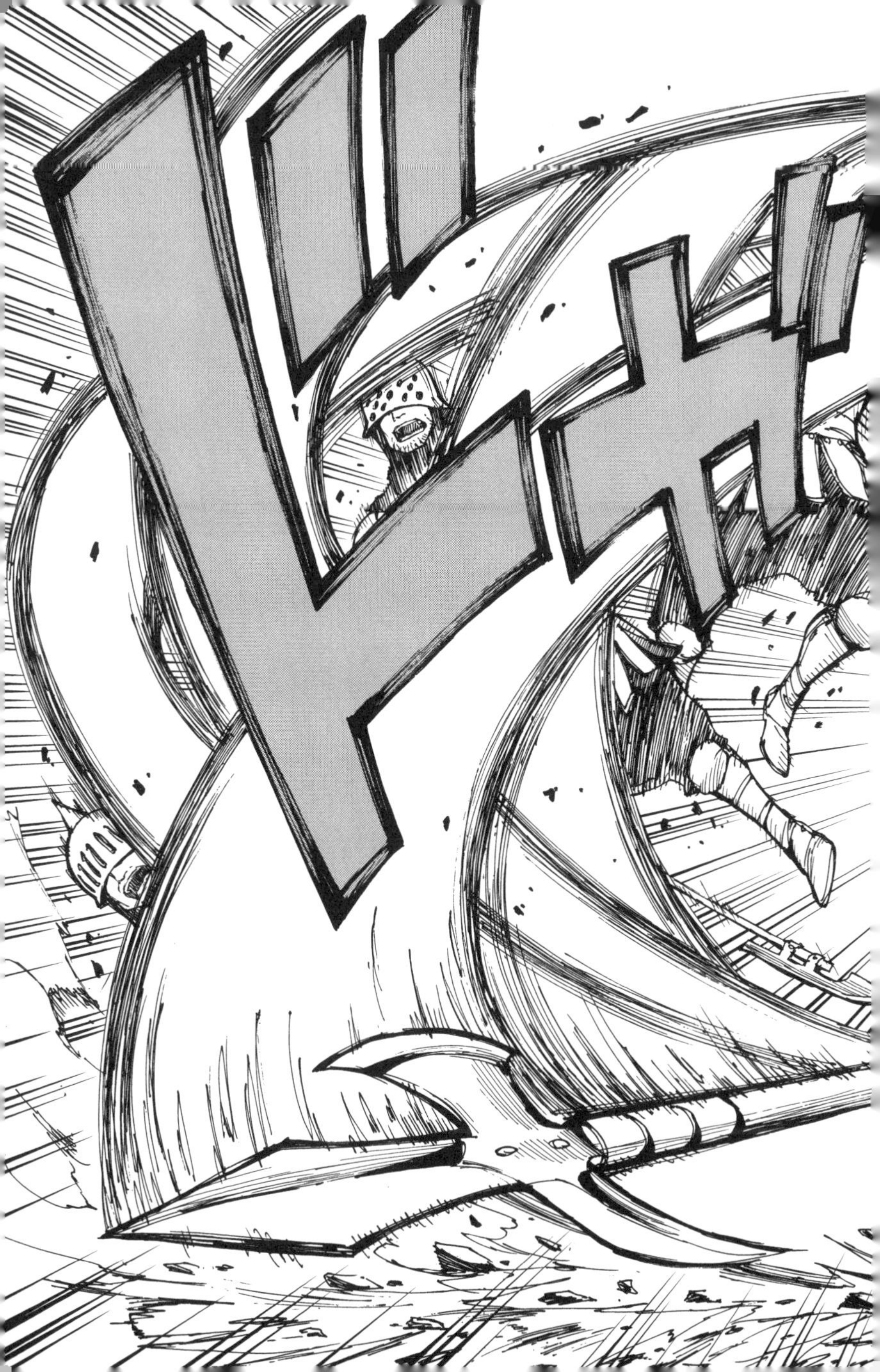
ビ

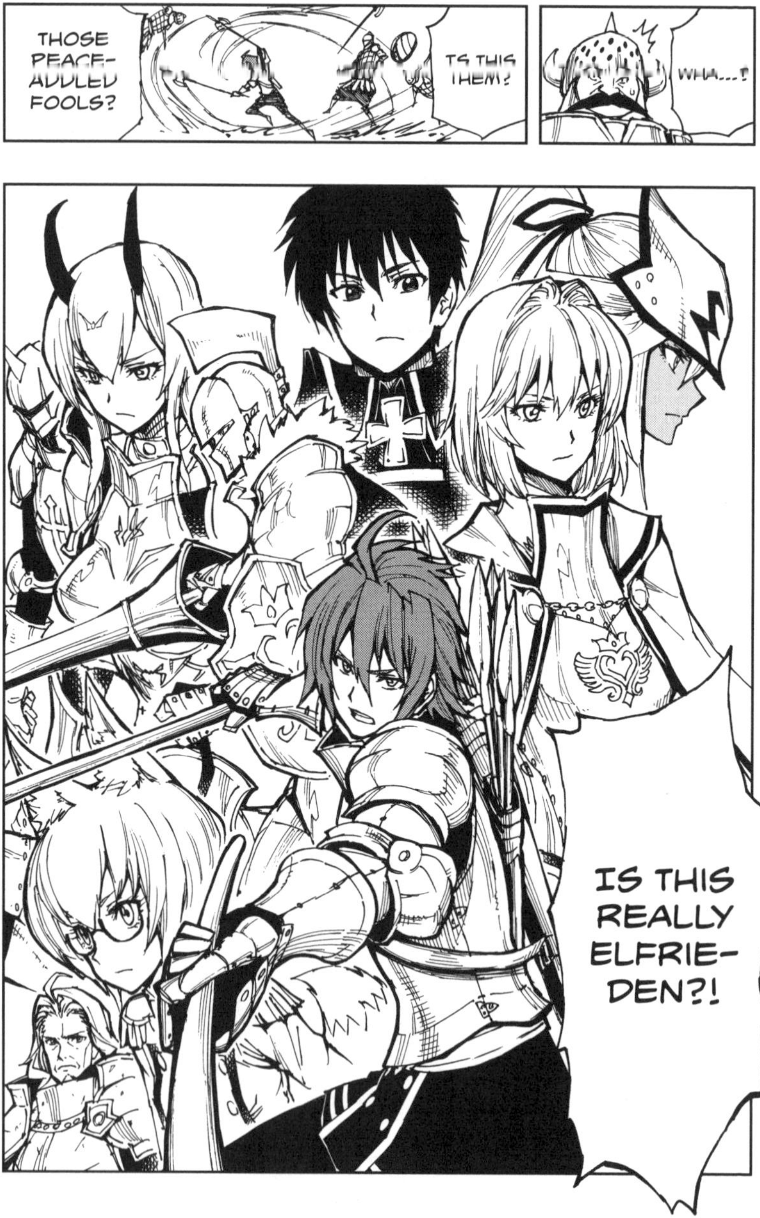
WHA...!
IS THIS THEM?
THOSE PEACE-ADDLED FOOLS?
IS THIS REALLY ELFRIE-DEN?!

Chapter 24: The Final Battle (2)

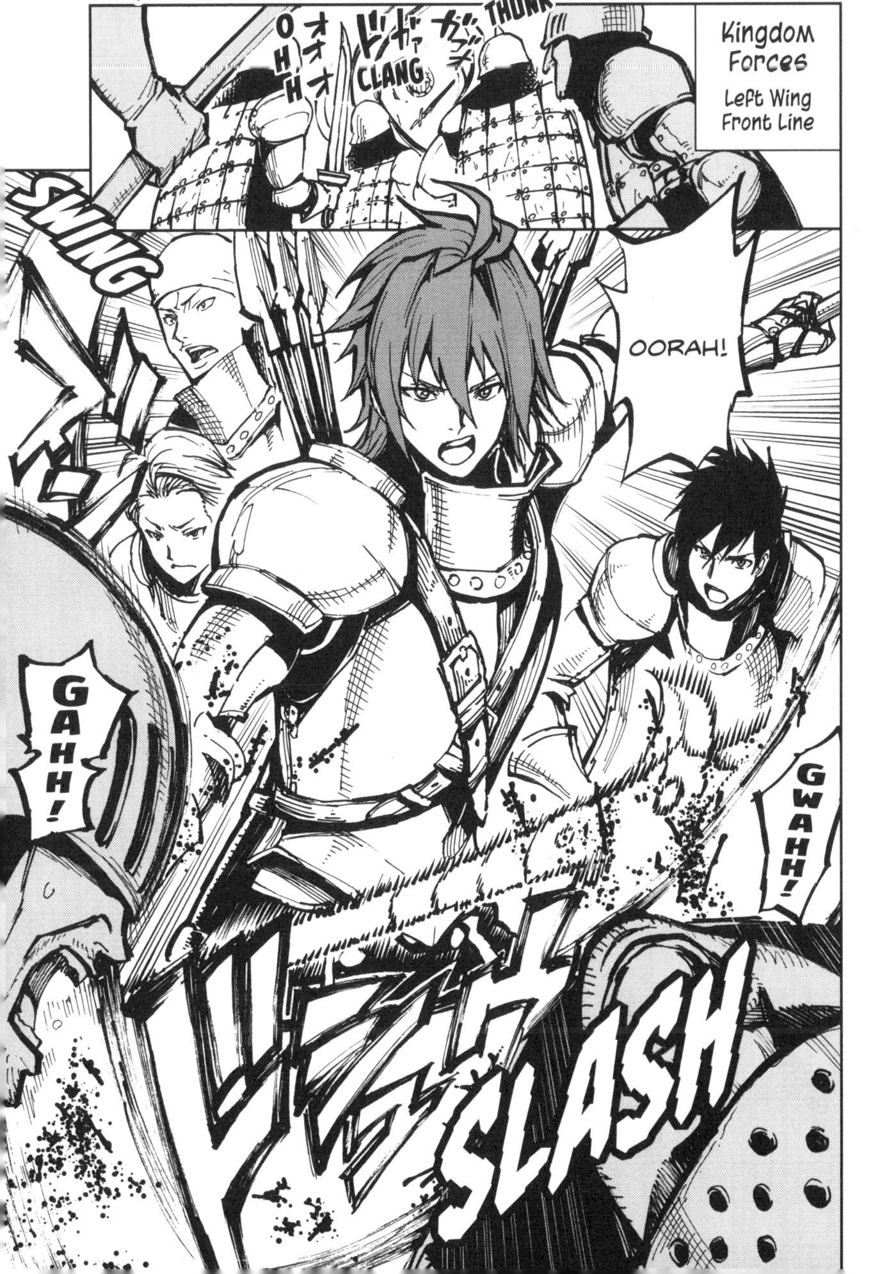
Kingdom Forces
Left Wing Front Line
THUNK
CLANG
OHH
OORAH!
GWAHH!
SLASH
GAHH!
SWING

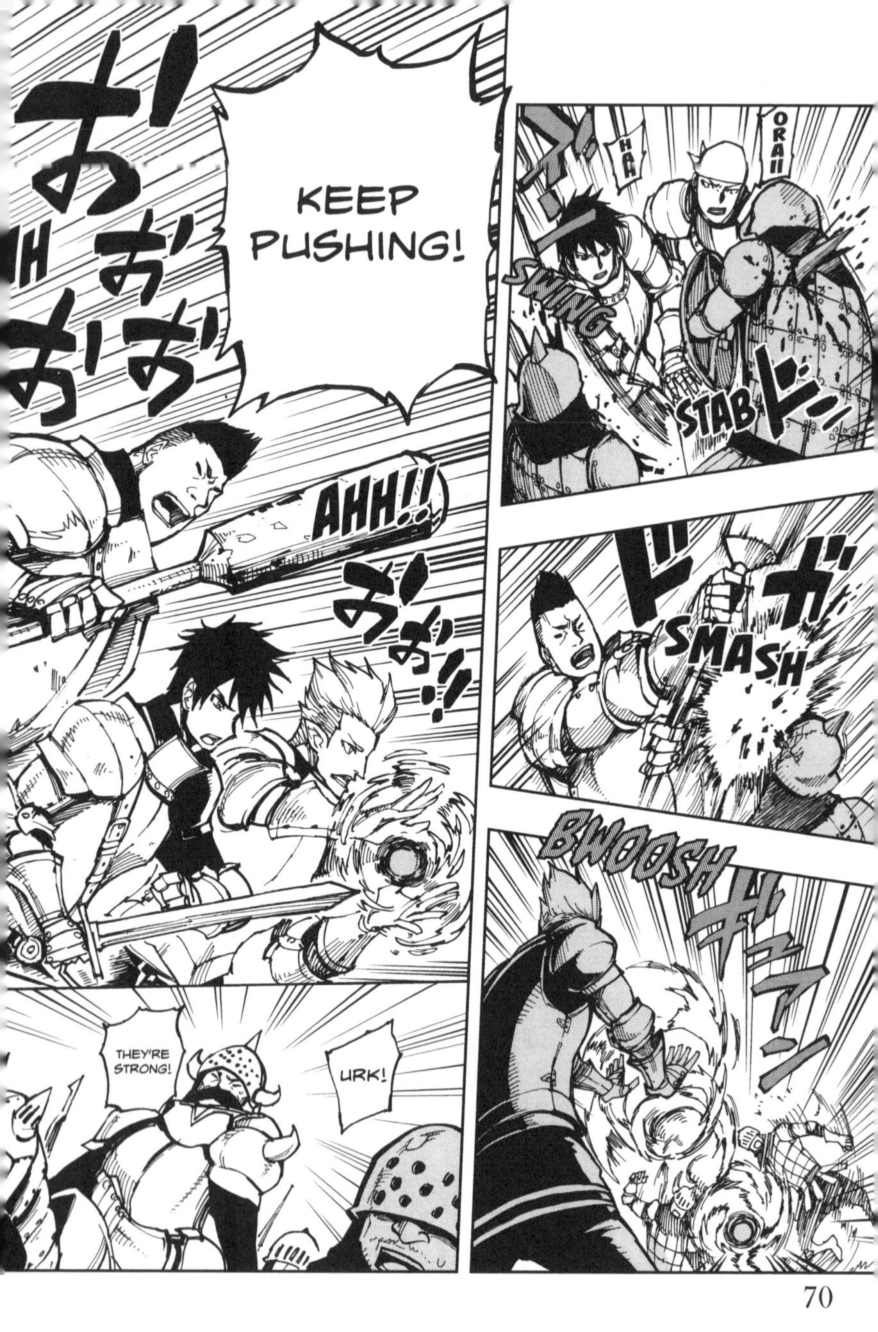
ORA!!
HAA
SWING
STAB
SMASH
BWOOSH
KEEP PUSHING!
AHH!!
URK!
THEY'RE STRONG!

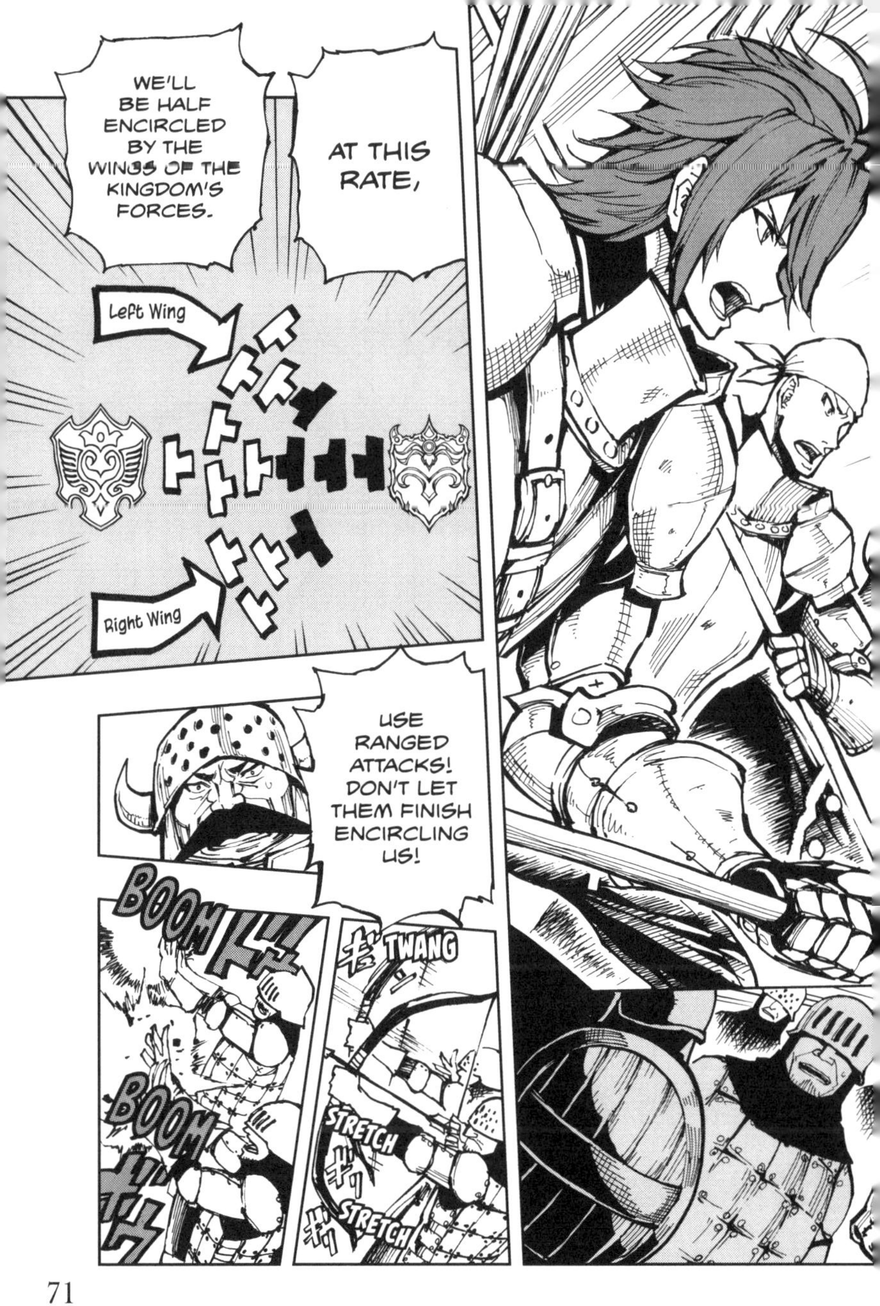
AT THIS RATE,
WE'LL BE HALF ENCIRCLED BY THE WINGS OF THE KINGDOM'S FORCES.
Left Wing
Right Wing
USE RANGED ATTACKS! DON'T LET THEM FINISH ENCIRCLING US!
TWANG
STRETCH
STRETCH
BOOM
BOOM

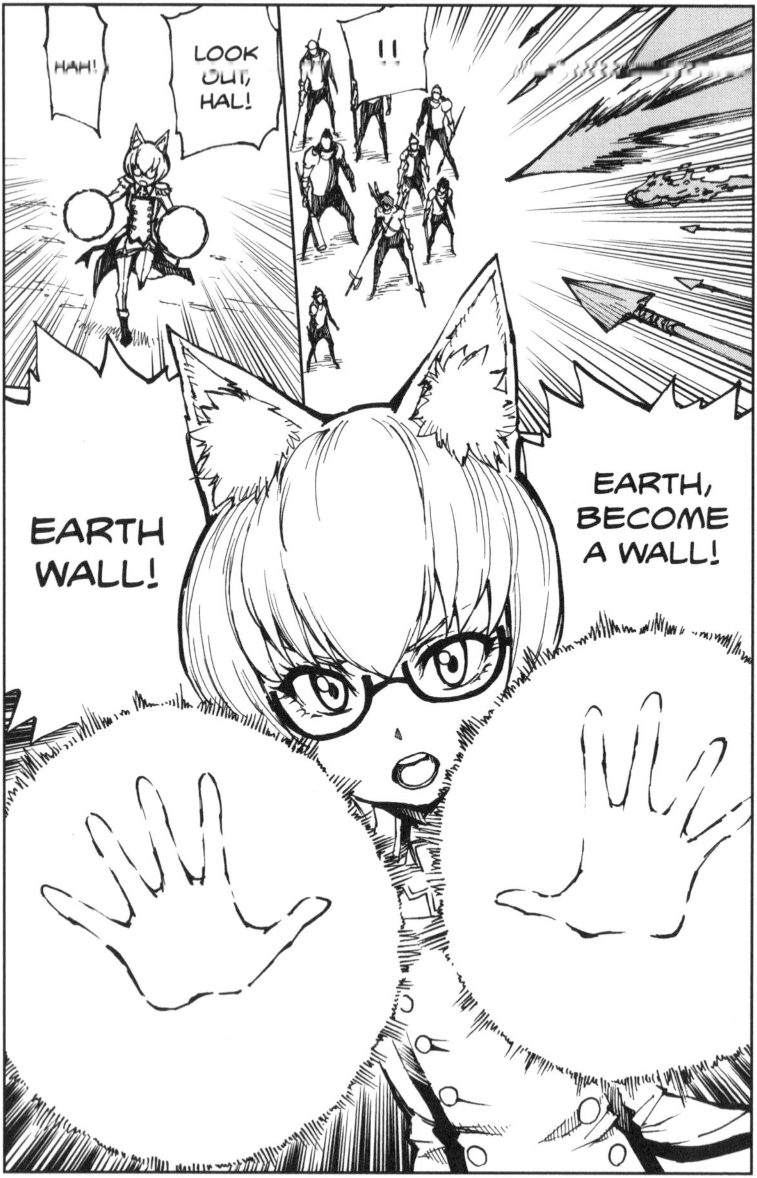
!!
LOOK OUT, HAL!
HAH!
EARTH, BECOME A WALL!
EARTH WALL!

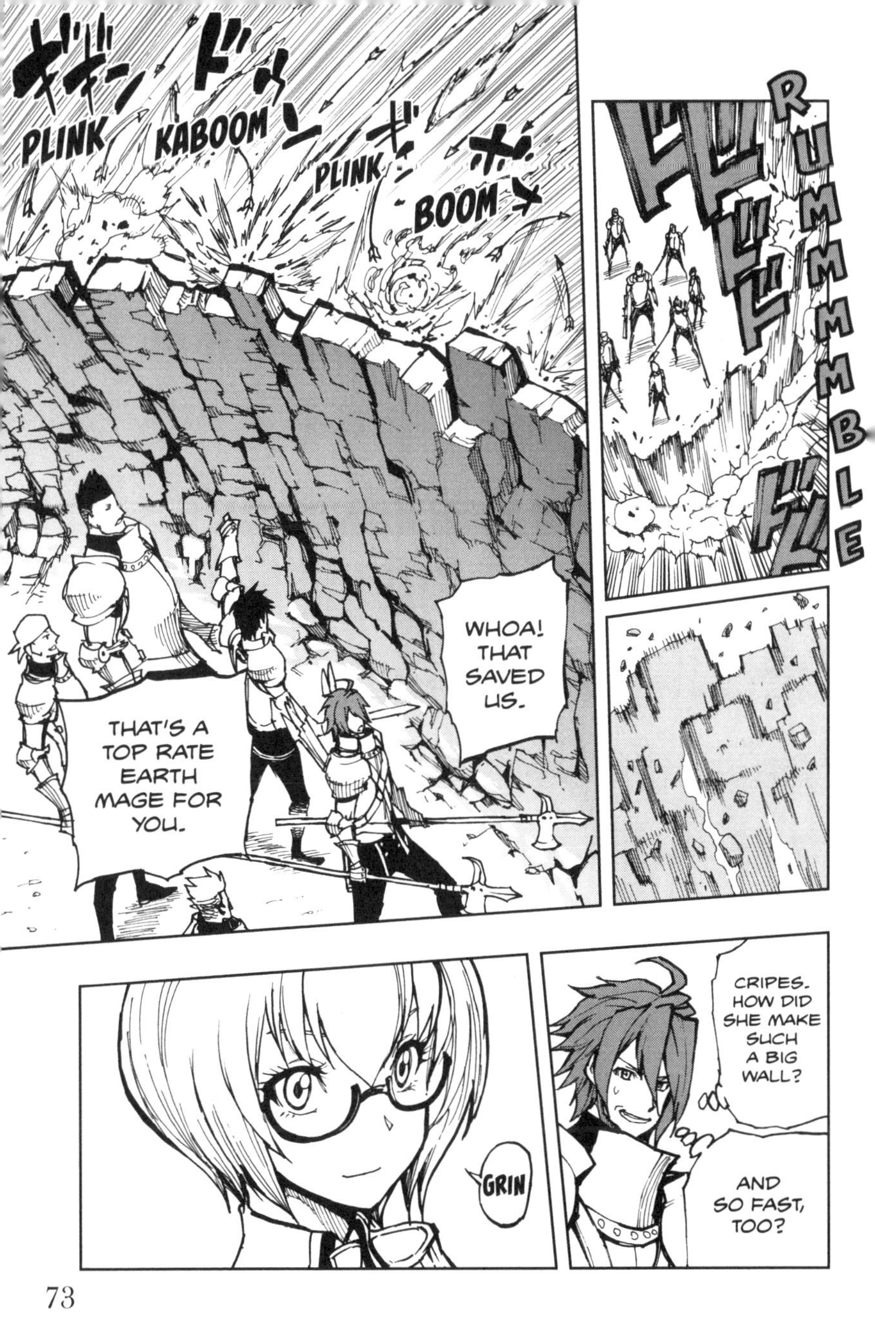
RUMMMMBLE
PLINK
KABOOM
PLINK
BOOM
WHOA! THAT SAVED US.
THAT'S A TOP RATE EARTH MAGE FOR YOU.
CRIPES. HOW DID SHE MAKE SUCH A BIG WALL?
AND SO FAST, TOO?
GRIN

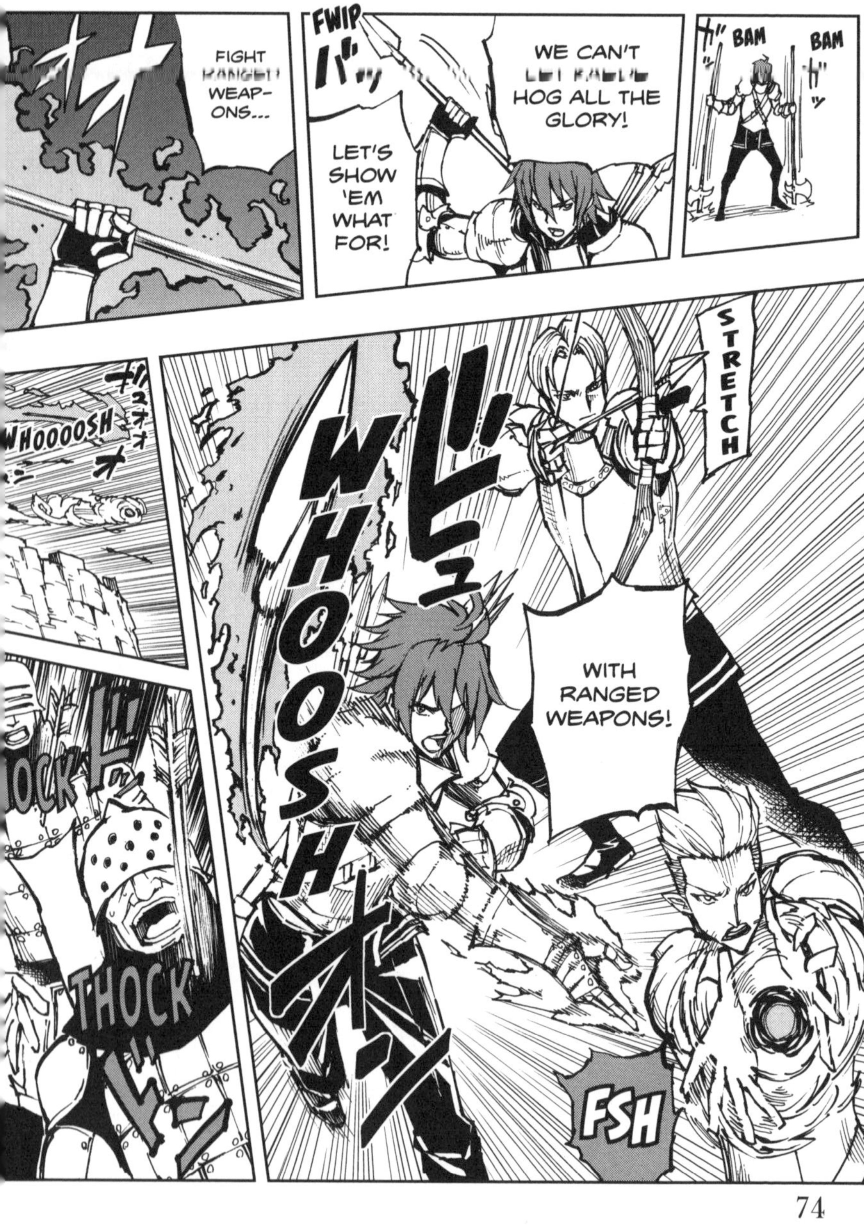
BAM
BAM
WE CAN'T
HOG ALL THE GLORY!
LET'S SHOW 'EM WHAT FOR!
FWIP
FIGHT
WEAP-ONS...
STRETCH
WHOOOSH
WITH RANGED WEAPONS!
FSH
WHOOOOSH
THOCK
THOCK

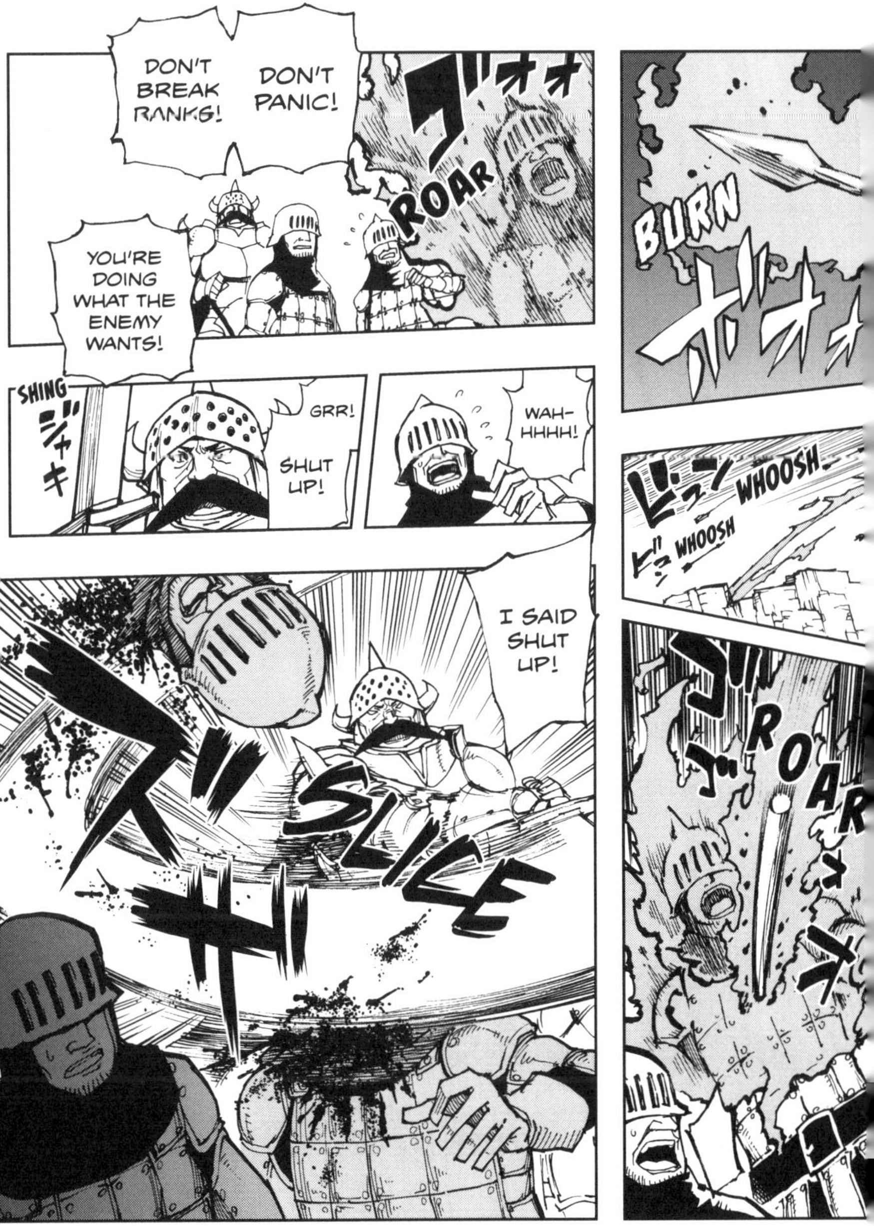
BURN
WHOOSH
WHOOSH
ROAR
DON'T PANIC!
DON'T BREAK RANKS!
ROAR
YOU'RE DOING WHAT THE ENEMY WANTS!
WAH-HHHH!
GRR!
SHUT UP!
SHING
ジャキ
I SAID SHUT UP!
SLICE

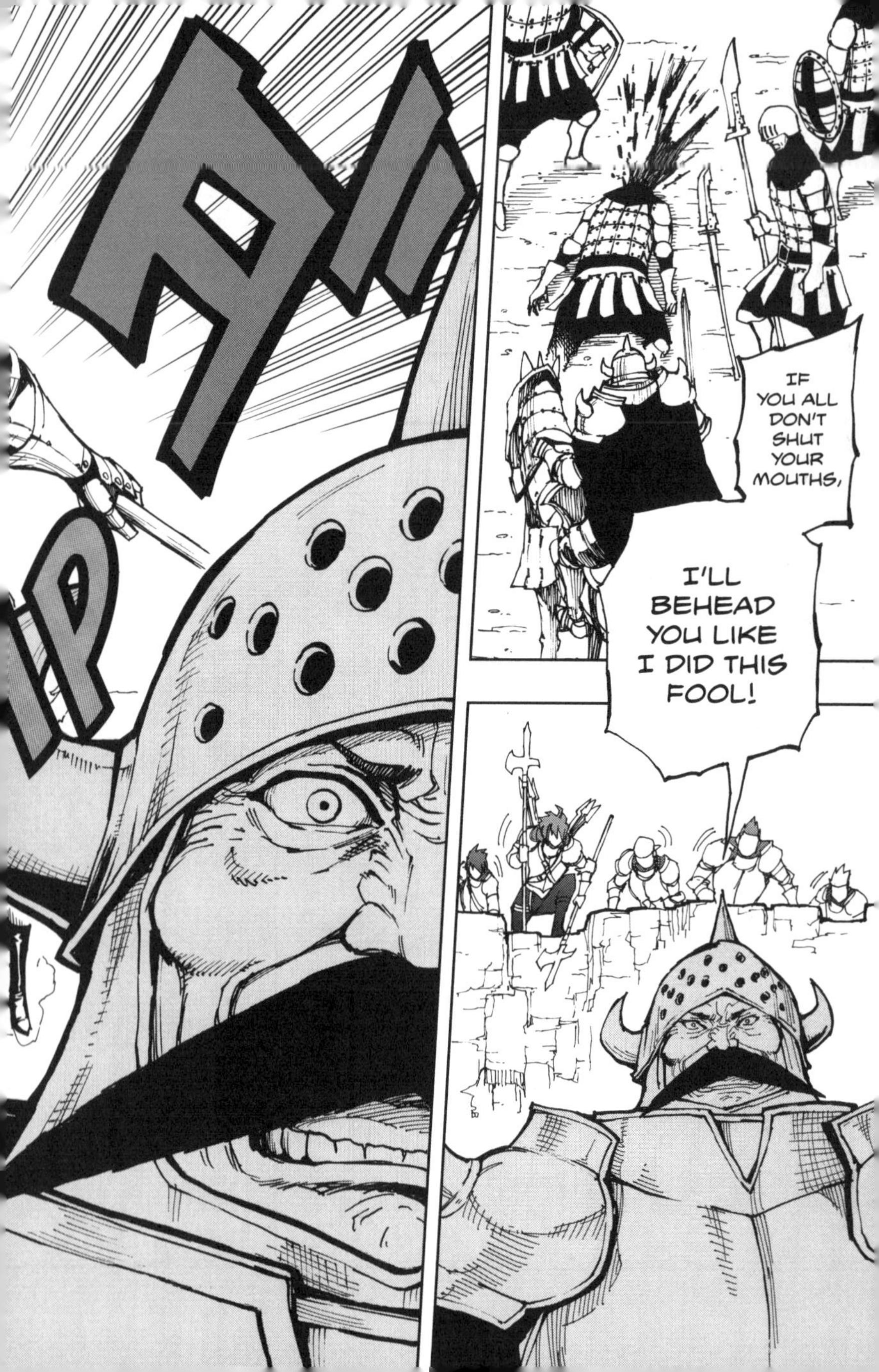
IF YOU ALL DON'T SHUT YOUR MOUTHS,
I'LL BEHEAD YOU LIKE I DID THIS FOOL!

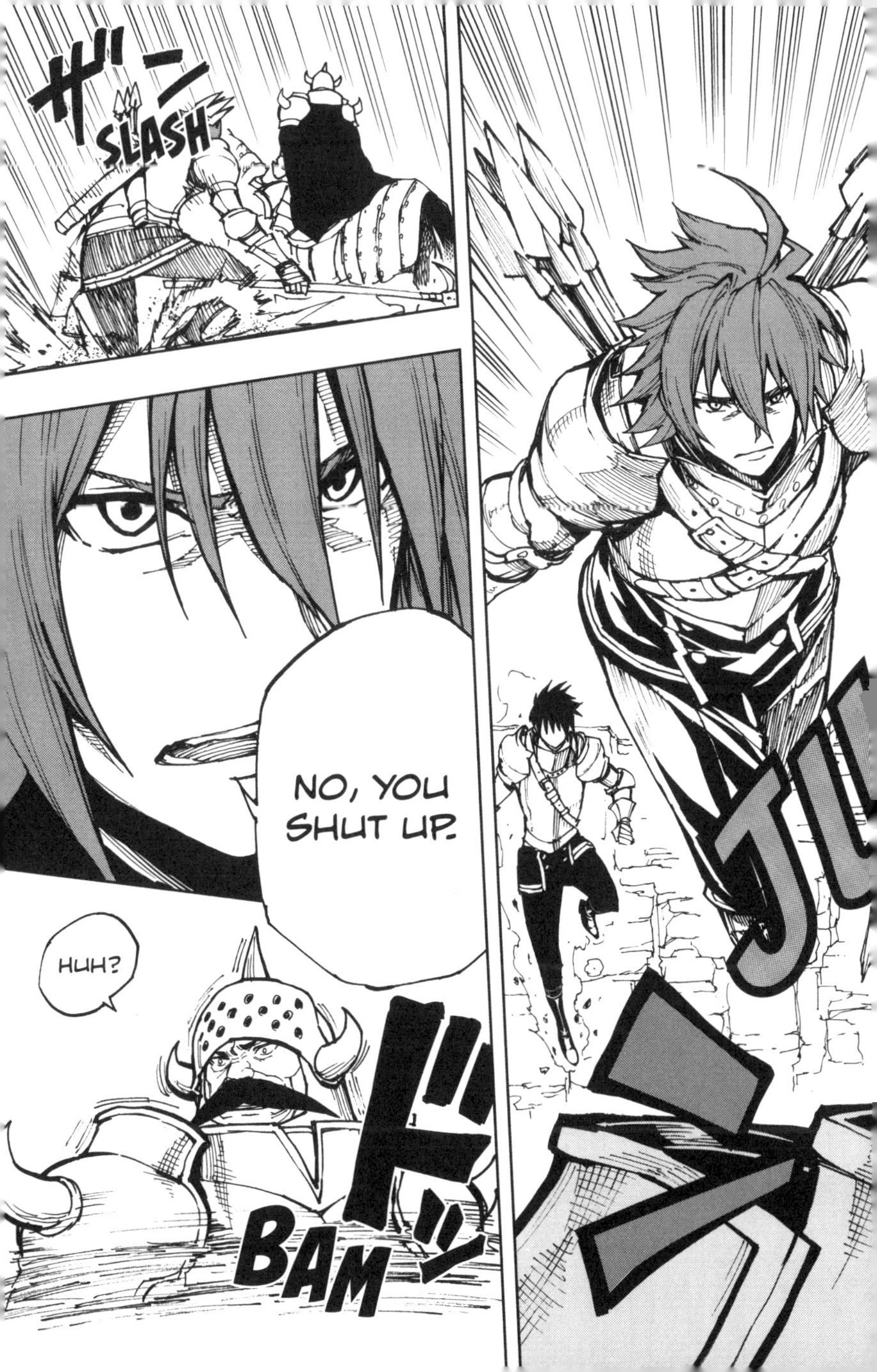
SLASH
NO, YOU SHUT UP.
HUH?
BAM

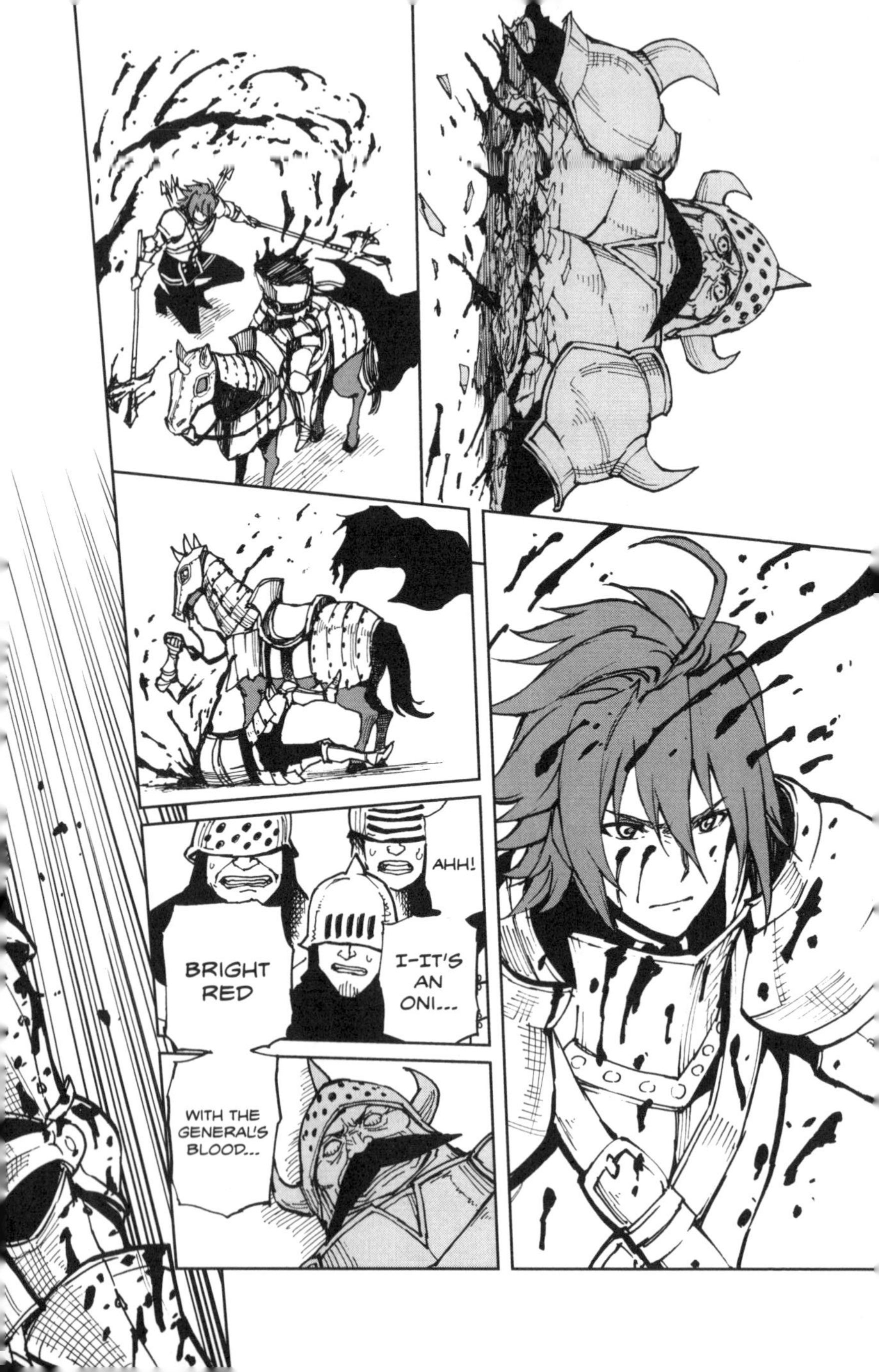
AHH!
I-IT'S AN ONI...
BRIGHT RED
WITH THE GENERAL'S BLOOD...

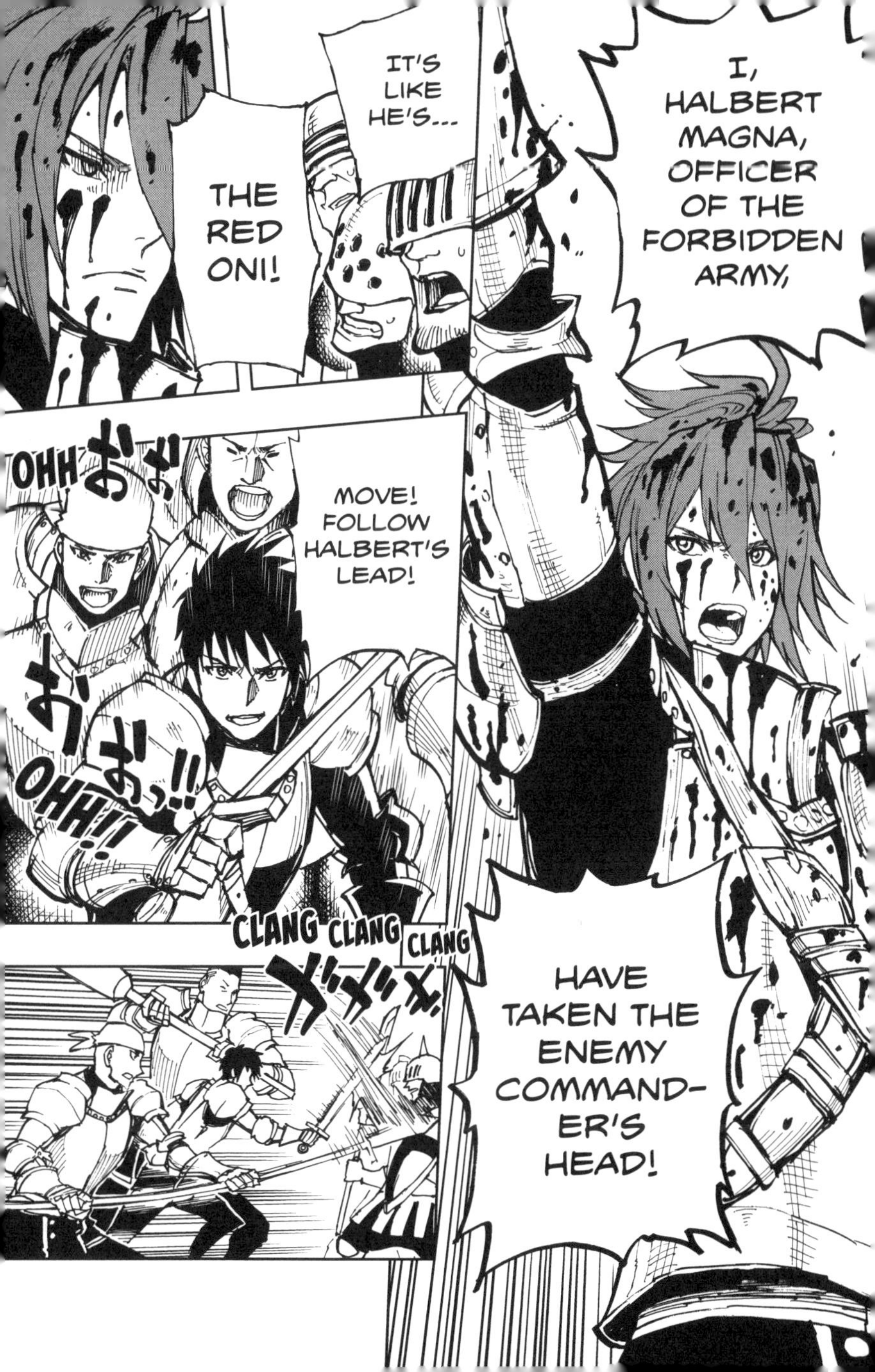

I, HALBERT MAGNA, OFFICER OF THE FORBIDDEN ARMY,
HAVE TAKEN THE ENEMY COMMANDER'S HEAD!
IT'S LIKE HE'S...
THE RED ONI!
MOVE! FOLLOW HALBERT'S LEAD!
OHH おぉ
おぉっ!! OHH!!
CLANG CLANG CLANG

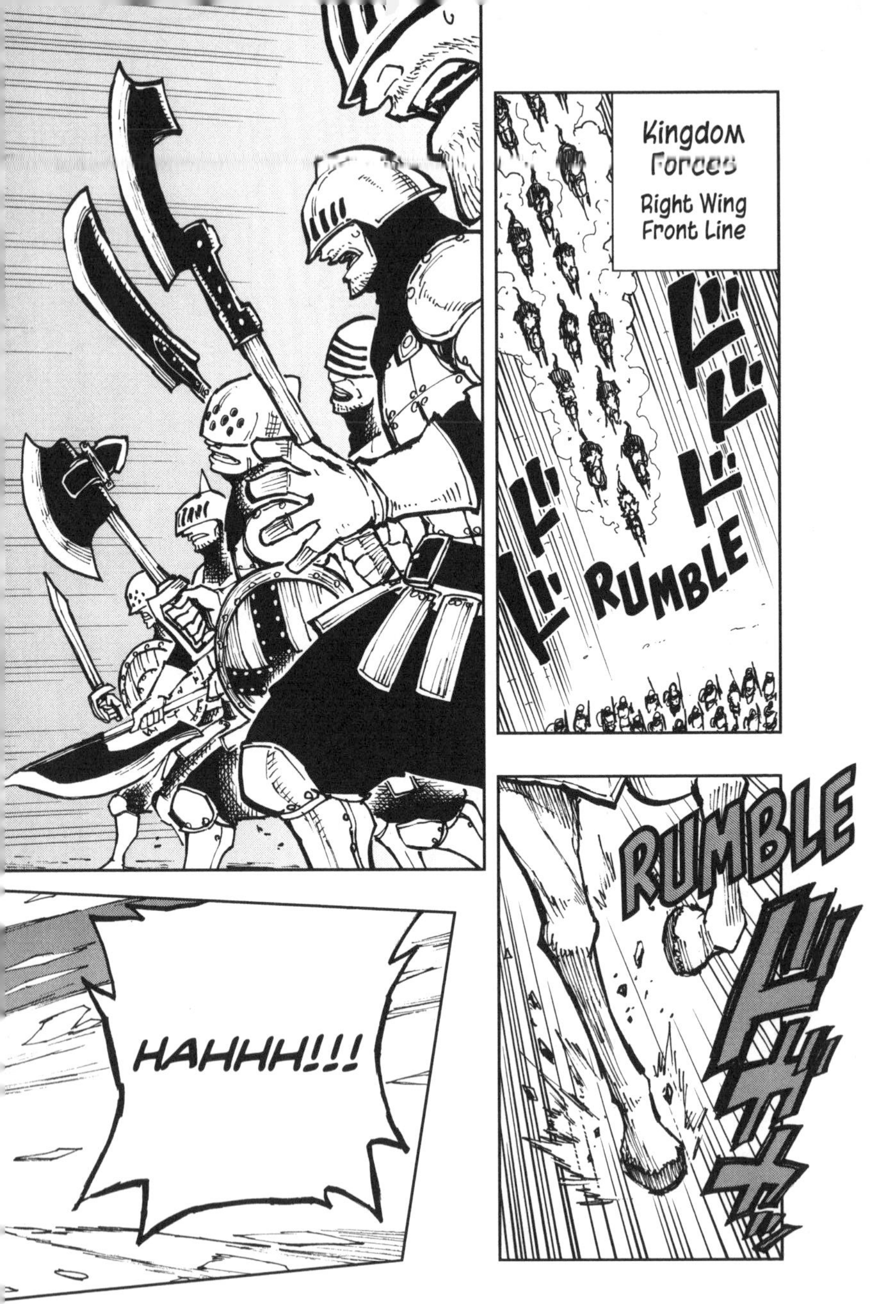
Kingdom Forces
Right Wing Front Line
RUMBLE
RUMBLE
HAHHH!!!

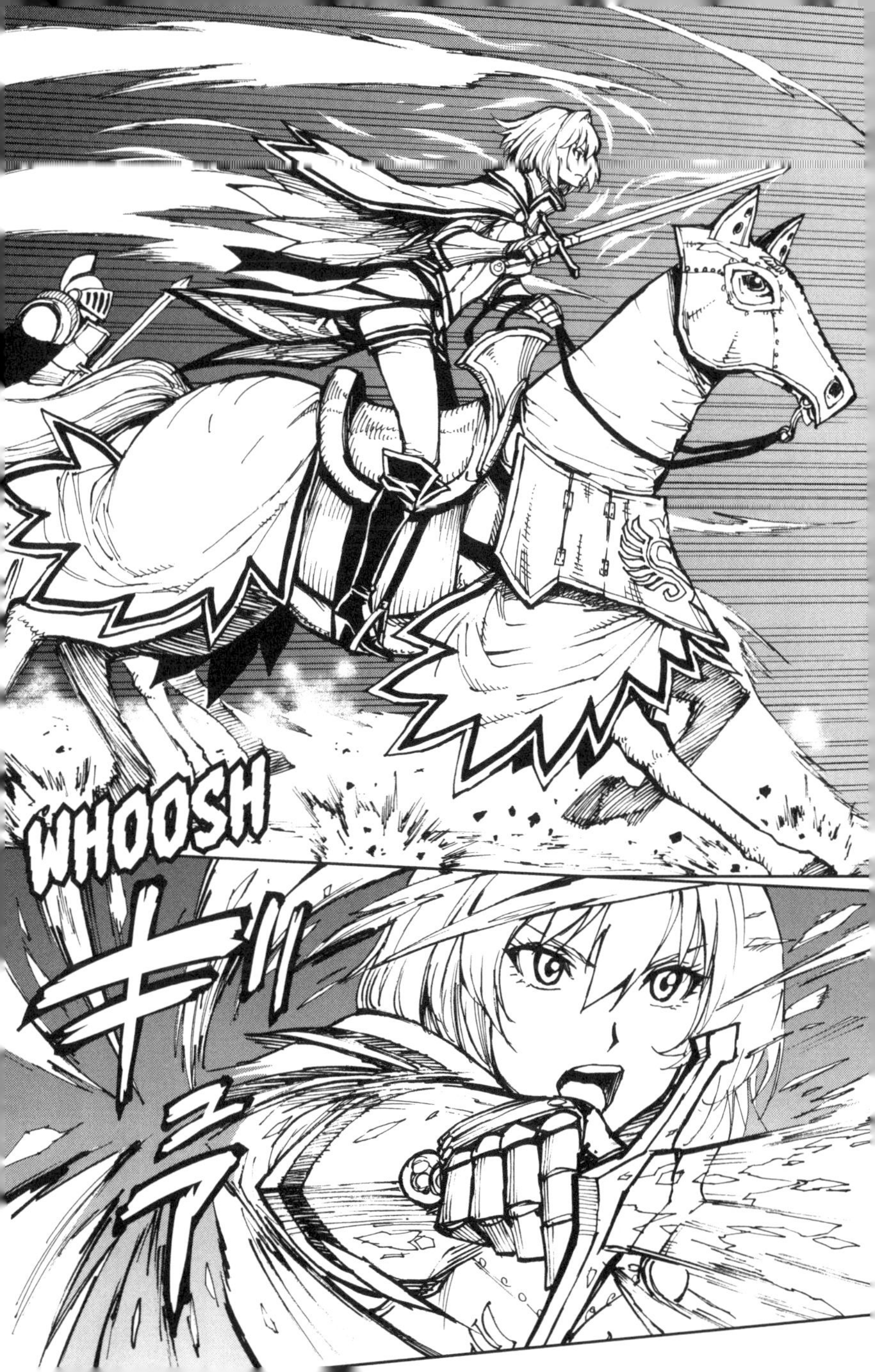
WHOOSH

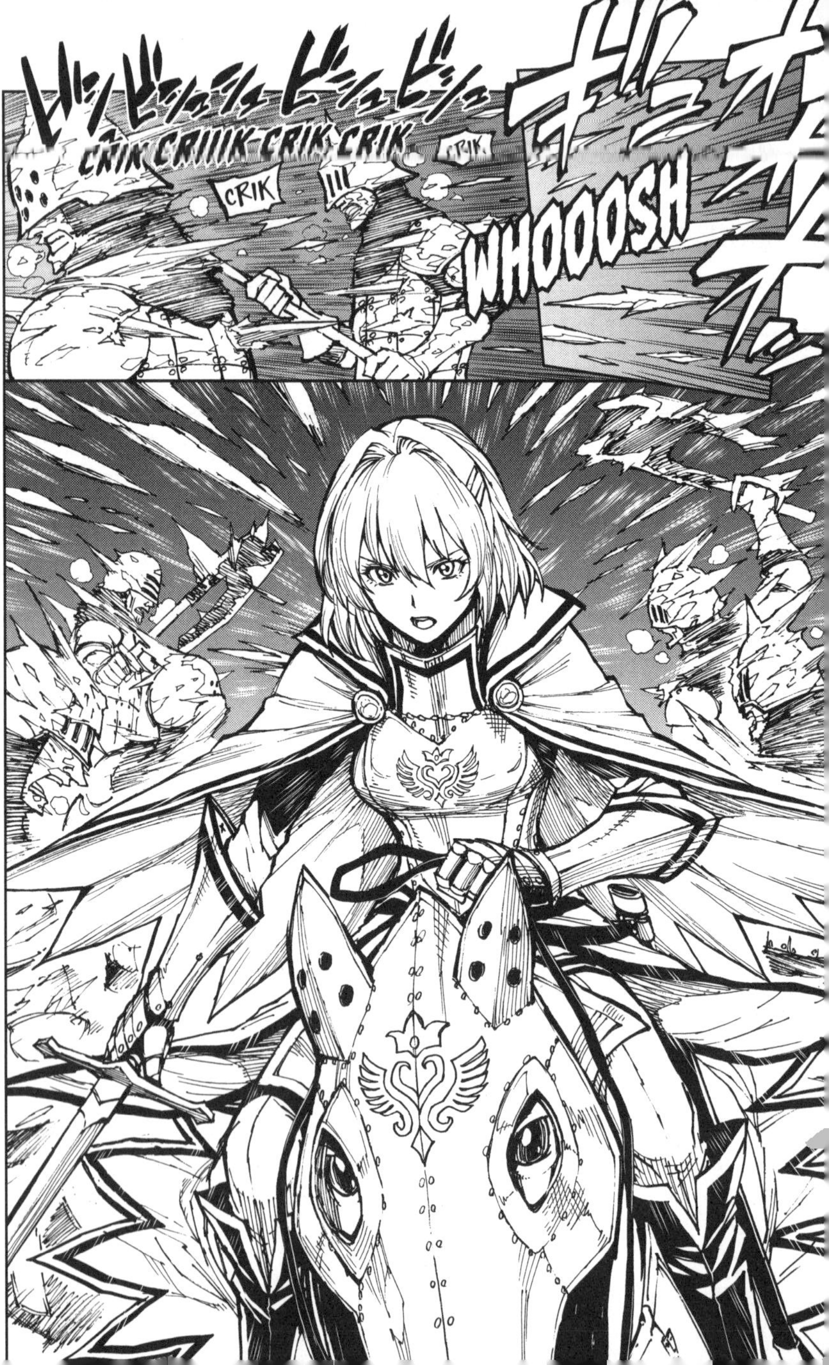
WHOOOSH
CRIK
CRIK CRIIIK CRIK CRIK
CRIK

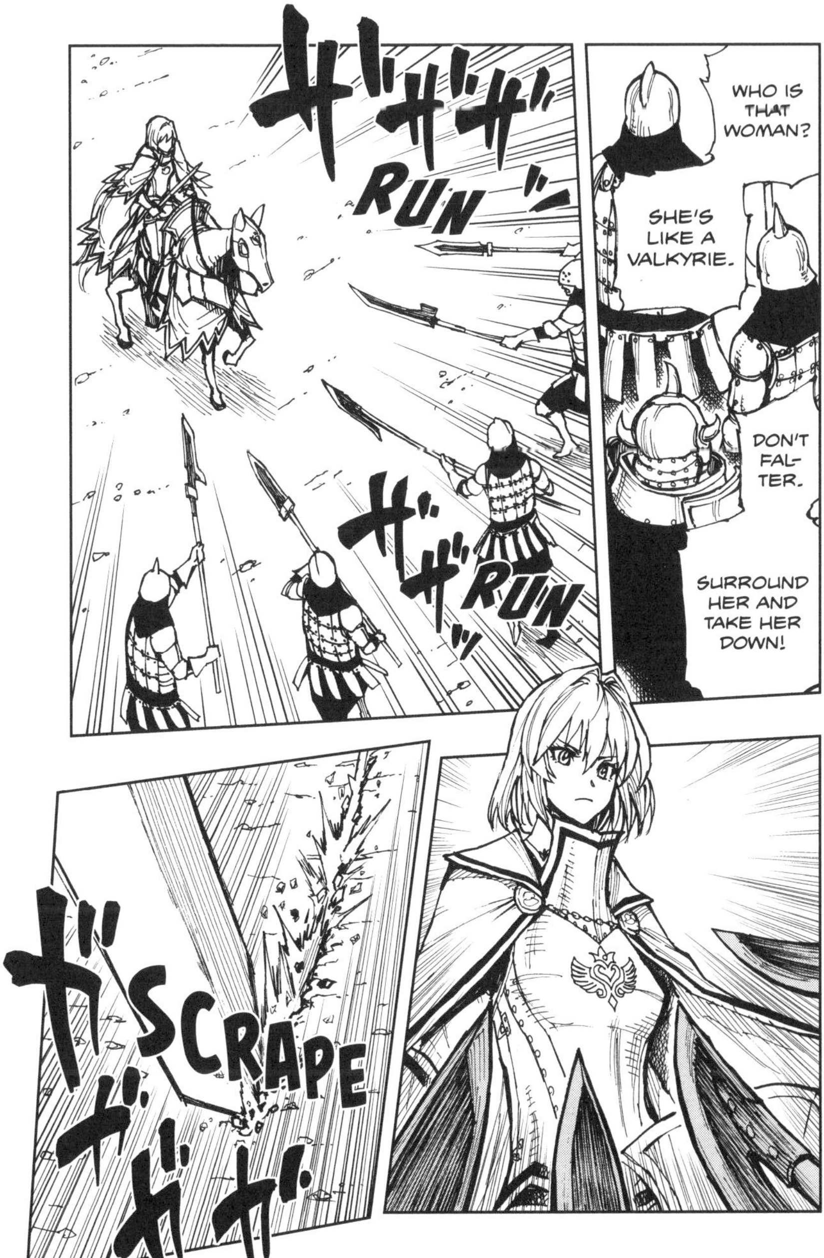
WHO IS THAT WOMAN?
SHE'S LIKE A VALKYRIE.
DON'T FAL-TER.
SURROUND HER AND TAKE HER DOWN!
RUN
RUN
SCRAPE

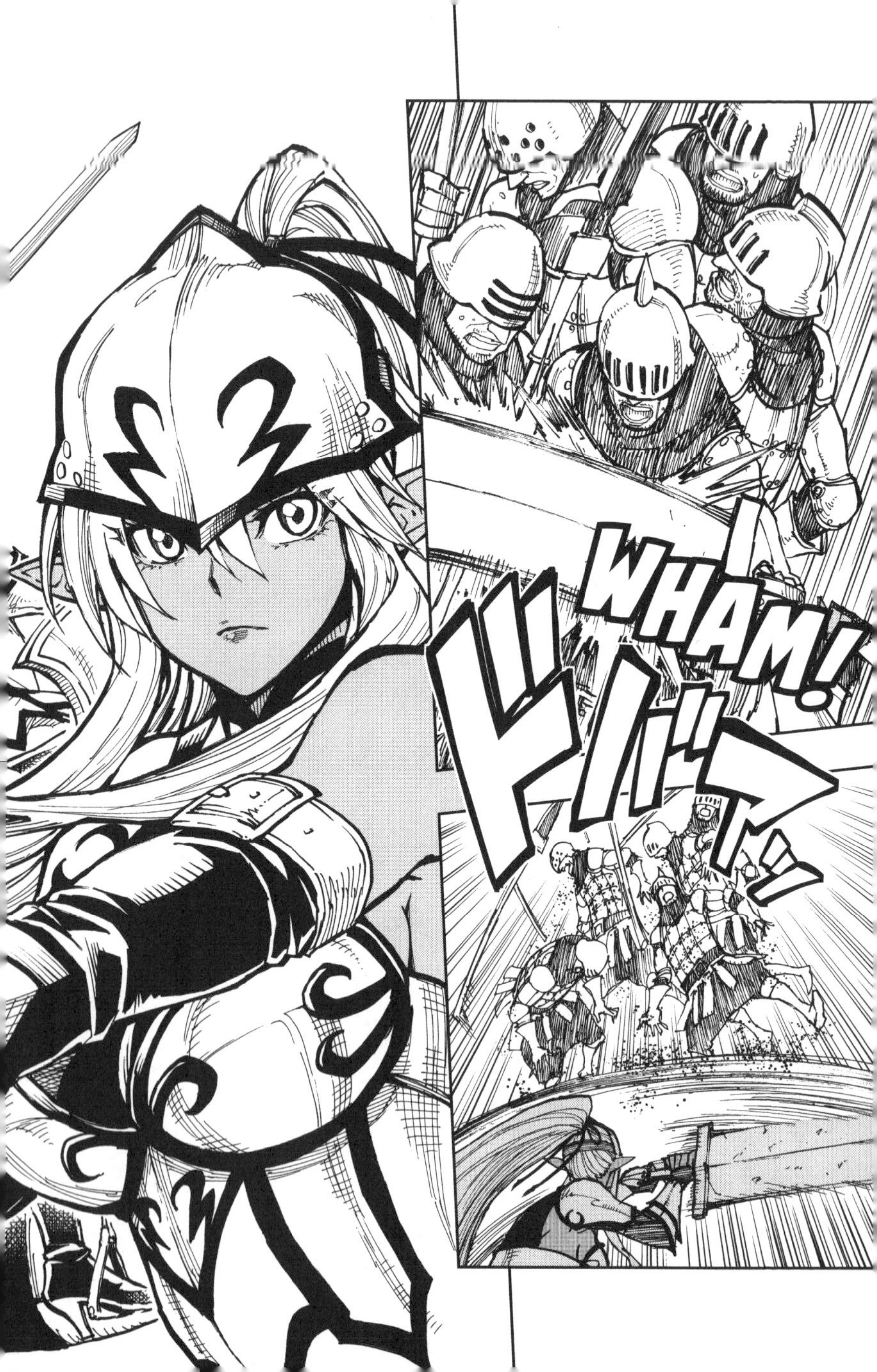
WHAM!
ドドドドーッ!!

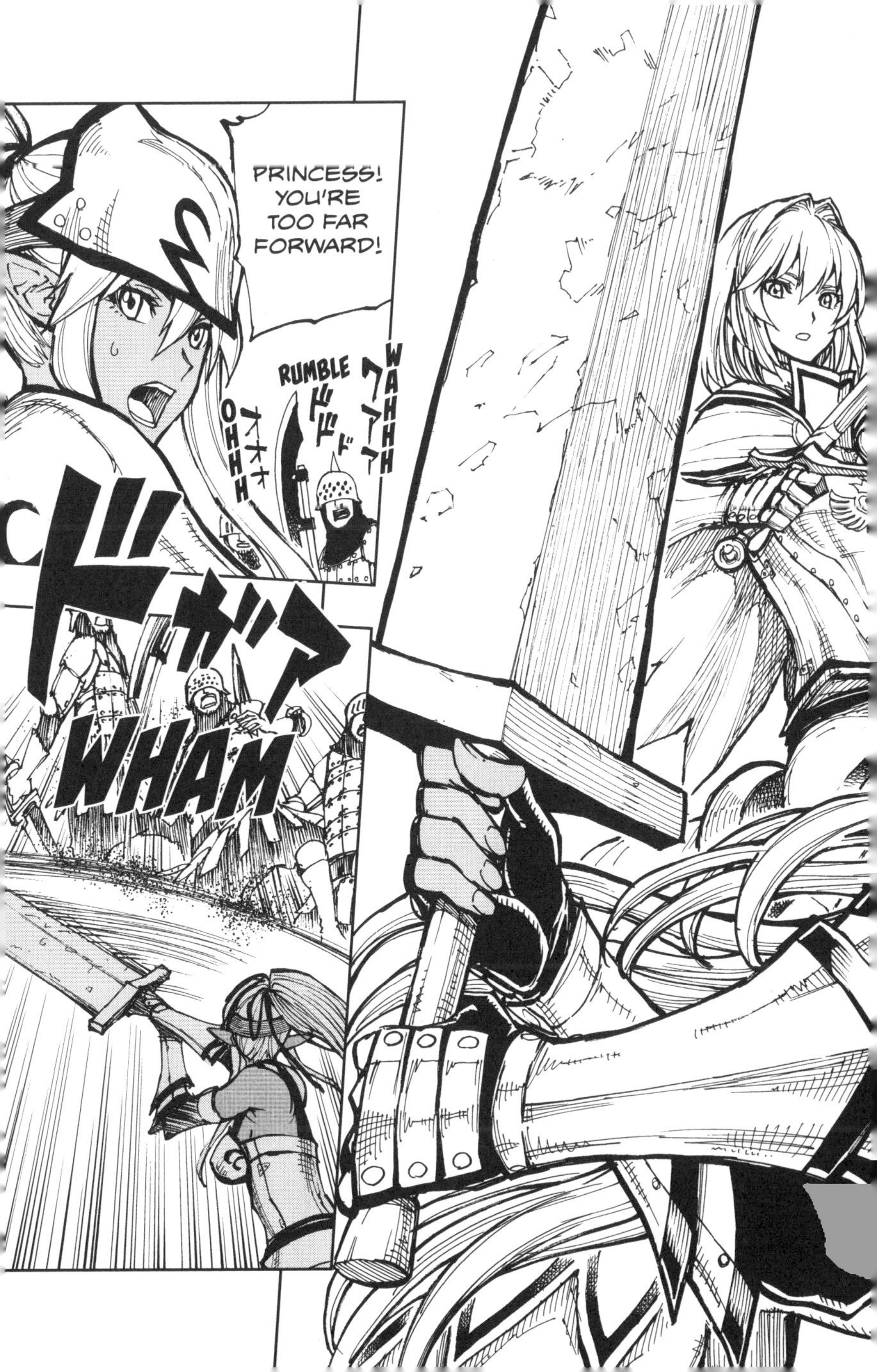
PRINCESS! YOU'RE TOO FAR FORWARD!
WAHHHH
ワァァァ
RUMBLE
ドドドド
OHHHH
オオオ
ドザァ
WHAM

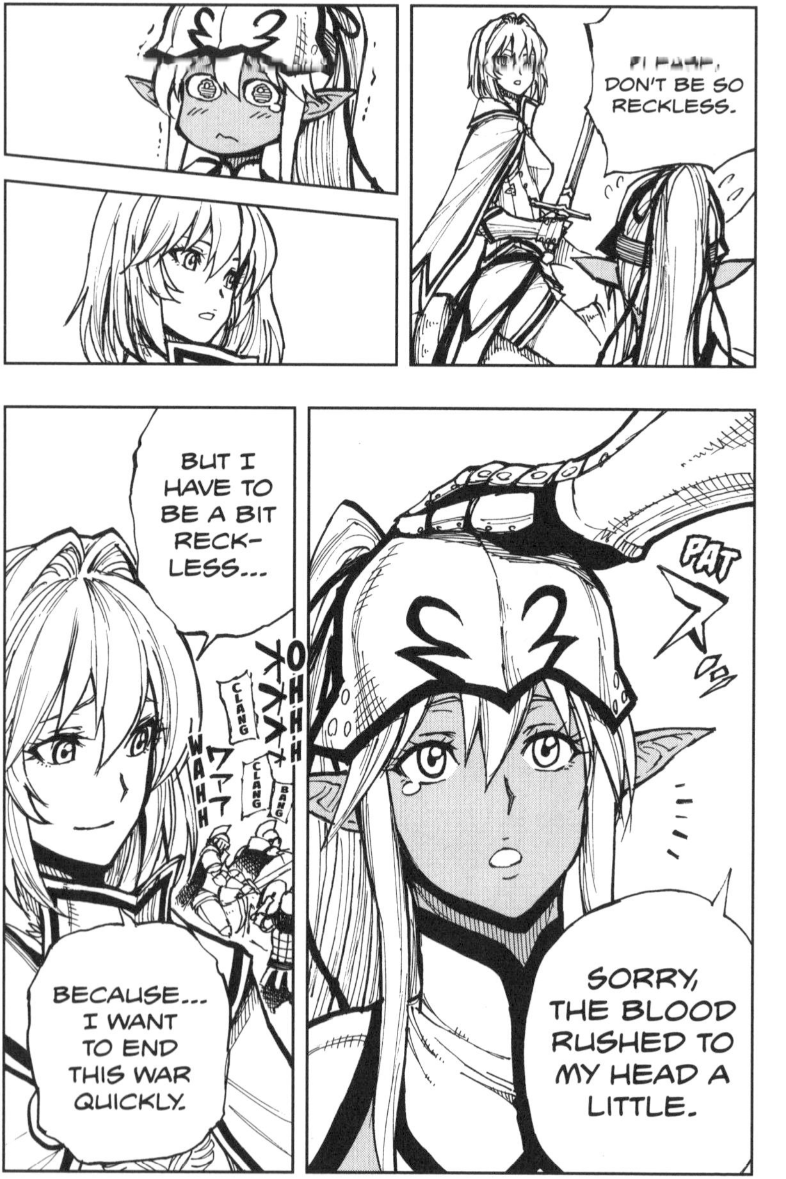
DON'T BE SO RECKLESS.
PAT
SORRY, THE BLOOD RUSHED TO MY HEAD A LITTLE.
BUT I HAVE TO BE A BIT RECK-LESS...
OHHHH
CLANG
WAHH
CLANG
BANG
BECAUSE... I WANT TO END THIS WAR QUICKLY.

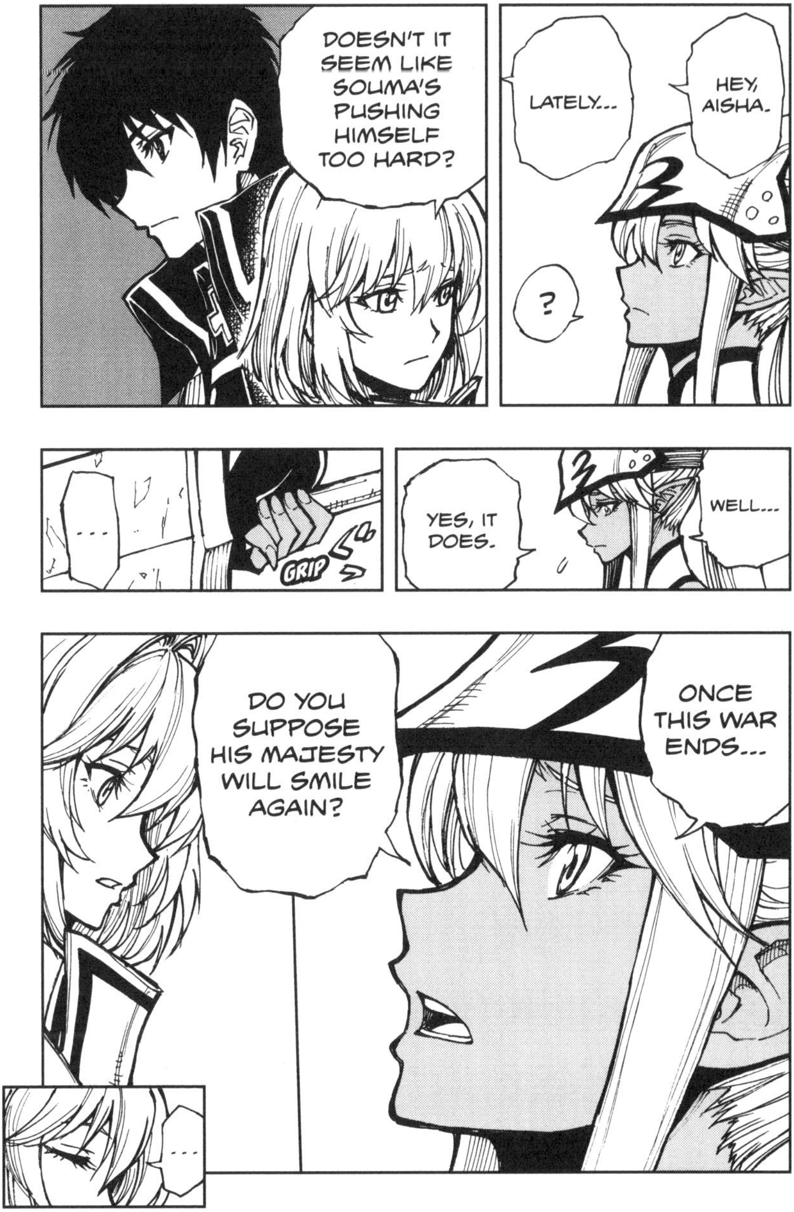
HEY, AISHA.
LATELY...
?
DOESN'T IT SEEM LIKE SOUMA'S PUSHING HIMSELF TOO HARD?
WELL...
YES, IT DOES.
...
GRIP
ONCE THIS WAR ENDS...
DO YOU SUPPOSE HIS MAJESTY WILL SMILE AGAIN?
...

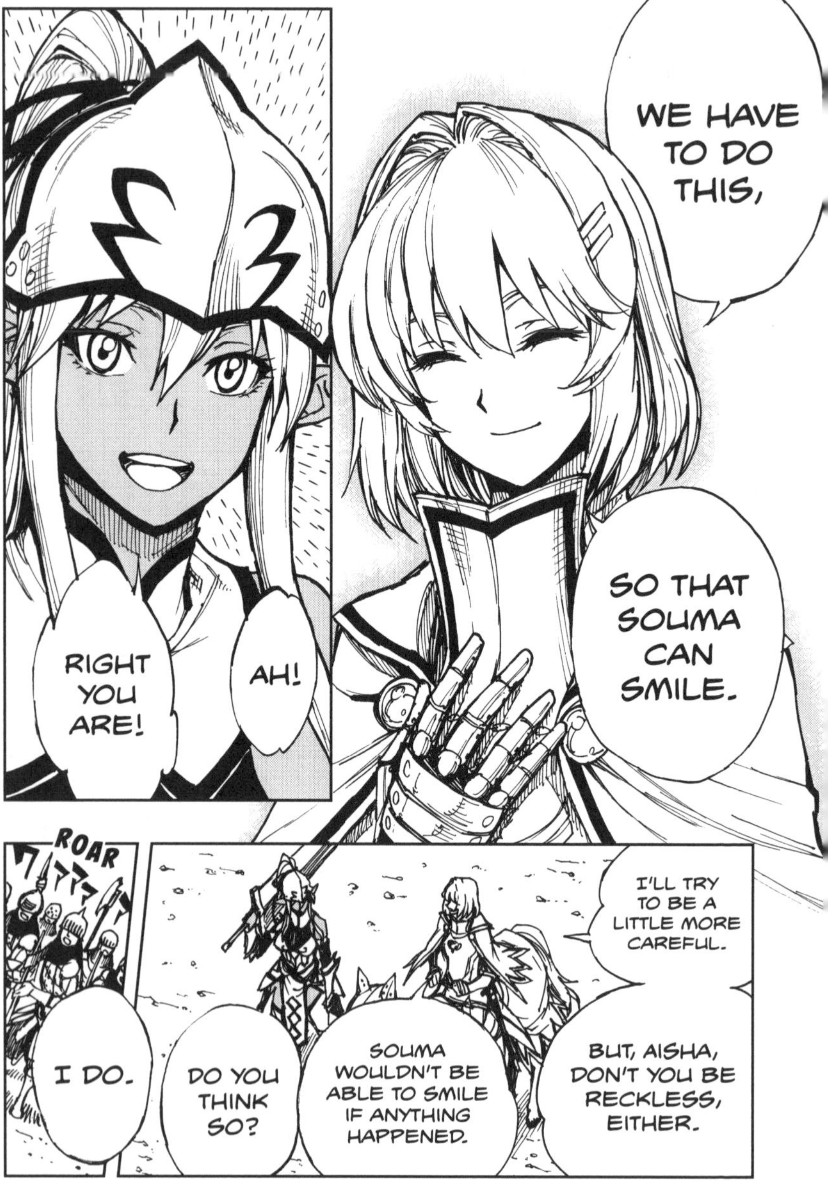
WE HAVE TO DO THIS,
SO THAT SOUMA CAN SMILE.
AH!
RIGHT YOU ARE!
I'LL TRY TO BE A LITTLE MORE CAREFUL.
BUT, AISHA, DON'T YOU BE RECKLESS, EITHER.
SOUMA WOULDN'T BE ABLE TO SMILE IF ANYTHING HAPPENED.
DO YOU THINK SO?
I DO.
ROAR

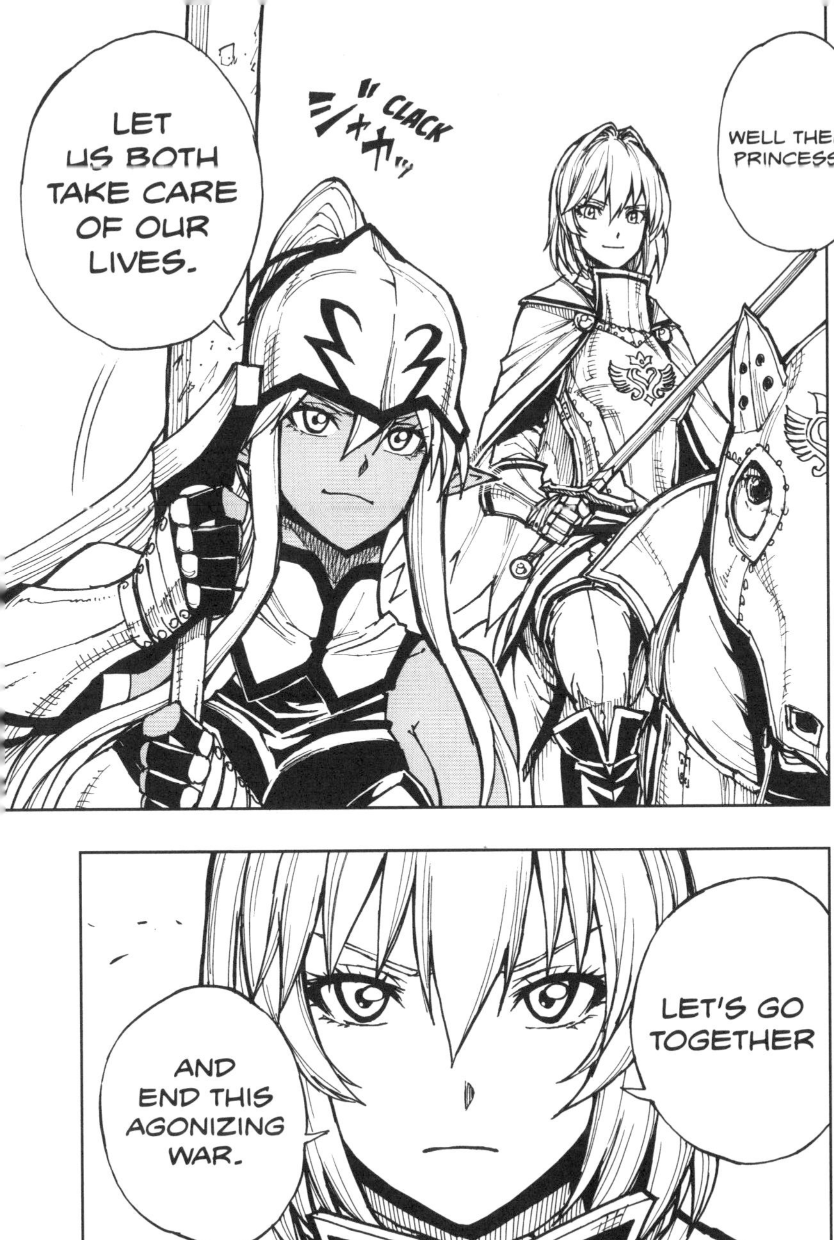
WELL THEN, PRINCESS.
CLACK
LET US BOTH TAKE CARE OF OUR LIVES.
LET'S GO TOGETHER
AND END THIS AGONIZING WAR.

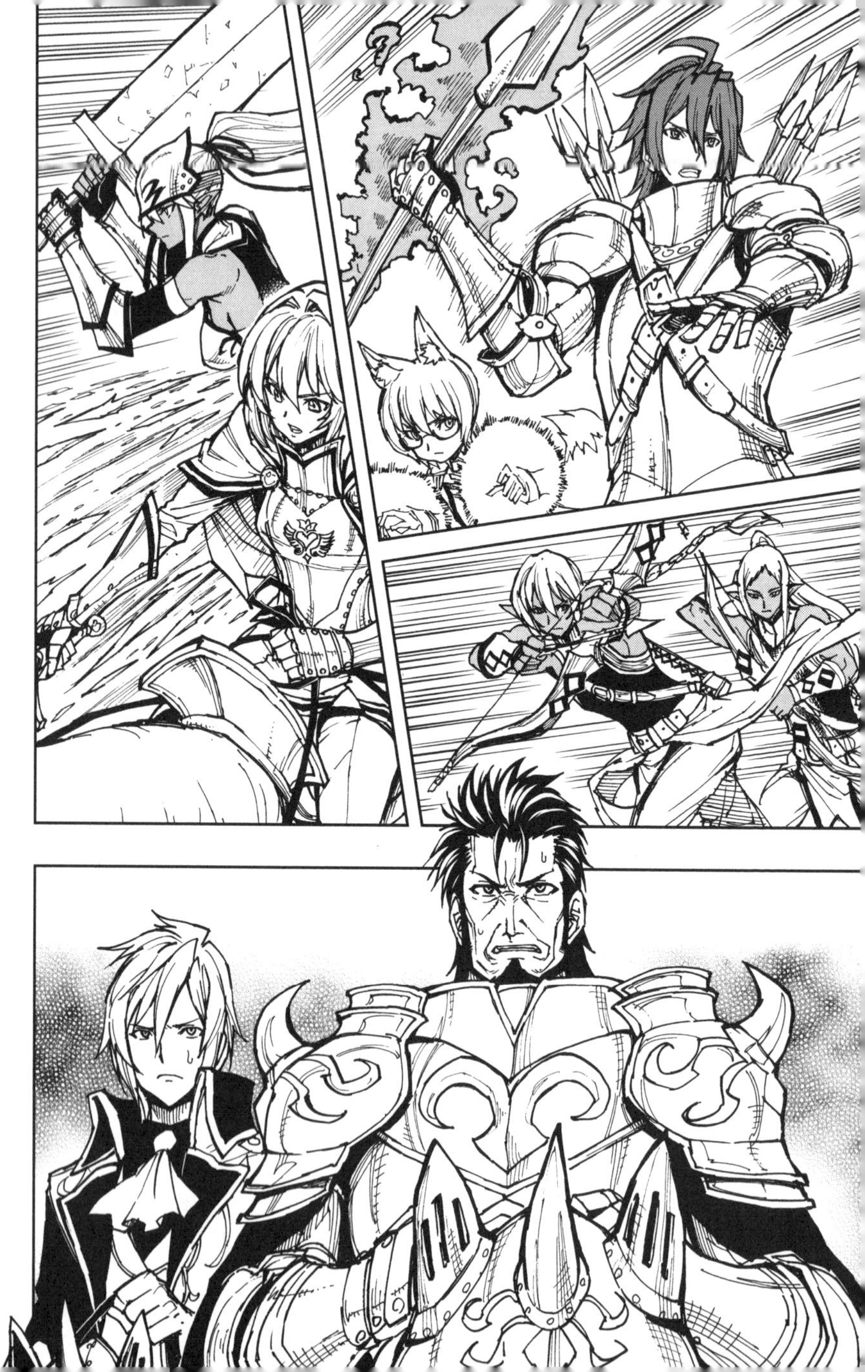

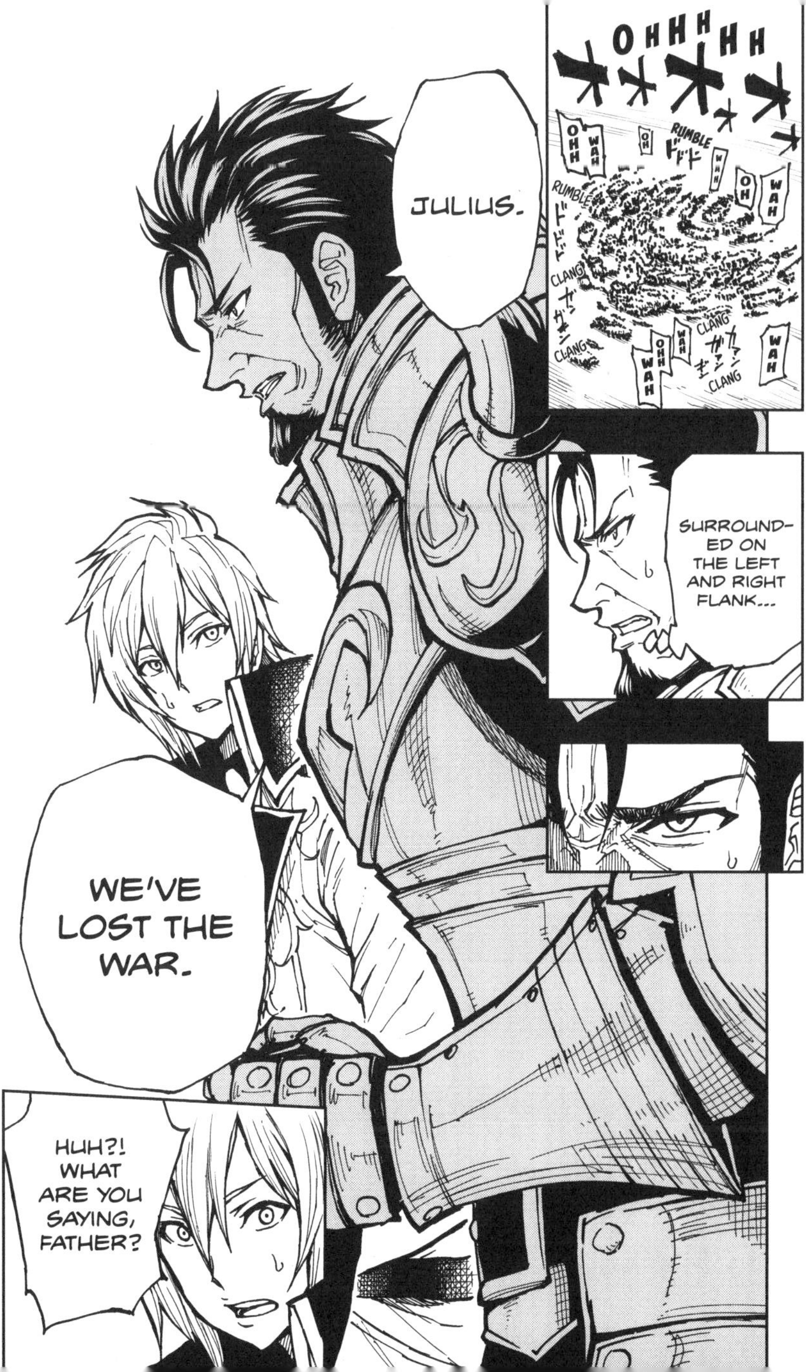
OHHHHH
OHH
WAH
OH
RUMBLE
WAH
OH
WAH
RUMBLE
CLANG
CLANG
OHH
WAH
CLANG
WAH
WAH
CLANG
SURROUNDED ON THE LEFT AND RIGHT FLANK...
JULIUS.
WE'VE LOST THE WAR.
HUH?! WHAT ARE YOU SAYING, FATHER?

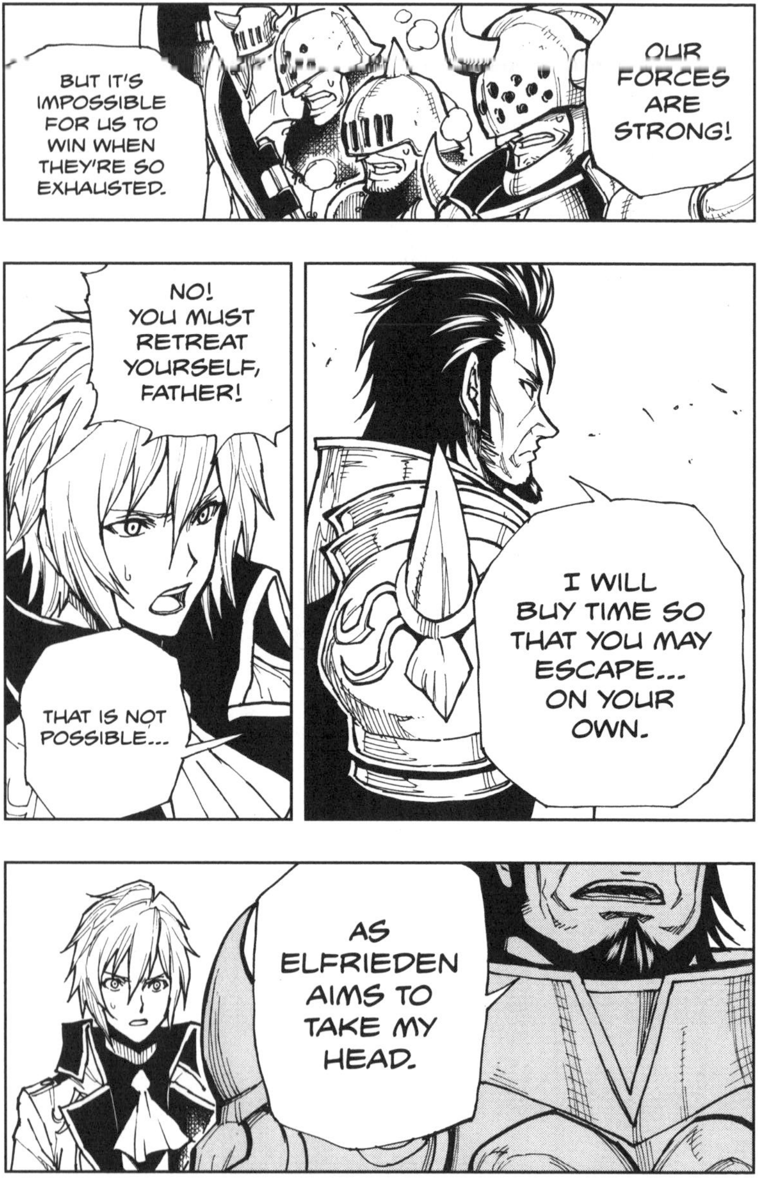
OUR FORCES ARE STRONG!
BUT IT'S IMPOSSIBLE FOR US TO WIN WHEN THEY'RE SO EXHAUSTED.
I WILL BUY TIME SO THAT YOU MAY ESCAPE... ON YOUR OWN.
NO! YOU MUST RETREAT YOURSELF, FATHER!
THAT IS NOT POSSIBLE...
AS ELFRIEDEN AIMS TO TAKE MY HEAD.

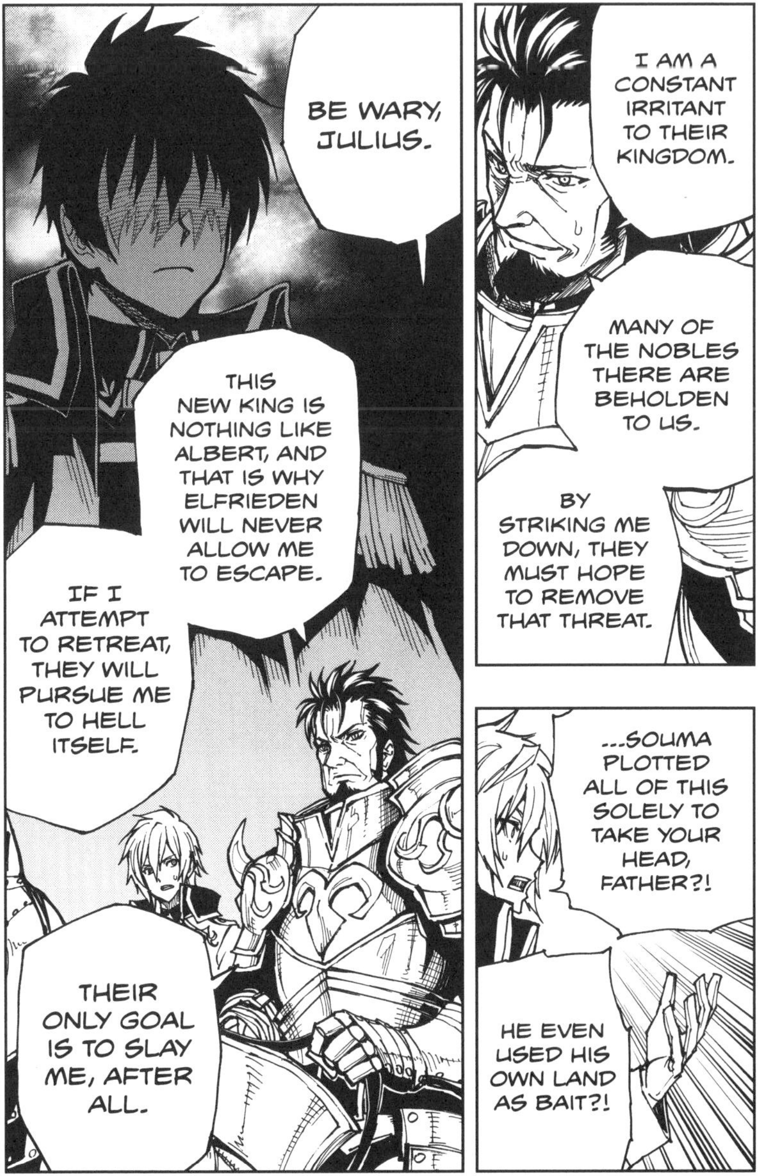
I AM A CONSTANT IRRITANT TO THEIR KINGDOM.
MANY OF THE NOBLES THERE ARE BEHOLDEN TO US.
BY STRIKING ME DOWN, THEY MUST HOPE TO REMOVE THAT THREAT.
...SOUMA PLOTTED ALL OF THIS SOLELY TO TAKE YOUR HEAD, FATHER?!
HE EVEN USED HIS OWN LAND AS BAIT?!
BE WARY, JULIUS.
THIS NEW KING IS NOTHING LIKE ALBERT, AND THAT IS WHY ELFRIEDEN WILL NEVER ALLOW ME TO ESCAPE.
IF I ATTEMPT TO RETREAT, THEY WILL PURSUE ME TO HELL ITSELF.
THEIR ONLY GOAL IS TO SLAY ME, AFTER ALL.

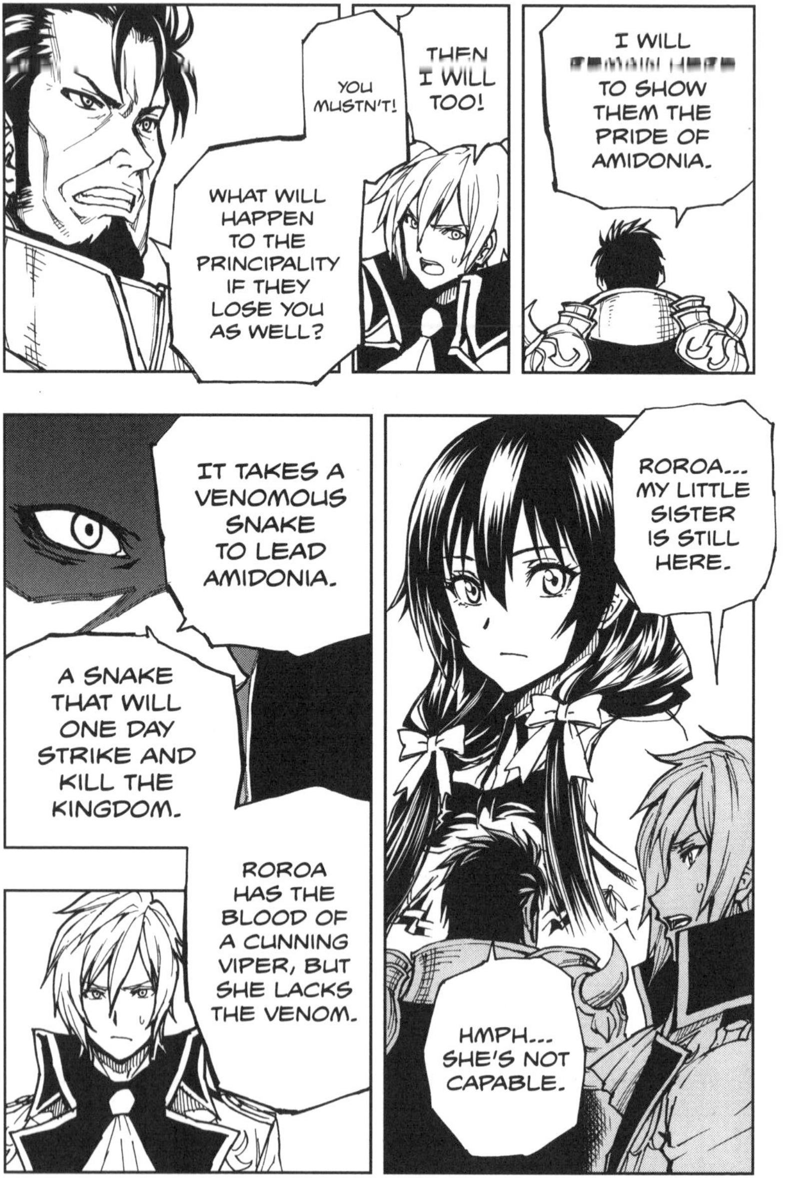
I WILL
TO SHOW THEM THE PRIDE OF AMIDONIA.
THEN I WILL TOO!
YOU MUSTN'T!
WHAT WILL HAPPEN TO THE PRINCIPALITY IF THEY LOSE YOU AS WELL?
ROROA... MY LITTLE SISTER IS STILL HERE.
HMPH... SHE'S NOT CAPABLE.
IT TAKES A VENOMOUS SNAKE TO LEAD AMIDONIA.
A SNAKE THAT WILL ONE DAY STRIKE AND KILL THE KINGDOM.
RORORA HAS THE BLOOD OF A CUNNING VIPER, BUT SHE LACKS THE VENOM.

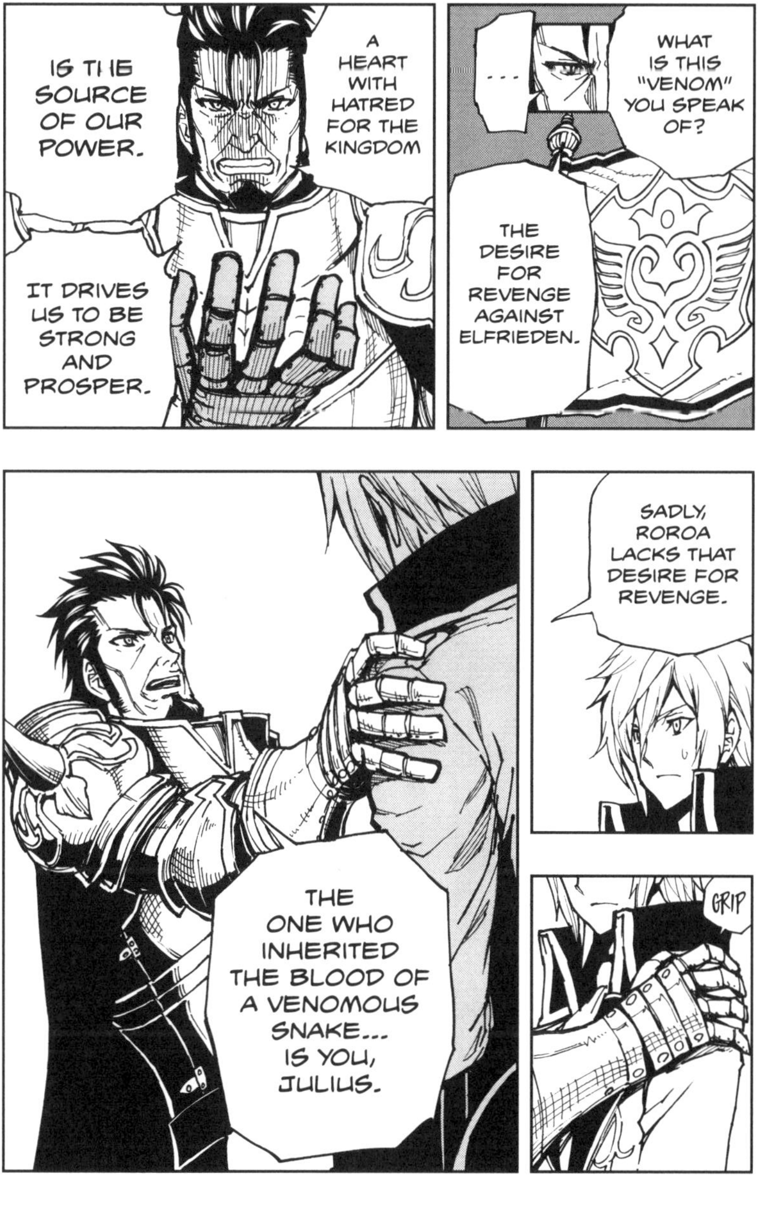
WHAT IS THIS "VENOM" YOU SPEAK OF?
...
THE DESIRE FOR REVENGE AGAINST ELFRIEDEN.
A HEART WITH HATRED FOR THE KINGDOM
IS THE SOURCE OF OUR POWER.
IT DRIVES US TO BE STRONG AND PROSPER.
SADLY, ROROA LACKS THAT DESIRE FOR REVENGE.
GRIP
THE ONE WHO INHERITED THE BLOOD OF A VENOMOUS SNAKE... IS YOU, JULIUS.

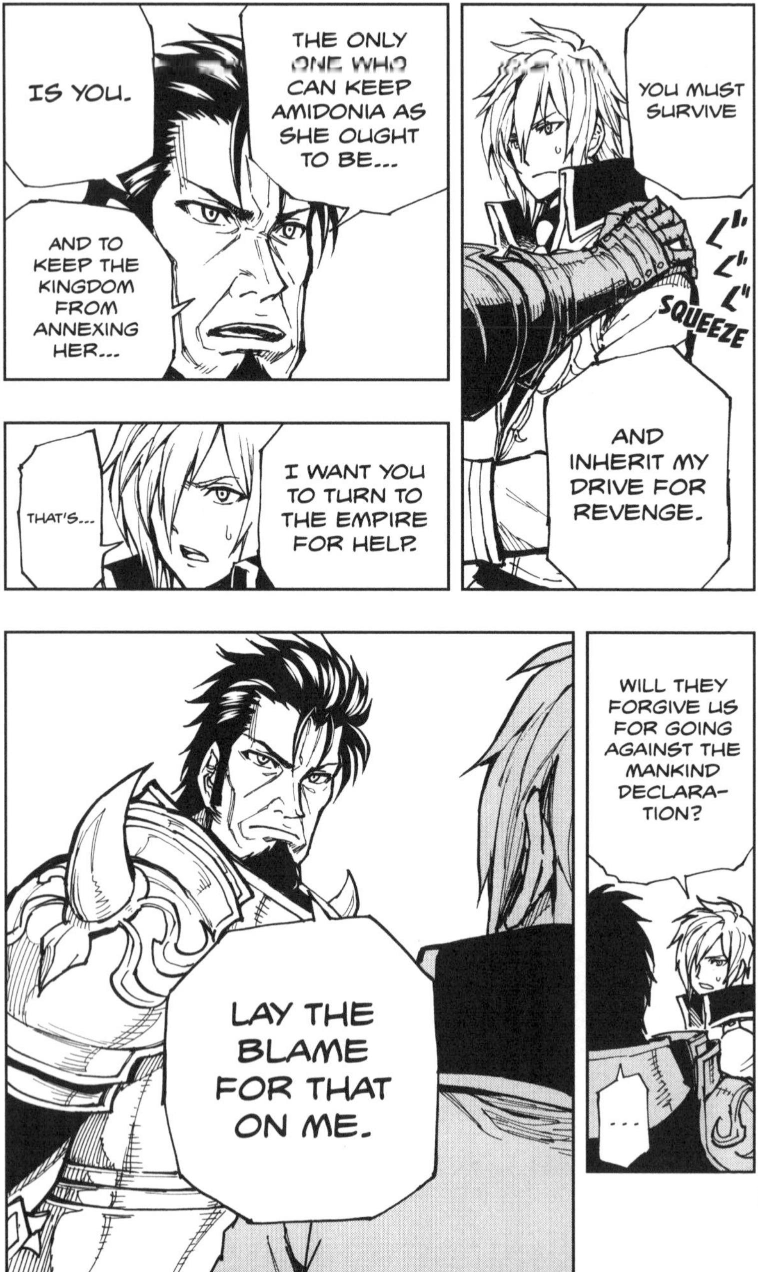
YOU MUST SURVIVE
ぐ ぐ ぐ
SQUEEZE
AND INHERIT MY DRIVE FOR REVENGE.
THE ONLY ONE WHO CAN KEEP AMIDONIA AS SHE OUGHT TO BE...
IS YOU.
AND TO KEEP THE KINGDOM FROM ANNEXING HER...
I WANT YOU TO TURN TO THE EMPIRE FOR HELP.
THAT'S...
WILL THEY FORGIVE US FOR GOING AGAINST THE MANKIND DECLARATION?
...
LAY THE BLAME FOR THAT ON ME.

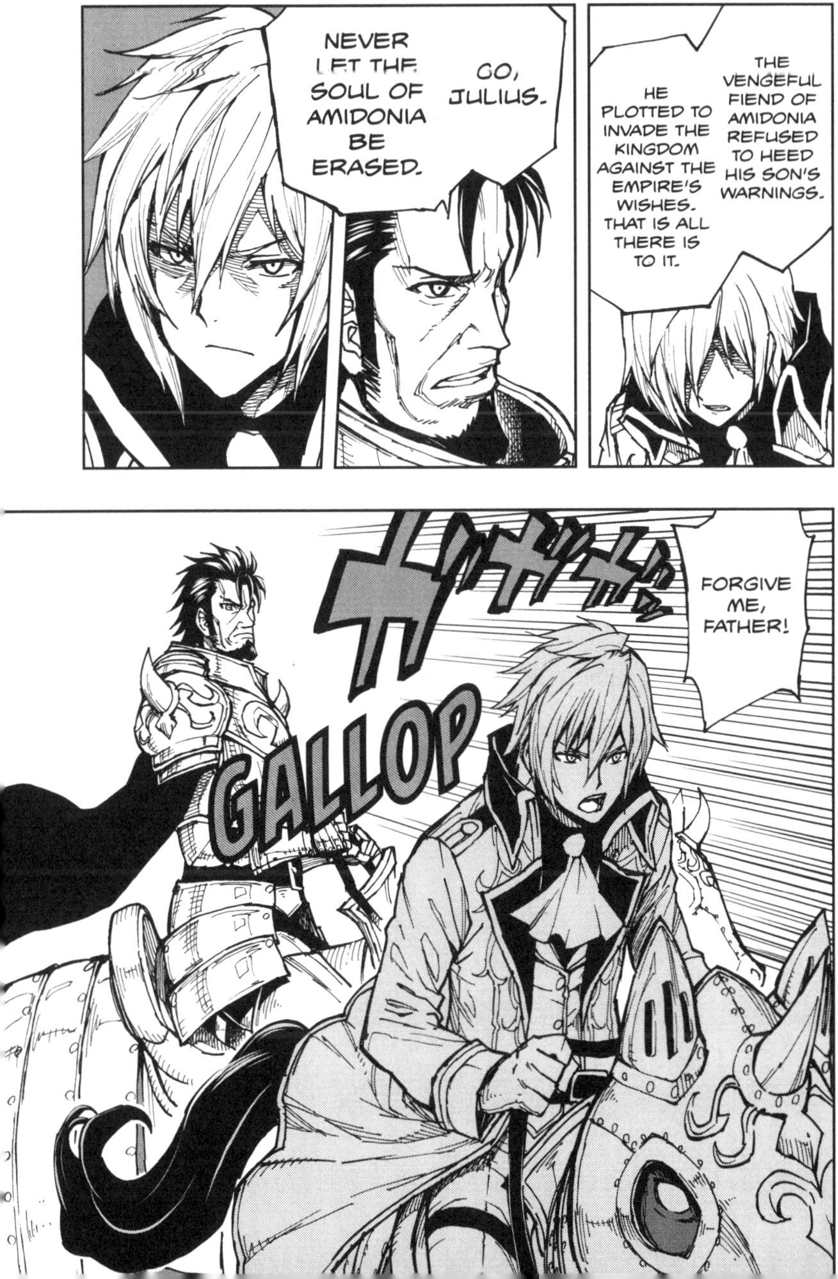
THE VENGEFUL FIEND OF AMIDONIA REFUSED TO HEED HIS SON'S WARNINGS.
HE PLOTTED TO INVADE THE KINGDOM AGAINST THE EMPIRE'S WISHES. THAT IS ALL THERE IS TO IT.
GO, JULIUS.
NEVER LET THE SOUL OF AMIDONIA BE ERASED.
FORGIVE ME, FATHER!
GALLOP

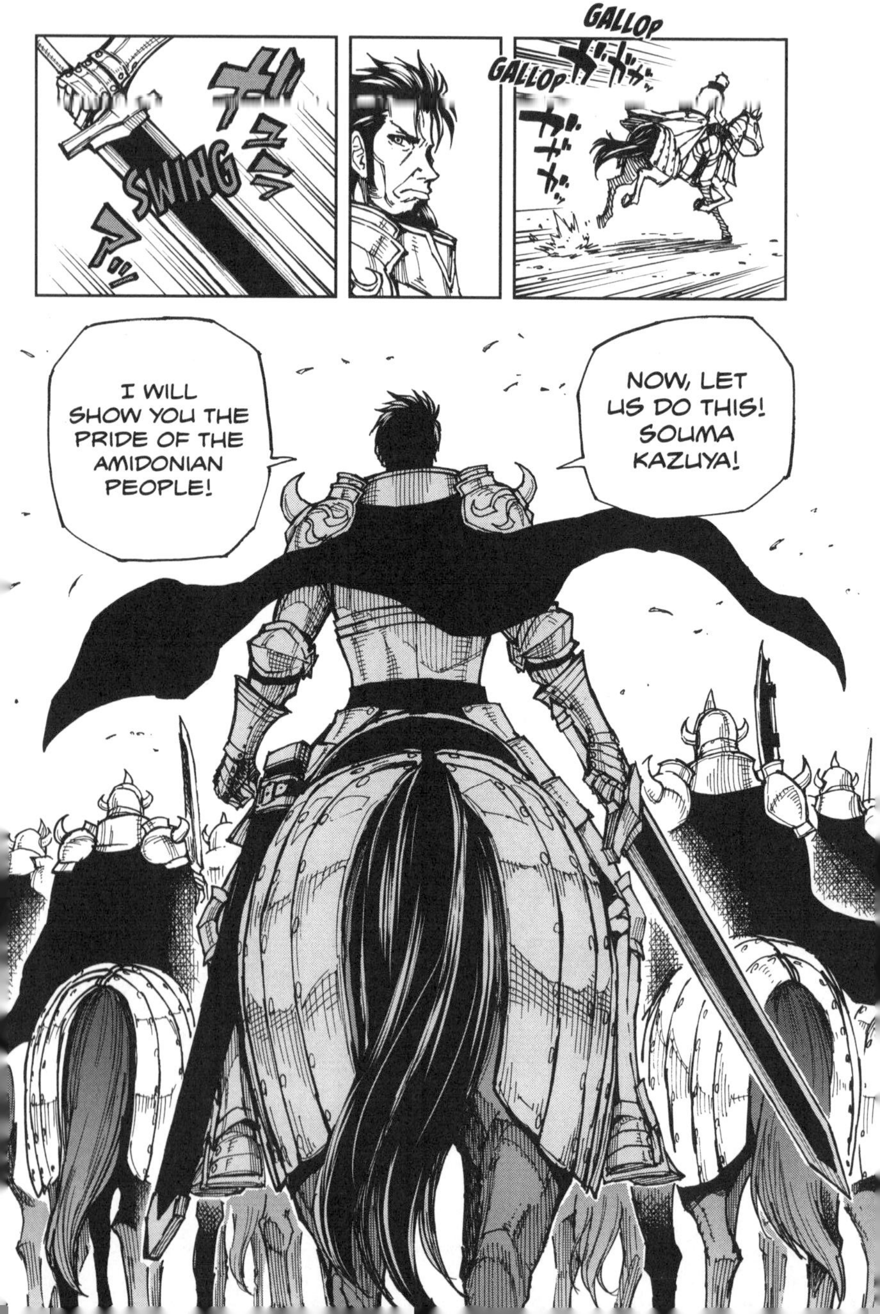
GALLOP
GALLOP
SWING
NOW, LET US DO THIS! SOUMA KAZUYA!
I WILL SHOW YOU THE PRIDE OF THE AMIDONIAN PEOPLE!

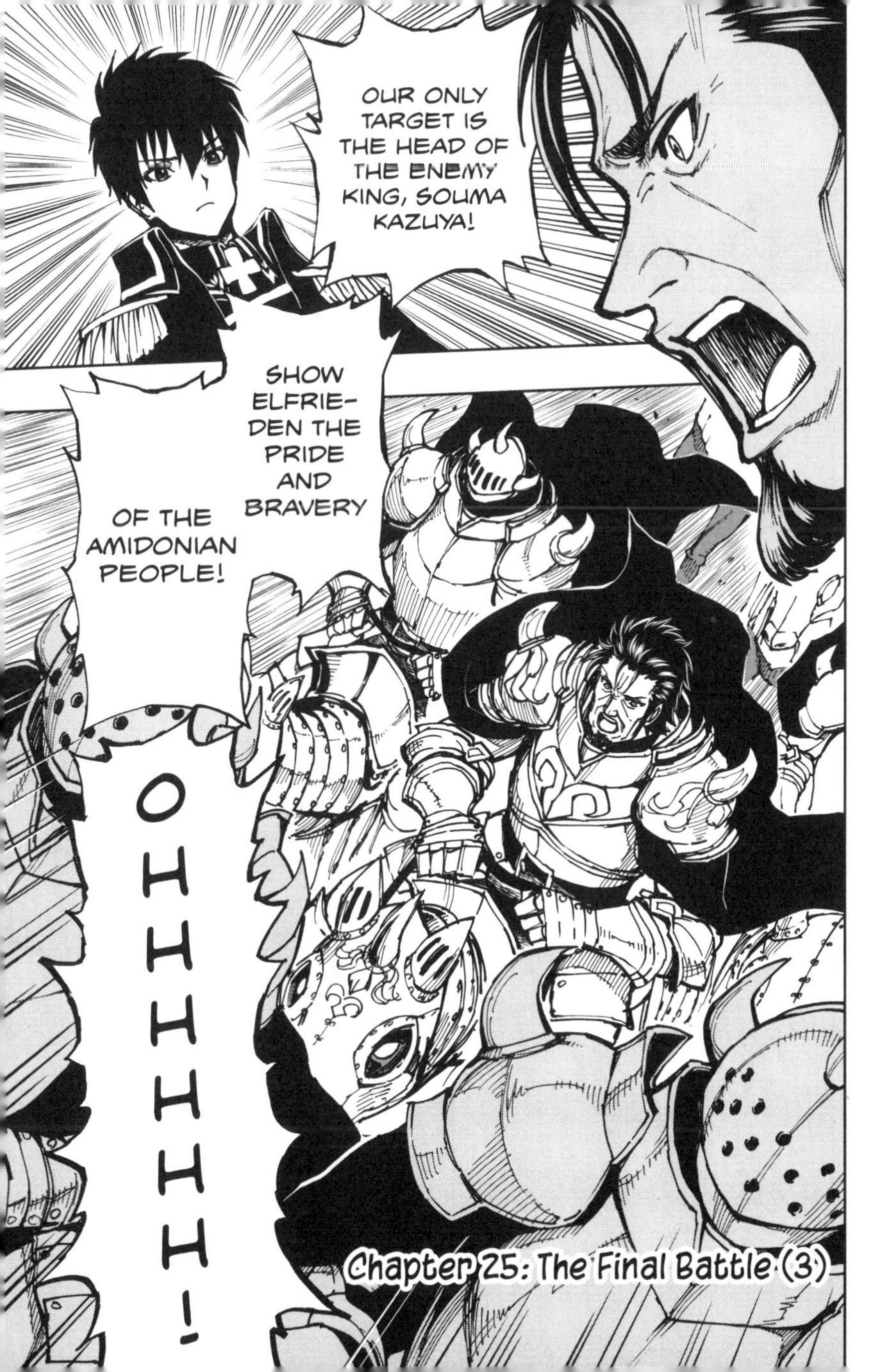
OUR ONLY TARGET IS THE HEAD OF THE ENEMY KING, SOUMA KAZUYA!
SHOW ELFRIEDEN THE PRIDE AND BRAVERY
OF THE AMIDONIAN PEOPLE!
OHHHHH!
Chapter 25: The Final Battle (3)

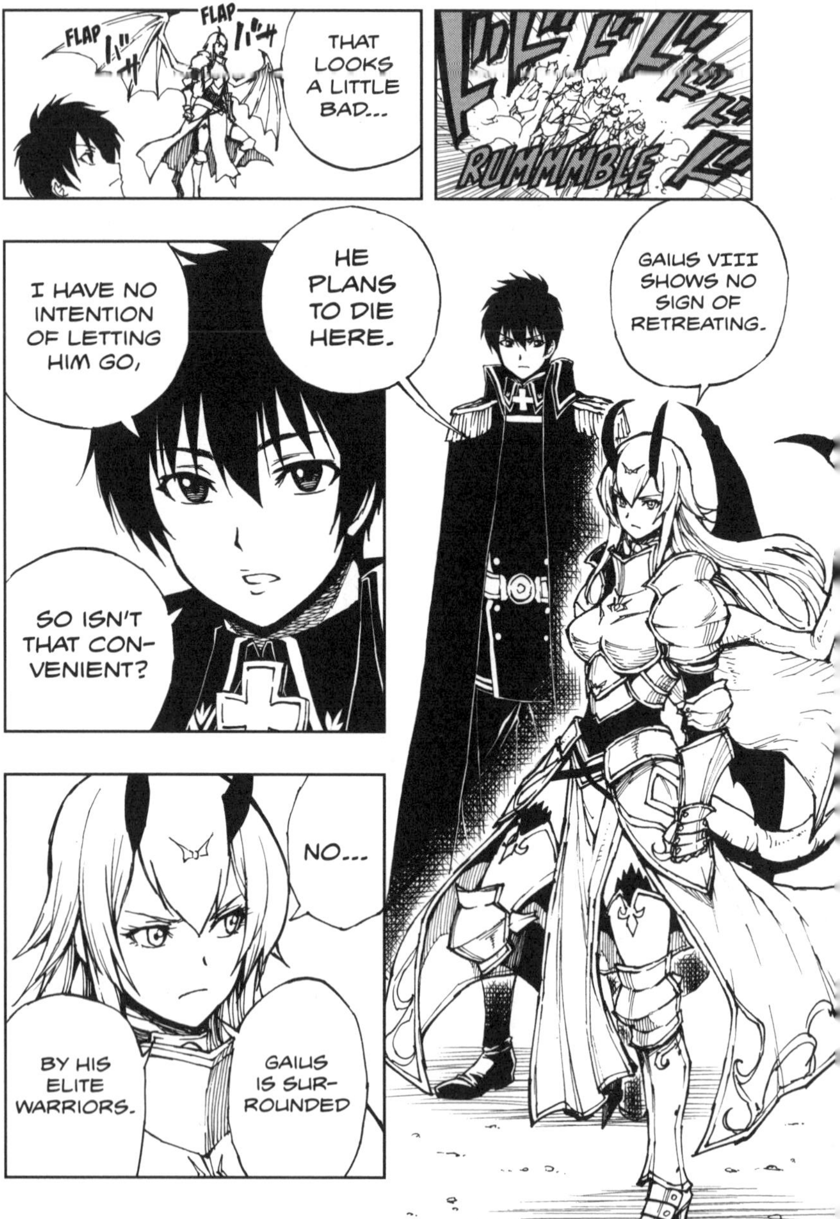
RUMMMBLE
FLAP
FLAP
THAT LOOKS A LITTLE BAD...
GAIUS VIII SHOWS NO SIGN OF RETREATING.
HE PLANS TO DIE HERE.
I HAVE NO INTENTION OF LETTING HIM GO,
SO ISN'T THAT CON-VENIENT?
NO...
GAIUS IS SUR-ROUNDED
BY HIS ELITE WARRIORS.

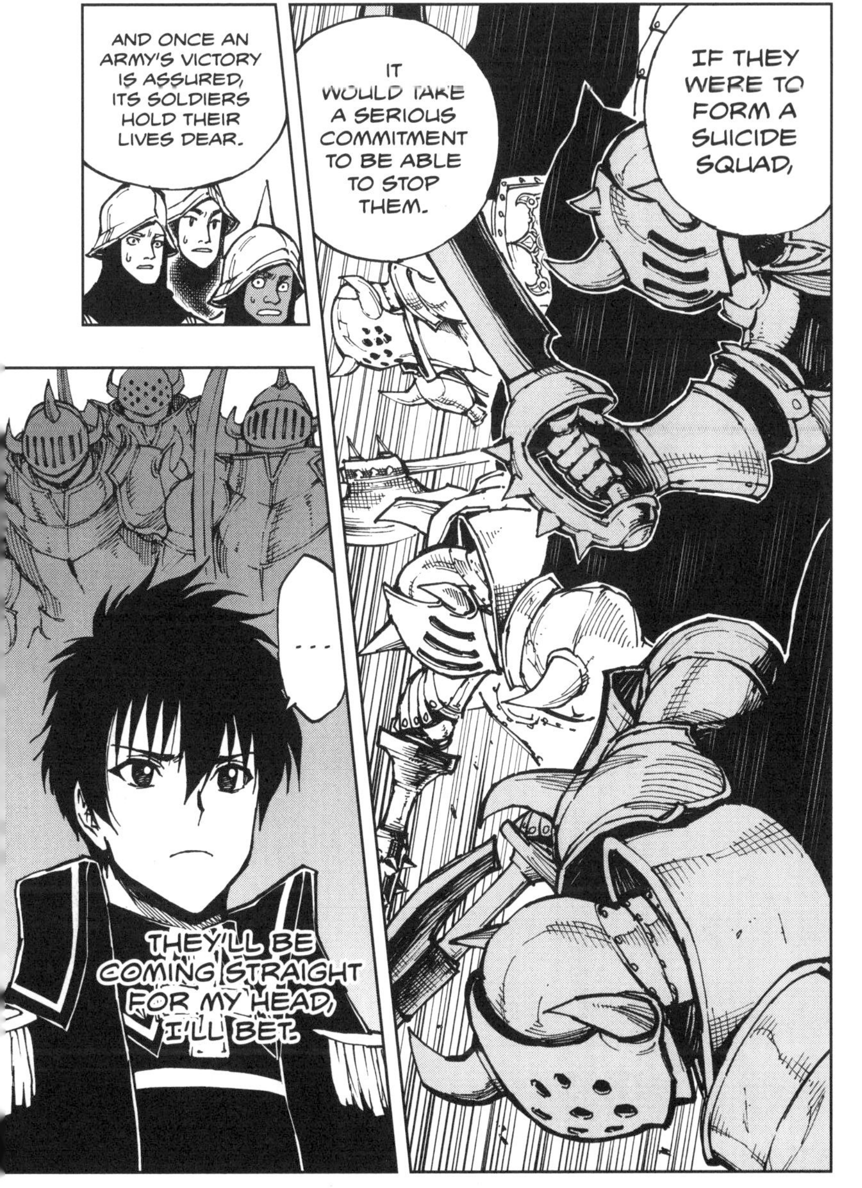
IF THEY WERE TO FORM A SUICIDE SQUAD,
IT WOULD TAKE A SERIOUS COMMITMENT TO BE ABLE TO STOP THEM.
AND ONCE AN ARMY'S VICTORY IS ASSURED, ITS SOLDIERS HOLD THEIR LIVES DEAR.
...
THEY'LL BE COMING STRAIGHT FOR MY HEAD, I'LL BET.

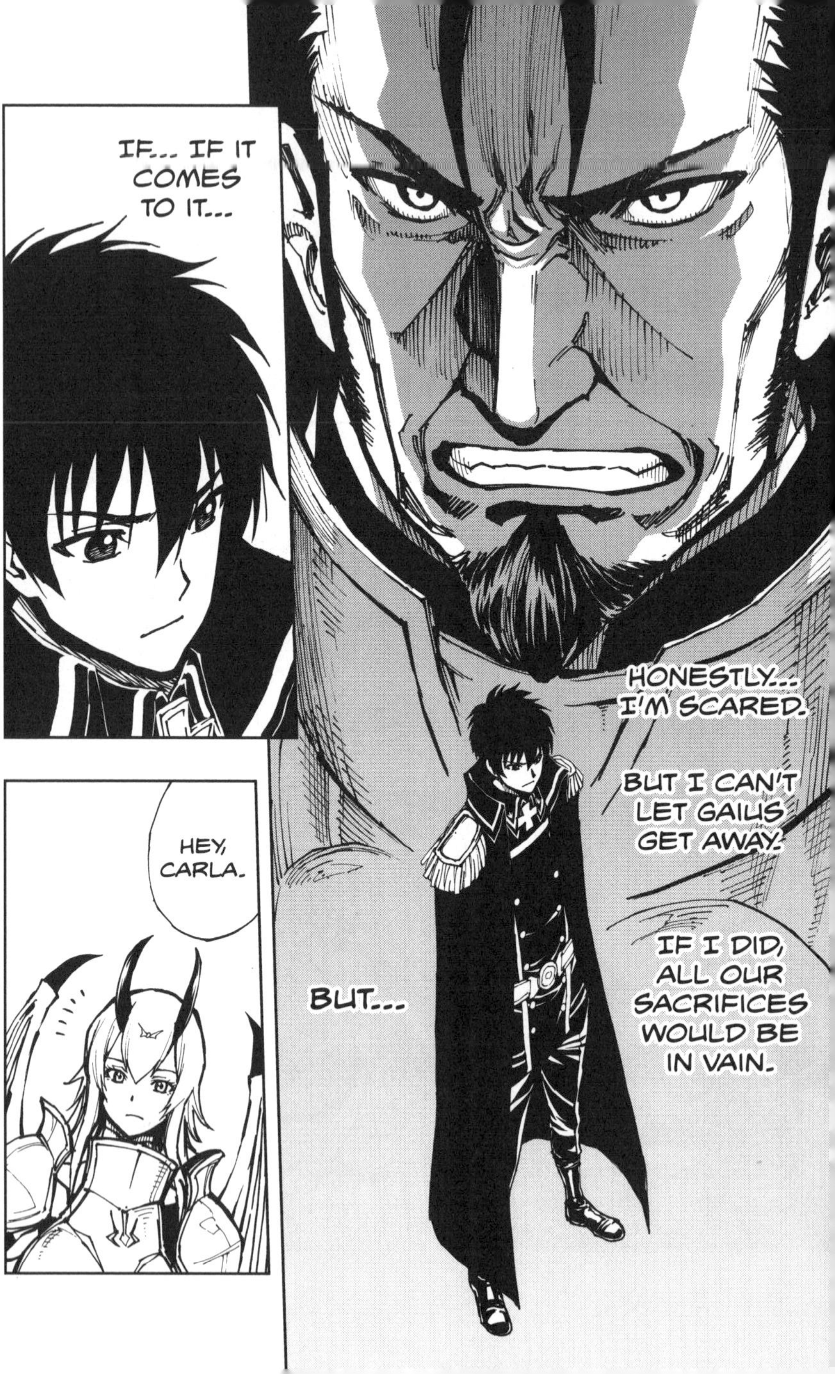
HONESTLY... I'M SCARED.
BUT I CAN'T LET GAILUS GET AWAY.
IF I DID, ALL OUR SACRIFICES WOULD BE IN VAIN.
BUT...
IF... IF IT COMES TO IT...
HEY, CARLA.

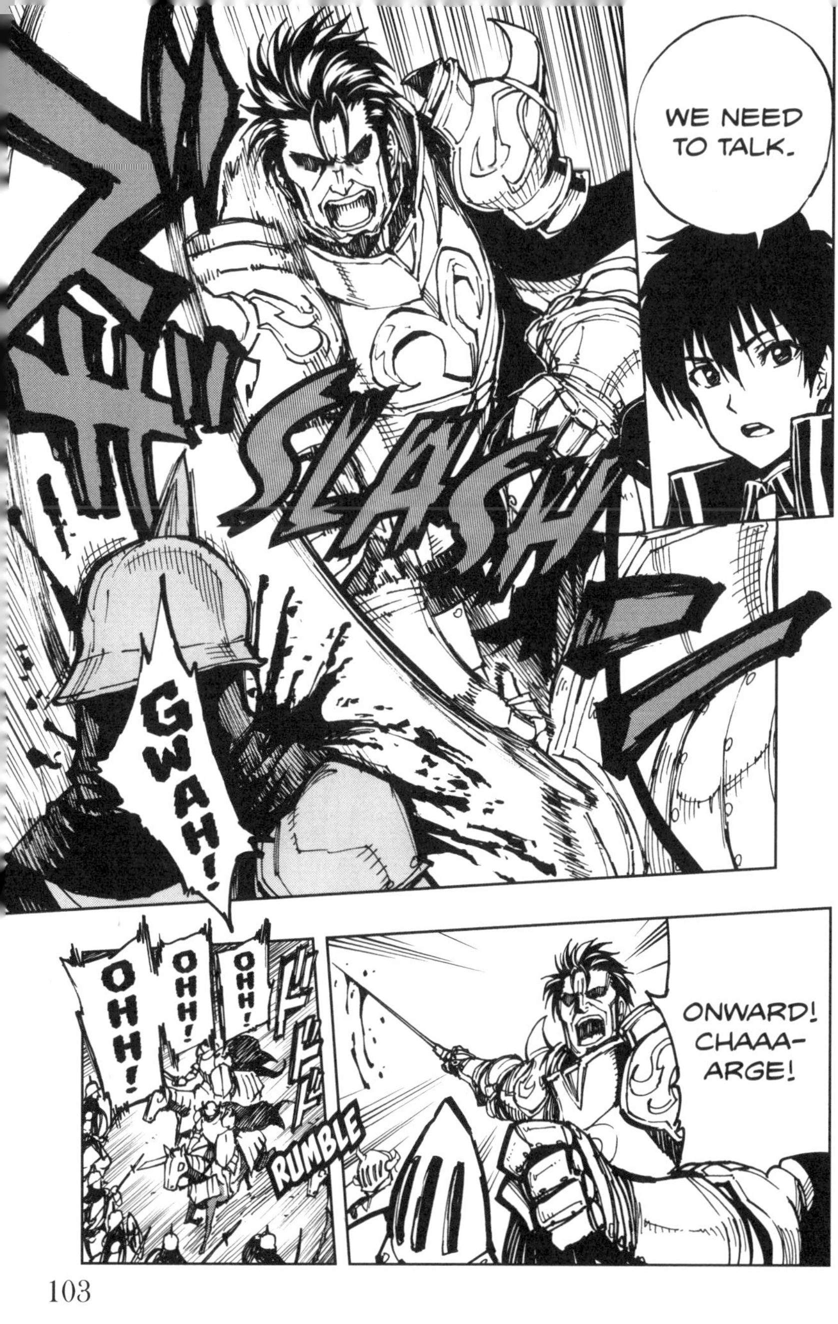
WE NEED TO TALK.
SLASH
GWAH!
ONWARD! CHAAA-ARGE!
OHH! OHH! OHH!
RUMBLE

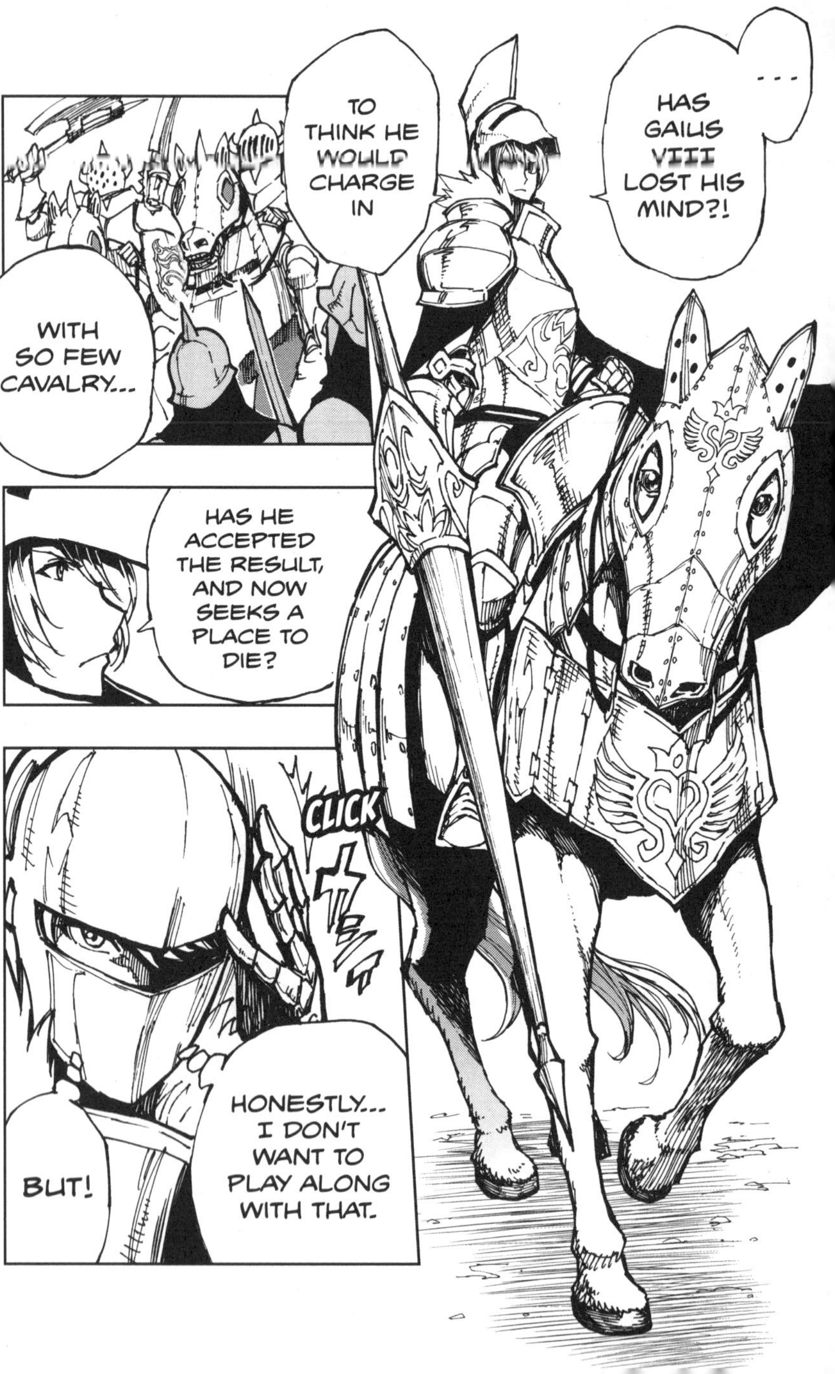
...
HAS GAIUS VIII LOST HIS MIND?!
TO THINK HE WOULD CHARGE IN
WITH SO FEW CAVALRY...
HAS HE ACCEPTED THE RESULT, AND NOW SEEKS A PLACE TO DIE?
CLICK
HONESTLY... I DON'T WANT TO PLAY ALONG WITH THAT.
BUT!

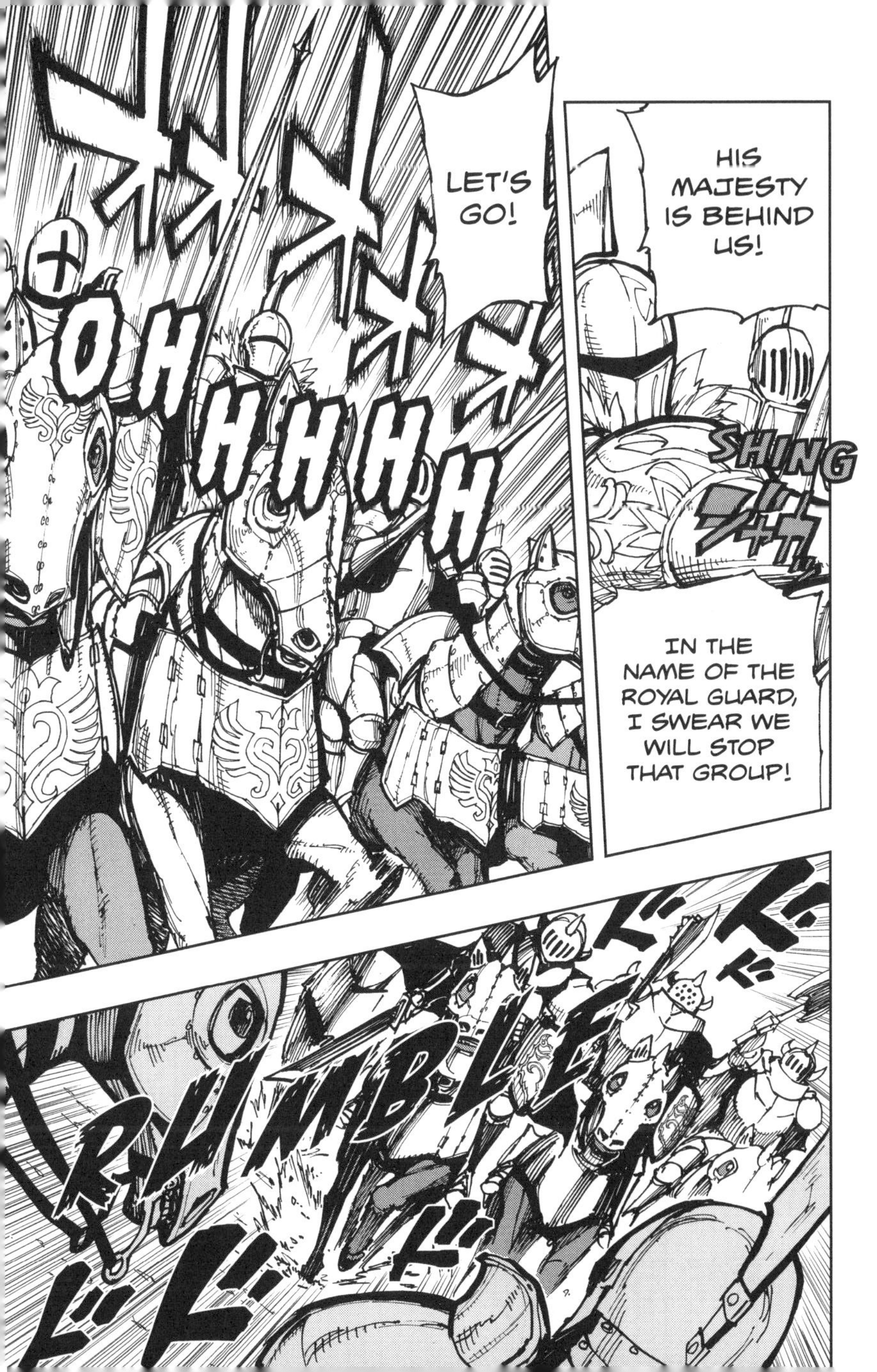
HIS MAJESTY IS BEHIND US!
SHING
IN THE NAME OF THE ROYAL GUARD, I SWEAR WE WILL STOP THAT GROUP!
LET'S GO!
OHHHHHH
RUMBLE

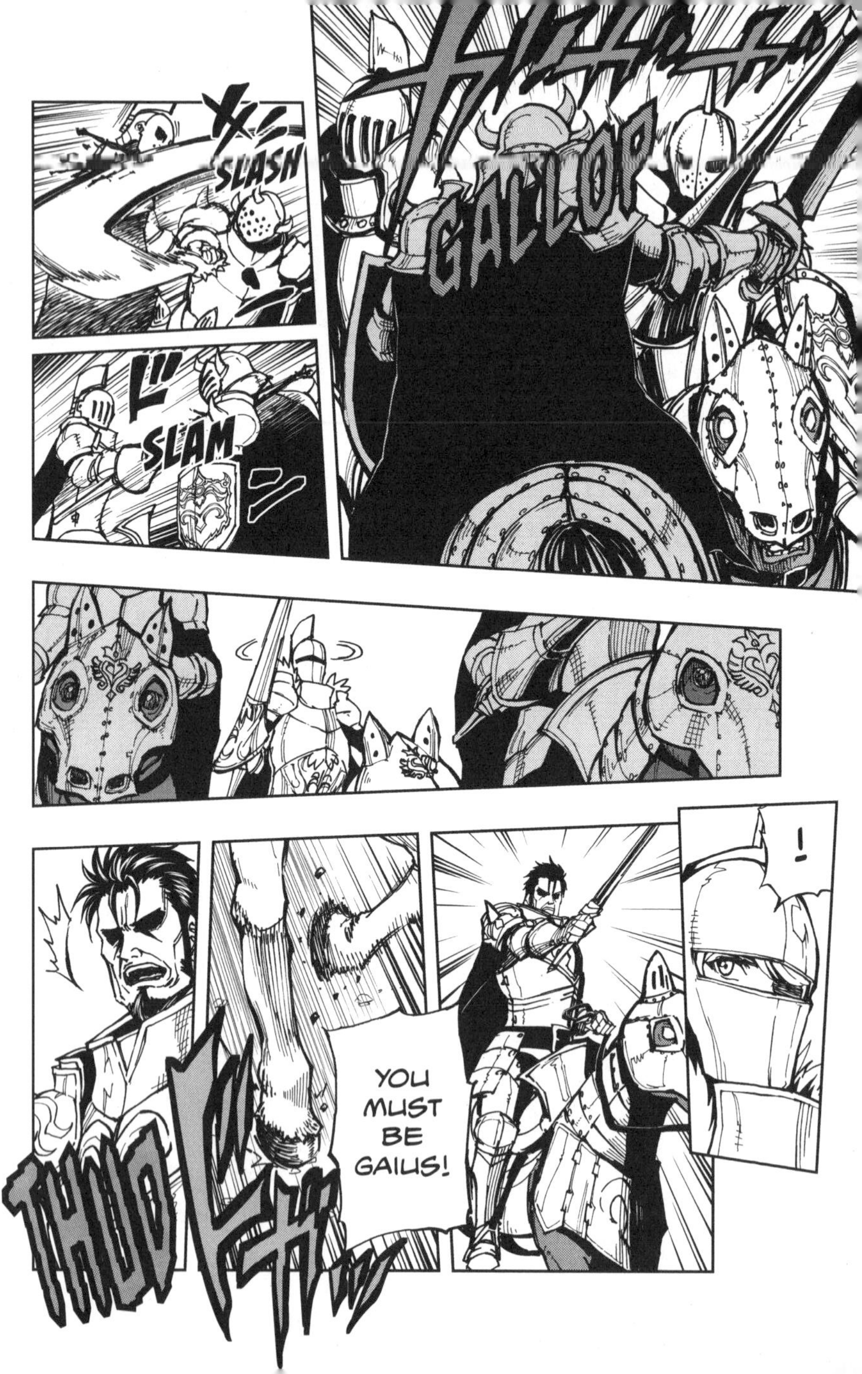
GALLOP
SLASH
SLAM
!
YOU MUST BE GAIUS!
THUD

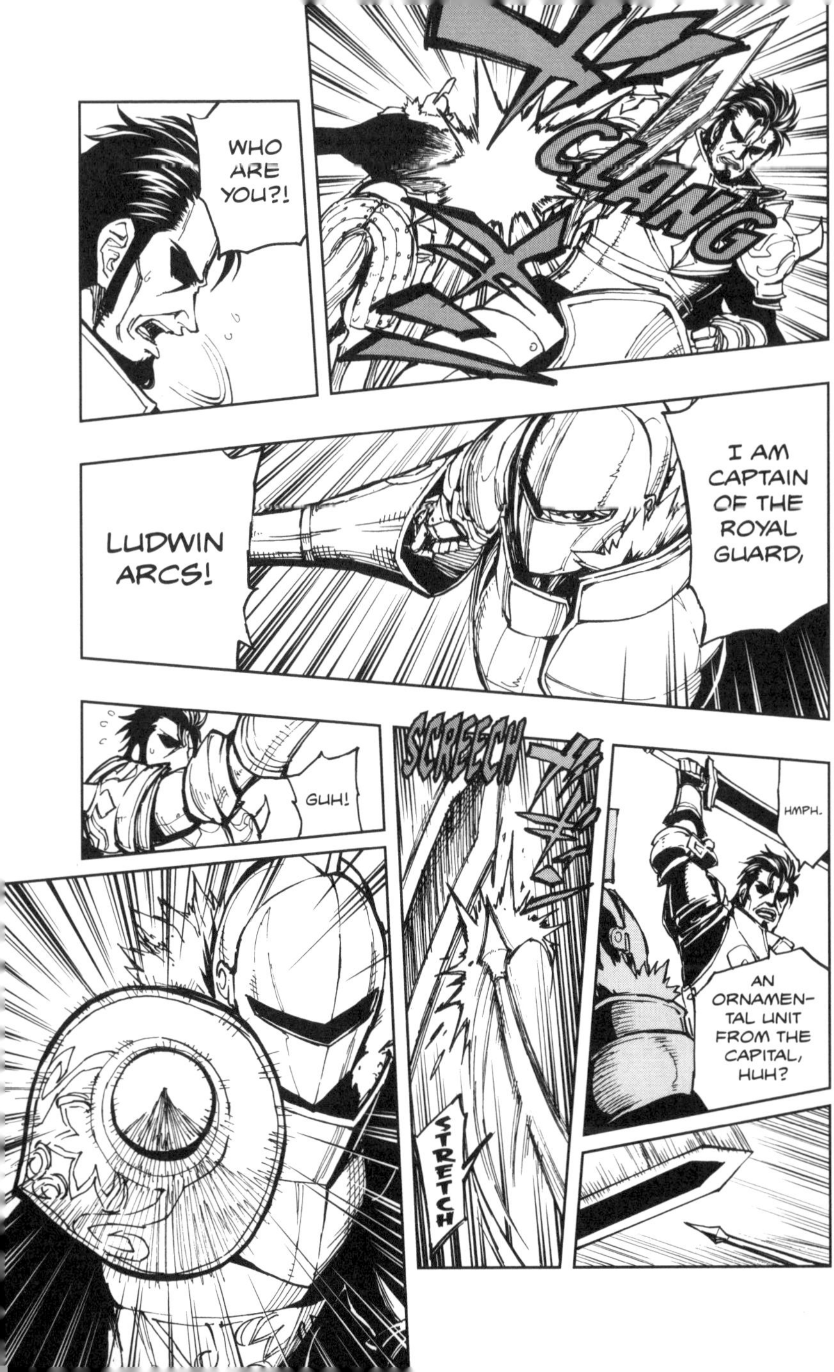
CLANG
WHO ARE YOU?!
I AM CAPTAIN OF THE ROYAL GUARD,
LUDWIN ARCS!
HMPH.
AN ORNAMEN-TAL UNIT FROM THE CAPITAL, HUH?
SCREECH
STRETCH
GUH!

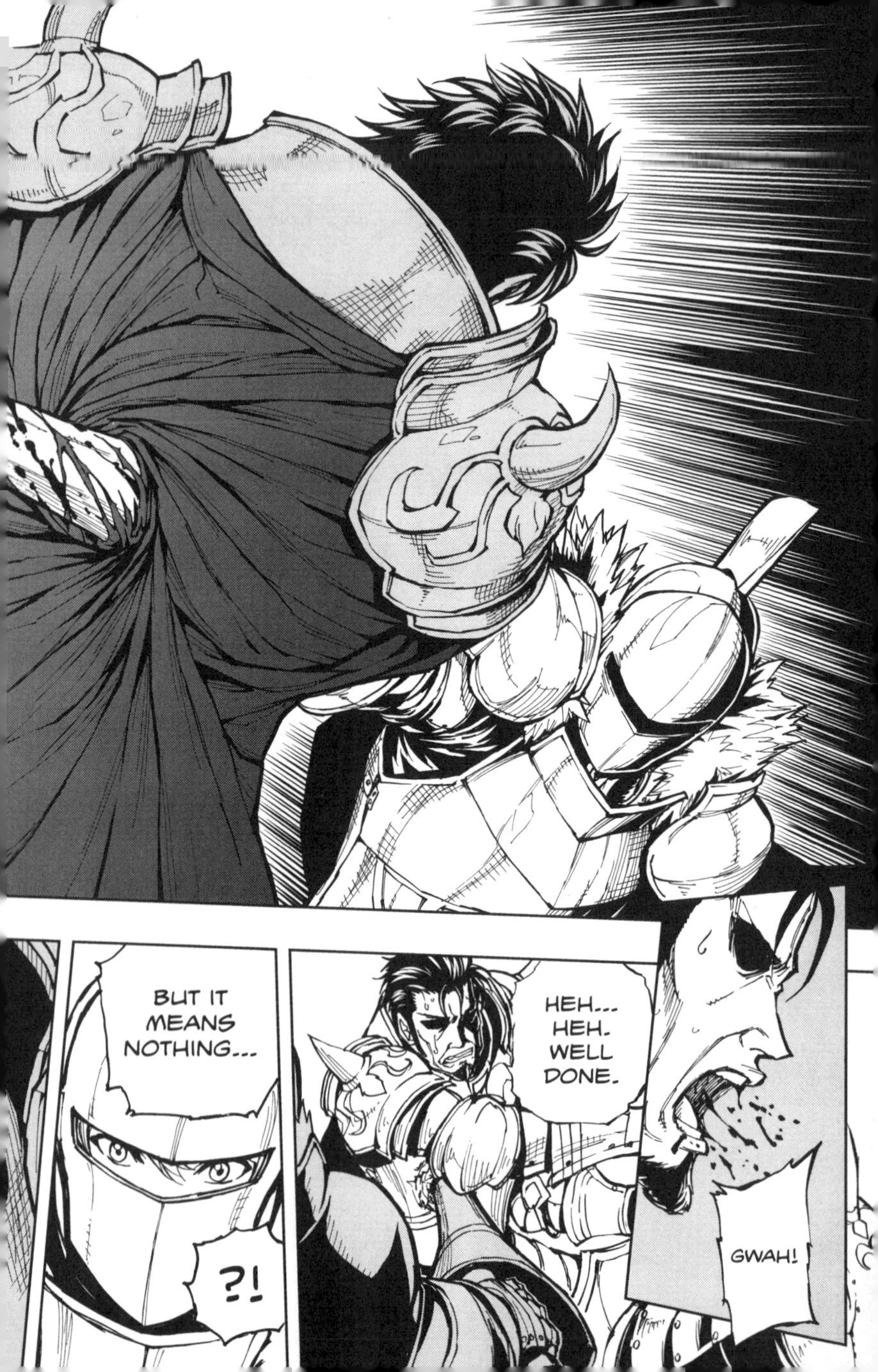
GWAH!
HEH... HEH. WELL DONE.
BUT IT MEANS NOTHING...
?!

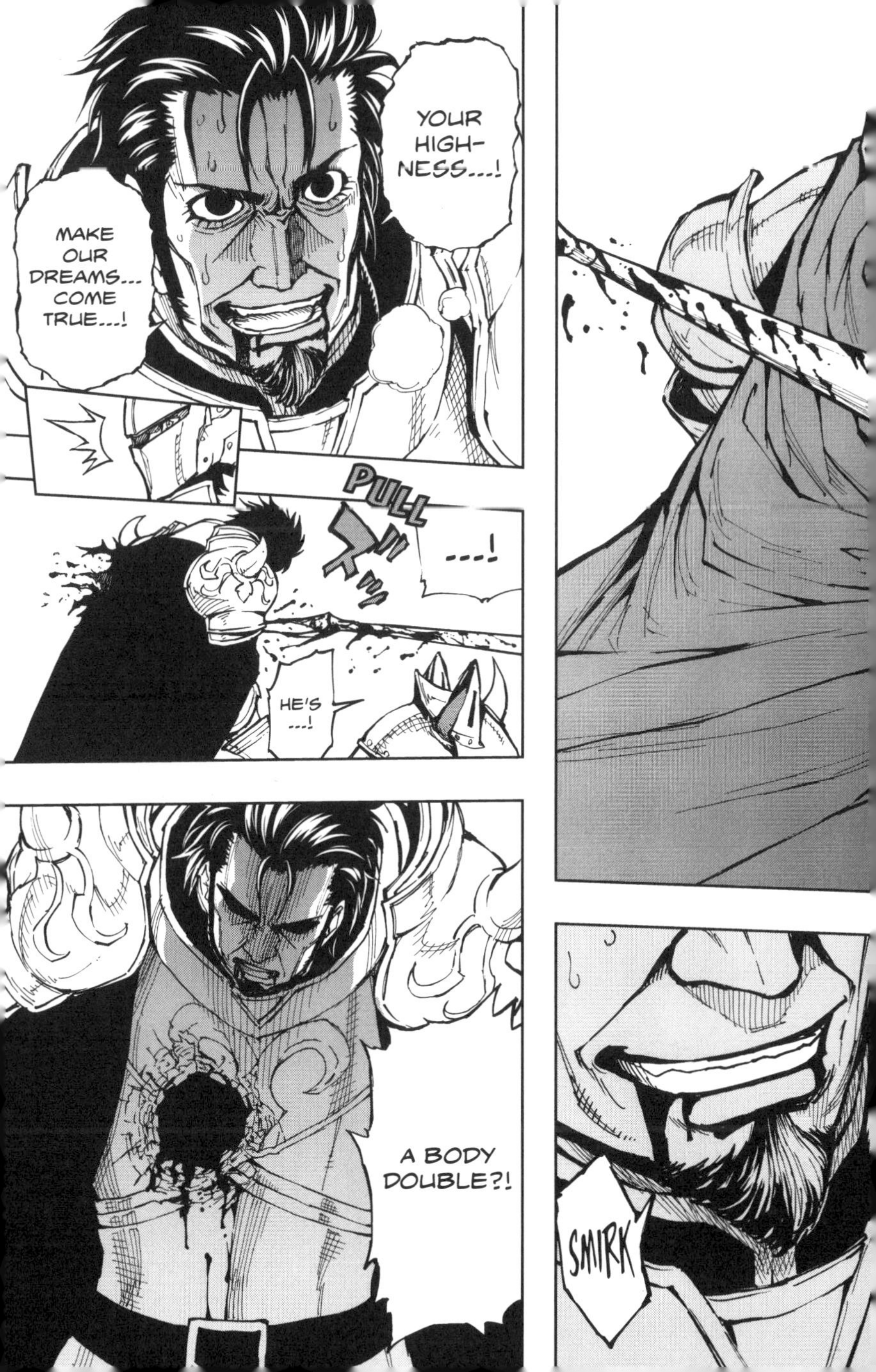
YOUR HIGH-NESS...!
MAKE OUR DREAMS... COME TRUE...!
PULL
---!
HE'S ---!
SMIRK
A BODY DOUBLE?!

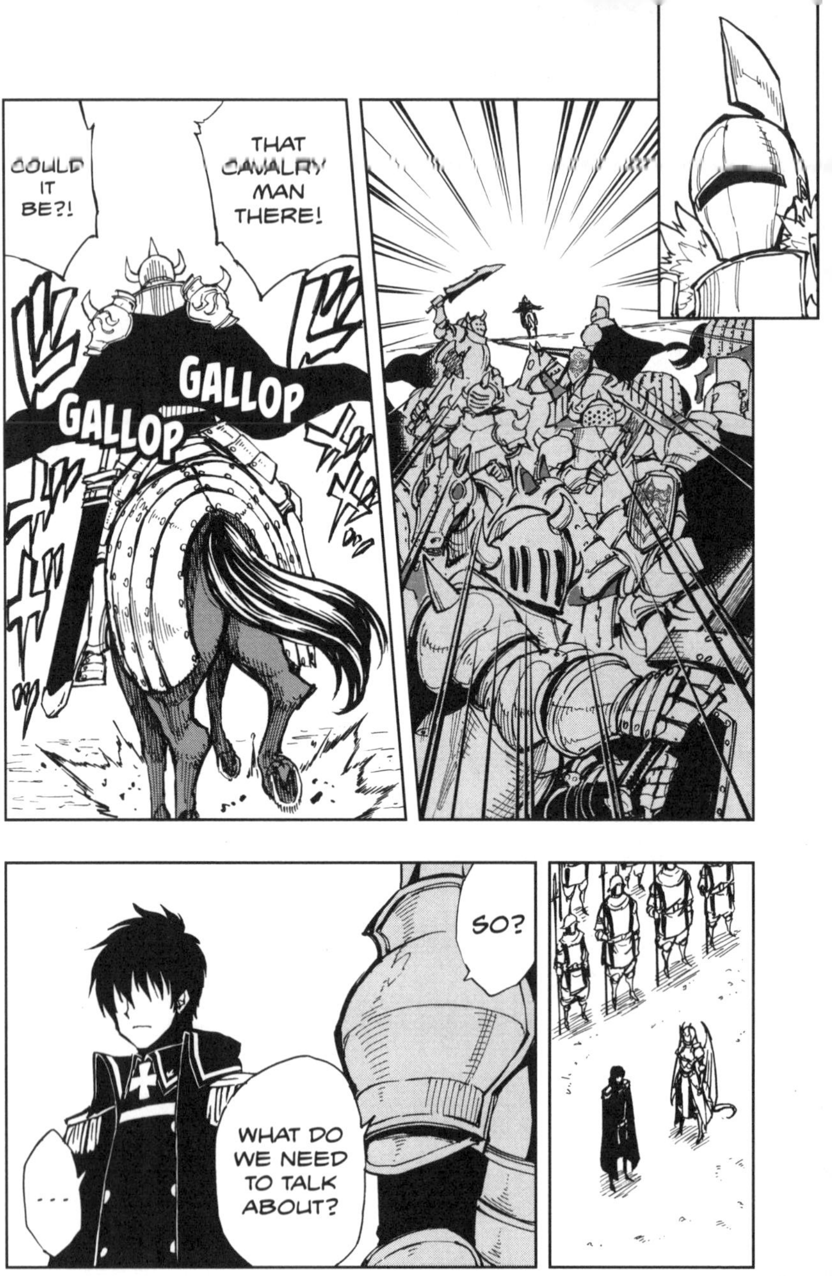
THAT CAVALRY MAN THERE!
COULD IT BE?!
GALLOP
GALLOP
SO?
WHAT DO WE NEED TO TALK ABOUT?
...

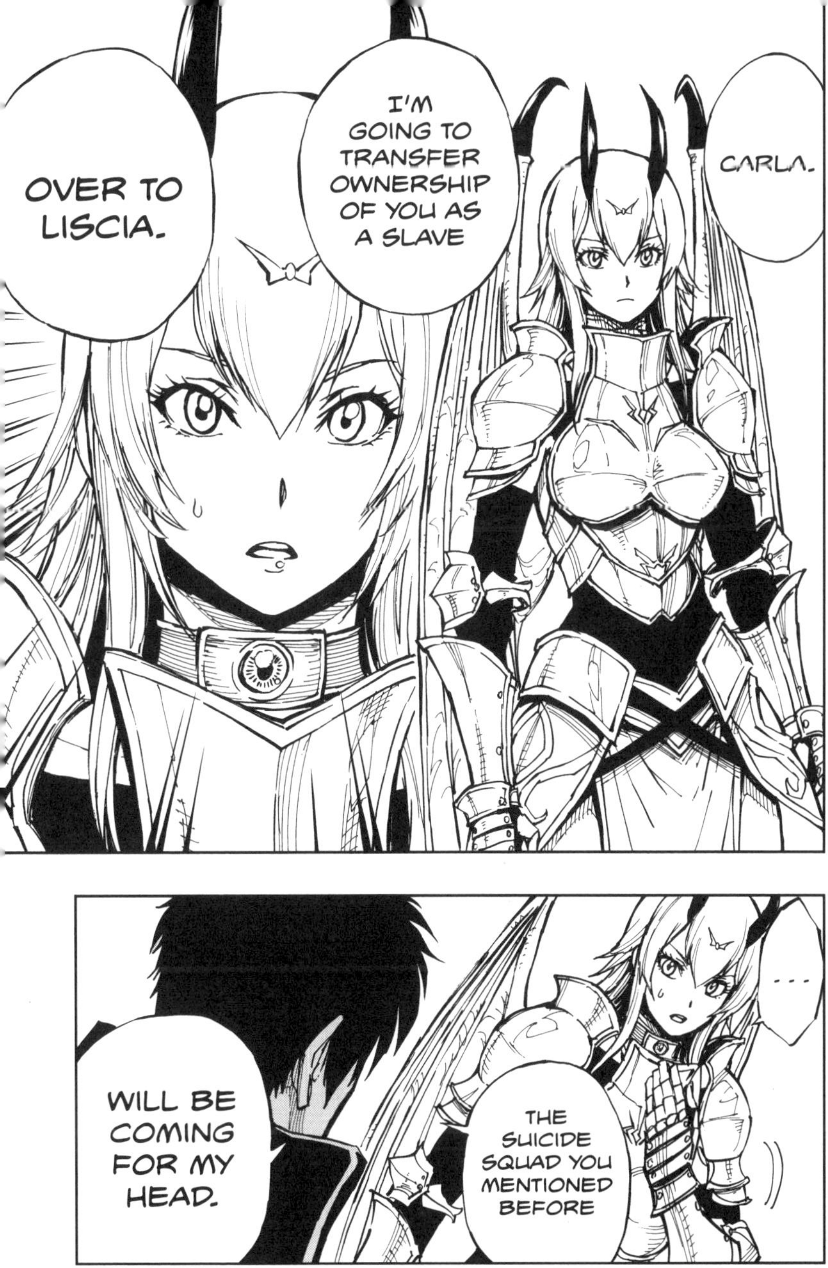
CARLA.
I'M GOING TO TRANSFER OWNERSHIP OF YOU AS A SLAVE
OVER TO LISCIA.
...
THE SUICIDE SQUAD YOU MENTIONED BEFORE
WILL BE COMING FOR MY HEAD.

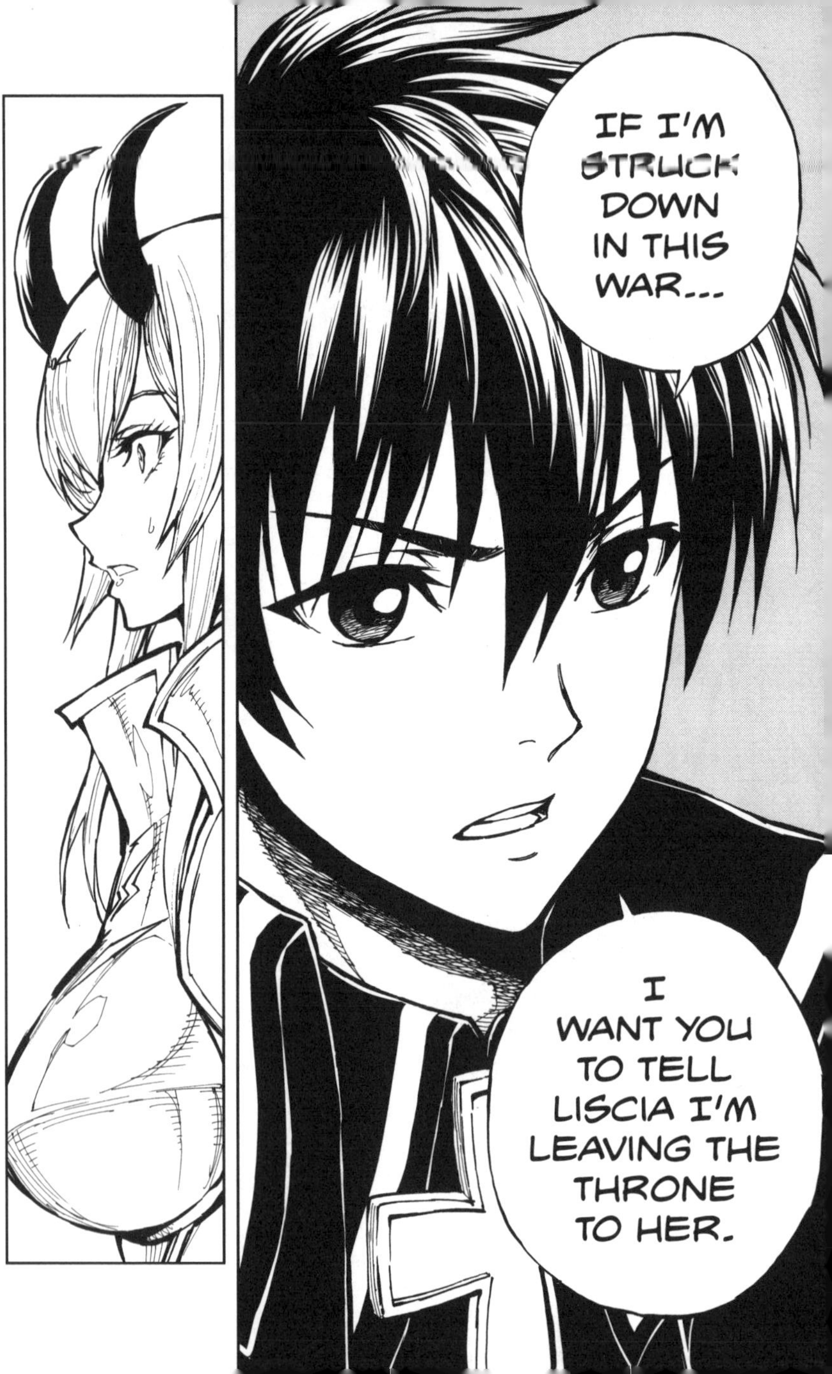
IF I'M STRUCK DOWN IN THIS WAR...
I WANT YOU TO TELL LISCIA I'M LEAVING THE THRONE TO HER.

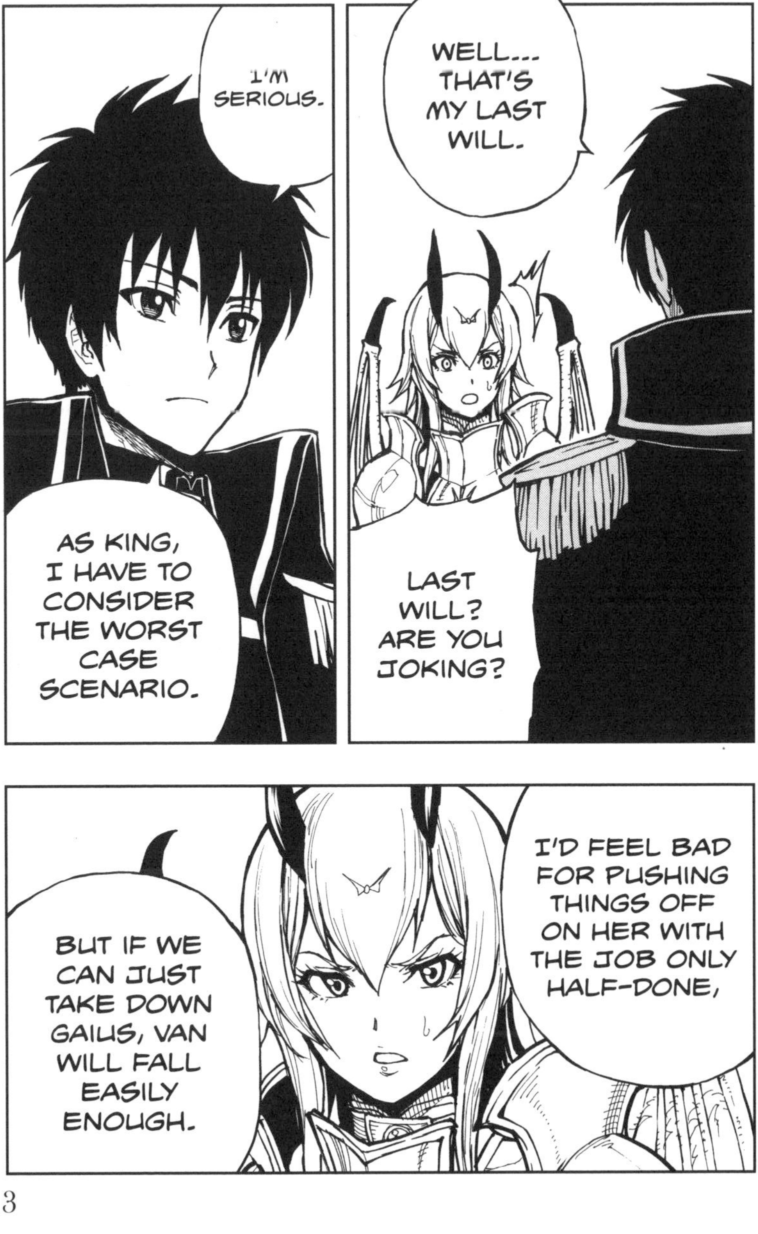
WELL... THAT'S MY LAST WILL.
LAST WILL? ARE YOU JOKING?
I'M SERIOUS.
AS KING, I HAVE TO CONSIDER THE WORST CASE SCENARIO.
I'D FEEL BAD FOR PUSHING THINGS OFF ON HER WITH THE JOB ONLY HALF-DONE,
BUT IF WE CAN JUST TAKE DOWN GAIUS, VAN WILL FALL EASILY ENOUGH.

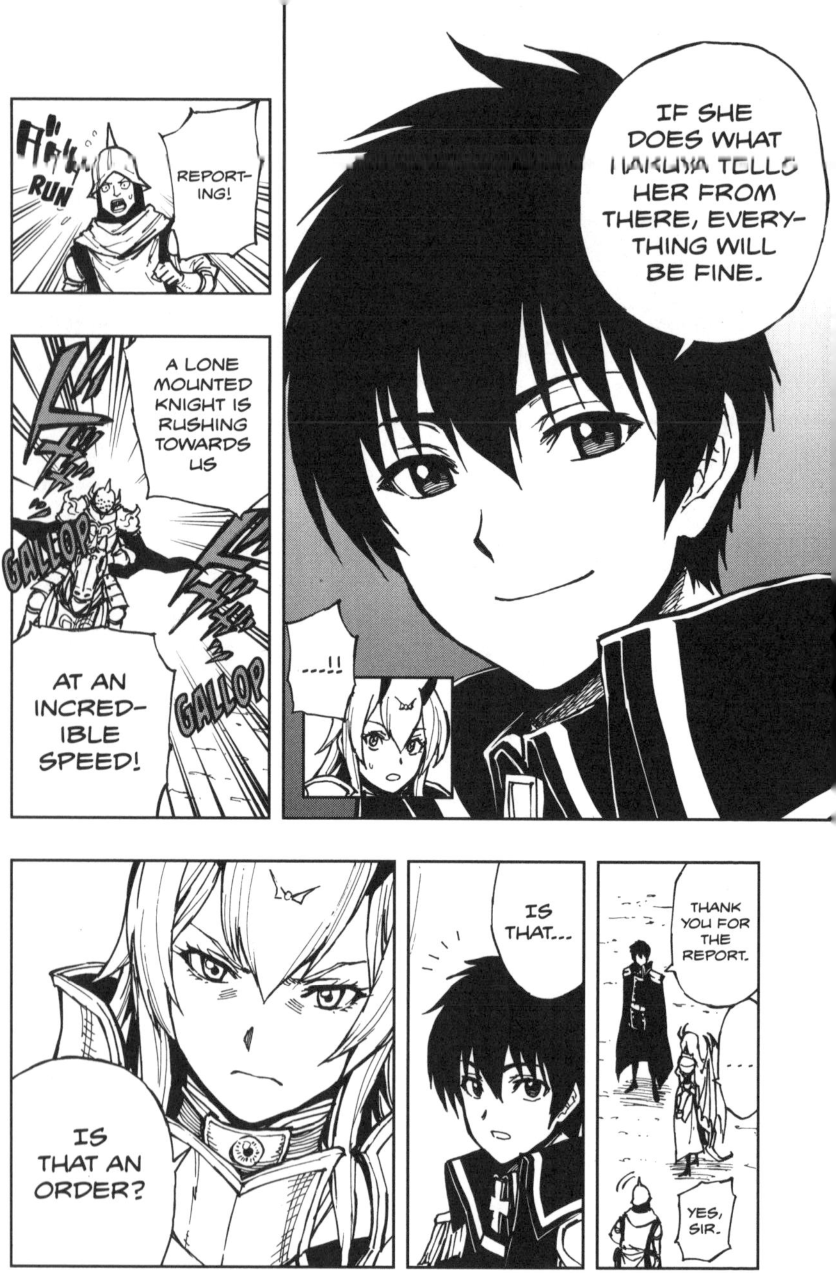
IF SHE DOES WHAT HAKUYA TELLS HER FROM THERE, EVERYTHING WILL BE FINE.
...!!
REPORTING!
RUN
A LONE MOUNTED KNIGHT IS RUSHING TOWARDS US
GALLOP
AT AN INCREDIBLE SPEED!
GALLOP
THANK YOU FOR THE REPORT.
...
YES, SIR.
IS THAT...
IS THAT AN ORDER?

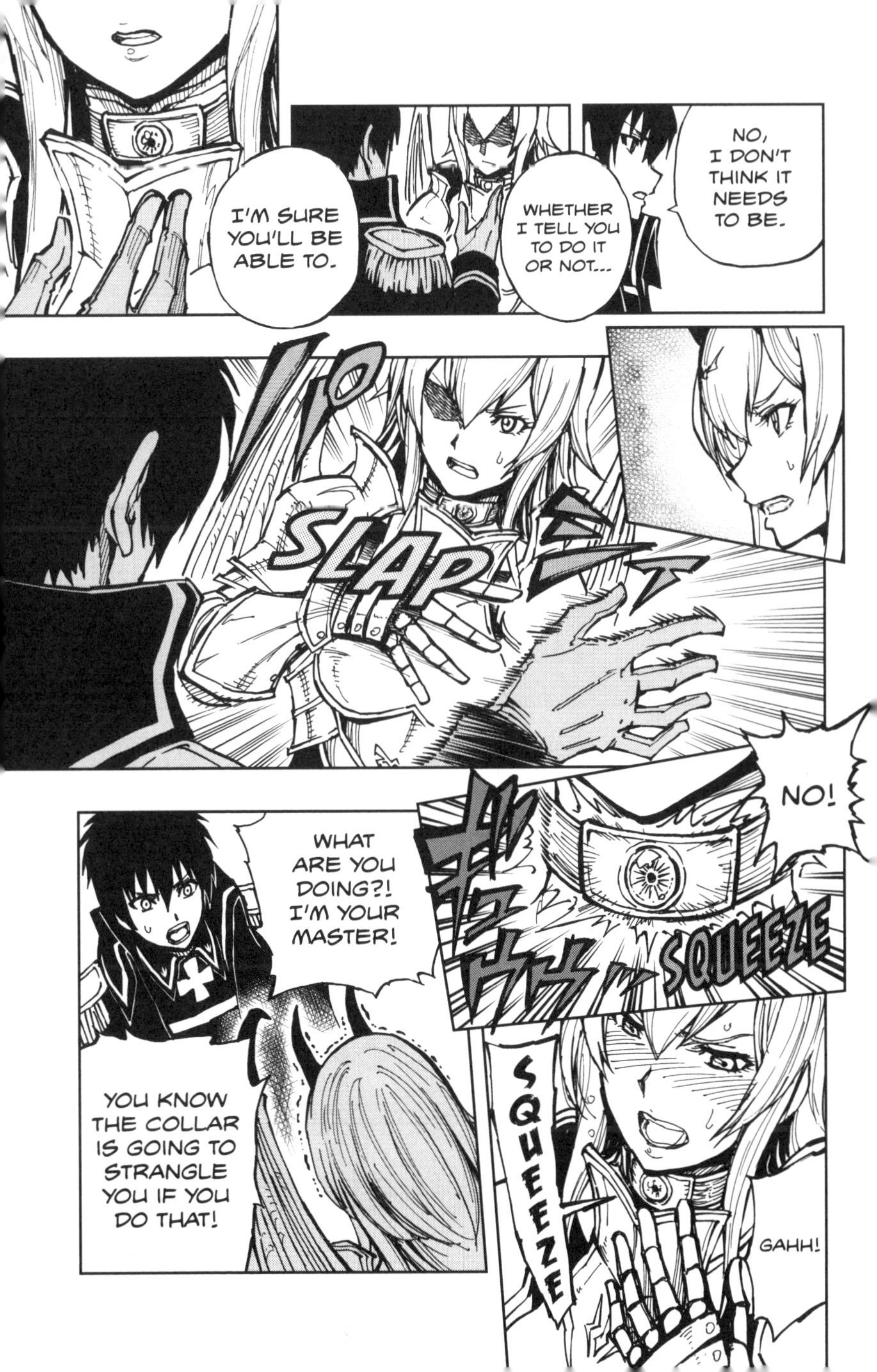
NO, I DON'T THINK IT NEEDS TO BE.
WHETHER I TELL YOU TO DO IT OR NOT...
I'M SURE YOU'LL BE ABLE TO.
SLAP
NO!
SQUEEZE
SQUEEZE
GAHH!
WHAT ARE YOU DOING?! I'M YOUR MASTER!
YOU KNOW THE COLLAR IS GOING TO STRANGLE YOU IF YOU DO THAT!

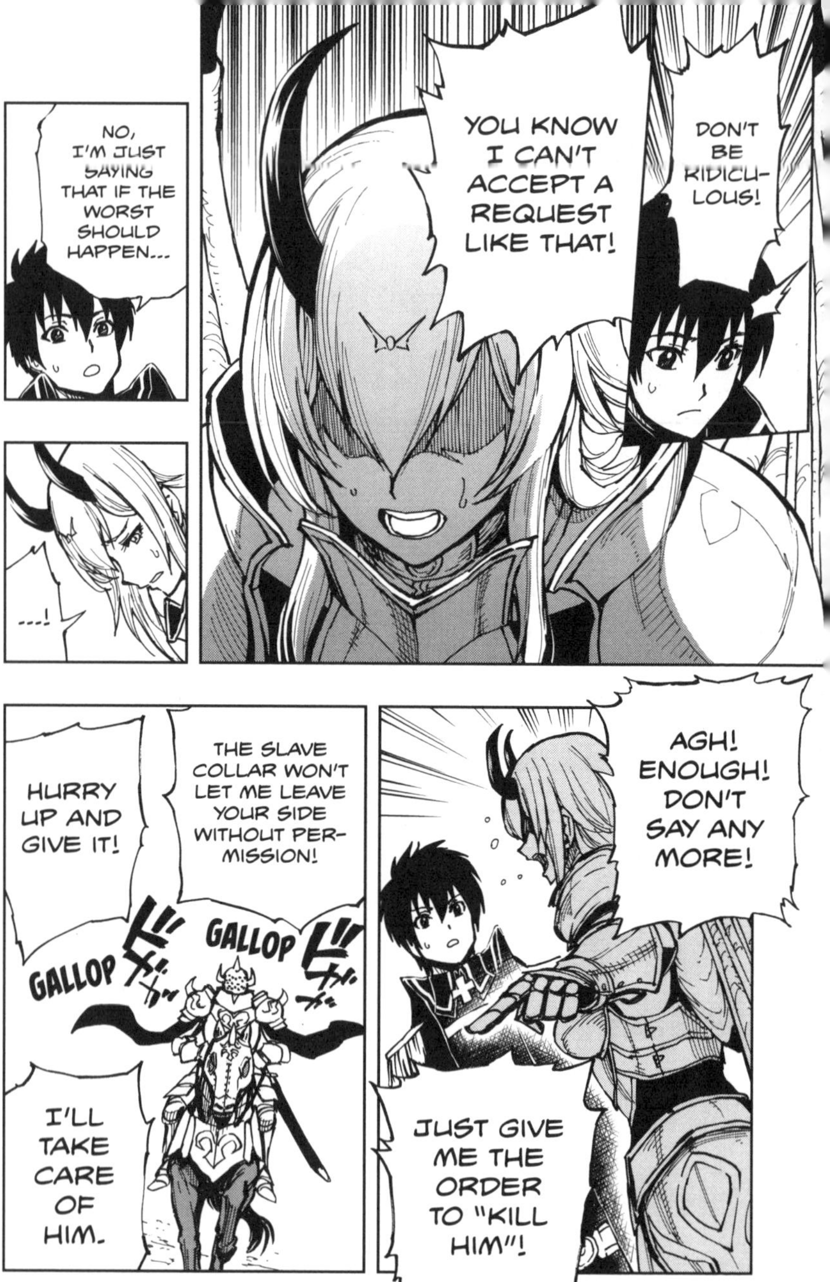
DON'T BE RIDICULOUS!
YOU KNOW I CAN'T ACCEPT A REQUEST LIKE THAT!
NO, I'M JUST SAYING THAT IF THE WORST SHOULD HAPPEN...
...!
AGH! ENOUGH! DON'T SAY ANY MORE!
JUST GIVE ME THE ORDER TO "KILL HIM"!
THE SLAVE COLLAR WON'T LET ME LEAVE YOUR SIDE WITHOUT PERMISSION!
HURRY UP AND GIVE IT!
GALLOP
GALLOP
I'LL TAKE CARE OF HIM.

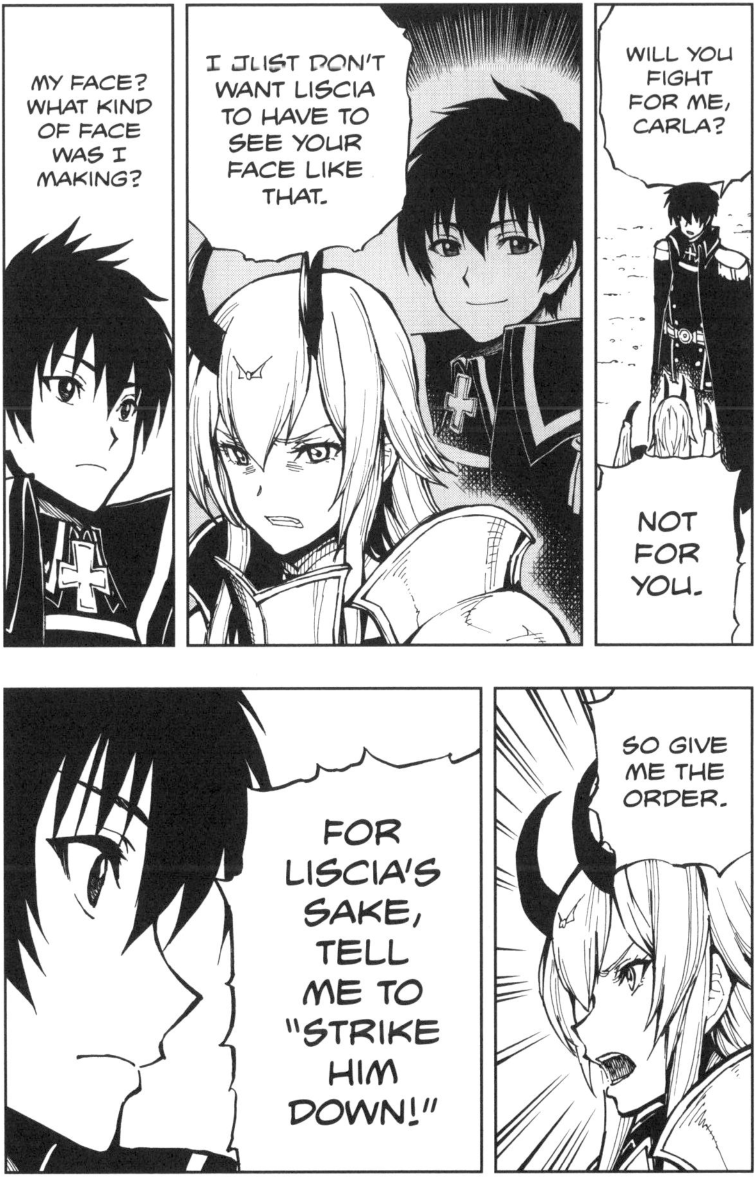
WILL YOU FIGHT FOR ME, CARLA?
NOT FOR YOU.
I JUST DON'T WANT LISCIA TO HAVE TO SEE YOUR FACE LIKE THAT.
MY FACE? WHAT KIND OF FACE WAS I MAKING?
SO GIVE ME THE ORDER.
FOR LISCIA'S SAKE, TELL ME TO "STRIKE HIM DOWN!"

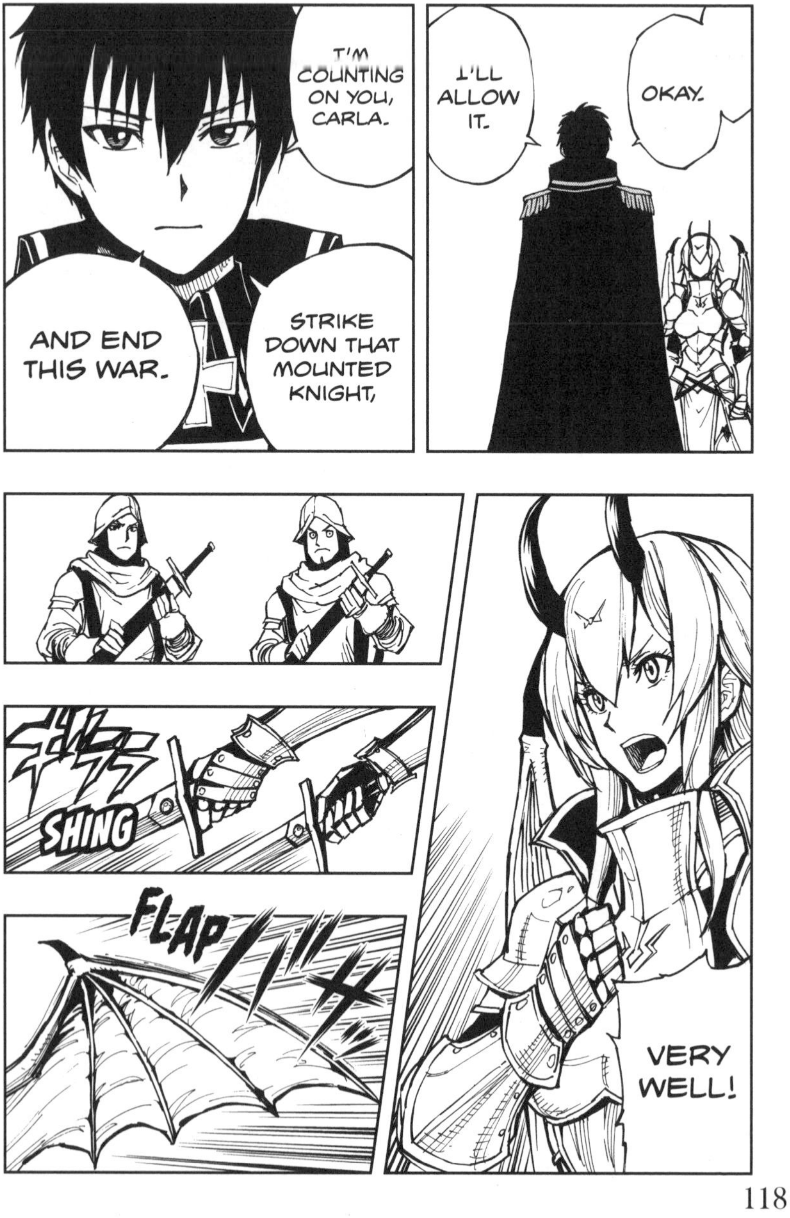
OKAY.
I'LL ALLOW IT.
I'M COUNTING ON YOU, CARLA.
STRIKE DOWN THAT MOUNTED KNIGHT,
AND END THIS WAR.
VERY WELL!
SHING
FLAP

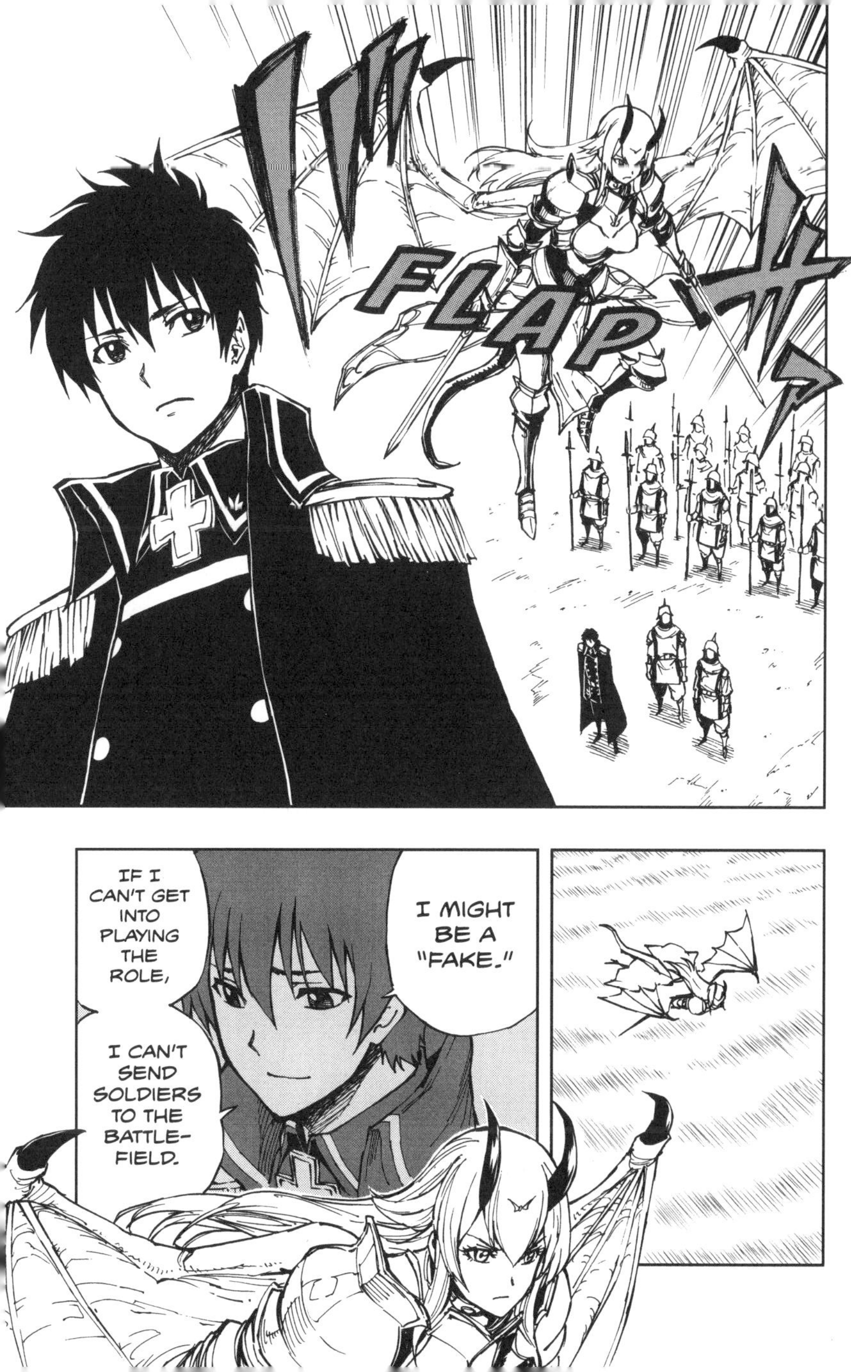
FLAP
I MIGHT BE A "FAKE."
IF I CAN'T GET INTO PLAYING THE ROLE,
I CAN'T SEND SOLDIERS TO THE BATTLE-FIELD.

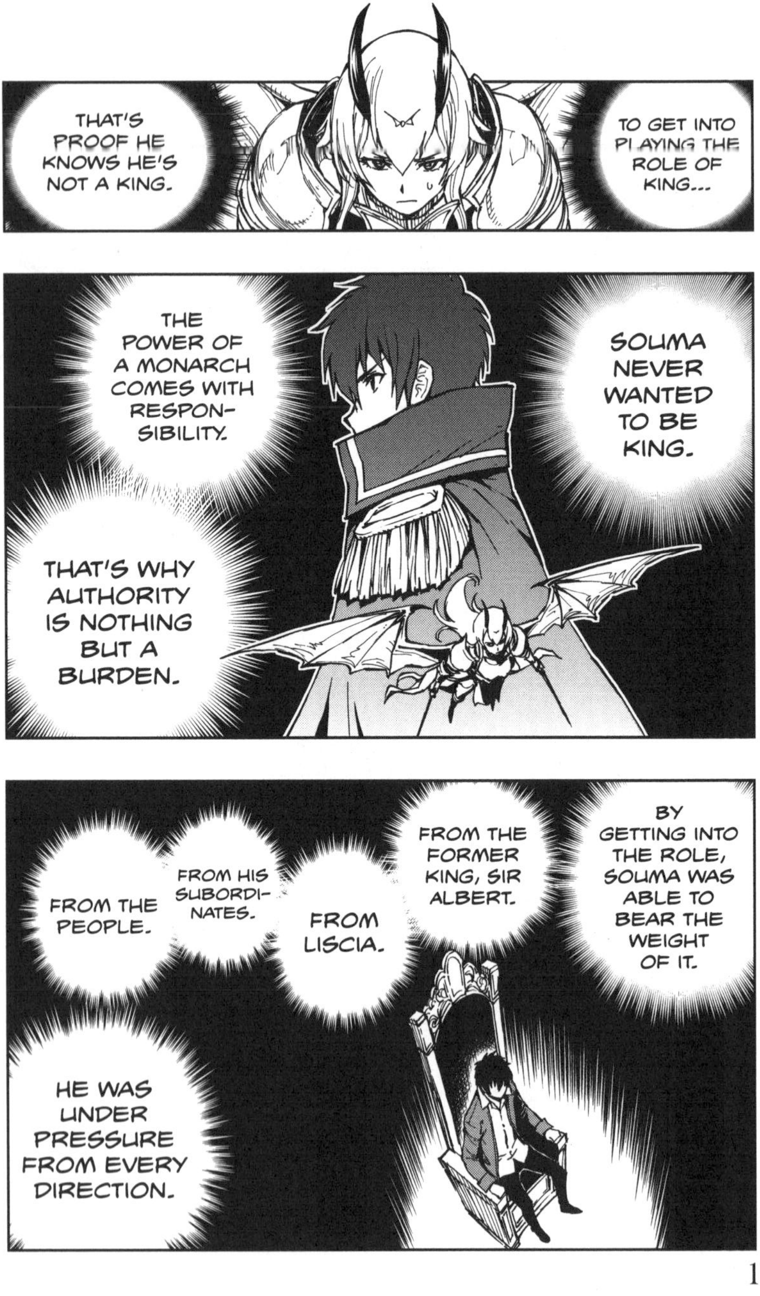
TO GET INTO PLAYING THE ROLE OF KING...
THAT'S PROOF HE KNOWS HE'S NOT A KING.
SOUMA NEVER WANTED TO BE KING.
THE POWER OF A MONARCH COMES WITH RESPON-SIBILITY.
THAT'S WHY AUTHORITY IS NOTHING BUT A BURDEN.
BY GETTING INTO THE ROLE, SOUMA WAS ABLE TO BEAR THE WEIGHT OF IT.
FROM THE FORMER KING, SIR ALBERT.
FROM LISCIA.
FROM HIS SUBORDI-NATES.
FROM THE PEOPLE.
HE WAS UNDER PRESSURE FROM EVERY DIRECTION.

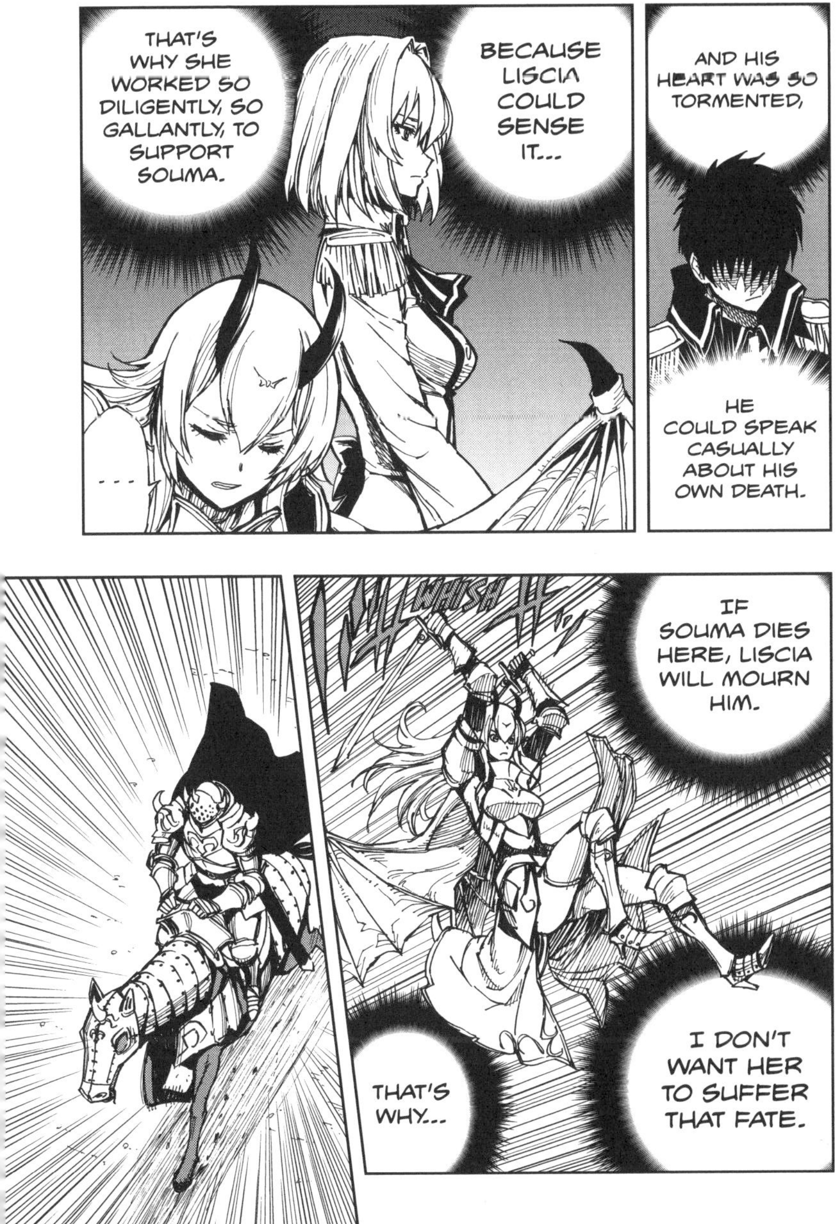
AND HIS HEART WAS SO TORMENTED,
HE COULD SPEAK CASUALLY ABOUT HIS OWN DEATH.
BECAUSE LISCIA COULD SENSE IT...
THAT'S WHY SHE WORKED SO DILIGENTLY, SO GALLANTLY, TO SUPPORT SOUMA.
...
WHISH
IF SOUMA DIES HERE, LISCIA WILL MOURN HIM.
I DON'T WANT HER TO SUFFER THAT FATE.
THAT'S WHY...

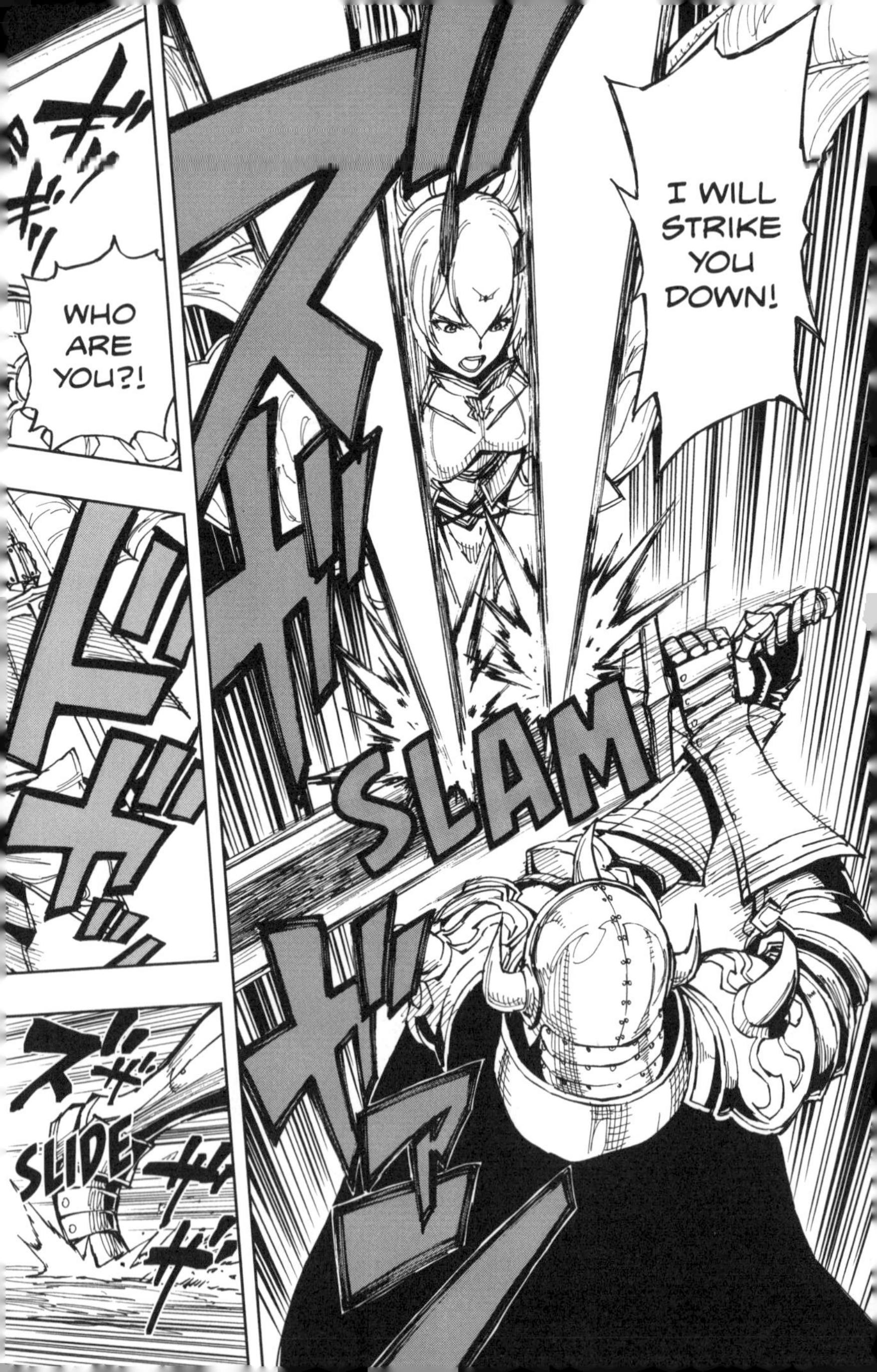
I WILL STRIKE YOU DOWN!
SLAM
WHO ARE YOU?!
SLIDE

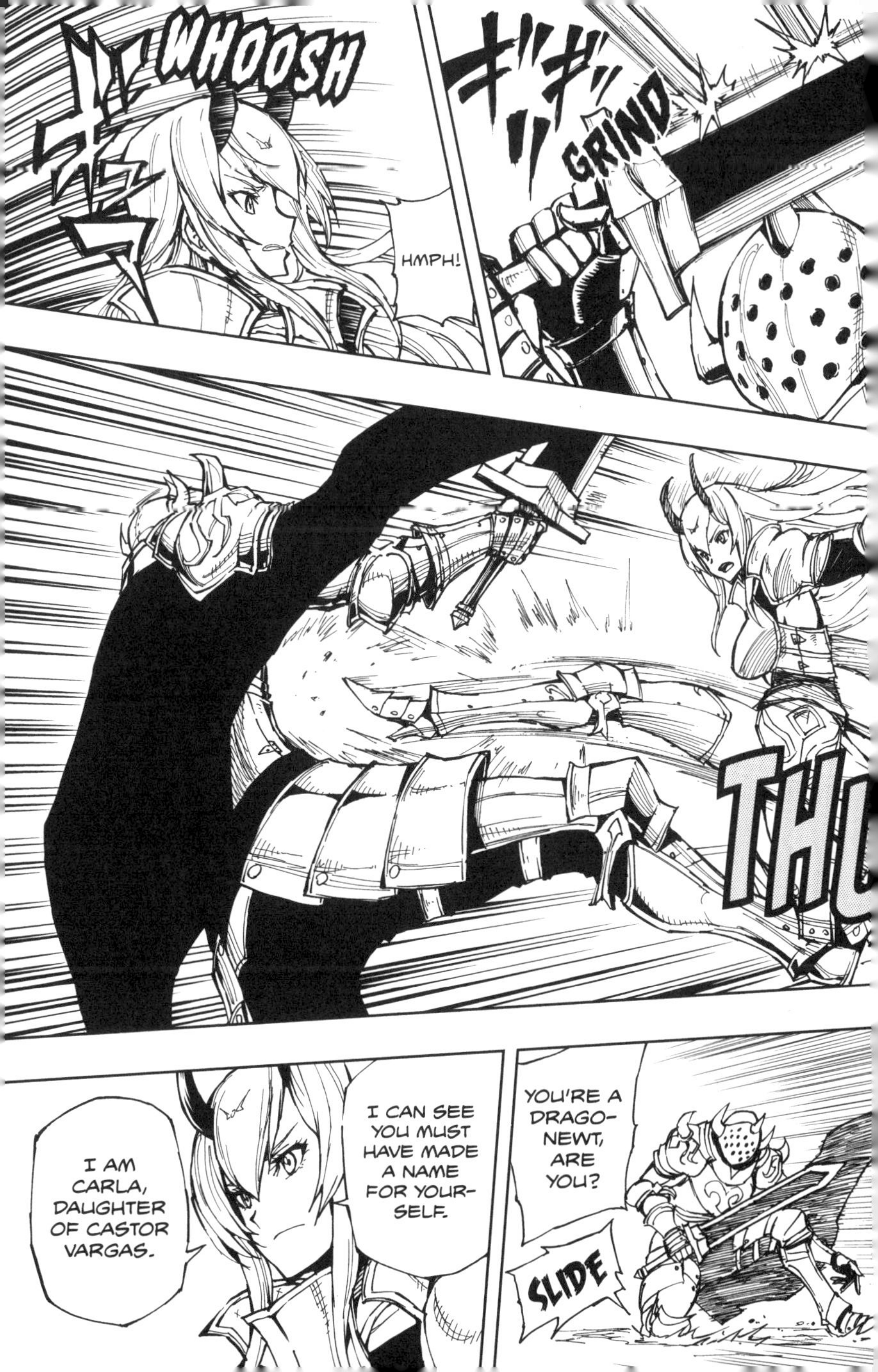
GRIND
WHOOSH
HMPH!
THU
YOU'RE A DRAGO-NEWT, ARE YOU?
SLIDE
I CAN SEE YOU MUST HAVE MADE A NAME FOR YOUR-SELF.
I AM CARLA, DAUGHTER OF CASTOR VARGAS.

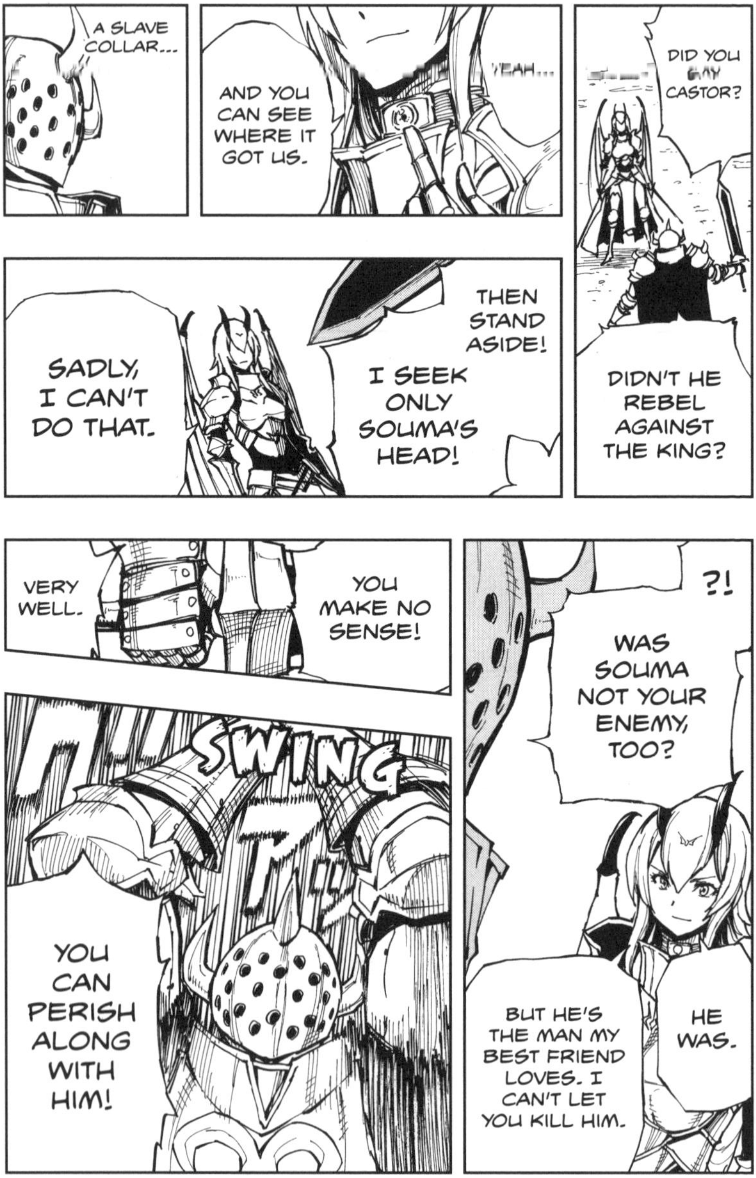
DID YOU SAY CASTOR?
DIDN'T HE REBEL AGAINST THE KING?
YEAH...
AND YOU CAN SEE WHERE IT GOT US.
A SLAVE COLLAR...
THEN STAND ASIDE!
I SEEK ONLY SOUMA'S HEAD!
SADLY, I CAN'T DO THAT.
?!
WAS SOUMA NOT YOUR ENEMY, TOO?
HE WAS.
BUT HE'S THE MAN MY BEST FRIEND LOVES. I CAN'T LET YOU KILL HIM.
YOU MAKE NO SENSE!
VERY WELL.
SWING
YOU CAN PERISH ALONG WITH HIM!

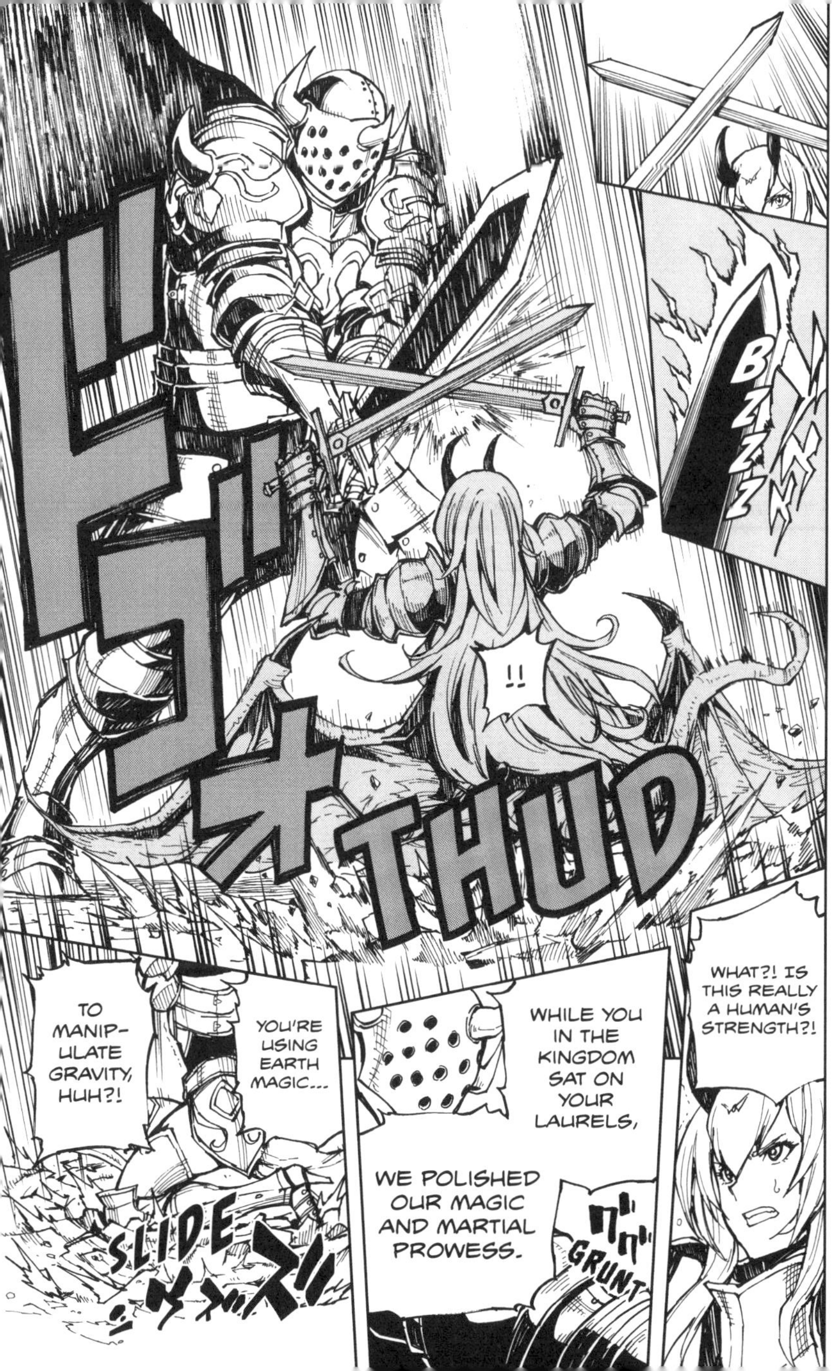
BZZZZ
!!
THUD
WHAT?! IS THIS REALLY A HUMAN'S STRENGTH?!
WHILE YOU IN THE KINGDOM SAT ON YOUR LAURELS,
WE POLISHED OUR MAGIC AND MARTIAL PROWESS.
GRUNT
YOU'RE USING EARTH MAGIC...
TO MANIP-ULATE GRAVITY, HUH?!
SLIDE

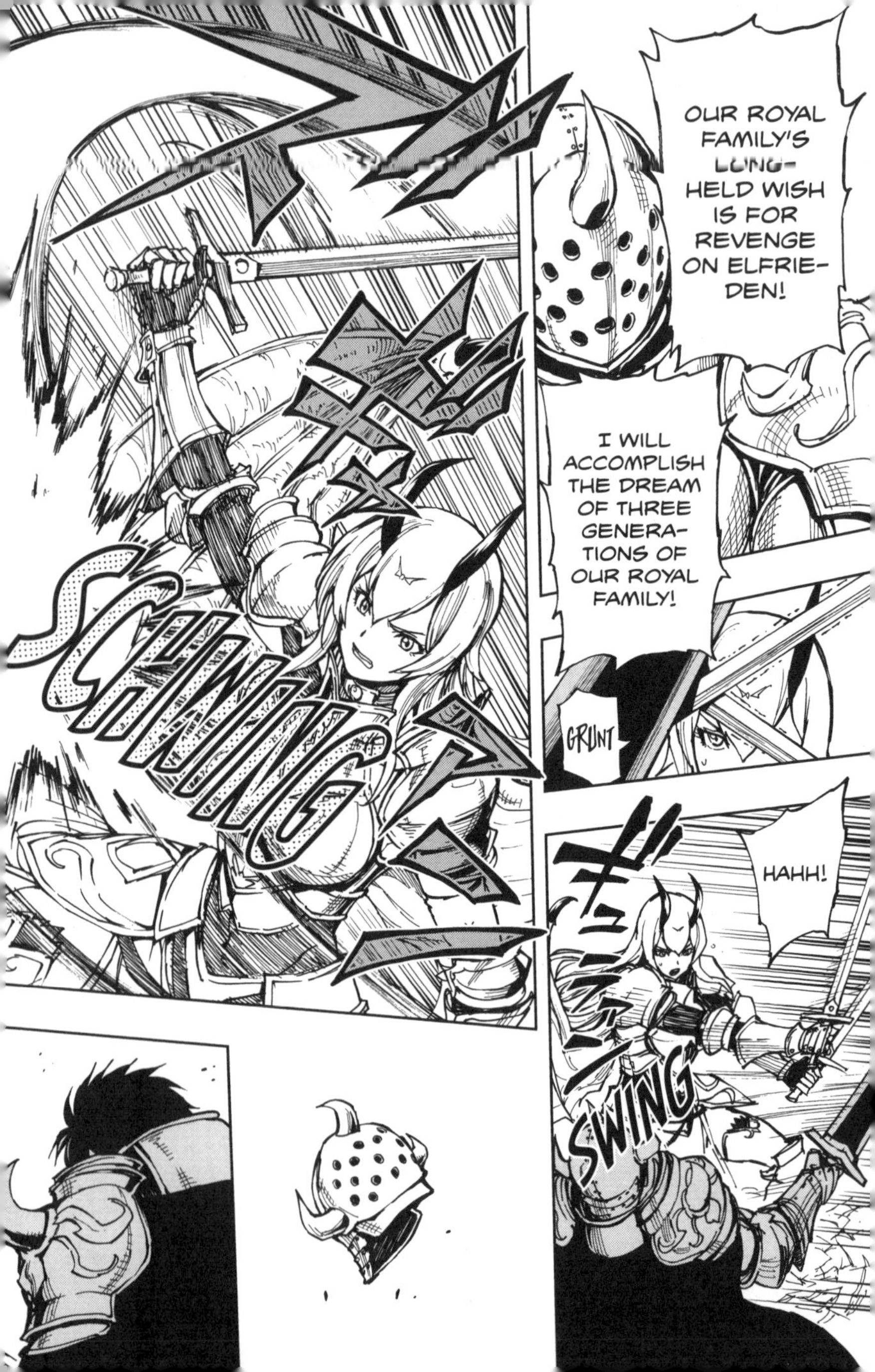
OUR ROYAL FAMILY'S LONG-HELD WISH IS FOR REVENGE ON ELFRIEDEN!
I WILL ACCOMPLISH THE DREAM OF THREE GENERATIONS OF OUR ROYAL FAMILY!
GRUNT
SCHWING
HAHH!
SWING

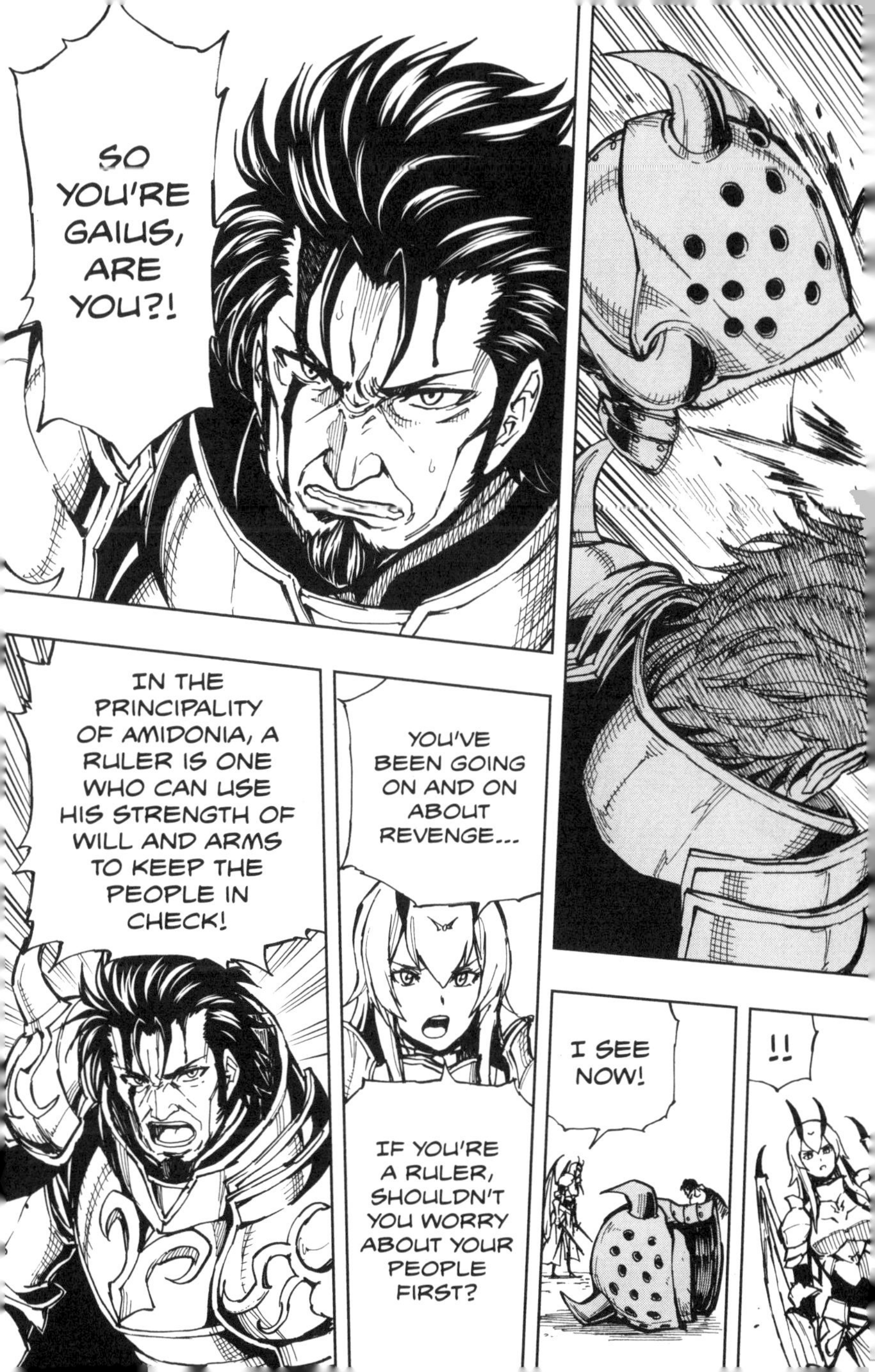
SO YOU'RE GAIUS, ARE YOU?!
YOU'VE BEEN GOING ON AND ON ABOUT REVENGE...
IF YOU'RE A RULER, SHOULDN'T YOU WORRY ABOUT YOUR PEOPLE FIRST?
IN THE PRINCIPALITY OF AMIDONIA, A RULER IS ONE WHO CAN USE HIS STRENGTH OF WILL AND ARMS TO KEEP THE PEOPLE IN CHECK!
!!
I SEE NOW!

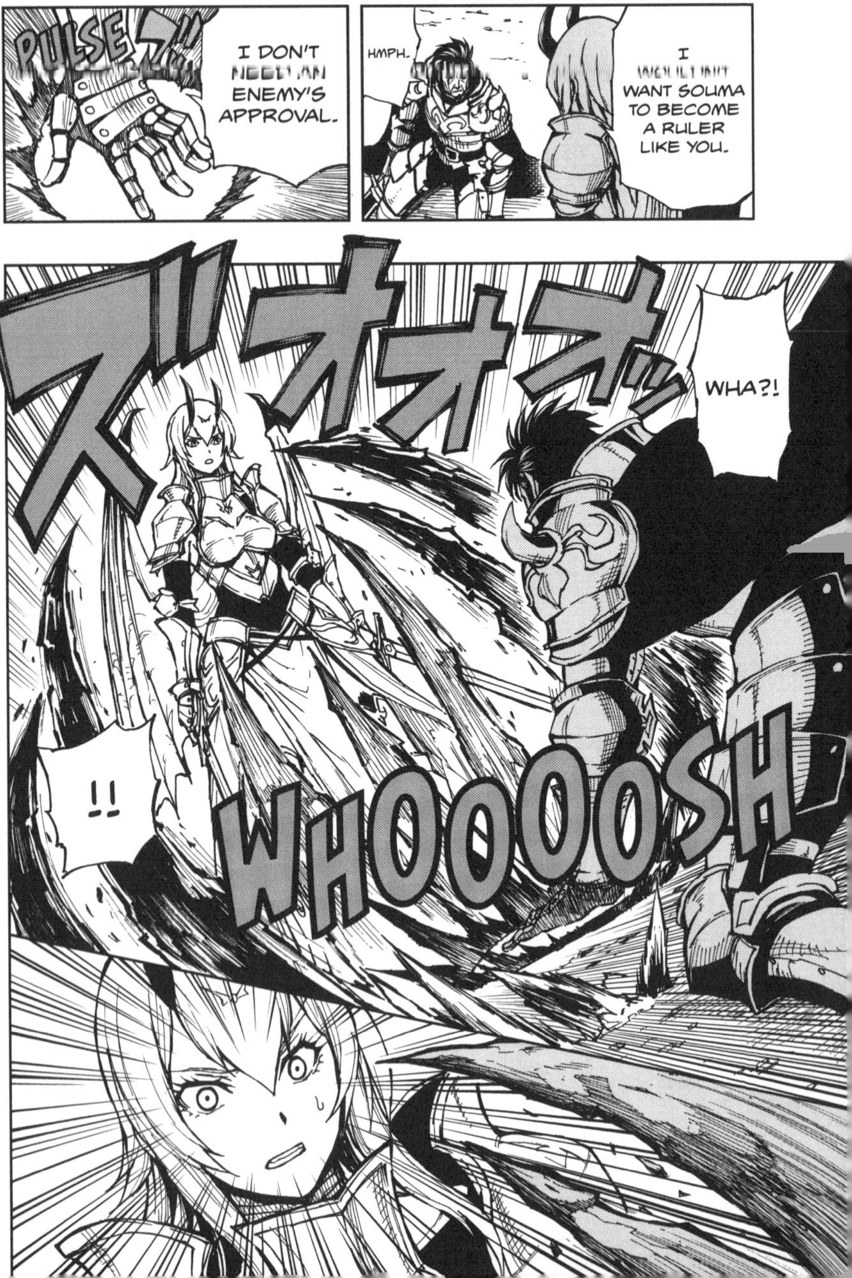
I
WANT SOUMA TO BECOME A RULER LIKE YOU.
HMPH.
PULSE
I DON'T
ENEMY'S APPROVAL.
ズオオオ
WHA?!
WHOOOOSH
!!

Chapter 26: The Final Battle (4)

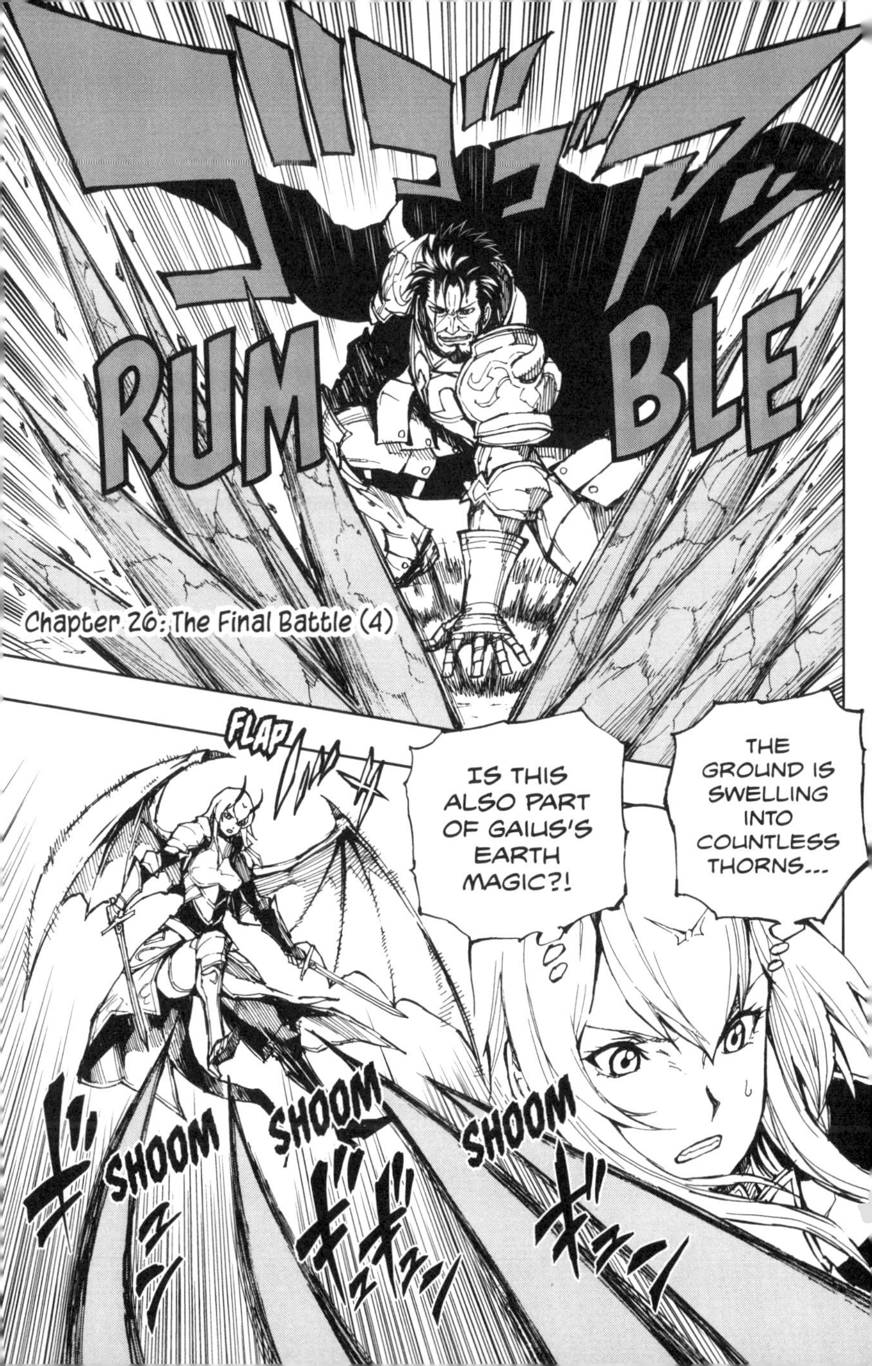
RUMBLE
THE GROUND IS SWELLING INTO COUNTLESS THORNS...
IS THIS ALSO PART OF GAILUS'S EARTH MAGIC?!
FLAP
SHOOM
SHOOM
SHOOM

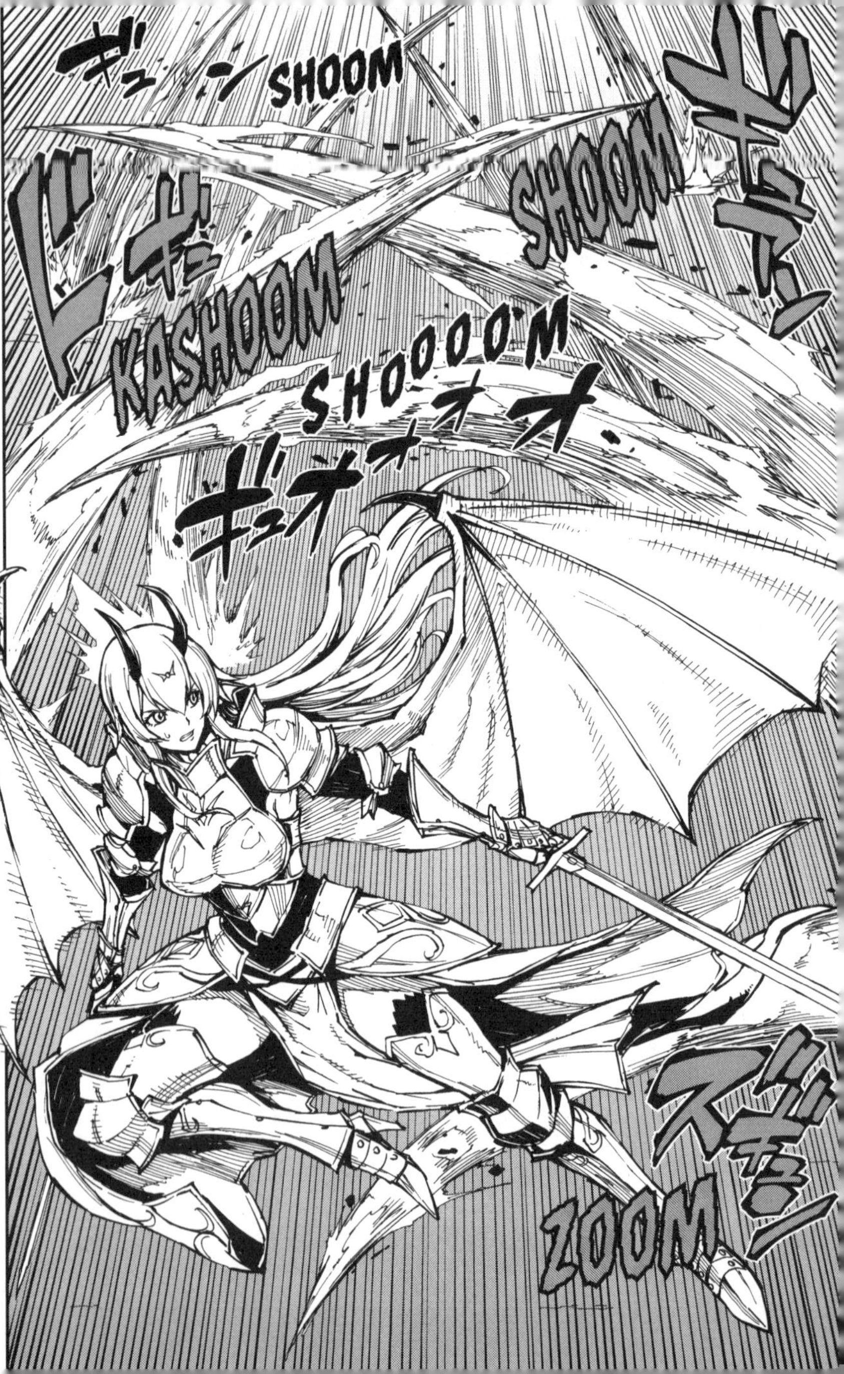
SHOOM
SHOOM
KASHOOM
SHOOOOM
ギュオオオオ
ZOOM

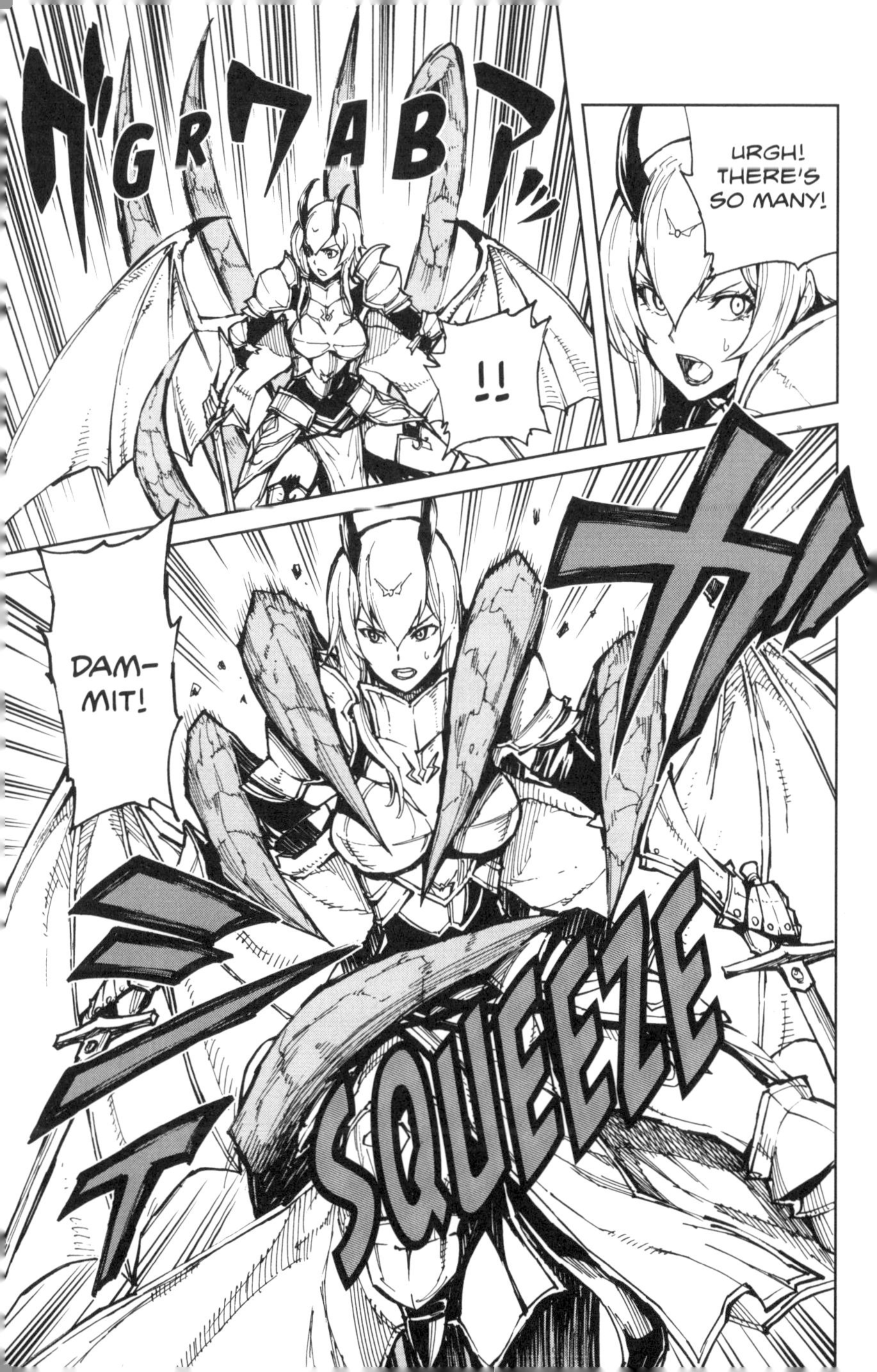
URGH! THERE'S SO MANY!
GRAB
!!
DAM-MIT!
SQUEEZE

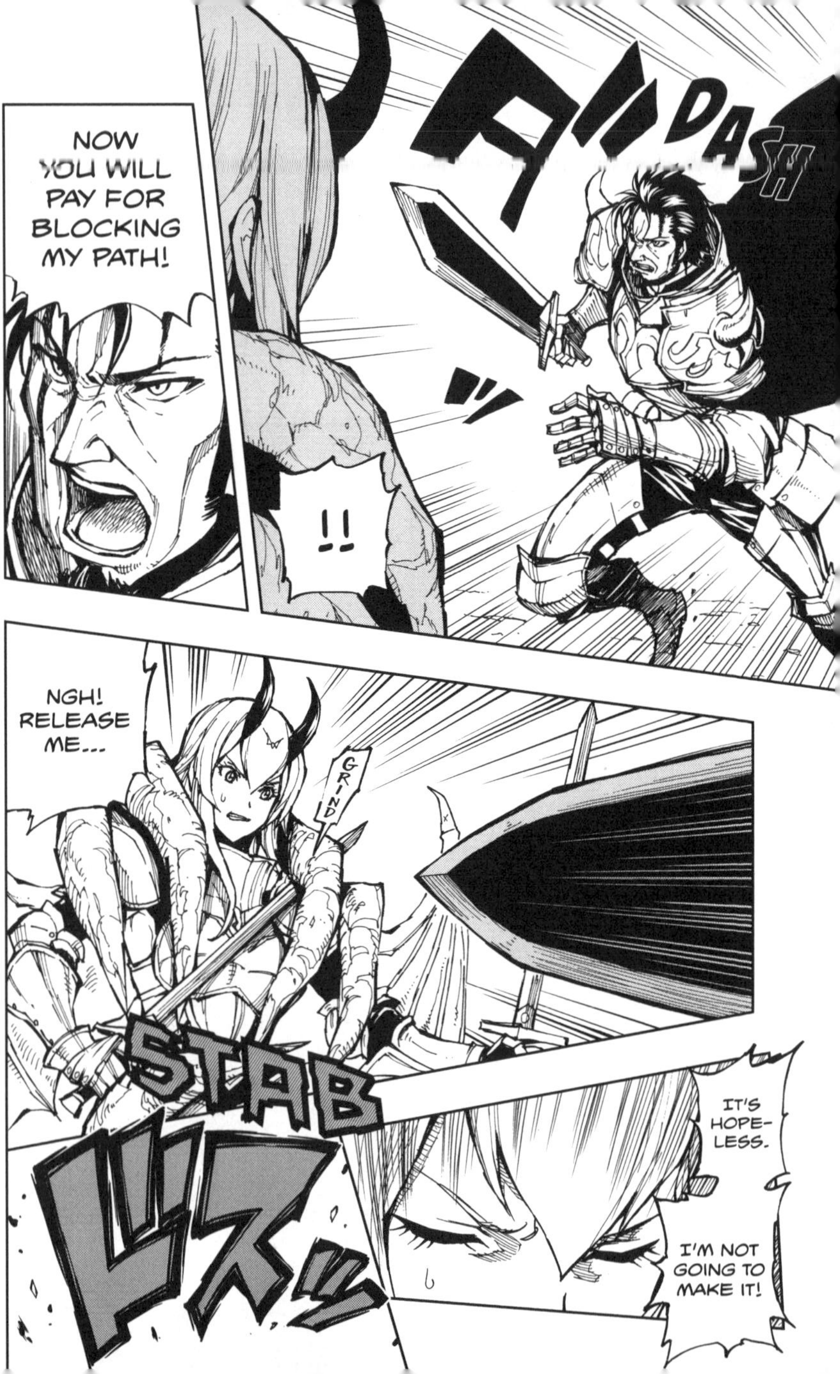
ダッ
DASH
!!
NOW YOU WILL PAY FOR BLOCKING MY PATH!
NGH! RELEASE ME...
GRIND
STAB
ドス!!
IT'S HOPE-LESS.
I'M NOT GOING TO MAKE IT!

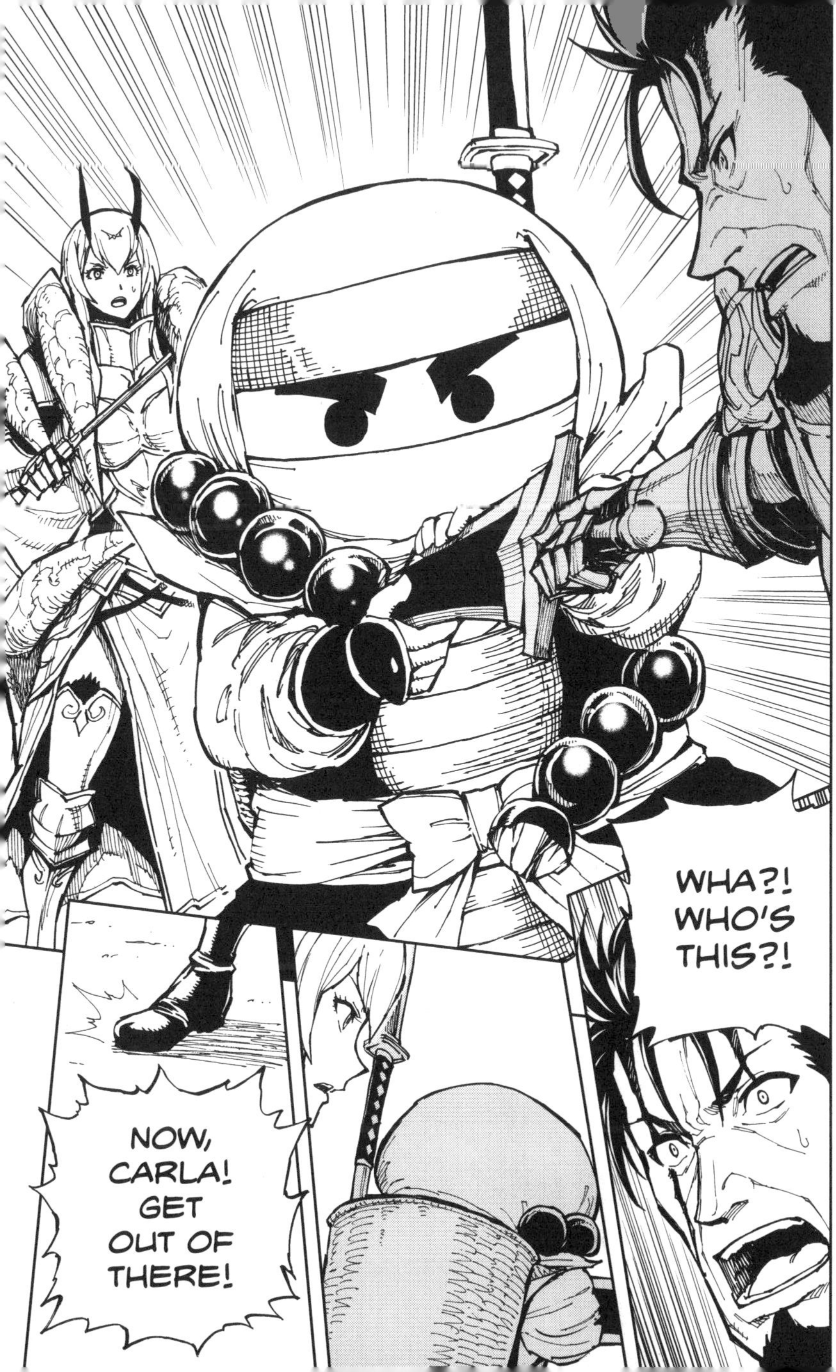
WHA?! WHO'S THIS?!
NOW, CARLA! GET OUT OF THERE!

SOUMA
KAZUYAAAA!!!

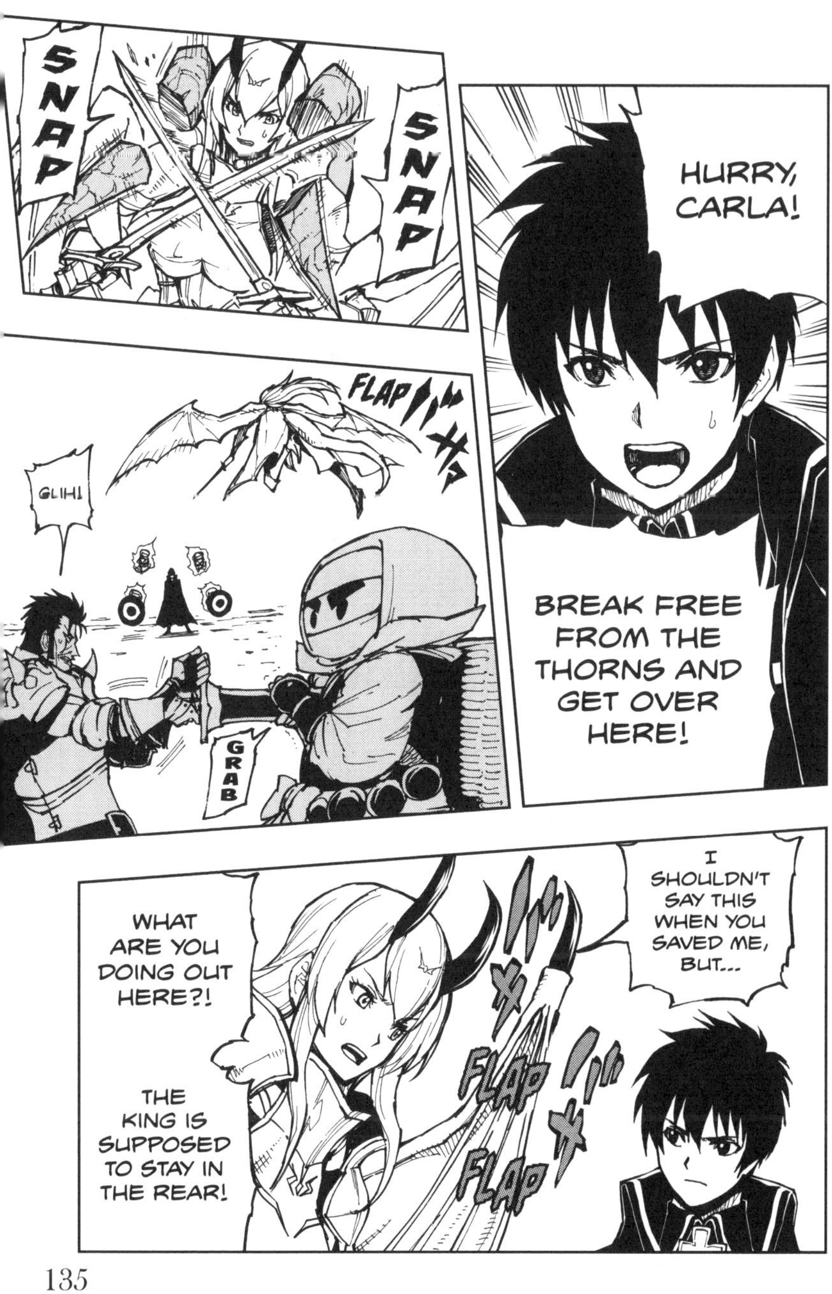
HURRY, CARLA!
BREAK FREE FROM THE THORNS AND GET OVER HERE!
SNAP
SNAP
FLAP
GLIH!
GRAB
I SHOULDN'T SAY THIS WHEN YOU SAVED ME, BUT...
FLAP
FLAP
WHAT ARE YOU DOING OUT HERE?!
THE KING IS SUPPOSED TO STAY IN THE REAR!

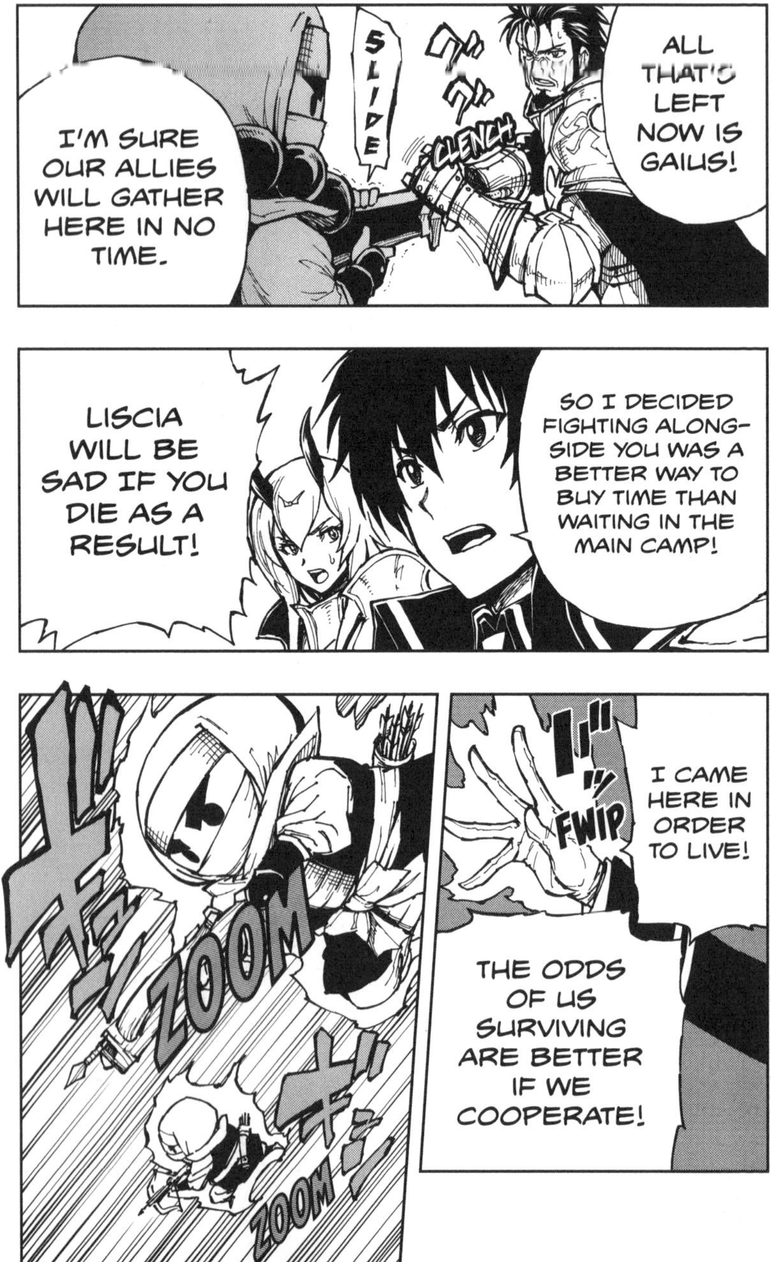

ALL THAT'S LEFT NOW IS GAIUS!
CLENCH
SLIDE
I'M SURE OUR ALLIES WILL GATHER HERE IN NO TIME.
SO I DECIDED FIGHTING ALONG-SIDE YOU WAS A BETTER WAY TO BUY TIME THAN WAITING IN THE MAIN CAMP!
LISCIA WILL BE SAD IF YOU DIE AS A RESULT!
I CAME HERE IN ORDER TO LIVE!
FWIP
THE ODDS OF US SURVIVING ARE BETTER IF WE COOPERATE!
ZOOM
ZOOM

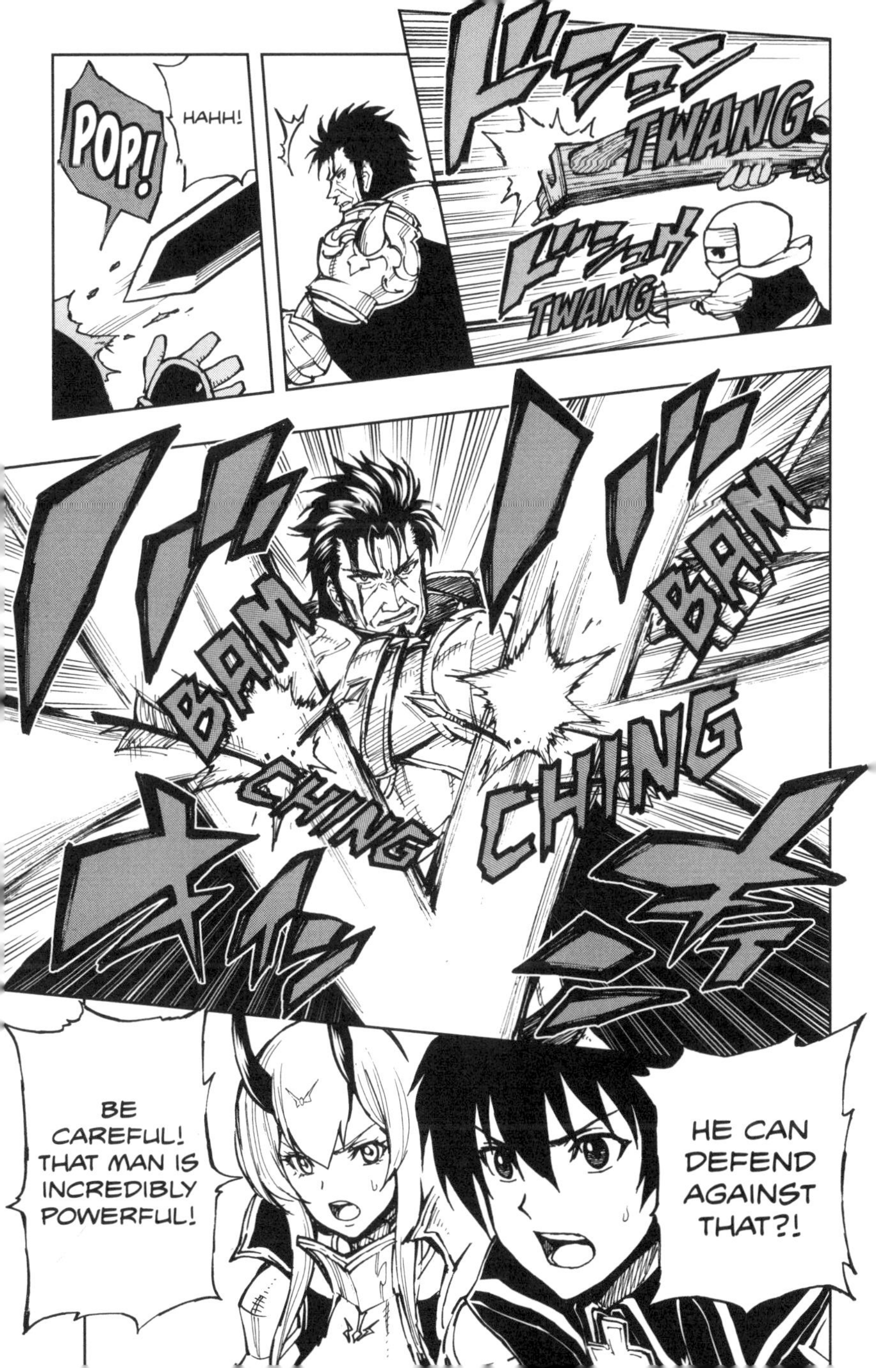
TWANG
TWANG
POP!
HAHH!
BAM
BAM
CHING
CHING
HE CAN DEFEND AGAINST THAT?!
BE CAREFUL! THAT MAN IS INCREDIBLY POWERFUL!

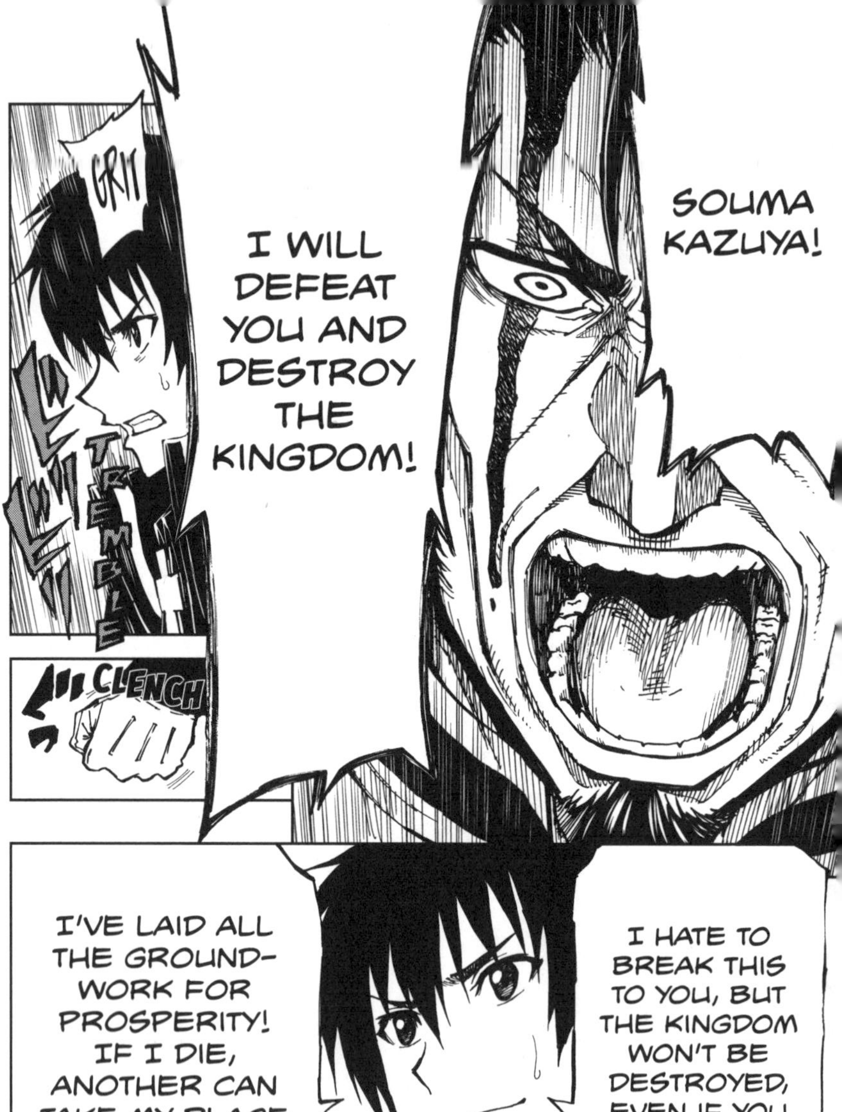
SOUMA KAZUYA!
I WILL DEFEAT YOU AND DESTROY THE KINGDOM!
GRIT
TREMBLE
CLENCH
I HATE TO BREAK THIS TO YOU, BUT THE KINGDOM WON'T BE DESTROYED, EVEN IF YOU DO KILL ME.
I'VE LAID ALL THE GROUND-WORK FOR PROSPERITY! IF I DIE, ANOTHER CAN TAKE MY PLACE AND RUN THINGS JUST AS WELL.

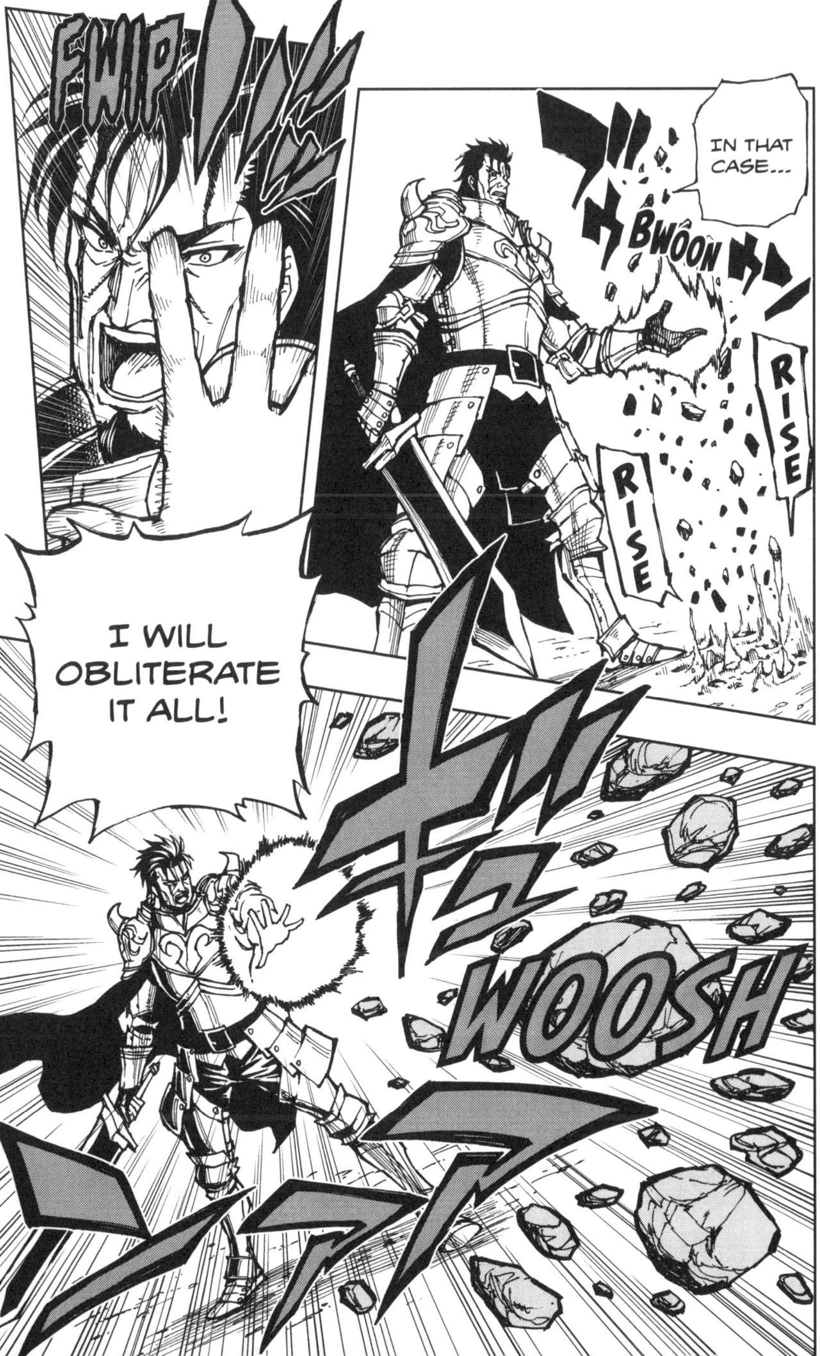
IN THAT CASE...
BWOON
RISE
RISE
FWIP
I WILL OBLITERATE IT ALL!
WOOSH

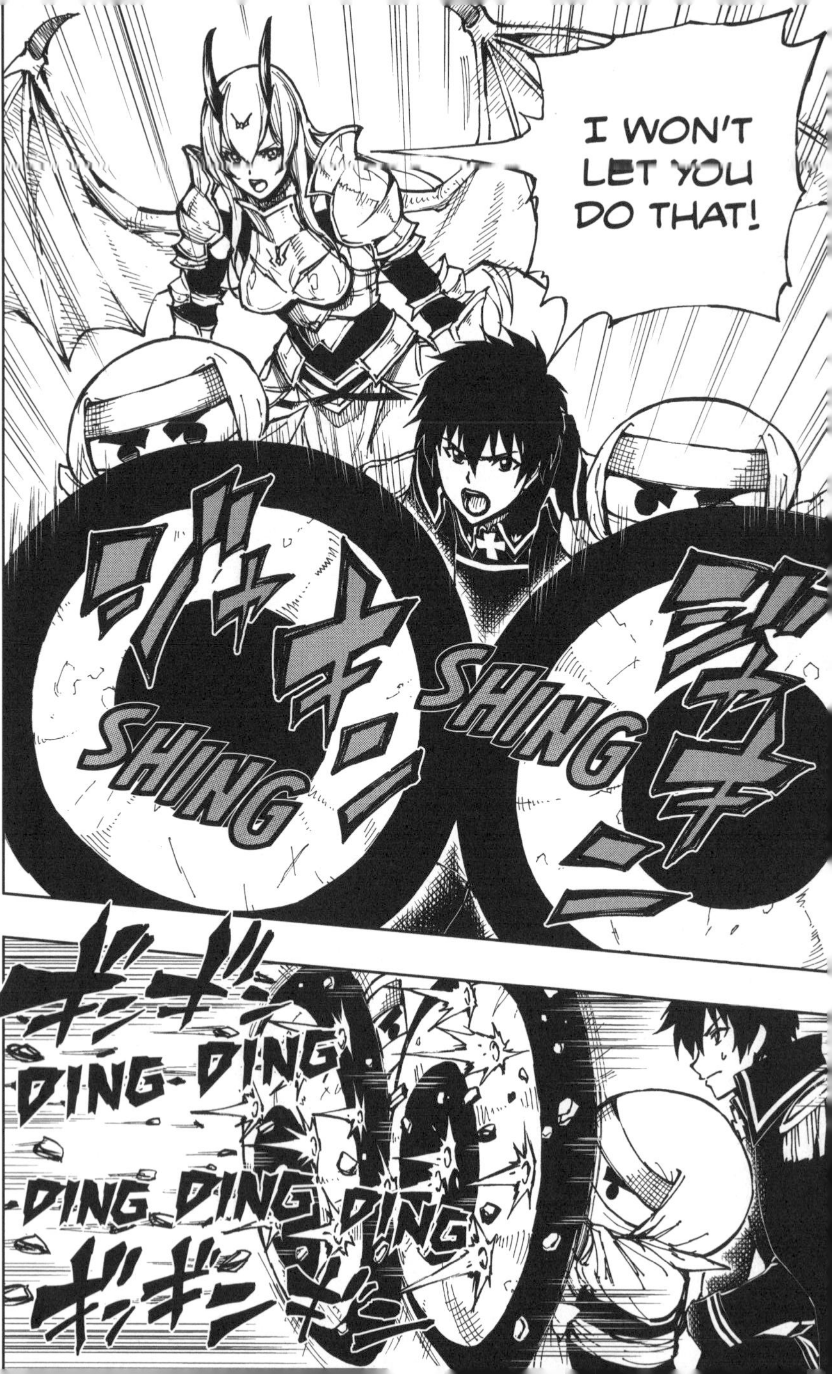
I WON'T LET YOU DO THAT!
SHING
SHING
DING DING
DING DING DING

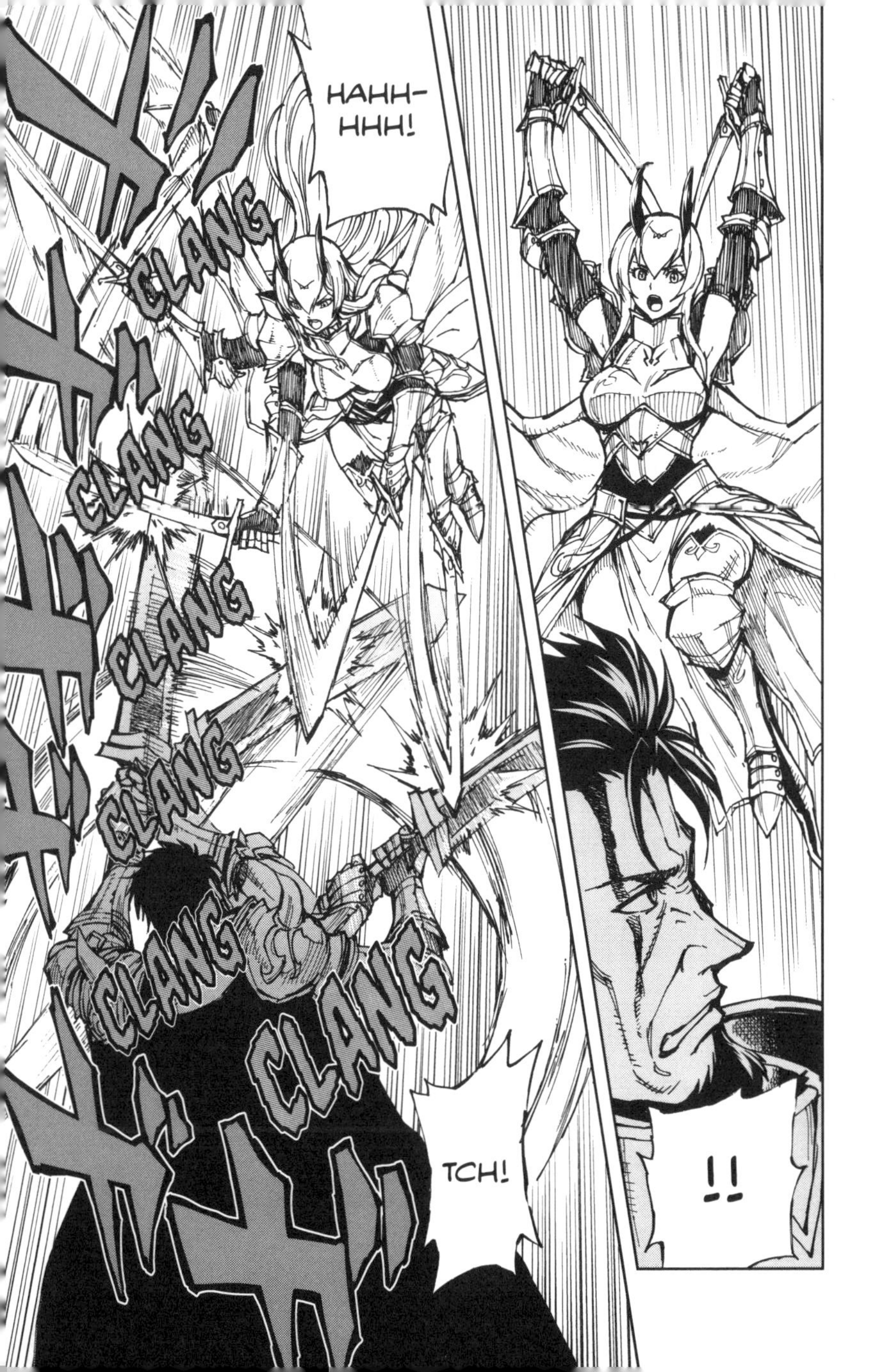
!!
HAHH-HHH!
CLANG
CLANG
CLANG
CLANG
CLANG
CLANG
TCH!

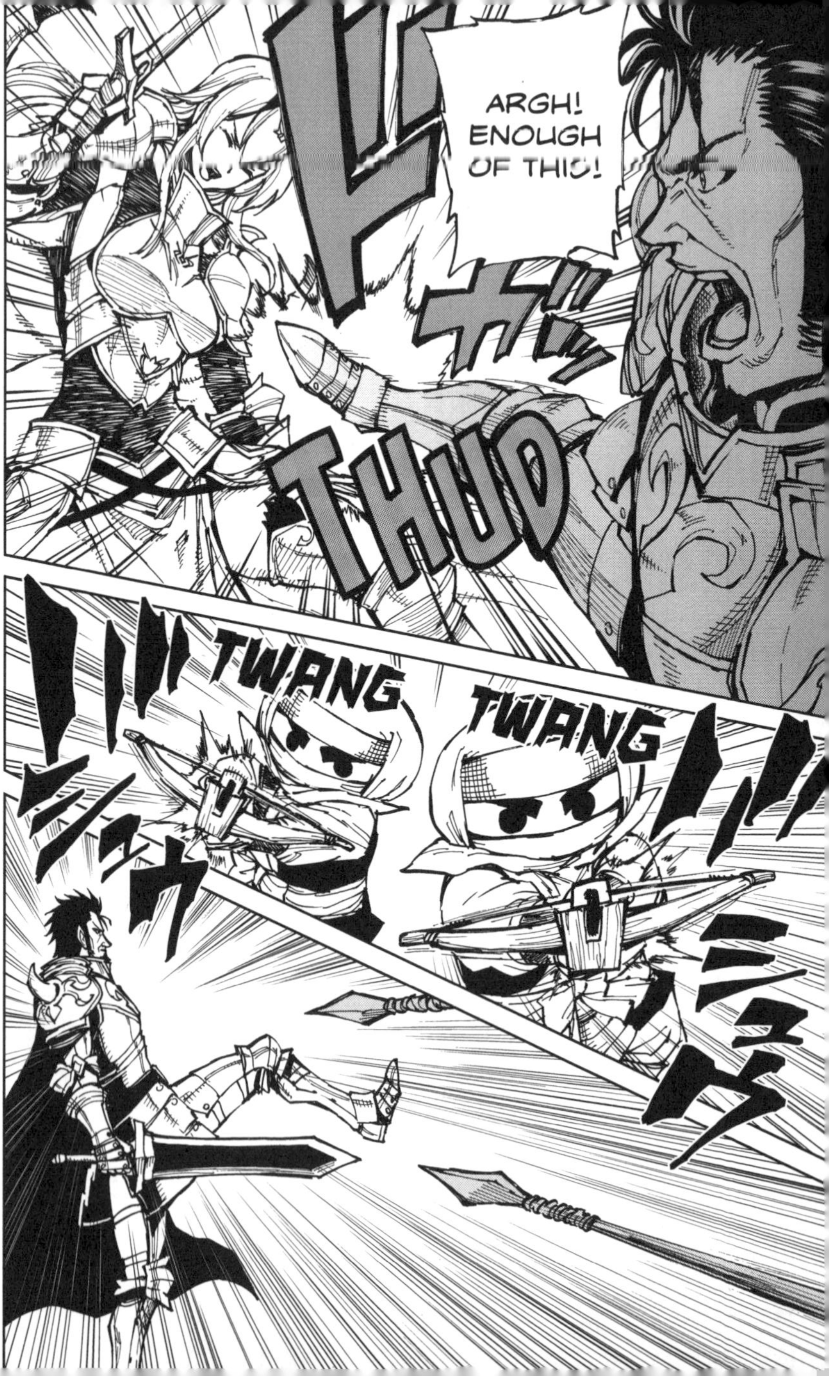
ARGH! ENOUGH OF THIS!
THUD
TWANG
TWANG

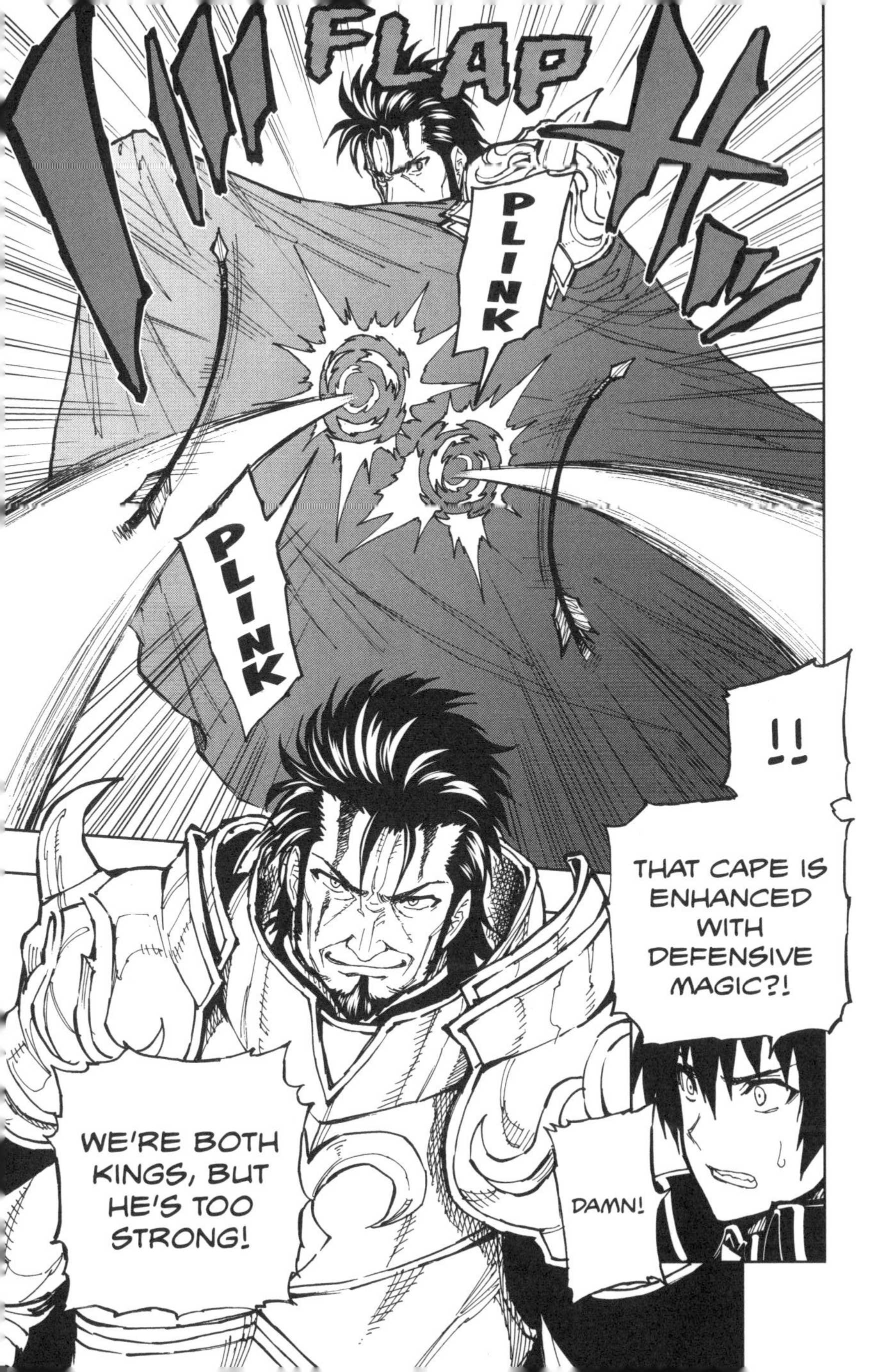
FLAP
PLINK
PLINK
!!
THAT CAPE IS ENHANCED WITH DEFENSIVE MAGIC?!
DAMN!
WE'RE BOTH KINGS, BUT HE'S TOO STRONG!

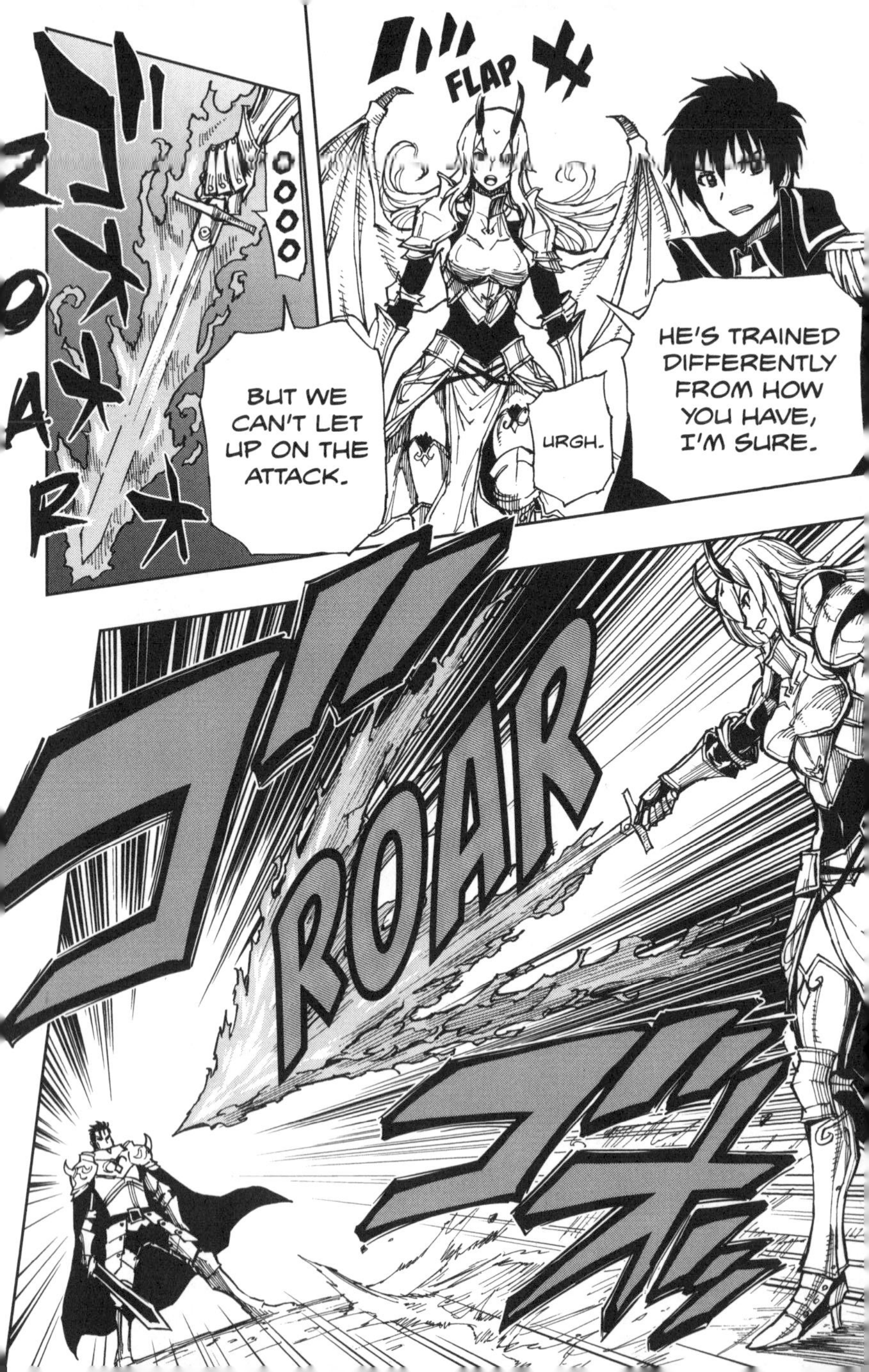

FLAP
HE'S TRAINED DIFFERENTLY FROM HOW YOU HAVE, I'M SURE.
URGH.
BUT WE CAN'T LET UP ON THE ATTACK.
OOOO
ROAR
ROAR

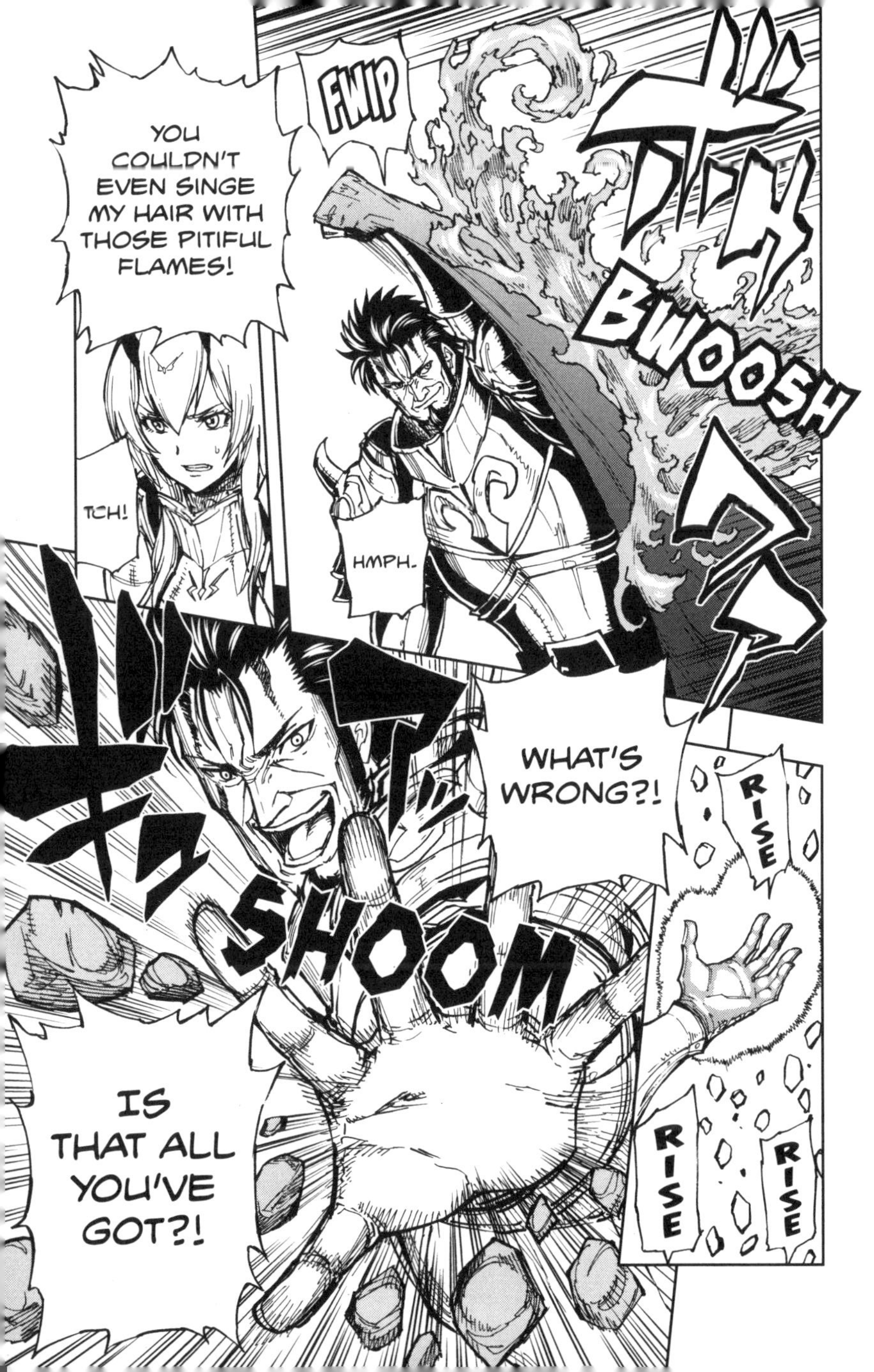
BWOOSH
FWIP
YOU COULDN'T EVEN SINGE MY HAIR WITH THOSE PITIFUL FLAMES!
HMPH.
TCH!
RISE
WHAT'S WRONG?!
SHOOM
RISE
RISE
IS THAT ALL YOU'VE GOT?!

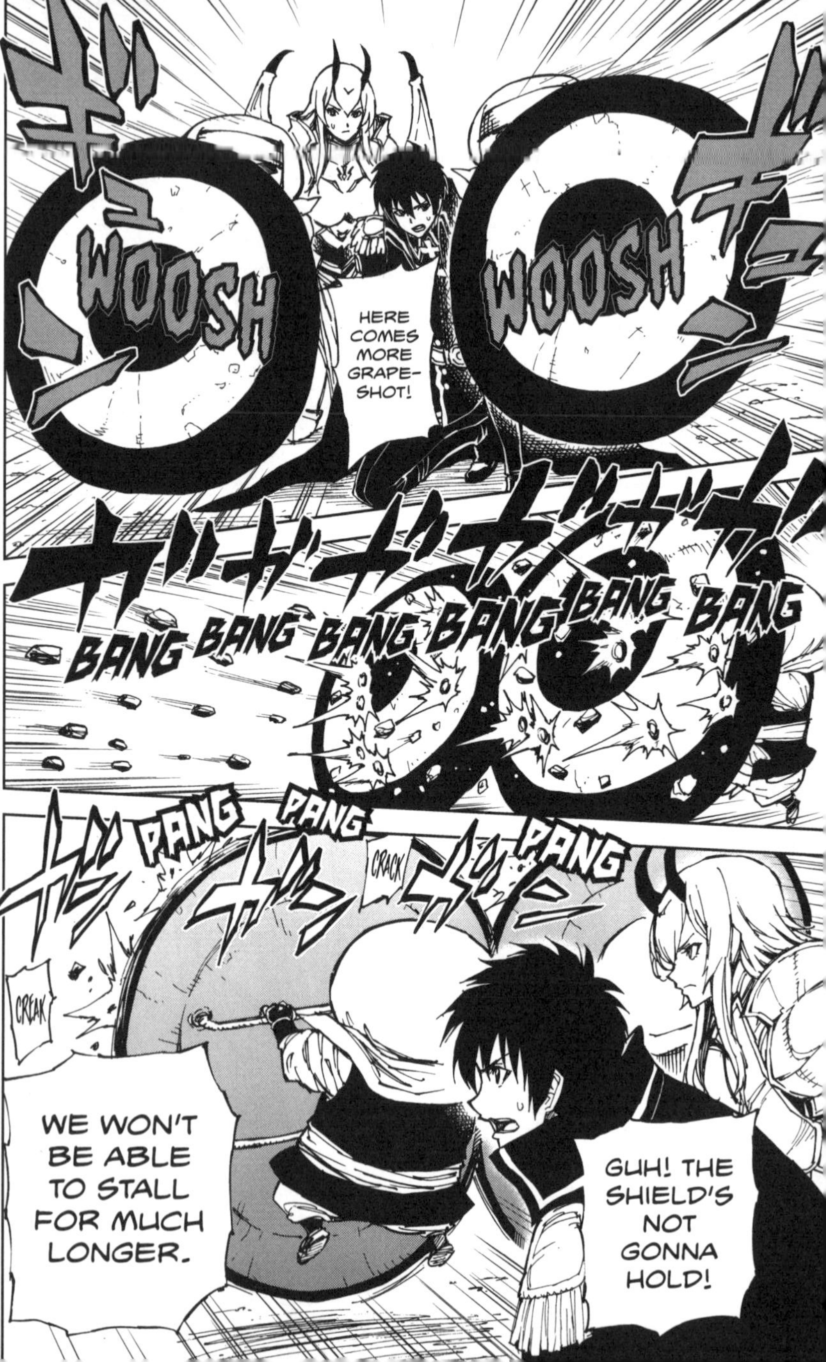
WOOSH
HERE COMES MORE GRAPE-SHOT!
WOOSH
BANG BANG BANG BANG BANG BANG
PANG
CRACK
PANG
PANG
CREAK
GUH! THE SHIELD'S NOT GONNA HOLD!
WE WON'T BE ABLE TO STALL FOR MUCH LONGER.

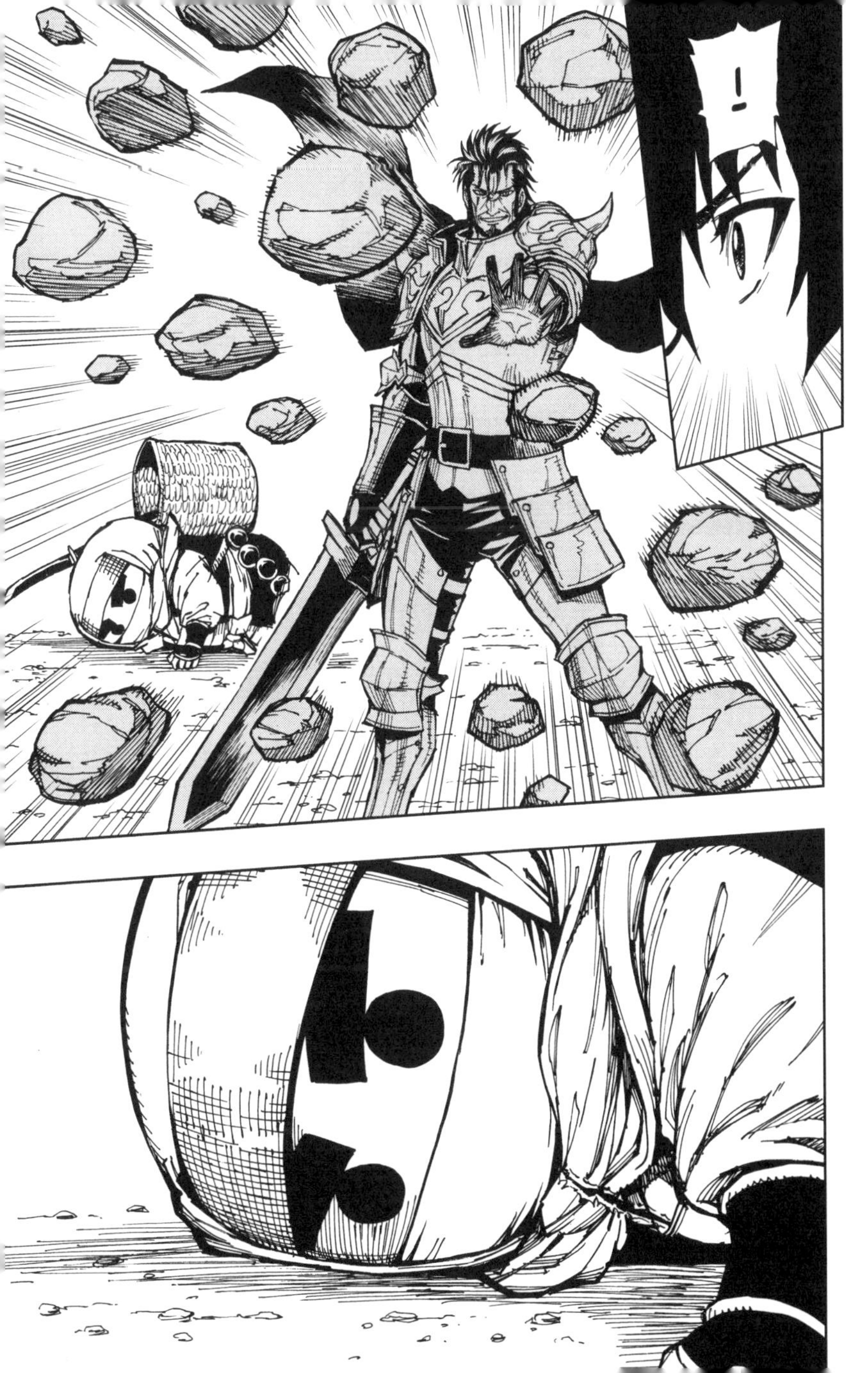
!

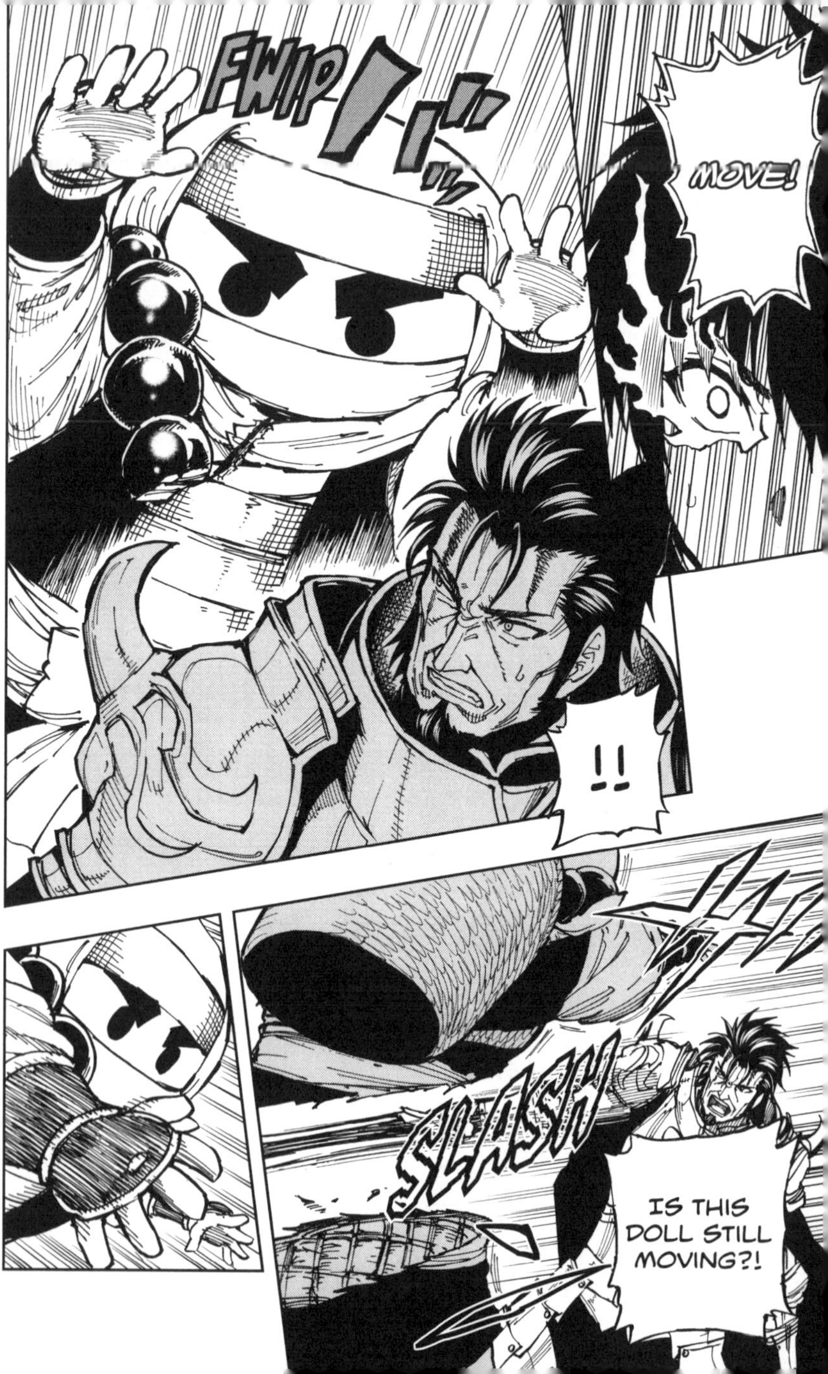
MOVE!
FWIP!
!!
SLASH
IS THIS DOLL STILL MOVING?!

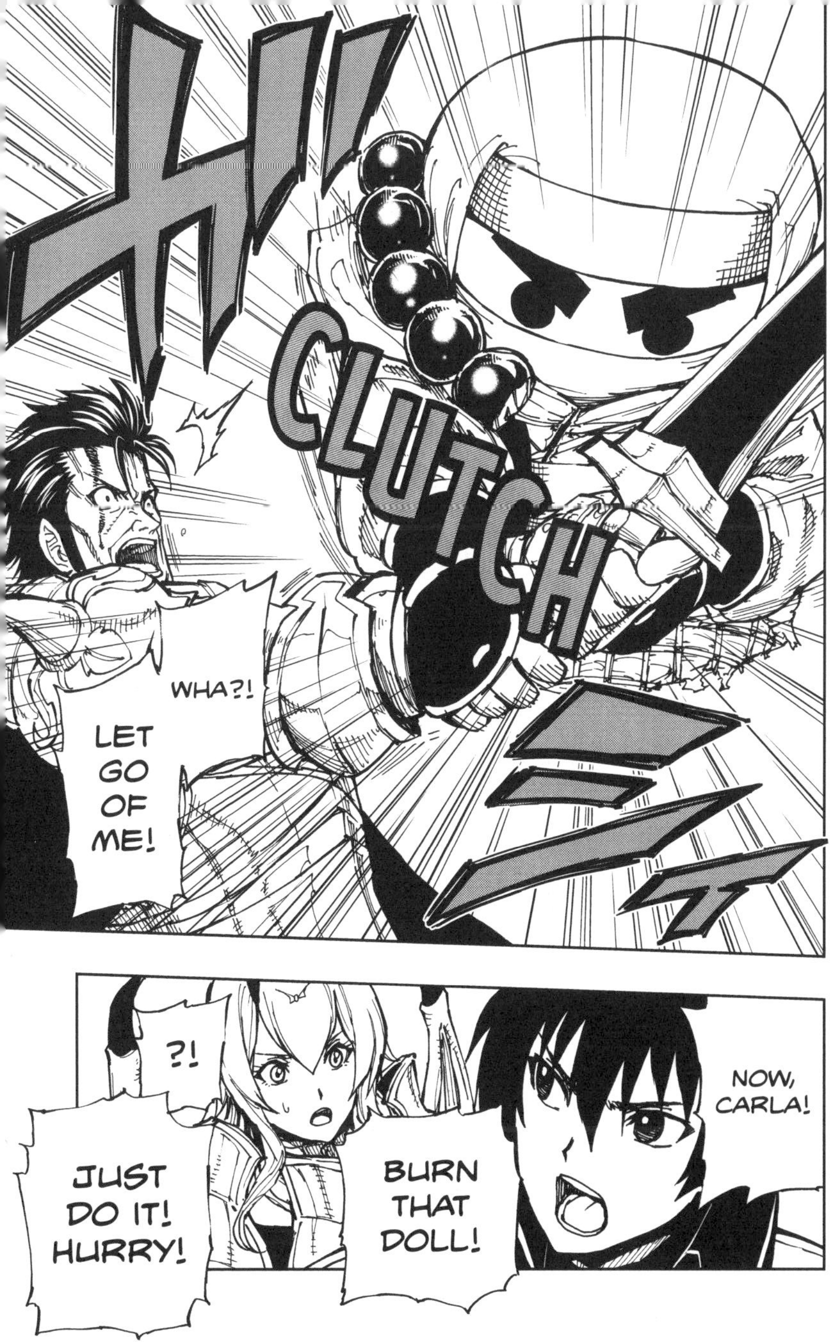
CLUTCH
WHA?!
LET GO OF ME!
NOW, CARLA!
BURN THAT DOLL!
?!
JUST DO IT! HURRY!

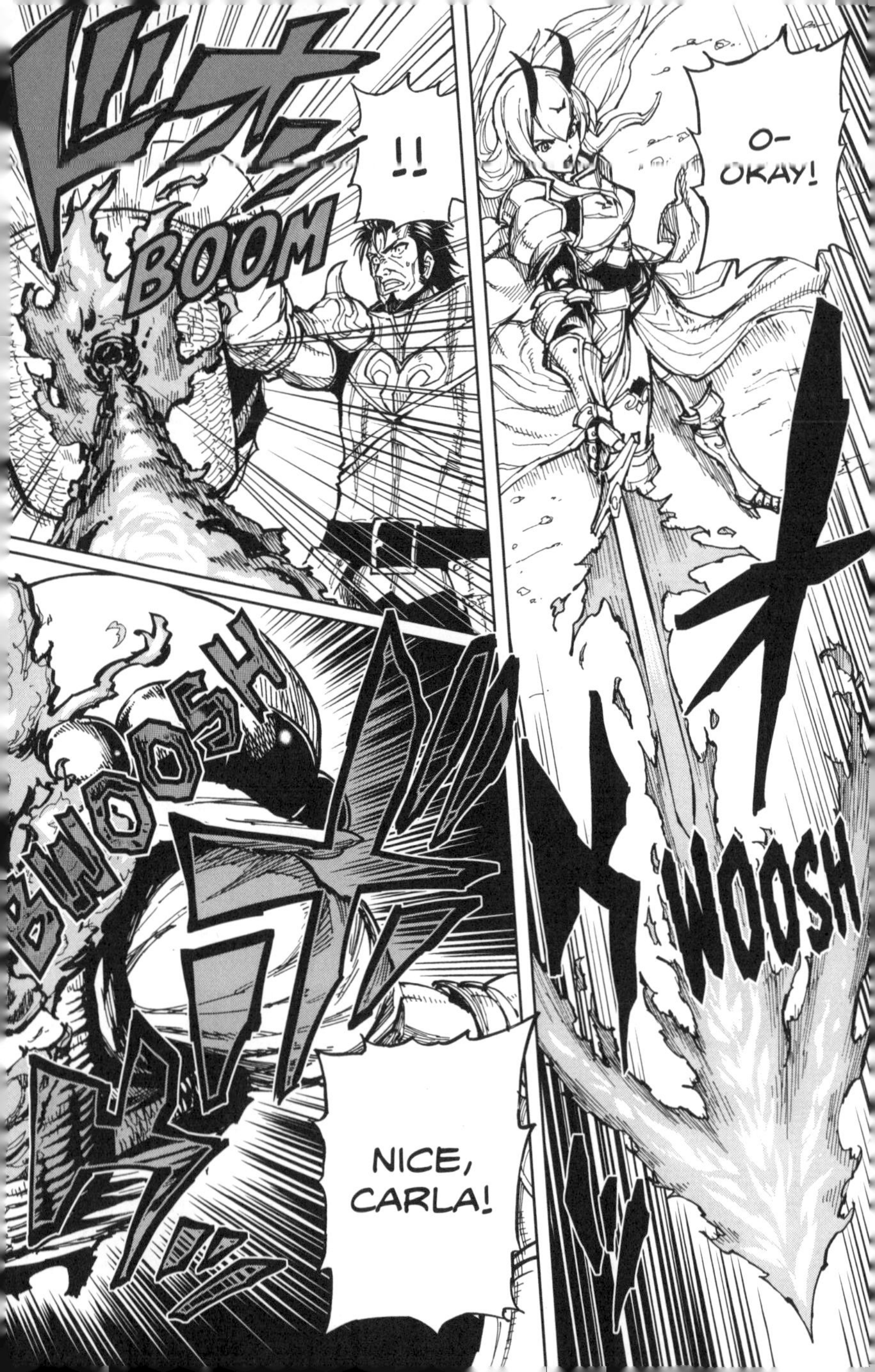
O-
OKAY!
WOOSH
!!
BOOM
WHOOSH
NICE,
CARLA!

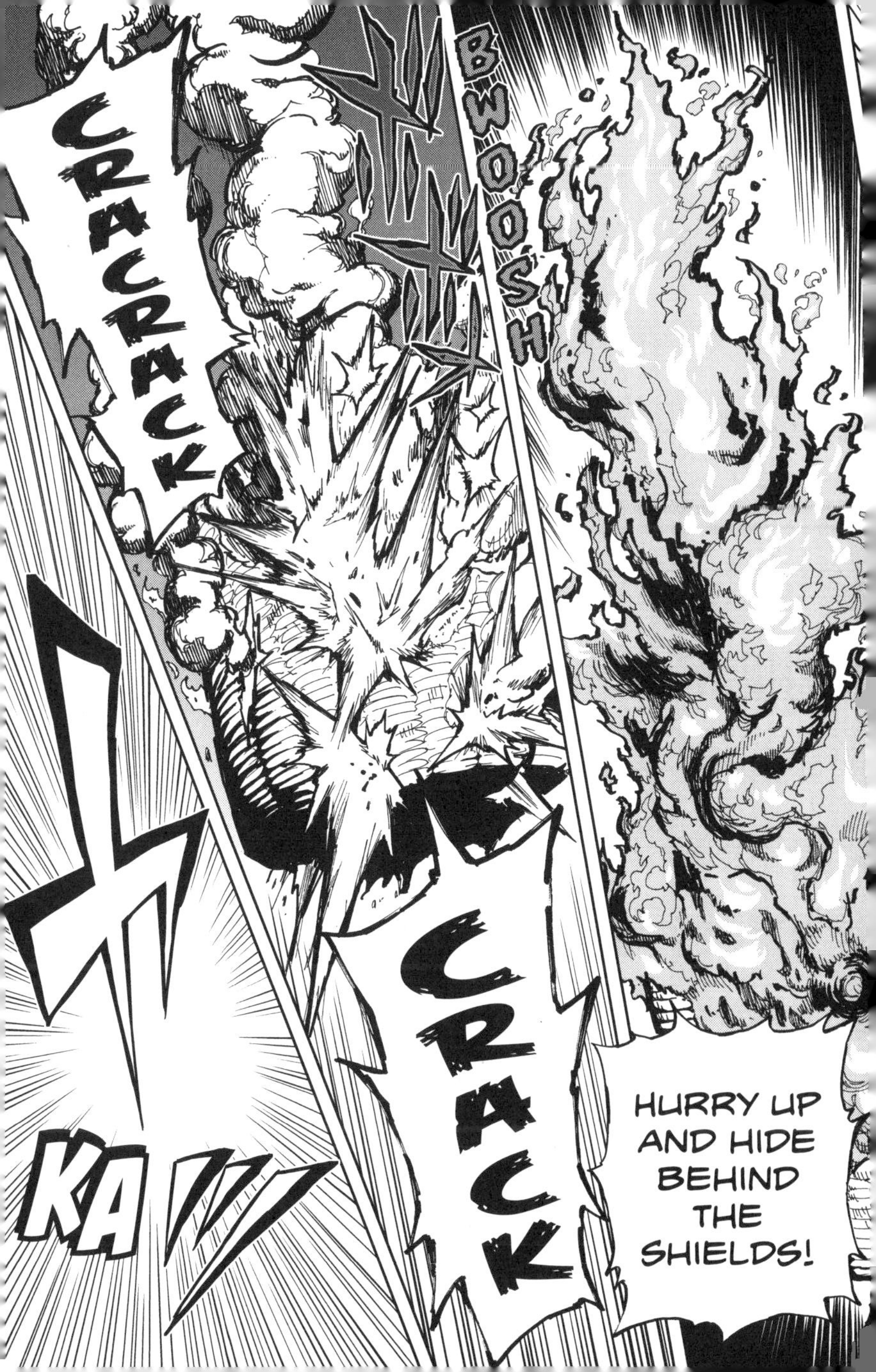
BWOOSH
HURRY UP AND HIDE BEHIND THE SHIELDS!
CRACK
CRACRACK
KA

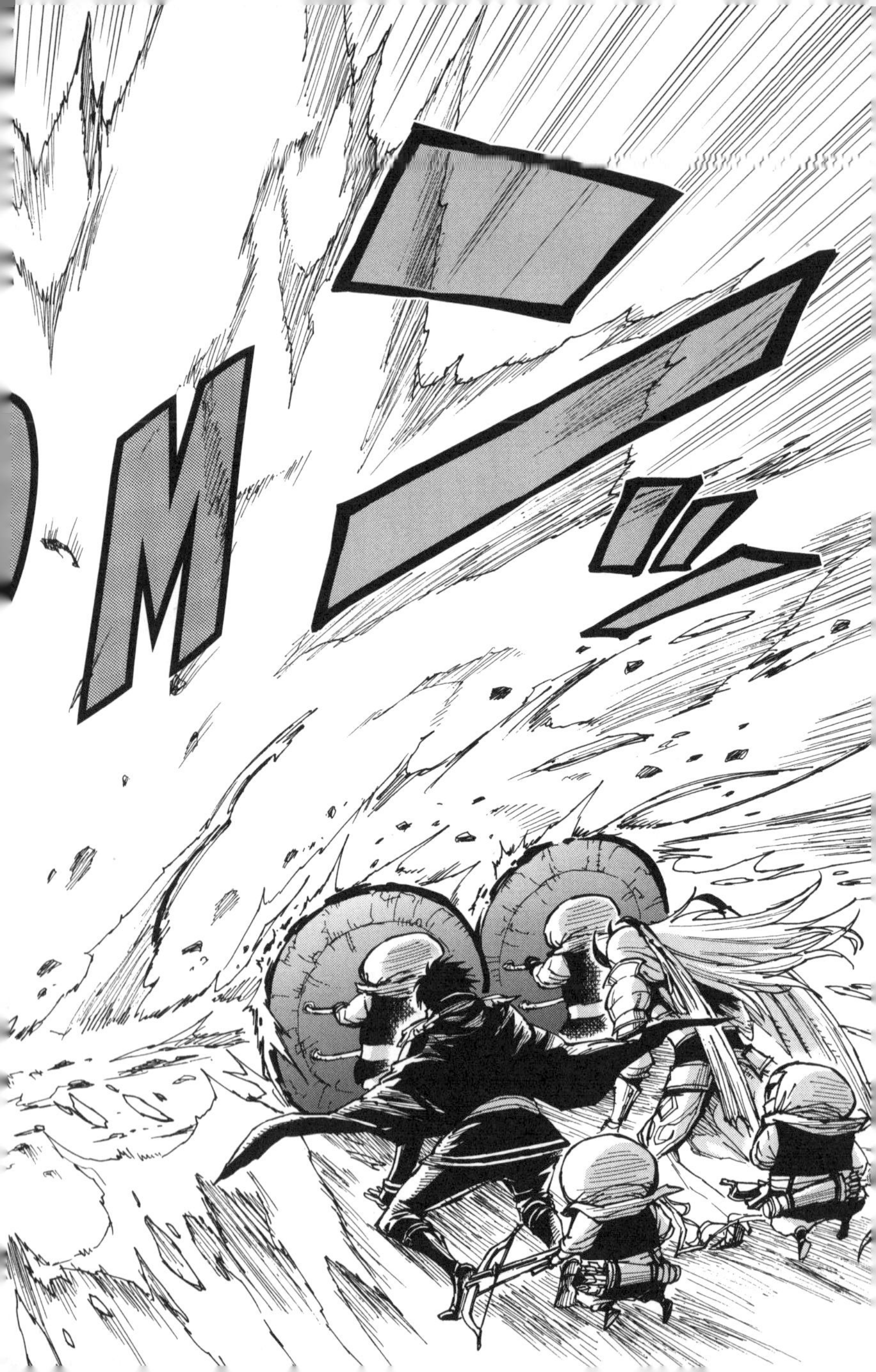
M

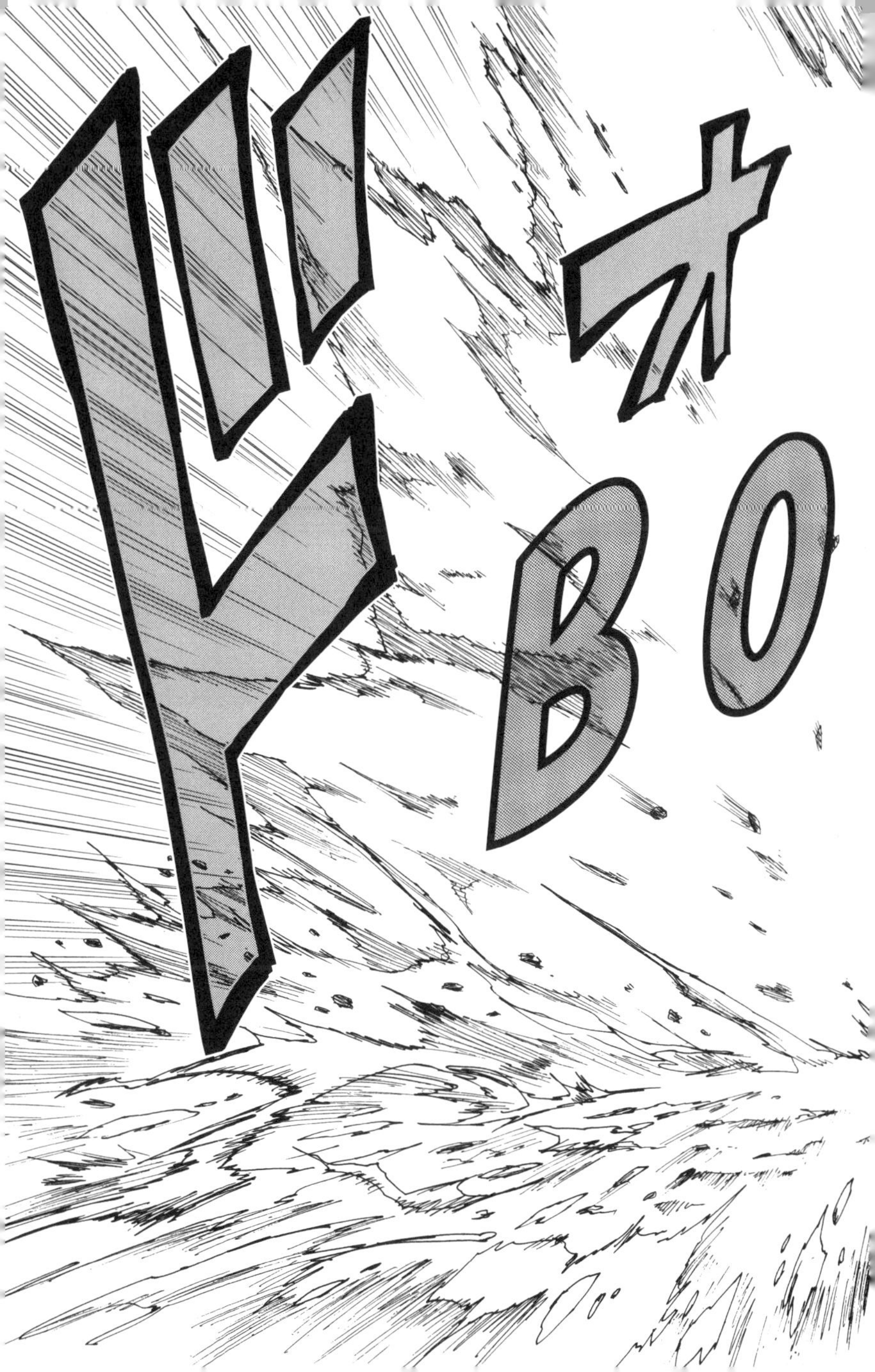
ドオ
BO

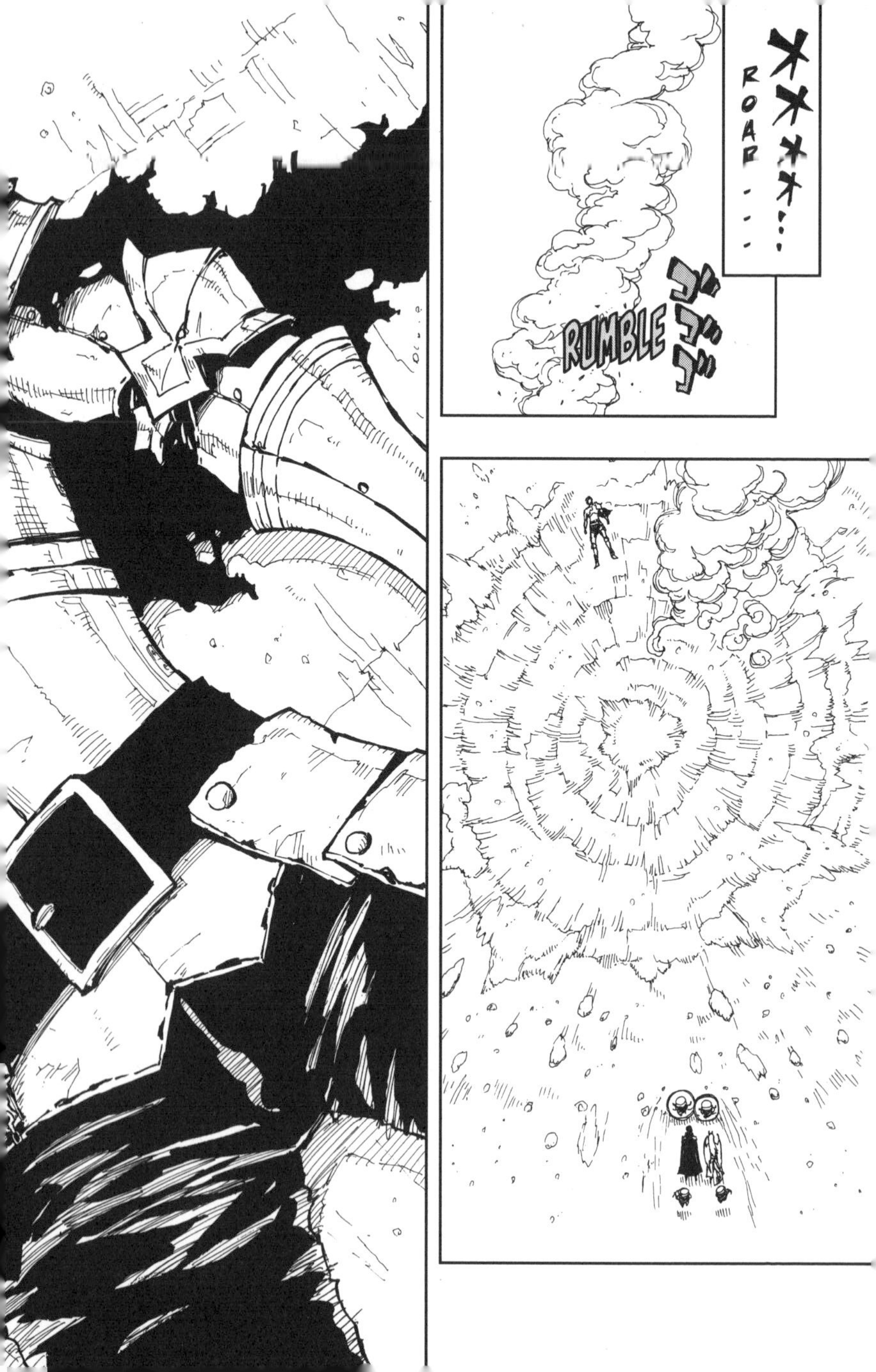
オオオオオ!!
ROAR...
ゴゴゴゴ
RUMBLE

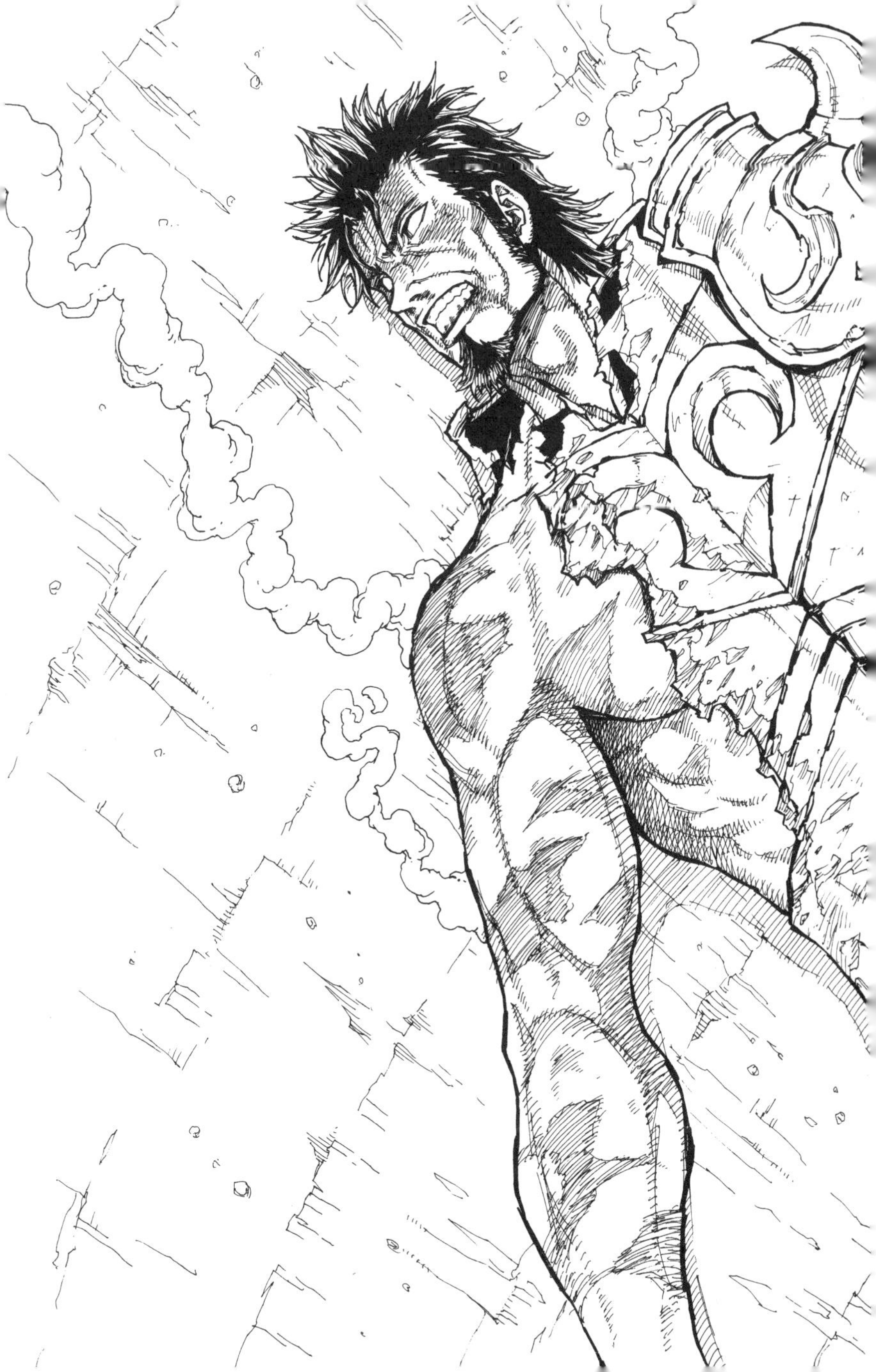

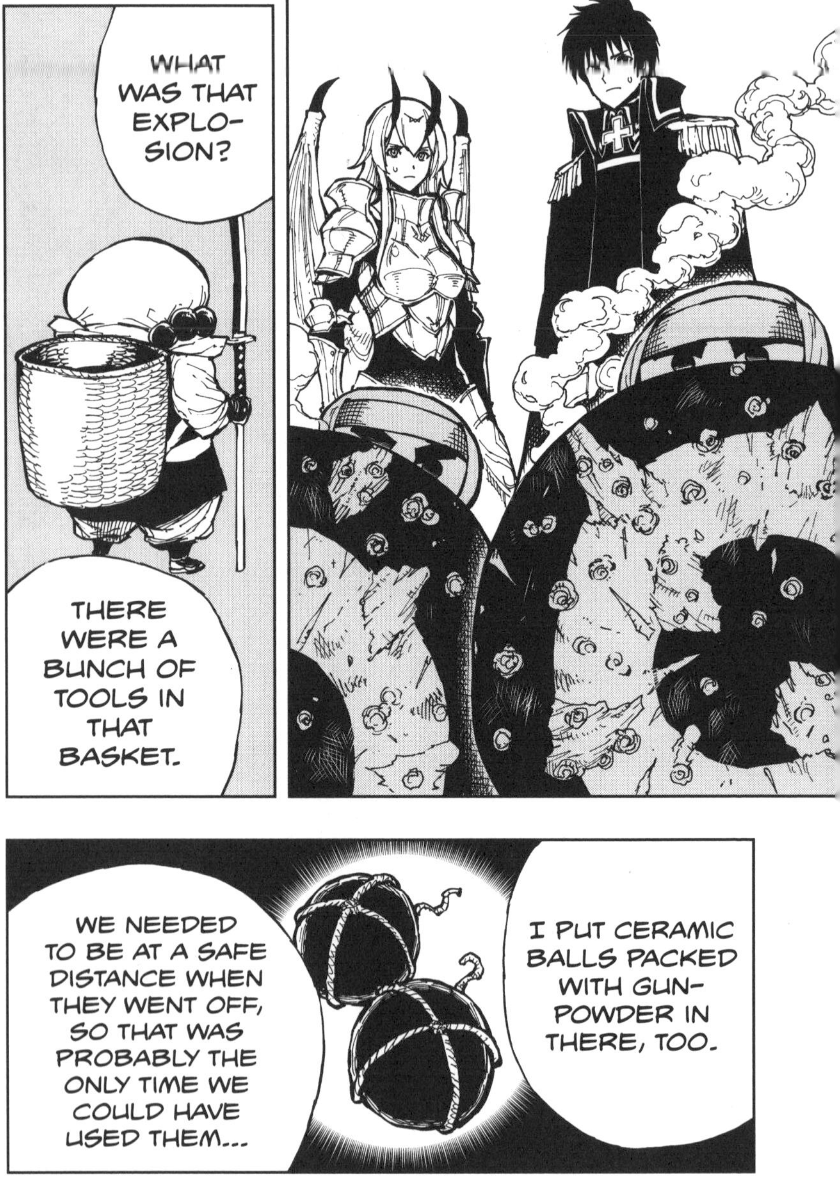
WHAT WAS THAT EXPLOSION?
THERE WERE A BUNCH OF TOOLS IN THAT BASKET.
I PUT CERAMIC BALLS PACKED WITH GUNPOWDER IN THERE, TOO.
WE NEEDED TO BE AT A SAFE DISTANCE WHEN THEY WENT OFF, SO THAT WAS PROBABLY THE ONLY TIME WE COULD HAVE USED THEM...

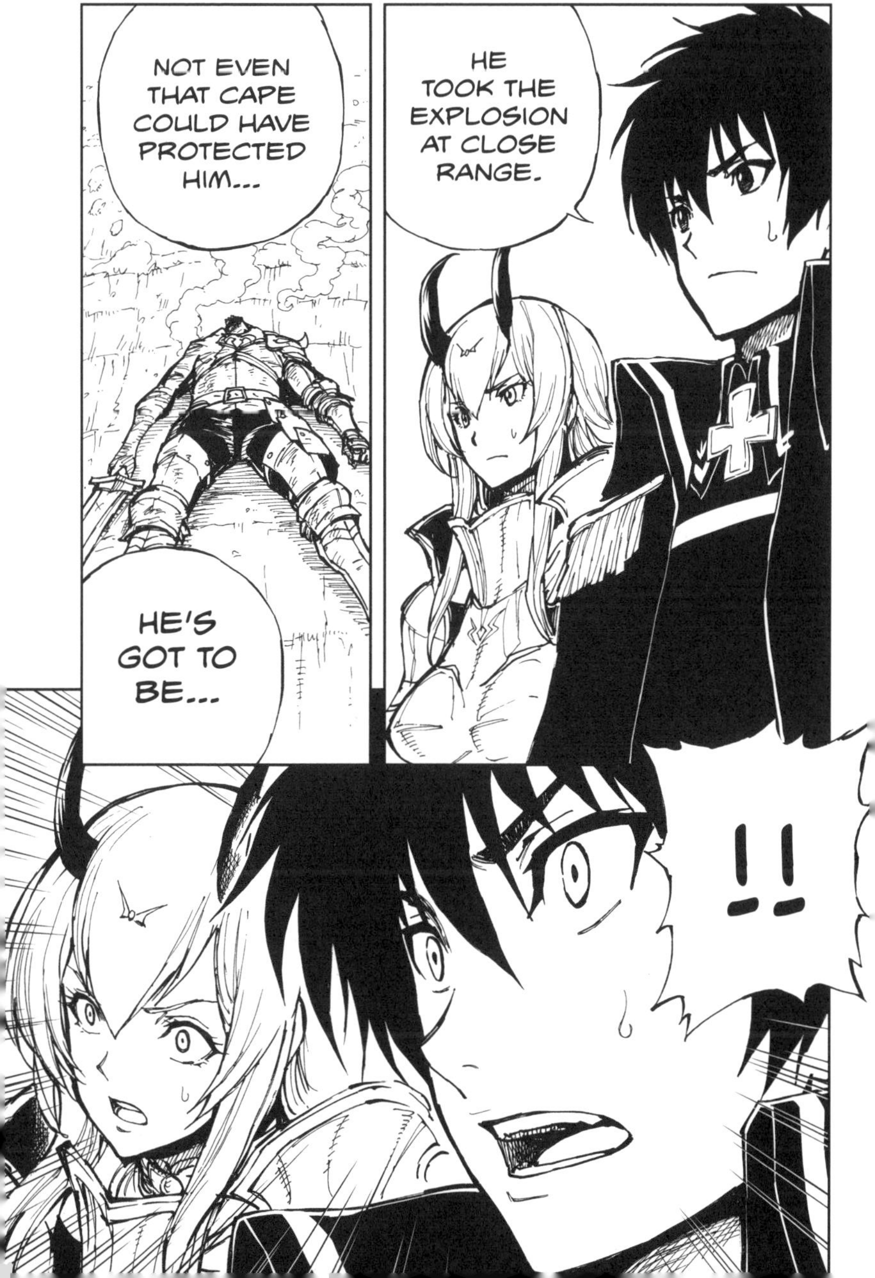
HE TOOK THE EXPLOSION AT CLOSE RANGE.
NOT EVEN THAT CAPE COULD HAVE PROTECTED HIM...
HE'S GOT TO BE...
!!

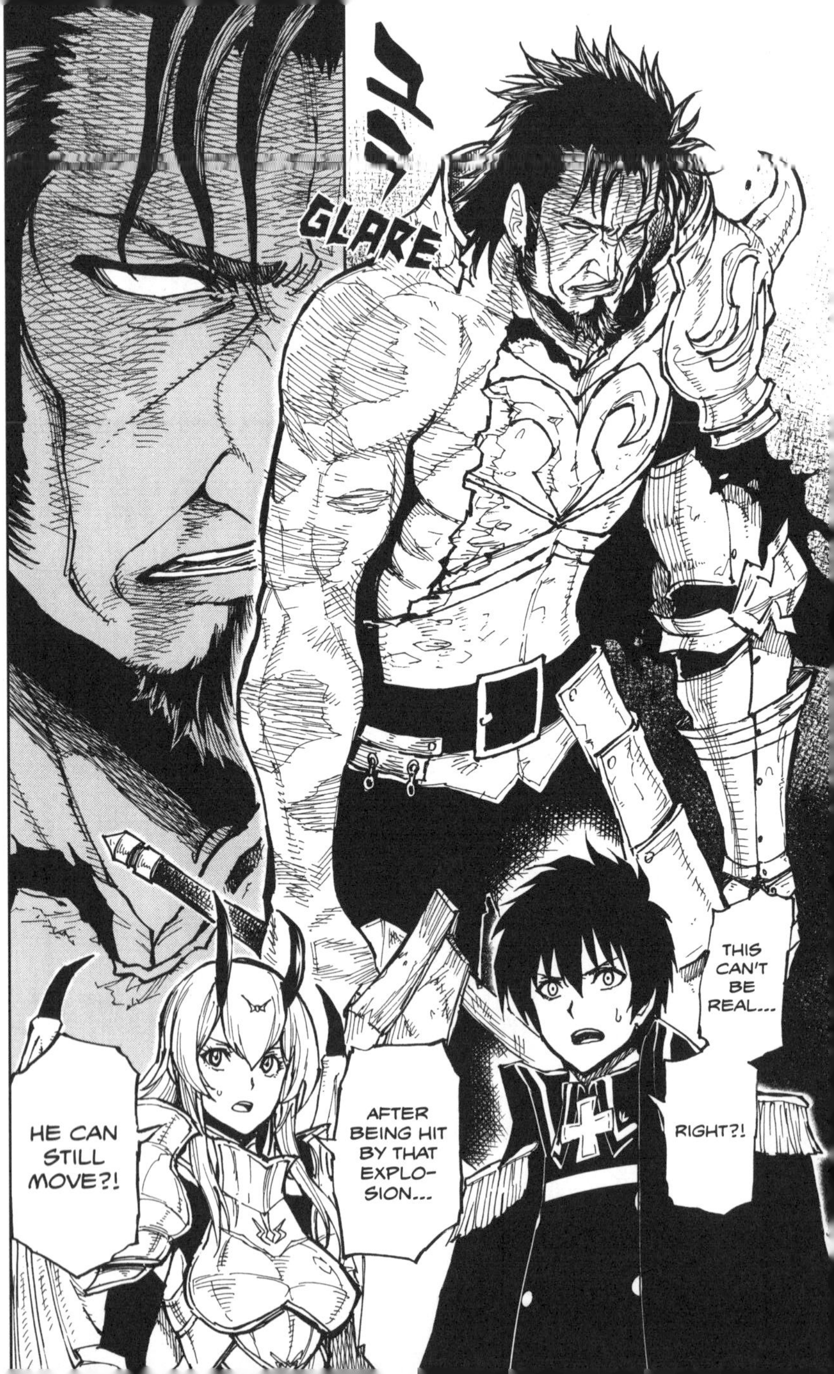
GLARE
THIS CAN'T BE REAL...
RIGHT?!
AFTER BEING HIT BY THAT EXPLOSION...
HE CAN STILL MOVE?!

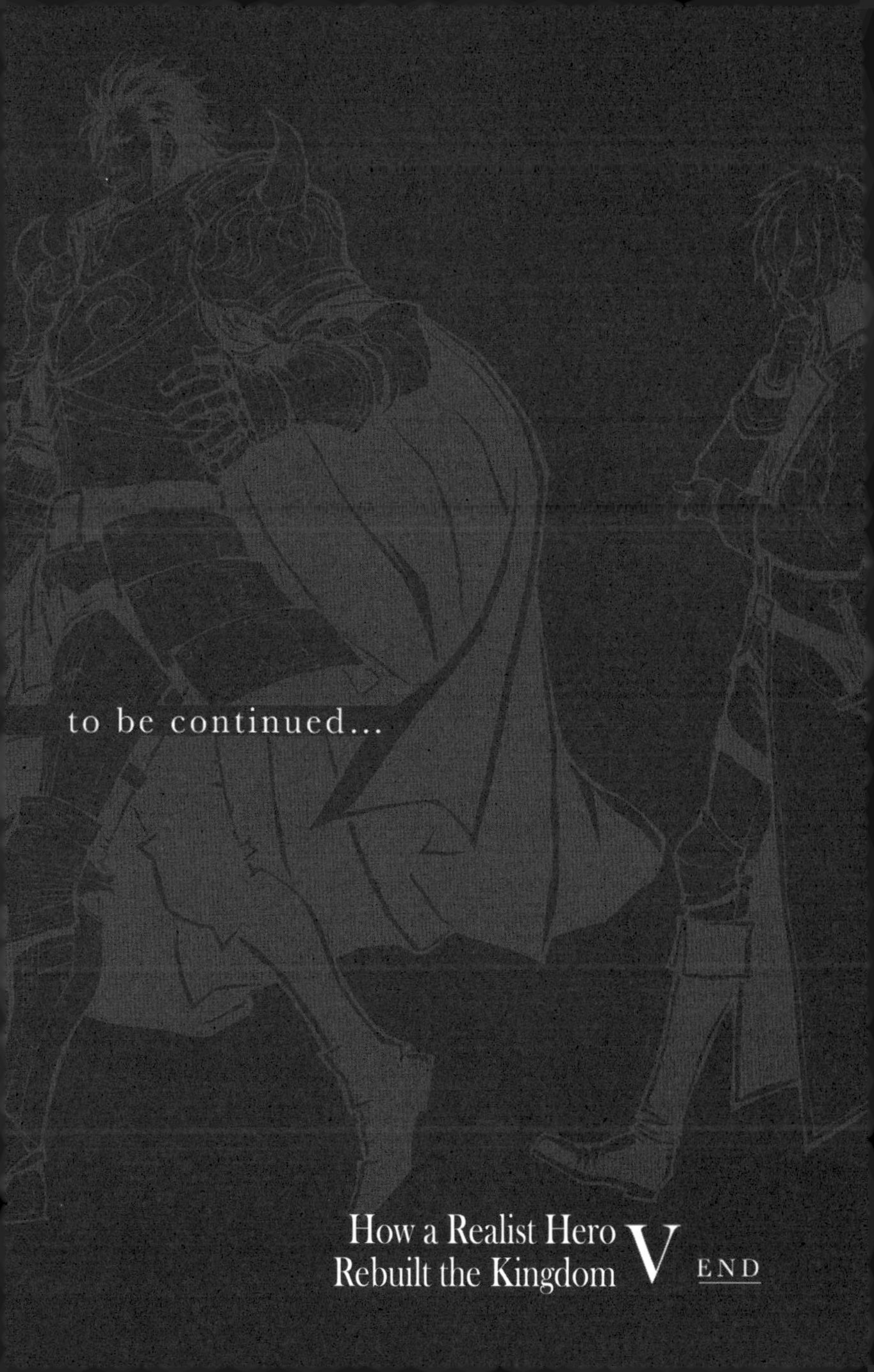
to be continued...
How a Realist Hero Rebuilt the Kingdom V
END

A Story from the Battlefield

The armed forces of the Elfrieden Kingdom led by Souma Kazuya were fighting the forces of the Principality of Amidonia led by Gaius VIII near Van, the capital of the Principality. Halbert, an officer in the Forbidden Army, was on the battlefield, wielding his twin spears once again. He impaled an enemy who stood in his way, planted his boot on the man as he tore his polearm free, then wiped the sweat from his chin.

"Damn, the Principality's troops are stubborn!"

The Kingdom held an overwhelming numerical advantage. On top of that, they were also relatively unspent, having had a full day to rest while the forces of the Principality rushed to return here. It looked like the Principality had drafted new troops on the way, so the quality of their soldiers was lower, too. Despite all of that, the Principality was putting up a good fight.

"Well... it shows they're just as desperate to win this as we are."

If they lost their main force, and Van fell, the Principality wouldn't have the endurance left to retake it. They were bordered by the theocratic Lunarian Orthodox Papal State to their north, and the Republic of Turgis to their south, who were pushing for northern expansion. The moment they showed weakness, these countries might move to prey on them. They had no choice but to fight desperately.

Enemy arrows soared towards Halbert. "Tch!"

He used his two spears to knock them out of the air, only to see many more coming from above. It looked like he'd gone too wild, leading the archers to focus him. One arrow that Halbert failed to knock down grazed his cheek, and another left a shallow gash in his upper arm. *This isn't good*, he thought.

Rumble, rumble. The ground rose up before Halbert to form a wall. As he took cover in the shadow of that earthen barrier, Kaede ran over to him.

"Hal, you're being reckless, you know!" she exclaimed.

"Sorry. You saved me there."

The dirt wall was the product of her earth magic.

Kaede wiped the sweat from Hal's brow with a handkerchief while saying, "The Principality is holding out well, but that can't last much longer. The mounting fatigue will exhaust them eventually. Until then, we should take our time, and attack them slowly."

"Yeah, but it's kinda frustrating," Halbert replied, spinning his arm around to loosen up his shoulder. "When we were at a disadvantage, holed up in that fort near Randel, I was thinking 'I'm not gonna let you beat us!' But now that we have the upper hand this time, I end up thinking, 'You're gonna lose anyway, so hurry up and run!'"

"That's just how it is. No one wants to lose, you know."

"Yeah..." Halbert sighed. "So... What's our next move once we win? Take all the territory we can off them?"

"After this battle, you mean? Well..." Kaede thought for a moment, then said, "More road work, I bet."

"Huh? Road work?" Halbert grunted in surprise.

"We expect the Gran Chaos Empire to make their appearance once this battle ends." Kaede smiled wryly. "Because under the Mankind Declaration, they will not accept changes to national borders caused by conflict between the nations of mankind."

"But our country isn't a signatory, right?"

"The Principality of Amidonia is. Though, despite that, they invade us under the pretext that we were a non-signatory state, so I'm sure the Empire won't be happy with them. At this rate, no matter how much of their territory we carve off now, we'll be forced into negotiations with the Empire. If they demand it be returned, all that effort will be for nothing."

"So there's no point seizing land now, is that it?"

"Yes." Kaede nodded. "So we'll start by hardening our position around here. Fortunately, Van was built with the intent of invading the Kingdom, so it's close to the border. There are currently no problems with our supply lines, but laying out a stronger transportation network never hurts."

"Which means we're back to working with dirt again, huh? Yeesh..."

Finally, unable to hold back the mounting pressure the Kingdom was putting on them, some of the Principality's troops broke. Seeing this from under the shadow of her dirt wall, Kaede said, "The battle's been decided now. Spread chaos through the enemy's forces."

"You want me to get in there and throw them into disarray, right?" Halbert stood up and readied his spears.

"Don't be reckless, Hal. I wouldn't want you to get hurt, you know."

"Yeah, I know. I've gotta build some roads after this, after all," he joked, but the look on Kaede's face was serious as she nodded.

"...Good luck out there, Hal."

"Yeah!"

Halbert headed towards the enemy with the other soldiers. After watching him go, Kaede turned to look back at the main camp.

This war will be over soon... But His Majesty's true battle will only begin after that. The pain and resentment left in people... As a king, he must find a way to tame those feelings, she thought.

Kaede was worried now, and turned her head. That was because she didn't have to worry about Souma. The people who worried for him were already at his side, and she realized that.

I'm worried for the person I care about, too, you know.

Kaede looked in the direction where Halbert had run.

THANK YOU FOR BUYING THE FIFTH VOLUME OF THE MANGA. THIS IS THE ORIGINAL CREATOR, DOJYOMARU.

I AM SURE YOU MUST HAVE NOTICED, BUT AS MR. UEDA DRAWS THE BATTLE SCENES, LISCIA AND THE OTHERS ARE GETTING NEW EQUIPMENT. ISN'T NEW EQUIPMENT NICE?

THE PANZER IV'S SCHÜRZEN SKIRT, THE DIVIDER'S HARMONICA CANNON, IT'S ALWAYS SO EXCITING.

I'M ALWAYS OVERWHELMED BY THE MANGA VERSION'S POWERFUL BATTLE SCENES, AND I HOPE EVERYONE ELSE IS, TOO. THIS HAS BEEN DOJYOMARU.

Dojyomaru

THANK YOU FOR BUYING
HOW A REALIST HERO REBUILT
THE KINGDOM V
-UEDA

*THIS DRAWING HAS NOTHING TO DO WITH THE MAIN STORY.

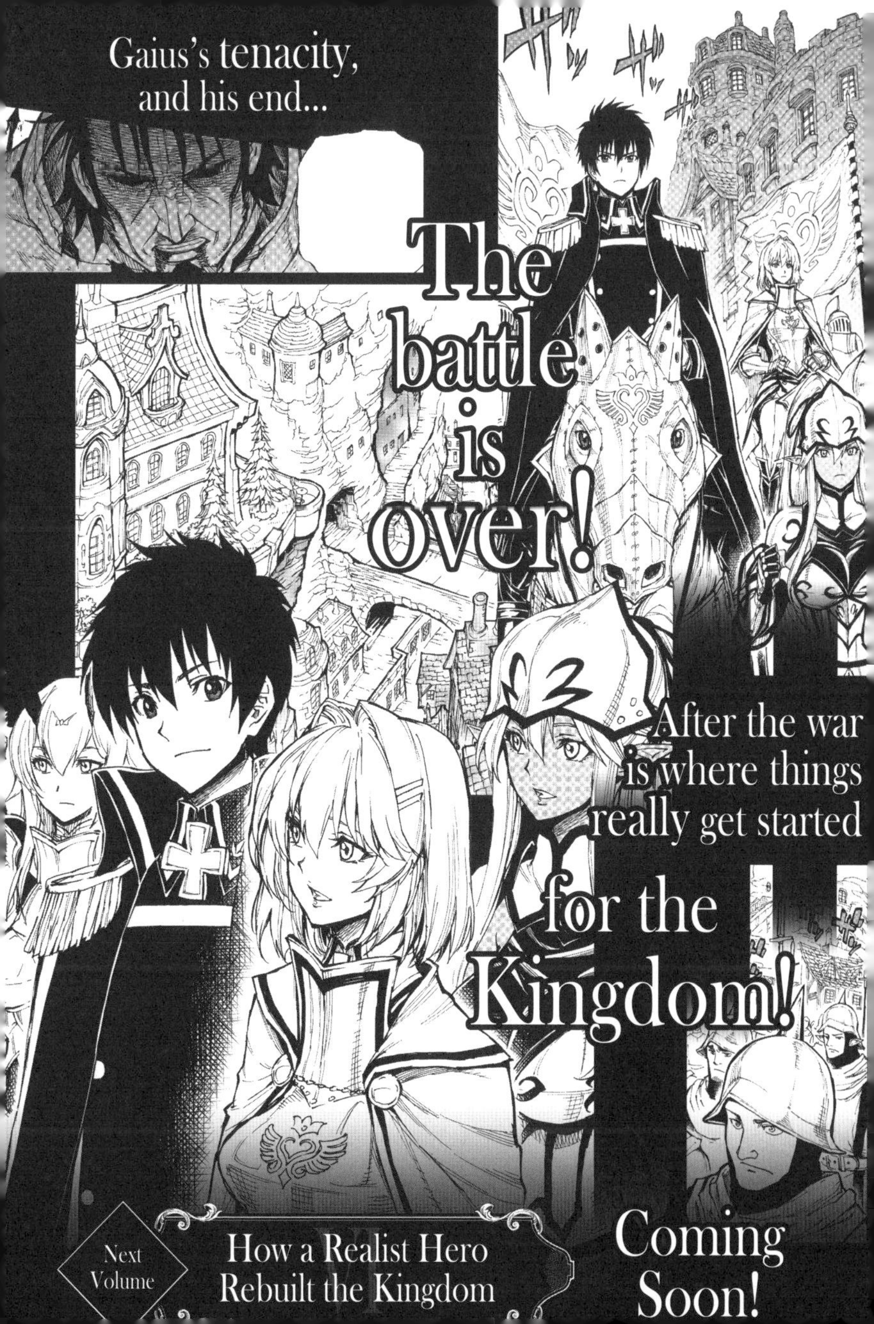
Gaius's tenacity, and his end...
The battle is over!
After the war is where things really get started for the Kingdom!
Next Volume
How a Realist Hero Rebuilt the Kingdom
Coming Soon!

VI

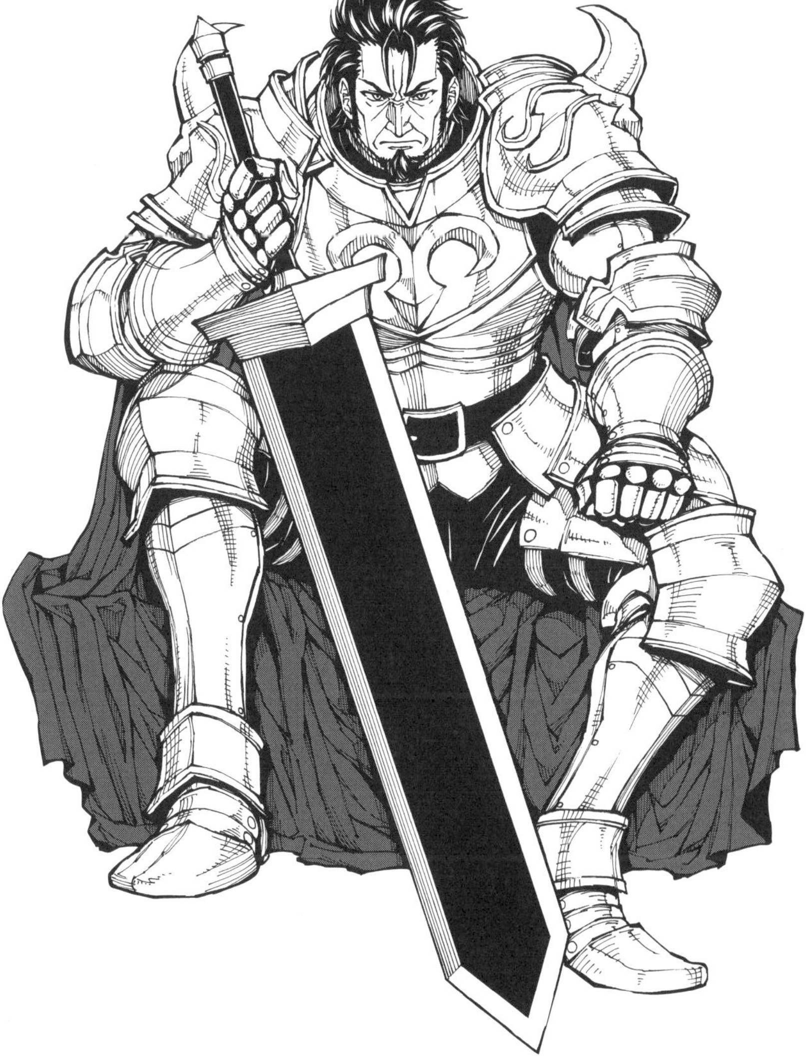

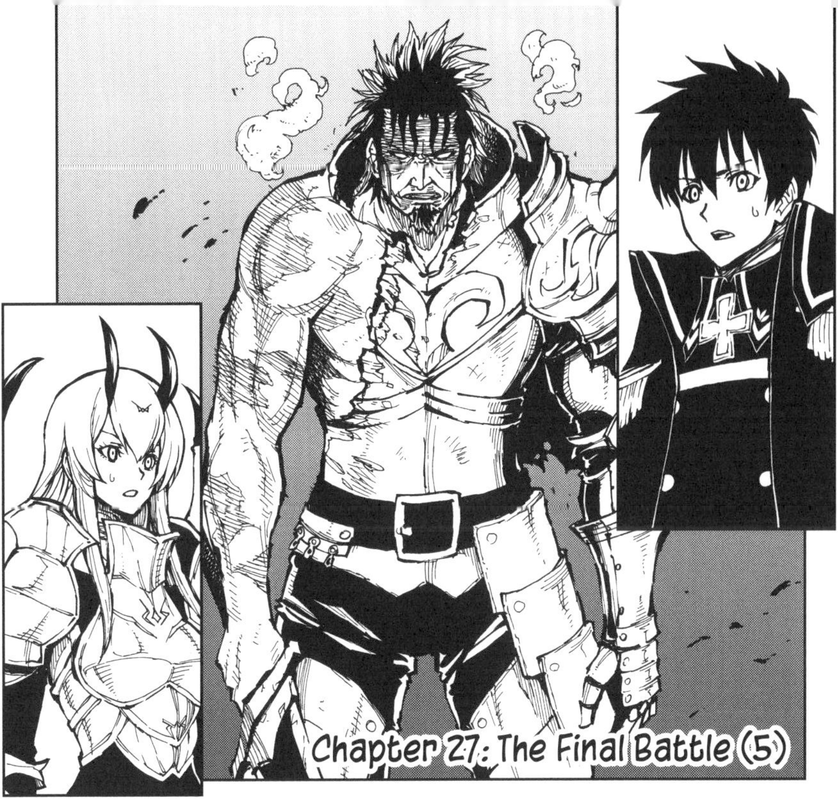
Chapter 27: The Final Battle (5)

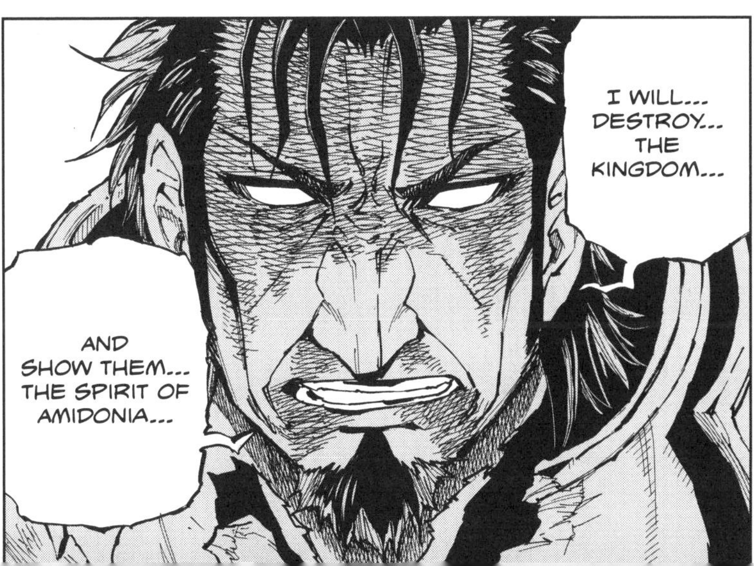
I WILL... DESTROY... THE KINGDOM...
AND SHOW THEM... THE SPIRIT OF AMIDONIA...

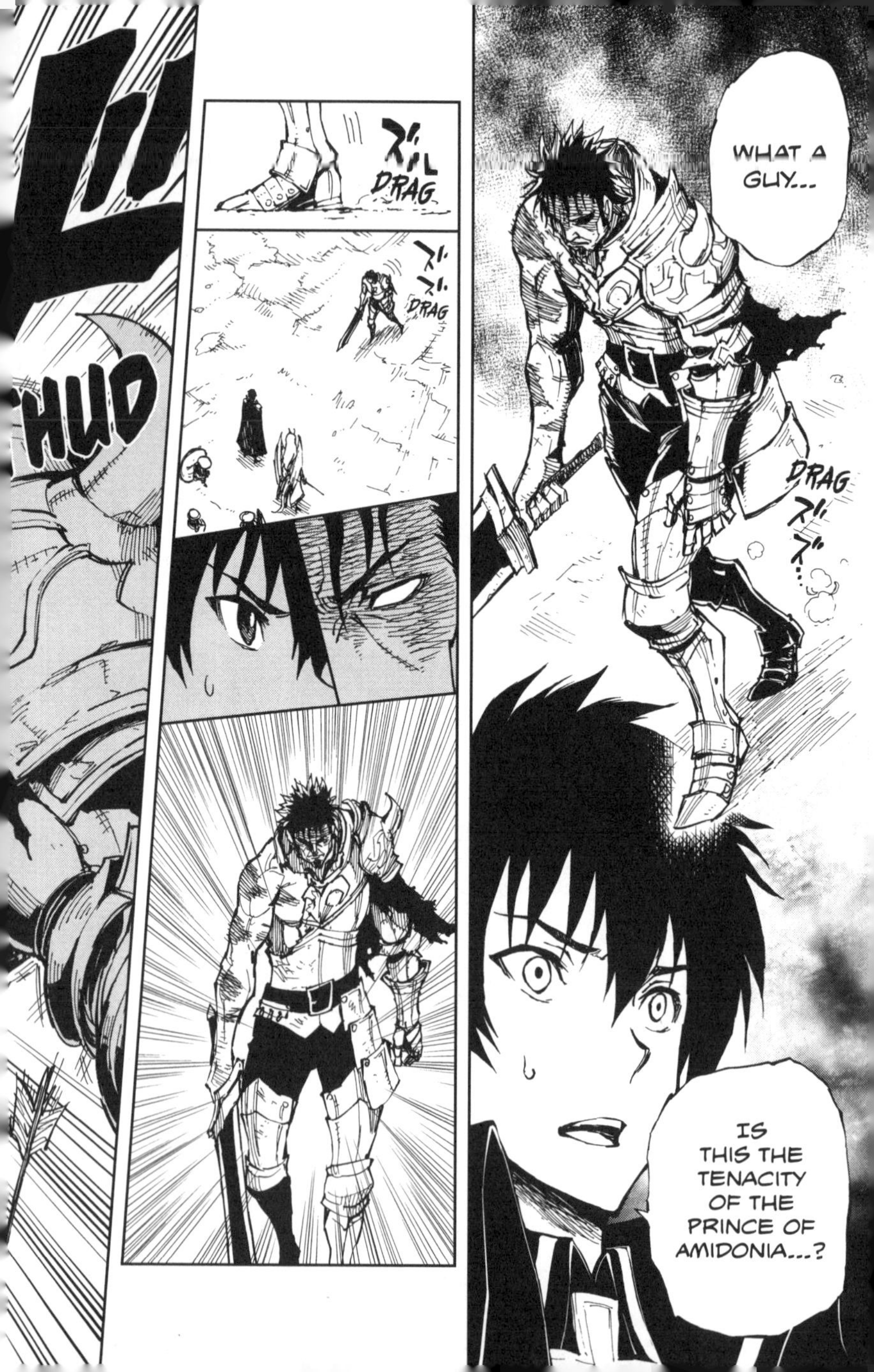
WHAT A GUY...
DRAG
ズズ...
IS THIS THE TENACITY OF THE PRINCE OF AMIDONIA...?
ズル
DRAG
ズズ
DRAG
HUD

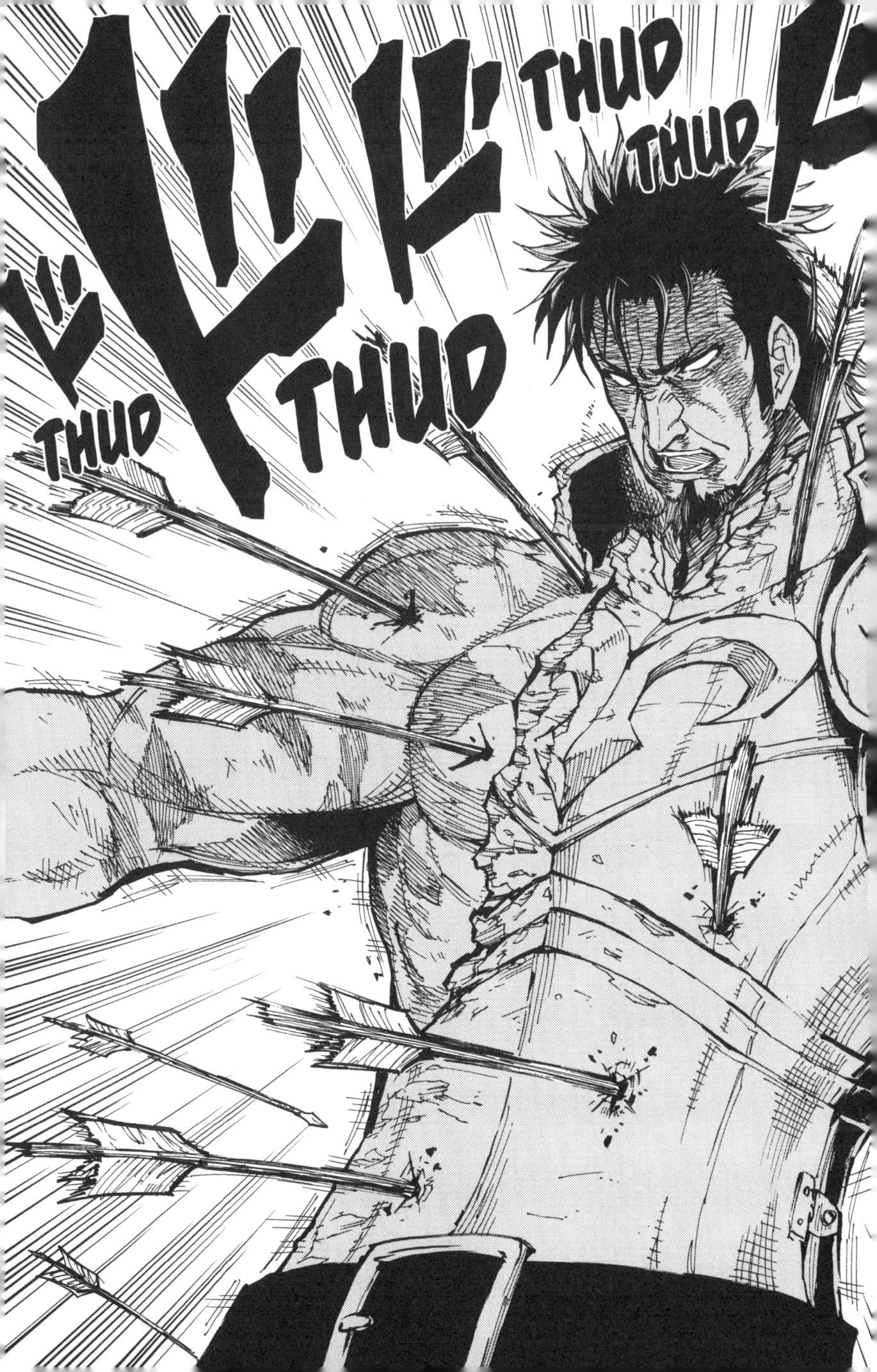
THUD
THUD
THUD
THUD

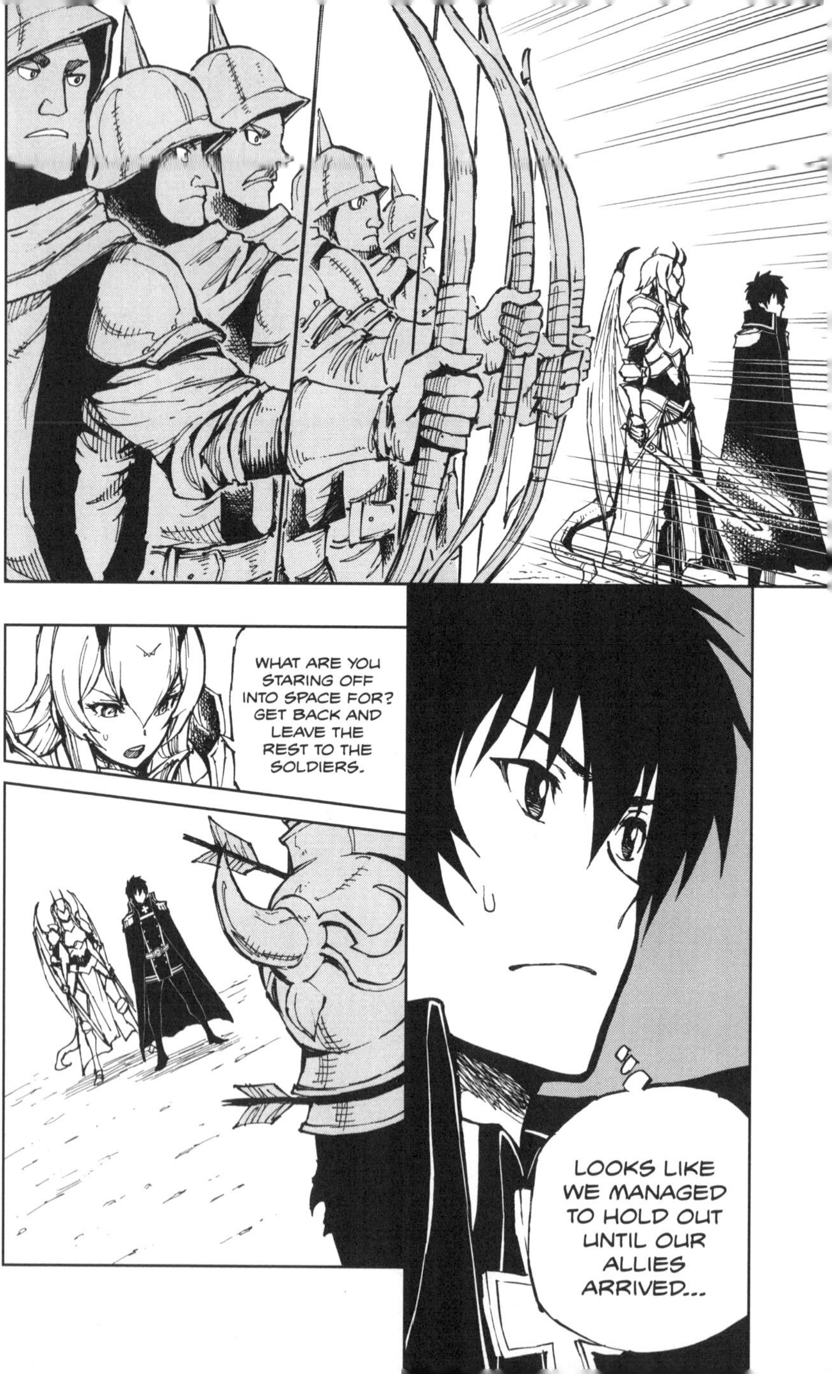
WHAT ARE YOU STARING OFF INTO SPACE FOR? GET BACK AND LEAVE THE REST TO THE SOLDIERS.
LOOKS LIKE WE MANAGED TO HOLD OUT UNTIL OUR ALLIES ARRIVED...

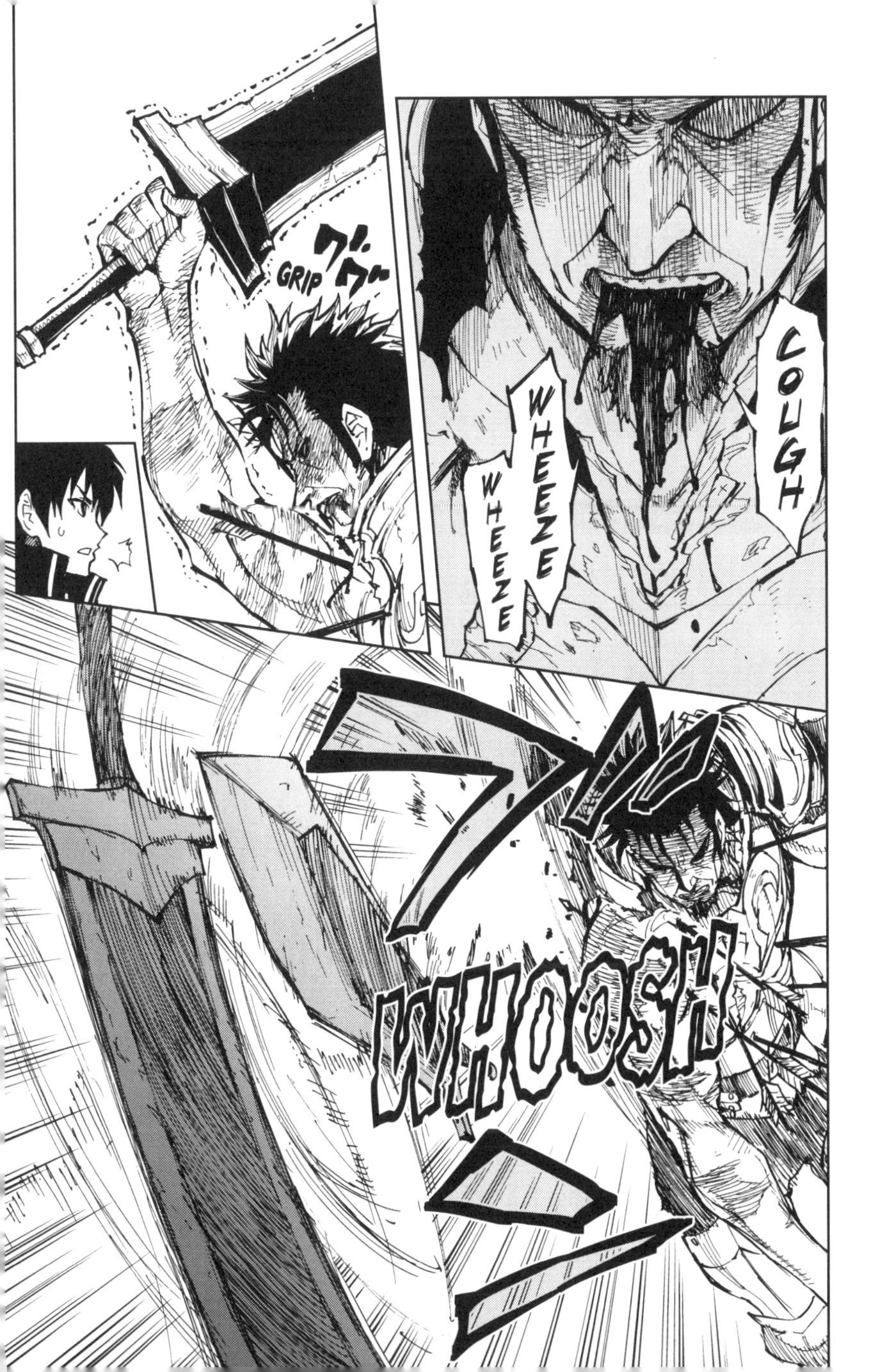
COUGH
WHEEZE
WHEEZE
GRIP
WHOOSH

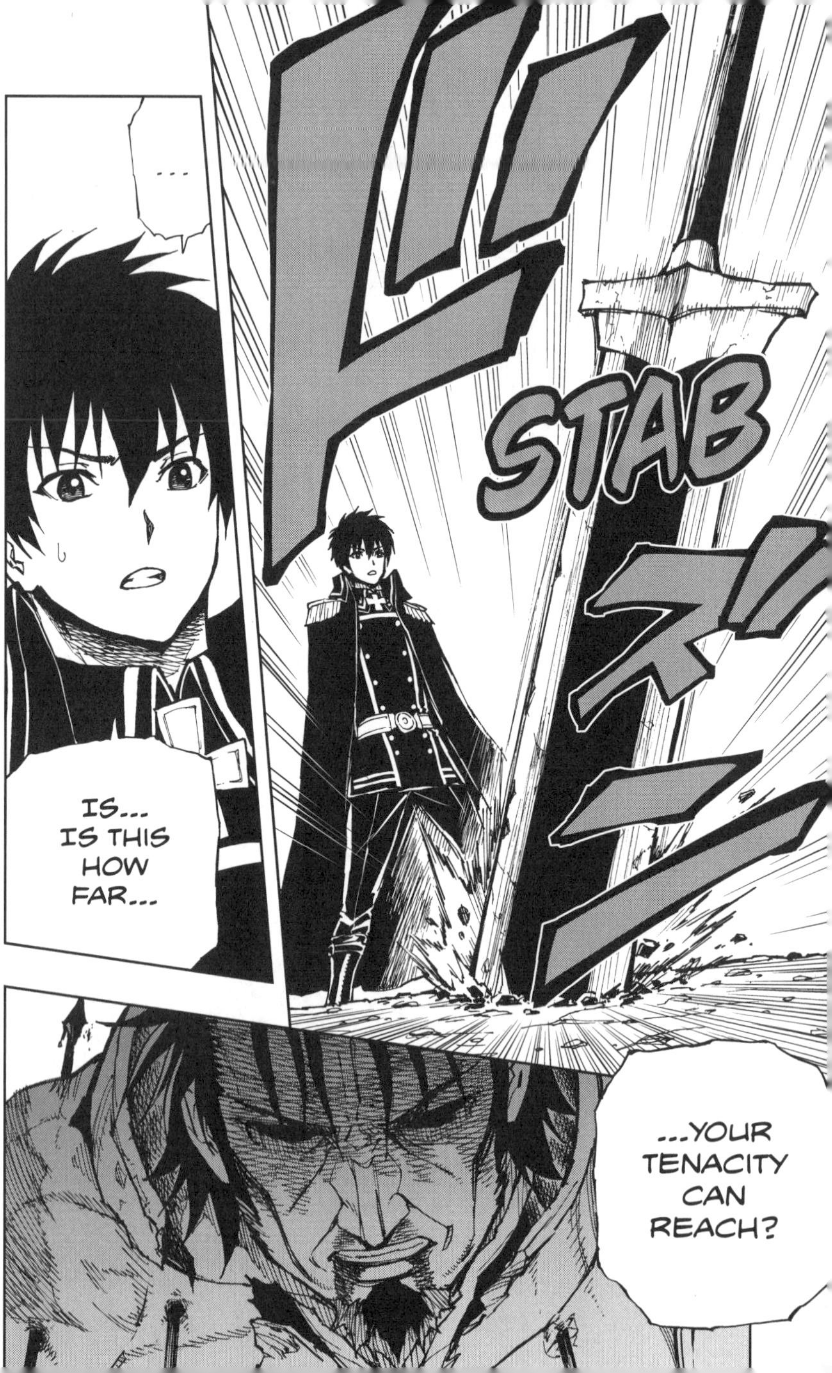
STAB
ズ
...
IS... IS THIS HOW FAR...
...YOUR TENACITY CAN REACH?

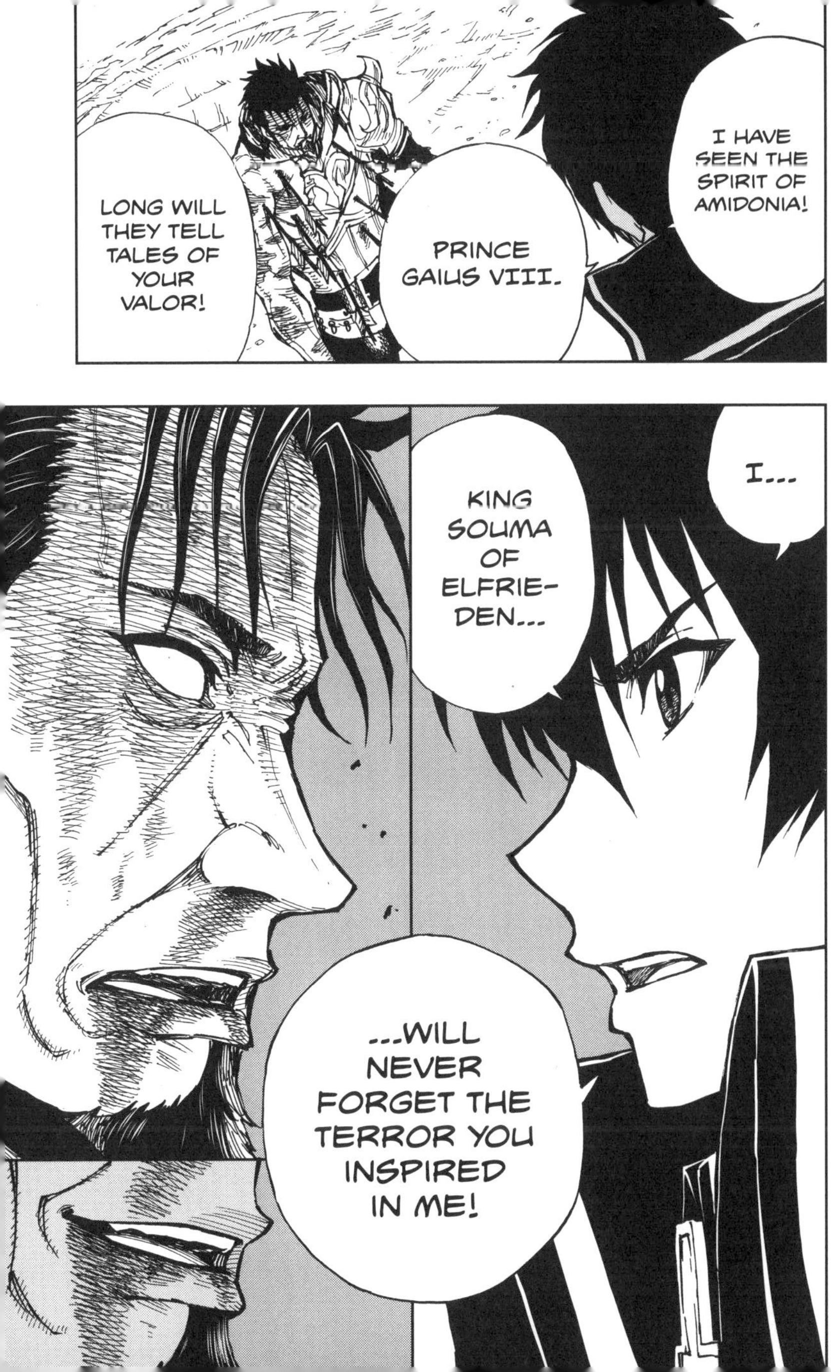
I HAVE SEEN THE SPIRIT OF AMIDONIA!
PRINCE GAIUS VIII.
LONG WILL THEY TELL TALES OF YOUR VALOR!
I...
KING SOUMA OF ELFRIE-DEN...
...WILL NEVER FORGET THE TERROR YOU INSPIRED IN ME!

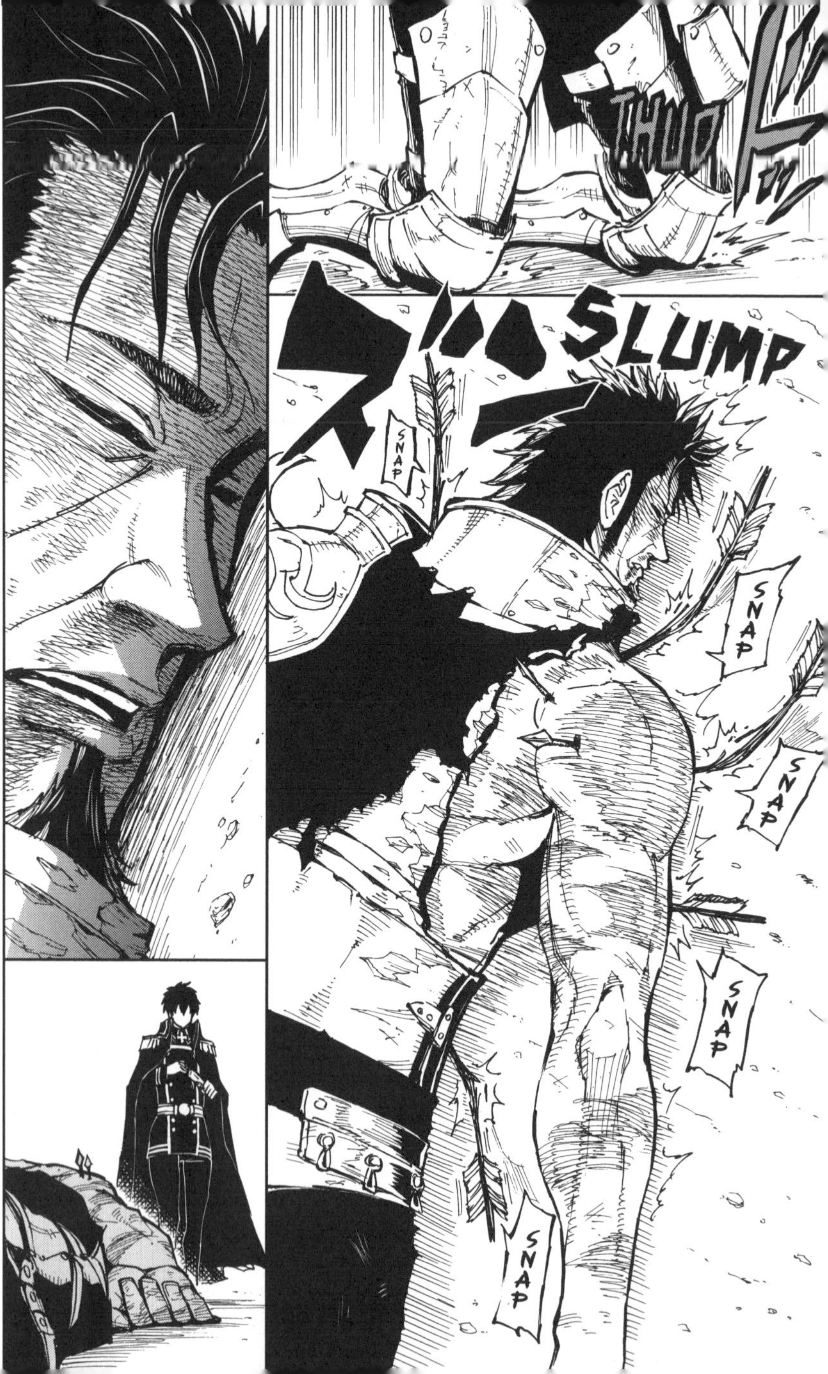
THUD
SLUMP
SNAP
SNAP
SNAP
SNAP
SNAP

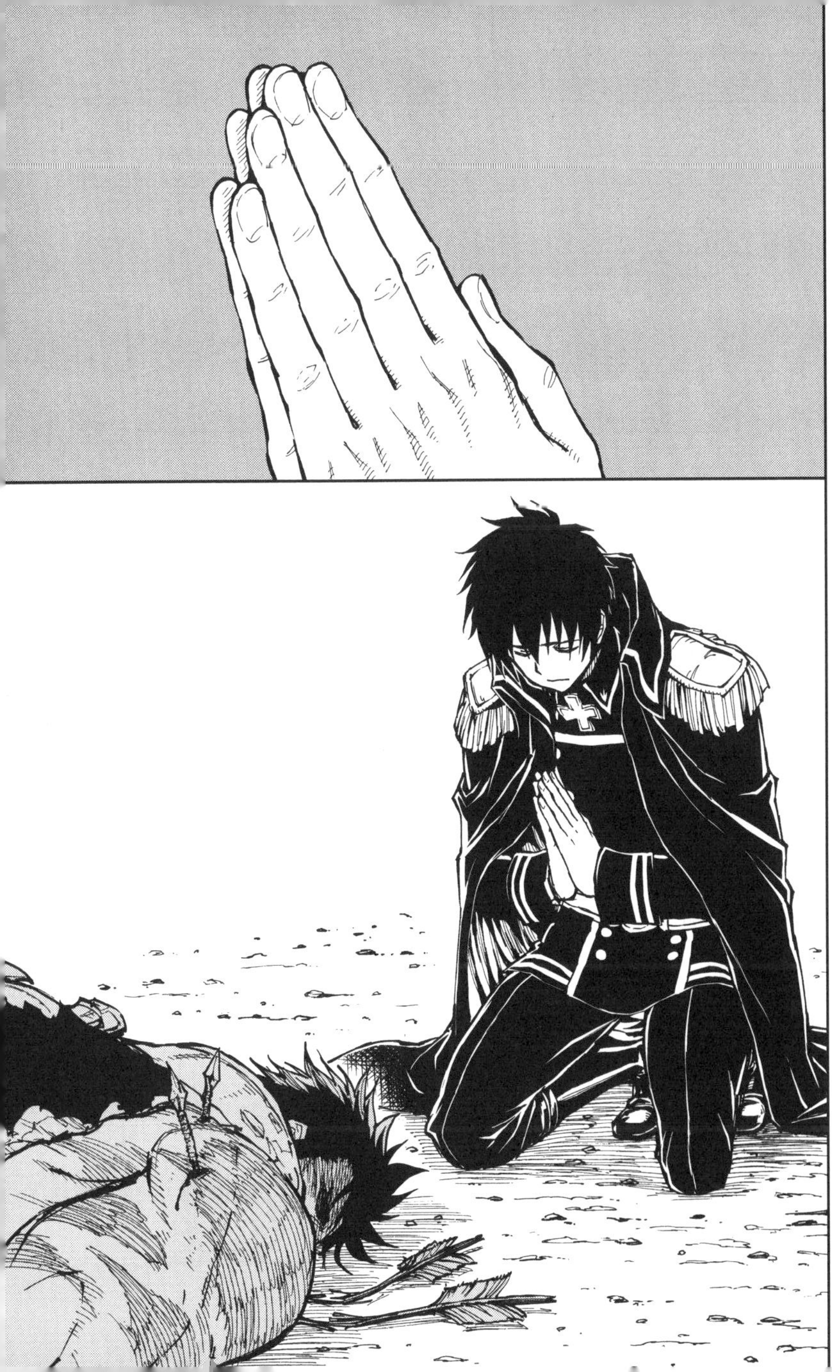

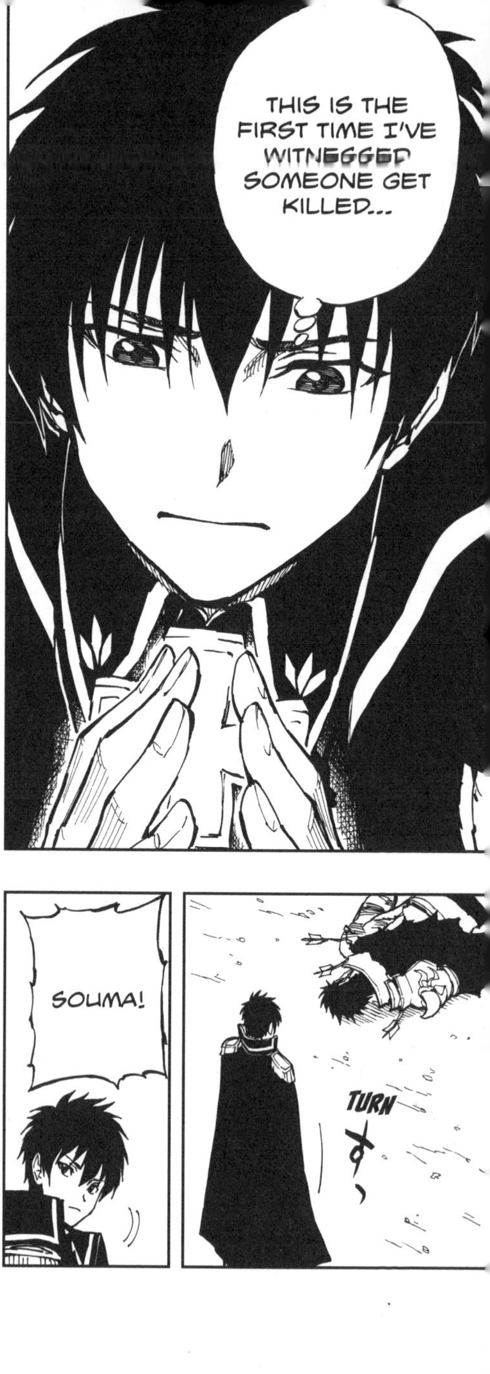
THIS IS THE FIRST TIME I'VE WITNESSED SOMEONE GET KILLED...
TURN
SOUMA!
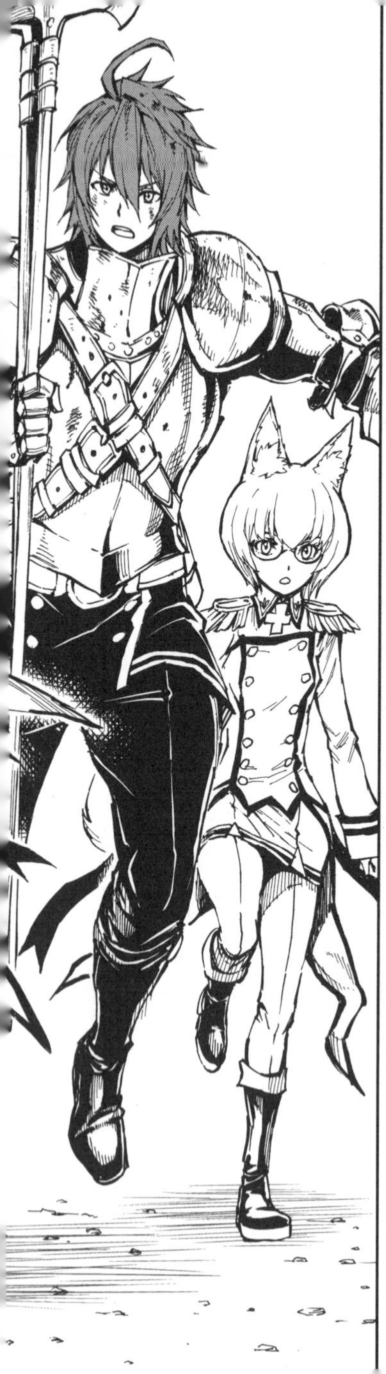

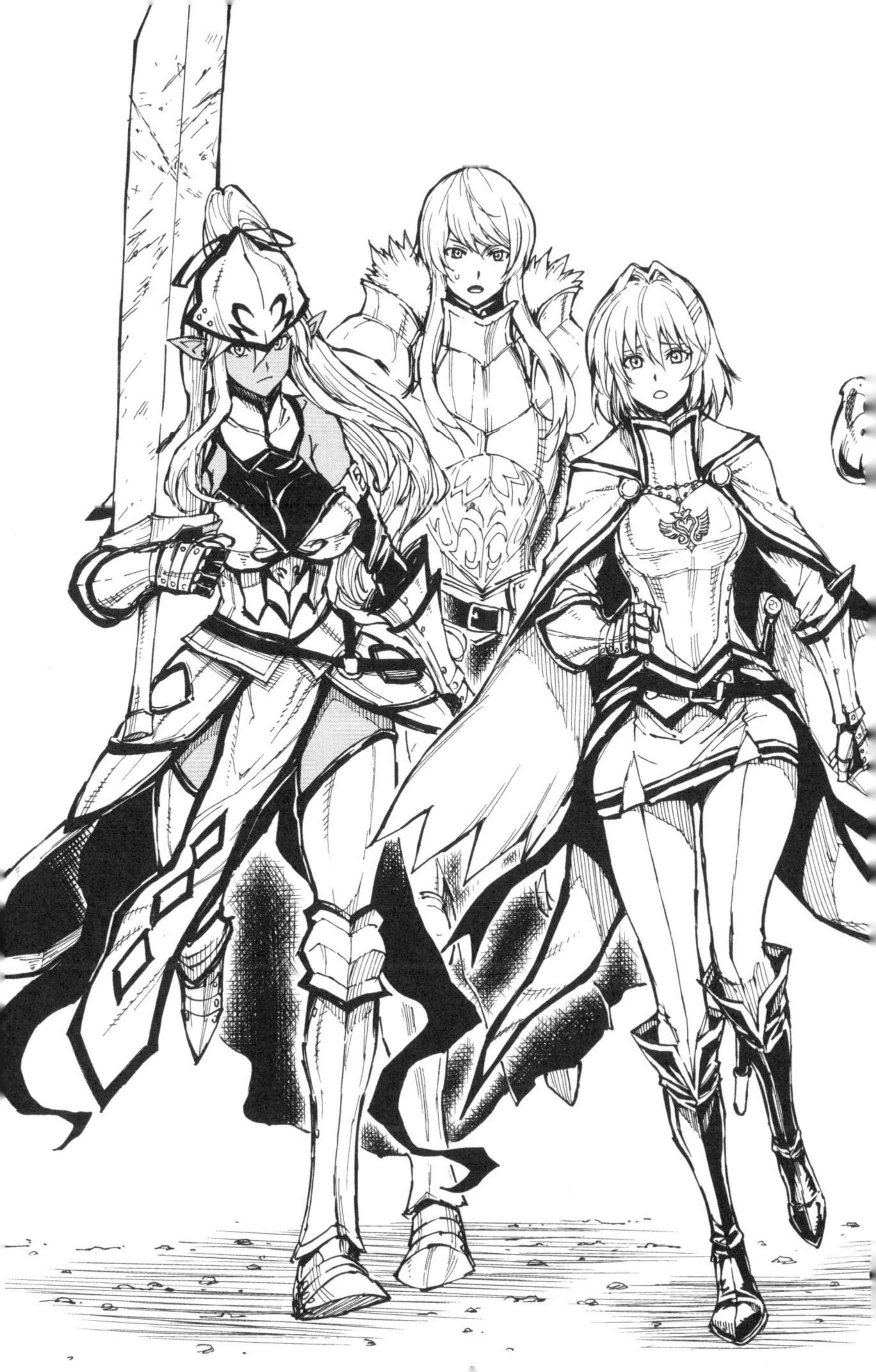

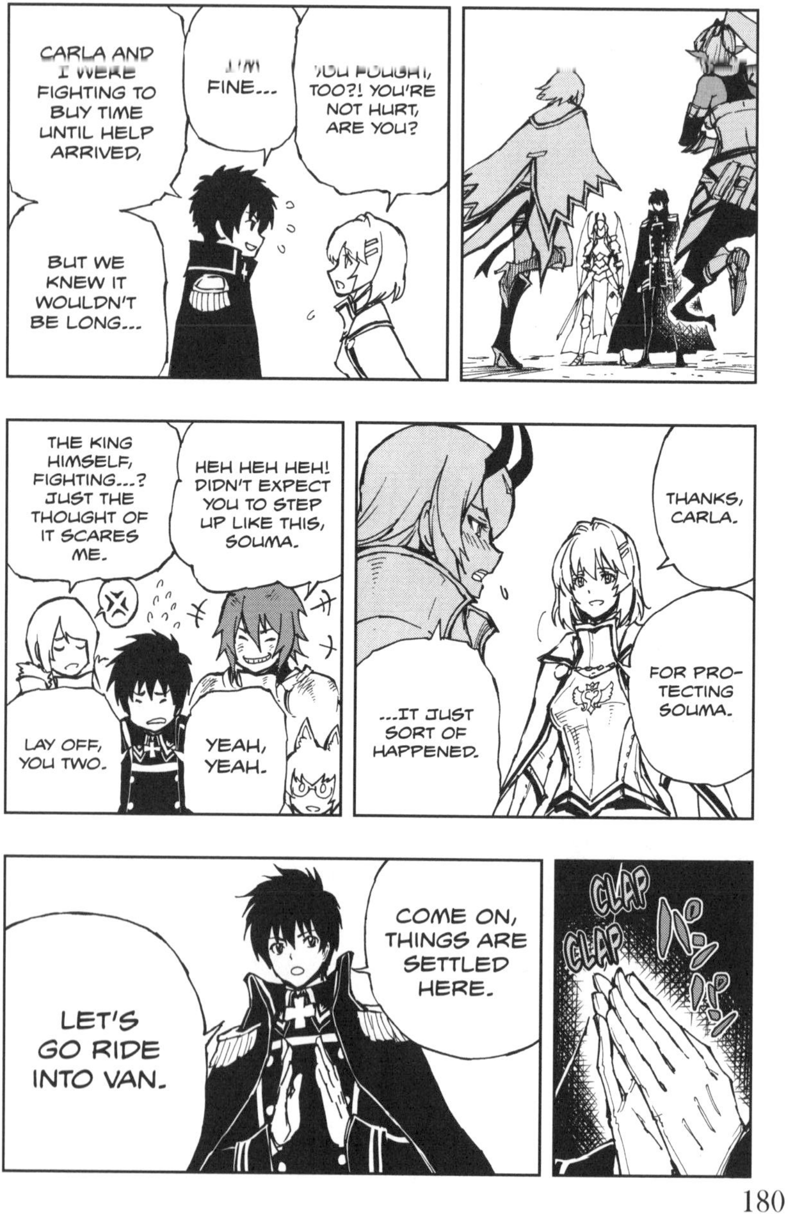
YOU FOUGHT, TOO?! YOU'RE NOT HURT, ARE YOU?
I'M FINE...
CARLA AND I WERE FIGHTING TO BUY TIME UNTIL HELP ARRIVED,
BUT WE KNEW IT WOULDN'T BE LONG...
THANKS, CARLA.
FOR PROTECTING SOUMA.
...IT JUST SORT OF HAPPENED.
HEH HEH HEH! DIDN'T EXPECT YOU TO STEP UP LIKE THIS, SOUMA.
THE KING HIMSELF, FIGHTING...? JUST THE THOUGHT OF IT SCARES ME.
YEAH, YEAH.
LAY OFF, YOU TWO.
CLAP
CLAP
パンパン!
COME ON, THINGS ARE SETTLED HERE.
LET'S GO RIDE INTO VAN.

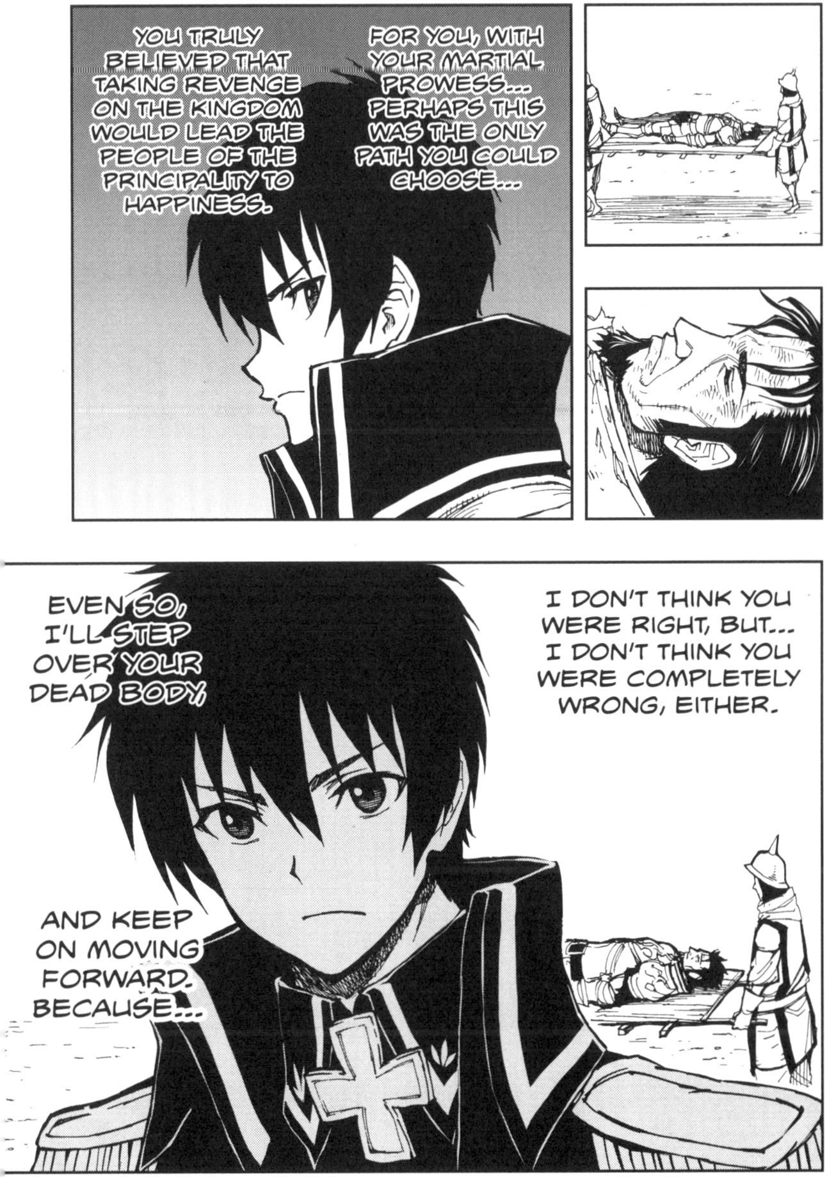
FOR YOU, WITH YOUR MARTIAL PROWESS... PERHAPS THIS WAS THE ONLY PATH YOU COULD CHOOSE...
YOU TRULY BELIEVED THAT TAKING REVENGE ON THE KINGDOM WOULD LEAD THE PEOPLE OF THE PRINCIPALITY TO HAPPINESS.
I DON'T THINK YOU WERE RIGHT, BUT... I DON'T THINK YOU WERE COMPLETELY WRONG, EITHER.
EVEN SO, I'LL STEP OVER YOUR DEAD BODY,
AND KEEP ON MOVING FORWARD. BECAUSE...

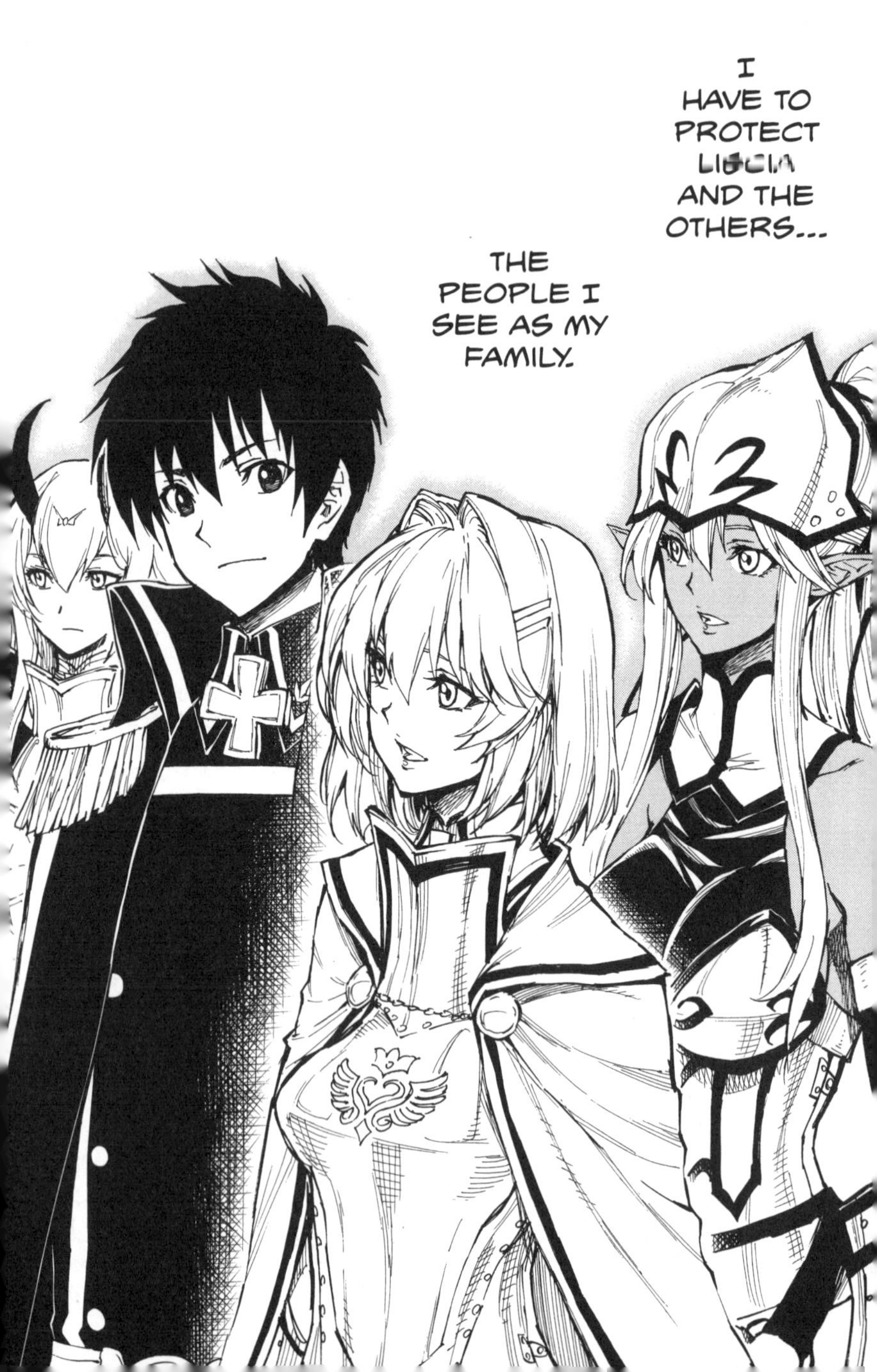
I HAVE TO PROTECT LI[illegible]IA AND THE OTHERS...
THE PEOPLE I SEE AS MY FAMILY.

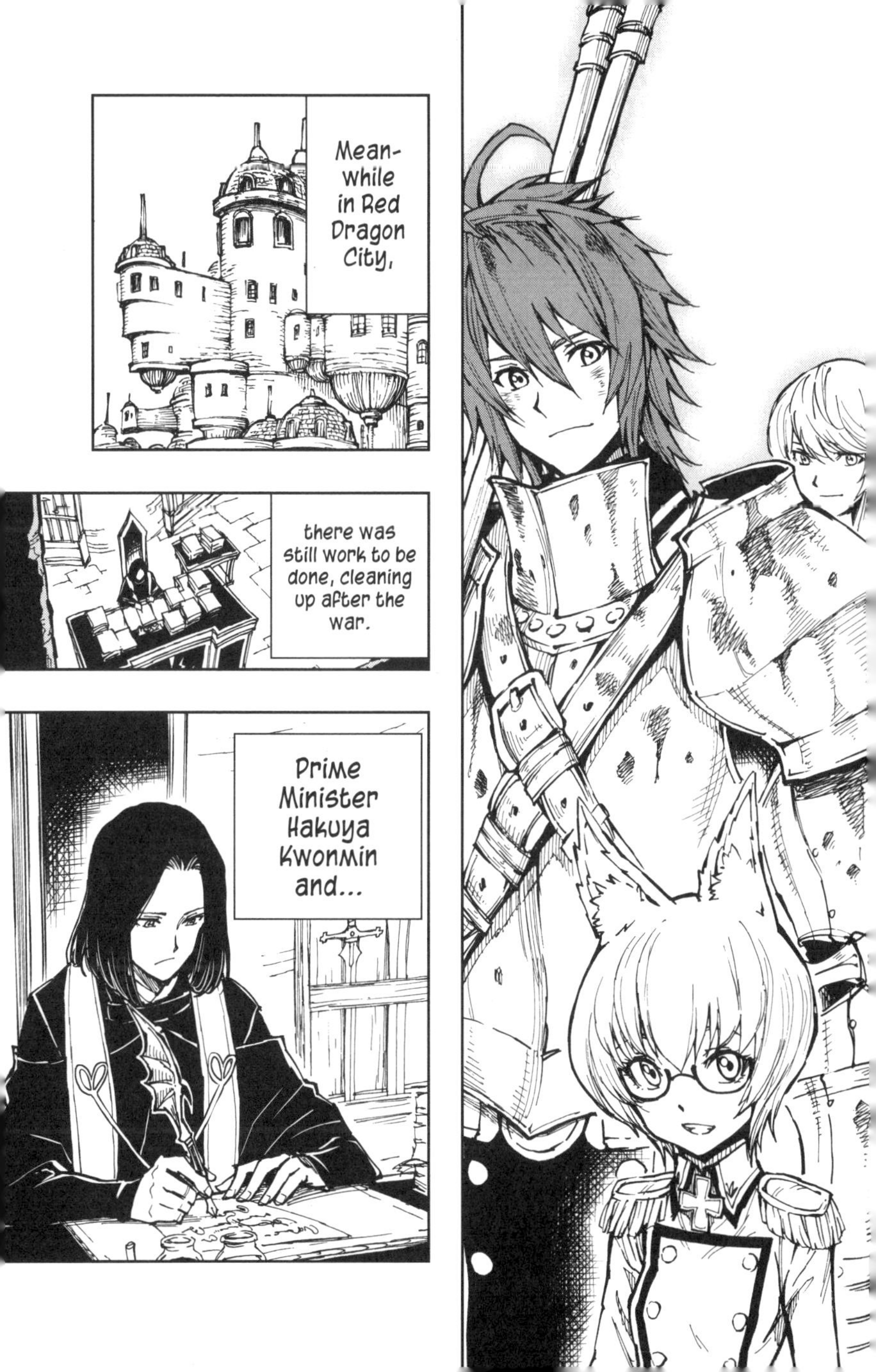
Mean-while in Red Dragon City,
there was still work to be done, cleaning up after the war.
Prime Minister Hakuya Kwonmin and...

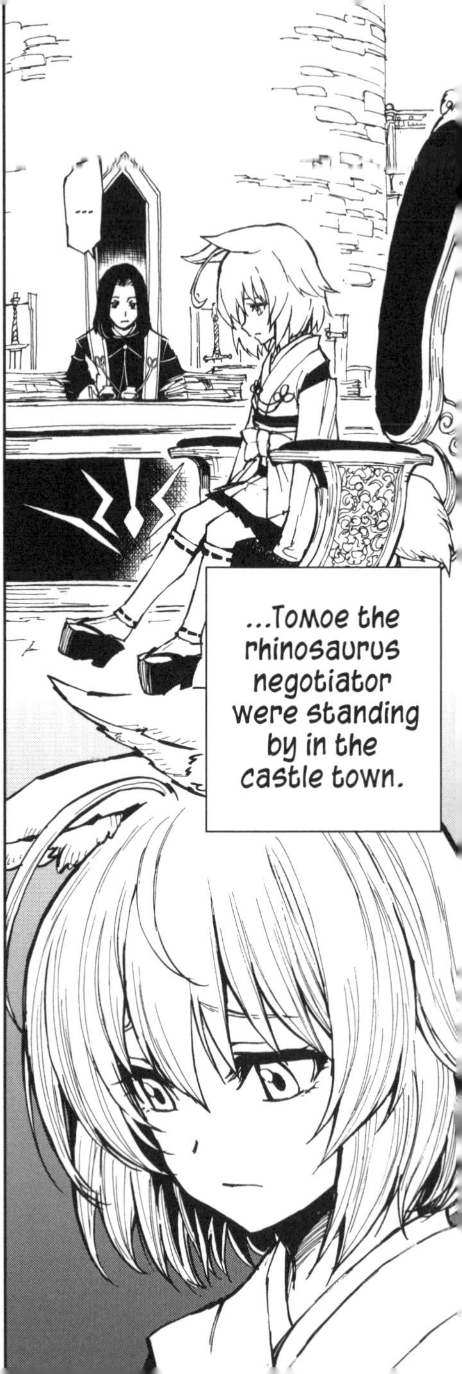
...
...Tomoe the rhinosaurus negotiator were standing by in the castle town.

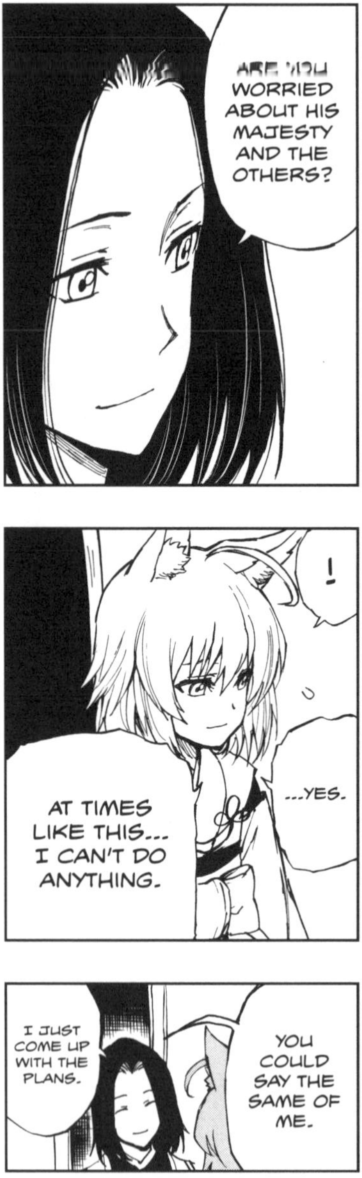
ARE YOU WORRIED ABOUT HIS MAJESTY AND THE OTHERS?
!
...YES.
AT TIMES LIKE THIS... I CAN'T DO ANYTHING.
YOU COULD SAY THE SAME OF ME.
I JUST COME UP WITH THE PLANS.

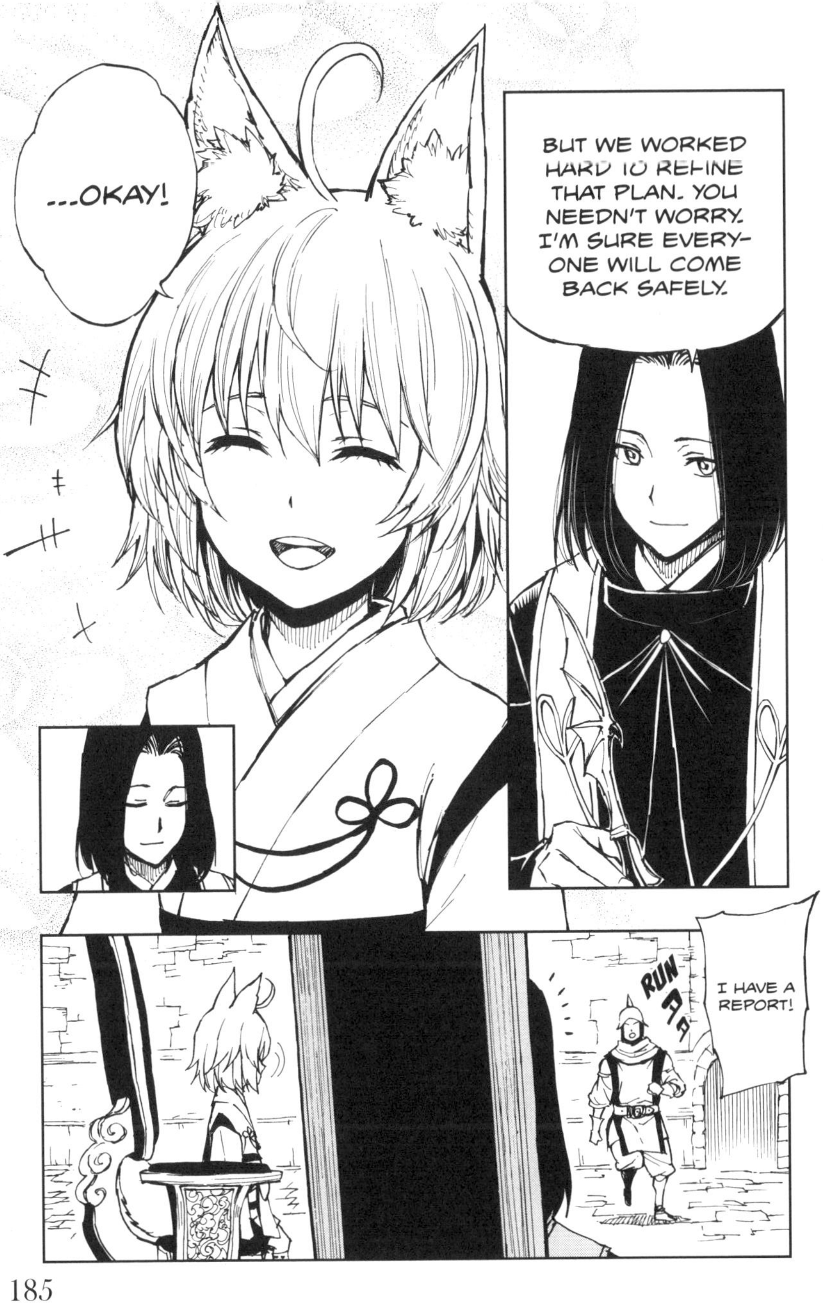
BUT WE WORKED HARD TO REFINE THAT PLAN. YOU NEEDN'T WORRY. I'M SURE EVERY-ONE WILL COME BACK SAFELY.
...OKAY!
RUN
I HAVE A REPORT!

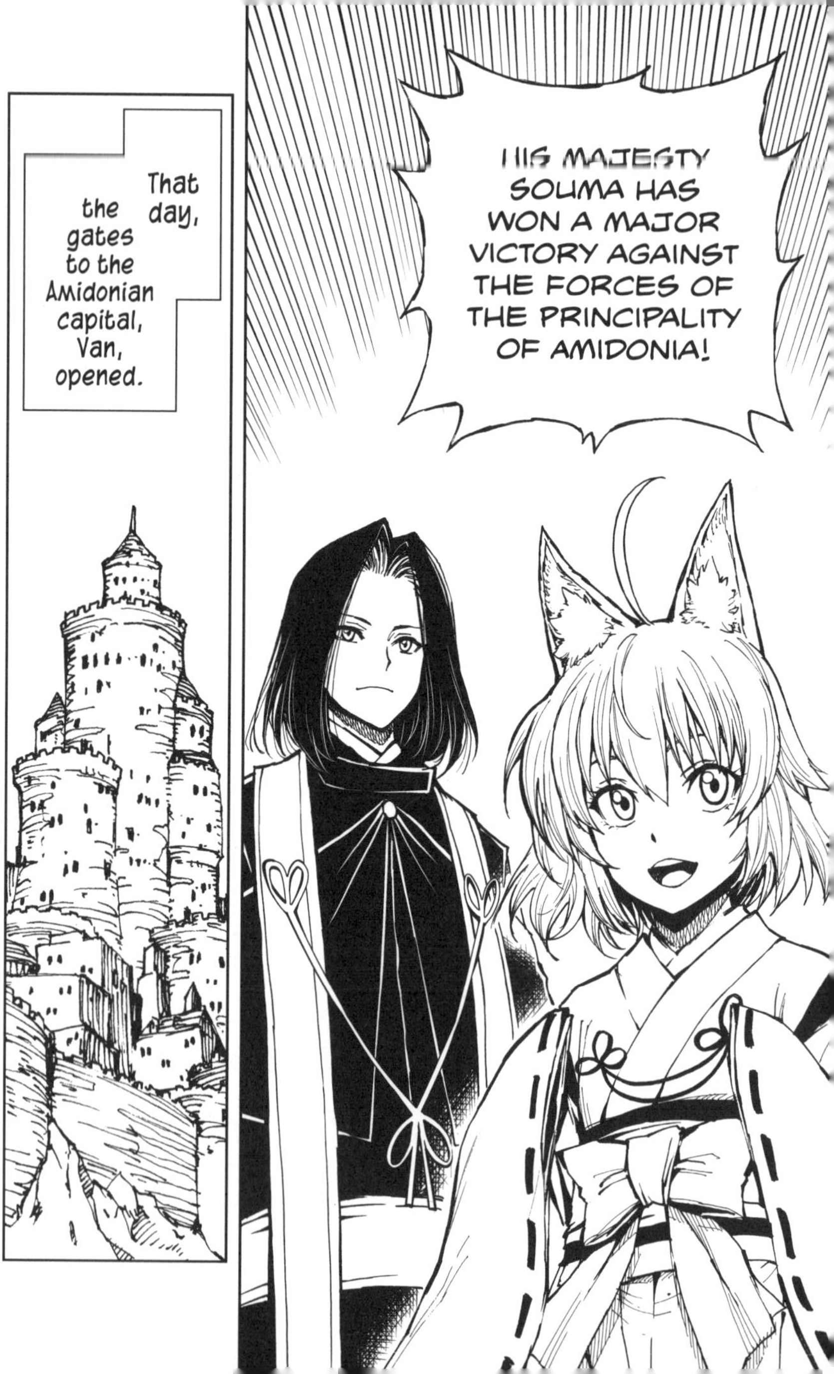
HIS MAJESTY SOUMA HAS WON A MAJOR VICTORY AGAINST THE FORCES OF THE PRINCIPALITY OF AMIDONIA!
That day, the gates to the Amidonian capital, Van, opened.

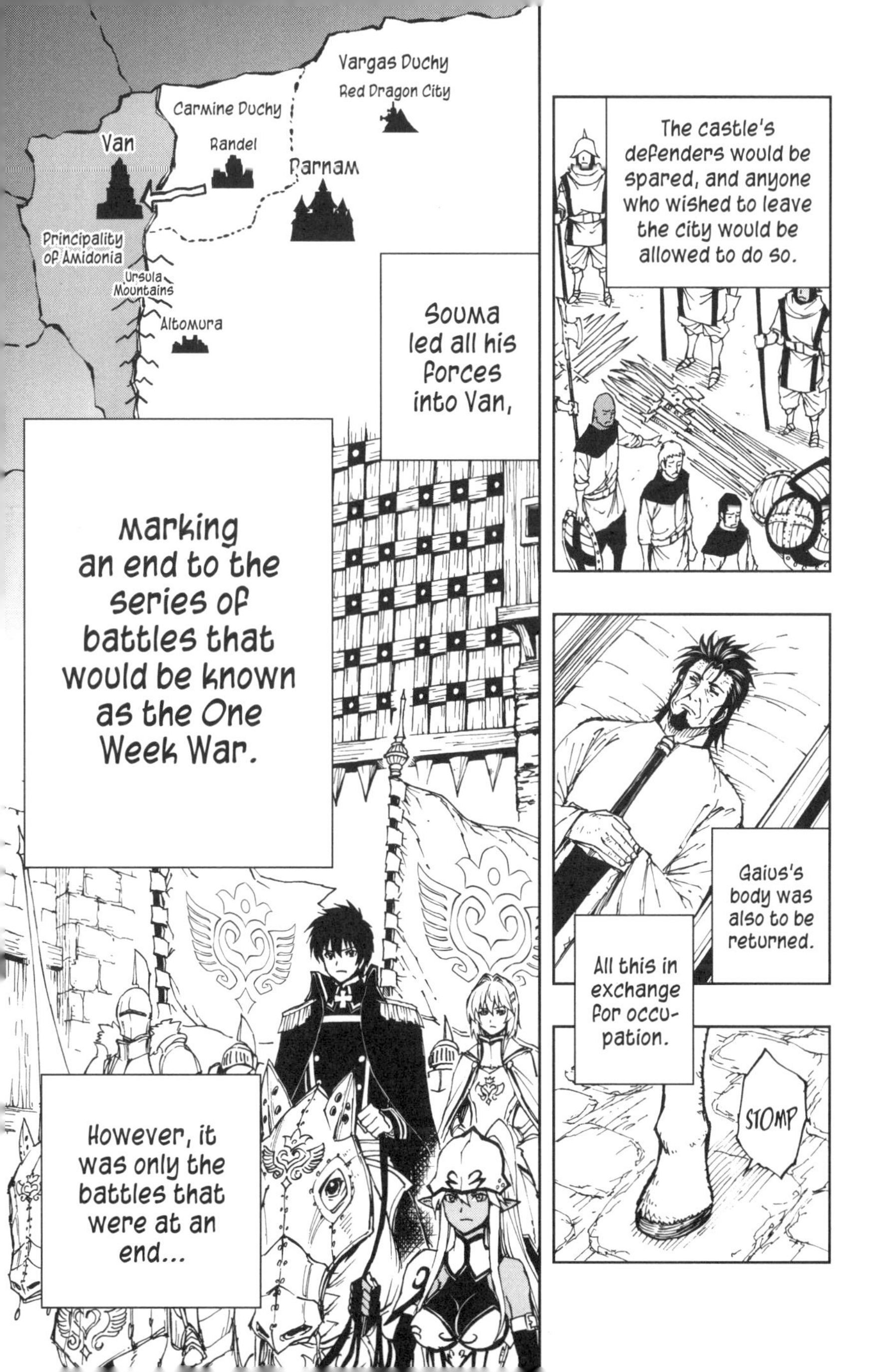
The castle's defenders would be spared, and anyone who wished to leave the city would be allowed to do so.
Gaius's body was also to be returned.
All this in exchange for occupation.
STOMP
Vargas Duchy
Red Dragon City
Carmine Duchy
Van
Randel
Parnam
Principality of Amidonia
Ursula Mountains
Altomura
Souma led all his forces into Van,
Marking an end to the series of battles that would be known as the One Week War.
However, it was only the battles that were at an end...

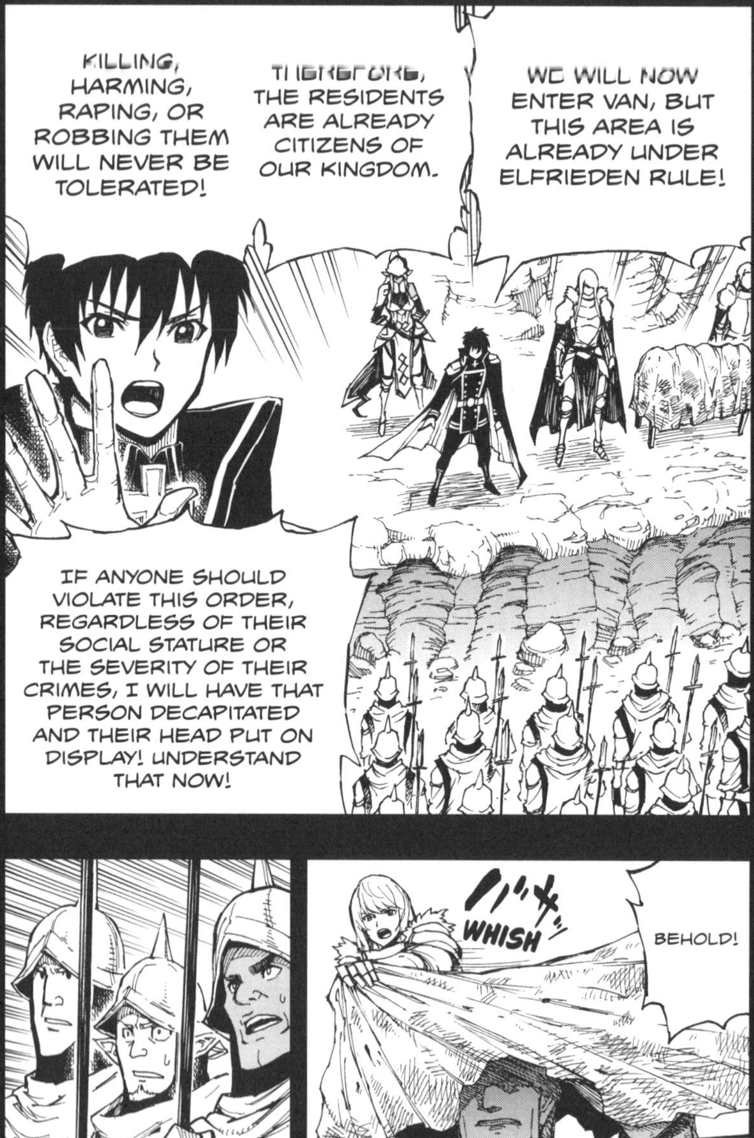
WE WILL NOW ENTER VAN, BUT THIS AREA IS ALREADY UNDER ELFRIEDEN RULE!
THEREFORE, THE RESIDENTS ARE ALREADY CITIZENS OF OUR KINGDOM.
KILLING, HARMING, RAPING, OR ROBBING THEM WILL NEVER BE TOLERATED!
IF ANYONE SHOULD VIOLATE THIS ORDER, REGARDLESS OF THEIR SOCIAL STATURE OR THE SEVERITY OF THEIR CRIMES, I WILL HAVE THAT PERSON DECAPITATED AND THEIR HEAD PUT ON DISPLAY! UNDERSTAND THAT NOW!
WHISH
BEHOLD!

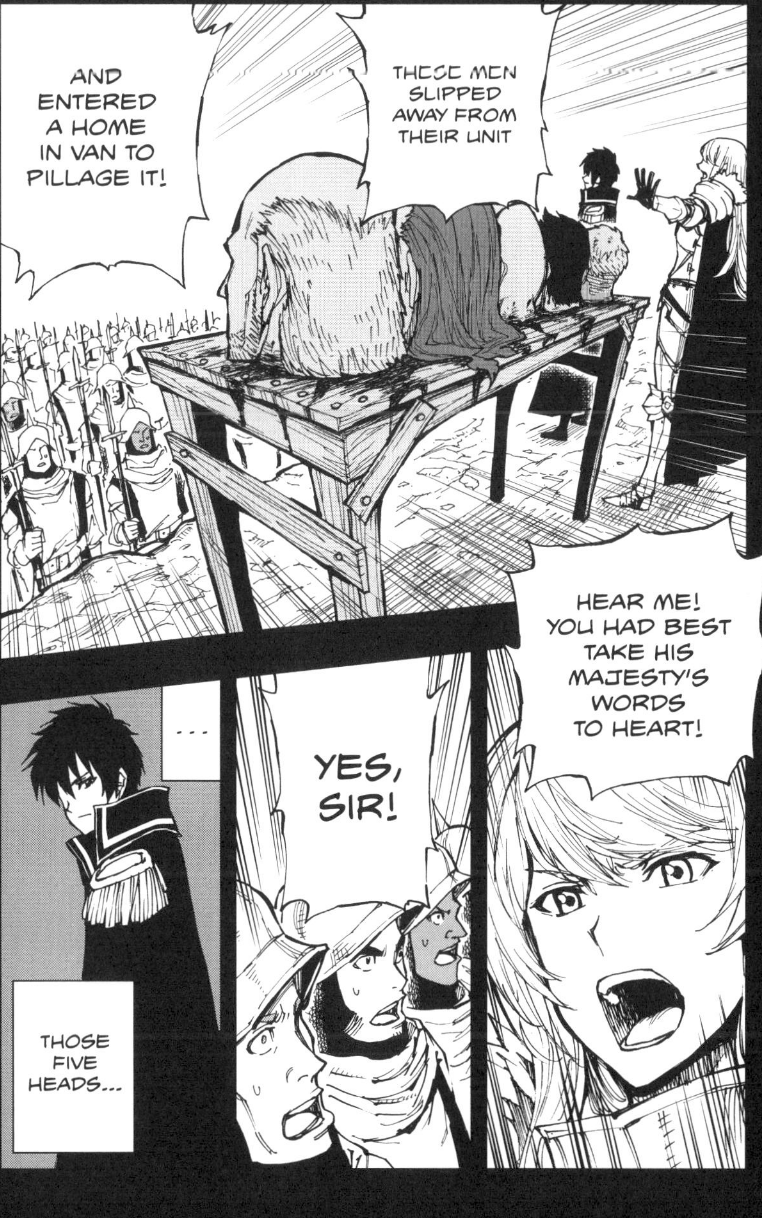

THESE MEN SLIPPED AWAY FROM THEIR UNIT
AND ENTERED A HOME IN VAN TO PILLAGE IT!
HEAR ME! YOU HAD BEST TAKE HIS MAJESTY'S WORDS TO HEART!
YES, SIR!
...
THOSE FIVE HEADS...

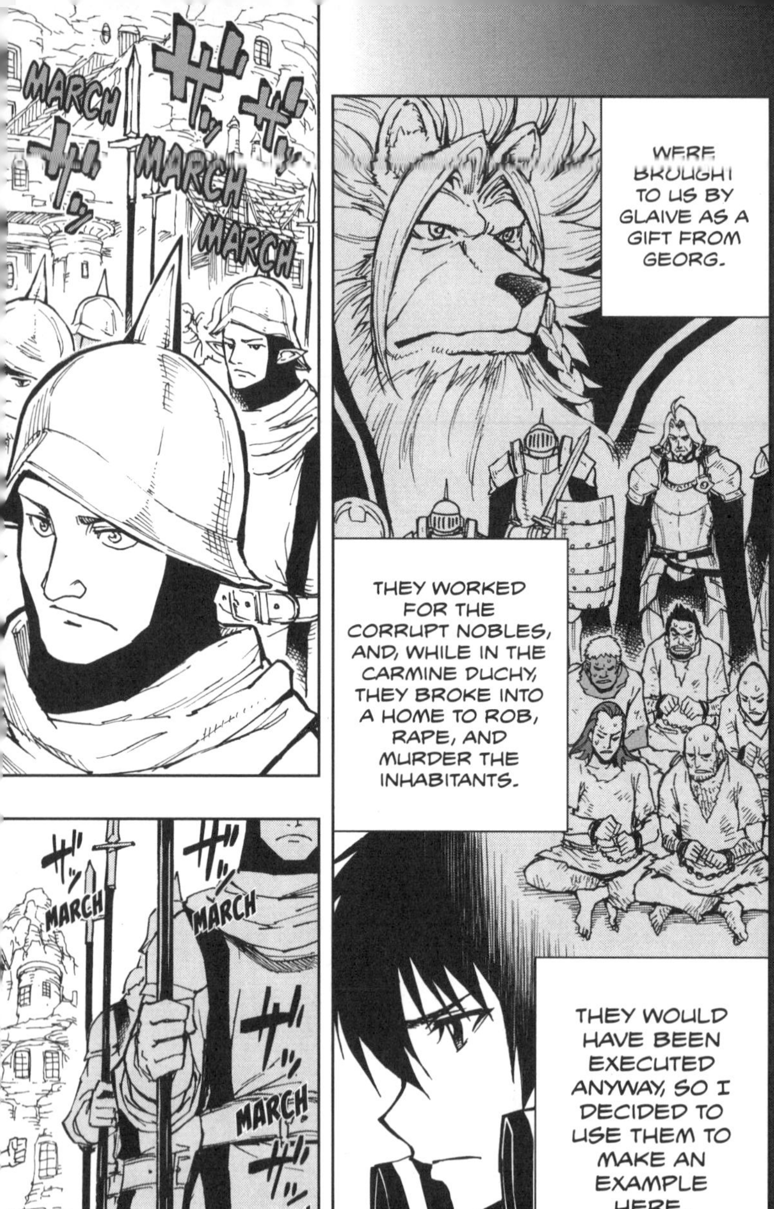
WERE BROUGHT TO US BY GLAIVE AS A GIFT FROM GEORG.
THEY WORKED FOR THE CORRUPT NOBLES, AND, WHILE IN THE CARMINE DUCHY, THEY BROKE INTO A HOME TO ROB, RAPE, AND MURDER THE INHABITANTS.
THEY WOULD HAVE BEEN EXECUTED ANYWAY, SO I DECIDED TO USE THEM TO MAKE AN EXAMPLE HERE.
MARCH
MARCH
MARCH
MARCH
MARCH
MARCH
MARCH

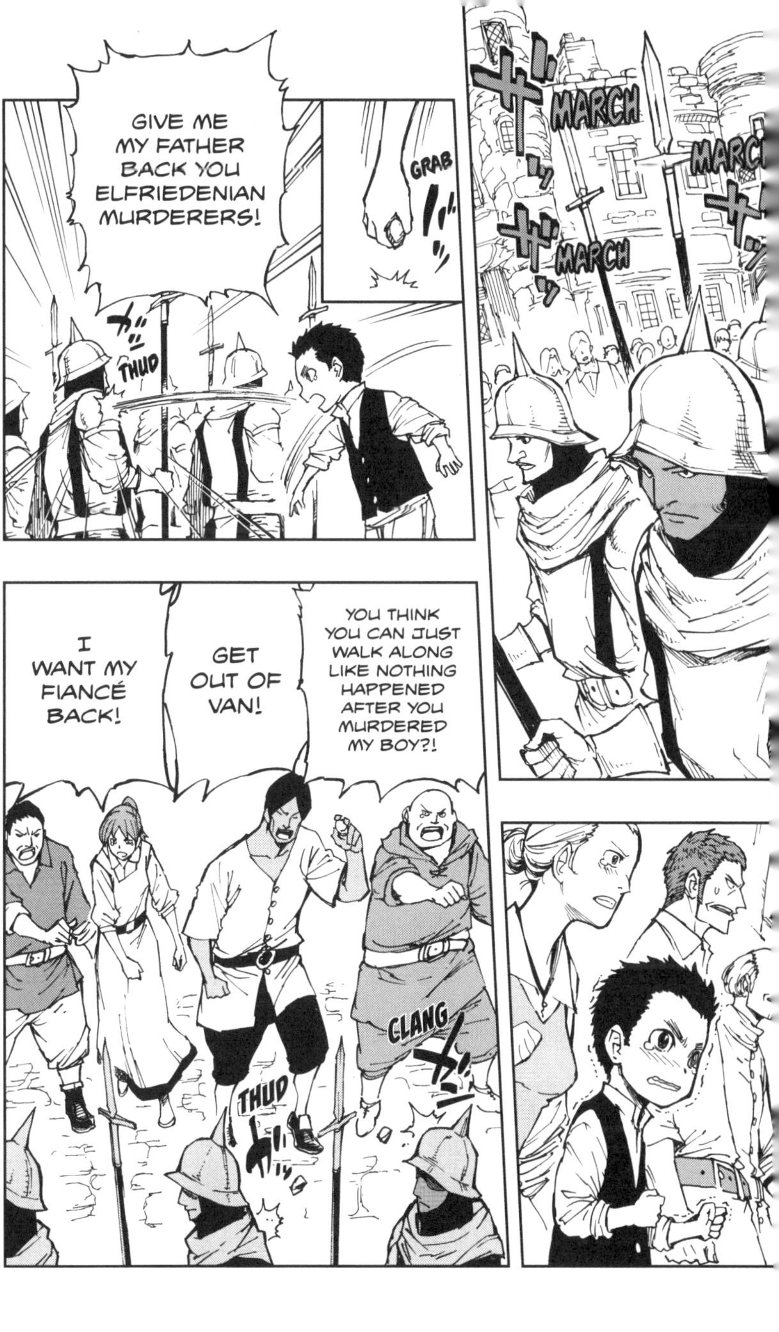
MARCH
MARCH
MARCH
GRAB
GIVE ME MY FATHER BACK YOU ELFRIEDENIAN MURDERERS!
THUD
YOU THINK YOU CAN JUST WALK ALONG LIKE NOTHING HAPPENED AFTER YOU MURDERED MY BOY?!
GET OUT OF VAN!
I WANT MY FIANCÉ BACK!
CLANG
THUD

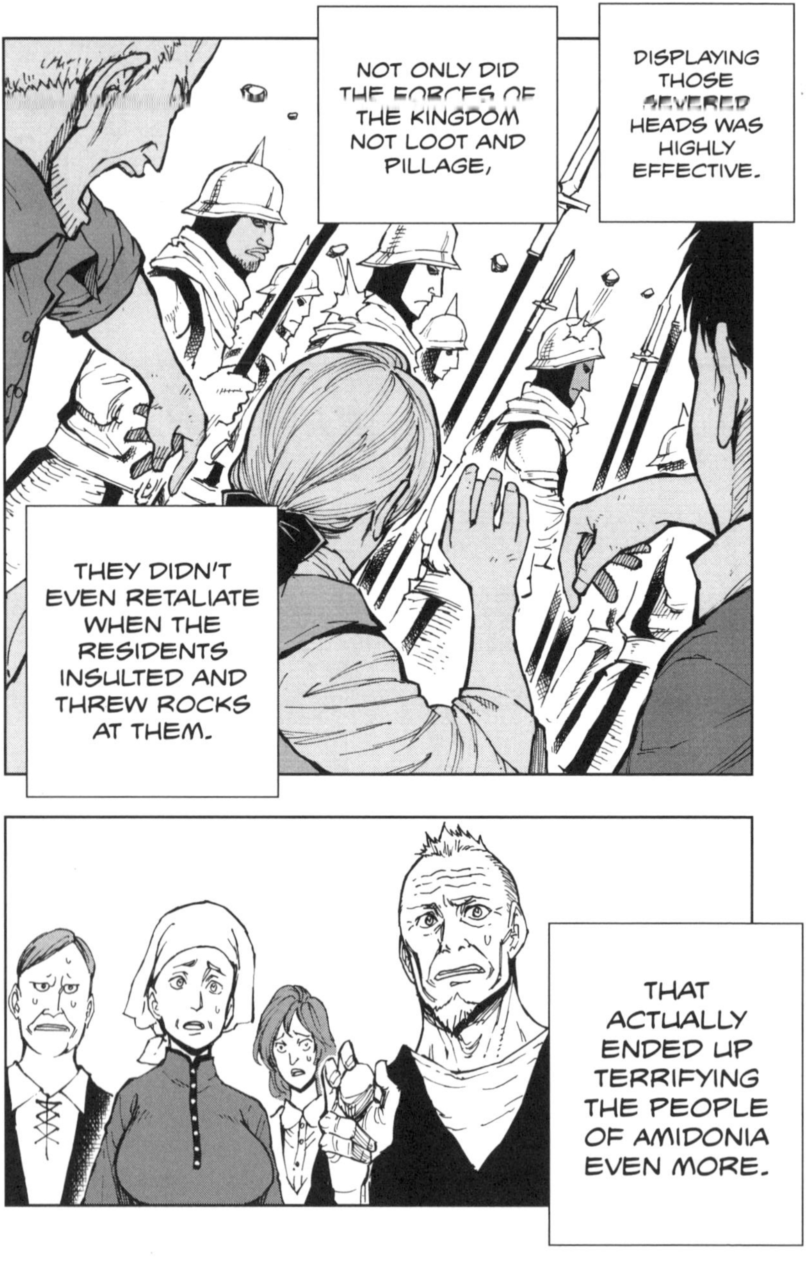
DISPLAYING THOSE SEVERED HEADS WAS HIGHLY EFFECTIVE.
NOT ONLY DID THE FORCES OF THE KINGDOM NOT LOOT AND PILLAGE,
THEY DIDN'T EVEN RETALIATE WHEN THE RESIDENTS INSULTED AND THREW ROCKS AT THEM.
THAT ACTUALLY ENDED UP TERRIFYING THE PEOPLE OF AMIDONIA EVEN MORE.

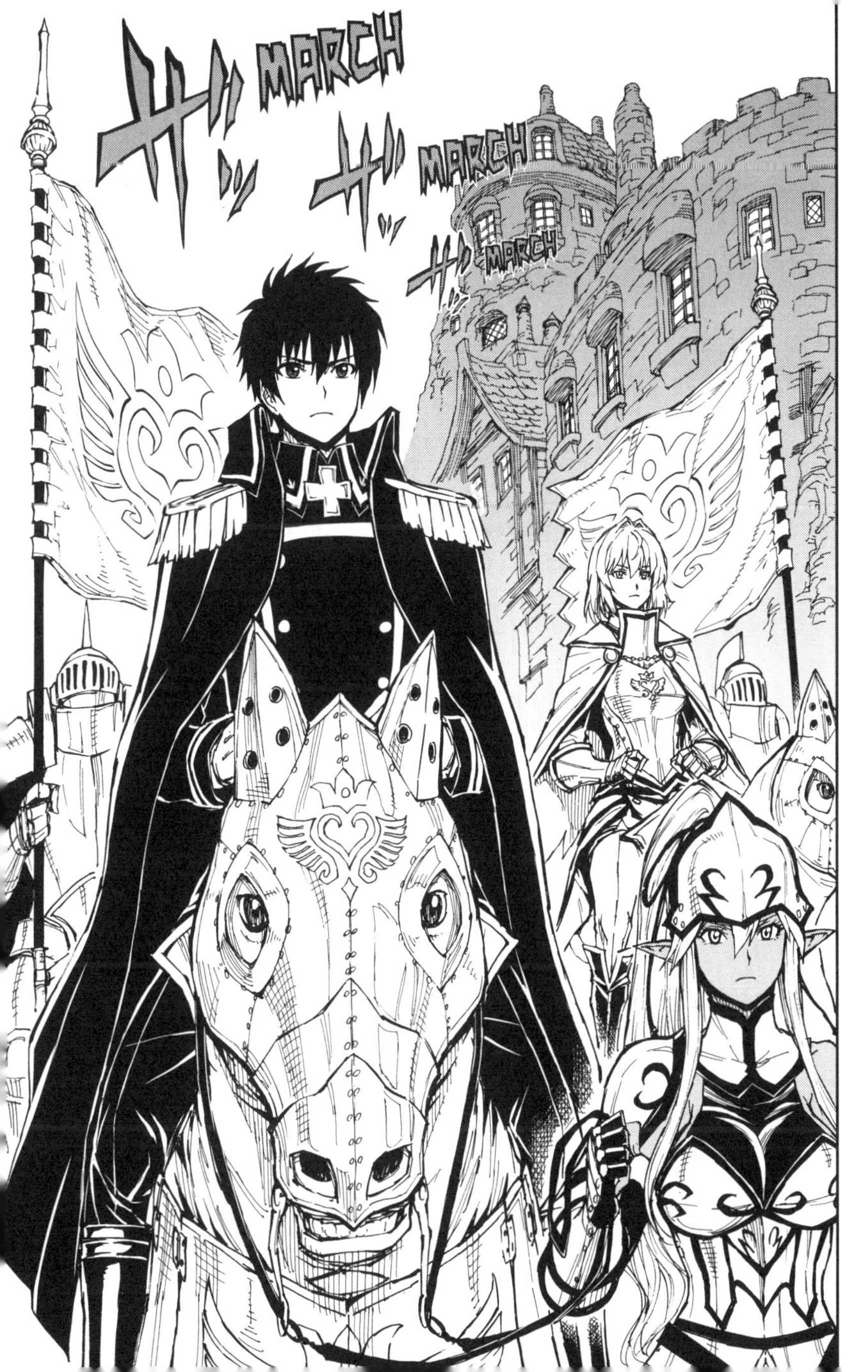
MARCH
MARCH
MARCH

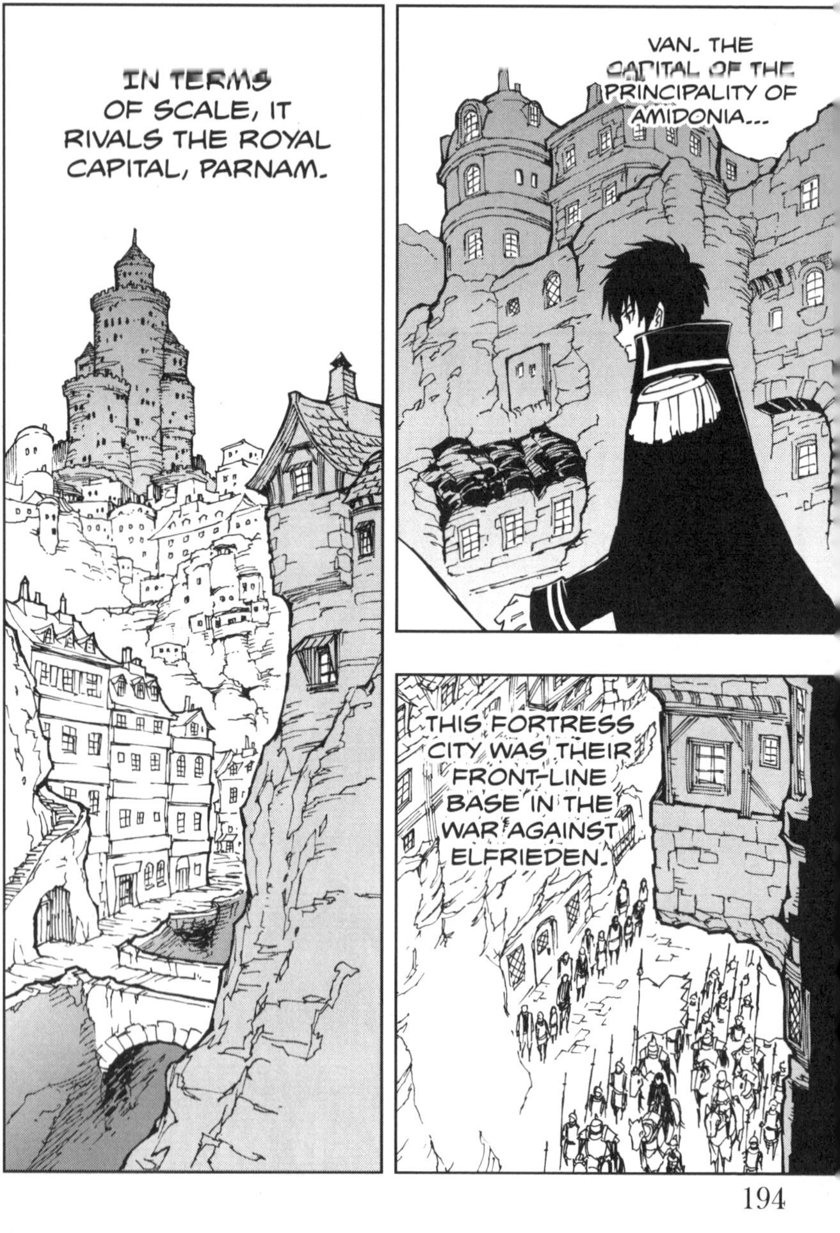
VAN. THE CAPITAL OF THE PRINCIPALITY OF AMIDONIA...
THIS FORTRESS CITY WAS THEIR FRONT-LINE BASE IN THE WAR AGAINST ELFRIEDEN.
IN TERMS OF SCALE, IT RIVALS THE ROYAL CAPITAL, PARNAM.

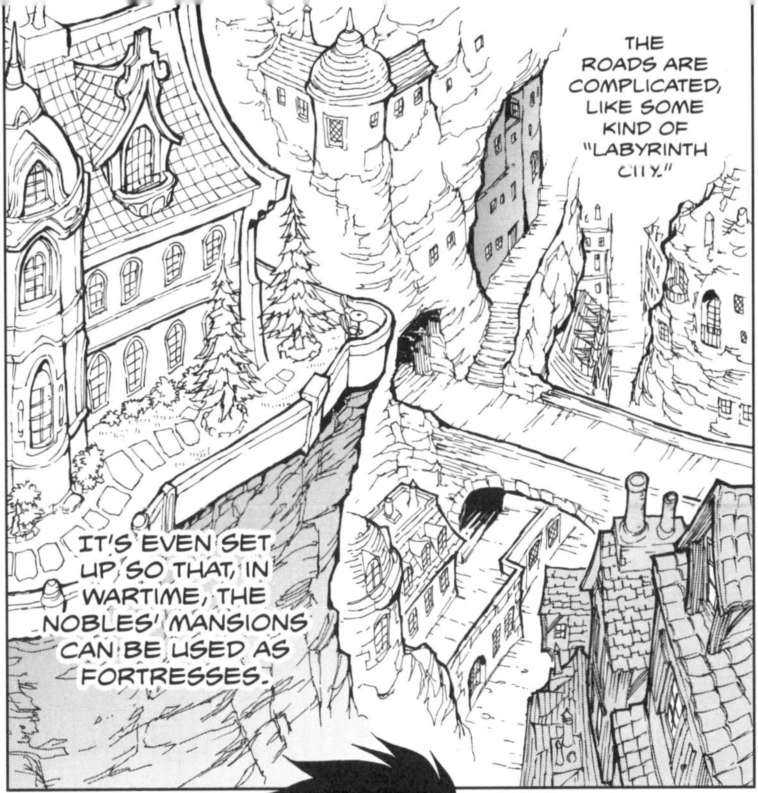
THE ROADS ARE COMPLICATED, LIKE SOME KIND OF "LABYRINTH CITY."
IT'S EVEN SET UP SO THAT, IN WARTIME, THE NOBLES' MANSIONS CAN BE USED AS FORTRESSES.

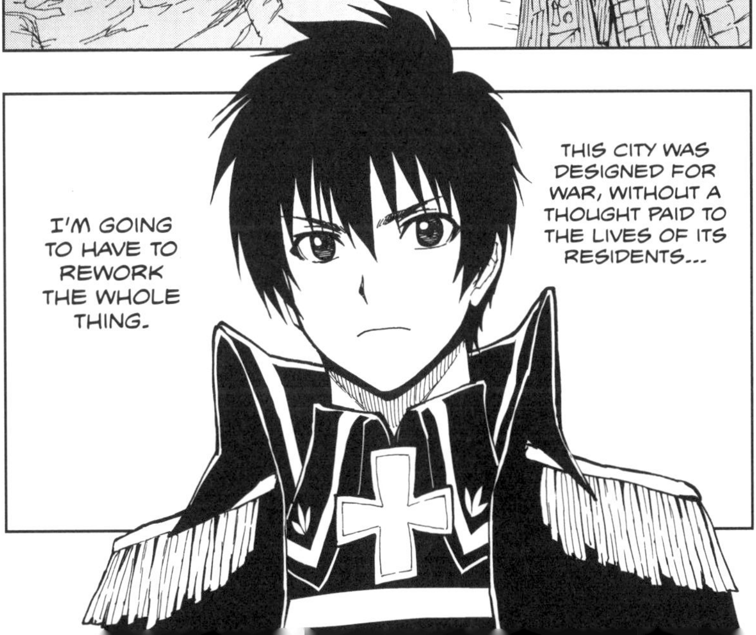
THIS CITY WAS DESIGNED FOR WAR, WITHOUT A THOUGHT PAID TO THE LIVES OF ITS RESIDENTS...
I'M GOING TO HAVE TO REWORK THE WHOLE THING.

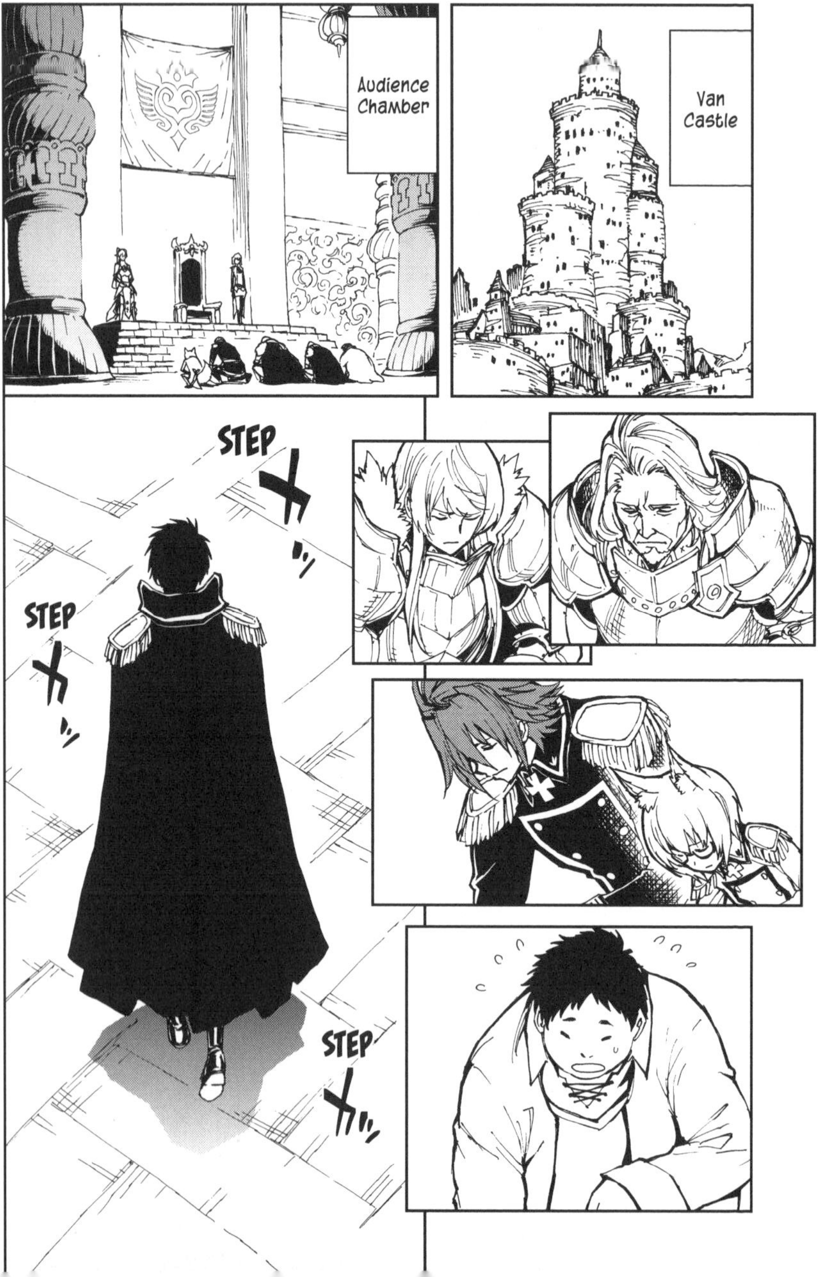
Van Castle
Audience Chamber
STEP
STEP
STEP

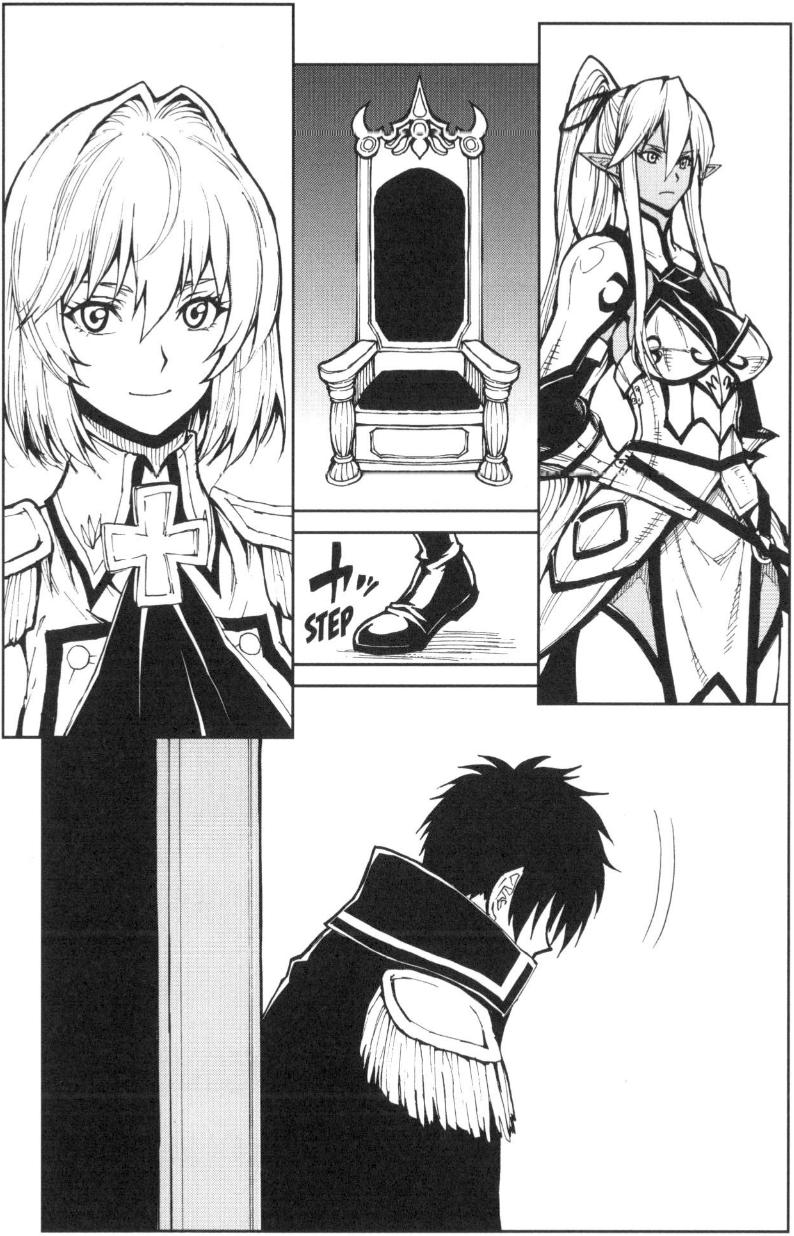
カッ
STEP

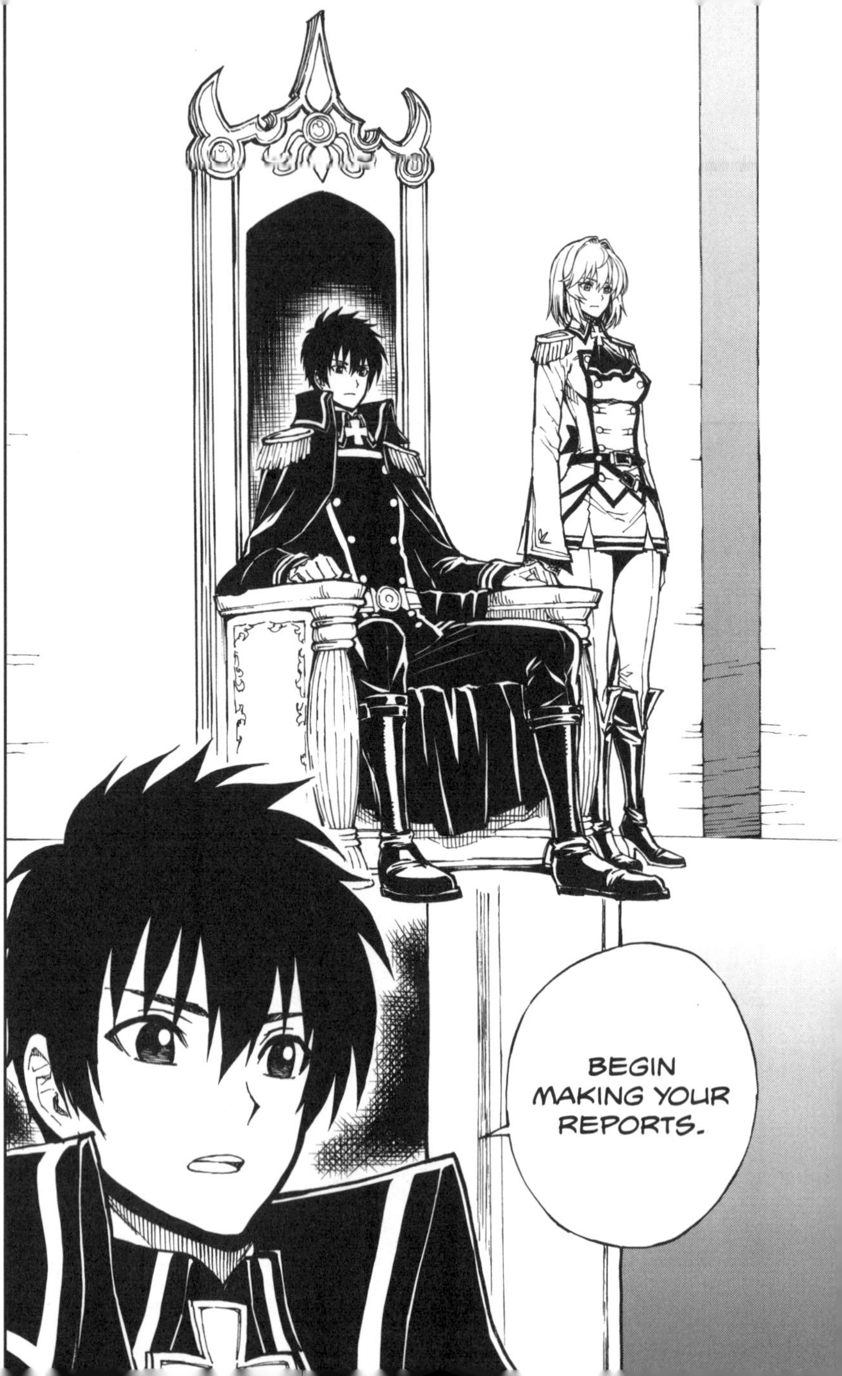
BEGIN MAKING YOUR REPORTS.

Chapter 28: Prologue to the Postwar Period

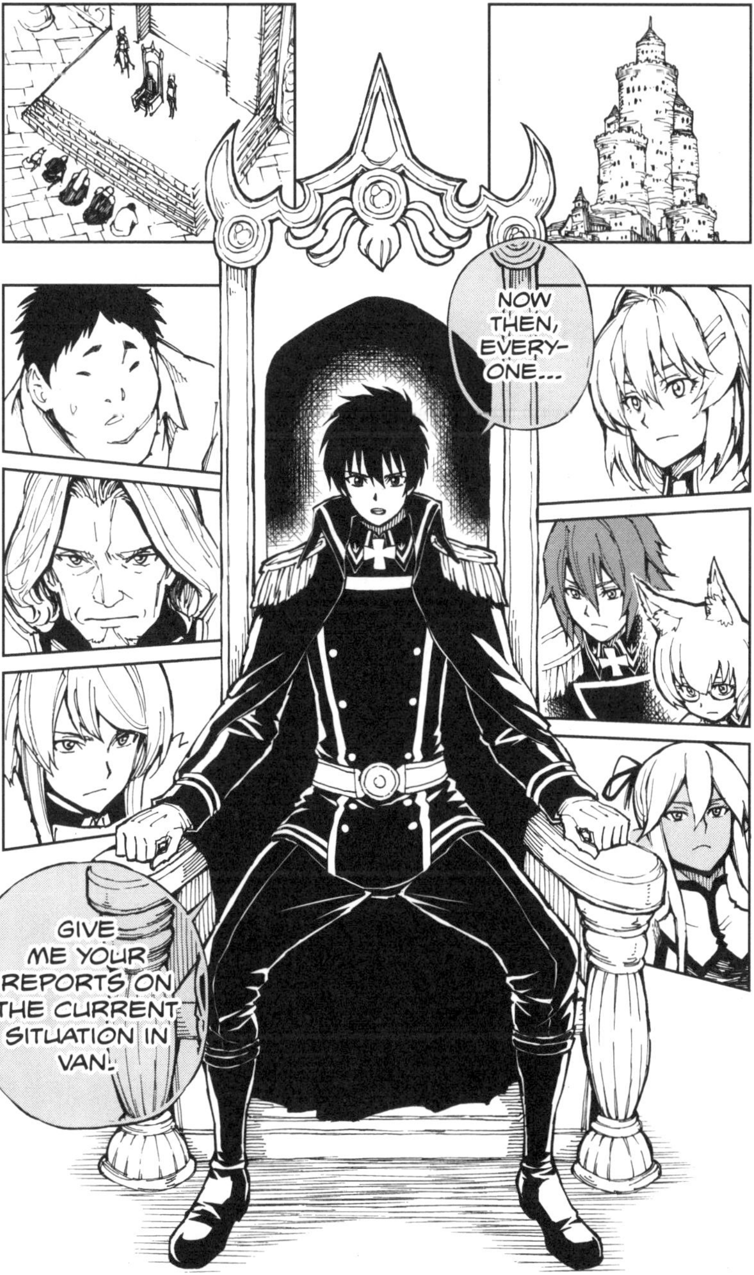
NOW THEN, EVERY-ONE...
GIVE ME YOUR REPORTS ON THE CURRENT SITUATION IN VAN.

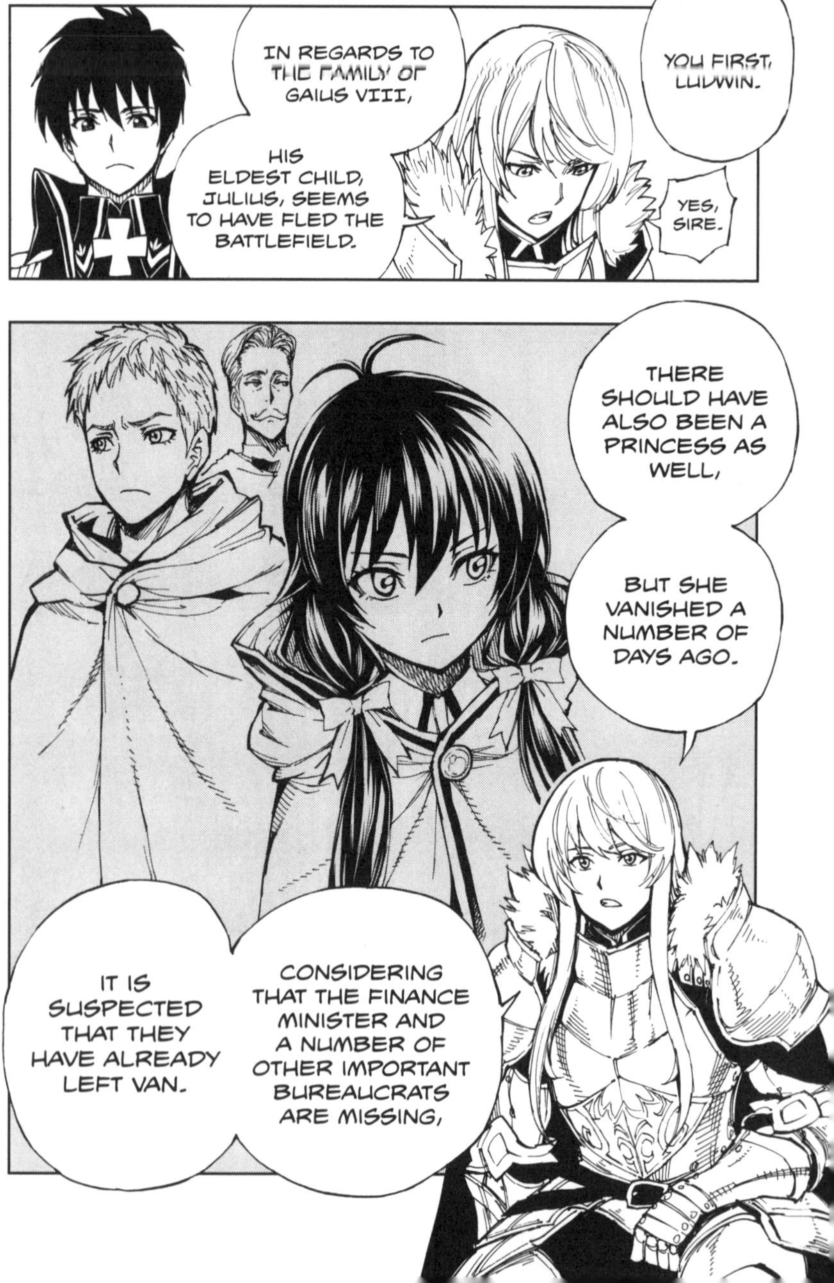

YOU FIRST, LUDWIN.
YES, SIRE.
IN REGARDS TO THE FAMILY OF GAIUS VIII,
HIS ELDEST CHILD, JULIUS, SEEMS TO HAVE FLED THE BATTLEFIELD.
THERE SHOULD HAVE ALSO BEEN A PRINCESS AS WELL,
BUT SHE VANISHED A NUMBER OF DAYS AGO.
CONSIDERING THAT THE FINANCE MINISTER AND A NUMBER OF OTHER IMPORTANT BUREAUCRATS ARE MISSING,
IT IS SUSPECTED THAT THEY HAVE ALREADY LEFT VAN.

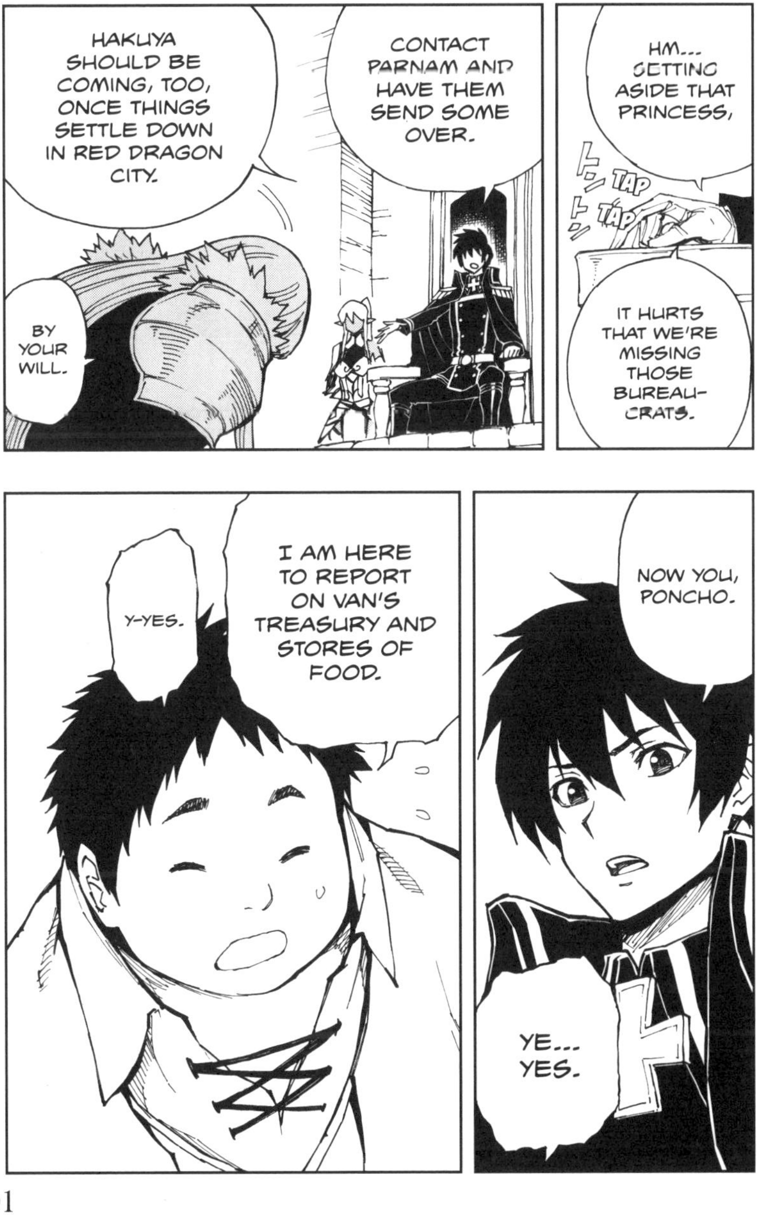
HM... SETTING ASIDE THAT PRINCESS,
TAP
TAP
IT HURTS THAT WE'RE MISSING THOSE BUREAU-CRATS.
CONTACT PARNAM AND HAVE THEM SEND SOME OVER.
HAKUYA SHOULD BE COMING, TOO, ONCE THINGS SETTLE DOWN IN RED DRAGON CITY.
BY YOUR WILL.
NOW YOU, PONCHO.
YE... YES.
I AM HERE TO REPORT ON VAN'S TREASURY AND STORES OF FOOD.
Y-YES.

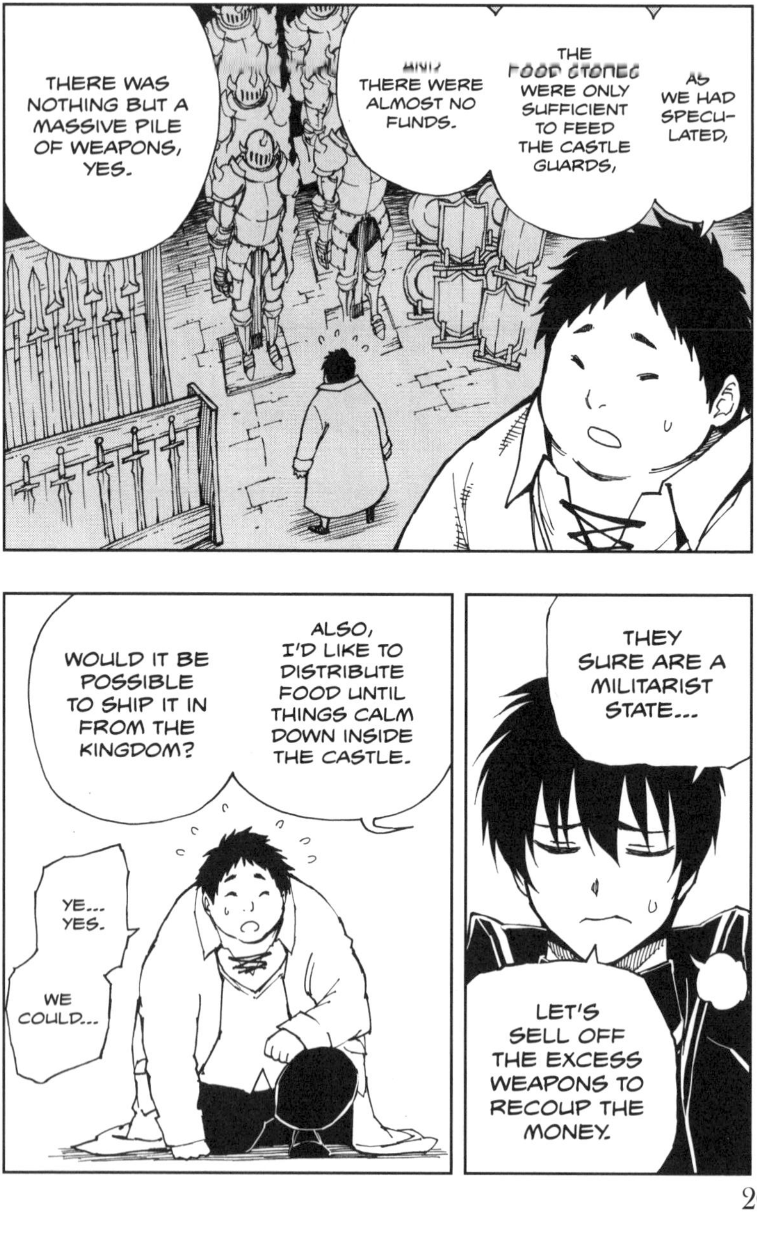
AS WE HAD SPECU-LATED,
THE FOOD STORES WERE ONLY SUFFICIENT TO FEED THE CASTLE GUARDS,
THERE WERE ALMOST NO FUNDS.
THERE WAS NOTHING BUT A MASSIVE PILE OF WEAPONS, YES.
THEY SURE ARE A MILITARIST STATE...
LET'S SELL OFF THE EXCESS WEAPONS TO RECOUP THE MONEY.
ALSO, I'D LIKE TO DISTRIBUTE FOOD UNTIL THINGS CALM DOWN INSIDE THE CASTLE.
WOULD IT BE POSSIBLE TO SHIP IT IN FROM THE KINGDOM?
YE... YES.
WE COULD...

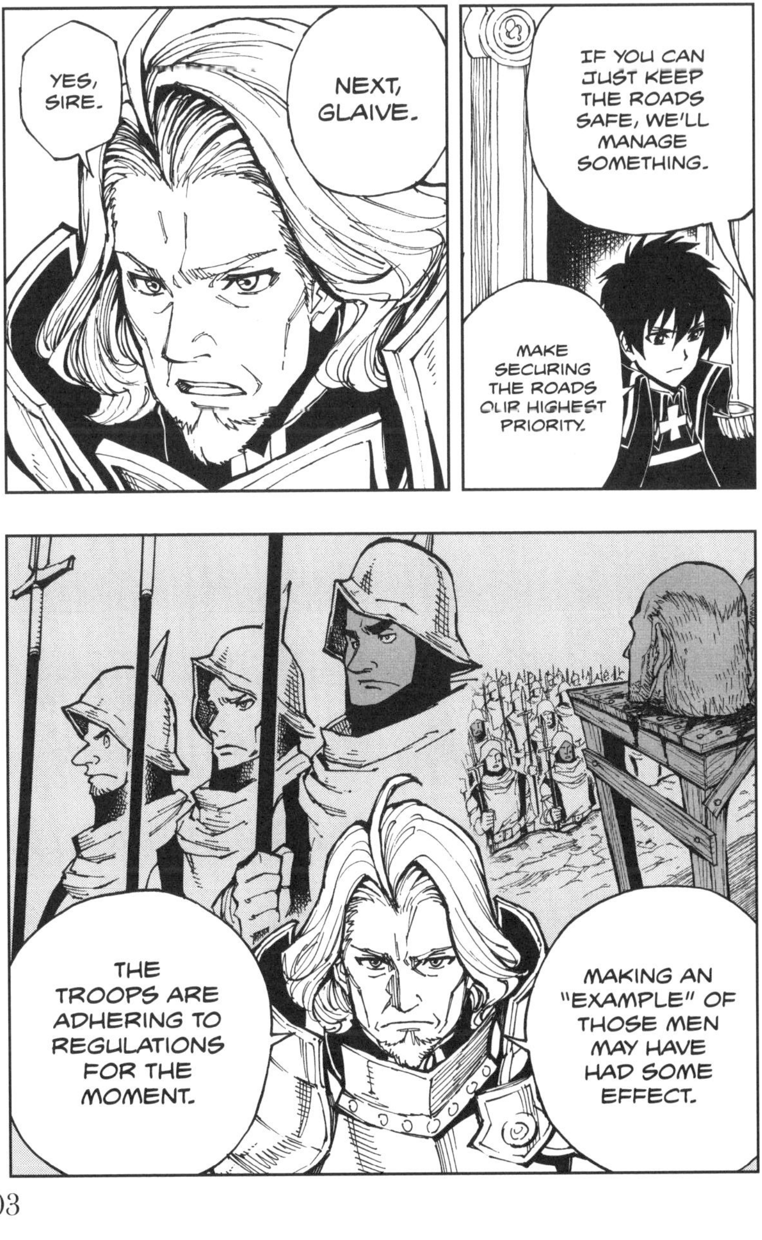
IF YOU CAN JUST KEEP THE ROADS SAFE, WE'LL MANAGE SOMETHING.
MAKE SECURING THE ROADS OUR HIGHEST PRIORITY.
NEXT, GLAIVE.
YES, SIRE.
MAKING AN "EXAMPLE" OF THOSE MEN MAY HAVE HAD SOME EFFECT.
THE TROOPS ARE ADHERING TO REGULATIONS FOR THE MOMENT.

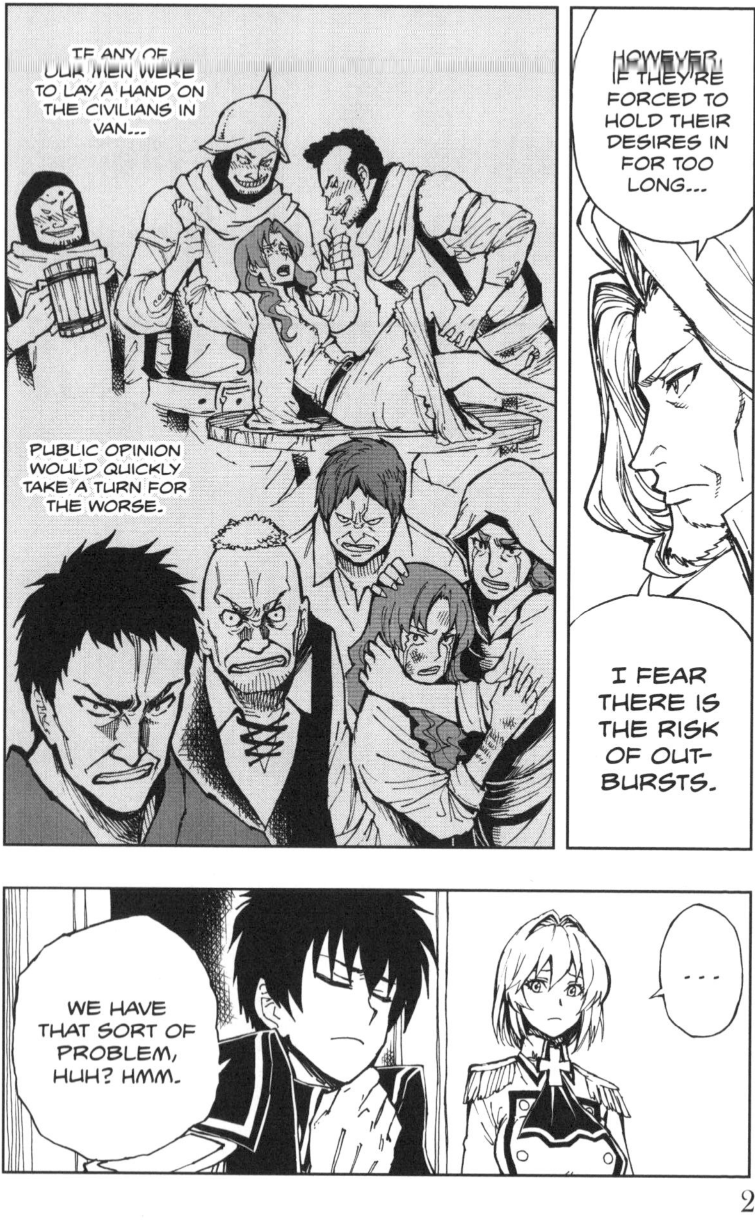
HOWEVER, IF THEY'RE FORCED TO HOLD THEIR DESIRES IN FOR TOO LONG...
I FEAR THERE IS THE RISK OF OUT-BURSTS.
IF ANY OF OUR MEN WERE TO LAY A HAND ON THE CIVILIANS IN VAN...
PUBLIC OPINION WOULD QUICKLY TAKE A TURN FOR THE WORSE.
...
WE HAVE THAT SORT OF PROBLEM, HUH? HMM.

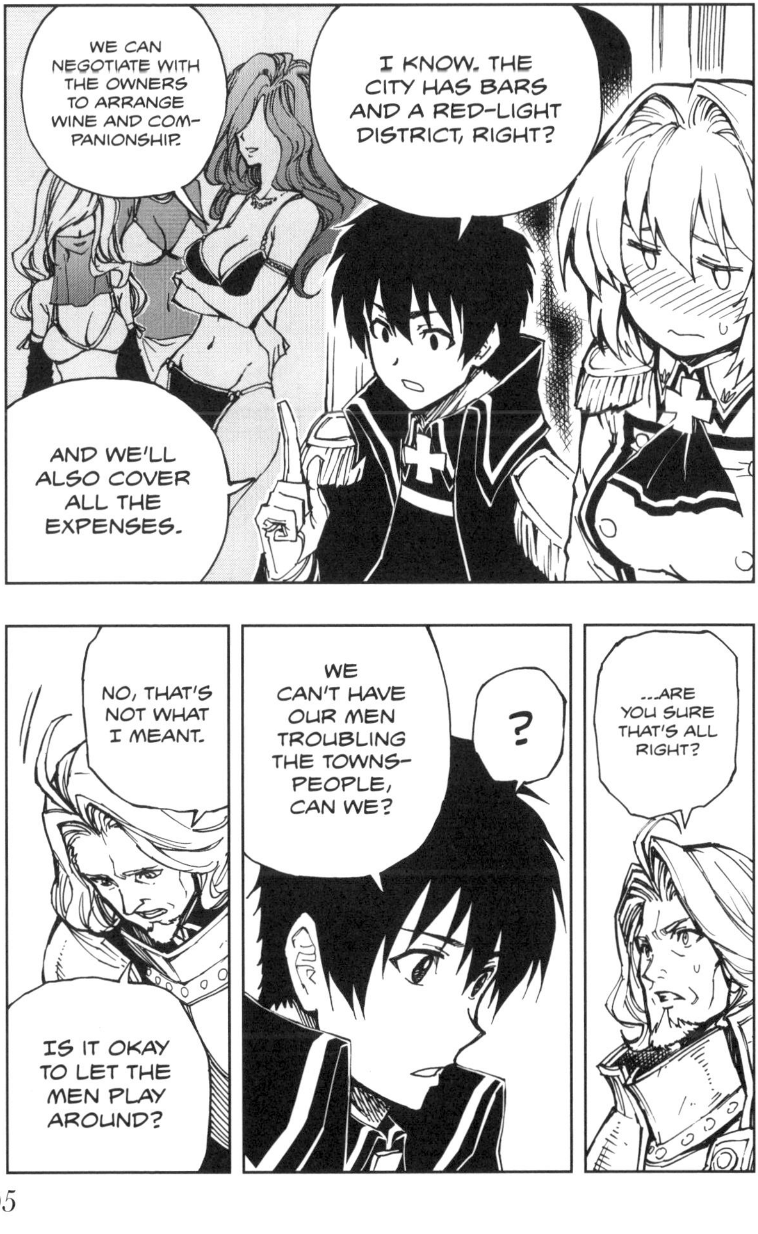
I KNOW. THE CITY HAS BARS AND A RED-LIGHT DISTRICT, RIGHT?
WE CAN NEGOTIATE WITH THE OWNERS TO ARRANGE WINE AND COM-PANIONSHIP.
AND WE'LL ALSO COVER ALL THE EXPENSES.
...ARE YOU SURE THAT'S ALL RIGHT?
?
WE CAN'T HAVE OUR MEN TROUBLING THE TOWNS-PEOPLE, CAN WE?
NO, THAT'S NOT WHAT I MEANT.
IS IT OKAY TO LET THE MEN PLAY AROUND?

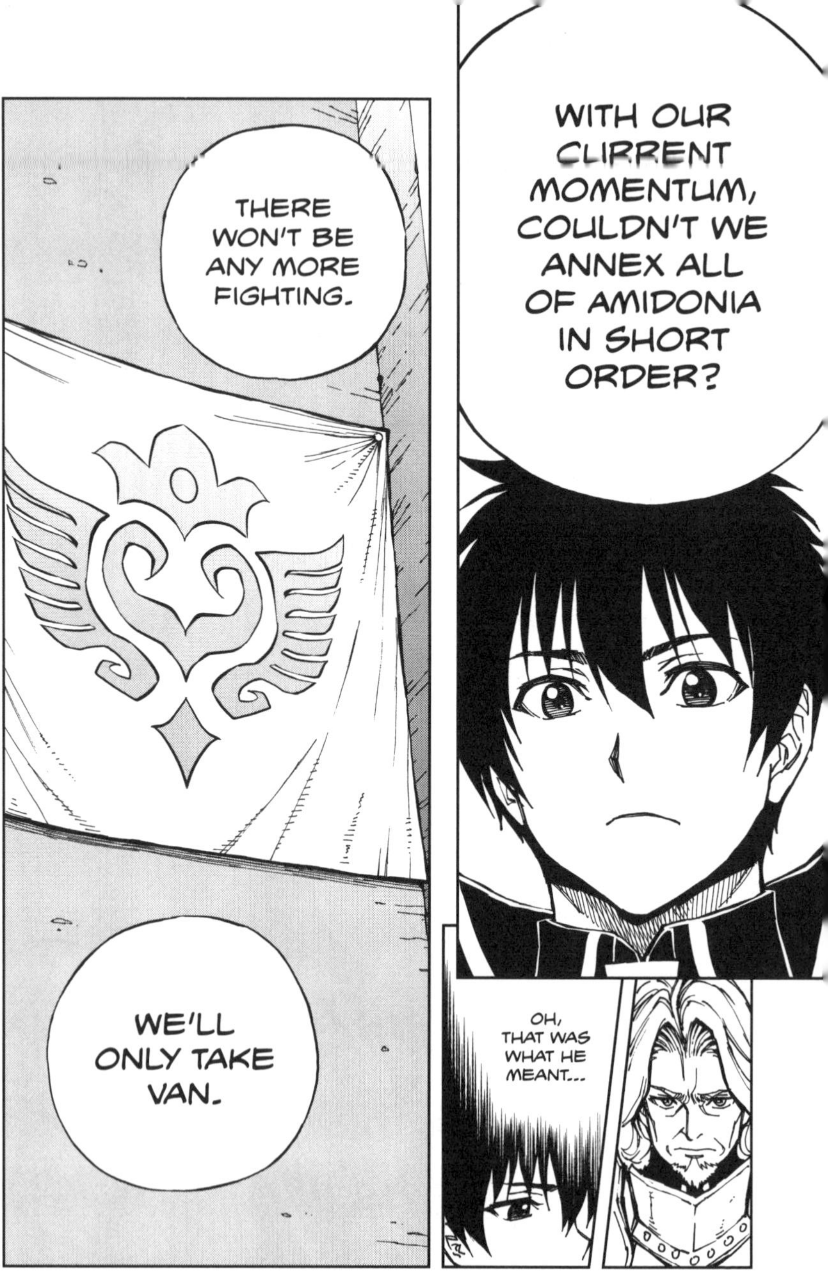
WITH OUR CURRENT MOMENTUM, COULDN'T WE ANNEX ALL OF AMIDONIA IN SHORT ORDER?
OH, THAT WAS WHAT HE MEANT...
THERE WON'T BE ANY MORE FIGHTING.
WE'LL ONLY TAKE VAN.

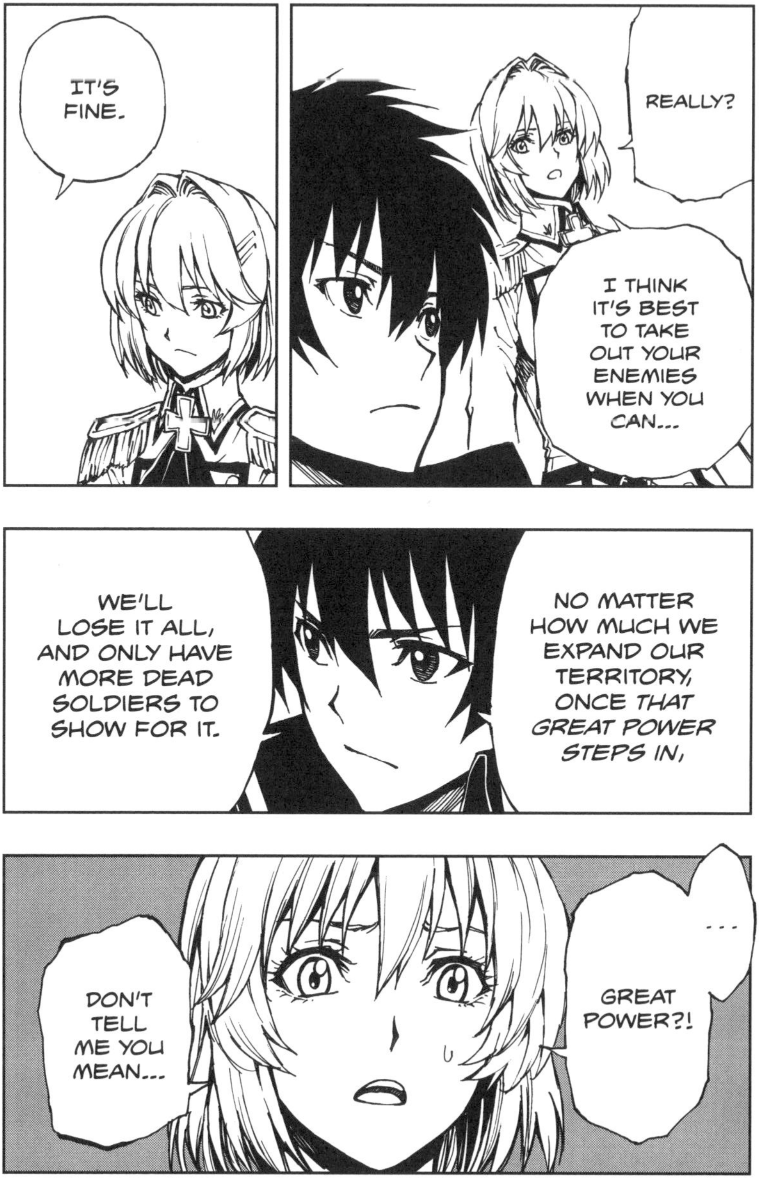
REALLY?
I THINK IT'S BEST TO TAKE OUT YOUR ENEMIES WHEN YOU CAN...
IT'S FINE.
NO MATTER HOW MUCH WE EXPAND OUR TERRITORY, ONCE *THAT* GREAT POWER STEPS IN,
WE'LL LOSE IT ALL, AND ONLY HAVE MORE DEAD SOLDIERS TO SHOW FOR IT.
... GREAT POWER?!
DON'T TELL ME YOU MEAN...

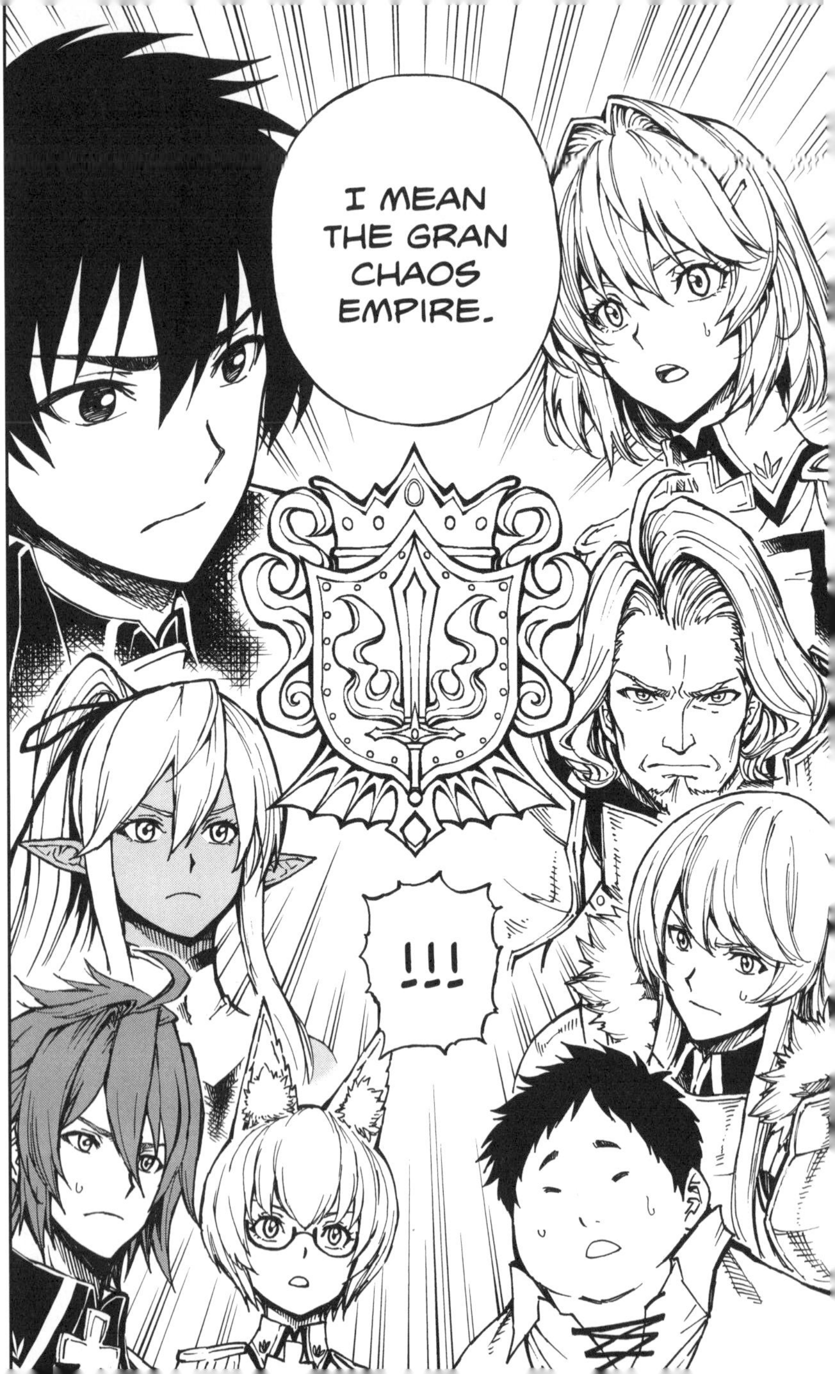
I MEAN THE GRAN CHAOS EMPIRE.
!!!

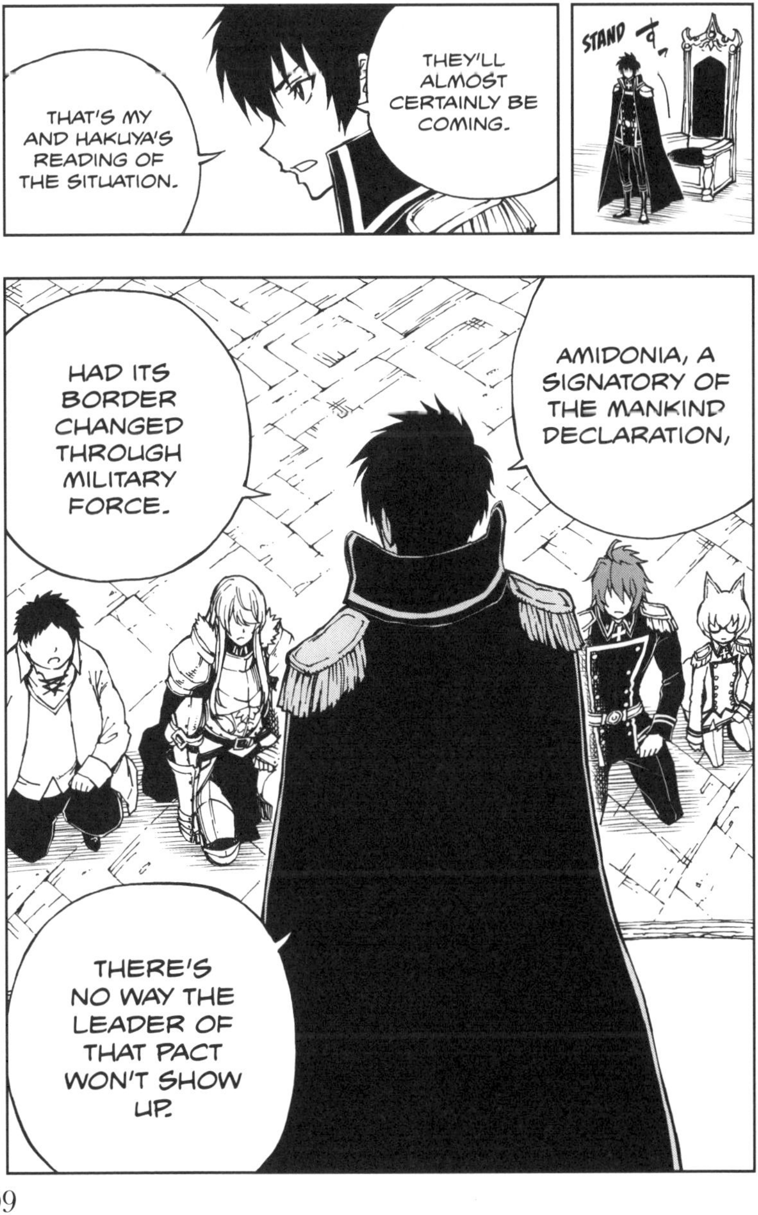
STAND
す
THEY'LL ALMOST CERTAINLY BE COMING.
THAT'S MY AND HAKUYA'S READING OF THE SITUATION.
AMIDONIA, A SIGNATORY OF THE MANKIND DECLARATION,
HAD ITS BORDER CHANGED THROUGH MILITARY FORCE.
THERE'S NO WAY THE LEADER OF THAT PACT WON'T SHOW UP.

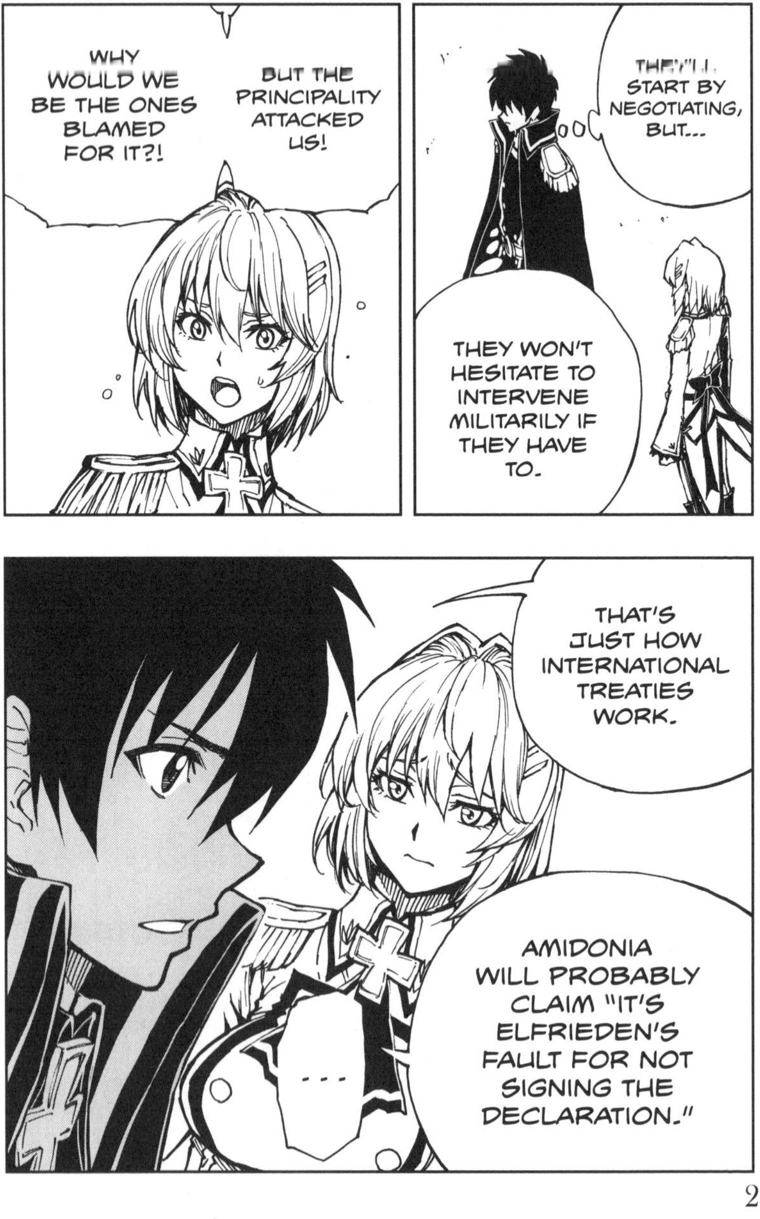
THEY'LL START BY NEGOTIATING, BUT...
THEY WON'T HESITATE TO INTERVENE MILITARILY IF THEY HAVE TO.
BUT THE PRINCIPALITY ATTACKED US!
WHY WOULD WE BE THE ONES BLAMED FOR IT?!
THAT'S JUST HOW INTERNATIONAL TREATIES WORK.
AMIDONIA WILL PROBABLY CLAIM "IT'S ELFRIEDEN'S FAULT FOR NOT SIGNING THE DECLARATION."
...

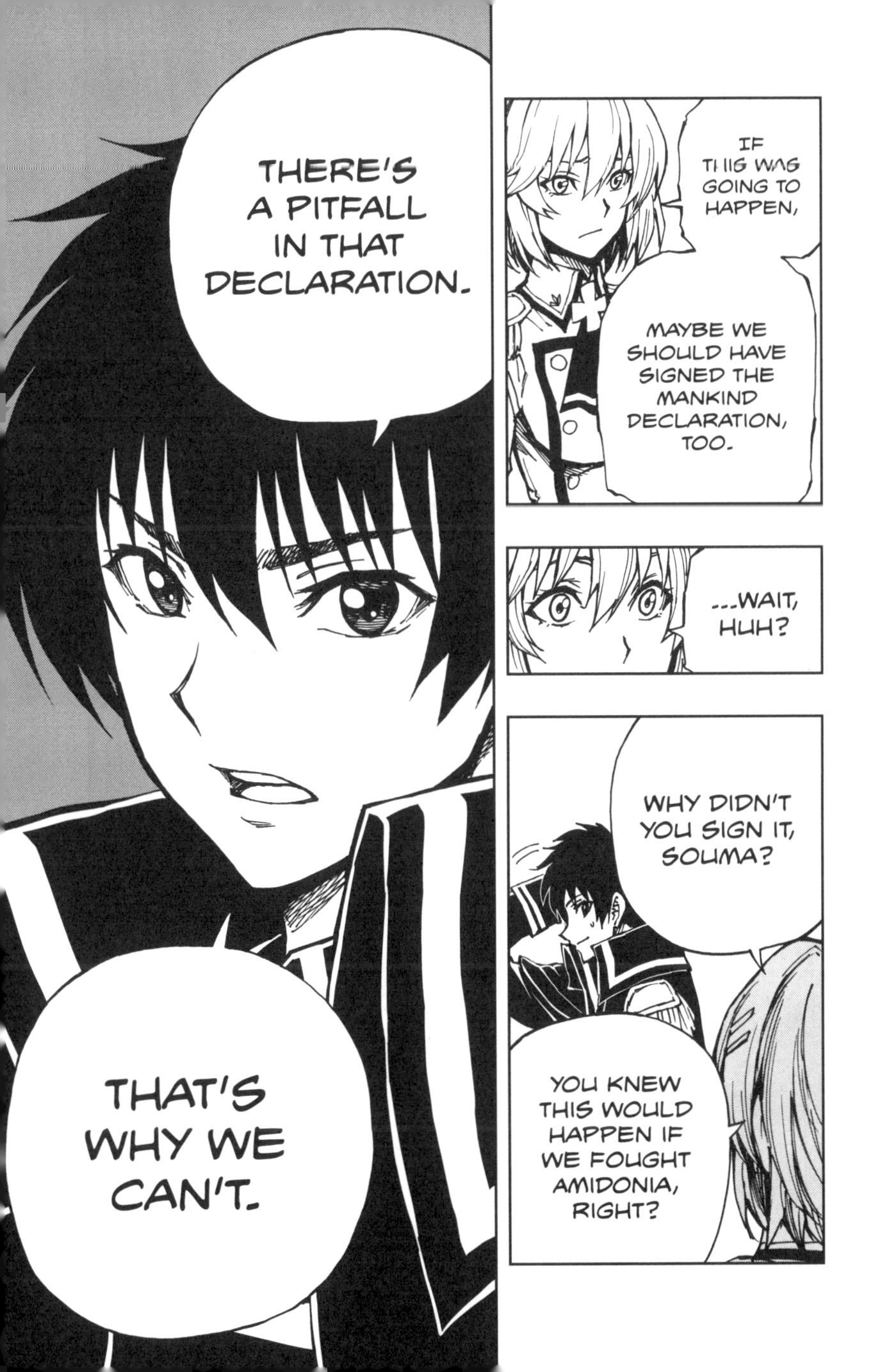
IF THIS WAS GOING TO HAPPEN,
MAYBE WE SHOULD HAVE SIGNED THE MANKIND DECLARATION, TOO.
...WAIT, HUH?
WHY DIDN'T YOU SIGN IT, SOUMA?
YOU KNEW THIS WOULD HAPPEN IF WE FOUGHT AMIDONIA, RIGHT?
THERE'S A PITFALL IN THAT DECLARATION.
THAT'S WHY WE CAN'T.

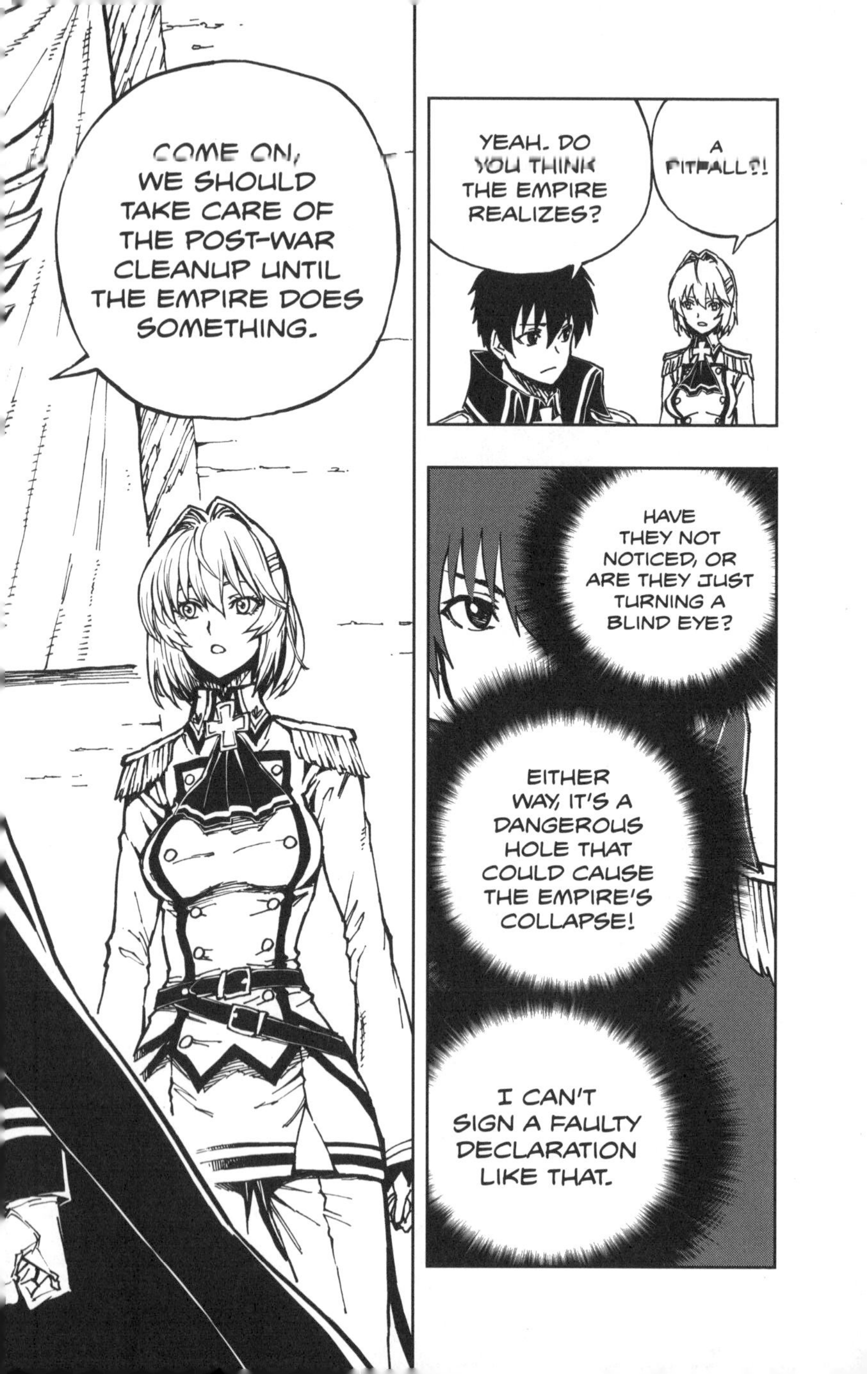
A PITFALL?!
YEAH. DO YOU THINK THE EMPIRE REALIZES?
HAVE THEY NOT NOTICED, OR ARE THEY JUST TURNING A BLIND EYE?
EITHER WAY, IT'S A DANGEROUS HOLE THAT COULD CAUSE THE EMPIRE'S COLLAPSE!
I CAN'T SIGN A FAULTY DECLARATION LIKE THAT.
COME ON, WE SHOULD TAKE CARE OF THE POST-WAR CLEANUP UNTIL THE EMPIRE DOES SOMETHING.

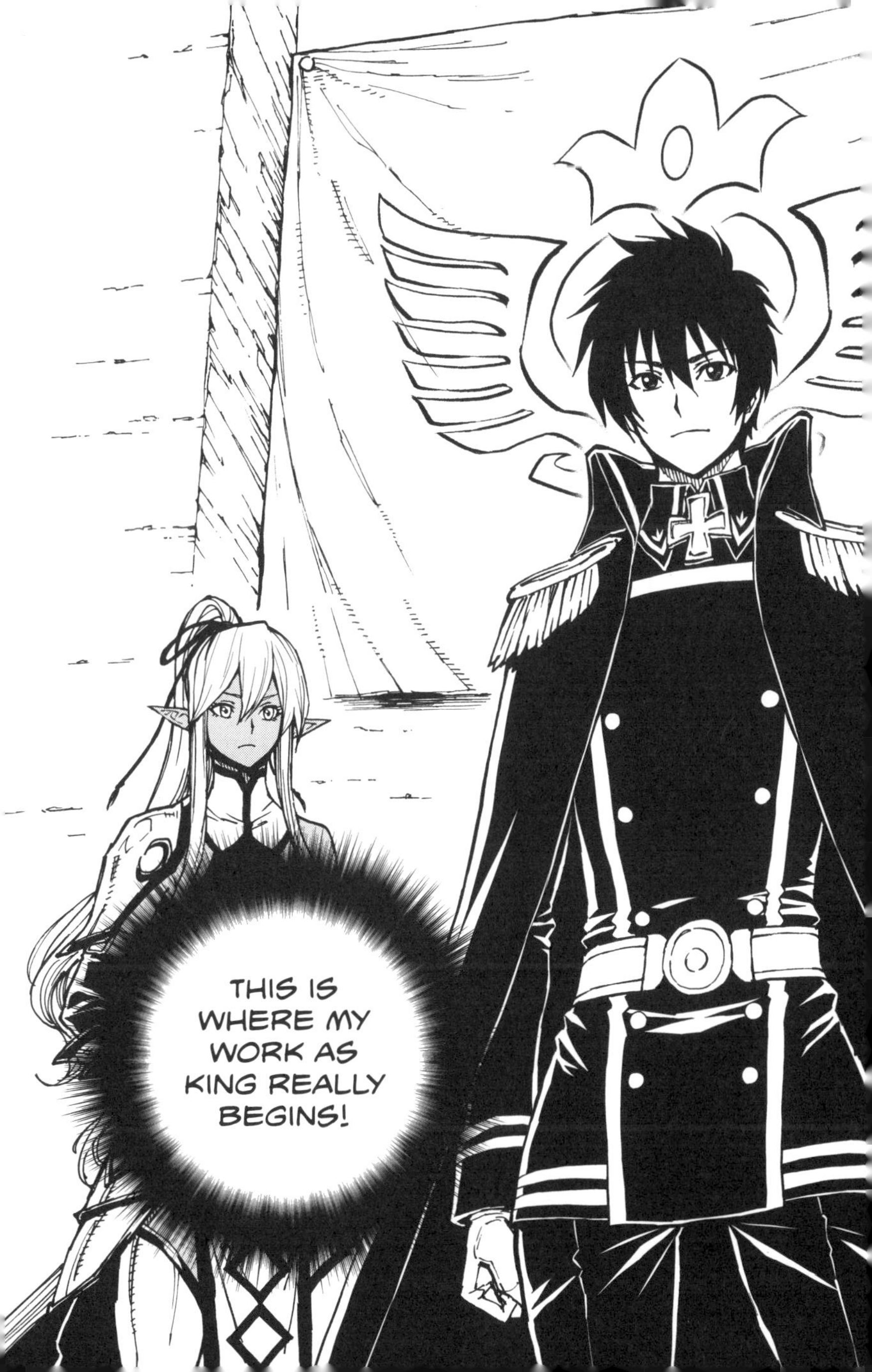
THIS IS WHERE MY WORK AS KING REALLY BEGINS!

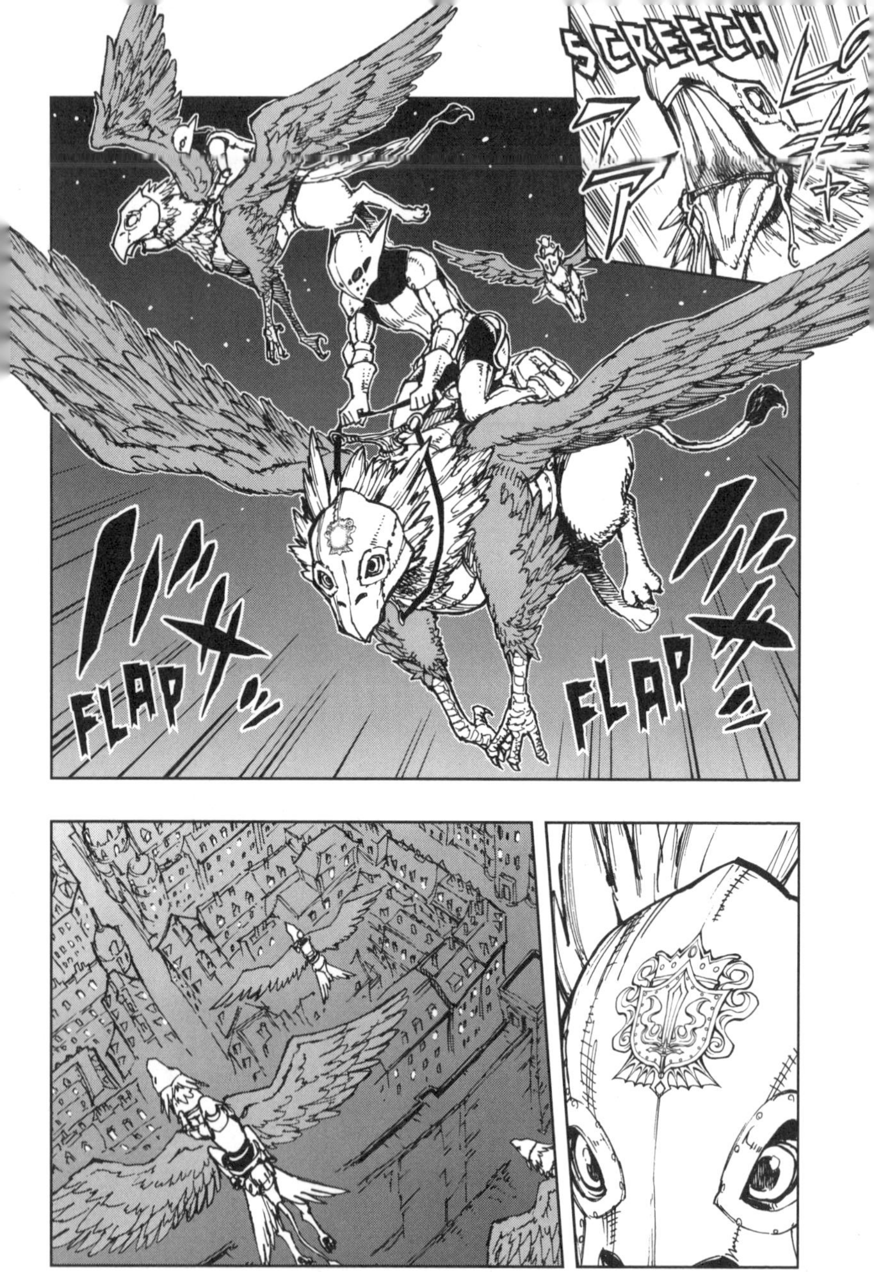
SCREECH
FLAP
FLAP

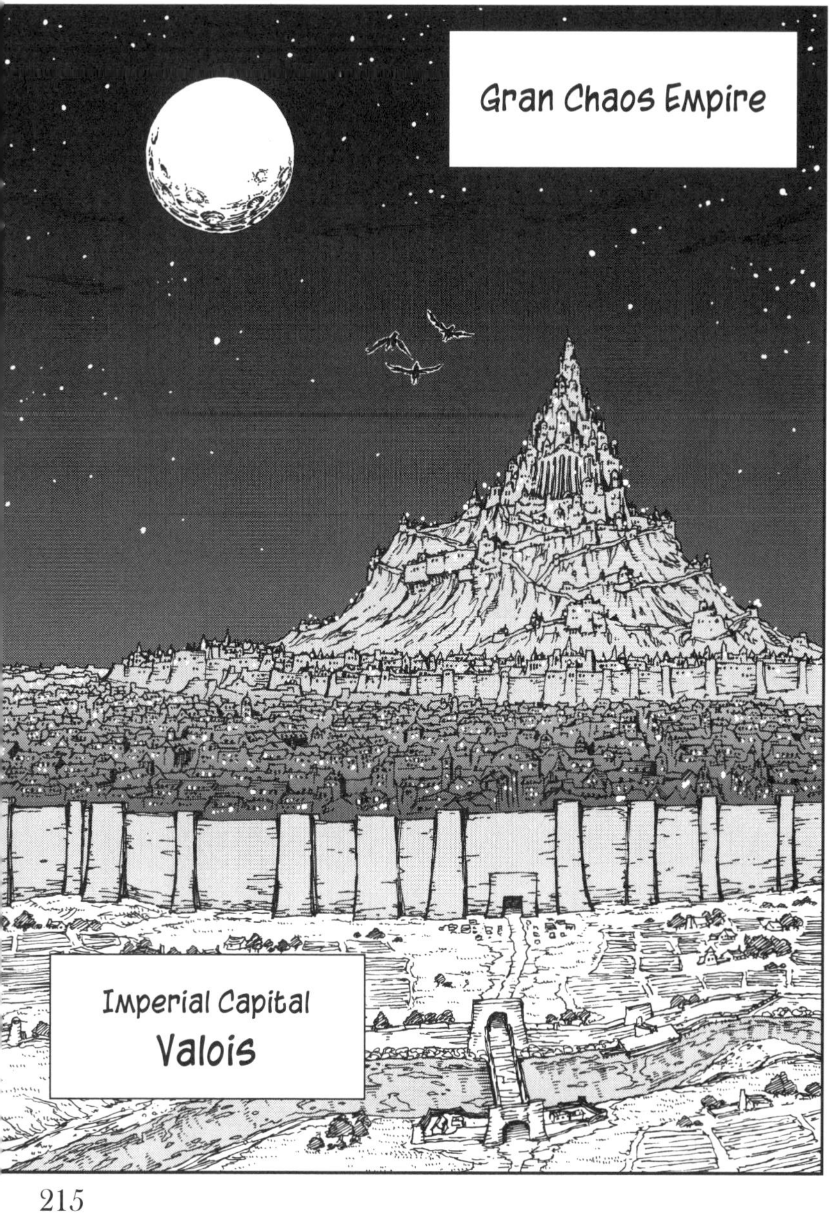
Gran Chaos Empire
Imperial Capital
Valois

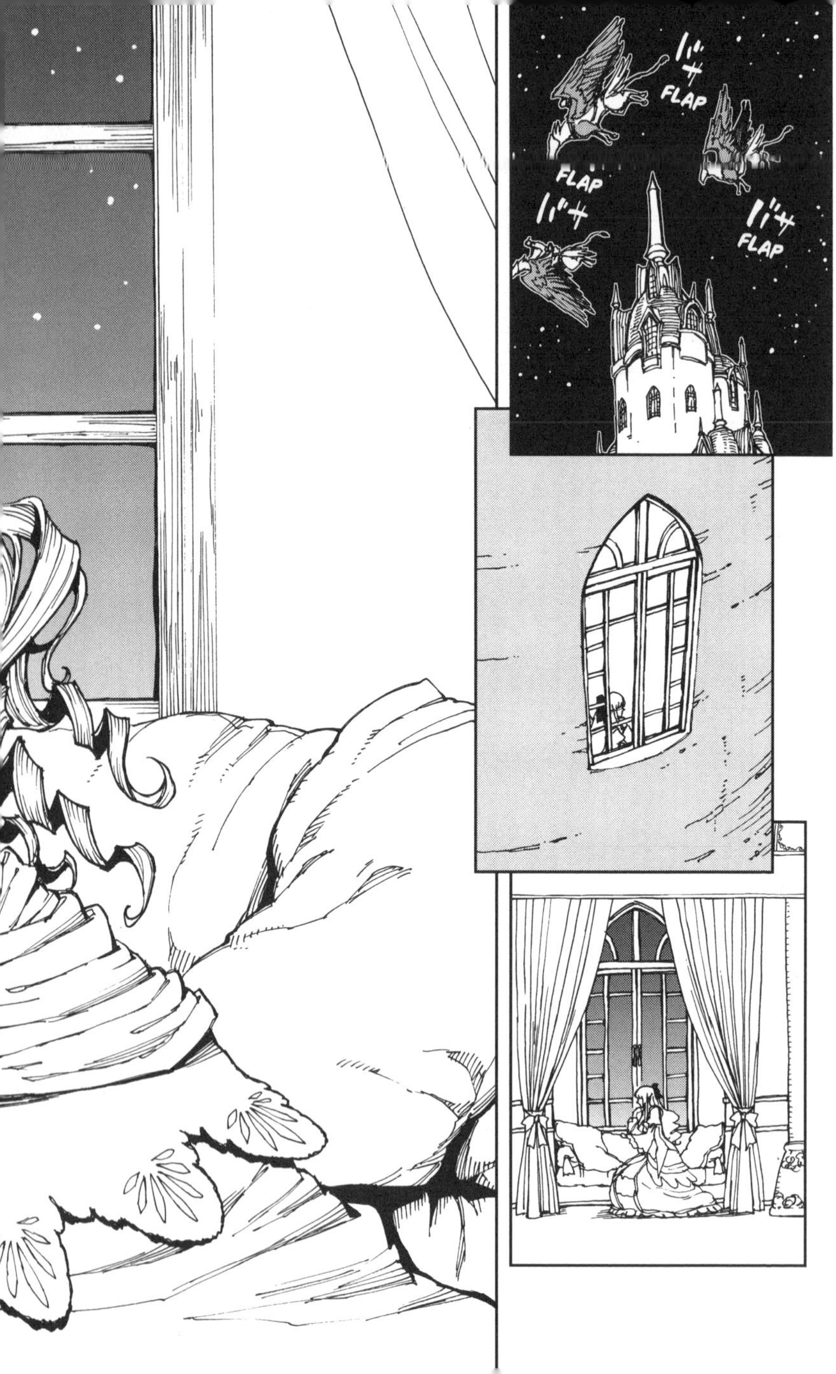
バサ
FLAP
バサ
FLAP
FLAP
バサ

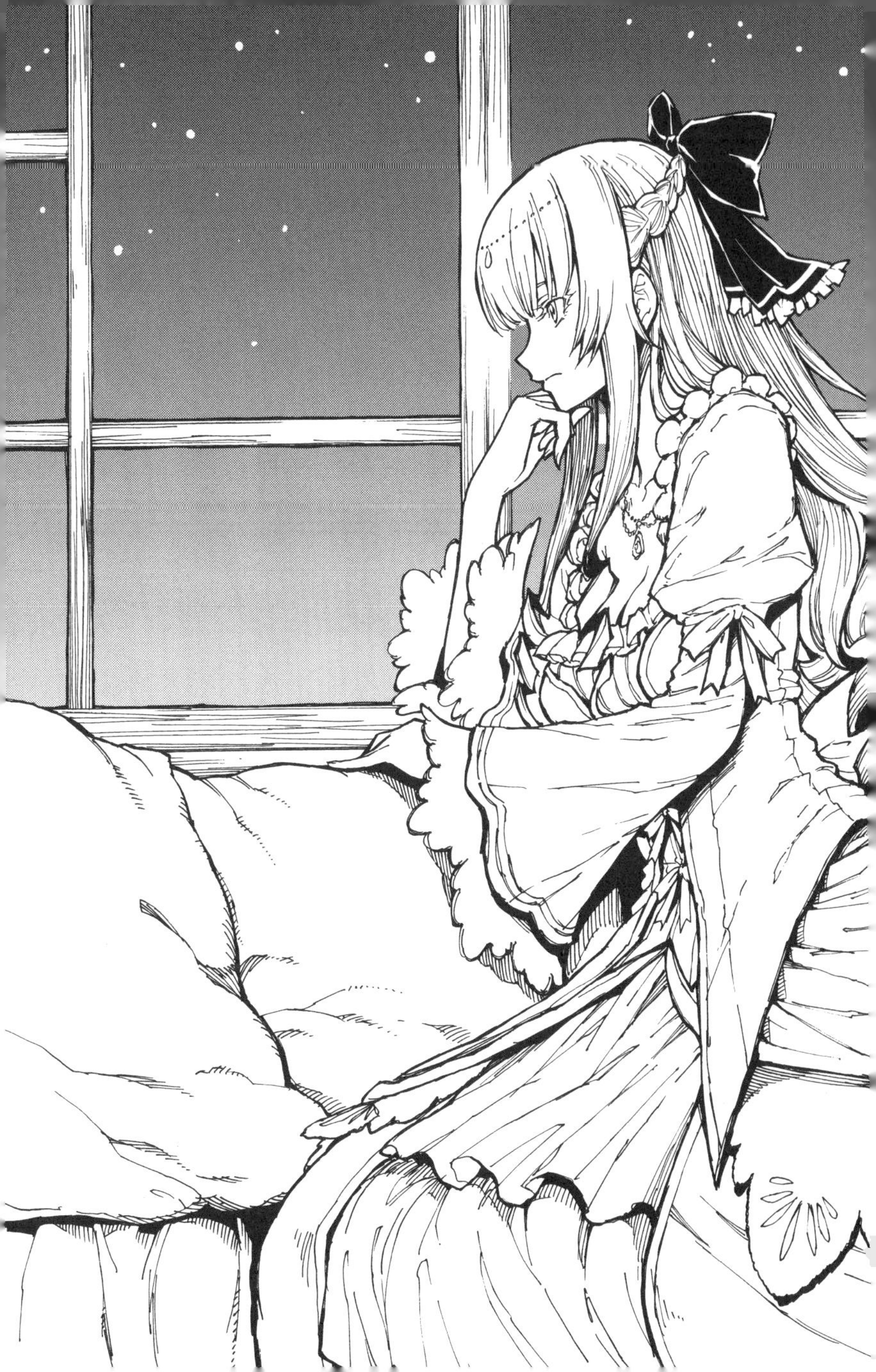

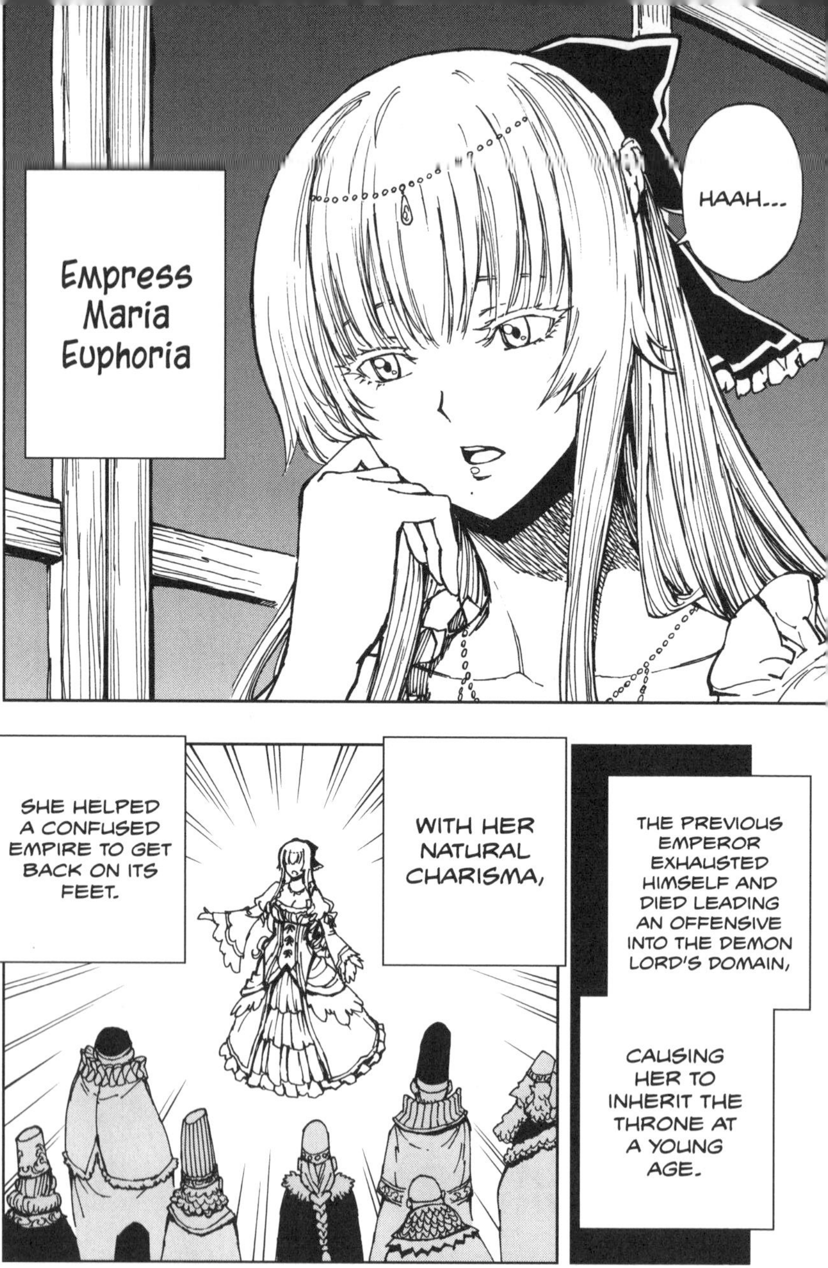
HAAH...
Empress Maria Euphoria
THE PREVIOUS EMPEROR EXHAUSTED HIMSELF AND DIED LEADING AN OFFENSIVE INTO THE DEMON LORD'S DOMAIN,
CAUSING HER TO INHERIT THE THRONE AT A YOUNG AGE.
WITH HER NATURAL CHARISMA,
SHE HELPED A CONFUSED EMPIRE TO GET BACK ON ITS FEET.

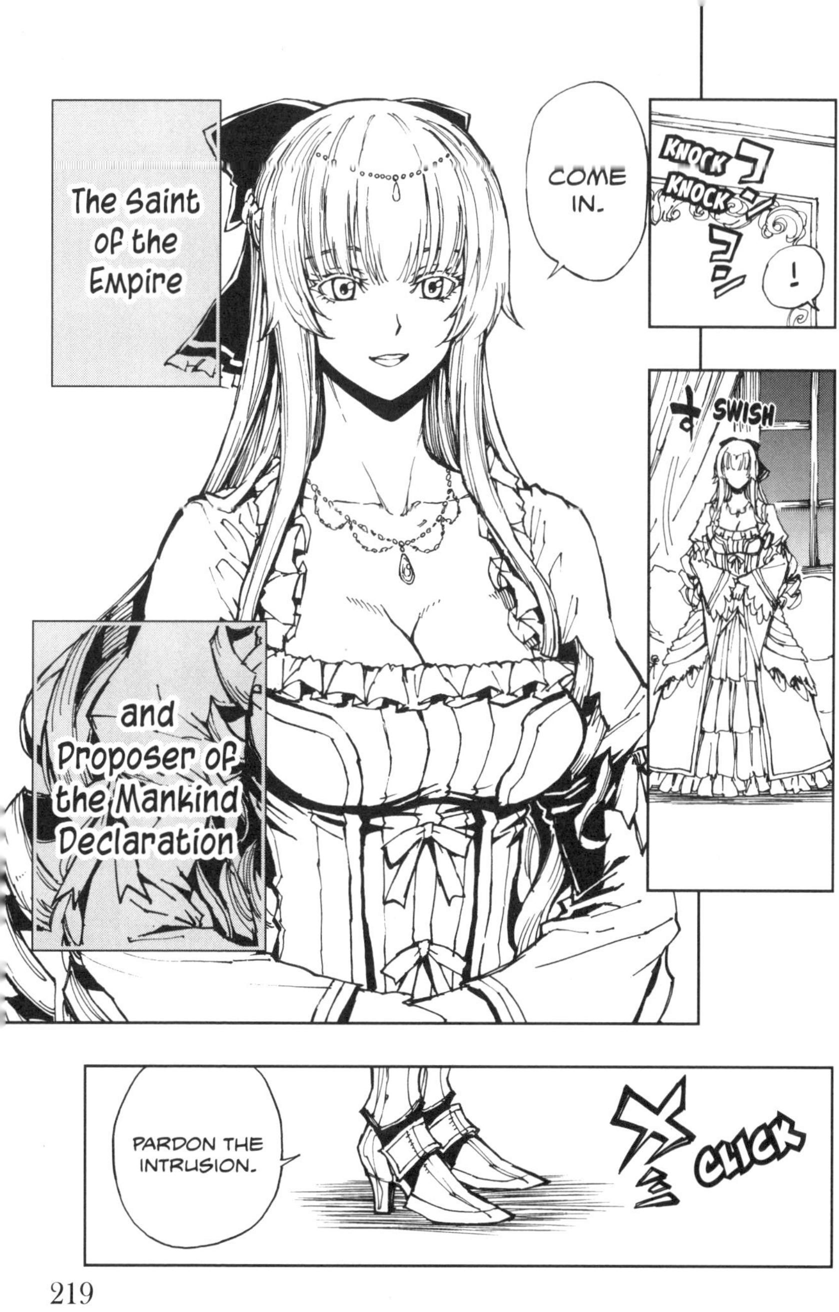
KNOCK KNOCK
!
COME IN.
SWISH
The Saint of the Empire
and Proposer of the Mankind Declaration
CLICK
PARDON THE INTRUSION.

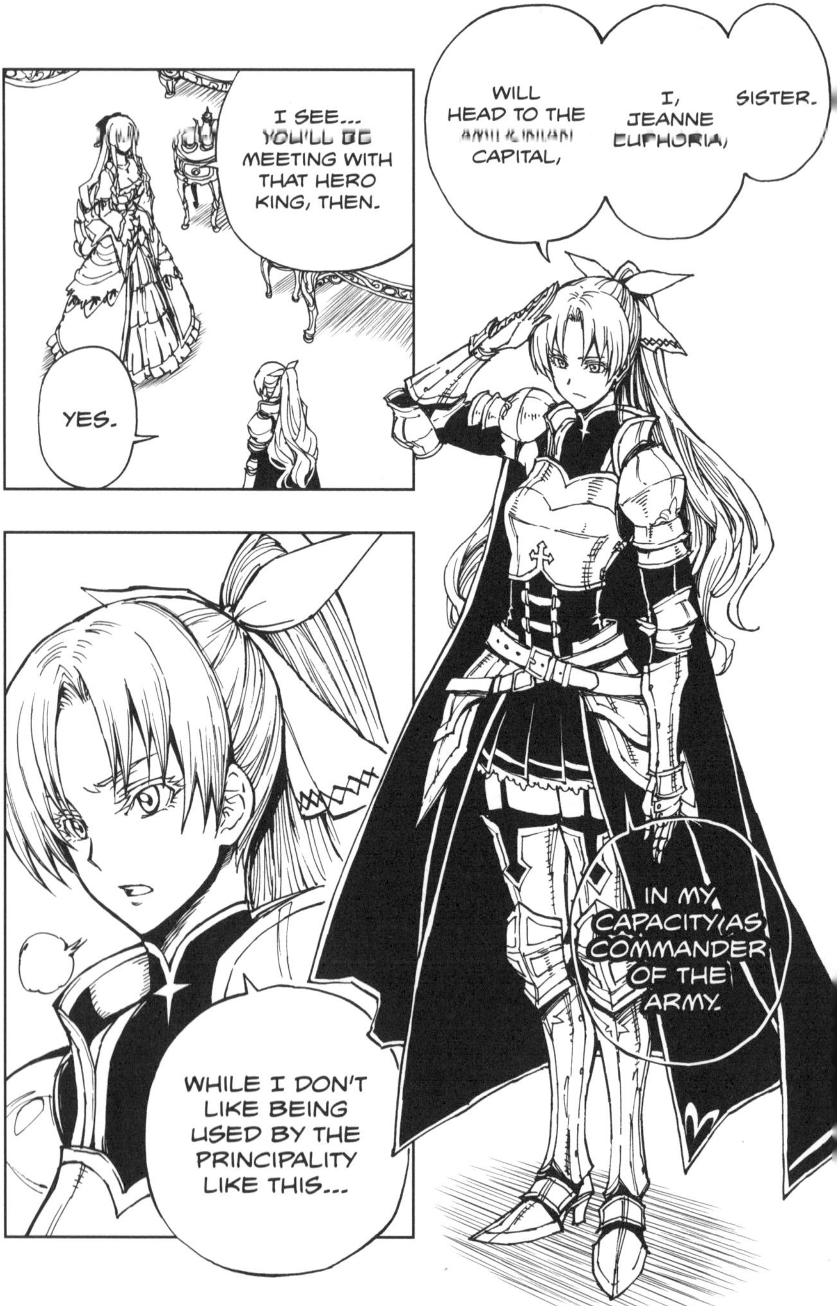
SISTER. I, JEANNE EUPHORIA, WILL HEAD TO THE CAPITAL,
IN MY CAPACITY AS COMMANDER OF THE ARMY.
I SEE... YOU'LL BE MEETING WITH THAT HERO KING, THEN.
YES.
WHILE I DON'T LIKE BEING USED BY THE PRINCIPALITY LIKE THIS...

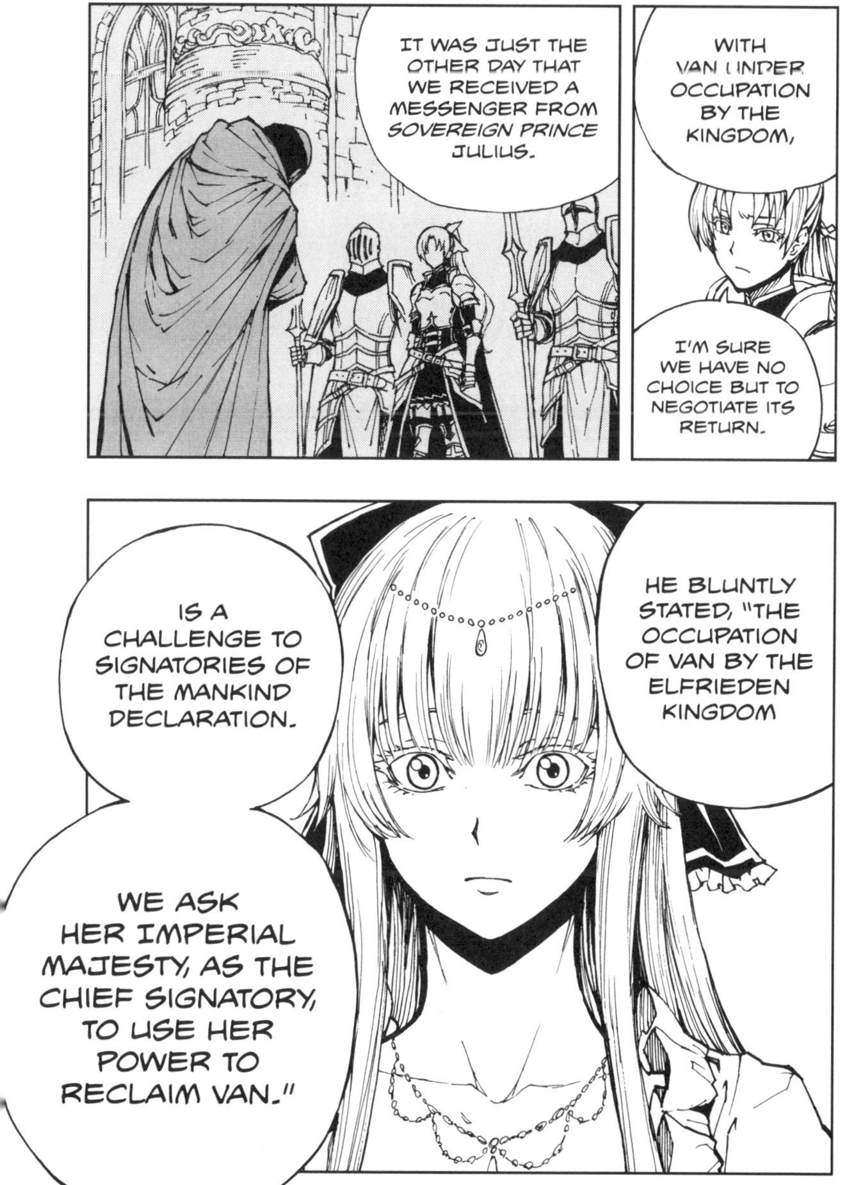
WITH VAN UNDER OCCUPATION BY THE KINGDOM,
I'M SURE WE HAVE NO CHOICE BUT TO NEGOTIATE ITS RETURN.
IT WAS JUST THE OTHER DAY THAT WE RECEIVED A MESSENGER FROM SOVEREIGN PRINCE JULIUS.
HE BLUNTLY STATED, "THE OCCUPATION OF VAN BY THE ELFRIEDEN KINGDOM
IS A CHALLENGE TO SIGNATORIES OF THE MANKIND DECLARATION.
WE ASK HER IMPERIAL MAJESTY, AS THE CHIEF SIGNATORY, TO USE HER POWER TO RECLAIM VAN."

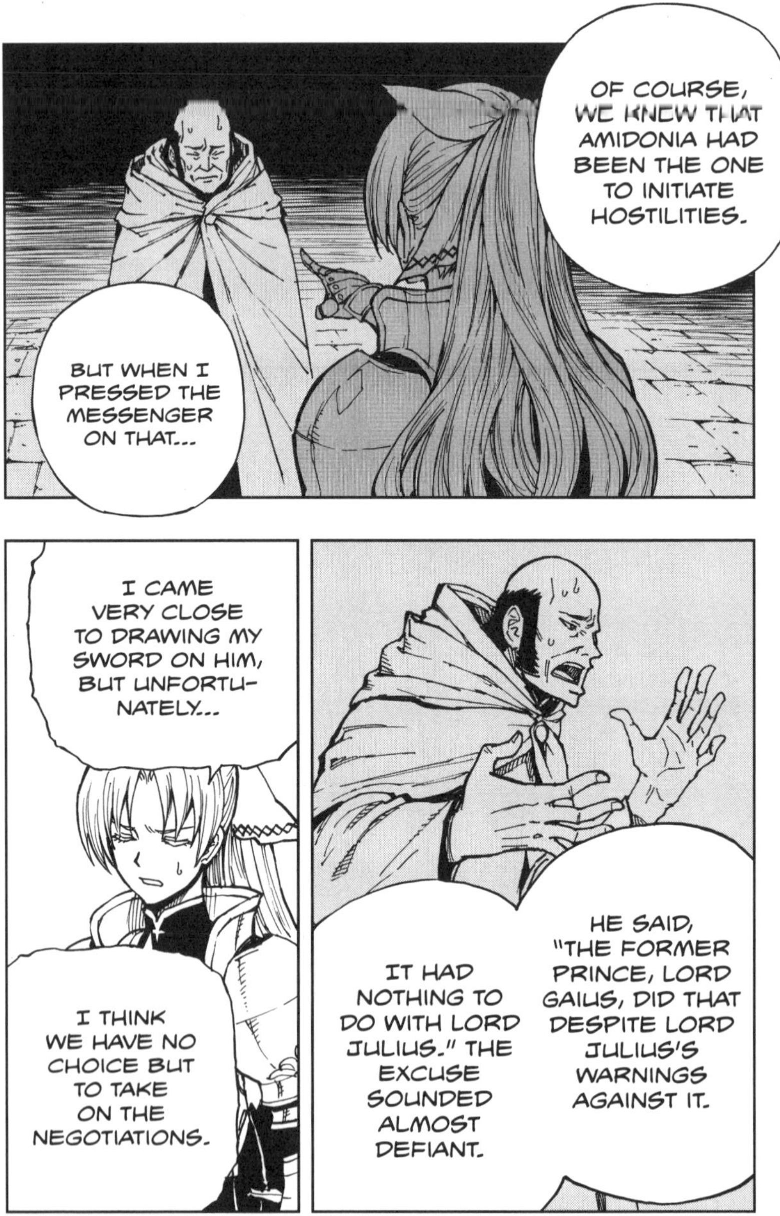
OF COURSE, WE KNEW THAT AMIDONIA HAD BEEN THE ONE TO INITIATE HOSTILITIES.
BUT WHEN I PRESSED THE MESSENGER ON THAT...
HE SAID, "THE FORMER PRINCE, LORD GAIUS, DID THAT DESPITE LORD JULIUS'S WARNINGS AGAINST IT.
IT HAD NOTHING TO DO WITH LORD JULIUS." THE EXCUSE SOUNDED ALMOST DEFIANT.
I CAME VERY CLOSE TO DRAWING MY SWORD ON HIM, BUT UNFORTU-NATELY...
I THINK WE HAVE NO CHOICE BUT TO TAKE ON THE NEGOTIATIONS.

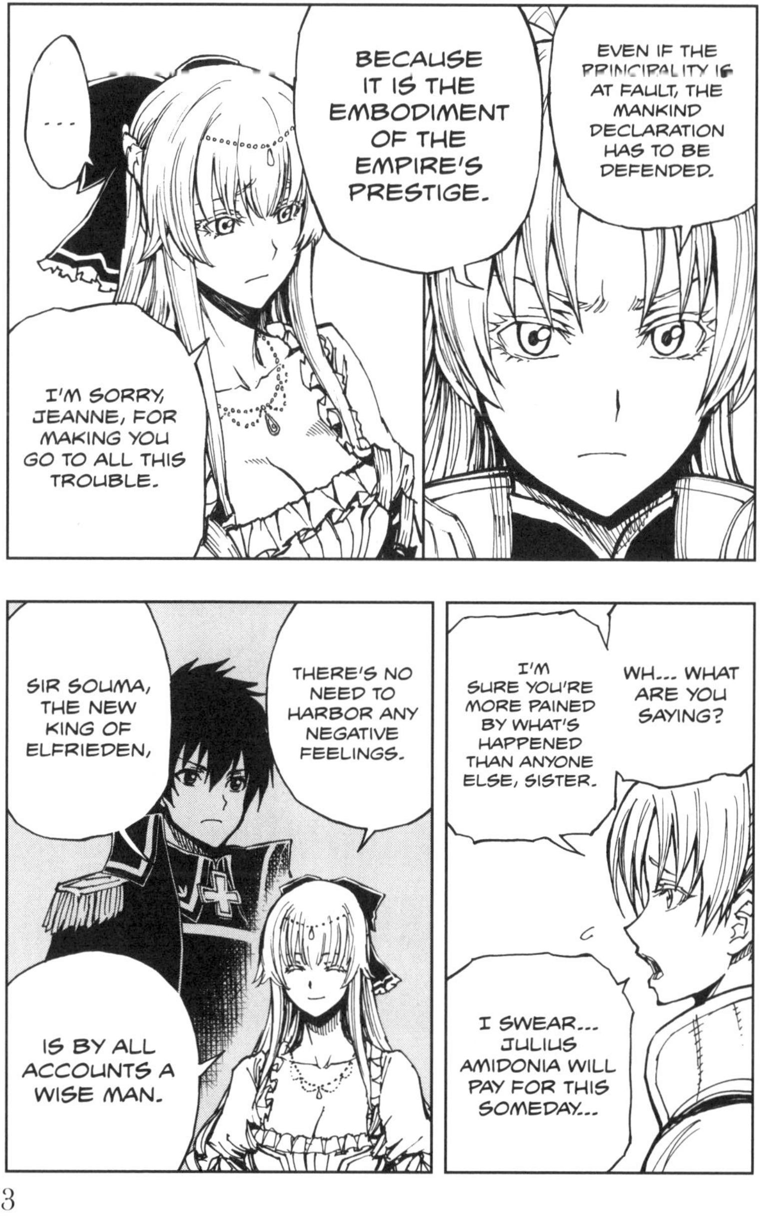
EVEN IF THE PRINCIPALITY IS AT FAULT, THE MANKIND DECLARATION HAS TO BE DEFENDED.
BECAUSE IT IS THE EMBODIMENT OF THE EMPIRE'S PRESTIGE.
...
I'M SORRY, JEANNE, FOR MAKING YOU GO TO ALL THIS TROUBLE.
WH... WHAT ARE YOU SAYING?
I'M SURE YOU'RE MORE PAINED BY WHAT'S HAPPENED THAN ANYONE ELSE, SISTER.
I SWEAR... JULIUS AMIDONIA WILL PAY FOR THIS SOMEDAY...
THERE'S NO NEED TO HARBOR ANY NEGATIVE FEELINGS.
SIR SOUMA, THE NEW KING OF ELFRIEDEN,
IS BY ALL ACCOUNTS A WISE MAN.

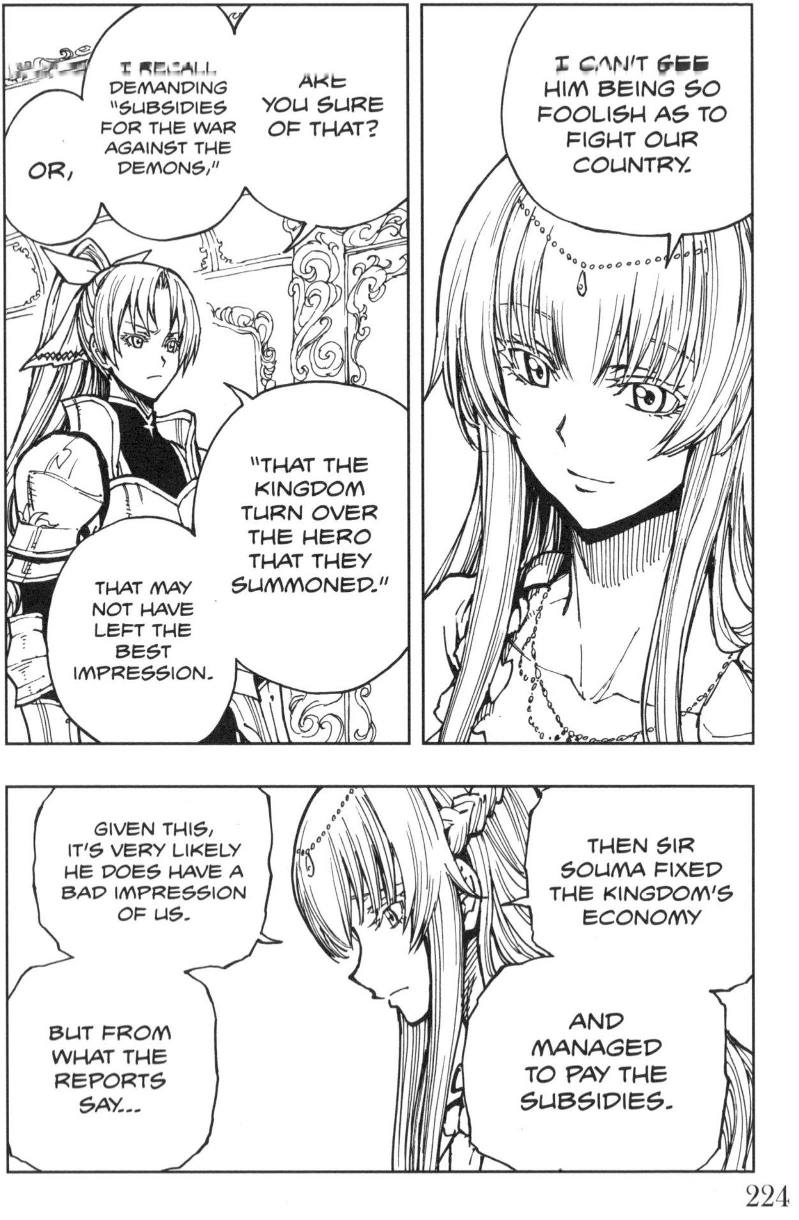
I CAN'T SEE HIM BEING SO FOOLISH AS TO FIGHT OUR COUNTRY.
ARE YOU SURE OF THAT?
OR, I RECALL DEMANDING "SUBSIDIES FOR THE WAR AGAINST THE DEMONS,"
"THAT THE KINGDOM TURN OVER THE HERO THAT THEY SUMMONED."
THAT MAY NOT HAVE LEFT THE BEST IMPRESSION.
THEN SIR SOUMA FIXED THE KINGDOM'S ECONOMY
AND MANAGED TO PAY THE SUBSIDIES.
GIVEN THIS, IT'S VERY LIKELY HE DOES HAVE A BAD IMPRESSION OF US.
BUT FROM WHAT THE REPORTS SAY...

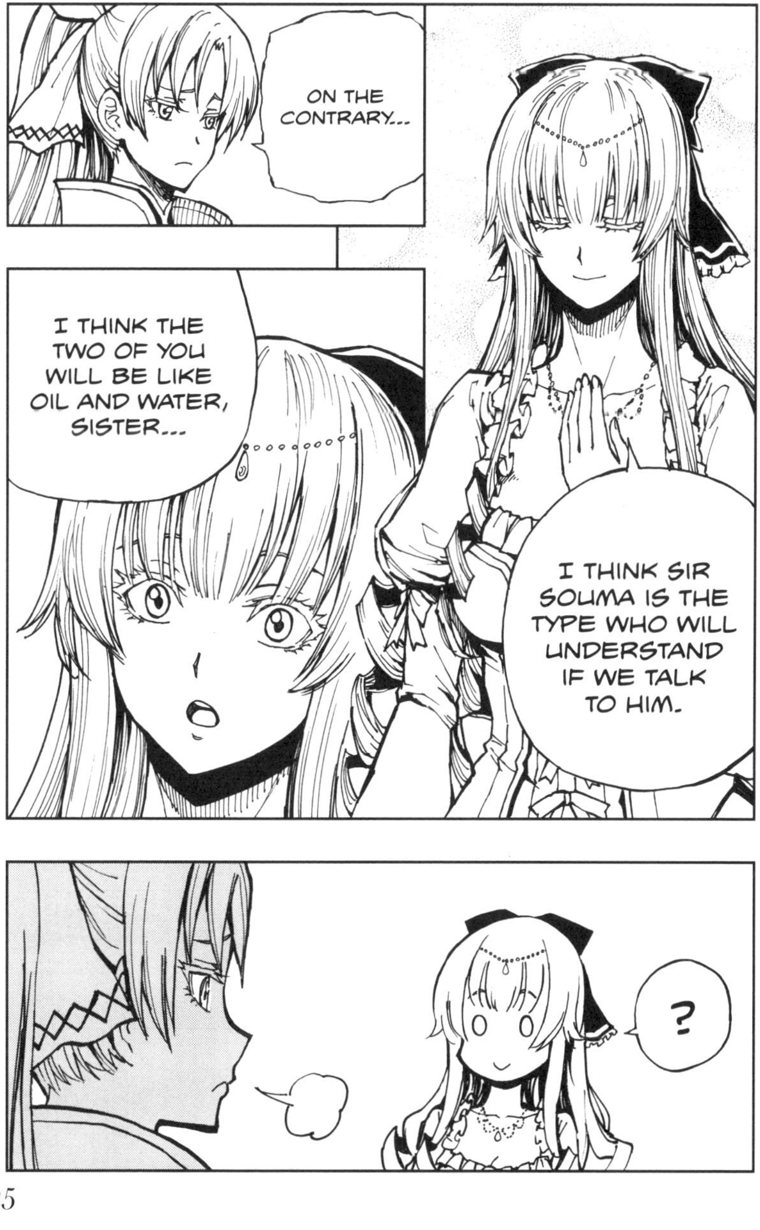
ON THE CONTRARY...
I THINK THE TWO OF YOU WILL BE LIKE OIL AND WATER, SISTER...
I THINK SIR SOUMA IS THE TYPE WHO WILL UNDERSTAND IF WE TALK TO HIM.
?

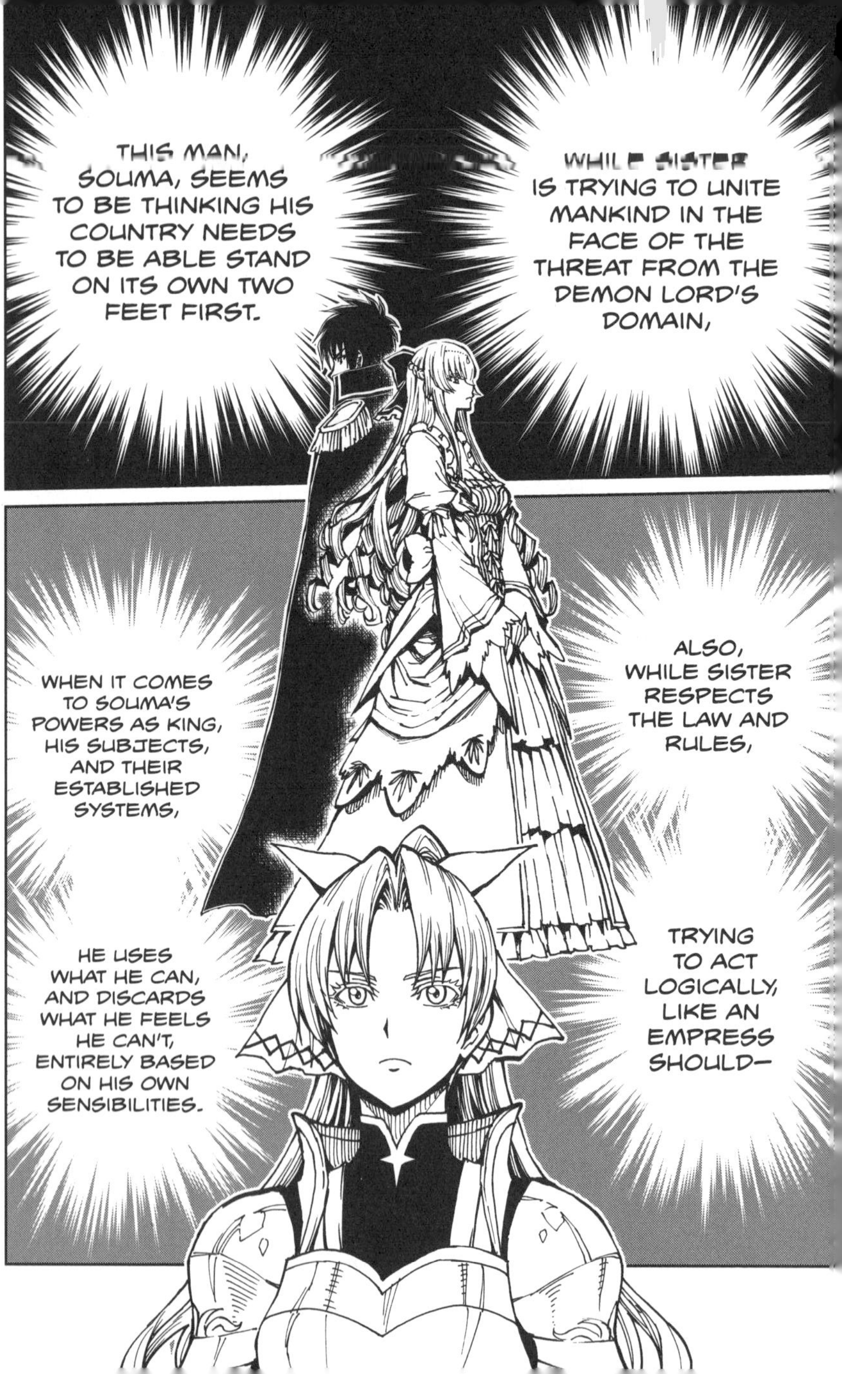
WHILE SISTER IS TRYING TO UNITE MANKIND IN THE FACE OF THE THREAT FROM THE DEMON LORD'S DOMAIN,
THIS MAN, SOUMA, SEEMS TO BE THINKING HIS COUNTRY NEEDS TO BE ABLE STAND ON ITS OWN TWO FEET FIRST.
ALSO, WHILE SISTER RESPECTS THE LAW AND RULES,
WHEN IT COMES TO SOUMA'S POWERS AS KING, HIS SUBJECTS, AND THEIR ESTABLISHED SYSTEMS,
TRYING TO ACT LOGICALLY, LIKE AN EMPRESS SHOULD—
HE USES WHAT HE CAN, AND DISCARDS WHAT HE FEELS HE CAN'T, ENTIRELY BASED ON HIS OWN SENSIBILITIES.

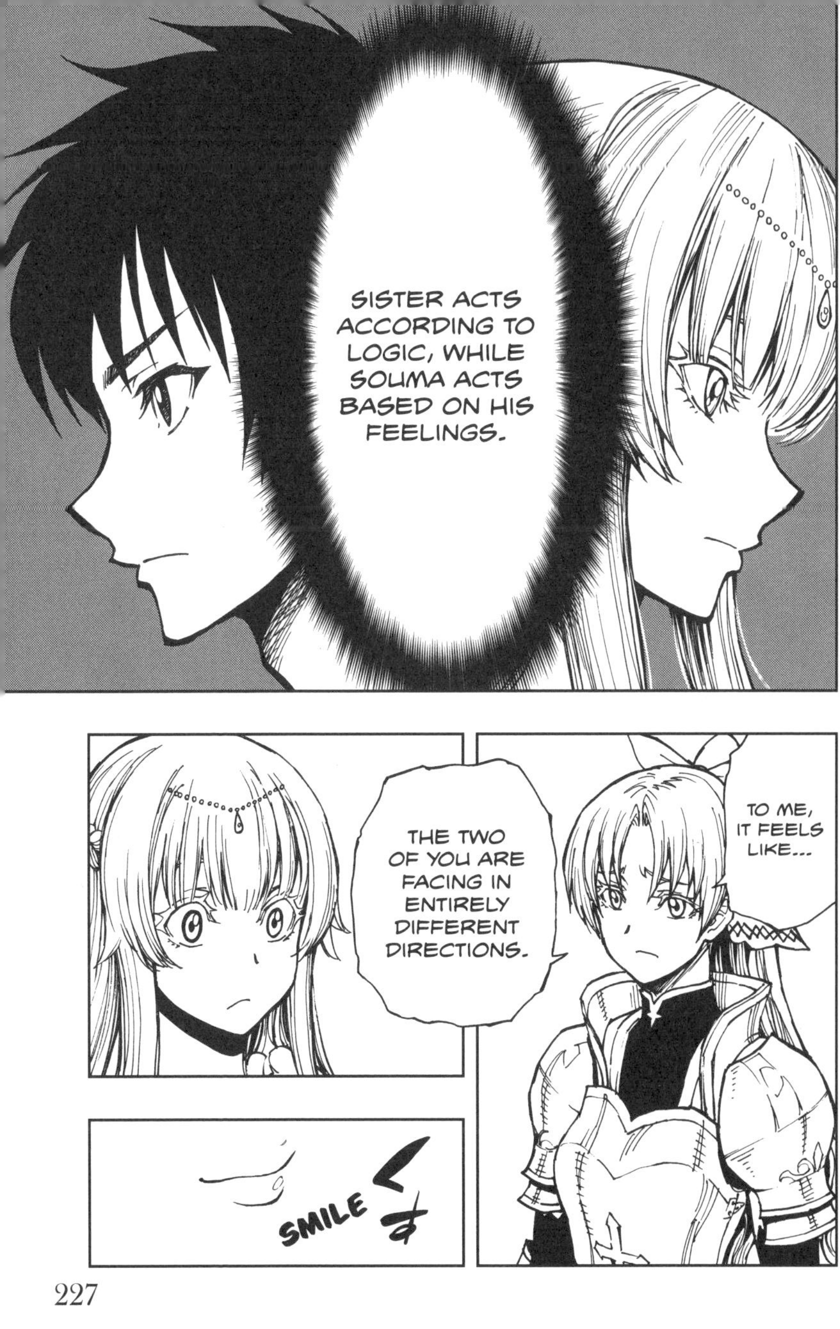
SISTER ACTS ACCORDING TO LOGIC, WHILE SOUMA ACTS BASED ON HIS FEELINGS.
TO ME, IT FEELS LIKE...
THE TWO OF YOU ARE FACING IN ENTIRELY DIFFERENT DIRECTIONS.
くす
SMILE

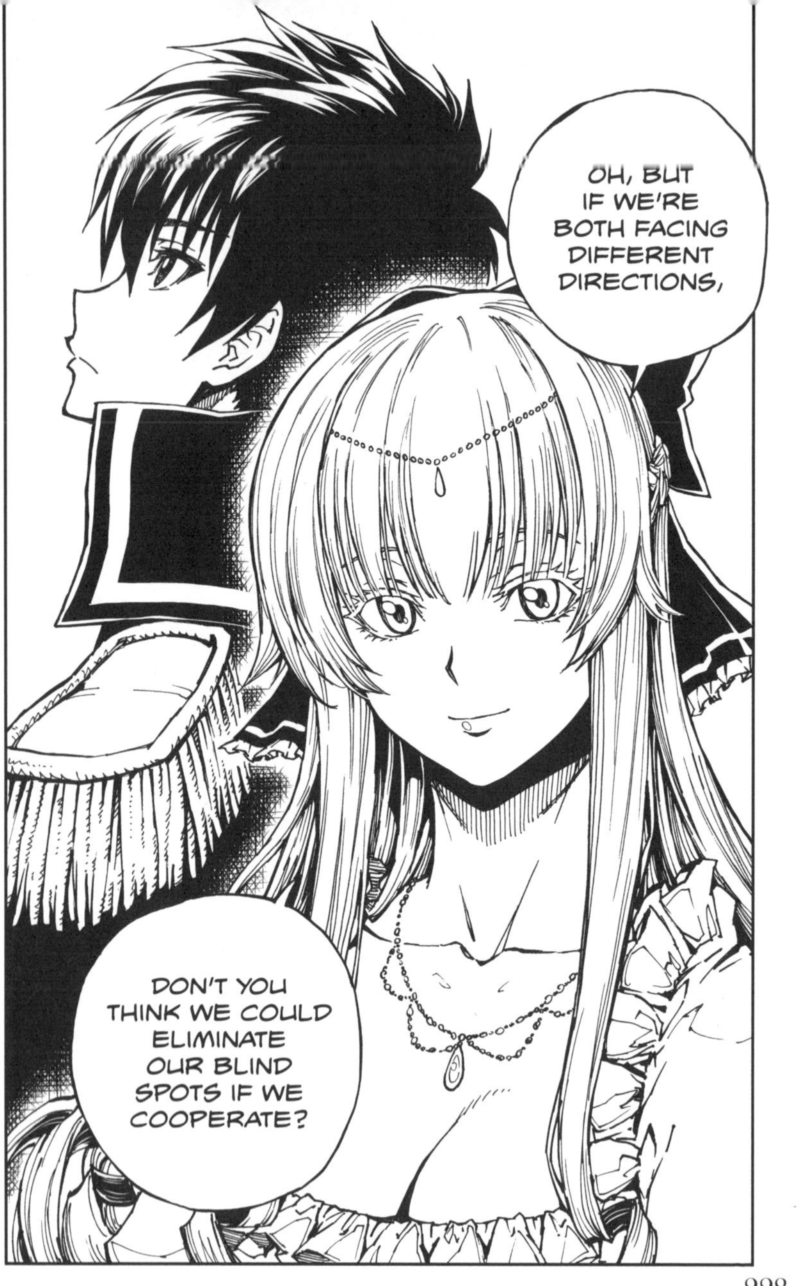
OH, BUT IF WE'RE BOTH FACING DIFFERENT DIRECTIONS,
DON'T YOU THINK WE COULD ELIMINATE OUR BLIND SPOTS IF WE COOPERATE?

Do you think this is enough gifts for Sir Souma?
Sister... I'm going there to negotiate with him.

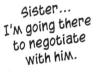

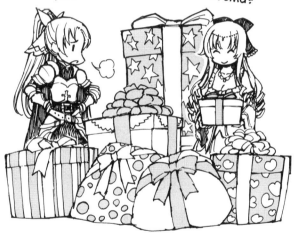

How a Realist Hero
Rebuilt the Kingdom

Chapter 29: Project Lorelei (1)

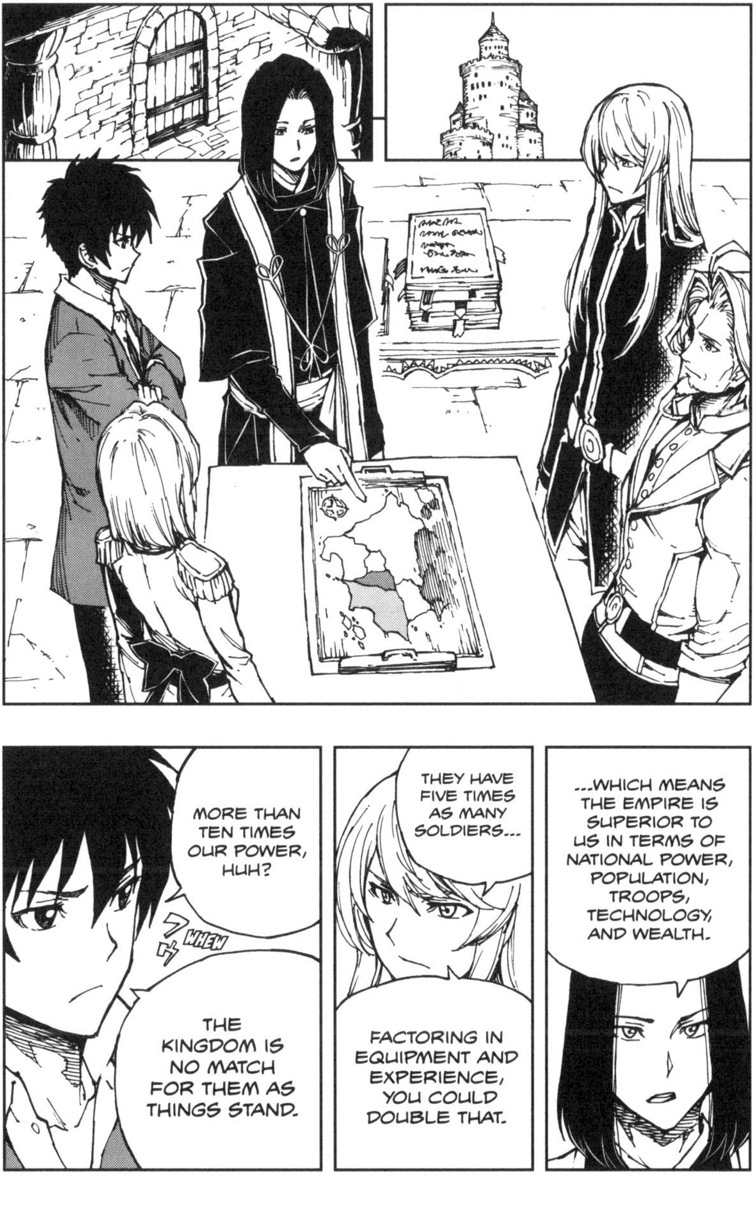
...WHICH MEANS THE EMPIRE IS SUPERIOR TO US IN TERMS OF NATIONAL POWER, POPULATION, TROOPS, TECHNOLOGY, AND WEALTH.
THEY HAVE FIVE TIMES AS MANY SOLDIERS...
FACTORING IN EQUIPMENT AND EXPERIENCE, YOU COULD DOUBLE THAT.
MORE THAN TEN TIMES OUR POWER, HUH?
WHEW
THE KINGDOM IS NO MATCH FOR THEM AS THINGS STAND.

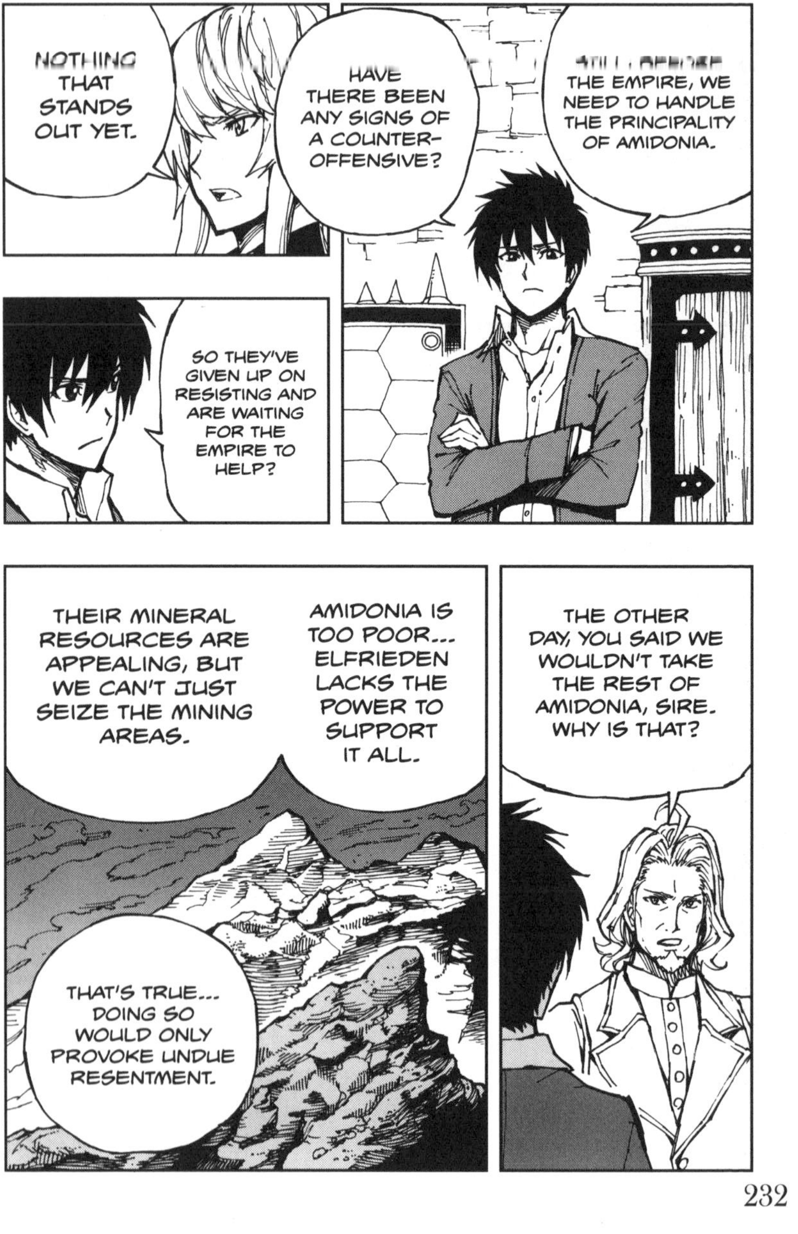
THE EMPIRE, WE NEED TO HANDLE THE PRINCIPALITY OF AMIDONIA.
HAVE THERE BEEN ANY SIGNS OF A COUNTER-OFFENSIVE?
THAT STANDS OUT YET.
SO THEY'VE GIVEN UP ON RESISTING AND ARE WAITING FOR THE EMPIRE TO HELP?
THE OTHER DAY, YOU SAID WE WOULDN'T TAKE THE REST OF AMIDONIA, SIRE. WHY IS THAT?
AMIDONIA IS TOO POOR... ELFRIEDEN LACKS THE POWER TO SUPPORT IT ALL.
THEIR MINERAL RESOURCES ARE APPEALING, BUT WE CAN'T JUST SEIZE THE MINING AREAS.
THAT'S TRUE... DOING SO WOULD ONLY PROVOKE UNDUE RESENTMENT.

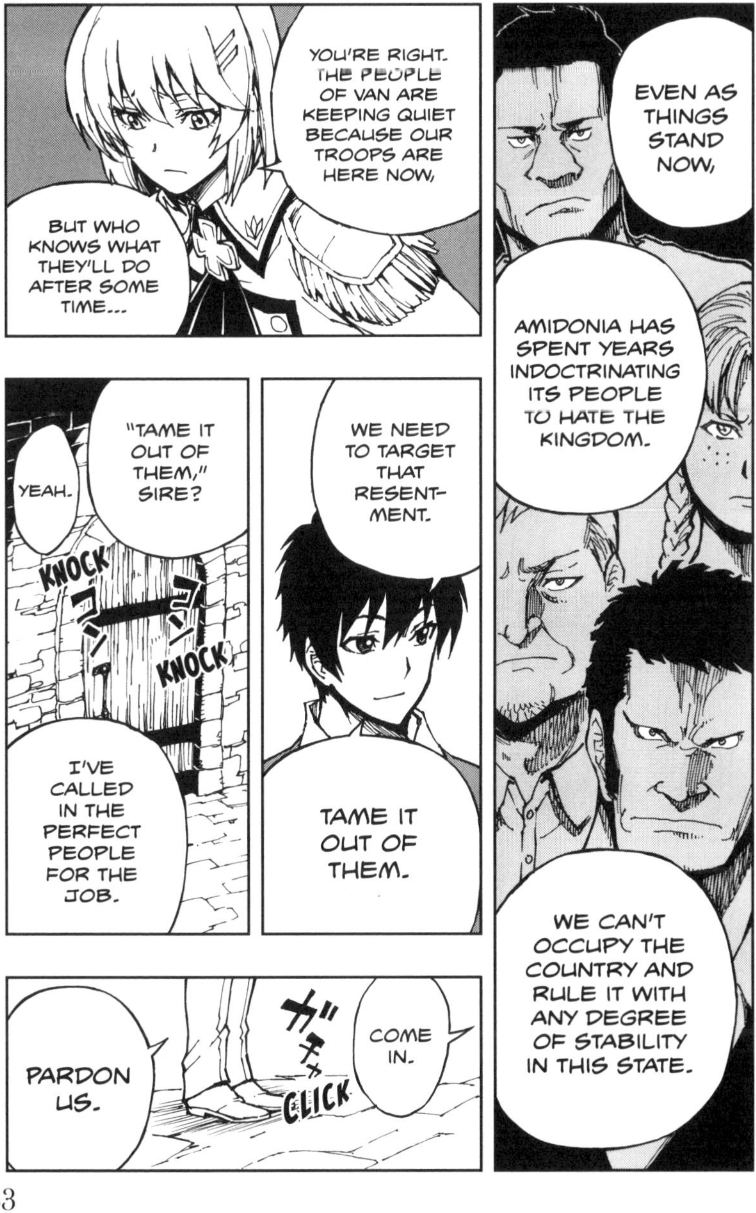
EVEN AS THINGS STAND NOW,
AMIDONIA HAS SPENT YEARS INDOCTRINATING ITS PEOPLE TO HATE THE KINGDOM.
WE CAN'T OCCUPY THE COUNTRY AND RULE IT WITH ANY DEGREE OF STABILITY IN THIS STATE.
YOU'RE RIGHT. THE PEOPLE OF VAN ARE KEEPING QUIET BECAUSE OUR TROOPS ARE HERE NOW,
BUT WHO KNOWS WHAT THEY'LL DO AFTER SOME TIME...
WE NEED TO TARGET THAT RESENTMENT.
TAME IT OUT OF THEM.
"TAME IT OUT OF THEM," SIRE?
YEAH.
KNOCK
KNOCK
I'VE CALLED IN THE PERFECT PEOPLE FOR THE JOB.
COME IN.
CLICK
PARDON US.

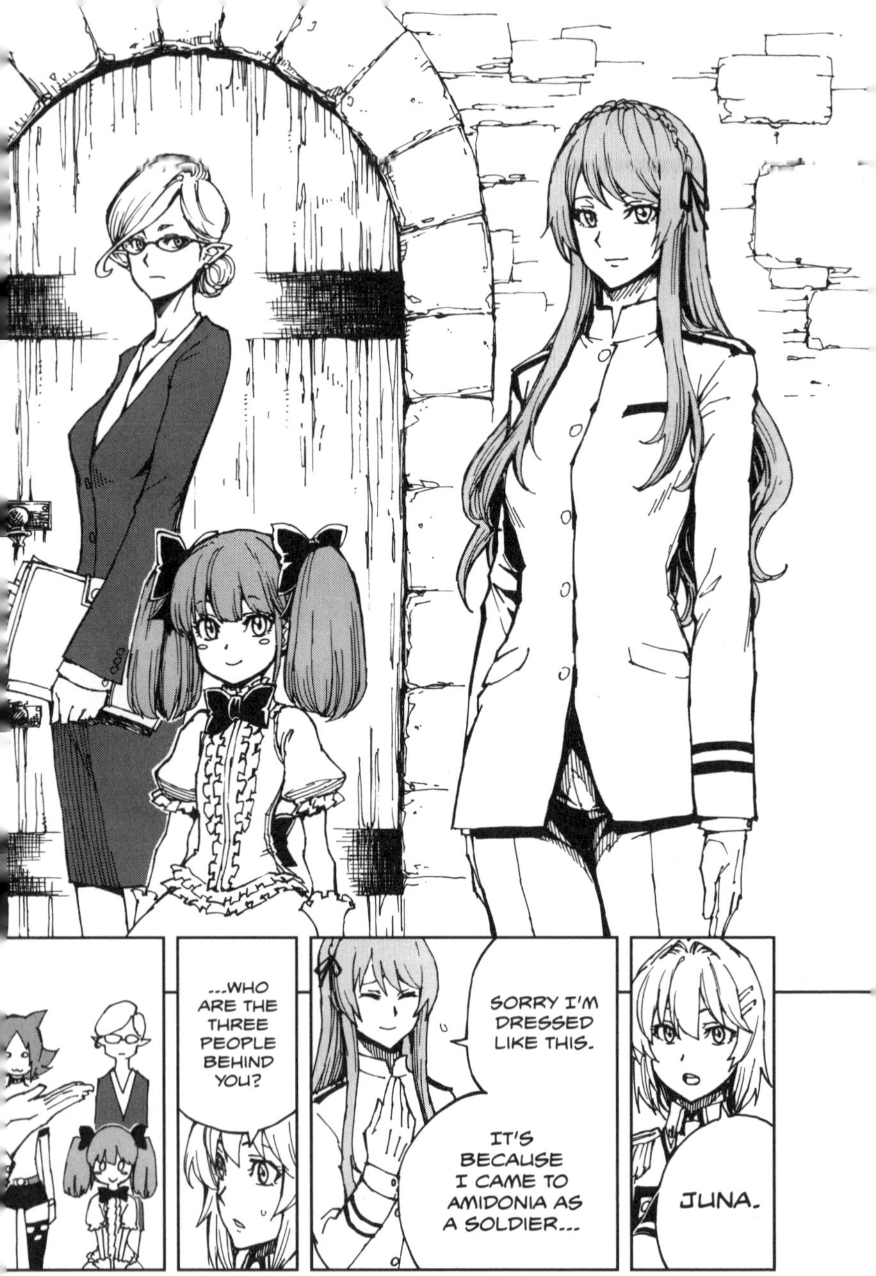
JUNA.
SORRY I'M DRESSED LIKE THIS.
IT'S BECAUSE I CAME TO AMIDONIA AS A SOLDIER...
...WHO ARE THE THREE PEOPLE BEHIND YOU?

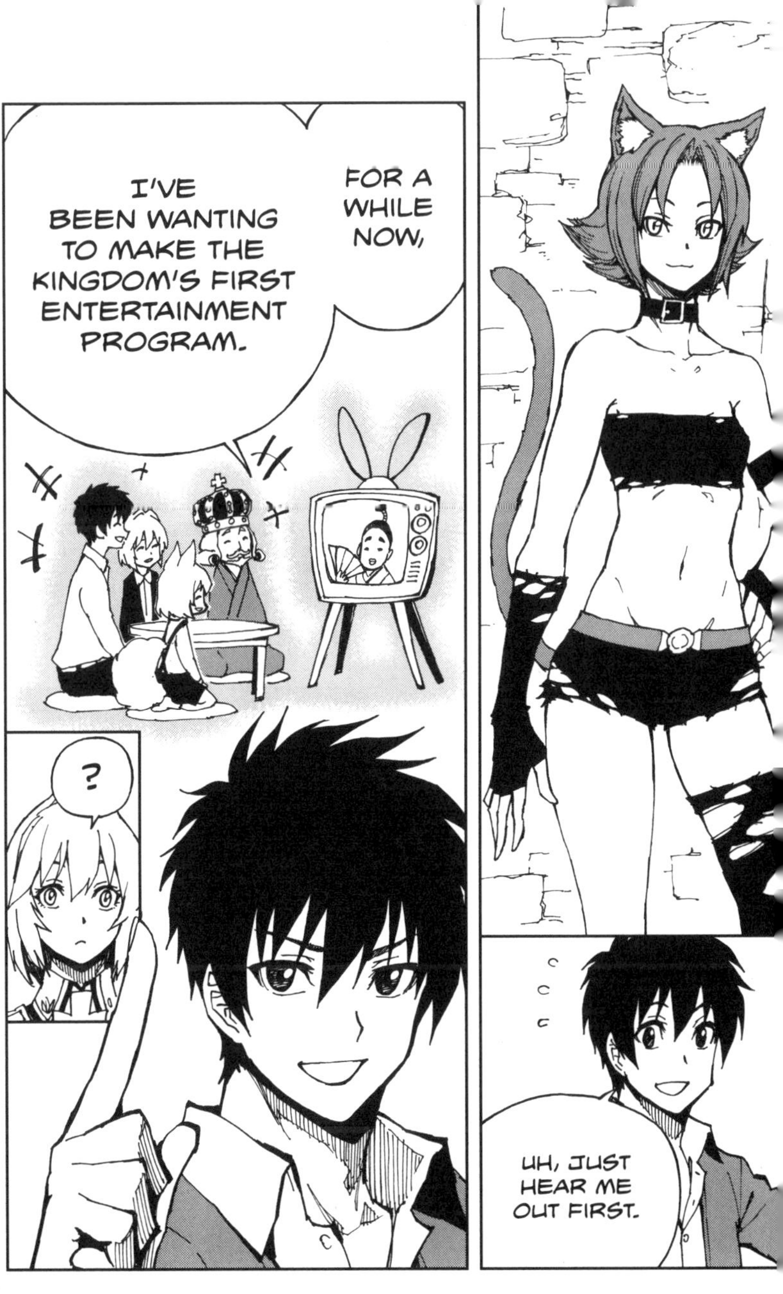
UH, JUST HEAR ME OUT FIRST.
FOR A WHILE NOW,
I'VE BEEN WANTING TO MAKE THE KINGDOM'S FIRST ENTERTAINMENT PROGRAM.
?

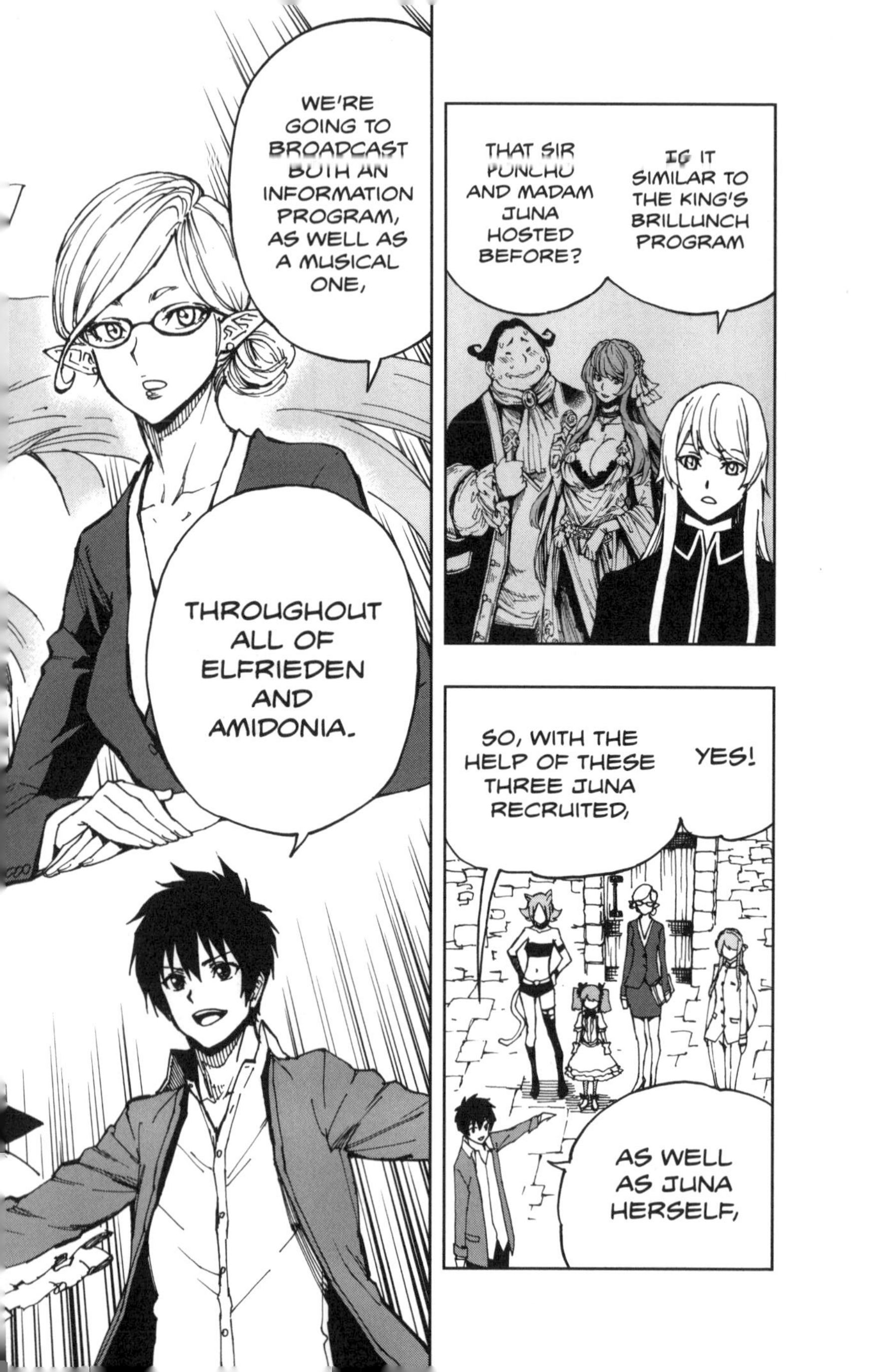
IS IT SIMILAR TO THE KING'S BRILLUNCH PROGRAM
THAT SIR PONCHO AND MADAM JUNA HOSTED BEFORE?
YES!
SO, WITH THE HELP OF THESE THREE JUNA RECRUITED,
AS WELL AS JUNA HERSELF,
WE'RE GOING TO BROADCAST BOTH AN INFORMATION PROGRAM, AS WELL AS A MUSICAL ONE,
THROUGHOUT ALL OF ELFRIEDEN AND AMIDONIA.

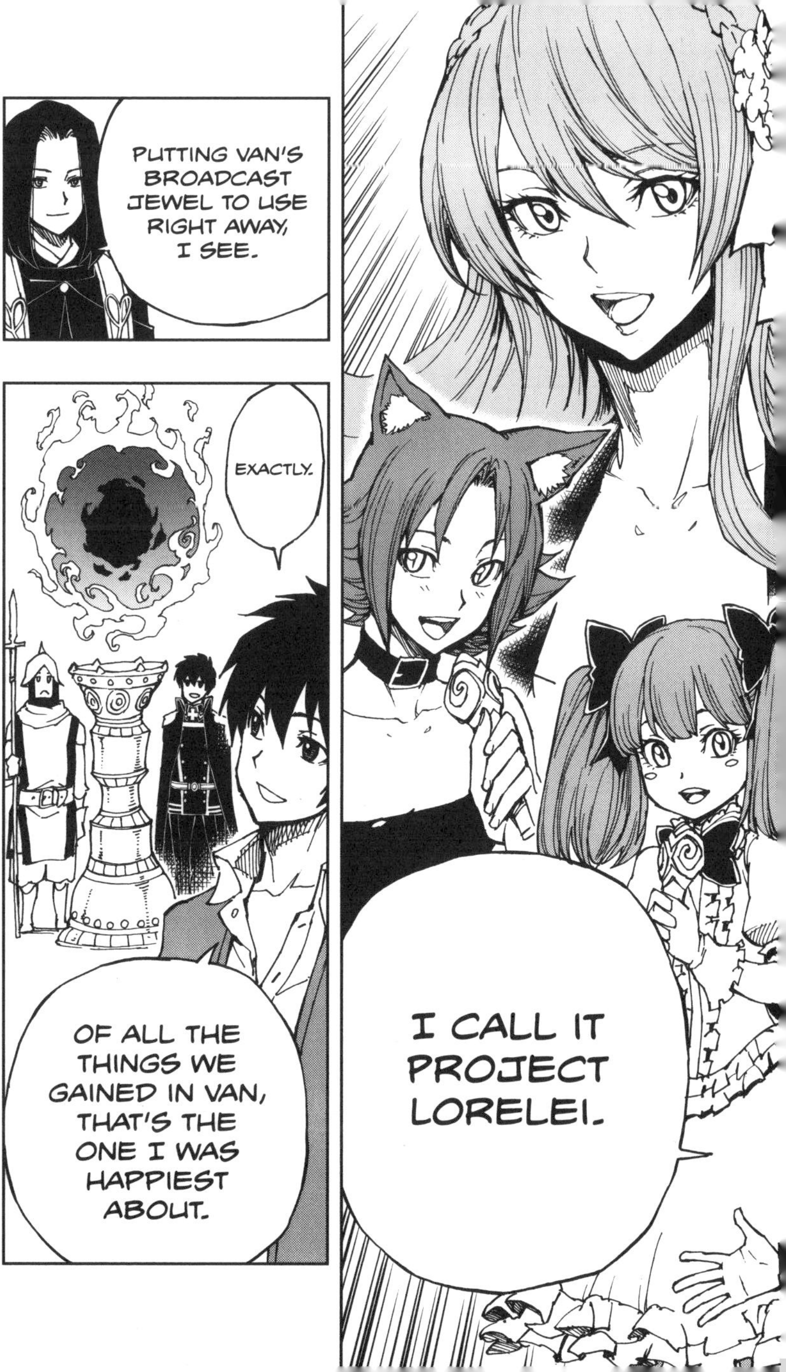
I CALL IT PROJECT LORELEI.
PUTTING VAN'S BROADCAST JEWEL TO USE RIGHT AWAY, I SEE.
EXACTLY.
OF ALL THE THINGS WE GAINED IN VAN, THAT'S THE ONE I WAS HAPPIEST ABOUT.

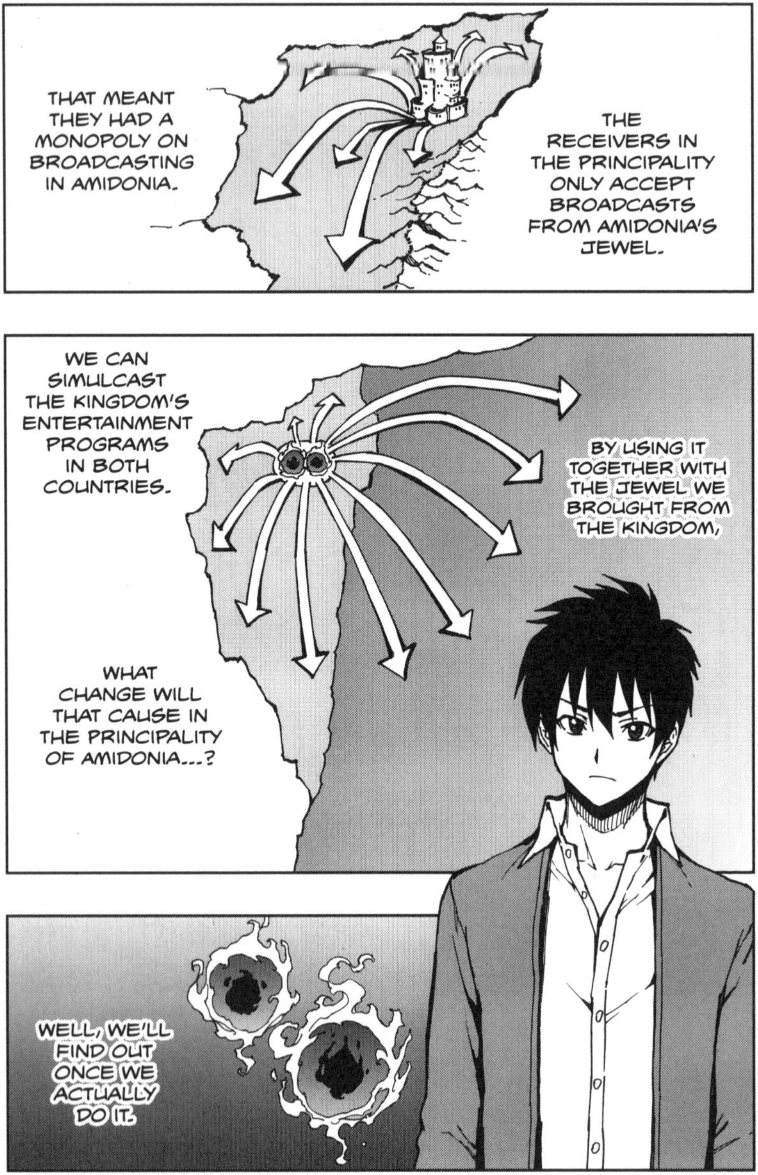
THE RECEIVERS IN THE PRINCIPALITY ONLY ACCEPT BROADCASTS FROM AMIDONIA'S JEWEL.
THAT MEANT THEY HAD A MONOPOLY ON BROADCASTING IN AMIDONIA.
BY USING IT TOGETHER WITH THE JEWEL WE BROUGHT FROM THE KINGDOM,
WE CAN SIMULCAST THE KINGDOM'S ENTERTAINMENT PROGRAMS IN BOTH COUNTRIES.
WHAT CHANGE WILL THAT CAUSE IN THE PRINCIPALITY OF AMIDONIA...?
WELL, WE'LL FIND OUT ONCE WE ACTUALLY DO IT.

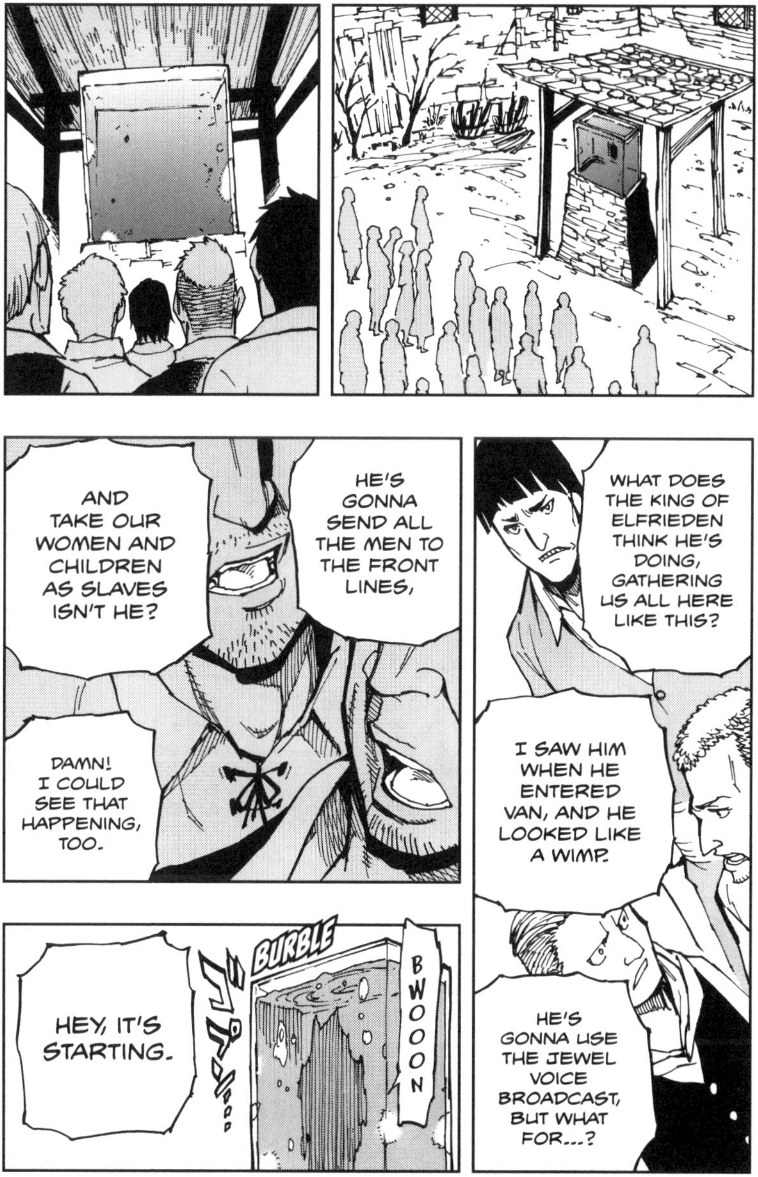

WHAT DOES THE KING OF ELFRIEDEN THINK HE'S DOING, GATHERING US ALL HERE LIKE THIS?
I SAW HIM WHEN HE ENTERED VAN, AND HE LOOKED LIKE A WIMP.
HE'S GONNA USE THE JEWEL VOICE BROADCAST, BUT WHAT FOR...?
HE'S GONNA SEND ALL THE MEN TO THE FRONT LINES,
AND TAKE OUR WOMEN AND CHILDREN AS SLAVES ISN'T HE?
DAMN! I COULD SEE THAT HAPPENING, TOO.
BWOOON
BURBLE
HEY, IT'S STARTING.

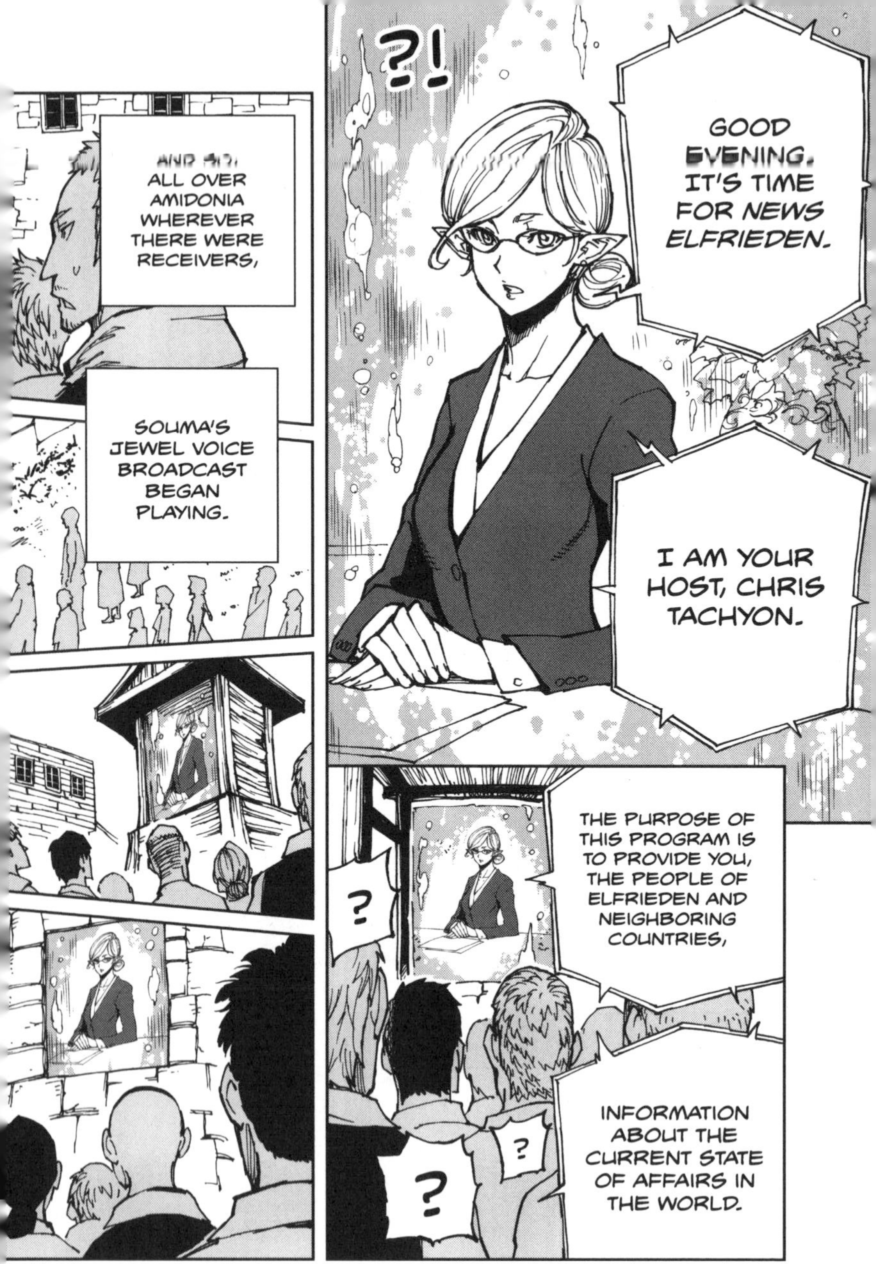
?!
GOOD EVENING. IT'S TIME FOR NEWS ELFRIEDEN.
I AM YOUR HOST, CHRIS TACHYON.
AND SO, ALL OVER AMIDONIA WHEREVER THERE WERE RECEIVERS,
SOUMA'S JEWEL VOICE BROADCAST BEGAN PLAYING.
THE PURPOSE OF THIS PROGRAM IS TO PROVIDE YOU, THE PEOPLE OF ELFRIEDEN AND NEIGHBORING COUNTRIES,
?
?
?
INFORMATION ABOUT THE CURRENT STATE OF AFFAIRS IN THE WORLD.

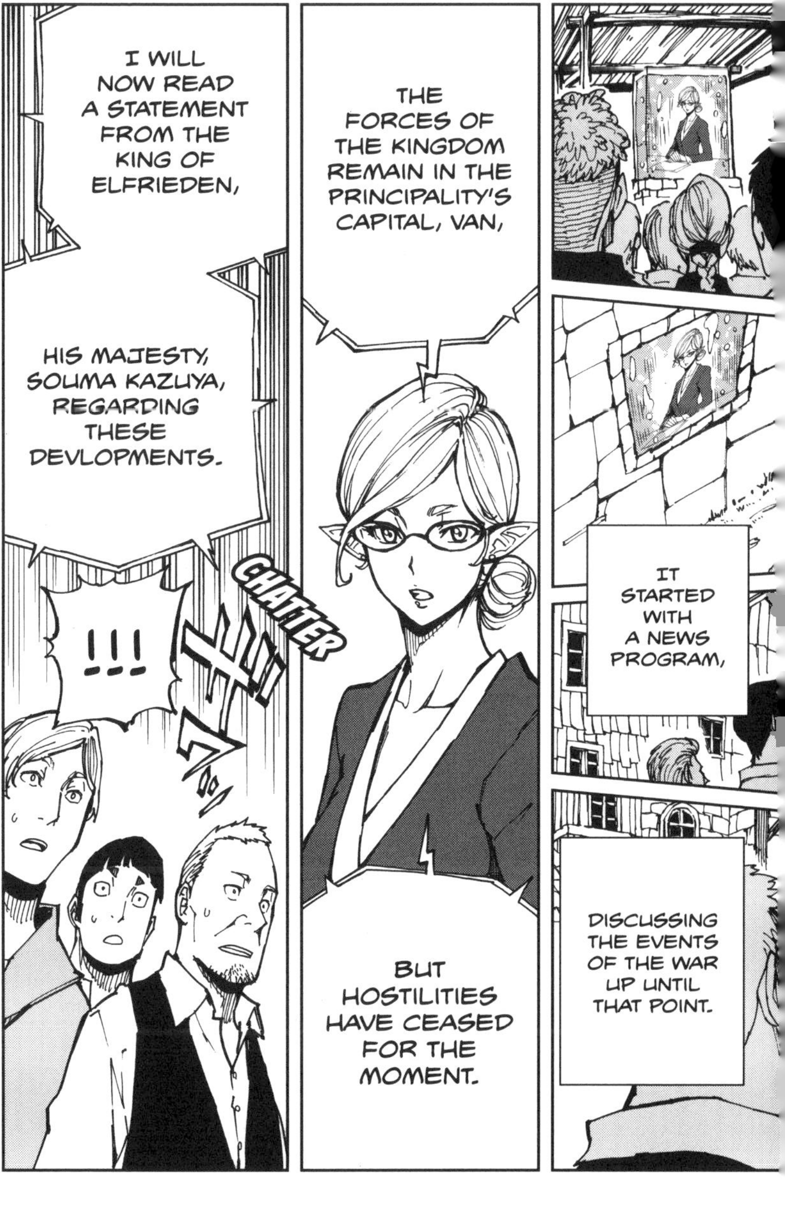
IT STARTED WITH A NEWS PROGRAM,
DISCUSSING THE EVENTS OF THE WAR UP UNTIL THAT POINT.
THE FORCES OF THE KINGDOM REMAIN IN THE PRINCIPALITY'S CAPITAL, VAN,
BUT HOSTILITIES HAVE CEASED FOR THE MOMENT.
I WILL NOW READ A STATEMENT FROM THE KING OF ELFRIEDEN,
HIS MAJESTY, SOUMA KAZUYA, REGARDING THESE DEVLOPMENTS.
!!!
CHATTER

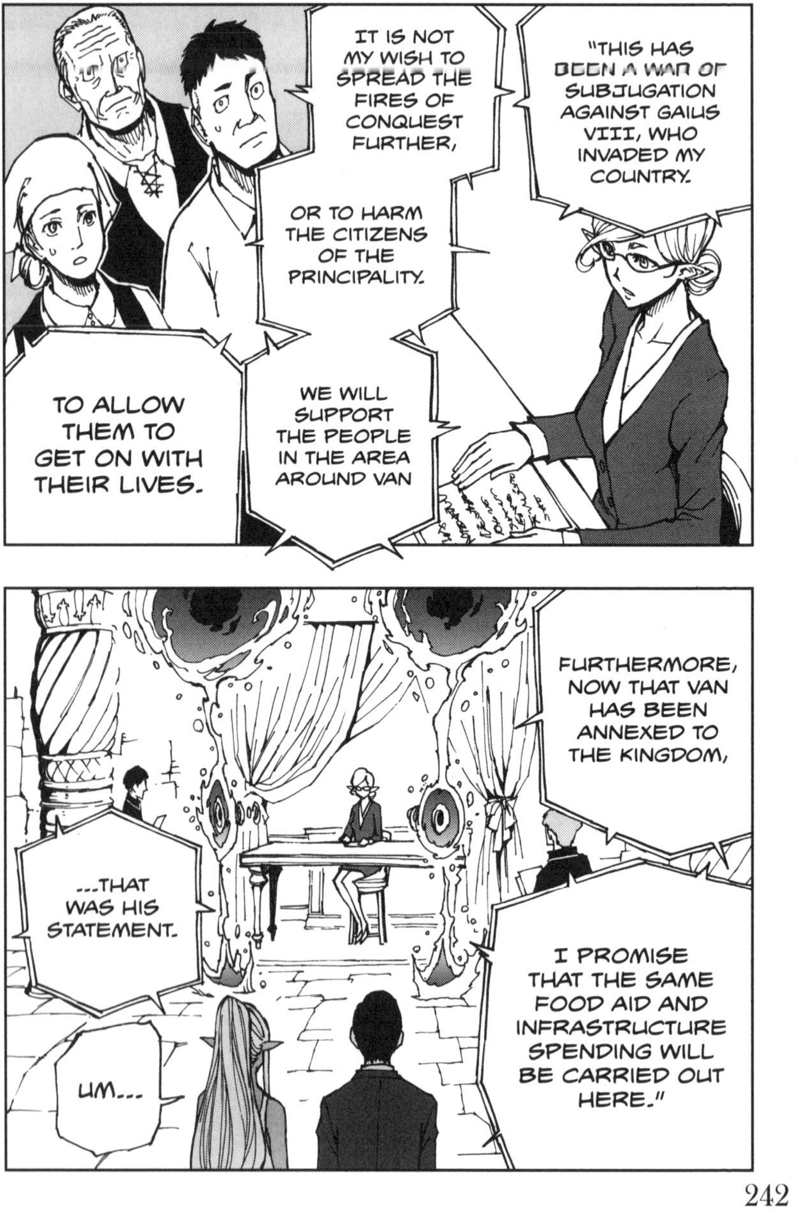
"THIS HAS BEEN A WAR OF SUBJUGATION AGAINST GAIUS VIII, WHO INVADED MY COUNTRY.
IT IS NOT MY WISH TO SPREAD THE FIRES OF CONQUEST FURTHER,
OR TO HARM THE CITIZENS OF THE PRINCIPALITY.
WE WILL SUPPORT THE PEOPLE IN THE AREA AROUND VAN
TO ALLOW THEM TO GET ON WITH THEIR LIVES.
FURTHERMORE, NOW THAT VAN HAS BEEN ANNEXED TO THE KINGDOM,
I PROMISE THAT THE SAME FOOD AID AND INFRASTRUCTURE SPENDING WILL BE CARRIED OUT HERE."
...THAT WAS HIS STATEMENT.
UM...

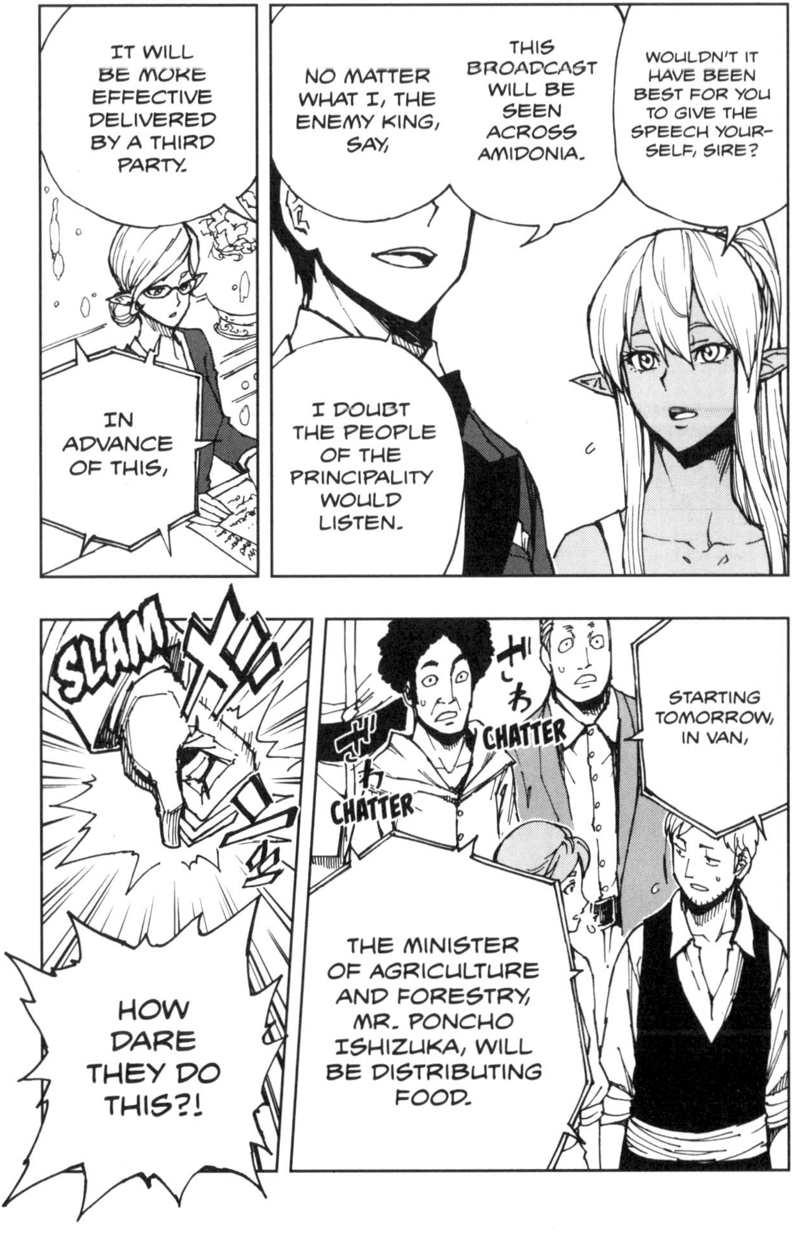
WOULDN'T IT HAVE BEEN BEST FOR YOU TO GIVE THE SPEECH YOURSELF, SIRE?
THIS BROADCAST WILL BE SEEN ACROSS AMIDONIA.
NO MATTER WHAT I, THE ENEMY KING, SAY,
I DOUBT THE PEOPLE OF THE PRINCIPALITY WOULD LISTEN.
IT WILL BE MORE EFFECTIVE DELIVERED BY A THIRD PARTY.
IN ADVANCE OF THIS,
STARTING TOMORROW, IN VAN,
CHATTER
CHATTER
THE MINISTER OF AGRICULTURE AND FORESTRY, MR. PONCHO ISHIZUKA, WILL BE DISTRIBUTING FOOD.
SLAM
HOW DARE THEY DO THIS?!

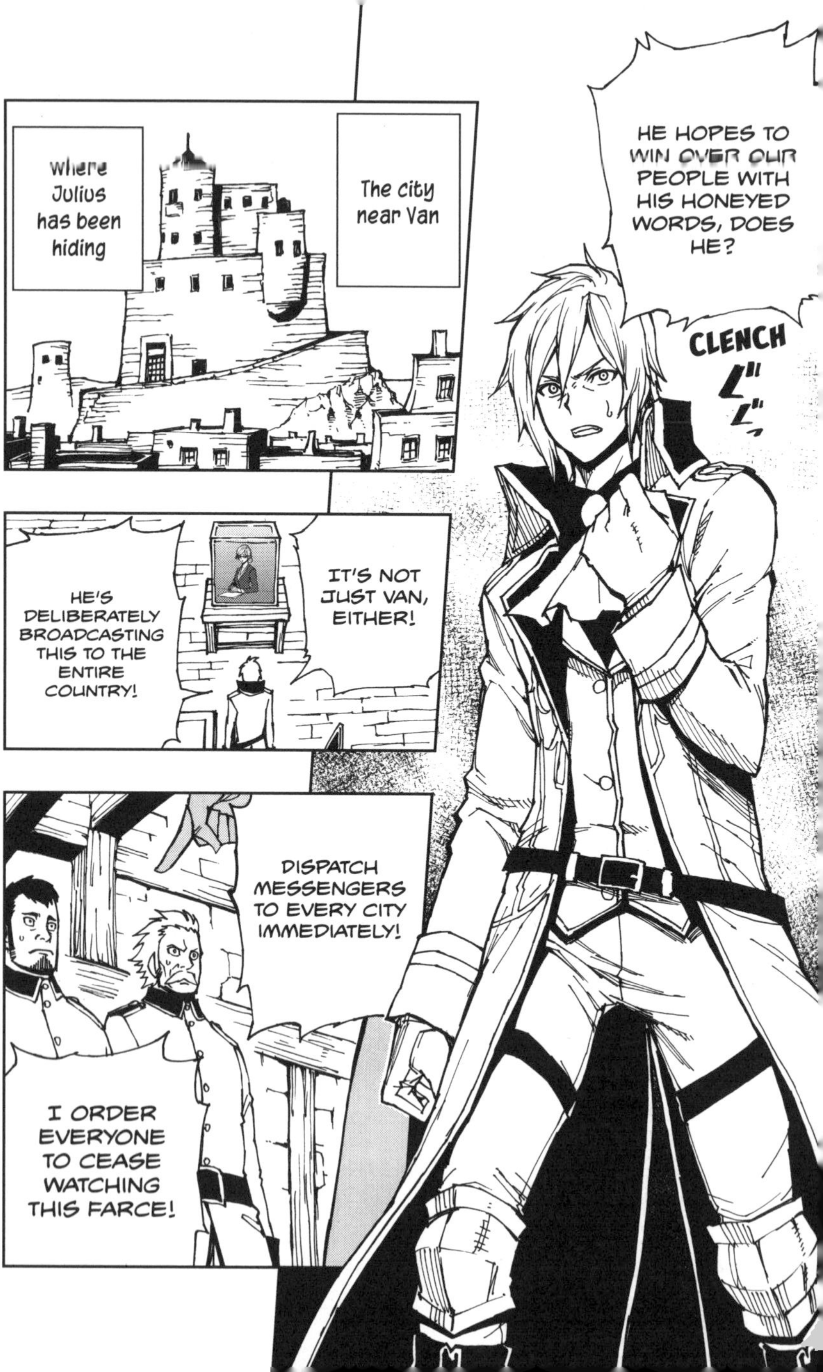
HE HOPES TO WIN OVER OUR PEOPLE WITH HIS HONEYED WORDS, DOES HE?
CLENCH
The city near Van
Where Julius has been hiding
IT'S NOT JUST VAN, EITHER!
HE'S DELIBERATELY BROADCASTING THIS TO THE ENTIRE COUNTRY!
DISPATCH MESSENGERS TO EVERY CITY IMMEDIATELY!
I ORDER EVERYONE TO CEASE WATCHING THIS FARCE!

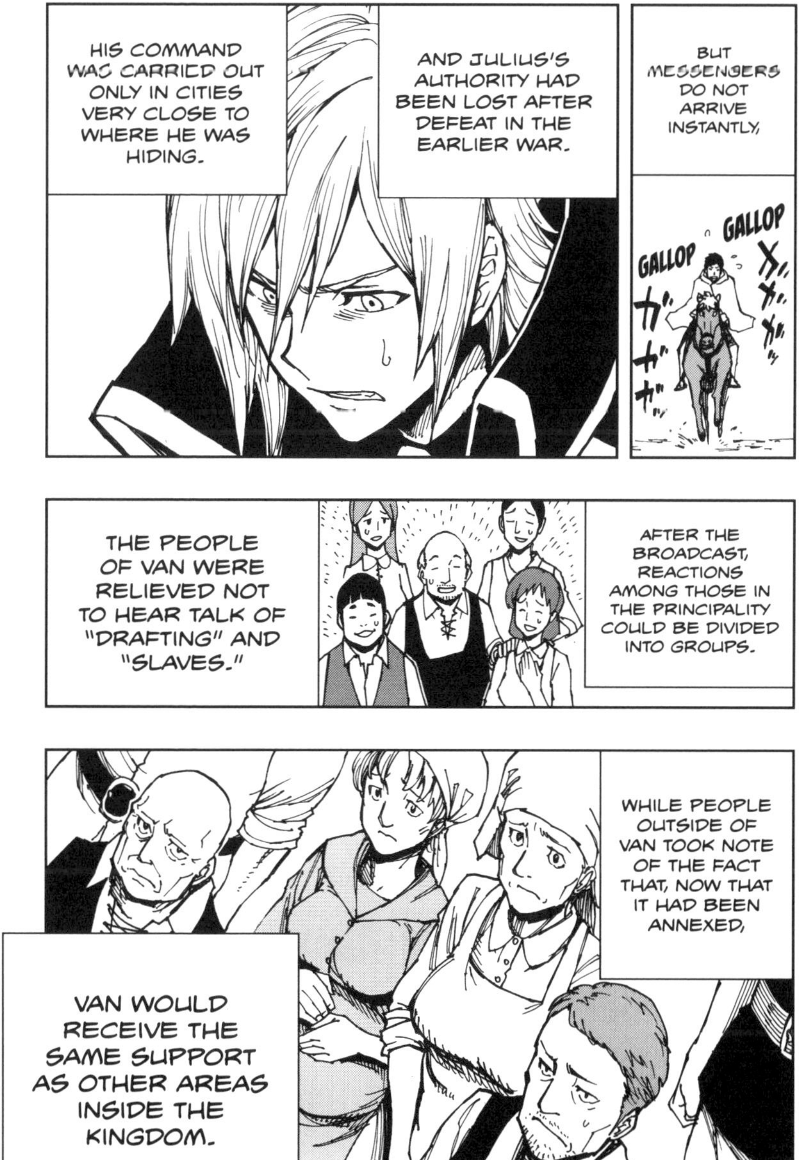
BUT MESSENGERS DO NOT ARRIVE INSTANTLY,
GALLOP
GALLOP
AND JULIUS'S AUTHORITY HAD BEEN LOST AFTER DEFEAT IN THE EARLIER WAR.
HIS COMMAND WAS CARRIED OUT ONLY IN CITIES VERY CLOSE TO WHERE HE WAS HIDING.
AFTER THE BROADCAST, REACTIONS AMONG THOSE IN THE PRINCIPALITY COULD BE DIVIDED INTO GROUPS.
THE PEOPLE OF VAN WERE RELIEVED NOT TO HEAR TALK OF "DRAFTING" AND "SLAVES."
WHILE PEOPLE OUTSIDE OF VAN TOOK NOTE OF THE FACT THAT, NOW THAT IT HAD BEEN ANNEXED,
VAN WOULD RECEIVE THE SAME SUPPORT AS OTHER AREAS INSIDE THE KINGDOM.

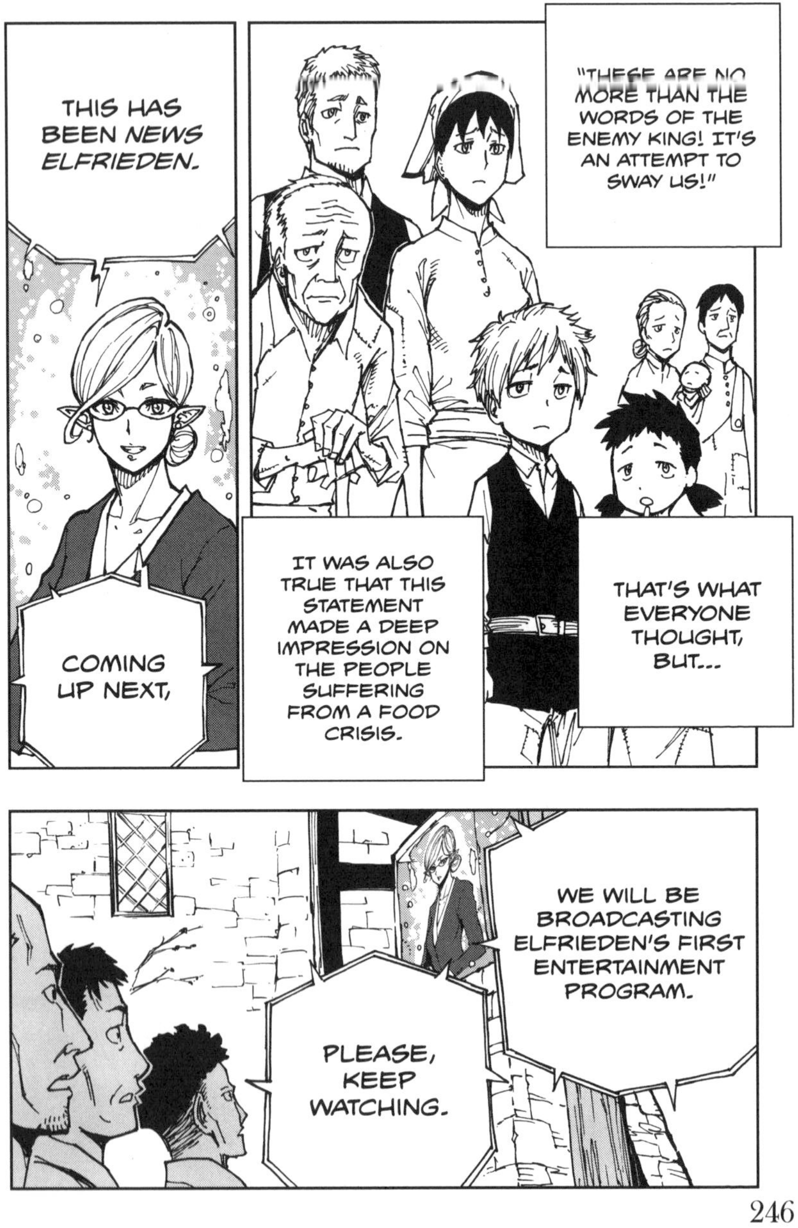
"THESE ARE NO MORE THAN THE WORDS OF THE ENEMY KING! IT'S AN ATTEMPT TO SWAY US!"
THAT'S WHAT EVERYONE THOUGHT, BUT...
IT WAS ALSO TRUE THAT THIS STATEMENT MADE A DEEP IMPRESSION ON THE PEOPLE SUFFERING FROM A FOOD CRISIS.
THIS HAS BEEN NEWS ELFRIEDEN.
COMING UP NEXT,
WE WILL BE BROADCASTING ELFRIEDEN'S FIRST ENTERTAINMENT PROGRAM.
PLEASE, KEEP WATCHING.

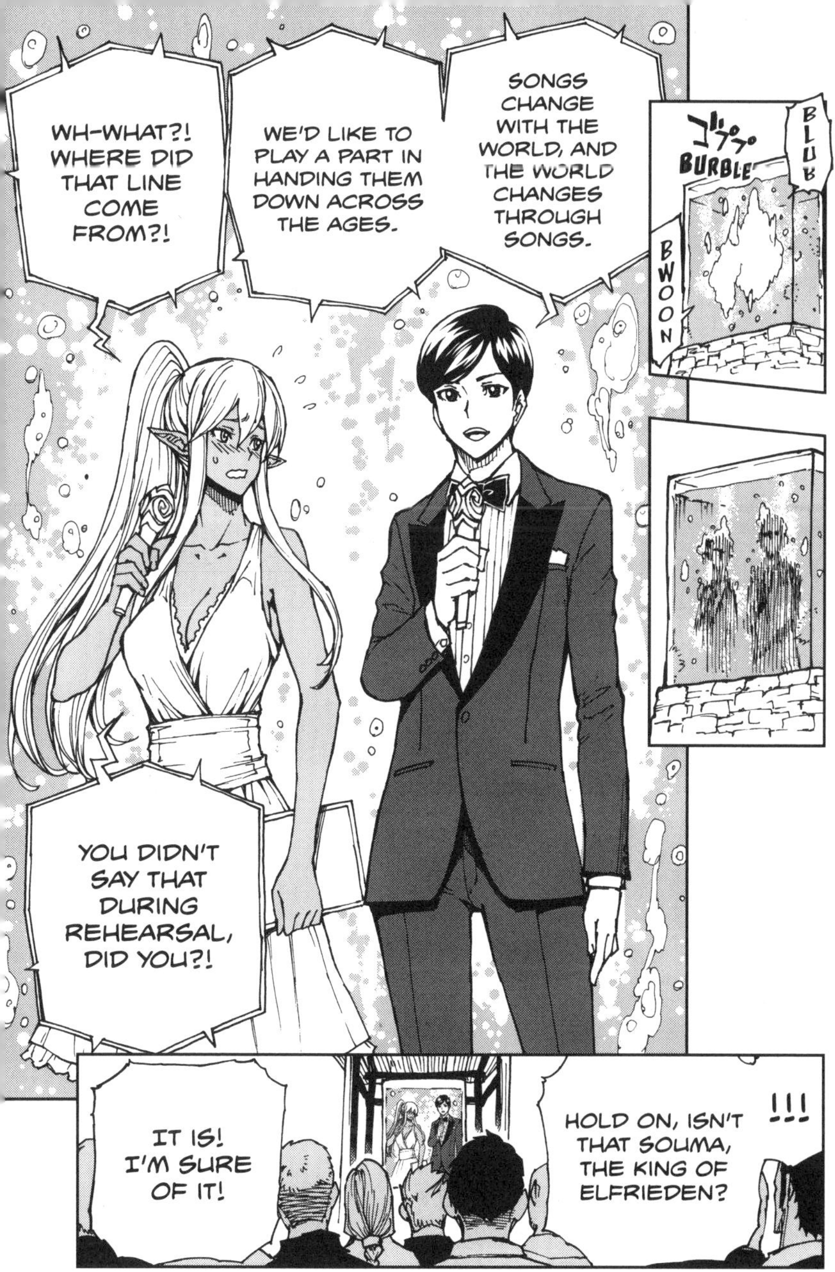
BLUB
BURBLE
BWOON
SONGS CHANGE WITH THE WORLD, AND THE WORLD CHANGES THROUGH SONGS.
WE'D LIKE TO PLAY A PART IN HANDING THEM DOWN ACROSS THE AGES.
WH-WHAT?! WHERE DID THAT LINE COME FROM?!
YOU DIDN'T SAY THAT DURING REHEARSAL, DID YOU?!
!!!
HOLD ON, ISN'T THAT SOUMA, THE KING OF ELFRIEDEN?
IT IS! I'M SURE OF IT!

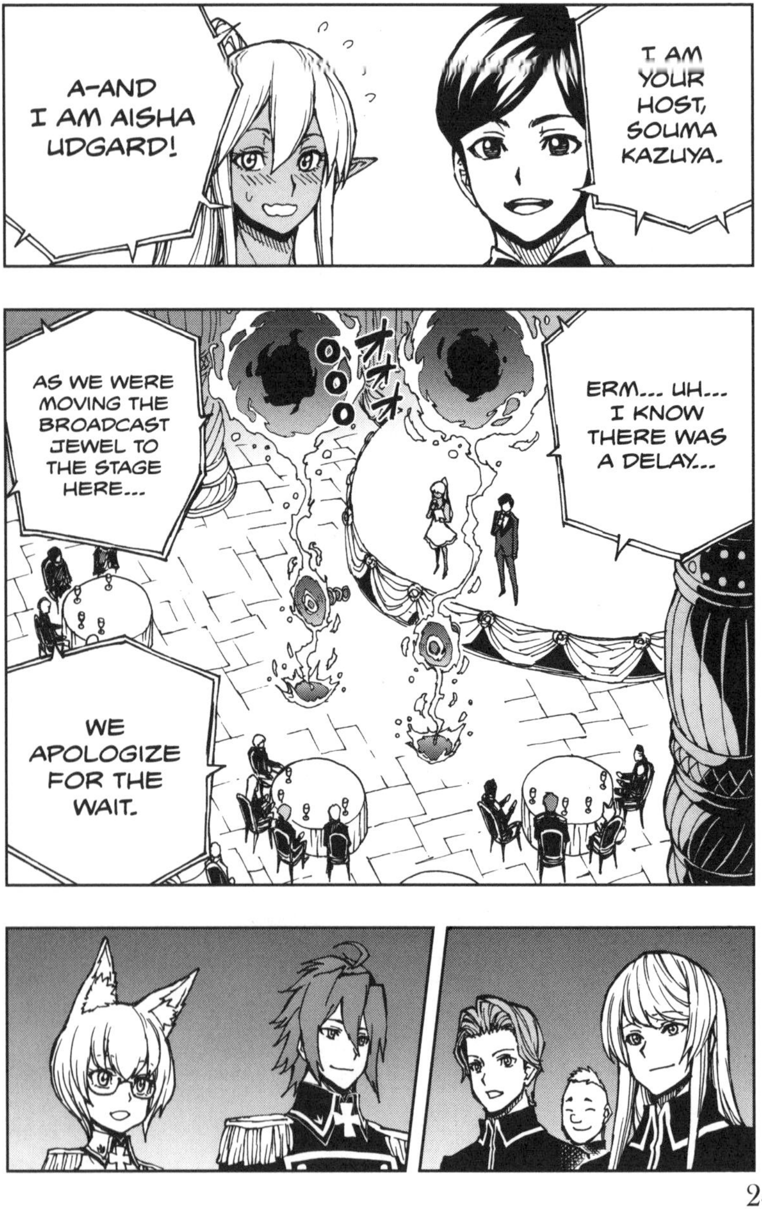
I AM YOUR HOST, SOUMA KAZUYA.
A-AND I AM AISHA UDGARD!
ERM... UH... I KNOW THERE WAS A DELAY...
オオオ
OOO.
AS WE WERE MOVING THE BROADCAST JEWEL TO THE STAGE HERE...
WE APOLOGIZE FOR THE WAIT.

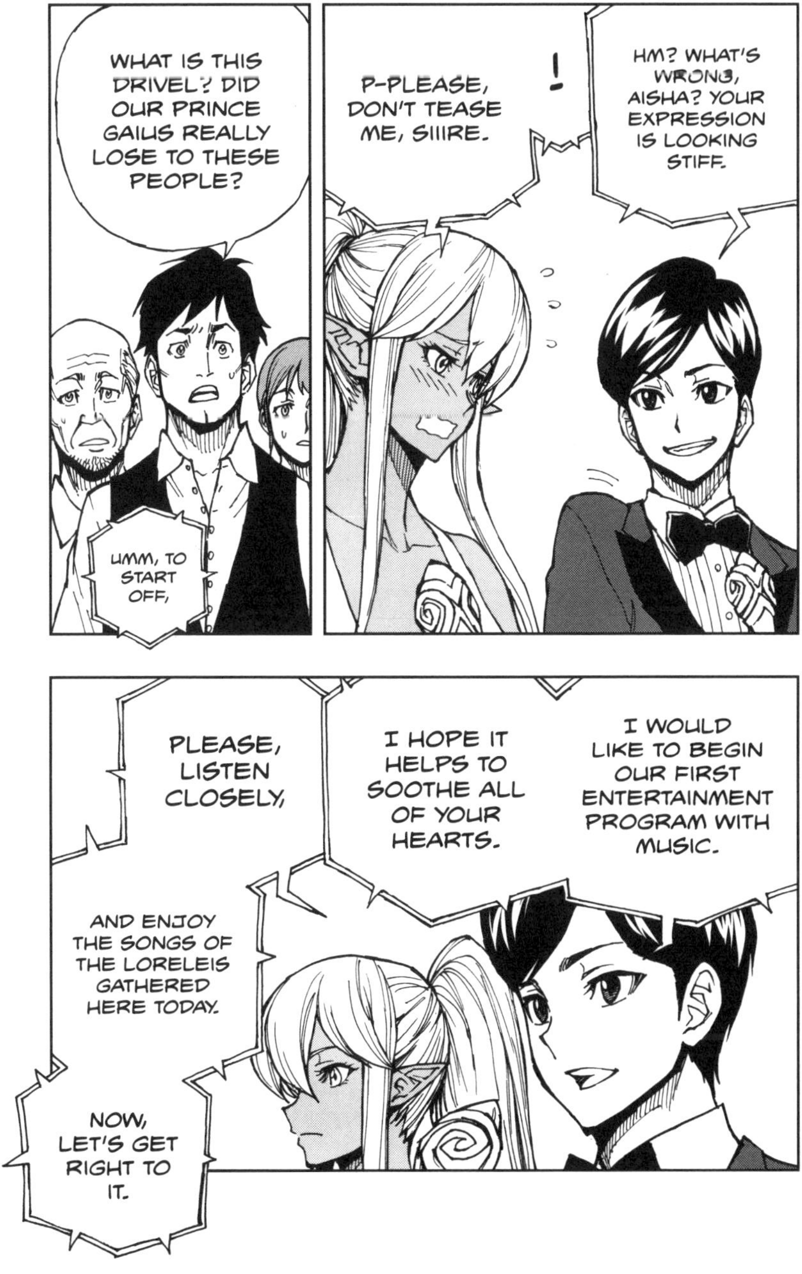
HM? WHAT'S WRONG, AISHA? YOUR EXPRESSION IS LOOKING STIFF.
!
P-PLEASE, DON'T TEASE ME, SIIIRE.
WHAT IS THIS DRIVEL? DID OUR PRINCE GAIUS REALLY LOSE TO THESE PEOPLE?
UMM, TO START OFF,
I WOULD LIKE TO BEGIN OUR FIRST ENTERTAINMENT PROGRAM WITH MUSIC.
I HOPE IT HELPS TO SOOTHE ALL OF YOUR HEARTS.
PLEASE, LISTEN CLOSELY,
AND ENJOY THE SONGS OF THE LORELEIS GATHERED HERE TODAY.
NOW, LET'S GET RIGHT TO IT.

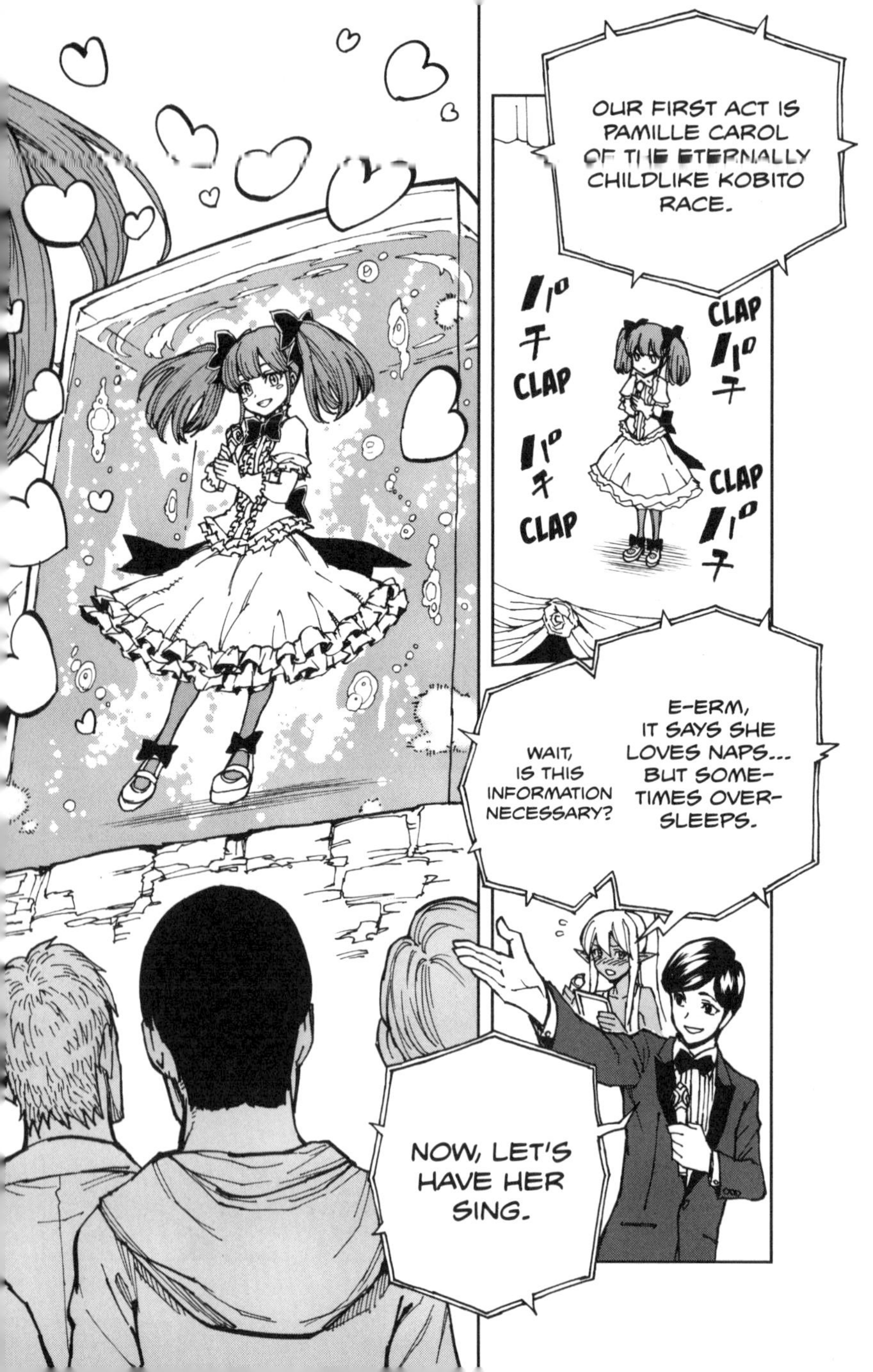
OUR FIRST ACT IS PAMILLE CAROL OF THE ETERNALLY CHILDLIKE KOBITO RACE.
パチ CLAP
パチ CLAP
パチ CLAP
パチ CLAP
E-ERM, IT SAYS SHE LOVES NAPS... BUT SOME-TIMES OVER-SLEEPS.
WAIT, IS THIS INFORMATION NECESSARY?
NOW, LET'S HAVE HER SING.

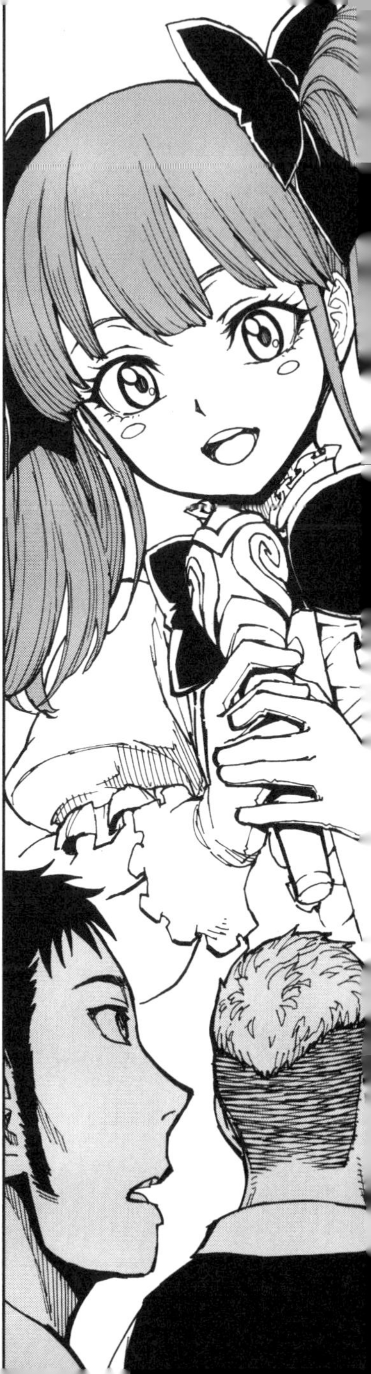

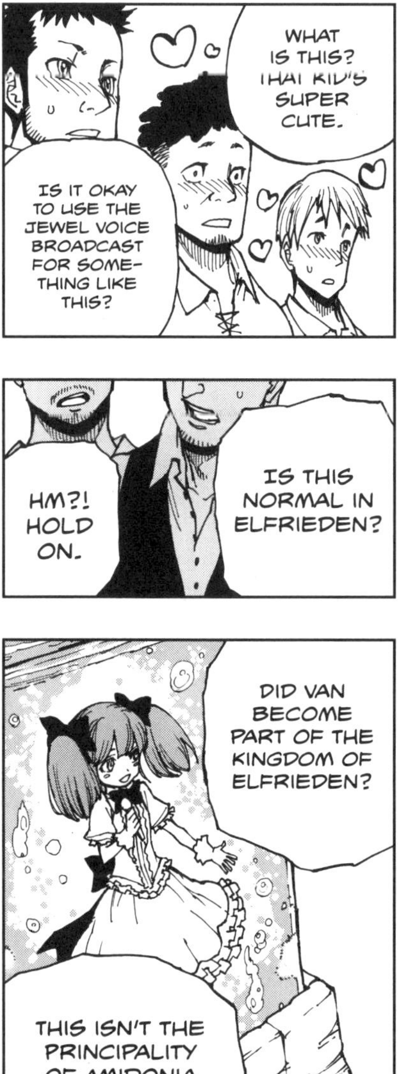
WHAT IS THIS? THAT KID'S SUPER CUTE.
IS IT OKAY TO USE THE JEWEL VOICE BROADCAST FOR SOME-THING LIKE THIS?
IS THIS NORMAL IN ELFRIEDEN?
HM?! HOLD ON.
DID VAN BECOME PART OF THE KINGDOM OF ELFRIEDEN?
THIS ISN'T THE PRINCIPALITY OF AMIDONIA ANYMORE, RIGHT...?

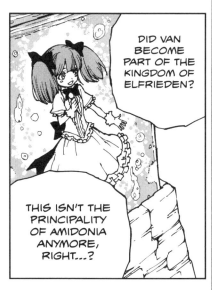

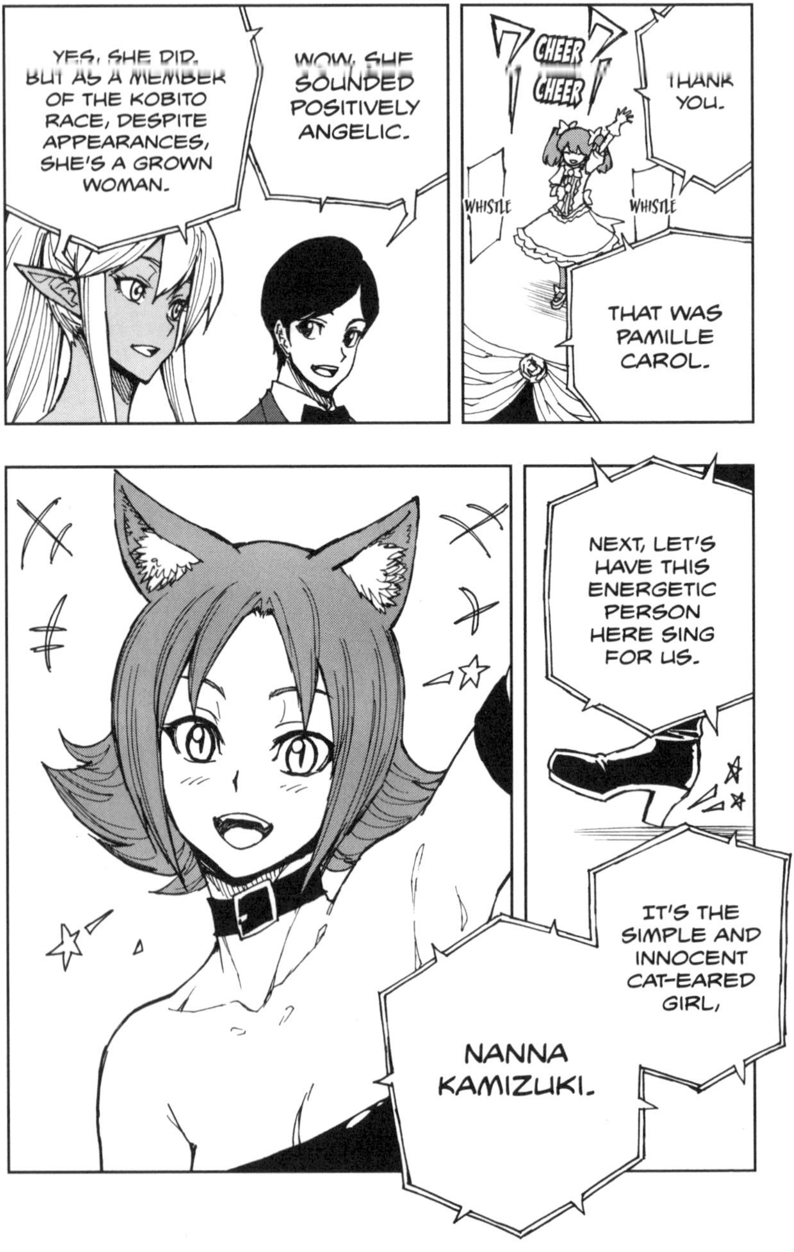

THANK YOU.
CHEER CHEER
WHISTLE
WHISTLE
THAT WAS PAMILLE CAROL.
WOW, SHE SOUNDED POSITIVELY ANGELIC.
YES, SHE DID. BUT AS A MEMBER OF THE KOBITO RACE, DESPITE APPEARANCES, SHE'S A GROWN WOMAN.
NEXT, LET'S HAVE THIS ENERGETIC PERSON HERE SING FOR US.
IT'S THE SIMPLE AND INNOCENT CAT-EARED GIRL,
NANNA KAMIZUKI.

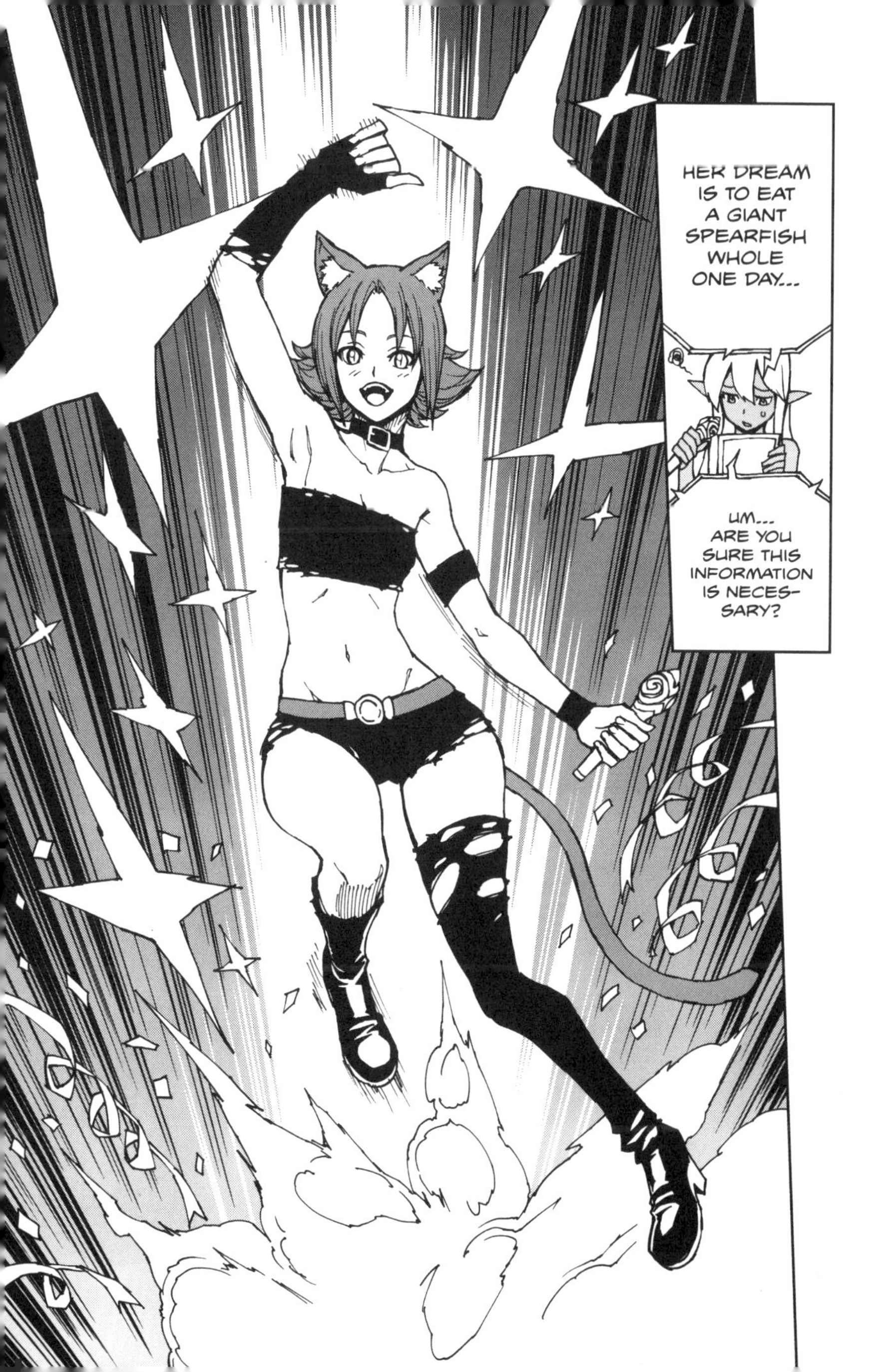
HER DREAM IS TO EAT A GIANT SPEARFISH WHOLE ONE DAY...
UM... ARE YOU SURE THIS INFORMATION IS NECES-SARY?

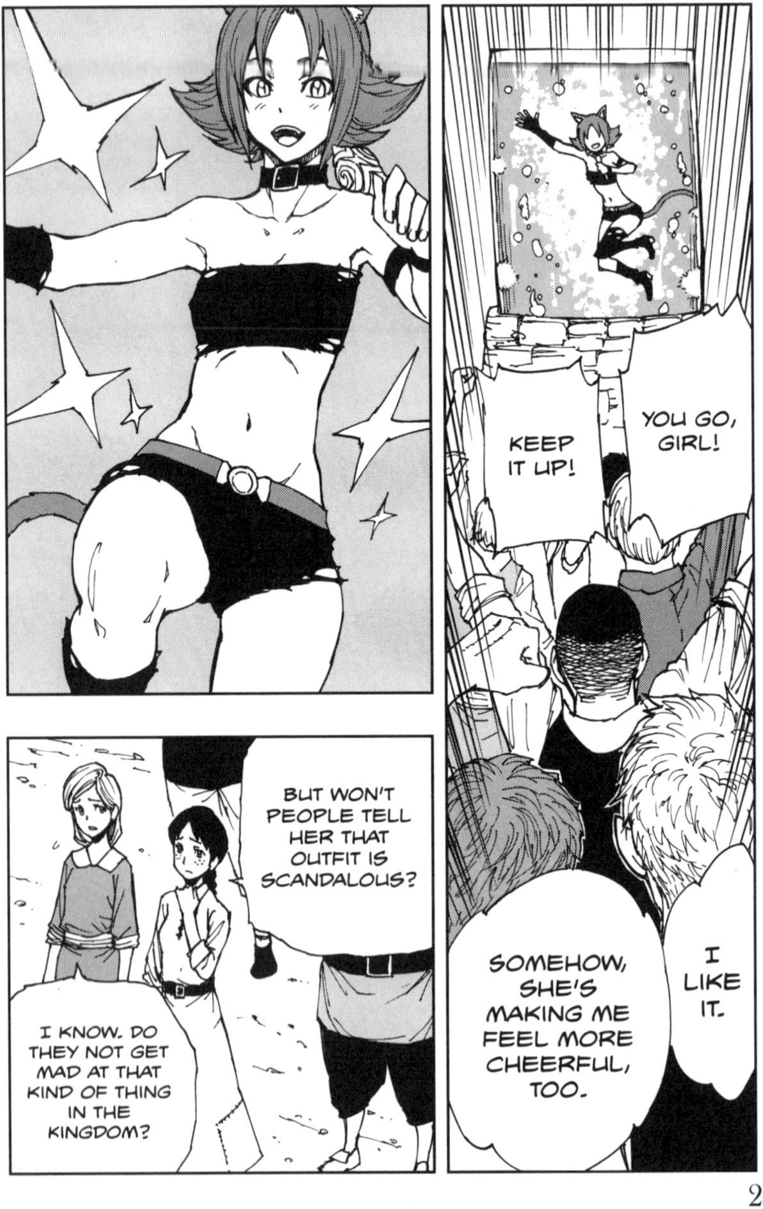
YOU GO, GIRL!
KEEP IT UP!
I LIKE IT.
SOMEHOW, SHE'S MAKING ME FEEL MORE CHEERFUL, TOO.
BUT WON'T PEOPLE TELL HER THAT OUTFIT IS SCANDALOUS?
I KNOW. DO THEY NOT GET MAD AT THAT KIND OF THING IN THE KINGDOM?

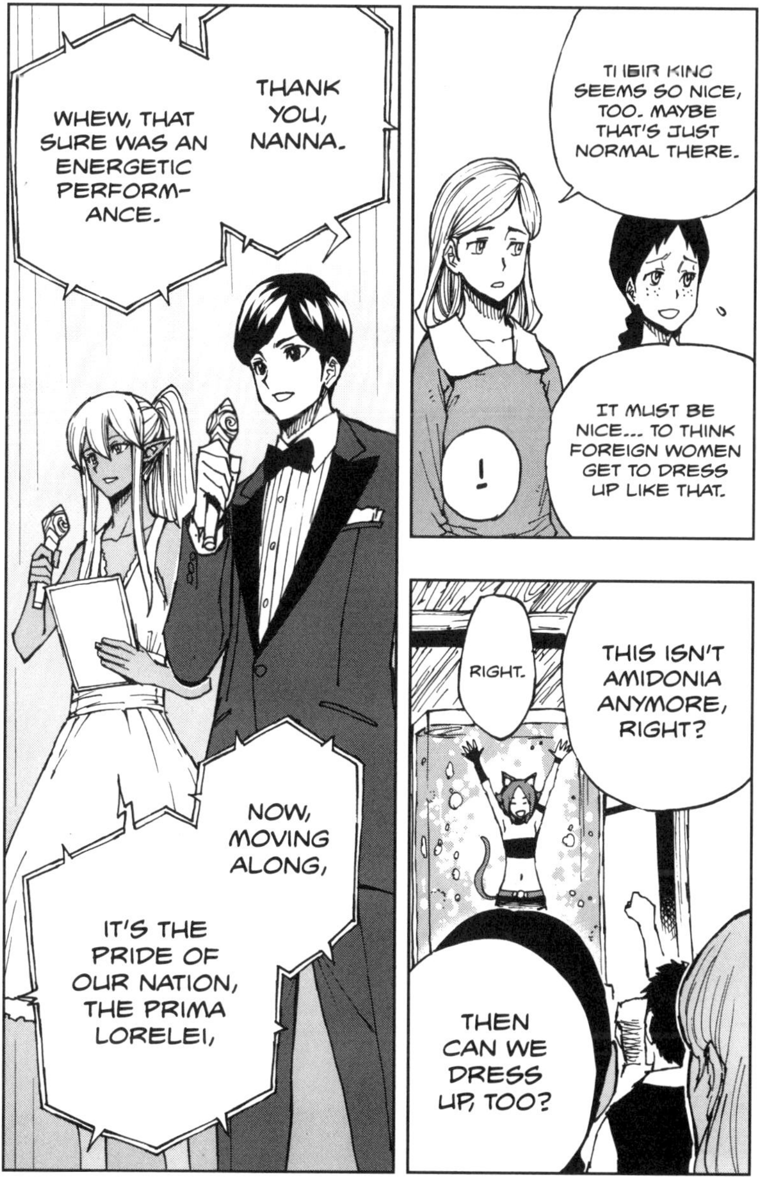
THEIR KING SEEMS SO NICE, TOO. MAYBE THAT'S JUST NORMAL THERE.
!
IT MUST BE NICE... TO THINK FOREIGN WOMEN GET TO DRESS UP LIKE THAT.
THIS ISN'T AMIDONIA ANYMORE, RIGHT?
RIGHT.
THEN CAN WE DRESS UP, TOO?
THANK YOU, NANNA.
WHEW, THAT SURE WAS AN ENERGETIC PERFORMANCE.
NOW, MOVING ALONG,
IT'S THE PRIDE OF OUR NATION, THE PRIMA LORELEI,

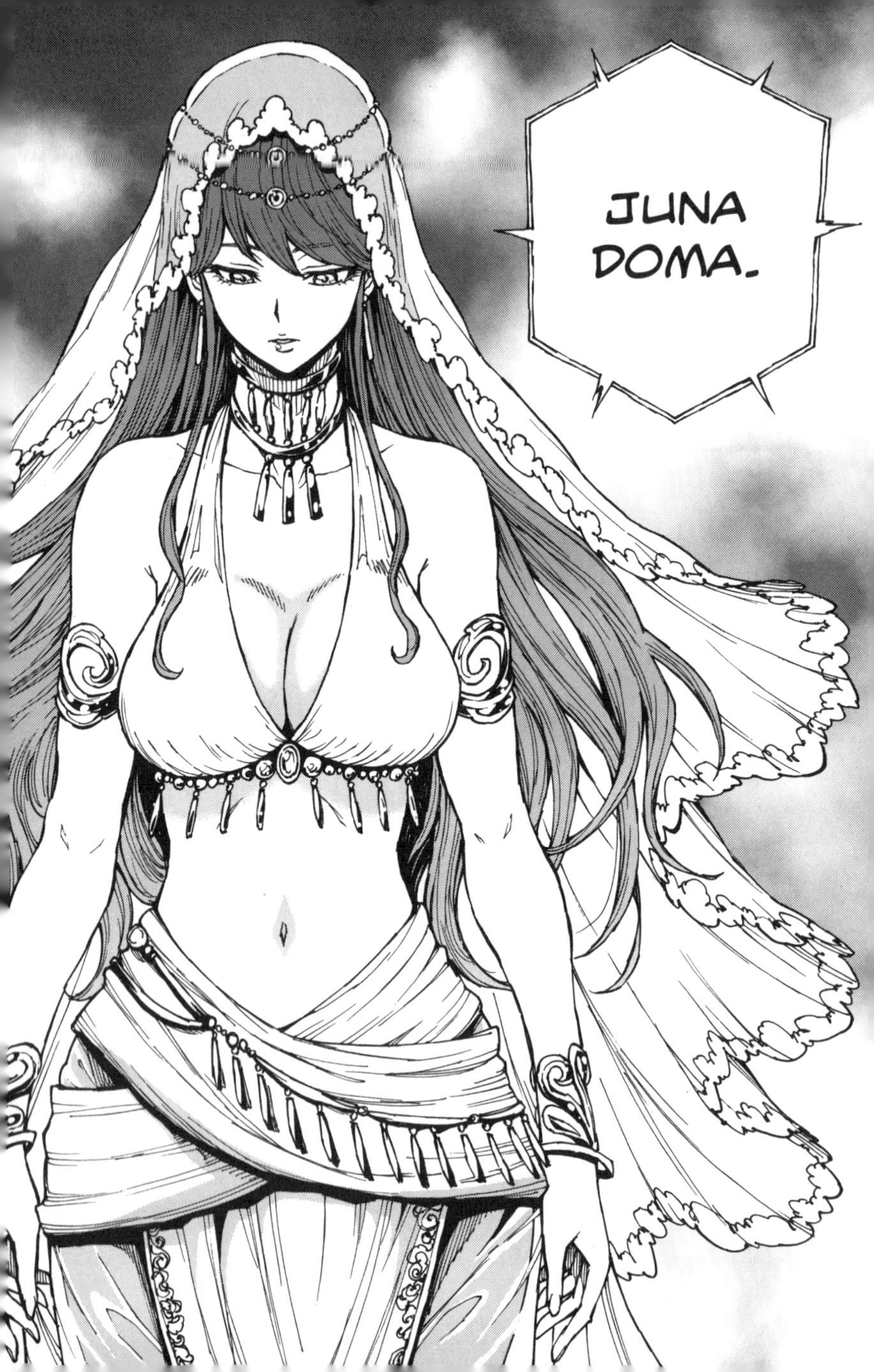
JUNA DOMA.

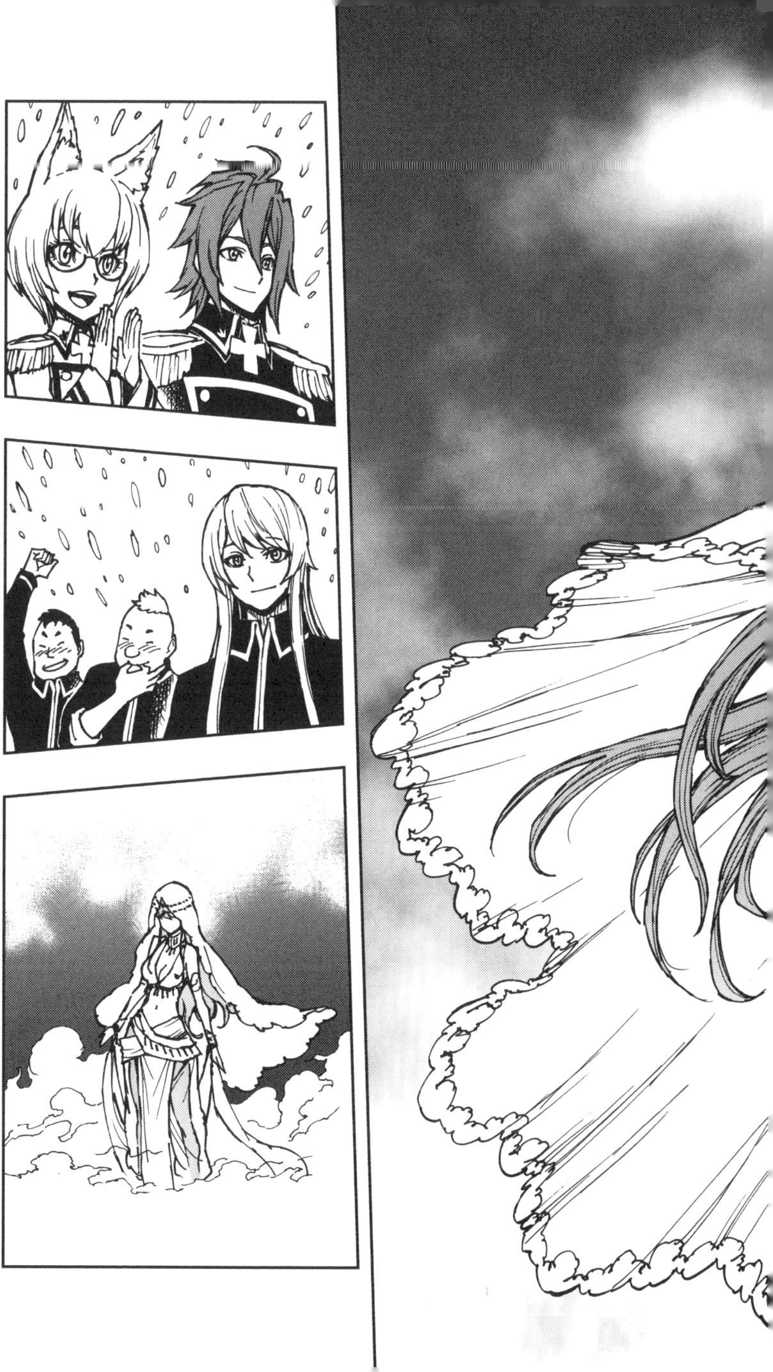

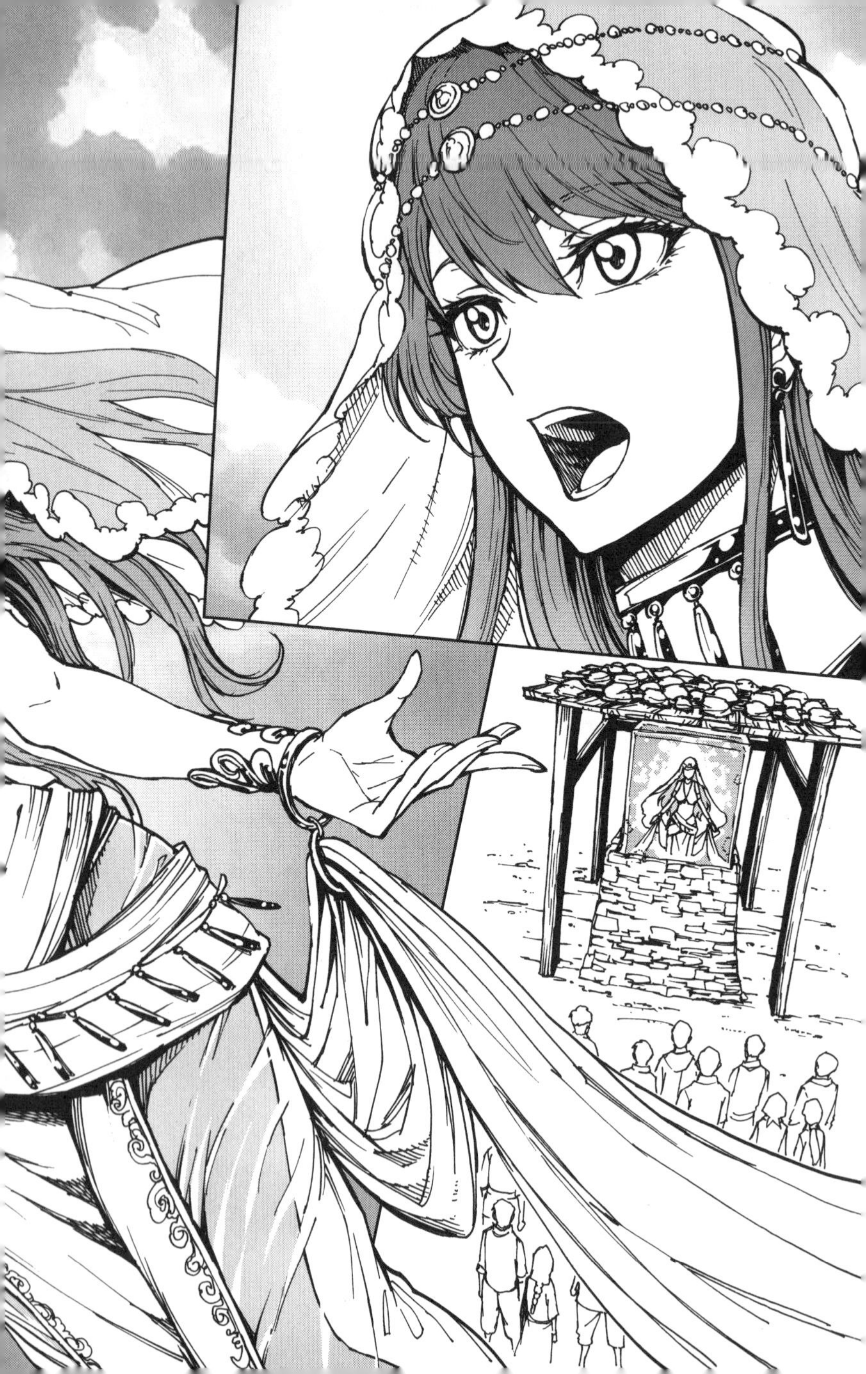

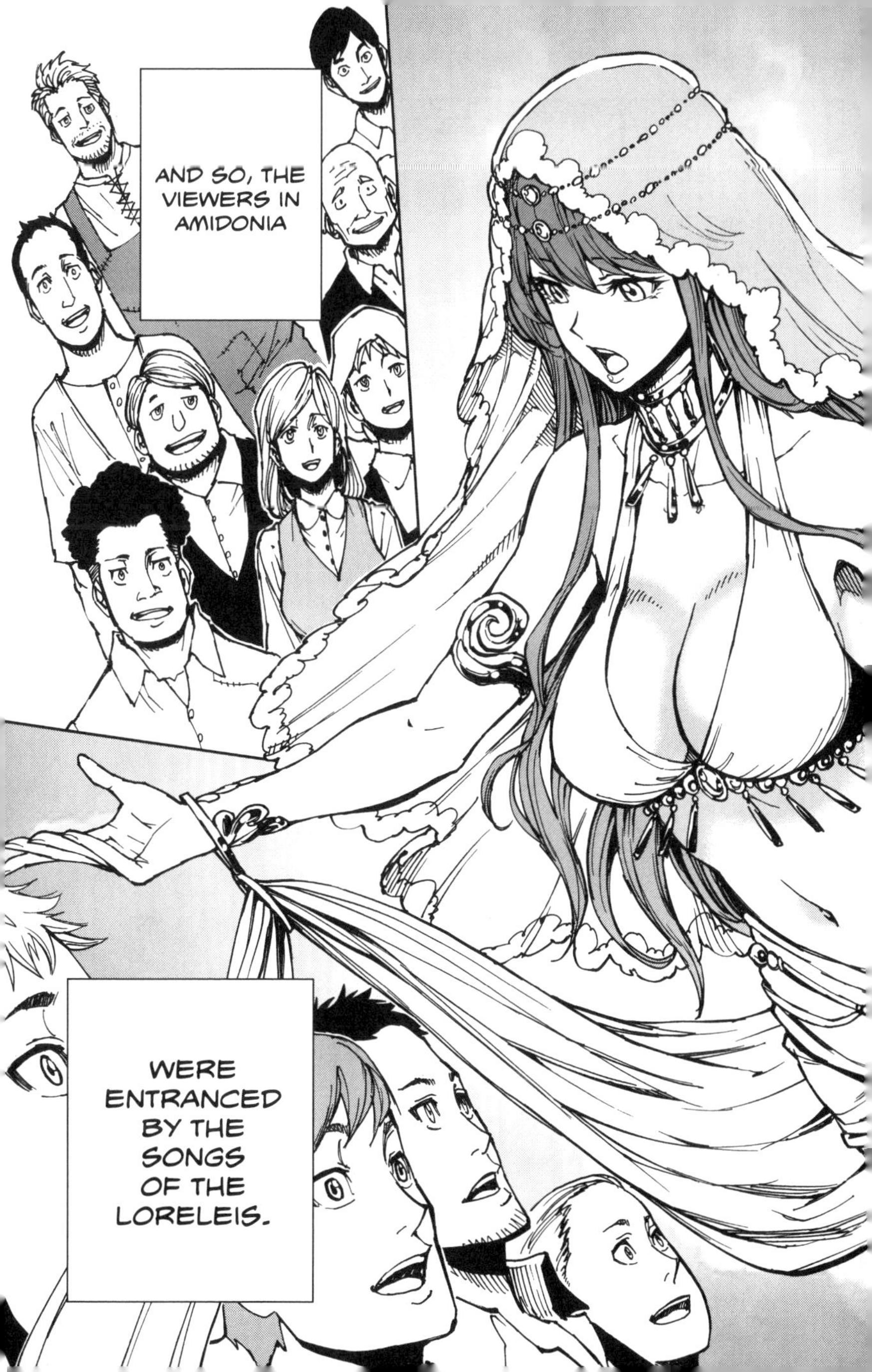
AND SO, THE VIEWERS IN AMIDONIA
WERE ENTRANCED BY THE SONGS OF THE LORELEIS.

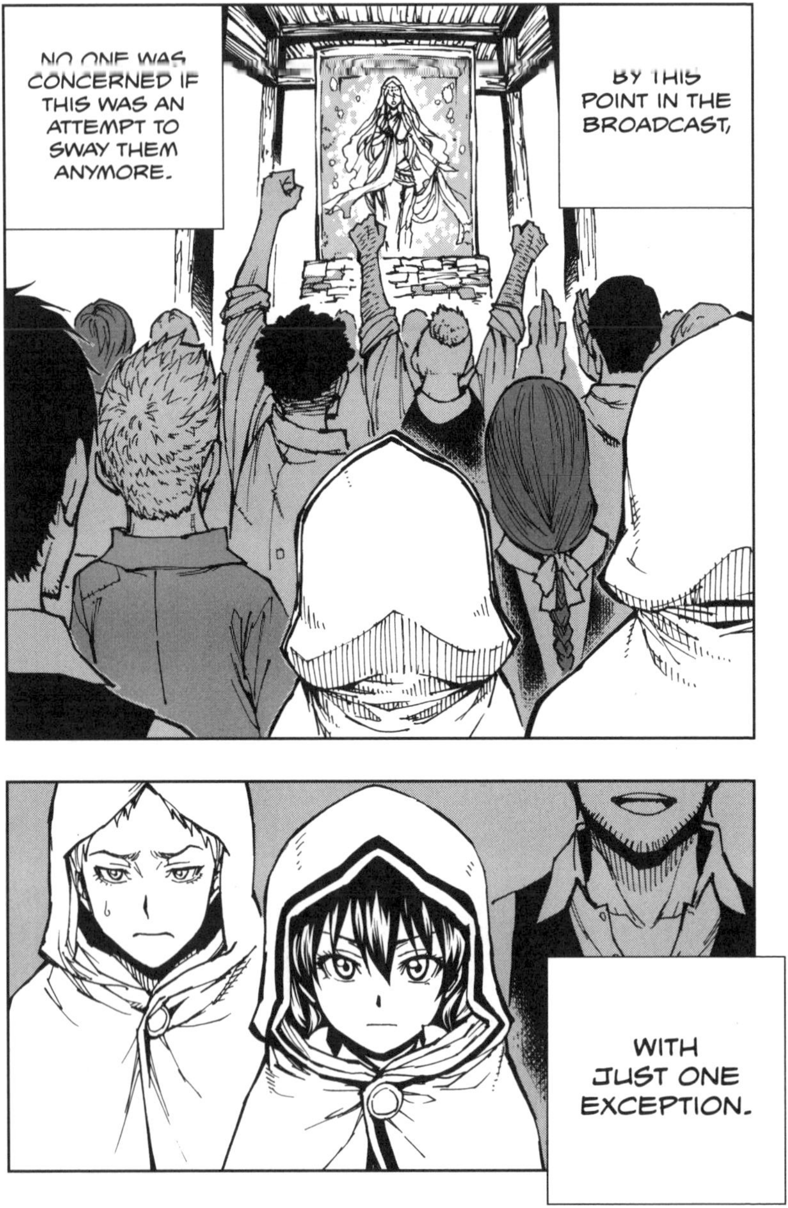
BY THIS POINT IN THE BROADCAST,
NO ONE WAS CONCERNED IF THIS WAS AN ATTEMPT TO SWAY THEM ANYMORE.
WITH JUST ONE EXCEPTION.

Chapter 30: Project Lorelei (2)

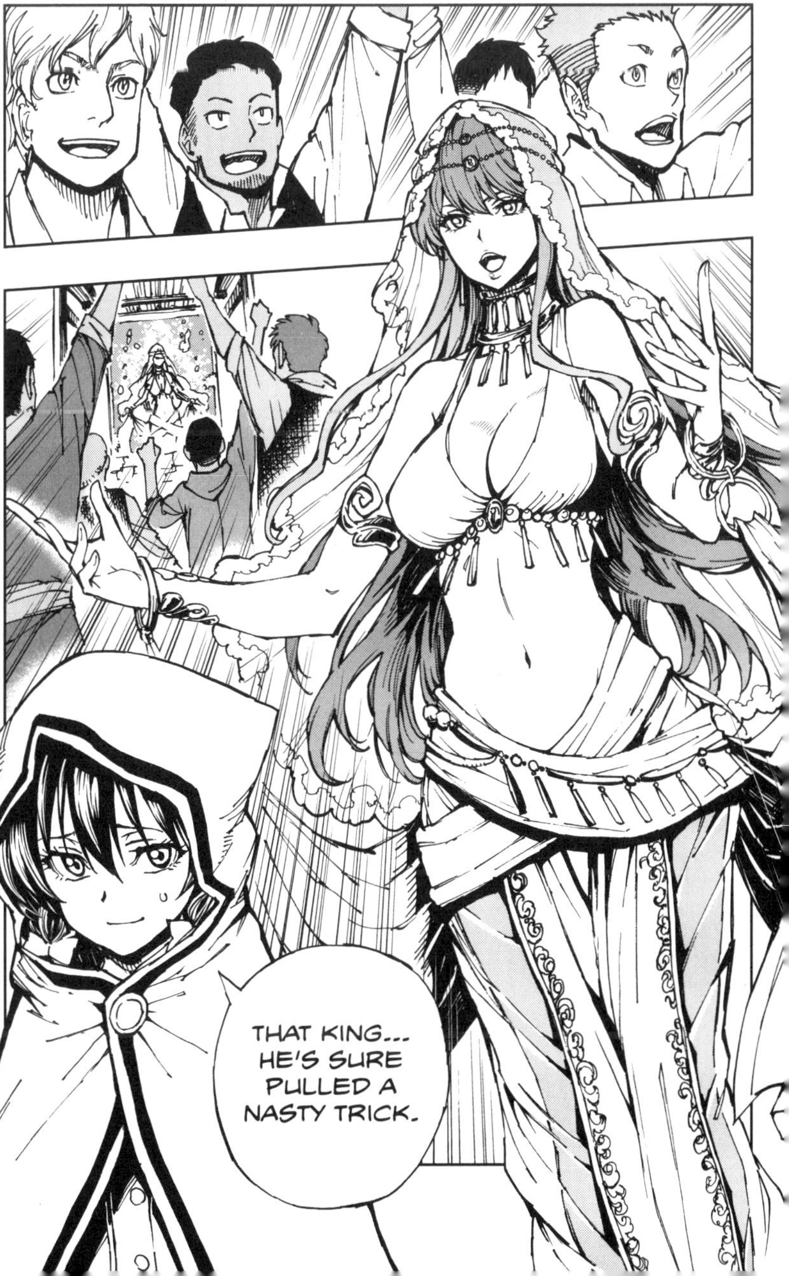
THAT KING... HE'S SURE PULLED A NASTY TRICK.

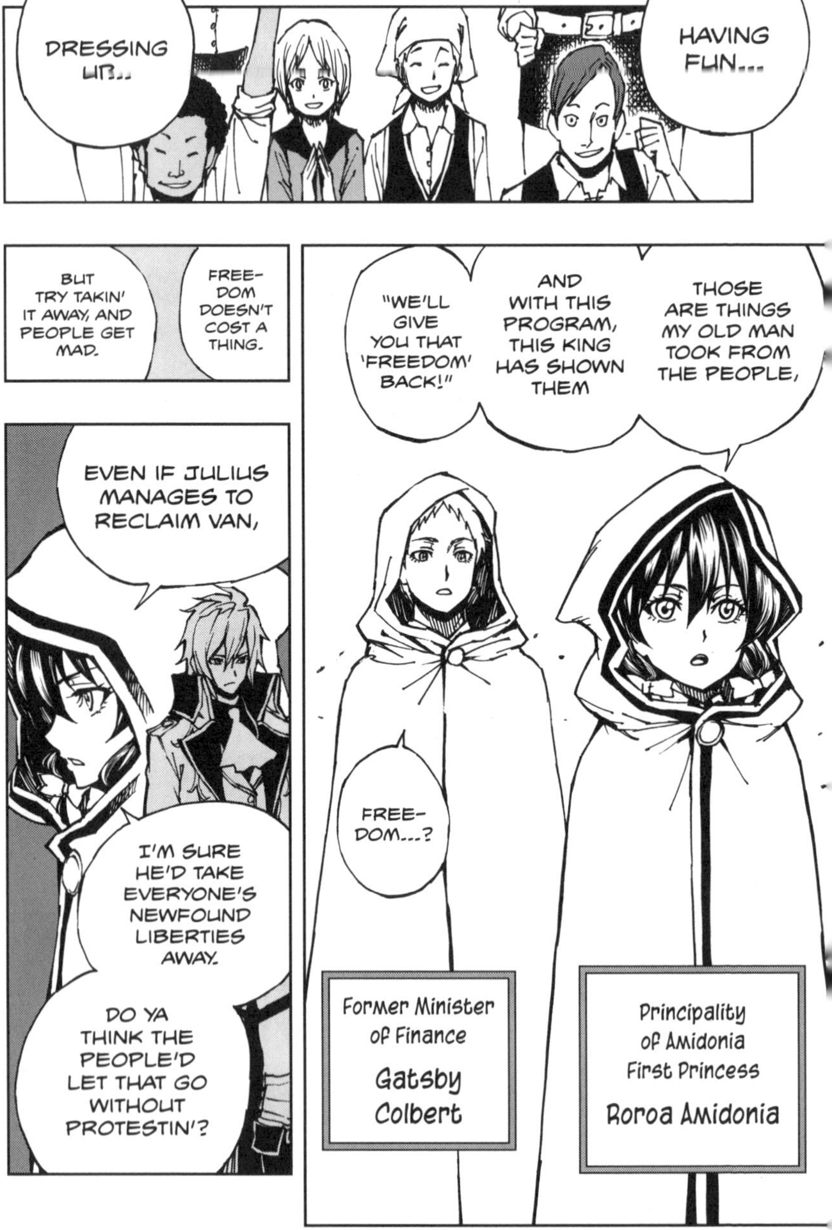
HAVING FUN...
DRESSING UP...
THOSE ARE THINGS MY OLD MAN TOOK FROM THE PEOPLE,
AND WITH THIS PROGRAM, THIS KING HAS SHOWN THEM
"WE'LL GIVE YOU THAT 'FREEDOM' BACK!"
FREE-DOM...?
Principality of Amidonia First Princess
Roroa Amidonia
Former Minister of Finance
Gatsby Colbert
FREE-DOM DOESN'T COST A THING.
BUT TRY TAKIN' IT AWAY, AND PEOPLE GET MAD.
EVEN IF JULIUS MANAGES TO RECLAIM VAN,
I'M SURE HE'D TAKE EVERYONE'S NEWFOUND LIBERTIES AWAY.
DO YA THINK THE PEOPLE'D LET THAT GO WITHOUT PROTESTIN'?

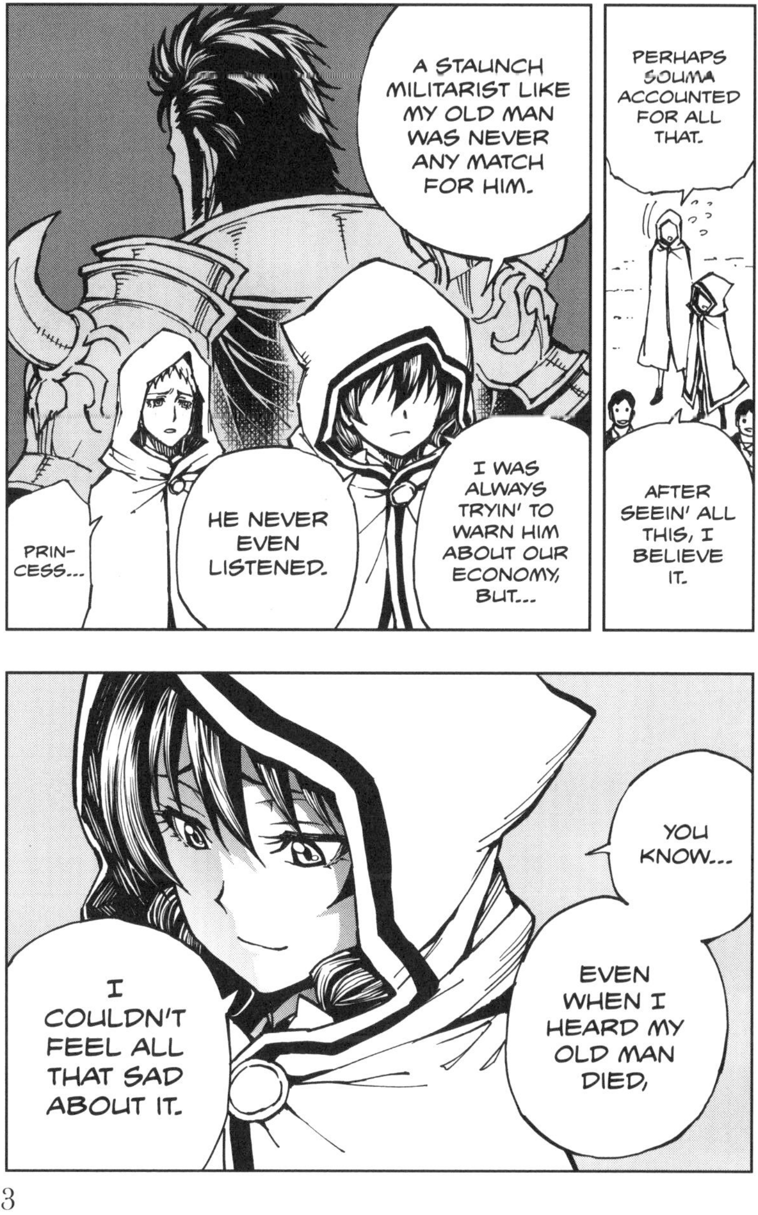
PERHAPS SOUMA ACCOUNTED FOR ALL THAT.
AFTER SEEIN' ALL THIS, I BELIEVE IT.
A STAUNCH MILITARIST LIKE MY OLD MAN WAS NEVER ANY MATCH FOR HIM.
I WAS ALWAYS TRYIN' TO WARN HIM ABOUT OUR ECONOMY, BUT...
HE NEVER EVEN LISTENED.
PRIN-CESS...
YOU KNOW...
EVEN WHEN I HEARD MY OLD MAN DIED,
I COULDN'T FEEL ALL THAT SAD ABOUT IT.

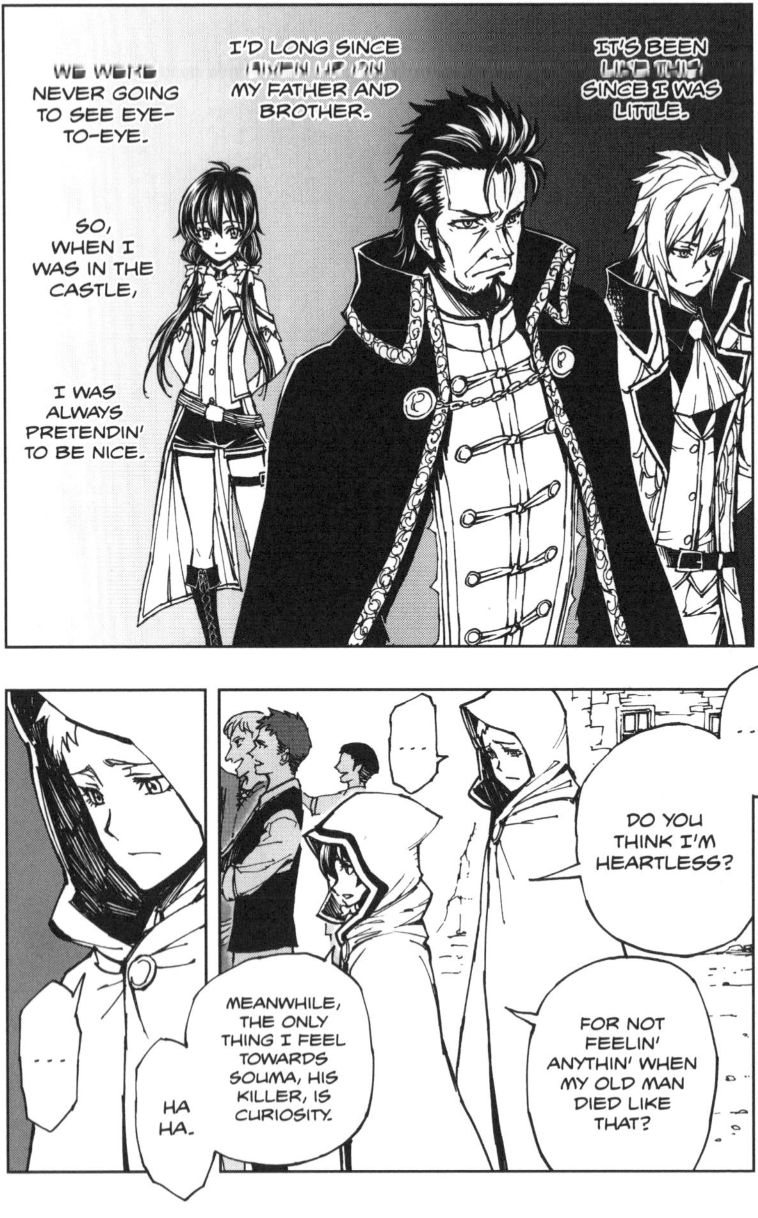
IT'S BEEN LIKE THIS SINCE I WAS LITTLE.
I'D LONG SINCE GIVEN UP ON MY FATHER AND BROTHER.
WE WERE NEVER GOING TO SEE EYE-TO-EYE.
SO, WHEN I WAS IN THE CASTLE,
I WAS ALWAYS PRETENDIN' TO BE NICE.
...
...
DO YOU THINK I'M HEARTLESS?
FOR NOT FEELIN' ANYTHIN' WHEN MY OLD MAN DIED LIKE THAT?
MEANWHILE, THE ONLY THING I FEEL TOWARDS SOUMA, HIS KILLER, IS CURIOSITY.
...
HA HA.

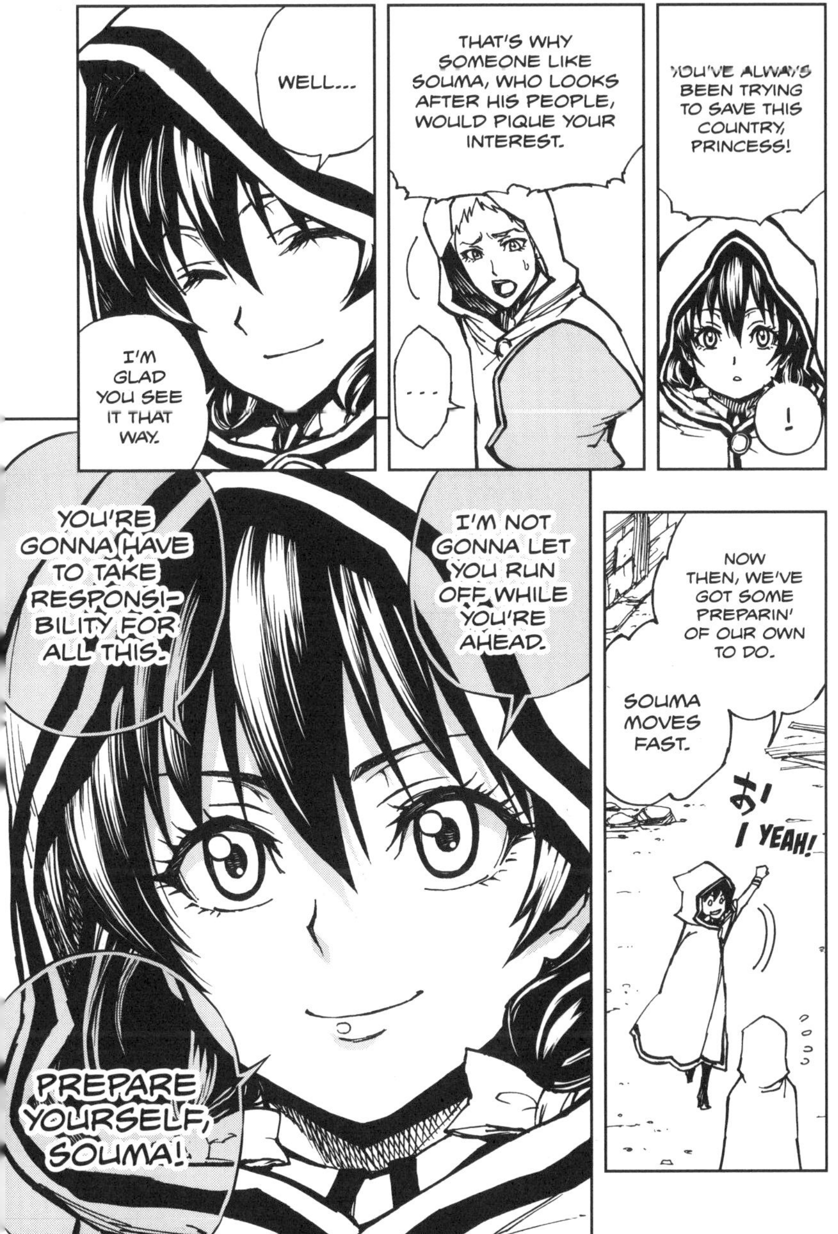
YOU'VE ALWAYS BEEN TRYING TO SAVE THIS COUNTRY, PRINCESS!
!
THAT'S WHY SOMEONE LIKE SOUMA, WHO LOOKS AFTER HIS PEOPLE, WOULD PIQUE YOUR INTEREST.
...
WELL...
I'M GLAD YOU SEE IT THAT WAY.
NOW THEN, WE'VE GOT SOME PREPARIN' OF OUR OWN TO DO.
SOUMA MOVES FAST.
I YEAH!
I'M NOT GONNA LET YOU RUN OFF WHILE YOU'RE AHEAD.
YOU'RE GONNA HAVE TO TAKE RESPONSI-BILITY FOR ALL THIS.
PREPARE YOURSELF, SOUMA!

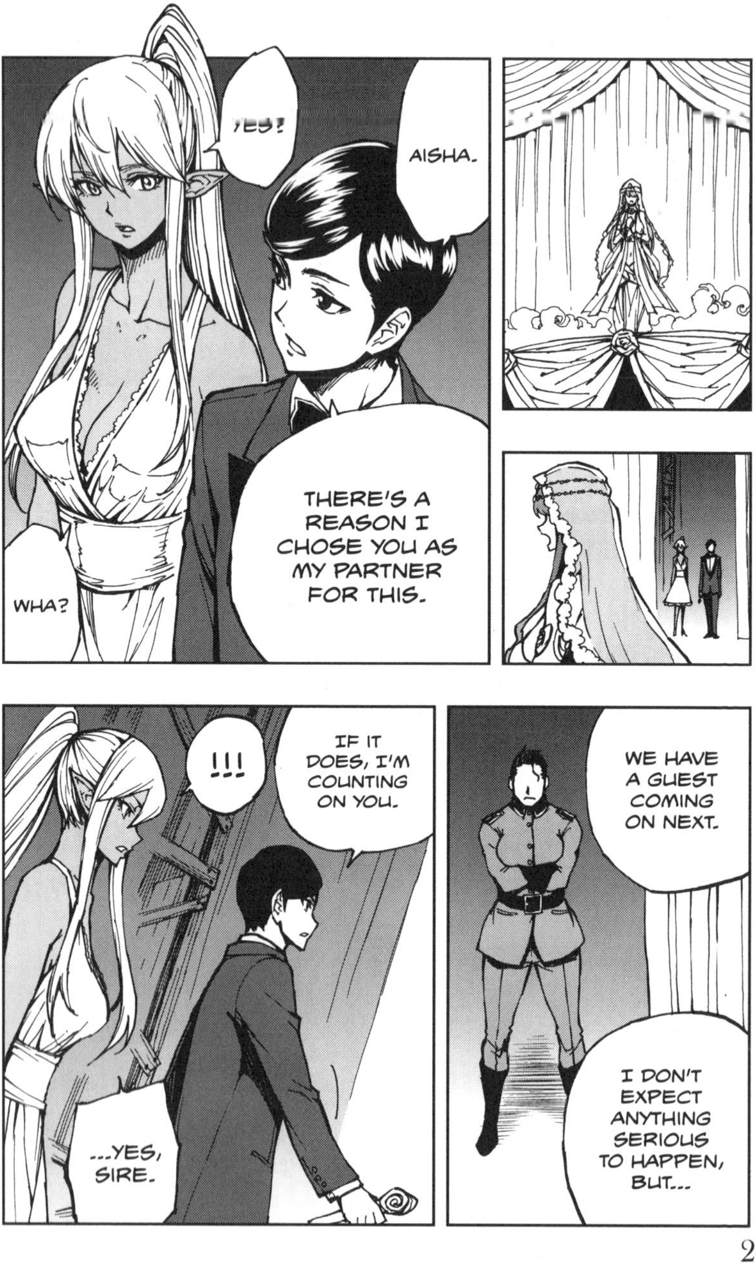
AISHA.
YES?
THERE'S A REASON I CHOSE YOU AS MY PARTNER FOR THIS.
WHA?
WE HAVE A GUEST COMING ON NEXT.
I DON'T EXPECT ANYTHING SERIOUS TO HAPPEN, BUT...
IF IT DOES, I'M COUNTING ON YOU.
!!!
...YES, SIRE.

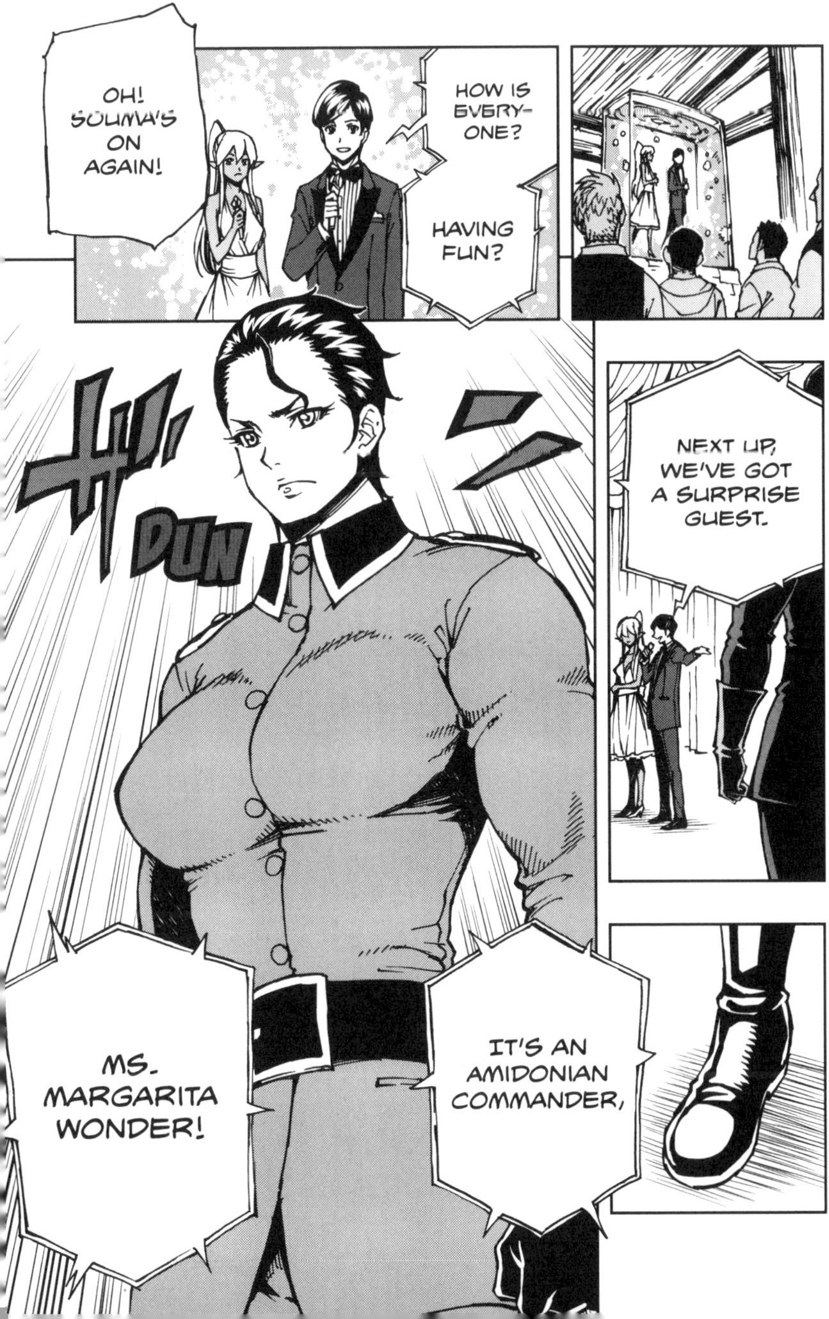
OH! SOUMA'S ON AGAIN!
HOW IS EVERY-ONE?
HAVING FUN?
NEXT UP, WE'VE GOT A SURPRISE GUEST.
ザッ
DUN
IT'S AN AMIDONIAN COMMANDER,
MS. MARGARITA WONDER!

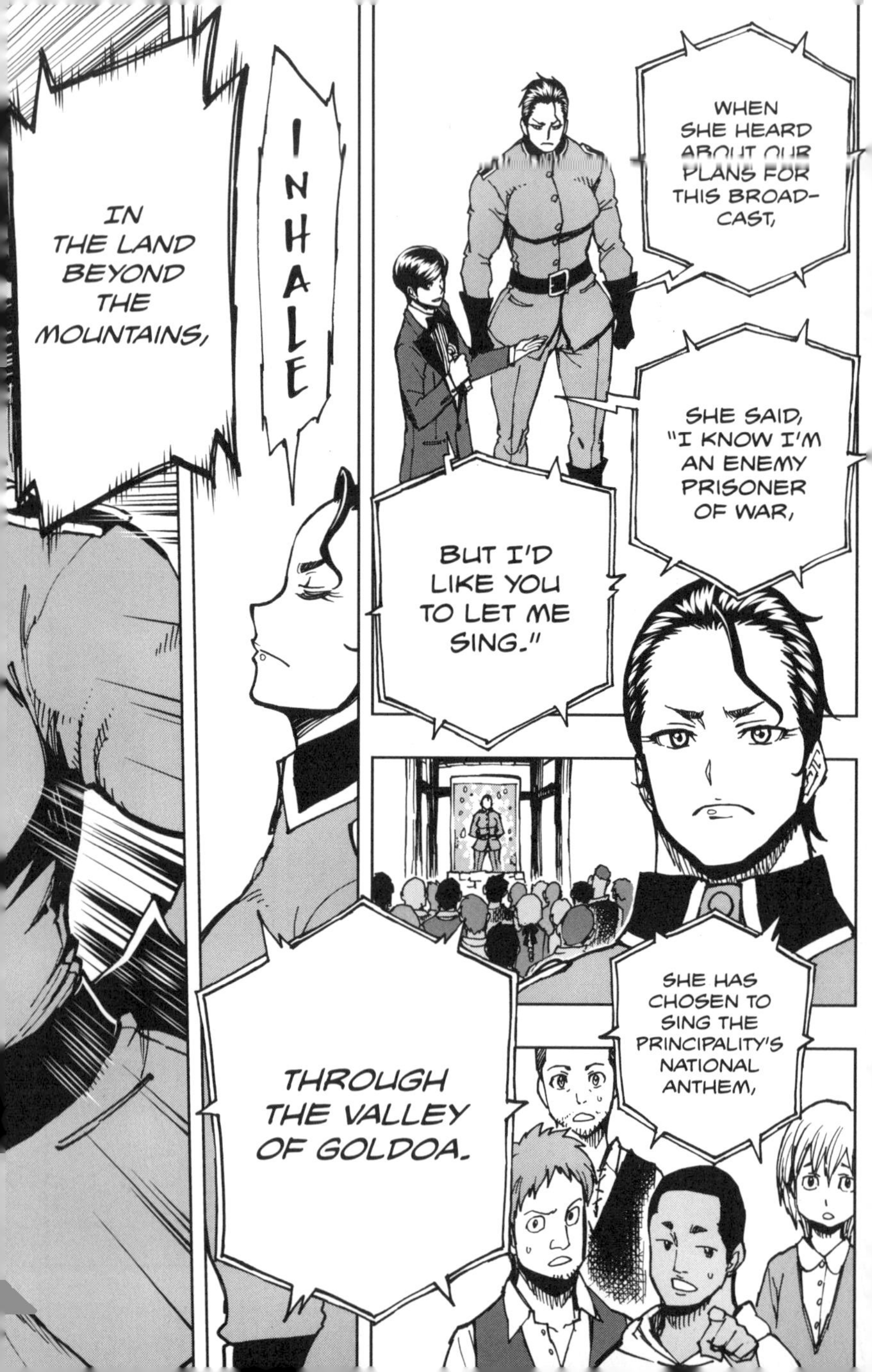
WHEN SHE HEARD ABOUT OUR PLANS FOR THIS BROAD-CAST,
SHE SAID, "I KNOW I'M AN ENEMY PRISONER OF WAR,
BUT I'D LIKE YOU TO LET ME SING."
SHE HAS CHOSEN TO SING THE PRINCIPALITY'S NATIONAL ANTHEM,
INHALE
IN THE LAND BEYOND THE MOUNTAINS,
THROUGH THE VALLEY OF GOLDOA.

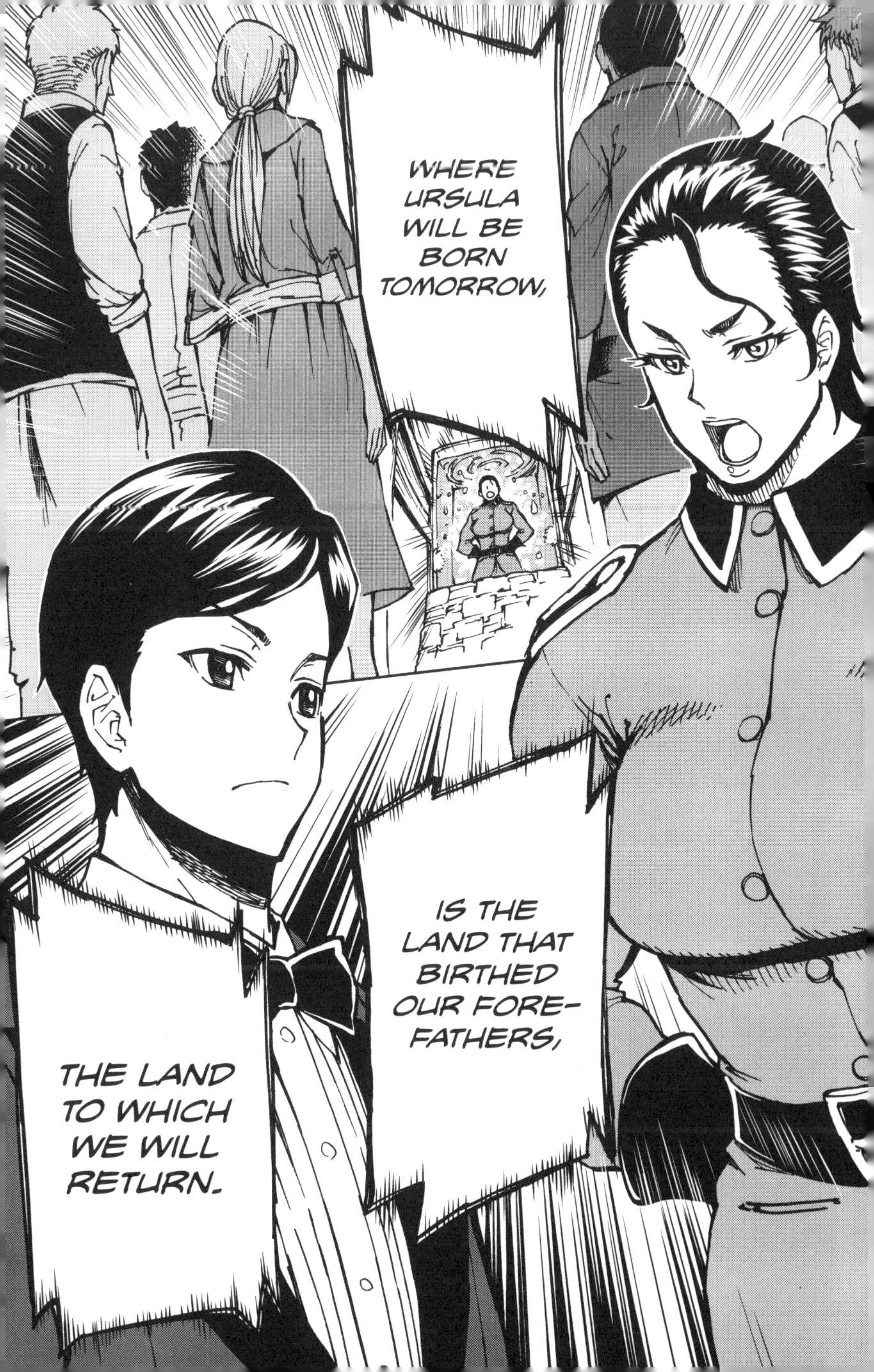
WHERE URSULA WILL BE BORN TOMORROW,
IS THE LAND THAT BIRTHED OUR FORE-FATHERS,
THE LAND TO WHICH WE WILL RETURN.

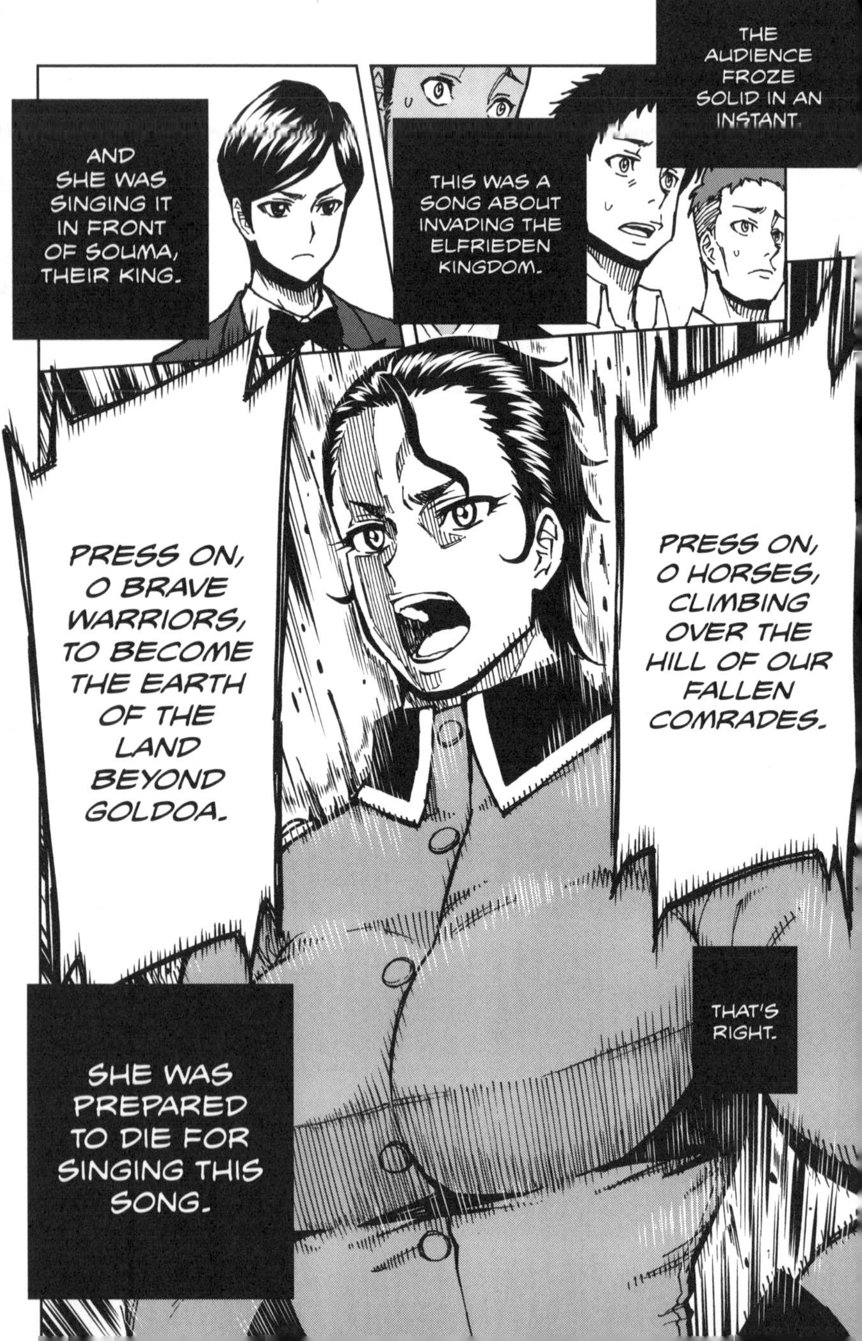
THE AUDIENCE FROZE SOLID IN AN INSTANT.
THIS WAS A SONG ABOUT INVADING THE ELFRIEDEN KINGDOM.
AND SHE WAS SINGING IT IN FRONT OF SOUMA, THEIR KING.
PRESS ON, O HORSES, CLIMBING OVER THE HILL OF OUR FALLEN COMRADES.
PRESS ON, O BRAVE WARRIORS, TO BECOME THE EARTH OF THE LAND BEYOND GOLDOA.
THAT'S RIGHT.
SHE WAS PREPARED TO DIE FOR SINGING THIS SONG.

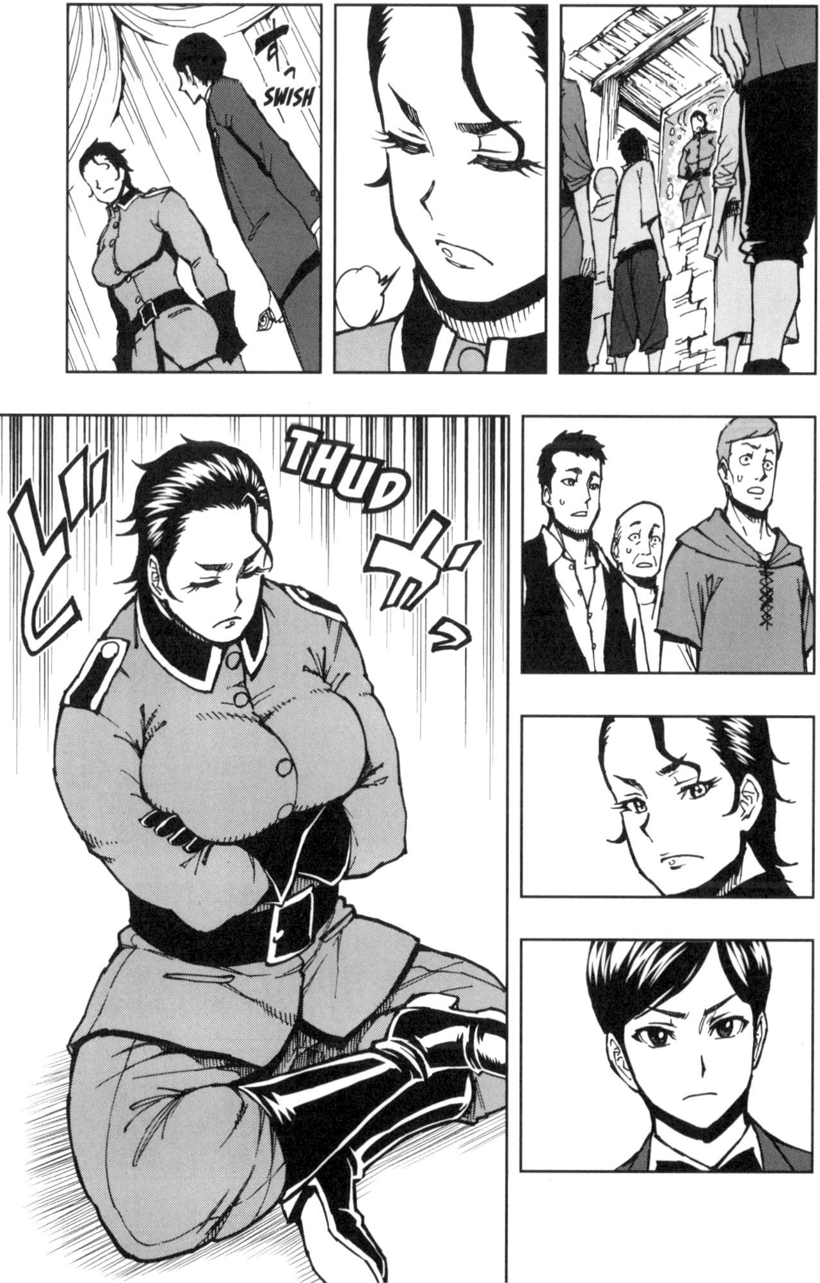
SWISH
THUD

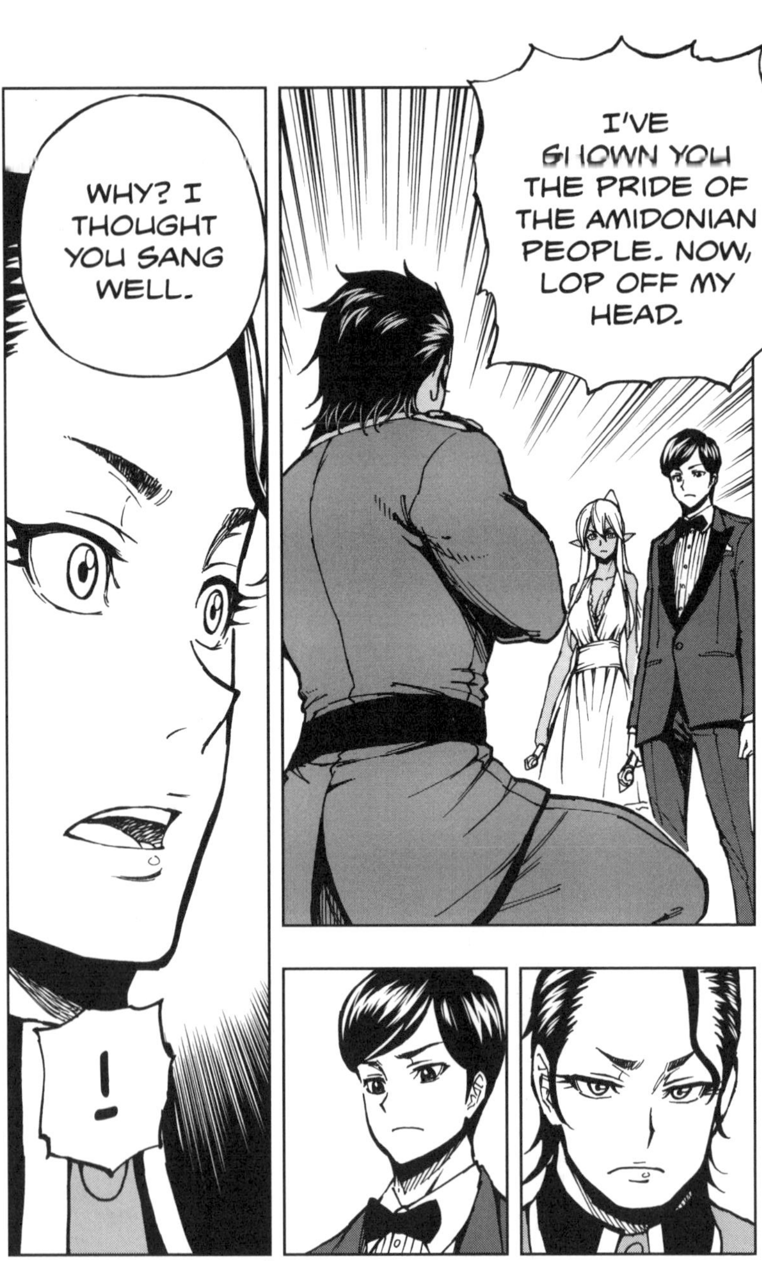
I'VE SHOWN YOU THE PRIDE OF THE AMIDONIAN PEOPLE. NOW, LOP OFF MY HEAD.
WHY? I THOUGHT YOU SANG WELL.
!

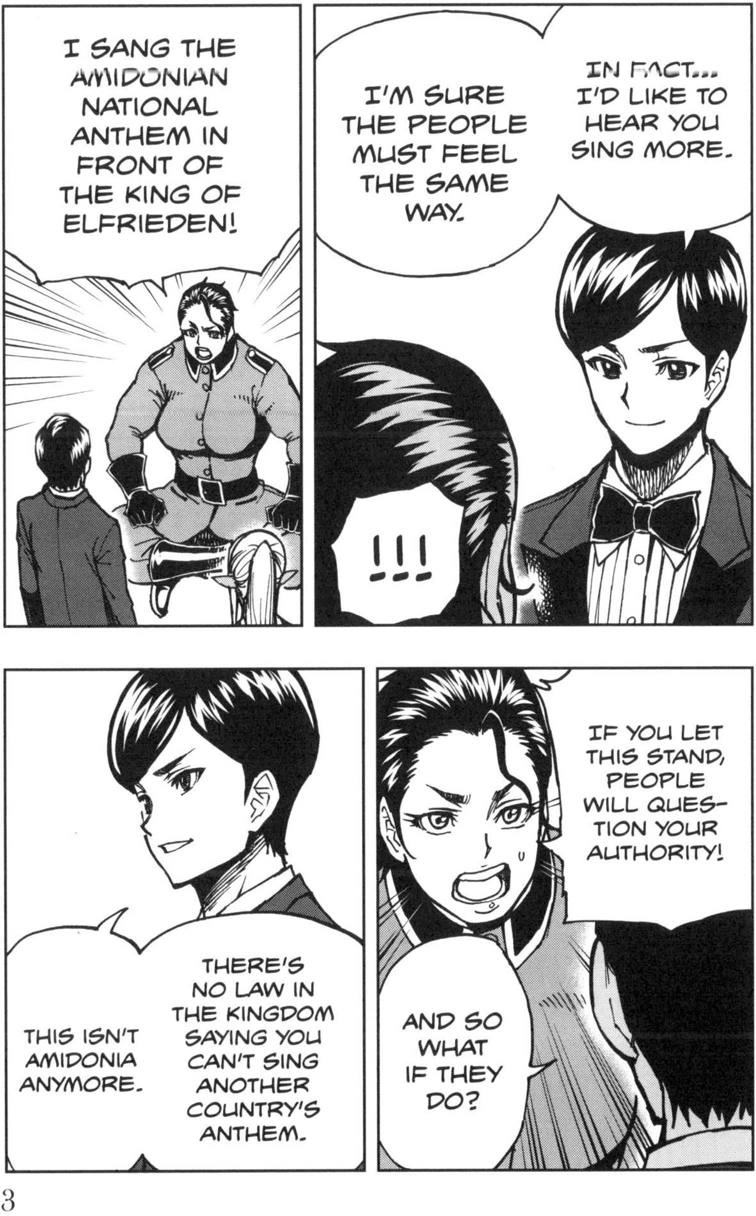
I'M SURE THE PEOPLE MUST FEEL THE SAME WAY. IN FACT... I'D LIKE TO HEAR YOU SING MORE.
!!!
I SANG THE AMIDONIAN NATIONAL ANTHEM IN FRONT OF THE KING OF ELFRIEDEN!
IF YOU LET THIS STAND, PEOPLE WILL QUES-TION YOUR AUTHORITY!
AND SO WHAT IF THEY DO?
THIS ISN'T AMIDONIA ANYMORE. THERE'S NO LAW IN THE KINGDOM SAYING YOU CAN'T SING ANOTHER COUNTRY'S ANTHEM.

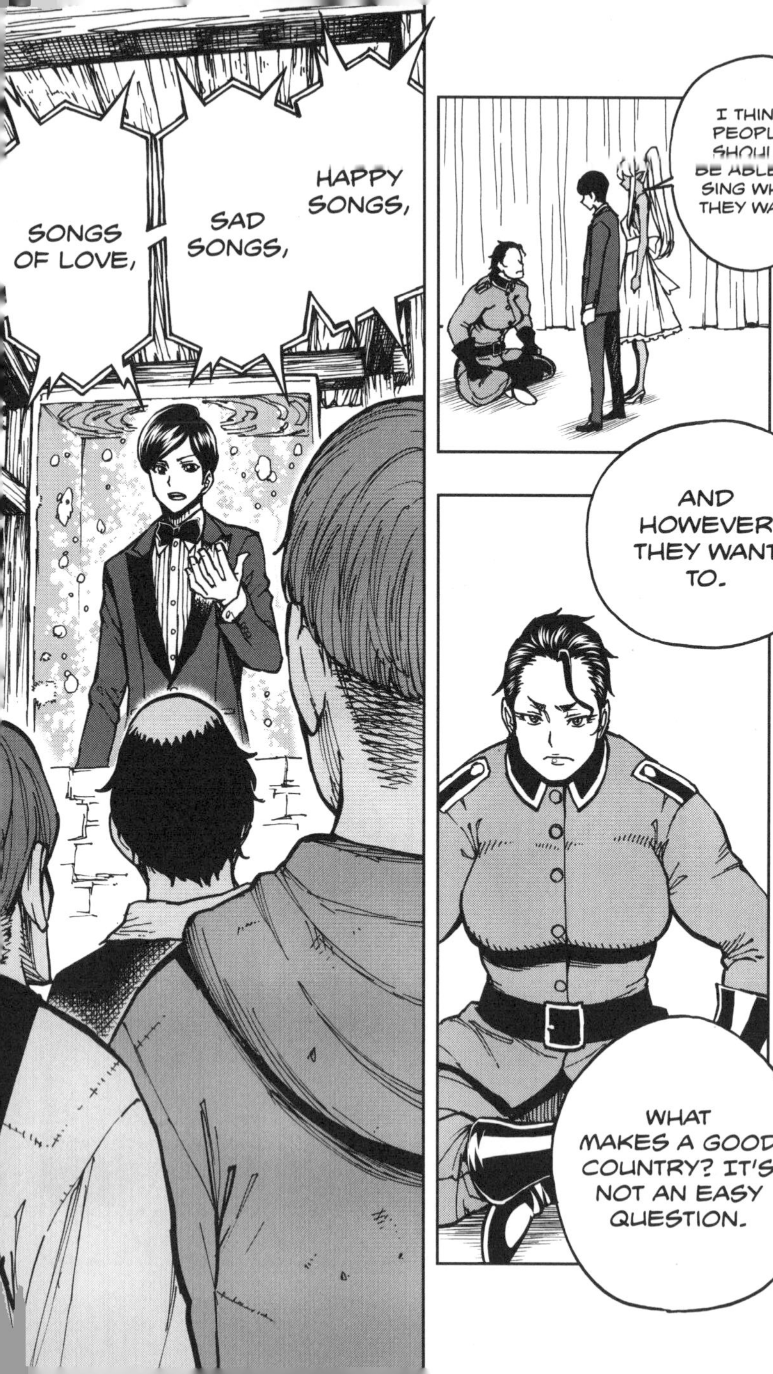
HAPPY SONGS,
SAD SONGS,
SONGS OF LOVE,
I THINK PEOPLE SHOULD BE ABLE TO SING WHAT THEY WANT,
AND HOWEVER THEY WANT TO.
WHAT MAKES A GOOD COUNTRY? IT'S NOT AN EASY QUESTION.

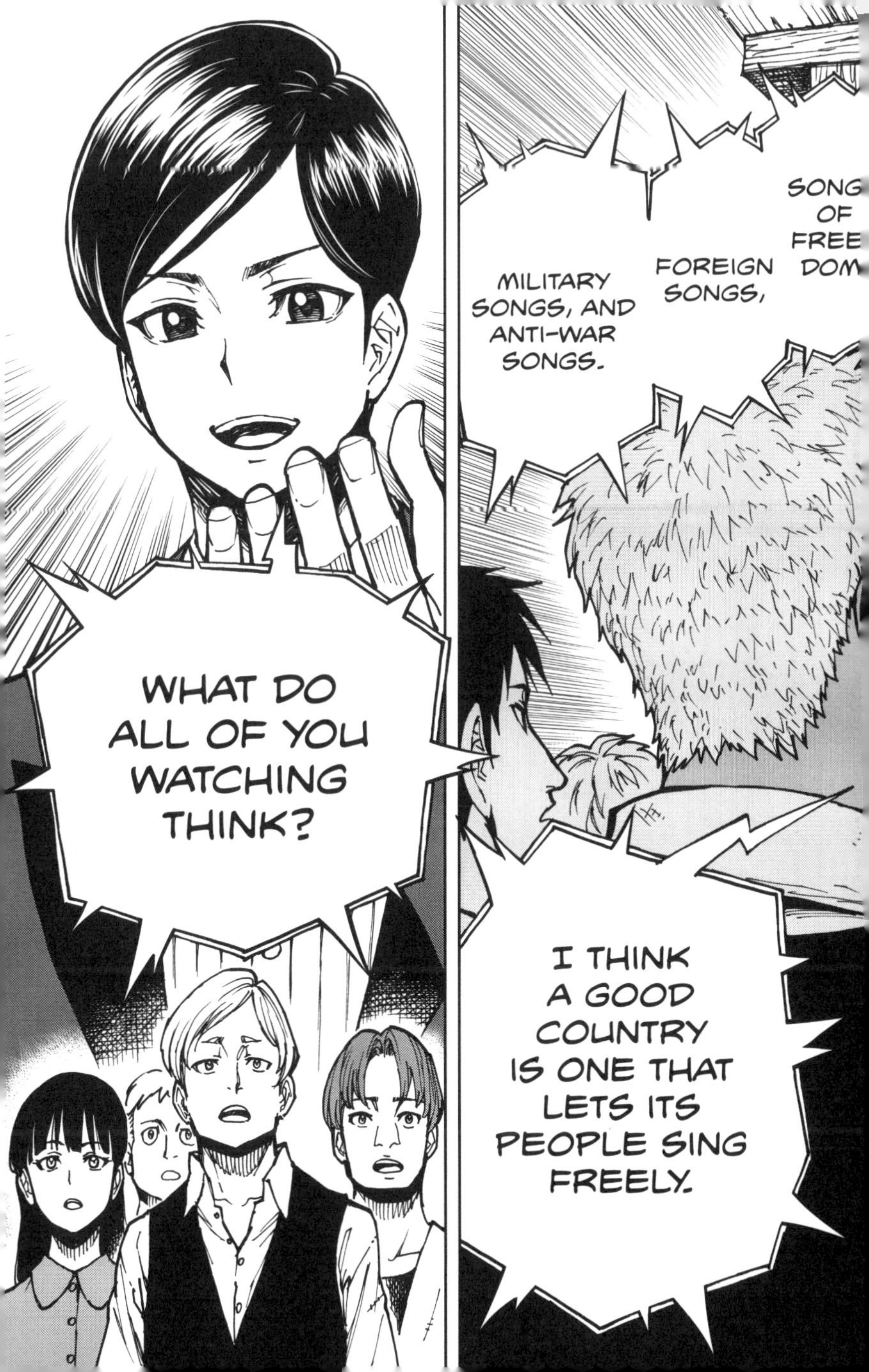
SONG OF FREEDOM
FOREIGN SONGS,
MILITARY SONGS, AND ANTI-WAR SONGS.
I THINK A GOOD COUNTRY IS ONE THAT LETS ITS PEOPLE SING FREELY.
WHAT DO ALL OF YOU WATCHING THINK?

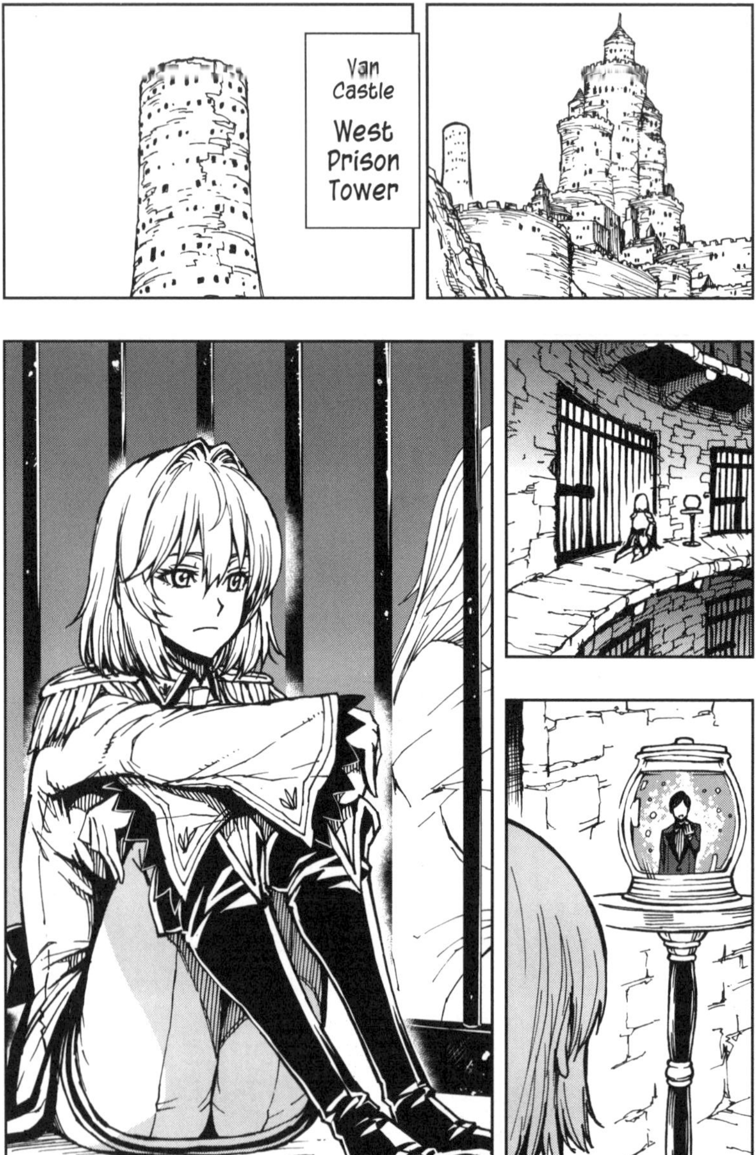
Van Castle
West Prison Tower

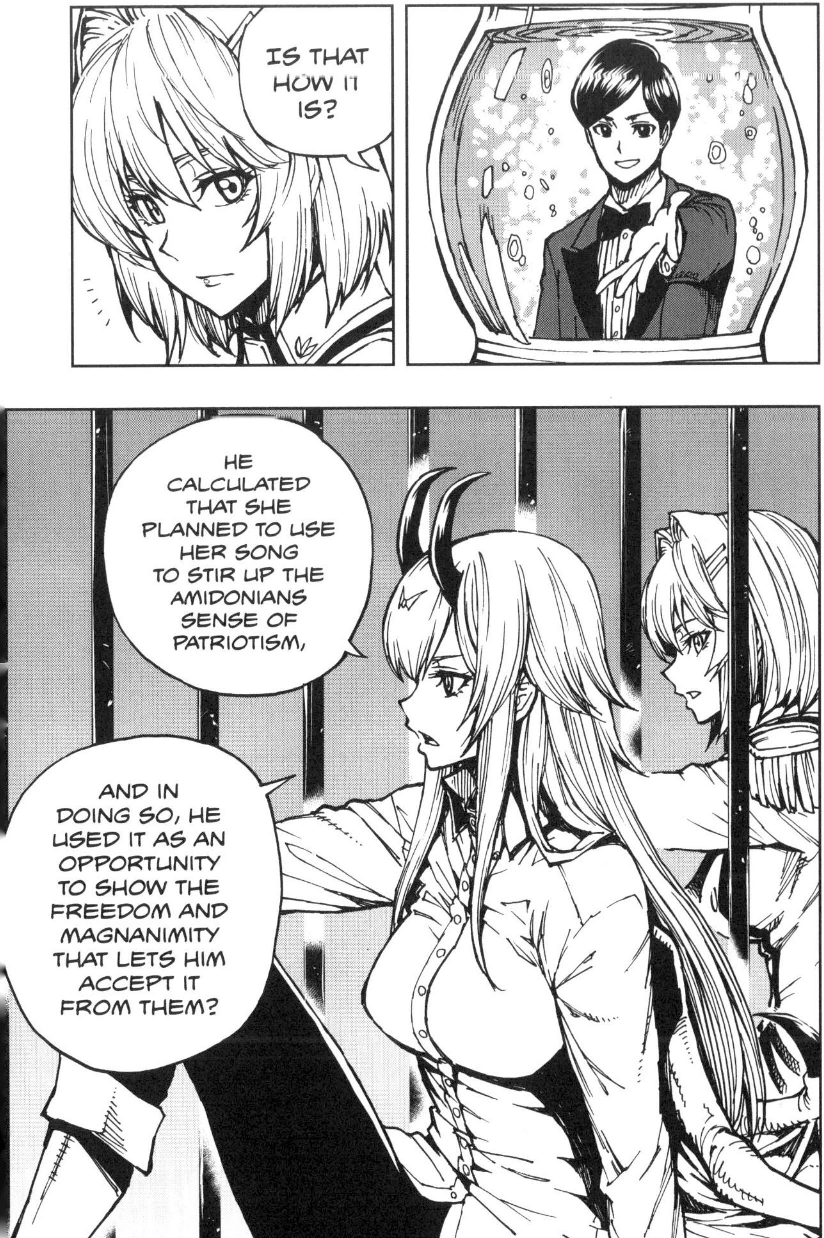
IS THAT HOW IT IS?
HE CALCULATED THAT SHE PLANNED TO USE HER SONG TO STIR UP THE AMIDONIANS SENSE OF PATRIOTISM,
AND IN DOING SO, HE USED IT AS AN OPPORTUNITY TO SHOW THE FREEDOM AND MAGNANIMITY THAT LETS HIM ACCEPT IT FROM THEM?

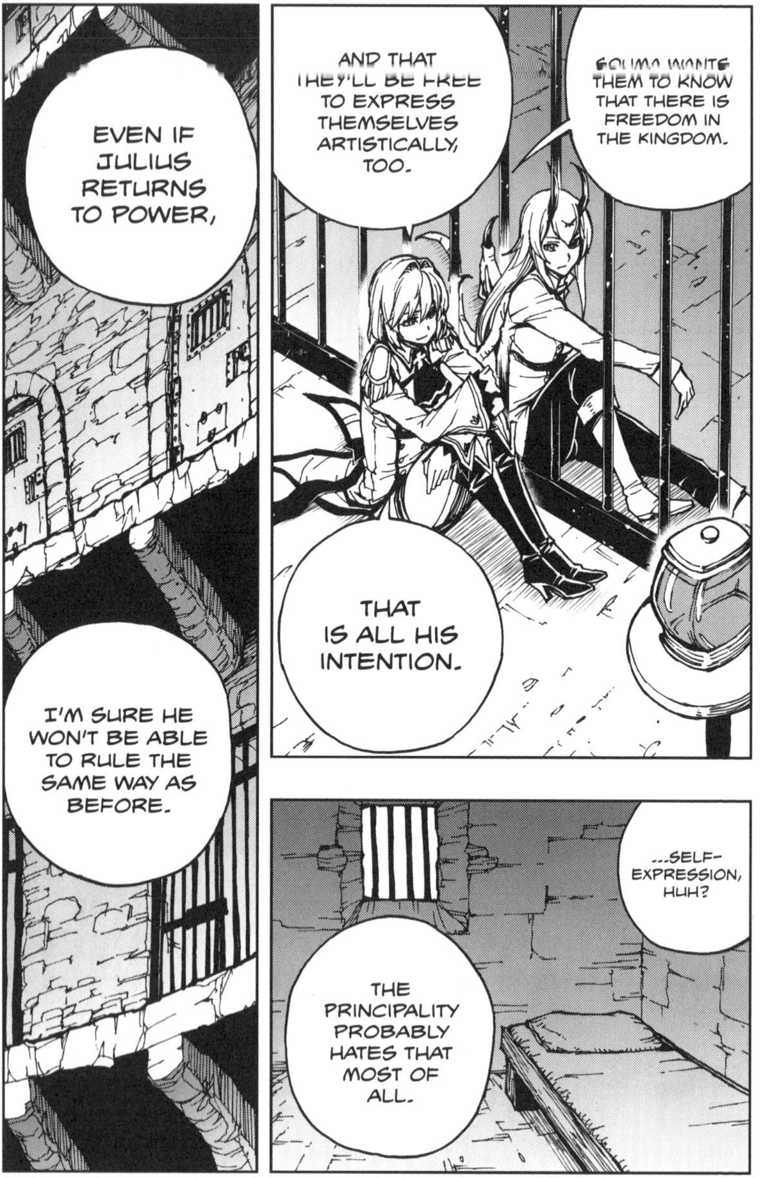
SOUMA WANTS THEM TO KNOW THAT THERE IS FREEDOM IN THE KINGDOM.
AND THAT THEY'LL BE FREE TO EXPRESS THEMSELVES ARTISTICALLY, TOO.
THAT IS ALL HIS INTENTION.
...SELF-EXPRESSION, HUH?
THE PRINCIPALITY PROBABLY HATES THAT MOST OF ALL.
EVEN IF JULIUS RETURNS TO POWER,
I'M SURE HE WON'T BE ABLE TO RULE THE SAME WAY AS BEFORE.

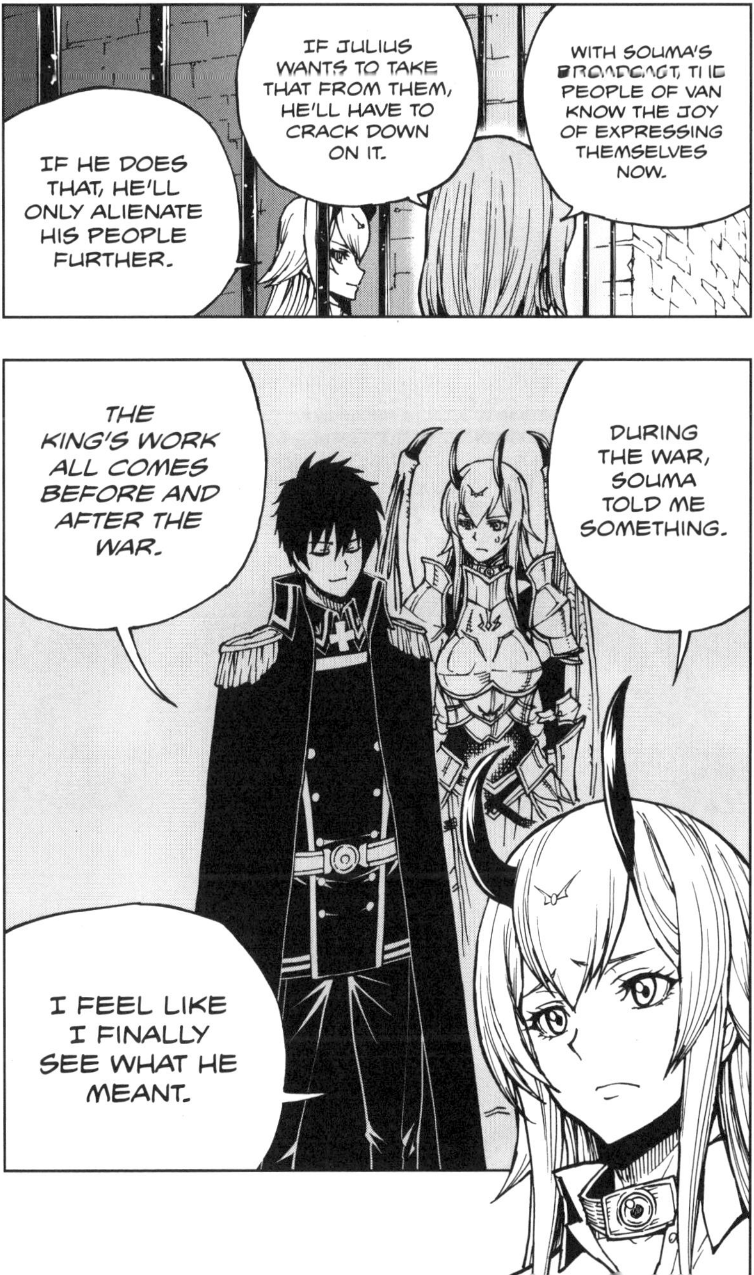
WITH SOUMA'S BROADCAST, THE PEOPLE OF VAN KNOW THE JOY OF EXPRESSING THEMSELVES NOW.
IF JULIUS WANTS TO TAKE THAT FROM THEM, HE'LL HAVE TO CRACK DOWN ON IT.
IF HE DOES THAT, HE'LL ONLY ALIENATE HIS PEOPLE FURTHER.
DURING THE WAR, SOUMA TOLD ME SOMETHING.
THE KING'S WORK ALL COMES BEFORE AND AFTER THE WAR.
I FEEL LIKE I FINALLY SEE WHAT HE MEANT.

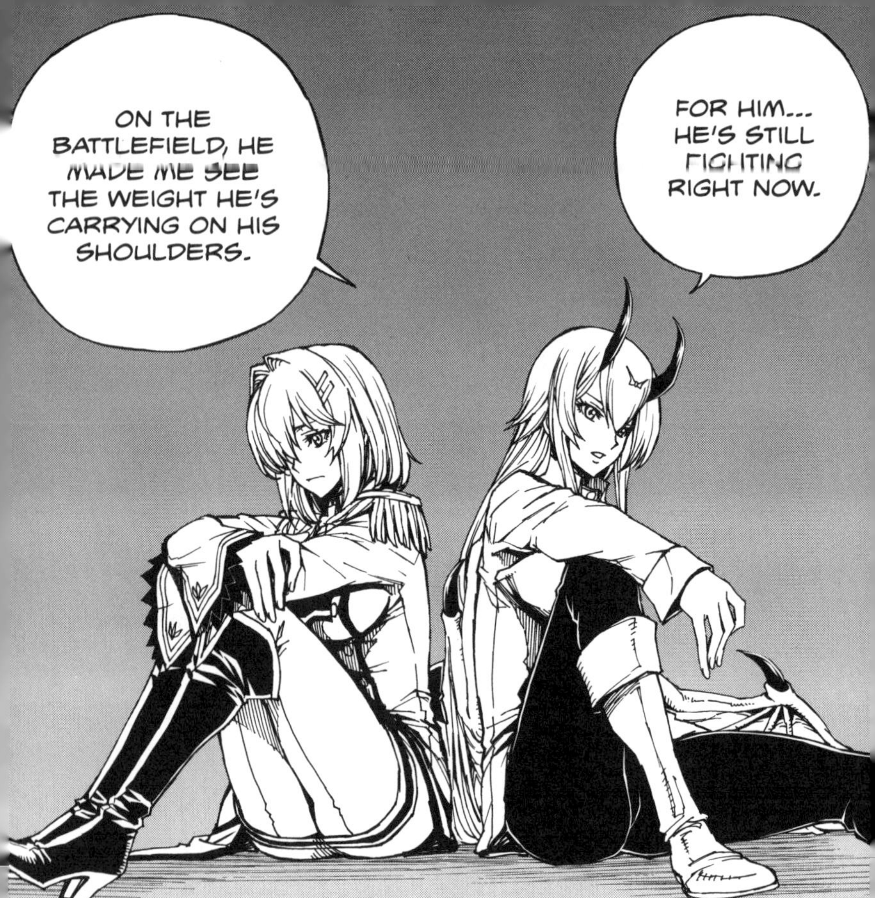
FOR HIM... HE'S STILL FIGHTING RIGHT NOW.
ON THE BATTLEFIELD, HE MADE ME SEE THE WEIGHT HE'S CARRYING ON HIS SHOULDERS.

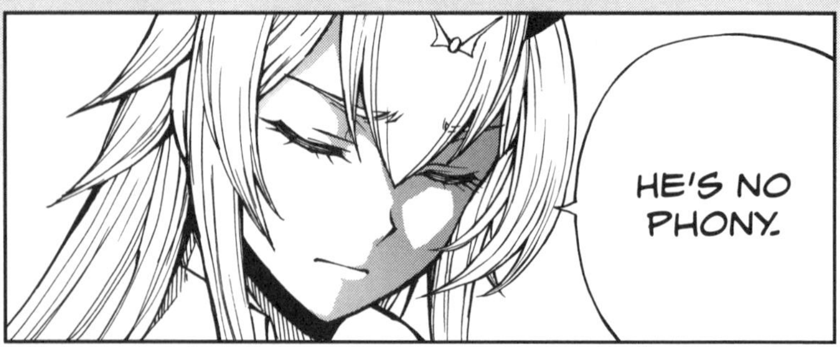
HE'S NO PHONY.

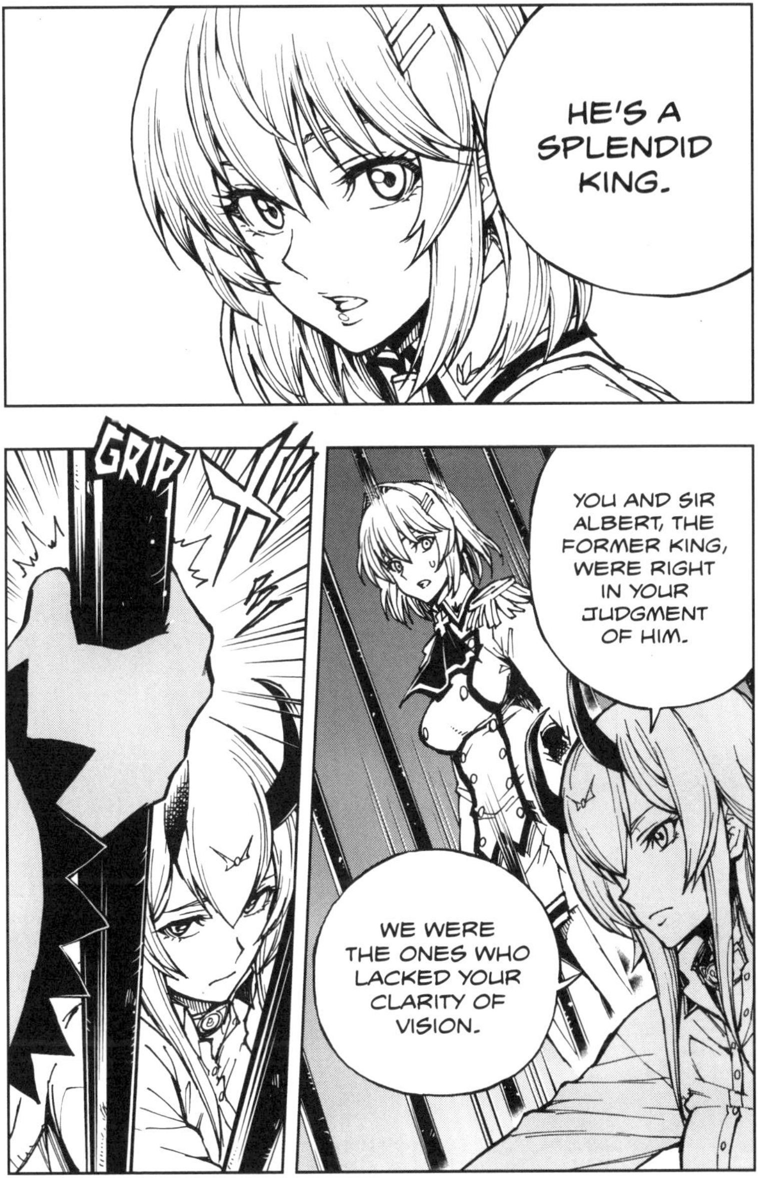
HE'S A SPLENDID KING.
YOU AND SIR ALBERT, THE FORMER KING, WERE RIGHT IN YOUR JUDGMENT OF HIM.
WE WERE THE ONES WHO LACKED YOUR CLARITY OF VISION.
GRIP

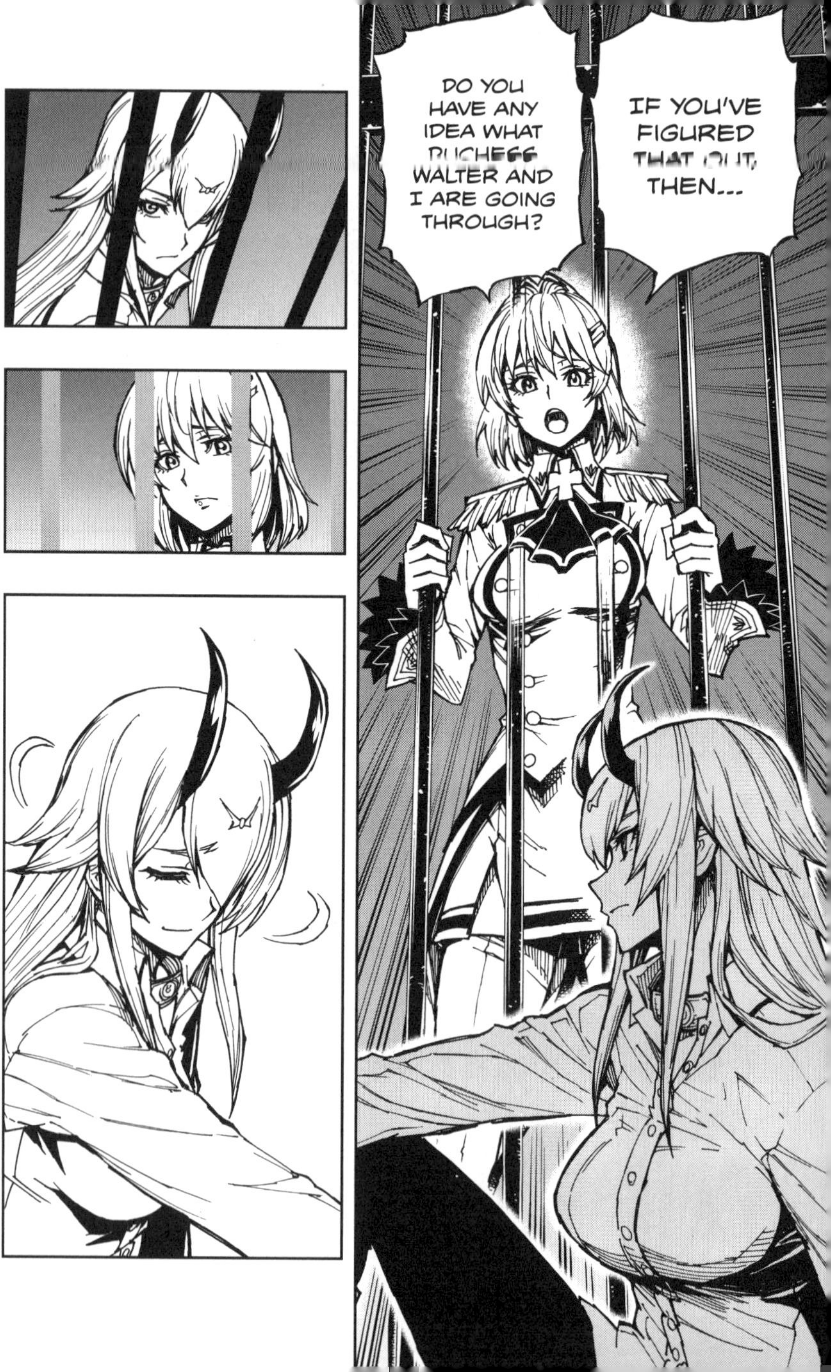
IF YOU'VE FIGURED THAT OUT, THEN...
DO YOU HAVE ANY IDEA WHAT DUCHESS WALTER AND I ARE GOING THROUGH?

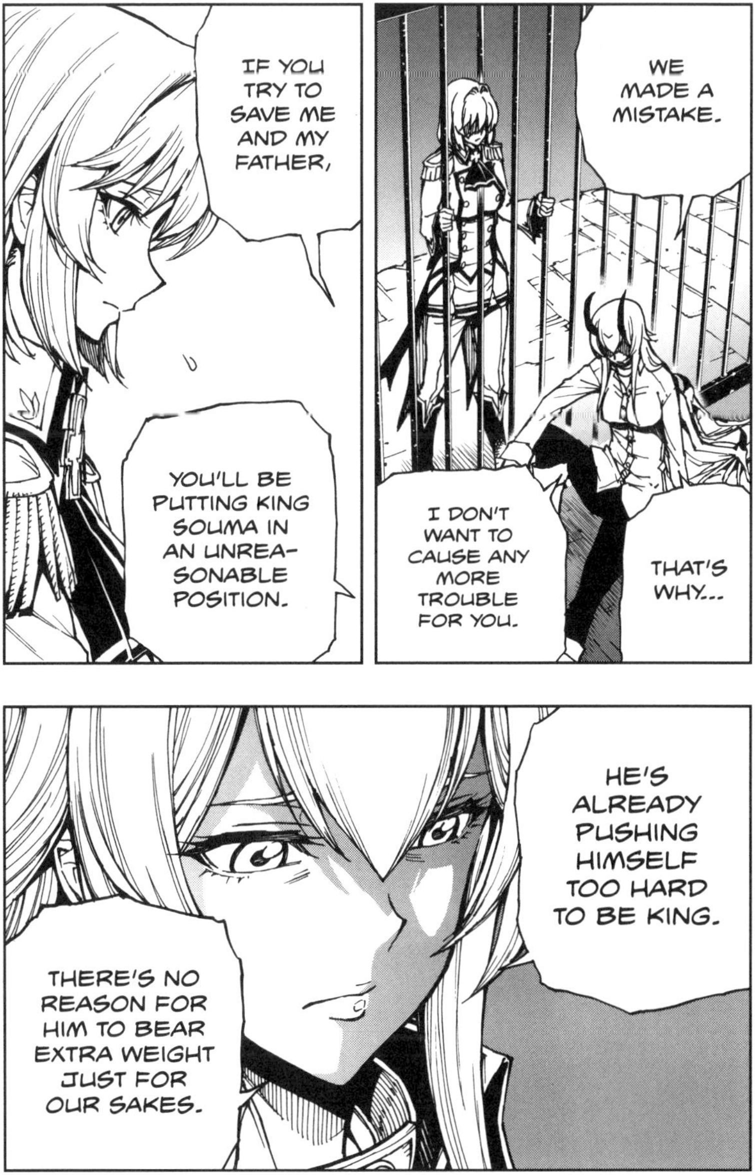
WE MADE A MISTAKE.
I DON'T WANT TO CAUSE ANY MORE TROUBLE FOR YOU.
THAT'S WHY...
IF YOU TRY TO SAVE ME AND MY FATHER,
YOU'LL BE PUTTING KING SOUMA IN AN UNREA-SONABLE POSITION.
HE'S ALREADY PUSHING HIMSELF TOO HARD TO BE KING.
THERE'S NO REASON FOR HIM TO BEAR EXTRA WEIGHT JUST FOR OUR SAKES.

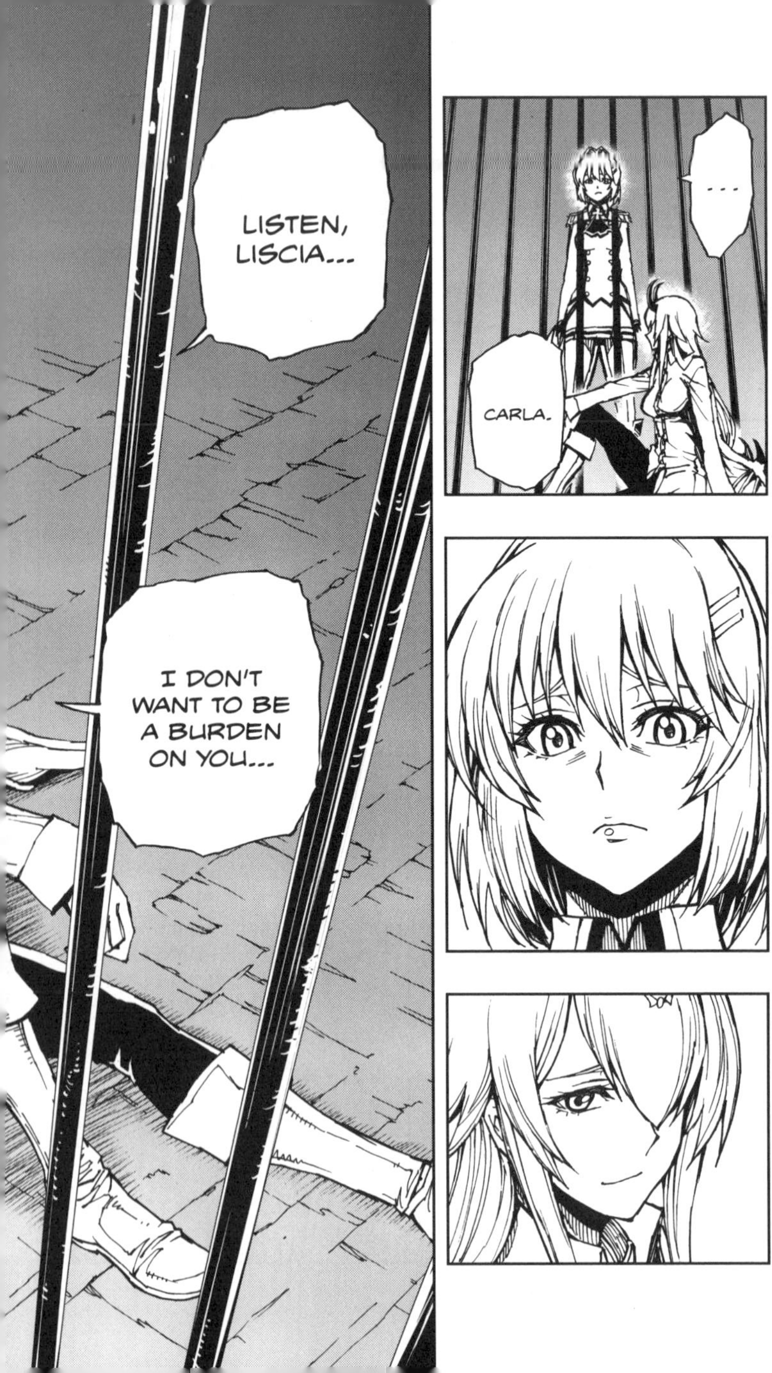
...
CARLA.
LISTEN, LISCIA...
I DON'T WANT TO BE A BURDEN ON YOU...

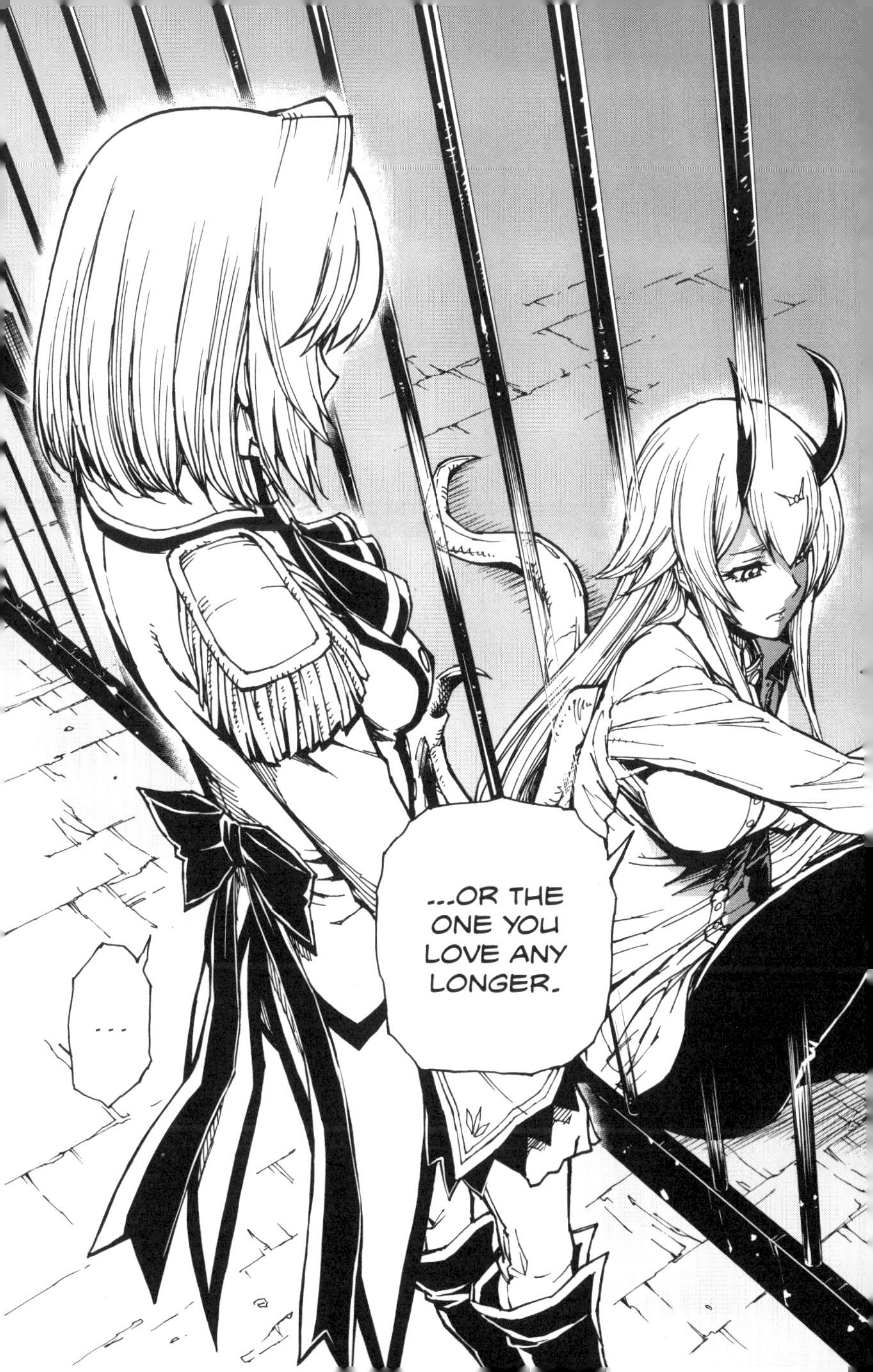
...OR THE ONE YOU LOVE ANY LONGER.
...

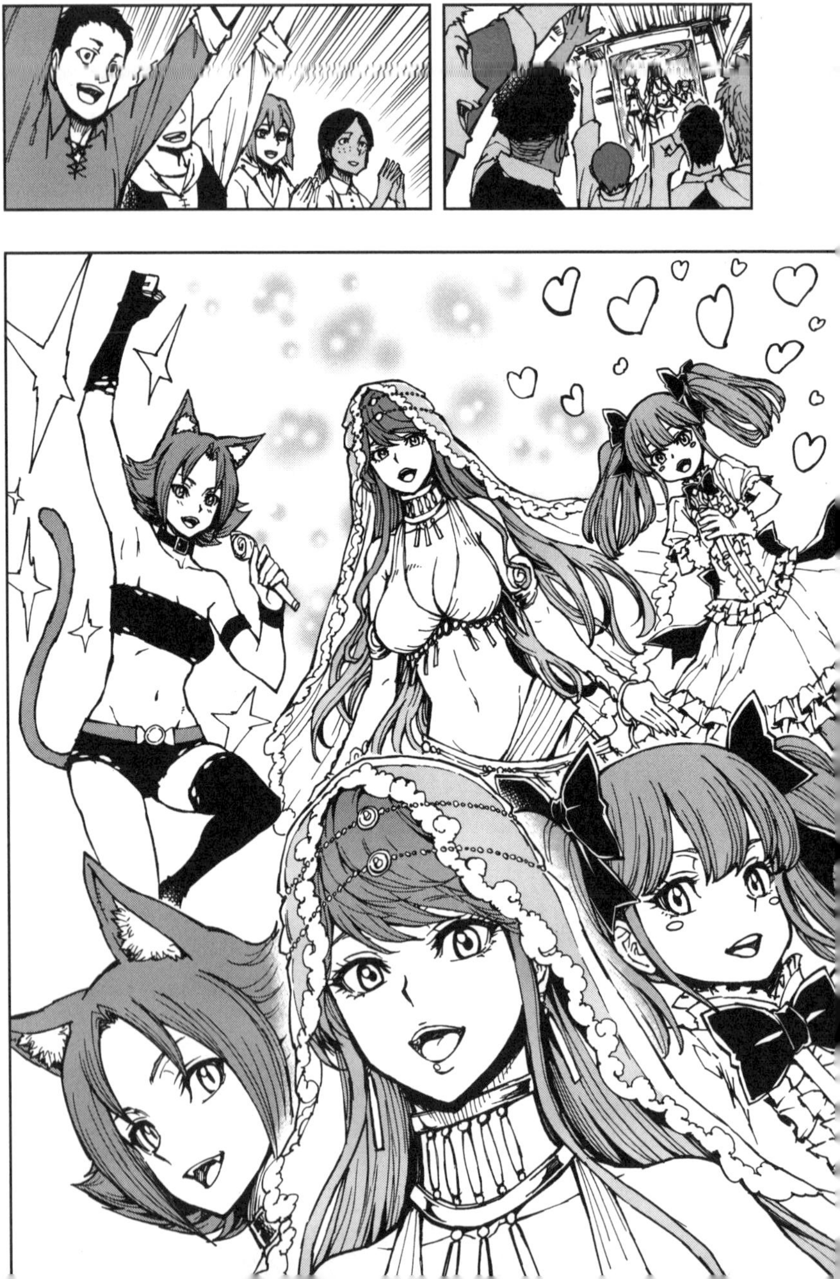

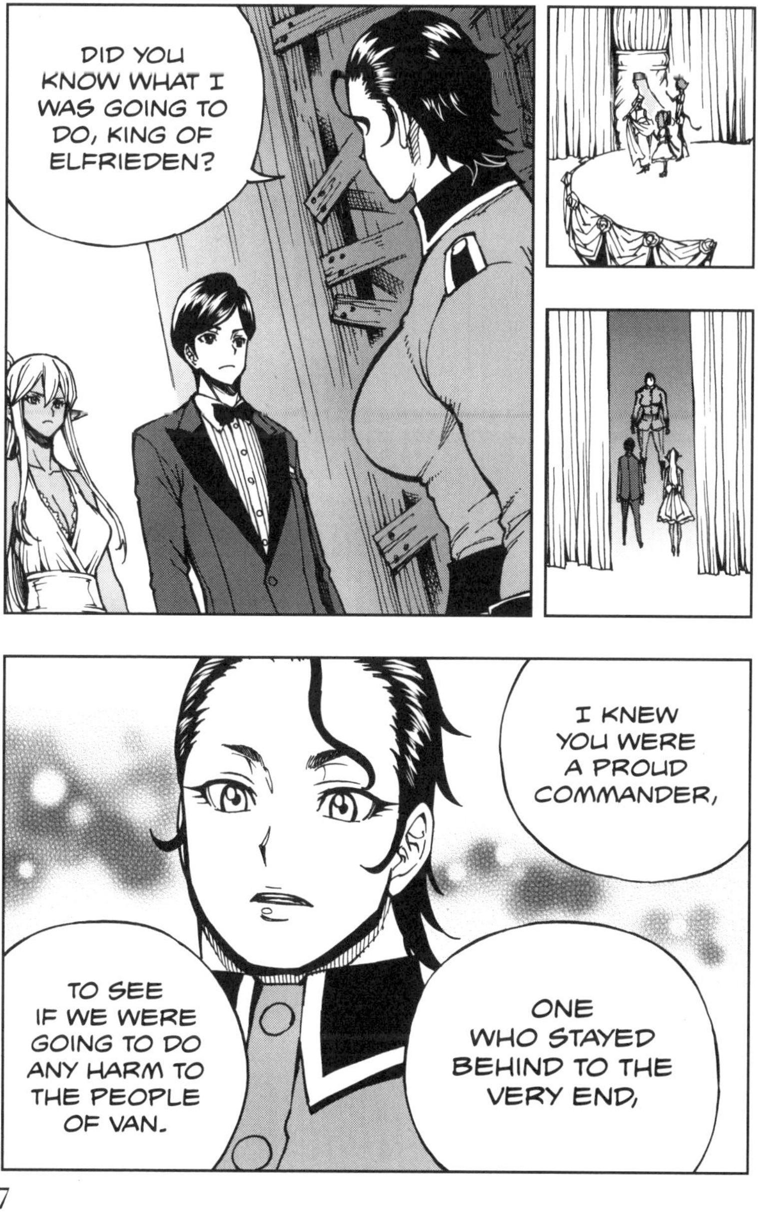
DID YOU KNOW WHAT I WAS GOING TO DO, KING OF ELFRIEDEN?
I KNEW YOU WERE A PROUD COMMANDER,
ONE WHO STAYED BEHIND TO THE VERY END,
TO SEE IF WE WERE GOING TO DO ANY HARM TO THE PEOPLE OF VAN.

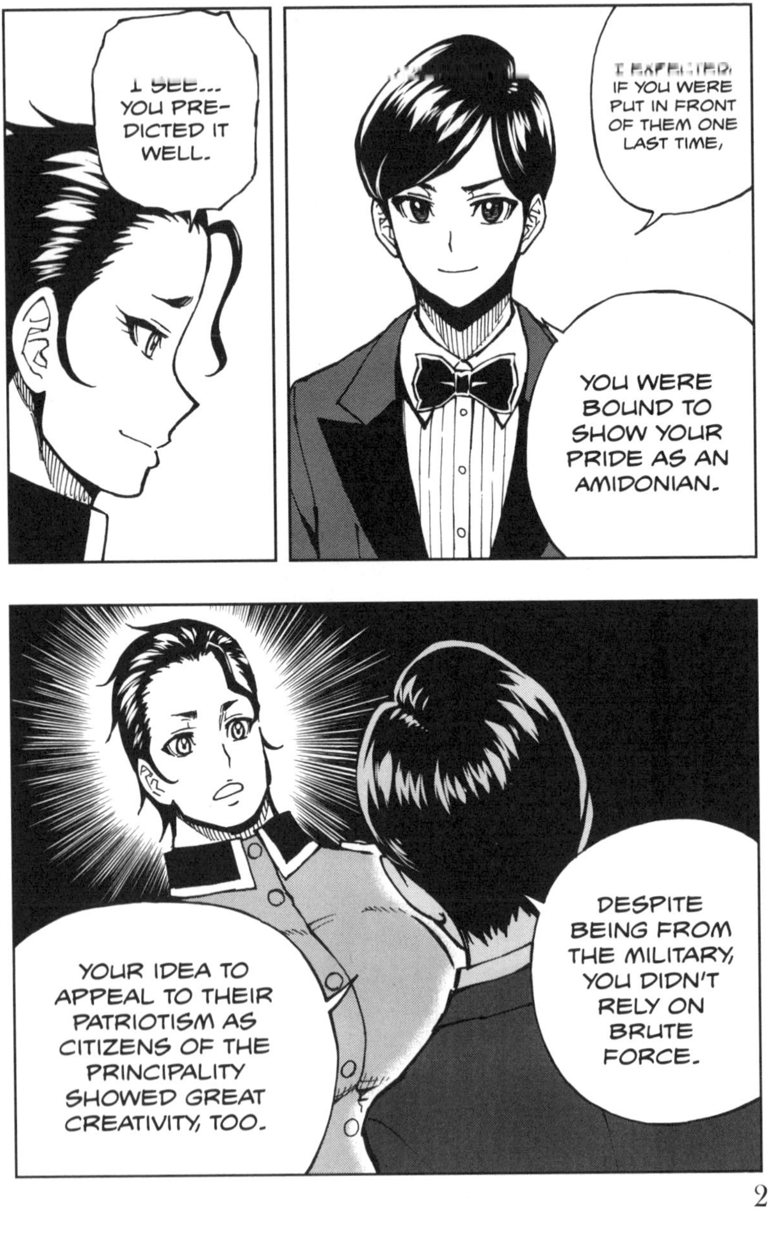

I EXPECTED, IF YOU WERE PUT IN FRONT OF THEM ONE LAST TIME,
YOU WERE BOUND TO SHOW YOUR PRIDE AS AN AMIDONIAN.
I SEE... YOU PRE-DICTED IT WELL.
DESPITE BEING FROM THE MILITARY, YOU DIDN'T RELY ON BRUTE FORCE.
YOUR IDEA TO APPEAL TO THEIR PATRIOTISM AS CITIZENS OF THE PRINCIPALITY SHOWED GREAT CREATIVITY, TOO.

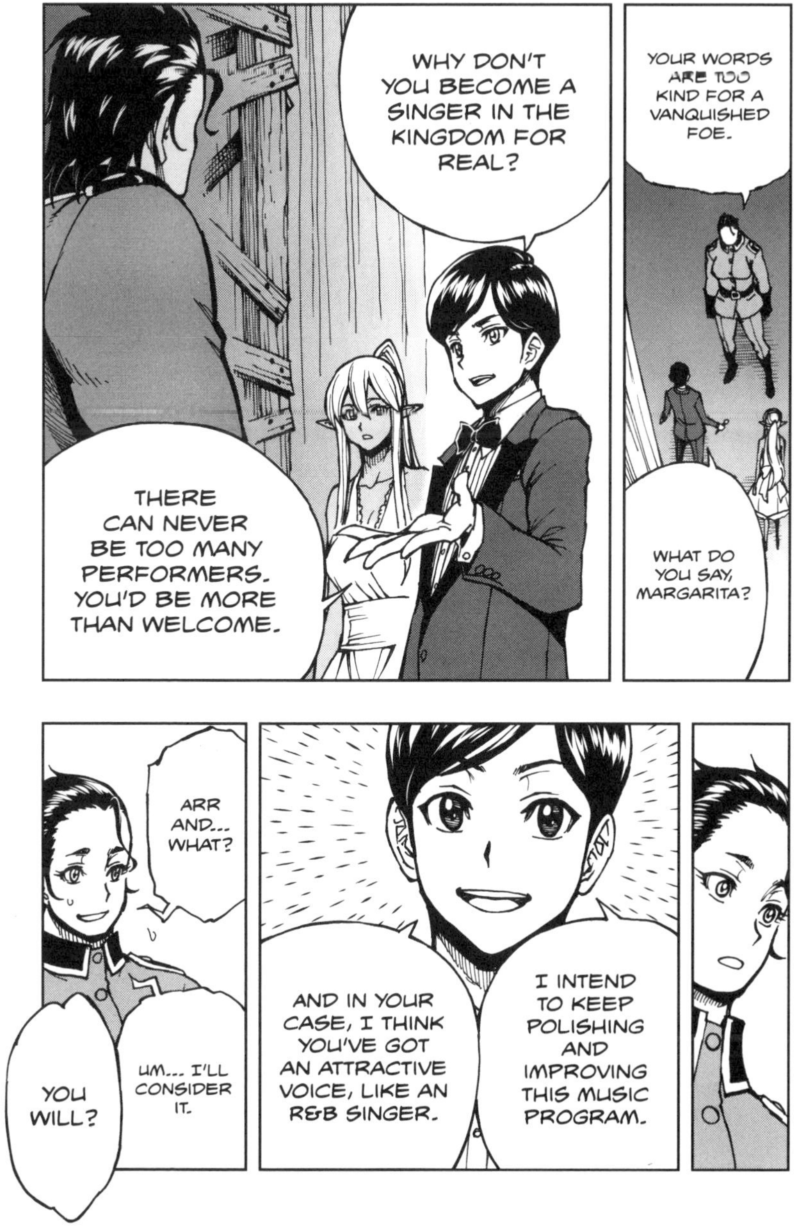
YOUR WORDS ARE TOO KIND FOR A VANQUISHED FOE.
WHAT DO YOU SAY, MARGARITA?
WHY DON'T YOU BECOME A SINGER IN THE KINGDOM FOR REAL?
THERE CAN NEVER BE TOO MANY PERFORMERS. YOU'D BE MORE THAN WELCOME.
I INTEND TO KEEP POLISHING AND IMPROVING THIS MUSIC PROGRAM.
AND IN YOUR CASE, I THINK YOU'VE GOT AN ATTRACTIVE VOICE, LIKE AN R&B SINGER.
ARR AND... WHAT?
UM... I'LL CONSIDER IT.
YOU WILL?

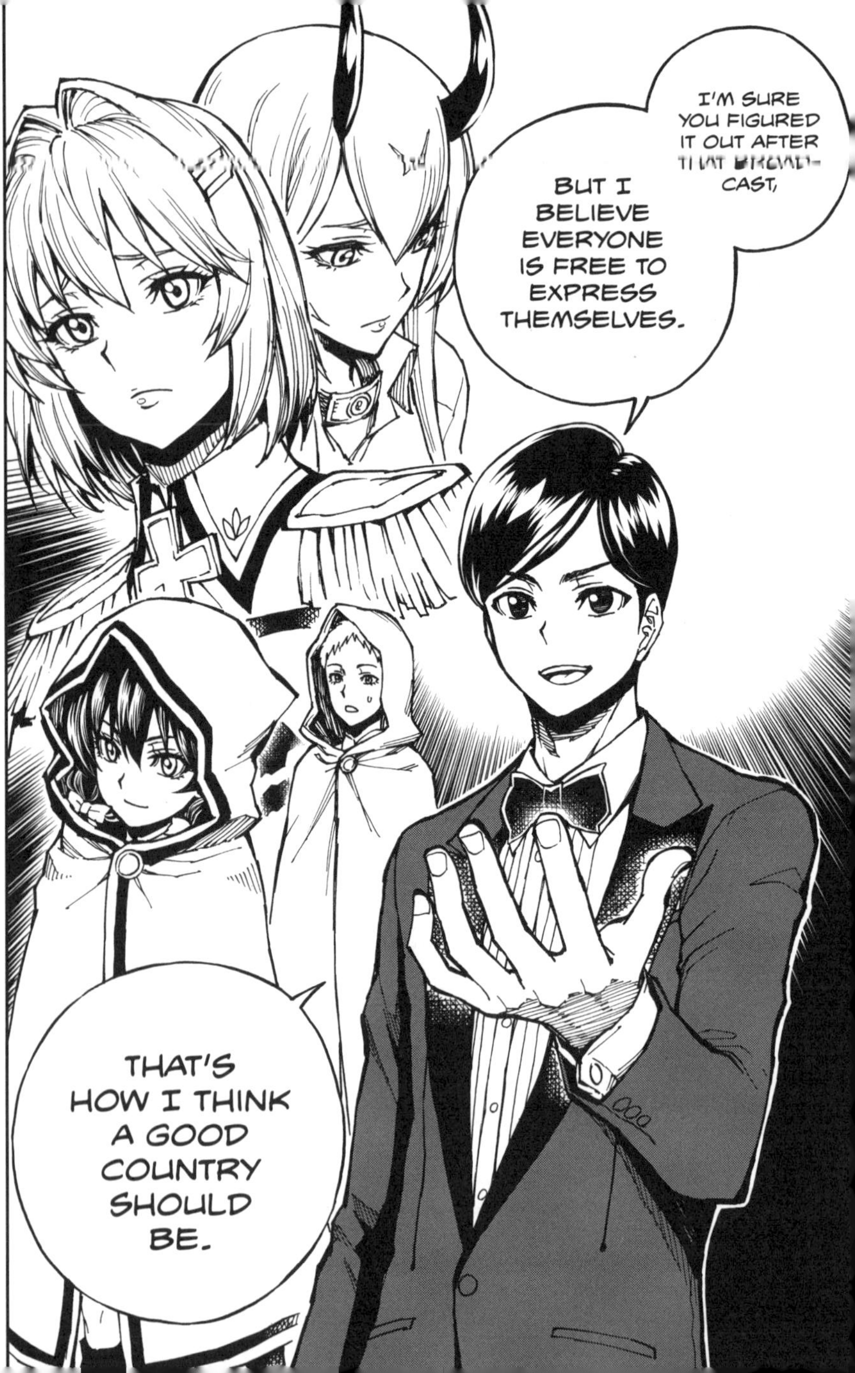
I'M SURE YOU FIGURED IT OUT AFTER THAT BROAD-CAST,
BUT I BELIEVE EVERYONE IS FREE TO EXPRESS THEMSELVES.
THAT'S HOW I THINK A GOOD COUNTRY SHOULD BE.

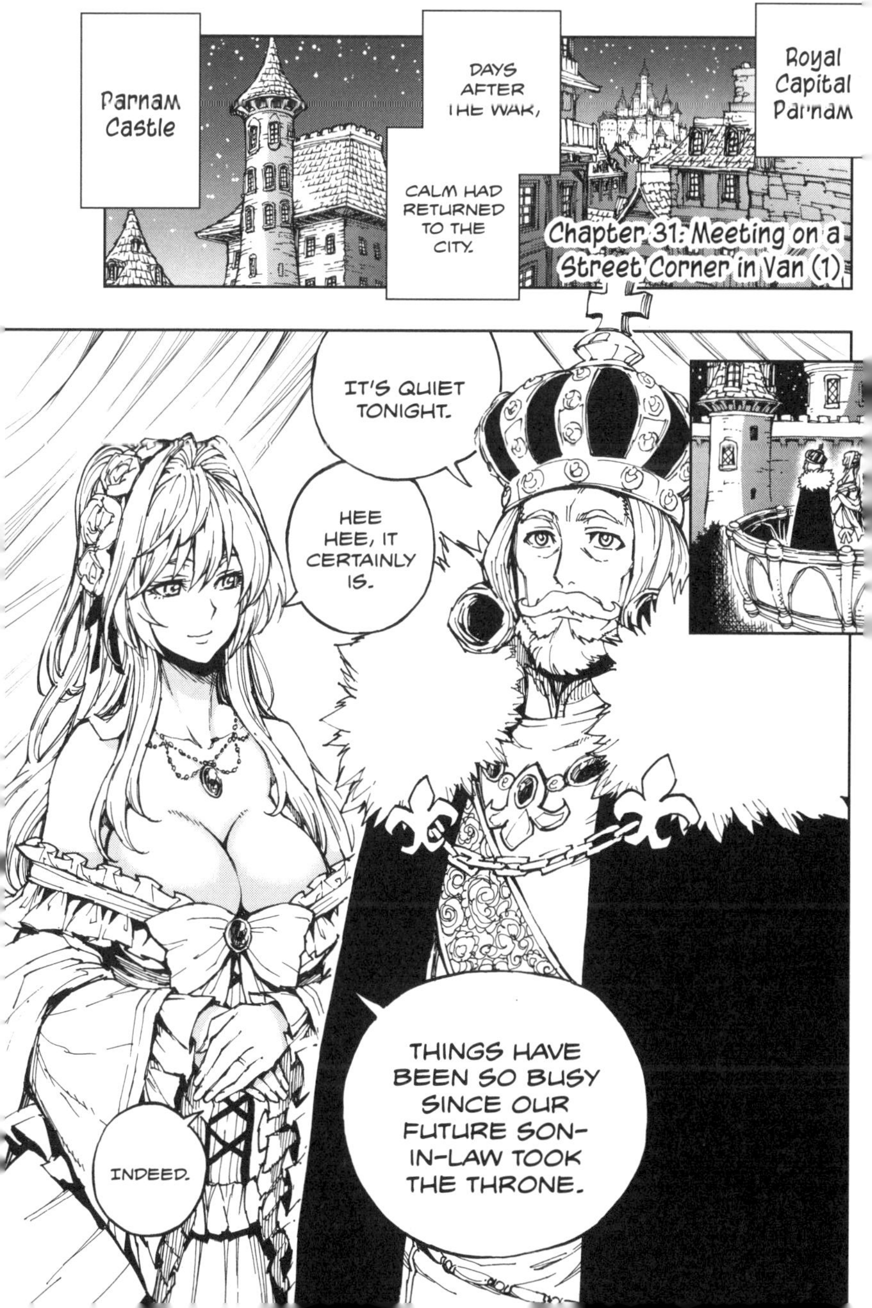
Royal Capital Parnam
Chapter 31: Meeting on a Street Corner in Van (1)
DAYS AFTER THE WAR,
CALM HAD RETURNED TO THE CITY.
Parnam Castle
IT'S QUIET TONIGHT.
HEE HEE, IT CERTAINLY IS.
THINGS HAVE BEEN SO BUSY SINCE OUR FUTURE SON-IN-LAW TOOK THE THRONE.
INDEED.

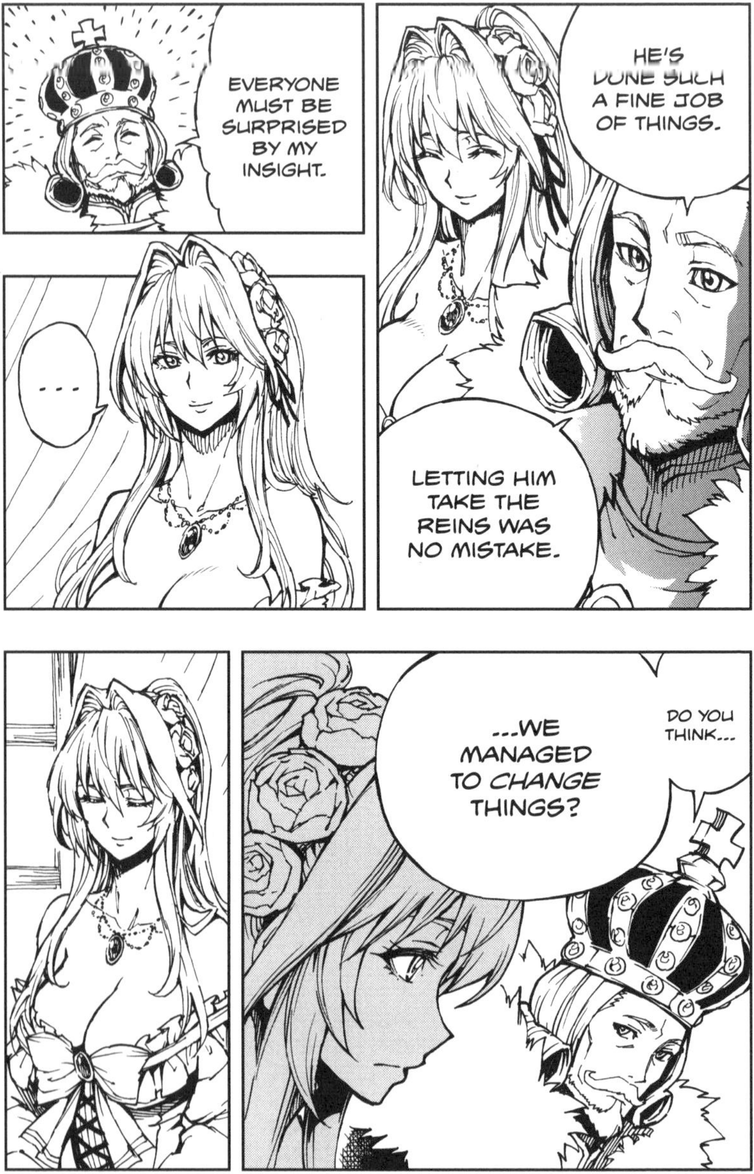
HE'S DONE SUCH A FINE JOB OF THINGS.
LETTING HIM TAKE THE REINS WAS NO MISTAKE.
EVERYONE MUST BE SURPRISED BY MY INSIGHT.
...
DO YOU THINK...
...WE MANAGED TO *CHANGE* THINGS?

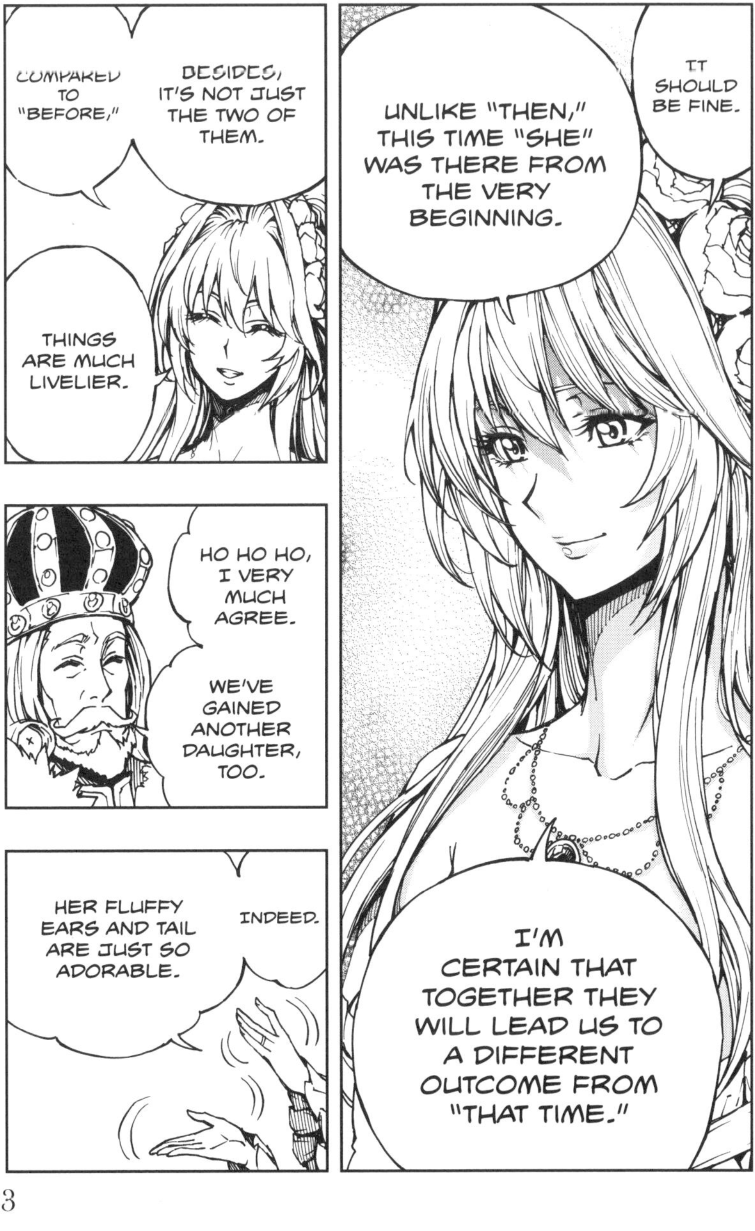
IT SHOULD BE FINE.
UNLIKE "THEN," THIS TIME "SHE" WAS THERE FROM THE VERY BEGINNING.
I'M CERTAIN THAT TOGETHER THEY WILL LEAD US TO A DIFFERENT OUTCOME FROM "THAT TIME."
BESIDES, IT'S NOT JUST THE TWO OF THEM.
COMPARED TO "BEFORE,"
THINGS ARE MUCH LIVELIER.
HO HO HO, I VERY MUCH AGREE.
WE'VE GAINED ANOTHER DAUGHTER, TOO.
INDEED.
HER FLUFFY EARS AND TAIL ARE JUST SO ADORABLE.

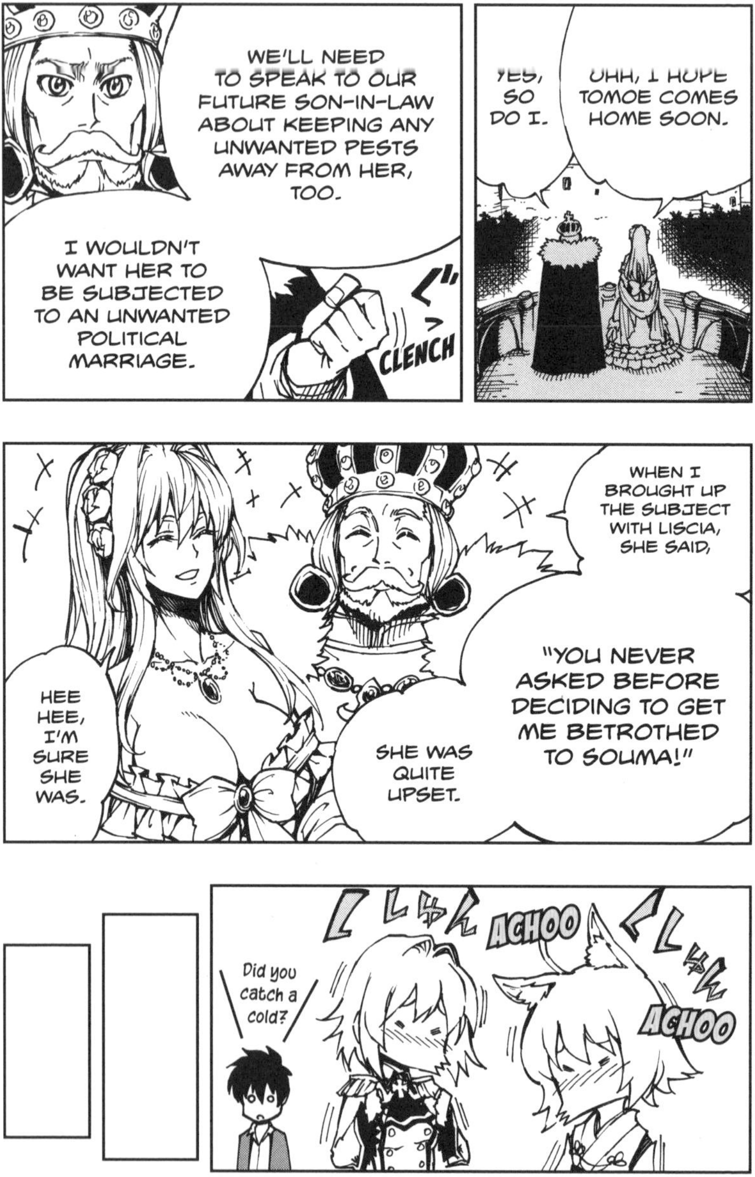
UHH, I HOPE TOMOE COMES HOME SOON.
YES, SO DO I.
WE'LL NEED TO SPEAK TO OUR FUTURE SON-IN-LAW ABOUT KEEPING ANY UNWANTED PESTS AWAY FROM HER, TOO.
CLENCH
I WOULDN'T WANT HER TO BE SUBJECTED TO AN UNWANTED POLITICAL MARRIAGE.
WHEN I BROUGHT UP THE SUBJECT WITH LISCIA, SHE SAID,
"YOU NEVER ASKED BEFORE DECIDING TO GET ME BETROTHED TO SOUMA!"
SHE WAS QUITE UPSET.
HEE HEE, I'M SURE SHE WAS.
ACHOO
ACHOO
Did you catch a cold?

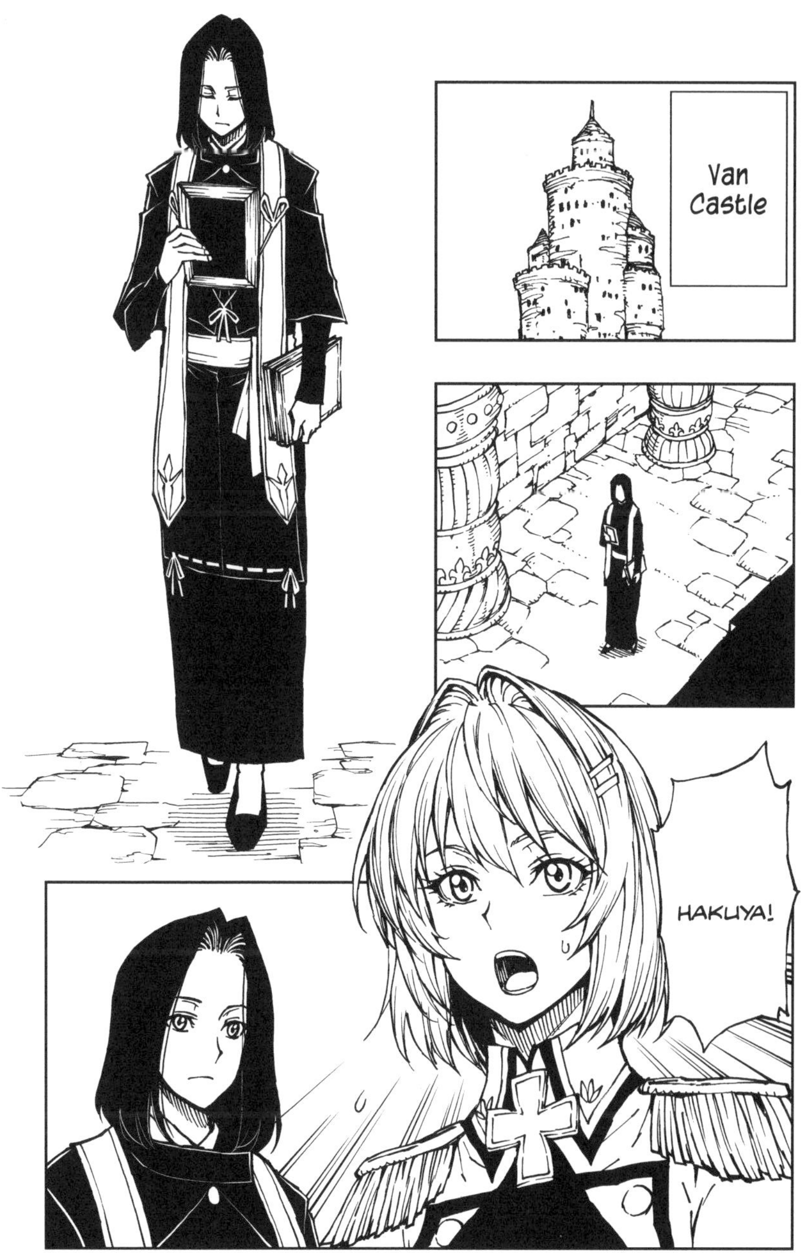
Van Castle
HAKUYA!

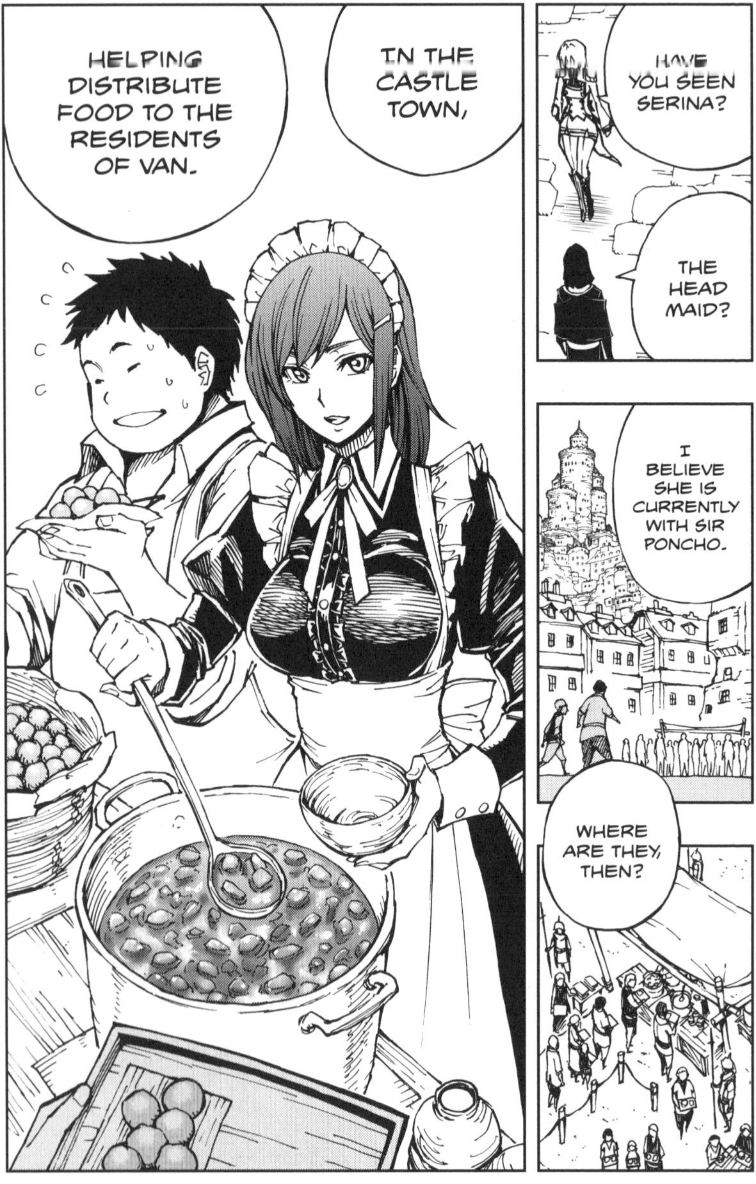
HAVE YOU SEEN SERINA?
THE HEAD MAID?
I BELIEVE SHE IS CURRENTLY WITH SIR PONCHO.
WHERE ARE THEY, THEN?
IN THE CASTLE TOWN,
HELPING DISTRIBUTE FOOD TO THE RESIDENTS OF VAN.

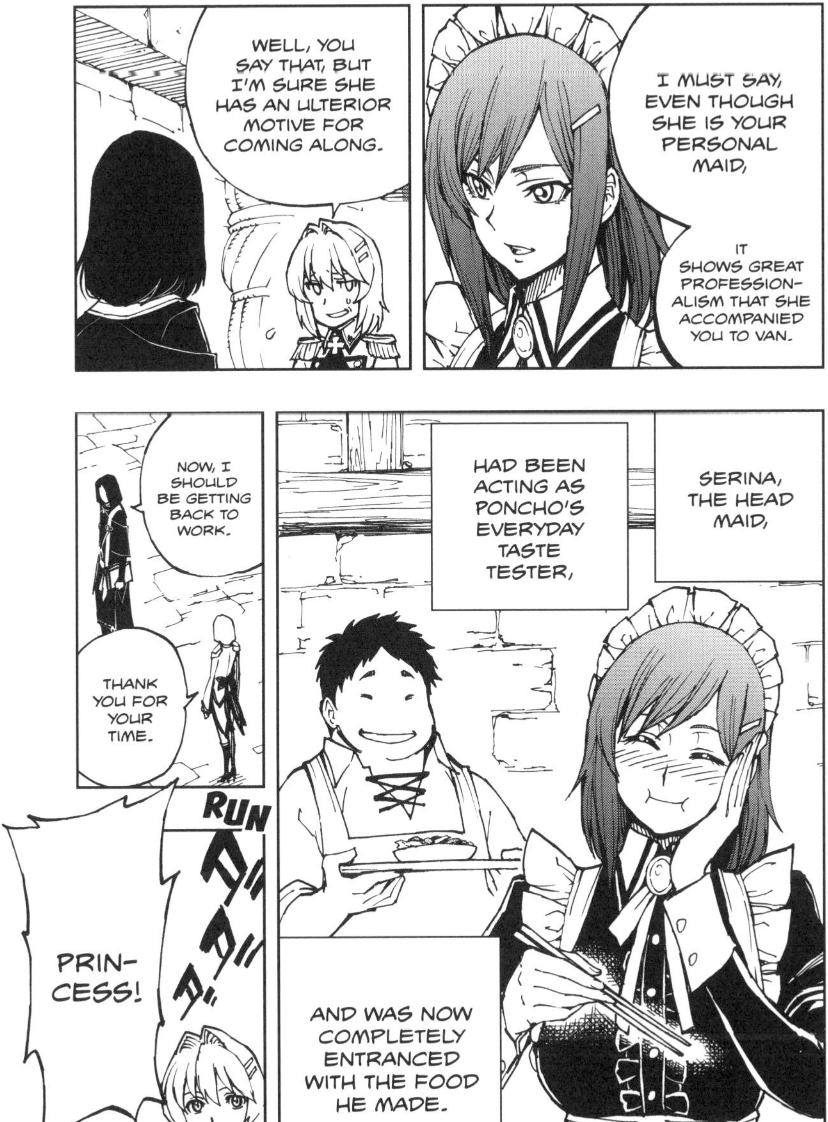
I MUST SAY, EVEN THOUGH SHE IS YOUR PERSONAL MAID,
IT SHOWS GREAT PROFESSION-ALISM THAT SHE ACCOMPANIED YOU TO VAN.
WELL, YOU SAY THAT, BUT I'M SURE SHE HAS AN ULTERIOR MOTIVE FOR COMING ALONG.
SERINA, THE HEAD MAID,
HAD BEEN ACTING AS PONCHO'S EVERYDAY TASTE TESTER,
AND WAS NOW COMPLETELY ENTRANCED WITH THE FOOD HE MADE.
NOW, I SHOULD BE GETTING BACK TO WORK.
THANK YOU FOR YOUR TIME.
RUN
PRIN-CESS!

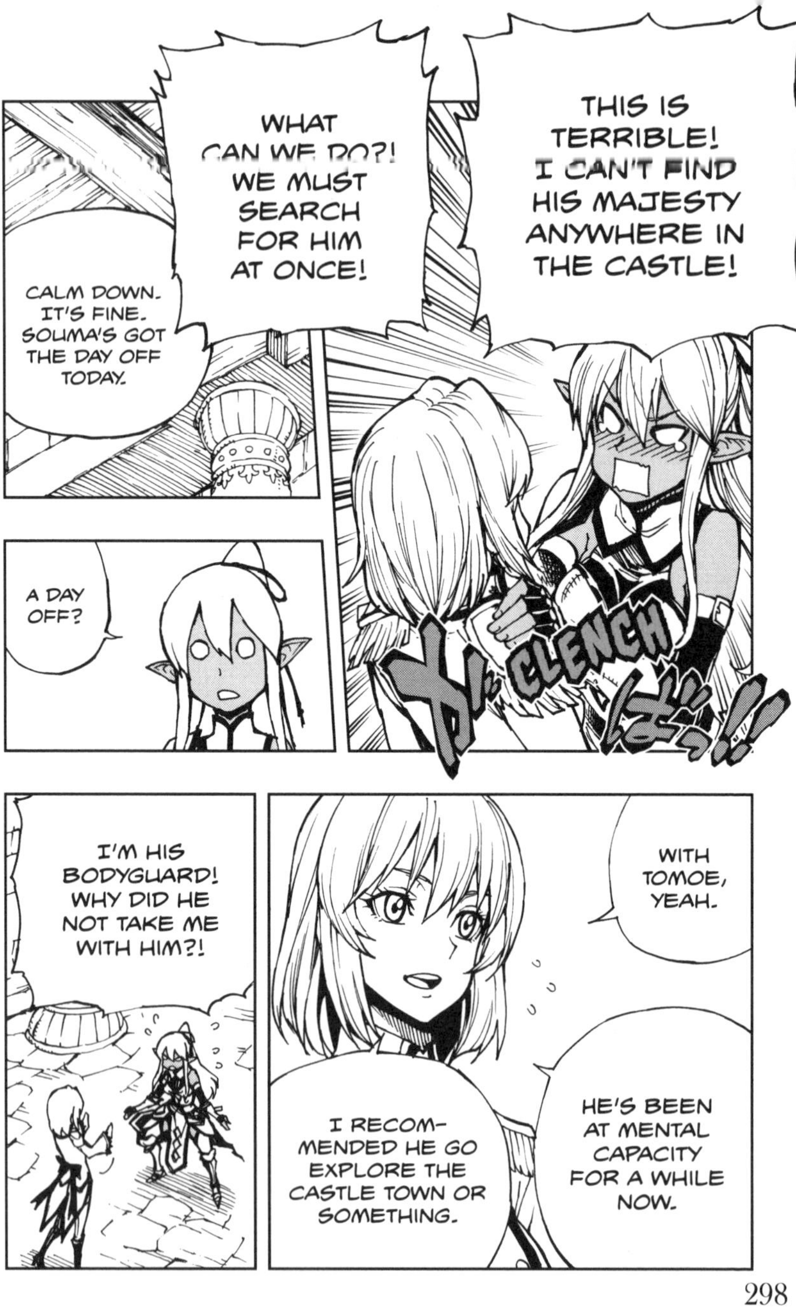
THIS IS TERRIBLE! I CAN'T FIND HIS MAJESTY ANYWHERE IN THE CASTLE!
WHAT CAN WE DO?! WE MUST SEARCH FOR HIM AT ONCE!
CLENCH
CALM DOWN. IT'S FINE. SOUMA'S GOT THE DAY OFF TODAY.
A DAY OFF?
WITH TOMOE, YEAH.
HE'S BEEN AT MENTAL CAPACITY FOR A WHILE NOW.
I RECOMMENDED HE GO EXPLORE THE CASTLE TOWN OR SOMETHING.
I'M HIS BODYGUARD! WHY DID HE NOT TAKE ME WITH HIM?!

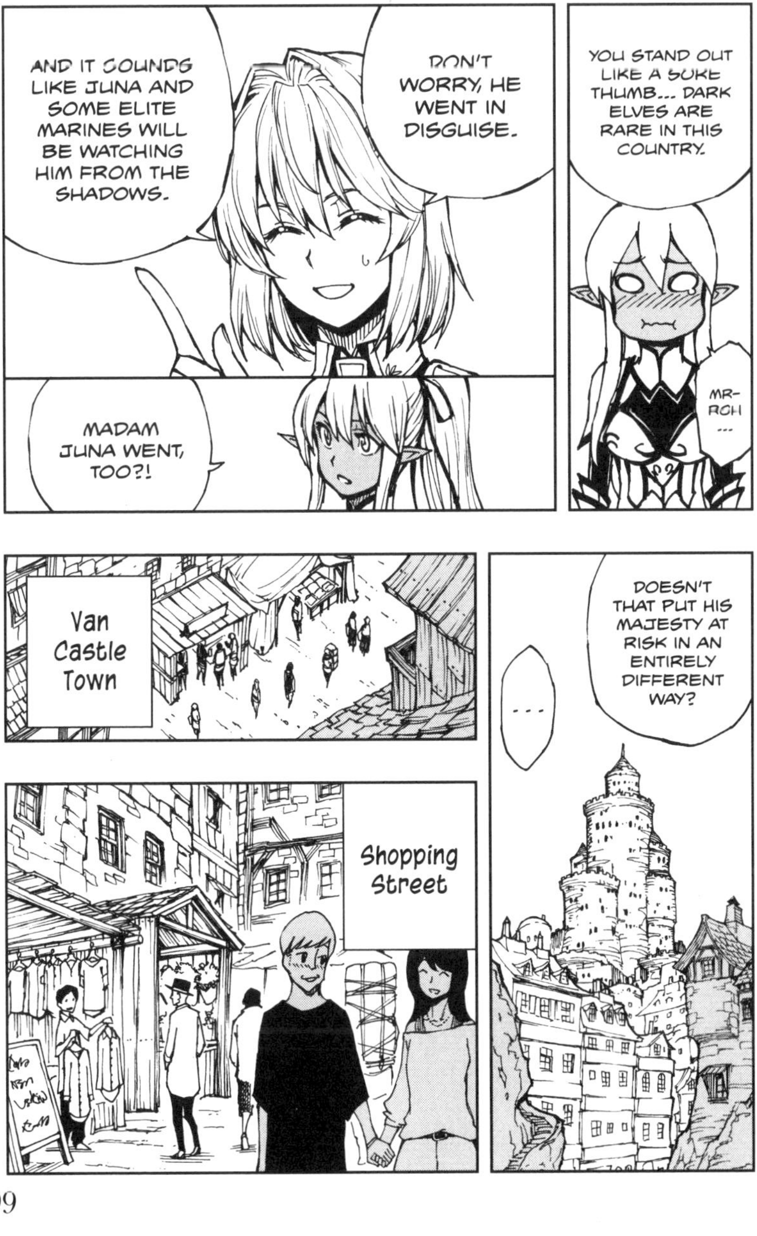
YOU STAND OUT LIKE A SORE THUMB... DARK ELVES ARE RARE IN THIS COUNTRY.
MR-ROH...
DON'T WORRY, HE WENT IN DISGUISE.
AND IT SOUNDS LIKE JUNA AND SOME ELITE MARINES WILL BE WATCHING HIM FROM THE SHADOWS.
MADAM JUNA WENT, TOO?!
DOESN'T THAT PUT HIS MAJESTY AT RISK IN AN ENTIRELY DIFFERENT WAY?
...
Van Castle Town
Shopping Street

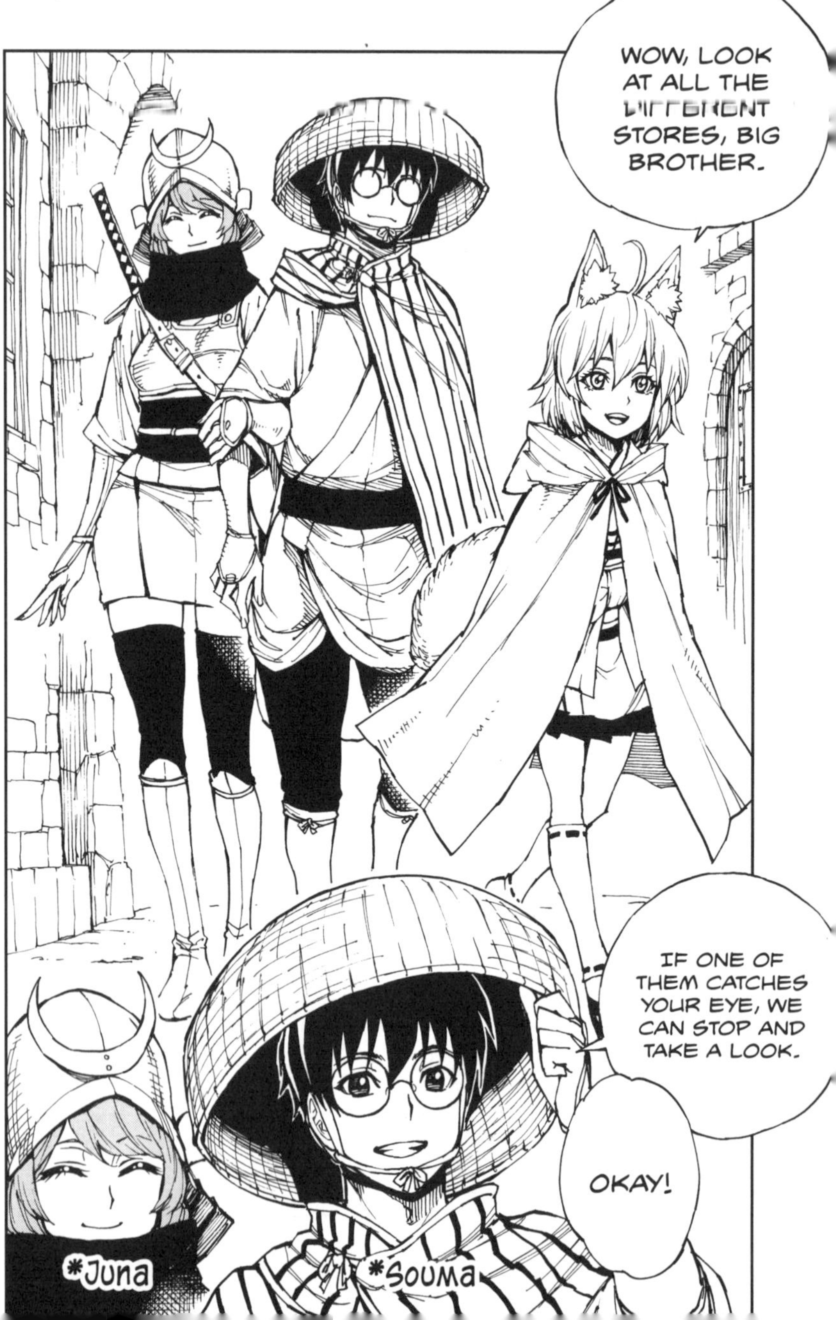
WOW, LOOK AT ALL THE DIFFERENT STORES, BIG BROTHER.
IF ONE OF THEM CATCHES YOUR EYE, WE CAN STOP AND TAKE A LOOK.
OKAY!
*Souma
*Juna

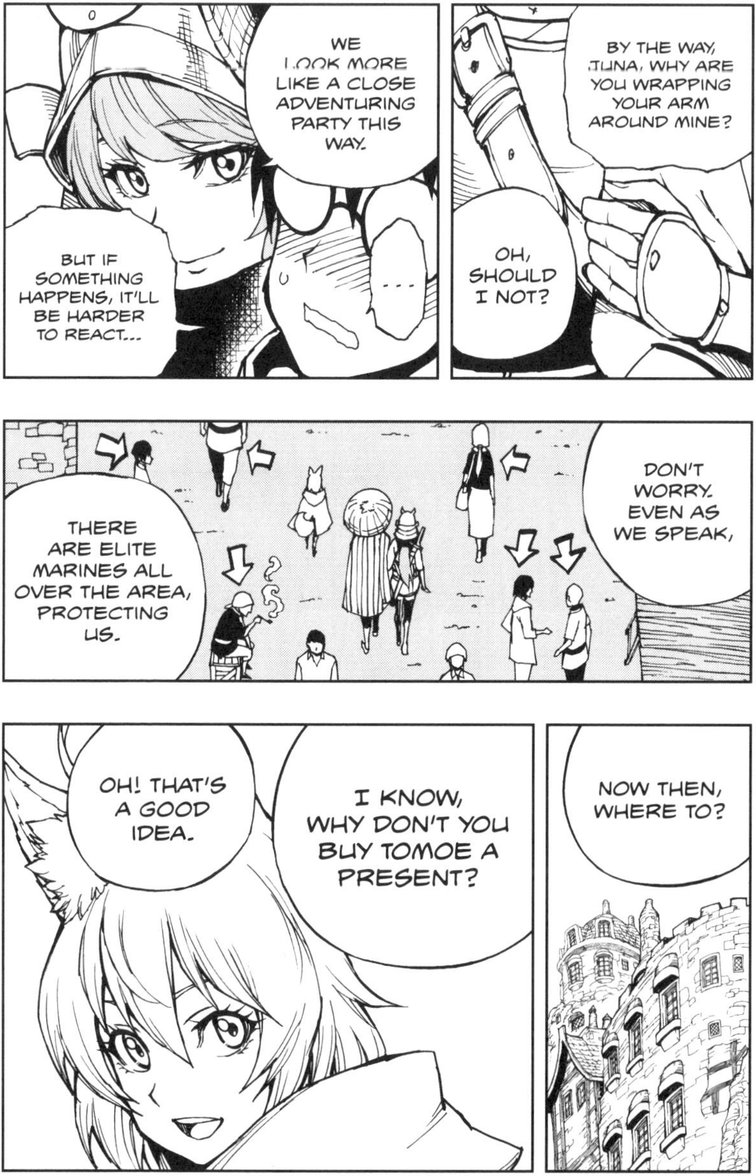
BY THE WAY, TUNA, WHY ARE YOU WRAPPING YOUR ARM AROUND MINE?
OH, SHOULD I NOT?
WE LOOK MORE LIKE A CLOSE ADVENTURING PARTY THIS WAY.
...
BUT IF SOMETHING HAPPENS, IT'LL BE HARDER TO REACT...
DON'T WORRY. EVEN AS WE SPEAK,
THERE ARE ELITE MARINES ALL OVER THE AREA, PROTECTING US.
NOW THEN, WHERE TO?
I KNOW, WHY DON'T YOU BUY TOMOE A PRESENT?
OH! THAT'S A GOOD IDEA.

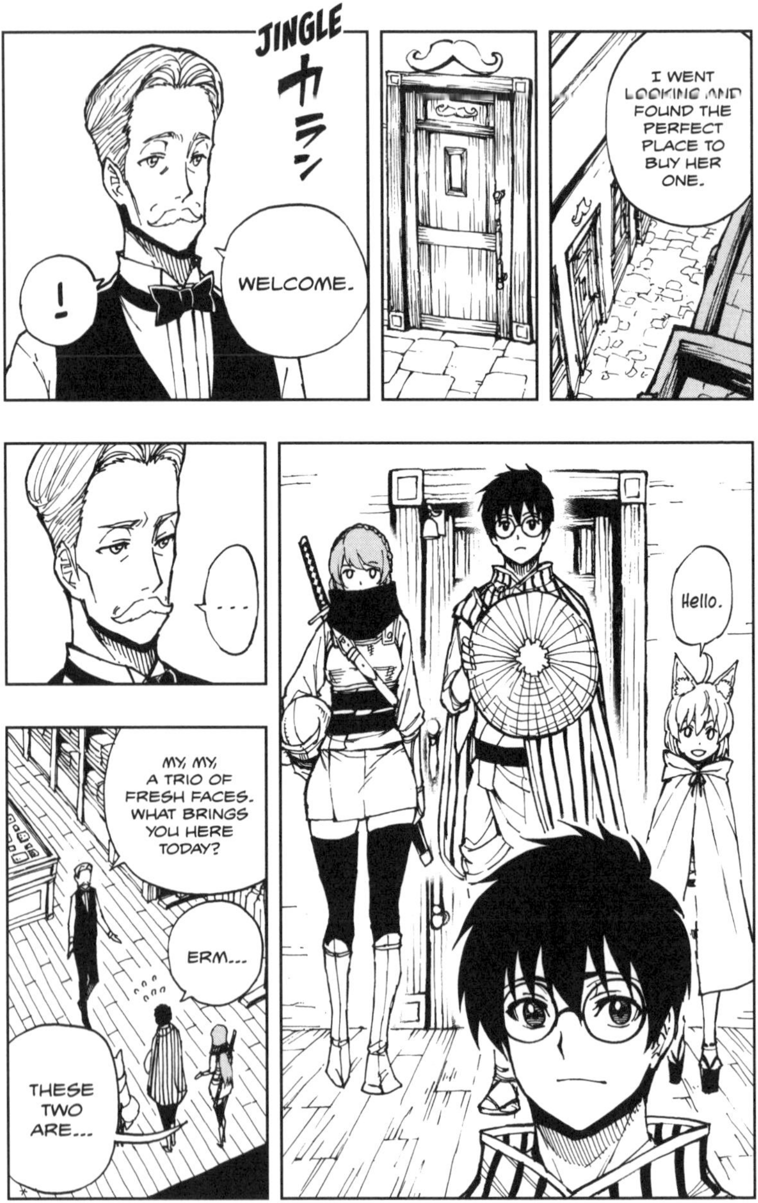

I WENT LOOKING AND FOUND THE PERFECT PLACE TO BUY HER ONE.
JINGLE
カラン
WELCOME.
!
Hello.
...
MY, MY, A TRIO OF FRESH FACES. WHAT BRINGS YOU HERE TODAY?
ERM...
THESE TWO ARE...

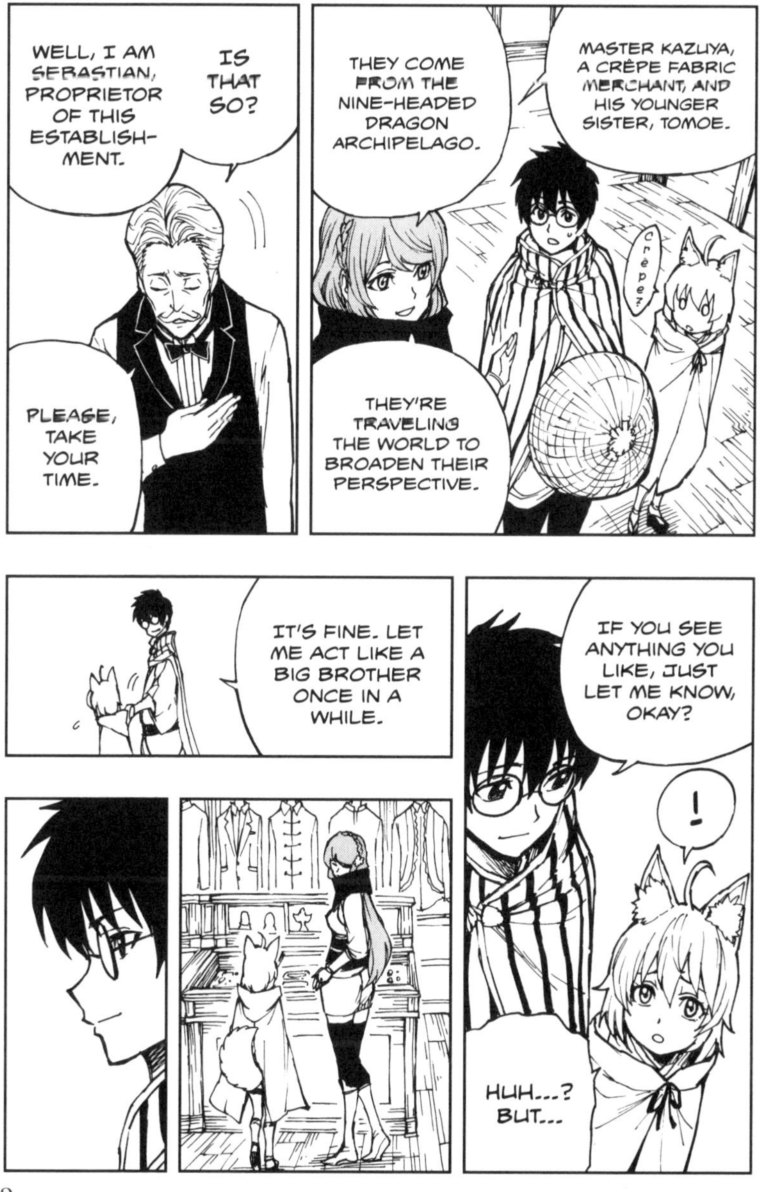
MASTER KAZUYA, A CRÊPE FABRIC MERCHANT, AND HIS YOUNGER SISTER, TOMOE.
THEY COME FROM THE NINE-HEADED DRAGON ARCHIPELAGO.
Crêpe?
THEY'RE TRAVELING THE WORLD TO BROADEN THEIR PERSPECTIVE.
IS THAT SO?
WELL, I AM SEBASTIAN, PROPRIETOR OF THIS ESTABLISHMENT.
PLEASE, TAKE YOUR TIME.
IF YOU SEE ANYTHING YOU LIKE, JUST LET ME KNOW, OKAY?
!
HUH...? BUT...
IT'S FINE. LET ME ACT LIKE A BIG BROTHER ONCE IN A WHILE.

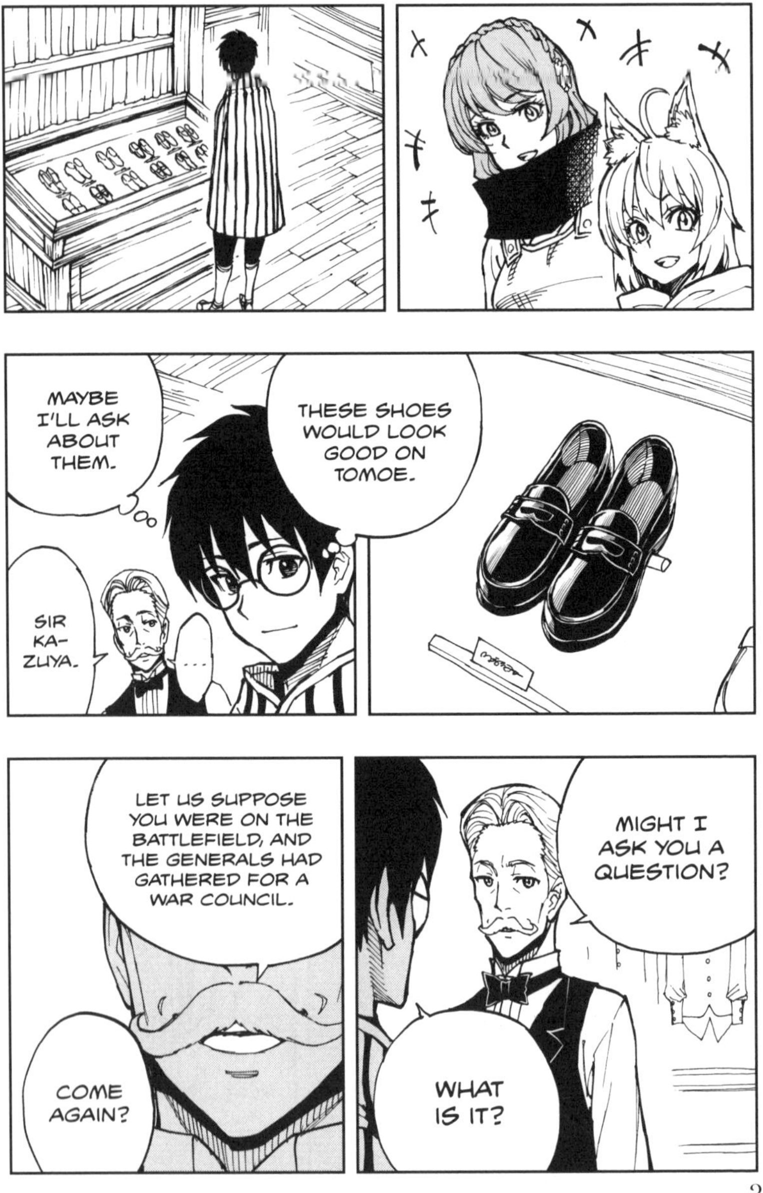
THESE SHOES WOULD LOOK GOOD ON TOMOE.
MAYBE I'LL ASK ABOUT THEM.
SIR KA-ZUYA.
...
MIGHT I ASK YOU A QUESTION?
WHAT IS IT?
LET US SUPPOSE YOU WERE ON THE BATTLEFIELD, AND THE GENERALS HAD GATHERED FOR A WAR COUNCIL.
COME AGAIN?

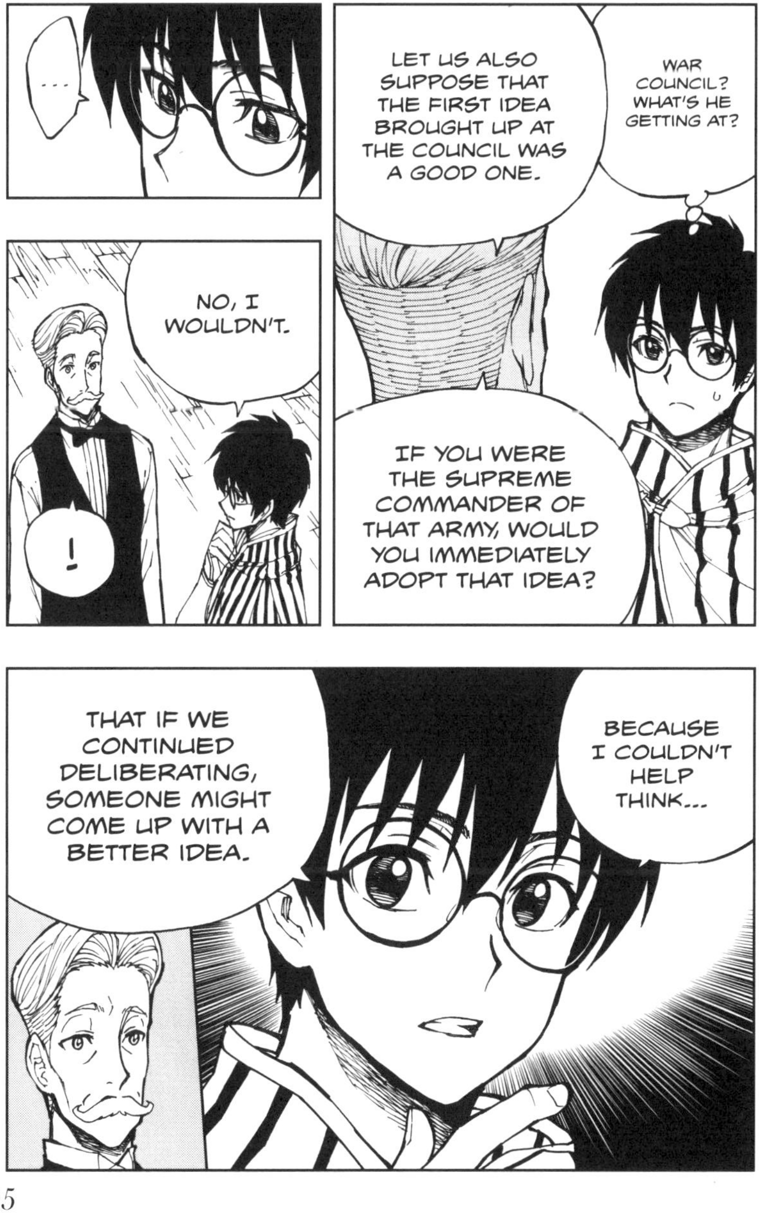

WAR COUNCIL? WHAT'S HE GETTING AT?
LET US ALSO SUPPOSE THAT THE FIRST IDEA BROUGHT UP AT THE COUNCIL WAS A GOOD ONE.
IF YOU WERE THE SUPREME COMMANDER OF THAT ARMY, WOULD YOU IMMEDIATELY ADOPT THAT IDEA?
...
NO, I WOULDN'T.
!
BECAUSE I COULDN'T HELP THINK...
THAT IF WE CONTINUED DELIBERATING, SOMEONE MIGHT COME UP WITH A BETTER IDEA.

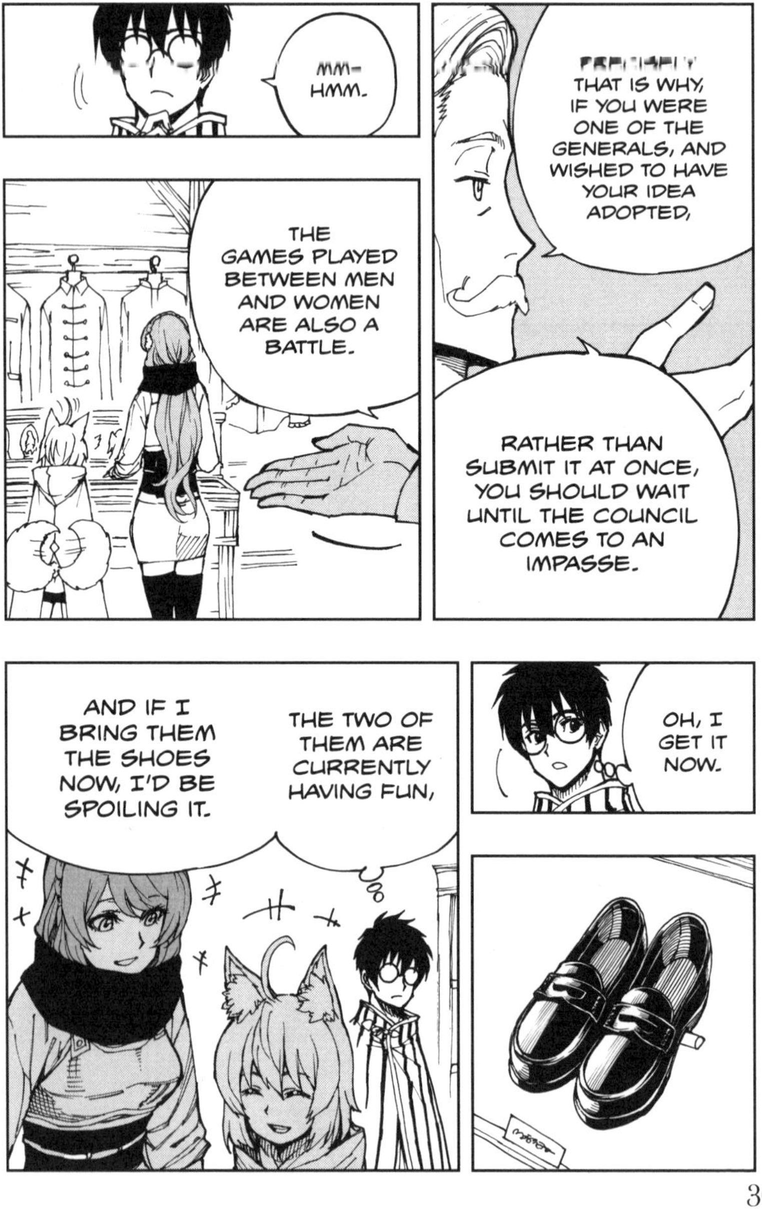
THAT IS WHY, IF YOU WERE ONE OF THE GENERALS, AND WISHED TO HAVE YOUR IDEA ADOPTED,
RATHER THAN SUBMIT IT AT ONCE, YOU SHOULD WAIT UNTIL THE COUNCIL COMES TO AN IMPASSE.
MM-HMM.
THE GAMES PLAYED BETWEEN MEN AND WOMEN ARE ALSO A BATTLE.
OH, I GET IT NOW.
THE TWO OF THEM ARE CURRENTLY HAVING FUN,
AND IF I BRING THEM THE SHOES NOW, I'D BE SPOILING IT.

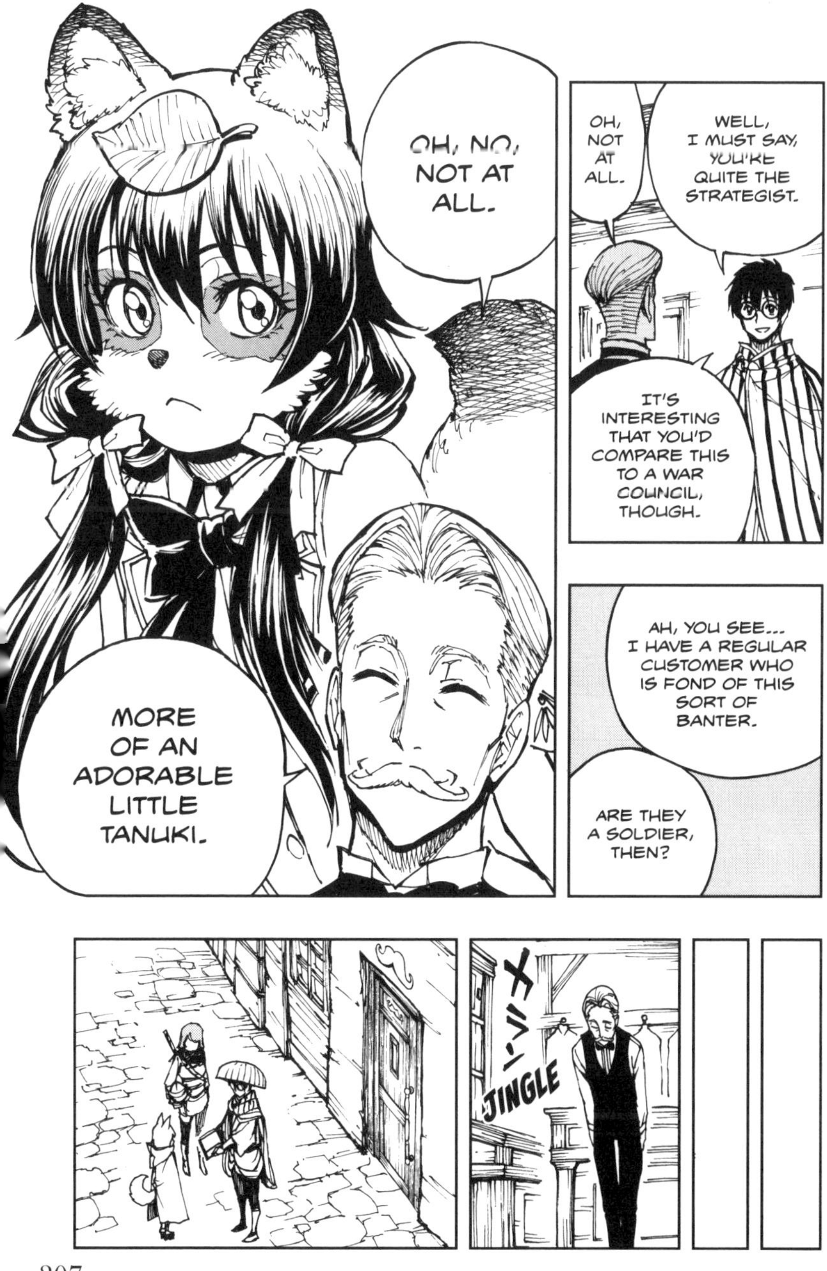
WELL, I MUST SAY, YOU'RE QUITE THE STRATEGIST.
OH, NOT AT ALL.
IT'S INTERESTING THAT YOU'D COMPARE THIS TO A WAR COUNCIL, THOUGH.
AH, YOU SEE... I HAVE A REGULAR CUSTOMER WHO IS FOND OF THIS SORT OF BANTER.
ARE THEY A SOLDIER, THEN?
OH, NO, NOT AT ALL.
MORE OF AN ADORABLE LITTLE TANUKI.
JINGLE

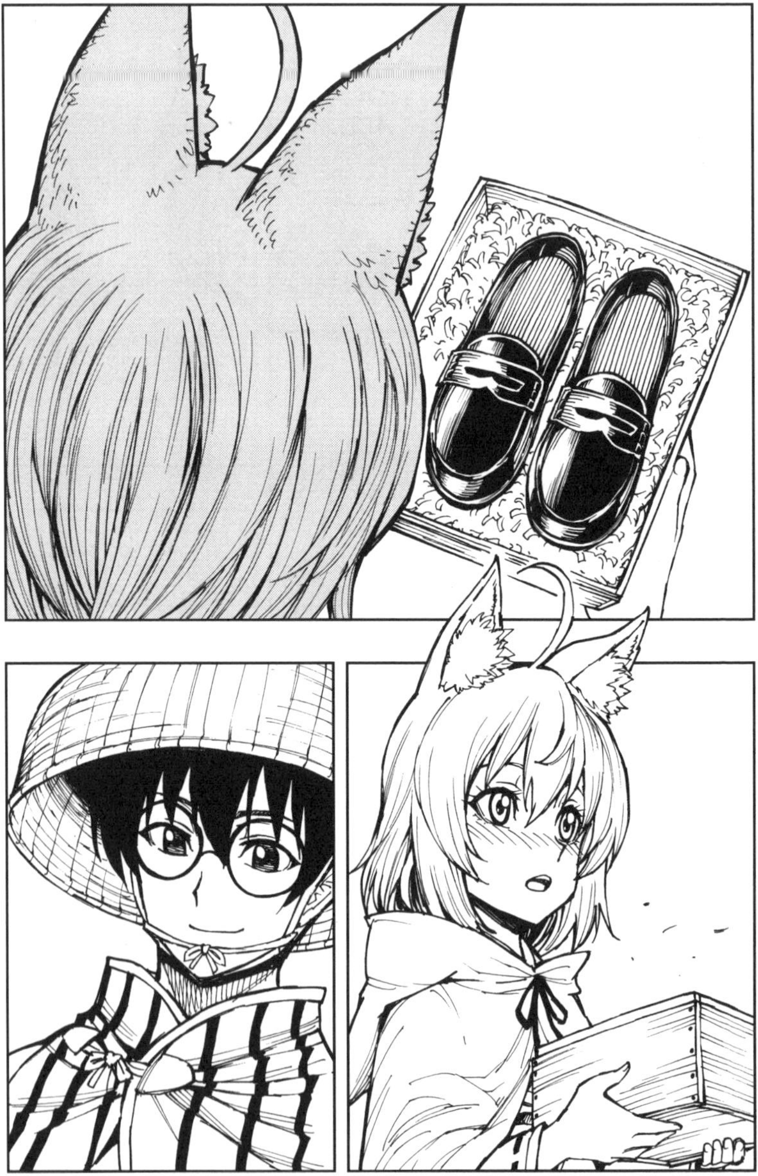

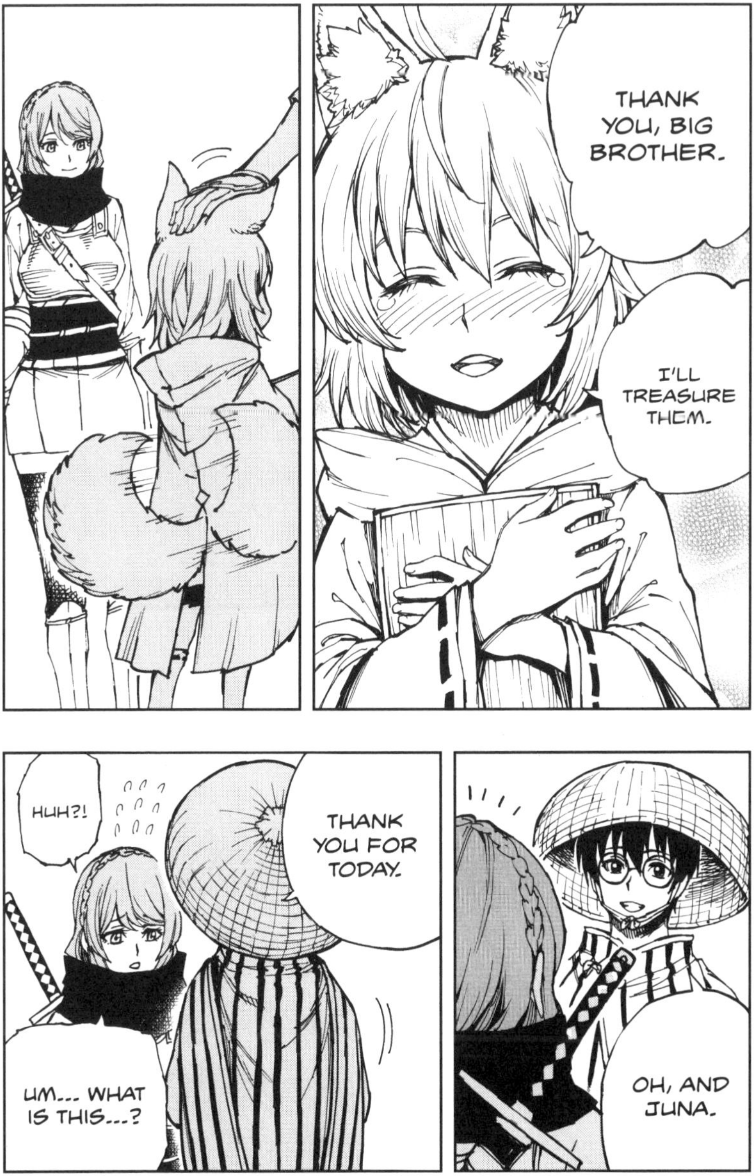
THANK YOU, BIG BROTHER.
I'LL TREASURE THEM.
OH, AND JUNA.
THANK YOU FOR TODAY.
HUH?!
UM... WHAT IS THIS...?

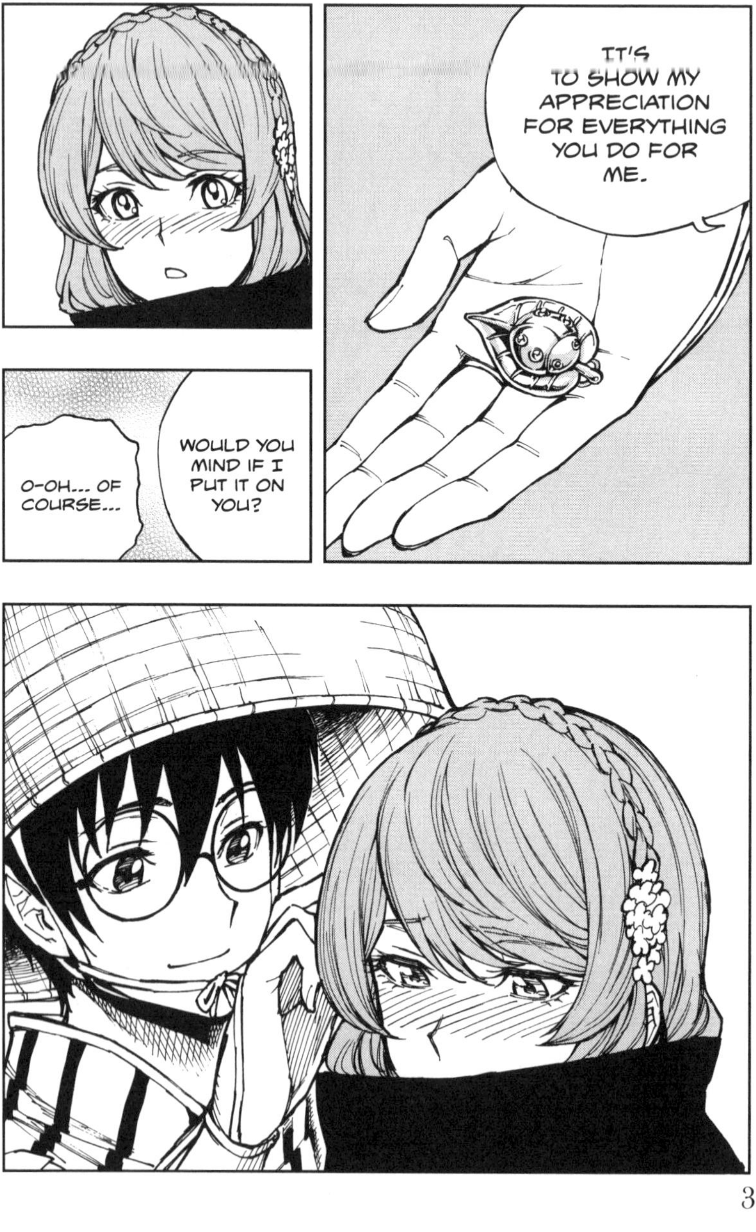
IT'S TO SHOW MY APPRECIATION FOR EVERYTHING YOU DO FOR ME.
WOULD YOU MIND IF I PUT IT ON YOU?
O-OH... OF COURSE...

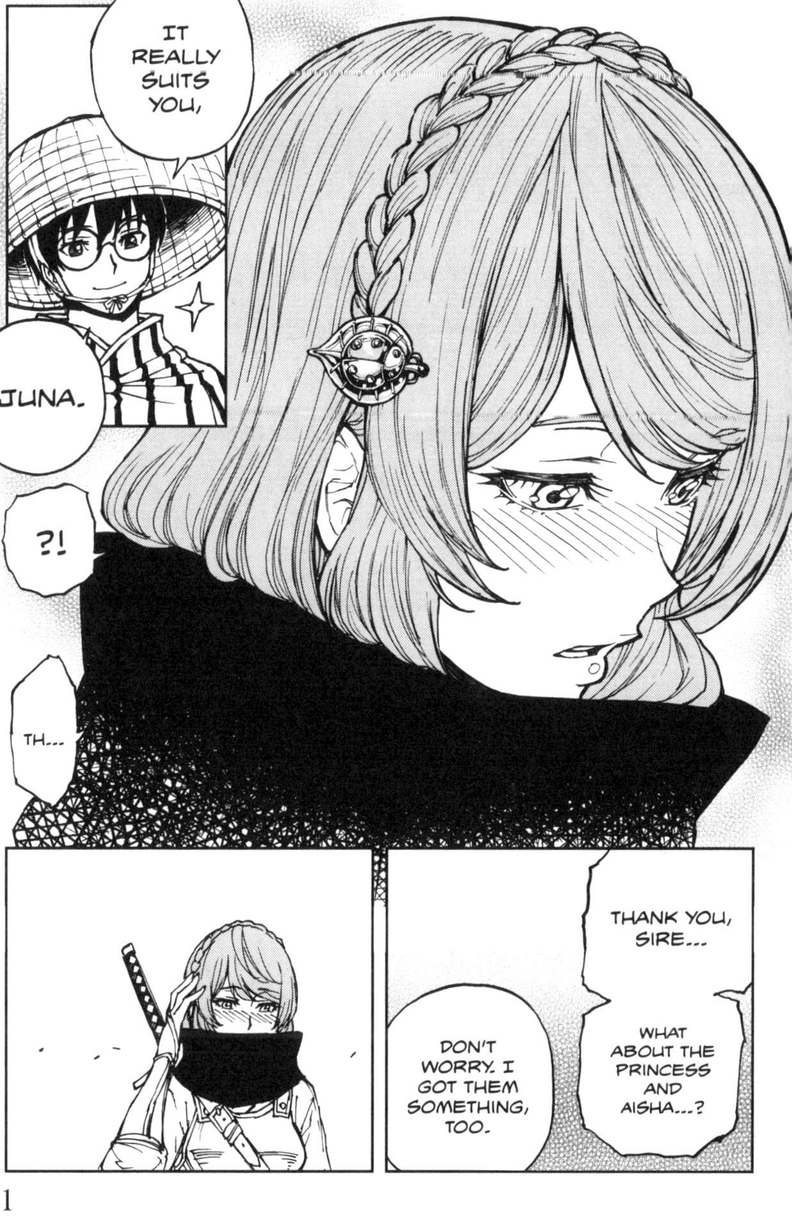
IT REALLY SUITS YOU,
JUNA.
?!
TH...
THANK YOU, SIRE...
WHAT ABOUT THE PRINCESS AND AISHA...?
DON'T WORRY. I GOT THEM SOMETHING, TOO.

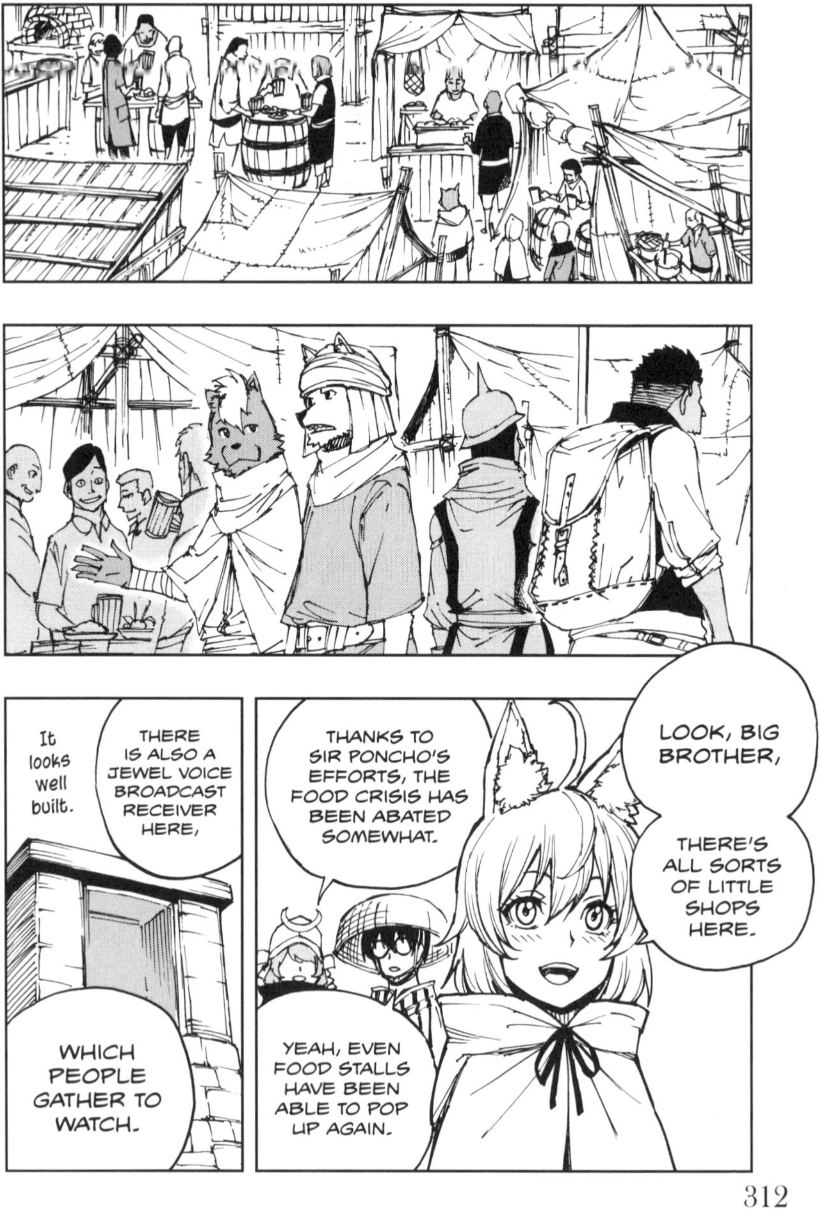
LOOK, BIG BROTHER,
THERE'S ALL SORTS OF LITTLE SHOPS HERE.
THANKS TO SIR PONCHO'S EFFORTS, THE FOOD CRISIS HAS BEEN ABATED SOMEWHAT.
YEAH, EVEN FOOD STALLS HAVE BEEN ABLE TO POP UP AGAIN.
THERE IS ALSO A JEWEL VOICE BROADCAST RECEIVER HERE,
It looks well built.
WHICH PEOPLE GATHER TO WATCH.

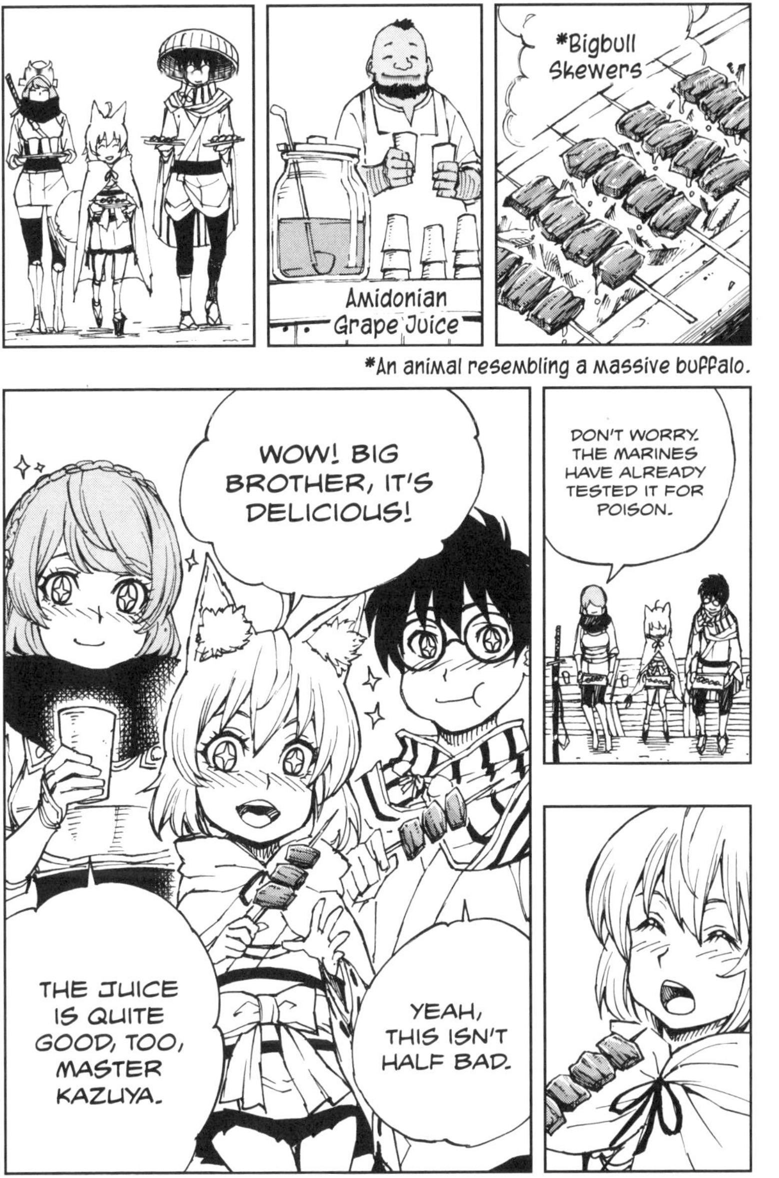
*Bigbull Skewers
Amidonian Grape Juice
*An animal resembling a massive buffalo.
DON'T WORRY. THE MARINES HAVE ALREADY TESTED IT FOR POISON.
WOW! BIG BROTHER, IT'S DELICIOUS!
YEAH, THIS ISN'T HALF BAD.
THE JUICE IS QUITE GOOD, TOO, MASTER KAZUYA.

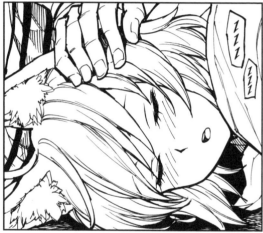

IF ONLY
EVERY DAY
COULD BE
LIKE TODAY...

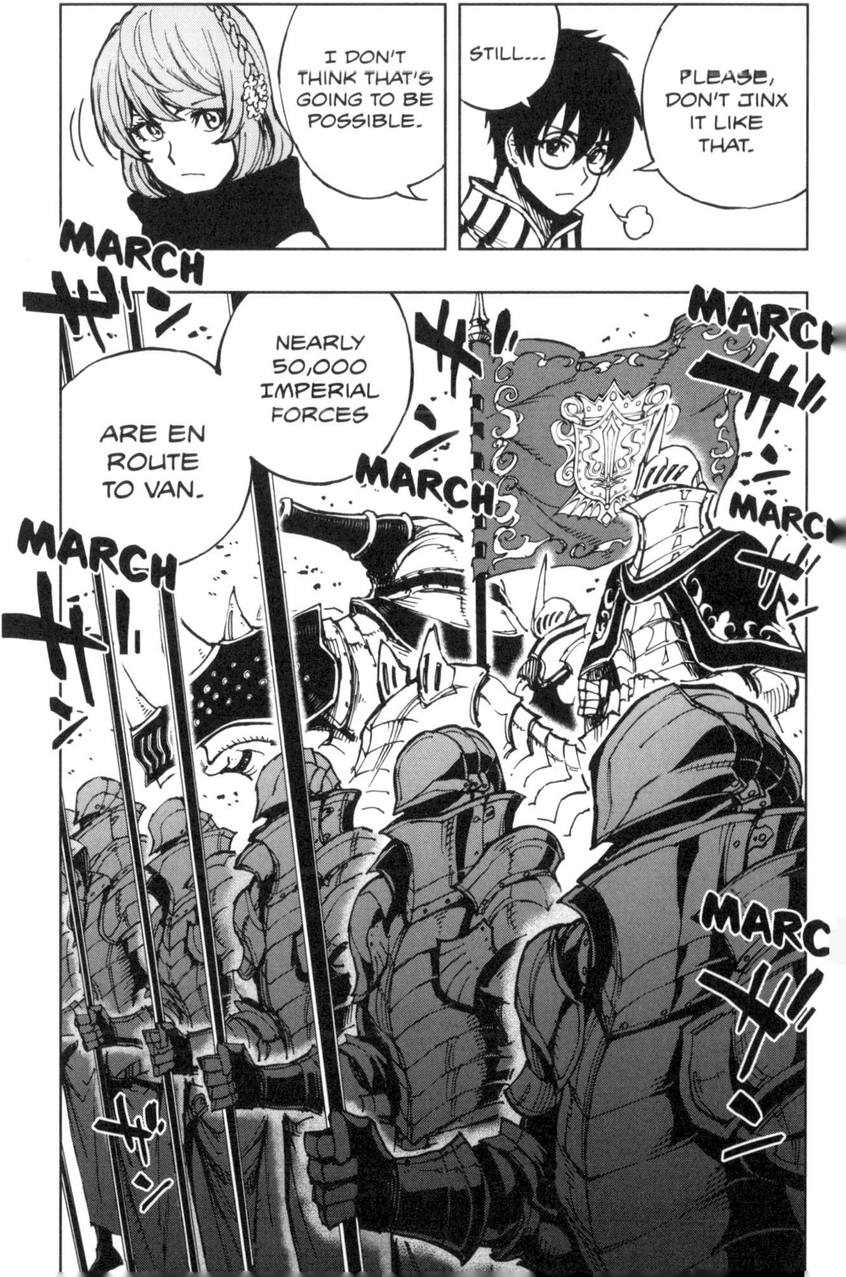
PLEASE, DON'T JINX IT LIKE THAT.
STILL...
I DON'T THINK THAT'S GOING TO BE POSSIBLE.
MARCH
MARCH
NEARLY 50,000 IMPERIAL FORCES
ARE EN ROUTE TO VAN.
MARCH
MARCH
MARCH
MARCH

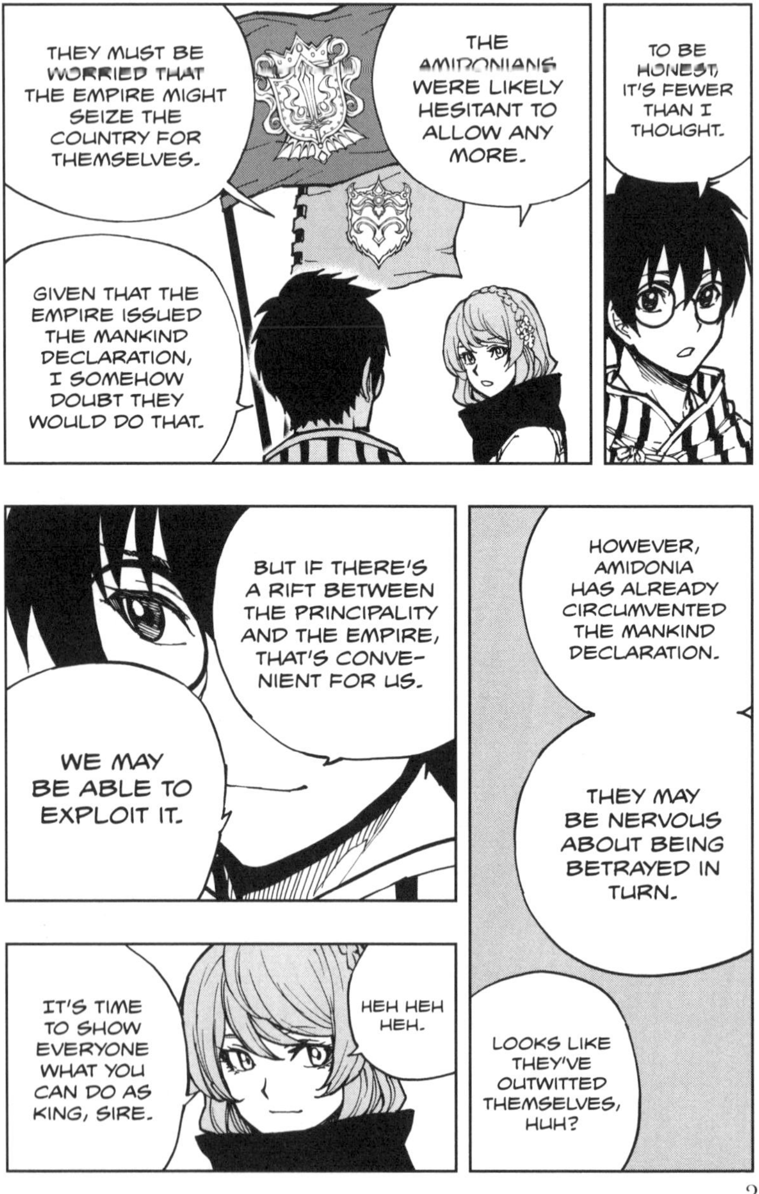
TO BE HONEST, IT'S FEWER THAN I THOUGHT.
THE AMIDONIANS WERE LIKELY HESITANT TO ALLOW ANY MORE.
THEY MUST BE WORRIED THAT THE EMPIRE MIGHT SEIZE THE COUNTRY FOR THEMSELVES.
GIVEN THAT THE EMPIRE ISSUED THE MANKIND DECLARATION, I SOMEHOW DOUBT THEY WOULD DO THAT.
HOWEVER, AMIDONIA HAS ALREADY CIRCUMVENTED THE MANKIND DECLARATION.
THEY MAY BE NERVOUS ABOUT BEING BETRAYED IN TURN.
LOOKS LIKE THEY'VE OUTWITTED THEMSELVES, HUH?
BUT IF THERE'S A RIFT BETWEEN THE PRINCIPALITY AND THE EMPIRE, THAT'S CONVE-NIENT FOR US.
WE MAY BE ABLE TO EXPLOIT IT.
HEH HEH HEH.
IT'S TIME TO SHOW EVERYONE WHAT YOU CAN DO AS KING, SIRE.

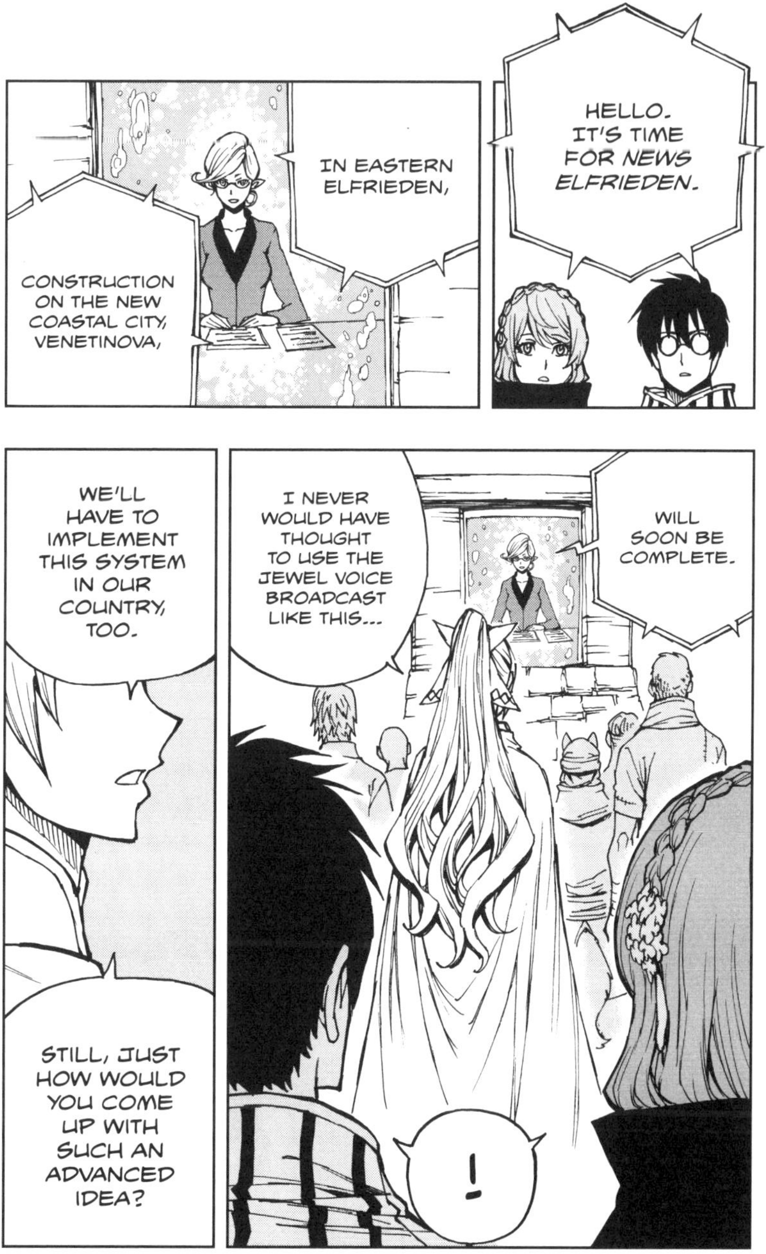
HELLO. IT'S TIME FOR NEWS ELFRIEDEN.
IN EASTERN ELFRIEDEN,
CONSTRUCTION ON THE NEW COASTAL CITY, VENETINOVA,
WILL SOON BE COMPLETE.
I NEVER WOULD HAVE THOUGHT TO USE THE JEWEL VOICE BROADCAST LIKE THIS...
!
WE'LL HAVE TO IMPLEMENT THIS SYSTEM IN OUR COUNTRY, TOO.
STILL, JUST HOW WOULD YOU COME UP WITH SUCH AN ADVANCED IDEA?

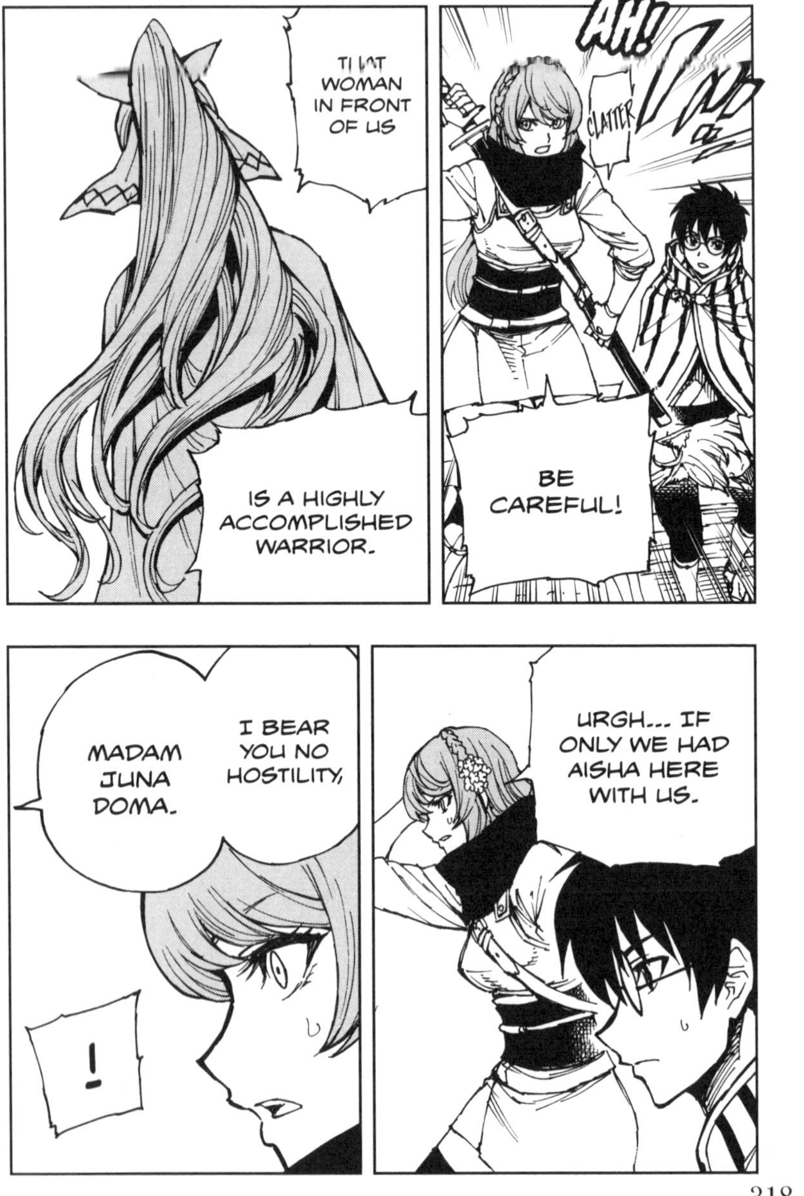
AH!
CLATTER
BE CAREFUL!
THAT WOMAN IN FRONT OF US
IS A HIGHLY ACCOMPLISHED WARRIOR.
URGH... IF ONLY WE HAD AISHA HERE WITH US.
I BEAR YOU NO HOSTILITY,
MADAM JUNA DOMA.
!

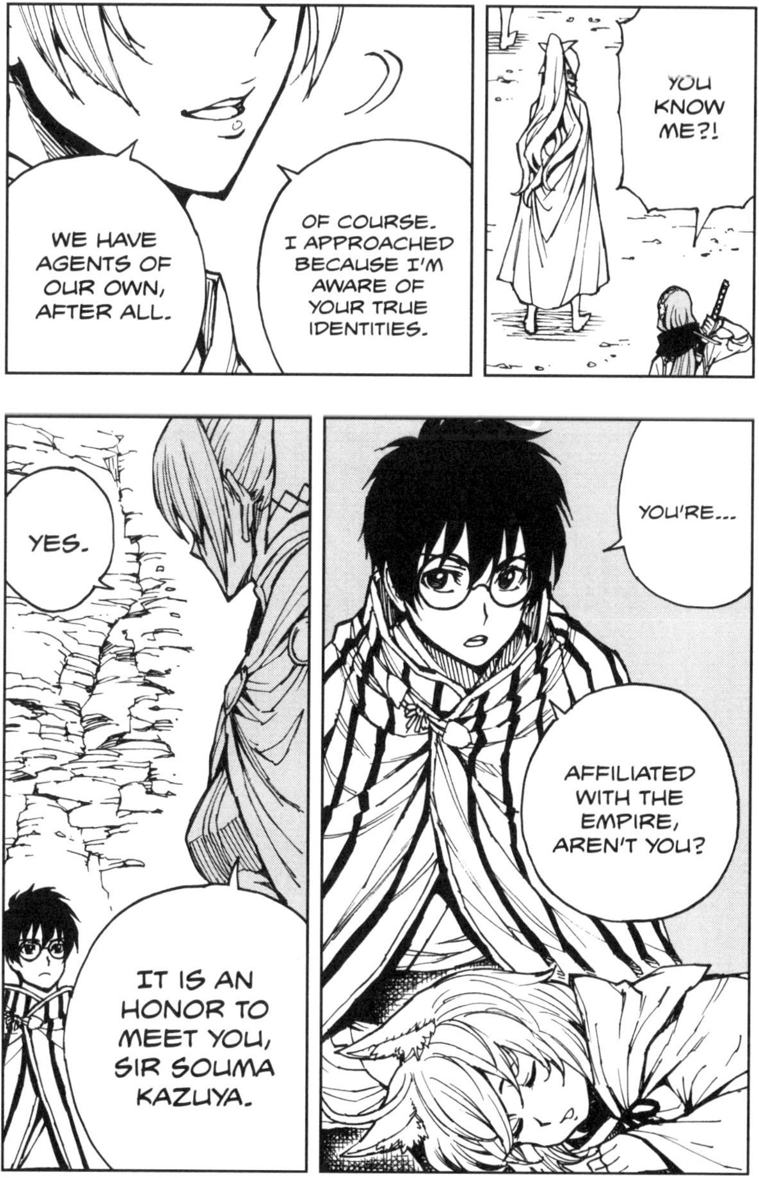
YOU KNOW ME?!
OF COURSE. I APPROACHED BECAUSE I'M AWARE OF YOUR TRUE IDENTITIES.
WE HAVE AGENTS OF OUR OWN, AFTER ALL.
YOU'RE...
AFFILIATED WITH THE EMPIRE, AREN'T YOU?
YES.
IT IS AN HONOR TO MEET YOU, SIR SOUMA KAZUYA.

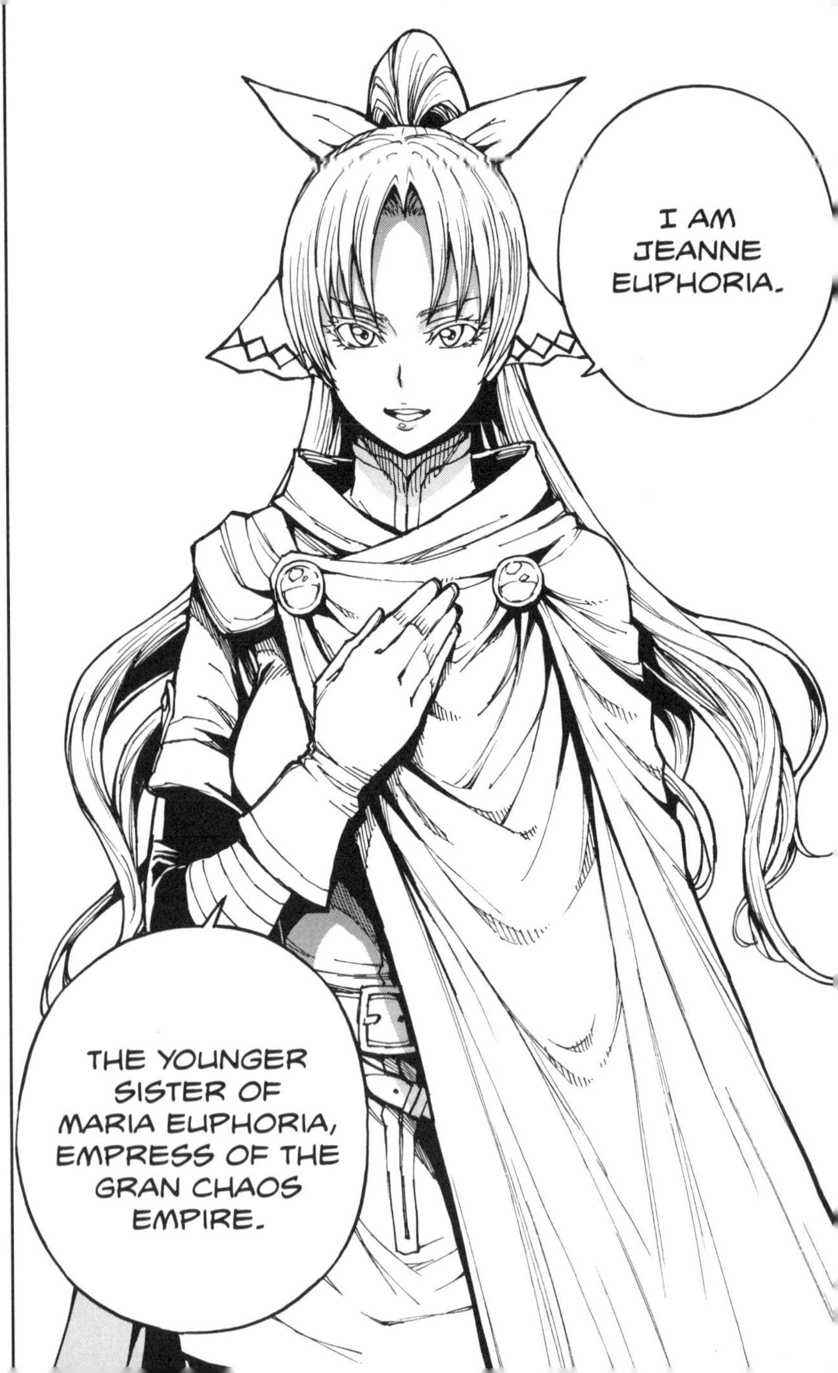
I AM JEANNE EUPHORIA.
THE YOUNGER SISTER OF MARIA EUPHORIA, EMPRESS OF THE GRAN CHAOS EMPIRE.

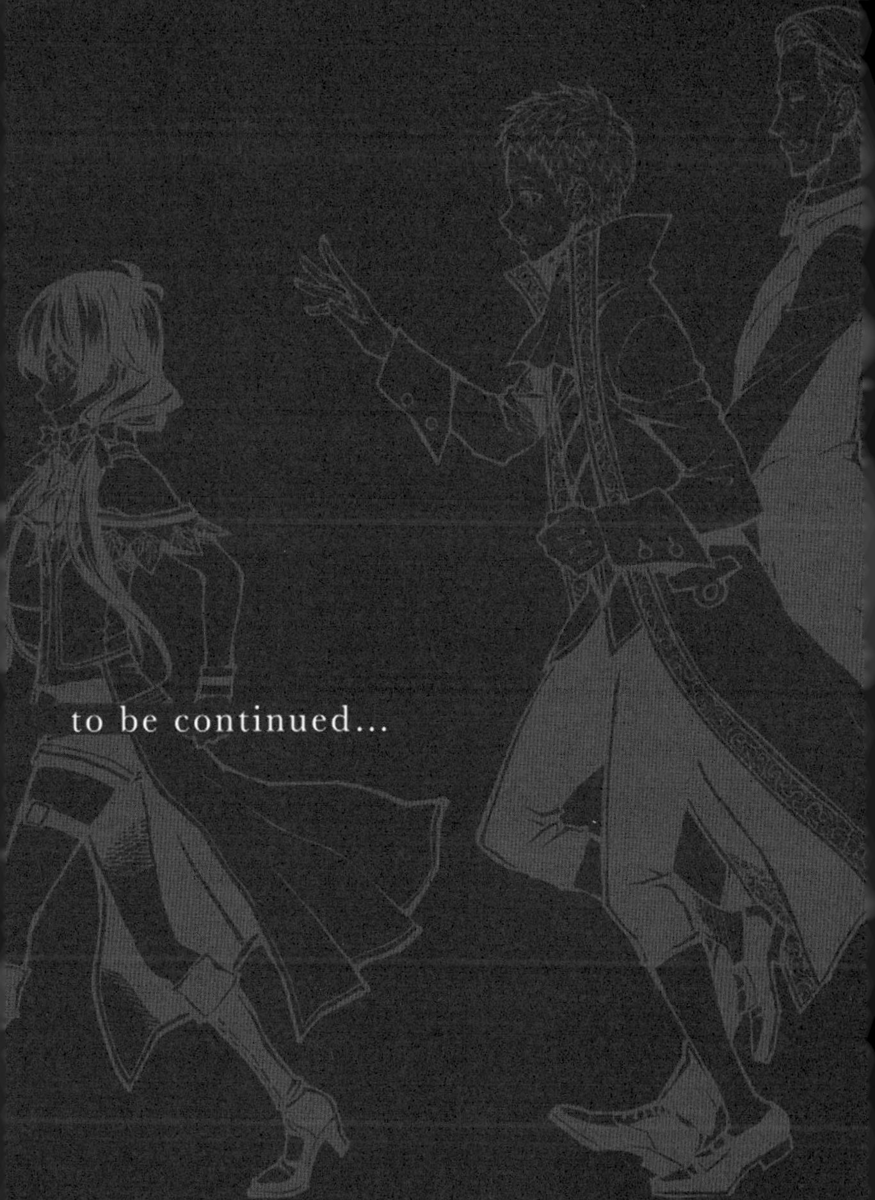
to be continued...

How a Realist Hero Rebuilt the Kingdom VI END

Which of Them Is Really on Top?

On a street corner in Van, currently under occupation by the Kingdom...

"W-We're handing out lily root dumplings here, yes."

Poncho, the Kingdom's Minister for the Food Crisis, was banging a ladle against the side of a cooking pot as he called out to passersby.

Souma had ordered Poncho to distribute meals to the citizens of Van in order to assuage the effects of the Amidonian food crisis, and also to win hearts and minds. Their trump card in this battle against hunger was the "beguiling lily," or more specifically, its roots. The beguiling lily was a plant native to the Principality of Amidonia, but it'd been largely ignored before now due to lack of knowledge in harvesting it for consumption. Fortunately, Poncho knew how to effectively utilize the plant—having learned so during his globetrotting culinary adventure. With this knowledge, he made dumplings from lily root and gave them out to the local populace. It was for this reason that people came to whisper about him as if he were a god.

Standing at Poncho's side as his support was a beautiful and intelligent maid.

"Sir Poncho, the third pot is empty. Please refill it," she said.

"Y-Yes! I'm on it. Please handle things here for a moment, Madam Serina."

"Leave it to me. But in return... You'll satisfy me tonight, won't you?" Serina smiled faintly as she said that.

"Y-Yes! Of course, yes!"

Poncho stood up ramrod straight as he replied. The people who overheard this conversation between the rotund man and the beautiful maid couldn't help but wonder what kind of relationship the two of them had.

That night, Serina spoke to Poncho with a lustful smile on her face.

"Come now, Sir Poncho, give it to me, like you promised."

She was sitting at the table, knife and fork in hand.

"Stuff my belly again tonight."

"Y-Yes, I will. Let's start you off with this."

Poncho laid a plate down in front of her with a clink. Serina cocked her head to the side as she looked at the golden brown objects on it.

"What are these?"

"Lily root dumplings fried in oil, yes," Poncho explained with a smile.

The two of them were working on developing a variation of the lily root dumplings that they had been handing out. Despite having enough ingredient excess to potentially end the food crisis, if it was always prepared the same way, people would quickly tire of it, which then would lead to depression in the populace. Because of this, there was a need to develop new recipes which would change up the taste and texture.

Though the duo was working on developing the new recipe "together," the actual cooking was Poncho's job. Serina was his taste tester. Her comments about "satisfying" her had been in regards to that.

"Will you be putting some sort of sauce on them?" Serina cocked her head to the side questioningly.

"No, no. I tried mixing a number of ingredients in, so try eating them as they are first."

"You did...? Well, then." Serina tossed a fried dumpling into her mouth. When she bit into it, a sweet flavor gently spread across her tongue. "...It's sweet. Delicious."

"I tried putting the anko paste that His Majesty taught me about in that one."

It was a fried dumpling with anko. The closest thing from Souma's world might have been sesame balls.

Serina chewed on it with a look of bliss on her face. Then, suddenly returning to her senses, she looked troubled.

"It's certainly delicious, but... this is a sweet, isn't it?"

"...I knew you would notice that, yes." Poncho sighed. He'd apparently anticipated this reaction. "I think it came out well, but it's a shame to turn the lily roots that we're counting on to serve as the main course into a snack. I think it will be fine once we have a more reliable supply of food, though, yes."

"I think so, too... What else did you try putting in these?"

"Things like cheese and nuts. I think these will still work as the main course, yes."

Once Poncho said that, Serina tried them.

"...These are good, too. They may not pack the punch that the anko did, but I wouldn't grow tired of either flavor. I suspect the cheese would work better if, instead of putting in large chunks, you were to finely grind it and knead it into the batter."

"I-I see! That could work, yes."

Poncho made a note of what Serina had said. She watched him with a serene expression, but suddenly seemed to realize something, and brought a finger to her lips.

"It... does work as a main course, but..."

"Hm? Is something bothering you?"

"I think it might be difficult for the common people to fry them in oil. Cooking oil is quite expensive, you see."

"You have a point, yes. With octopus, even if they can't fr it, it's still delicious raw, but lily root dumplings aren't very excit ing when all you do is boil them..." Poncho explained, using th octopus skewers Souma had made before as a point of compari son. "But if we're going to make them available at restaurants o food stalls, I think this should be fine. They can coat a large po with oil, and fry up a large batch all at once. That should bring th price down."

"I see. This might work as a recipe for restaurants," Serin agreed with a smile. "That aside, Sir Poncho... I'd like more of th anko ones."

"Ah, I'll have more ready in no time, yes." Poncho hurried ly prepared the next batch while Serina looked on.

The timid man who was not used to standing above others and the woman he'd caught firmly by the stomach. Which of then was the one on top? That was something that even the two of then didn't know.

THANK YOU FOR BUYING THE SIXTH VOLUME OF THE MANGA. THIS IS THE ORIGINAL CREATOR, DOJYOMARU.

FROM THIS VOLUME, THIS SERIES TRANSITIONS FROM BEING A STORY ABOUT WAR, TO BEING ABOUT WHAT COMES AFTER.

WHEN COMPARED TO RILING UP PEOPLE DURING THE WAR, CALMING BOTH SIDES DOWN AFTERWARDS IS MUCH MORE DIFFICULT, SO THE ORIGINAL WORK DEVOTES A CONSIDERABLE NUMBER OF PAGES TO IT.

THERE'S A LOT OF RATHER PLAIN MATERIAL COMING UP, BUT I'M SURE MR. UEDA'S IMPRESSIVE ARTWORK WILL MAKE IT SHINE. THANK YOU.

Dojyomaru

THANK YOU FOR BUYING HOW A REALIST HERO REBUILT THE KINGDOM VOLUME VI. -UEDA

*This drawing has nothing to do with the main story.

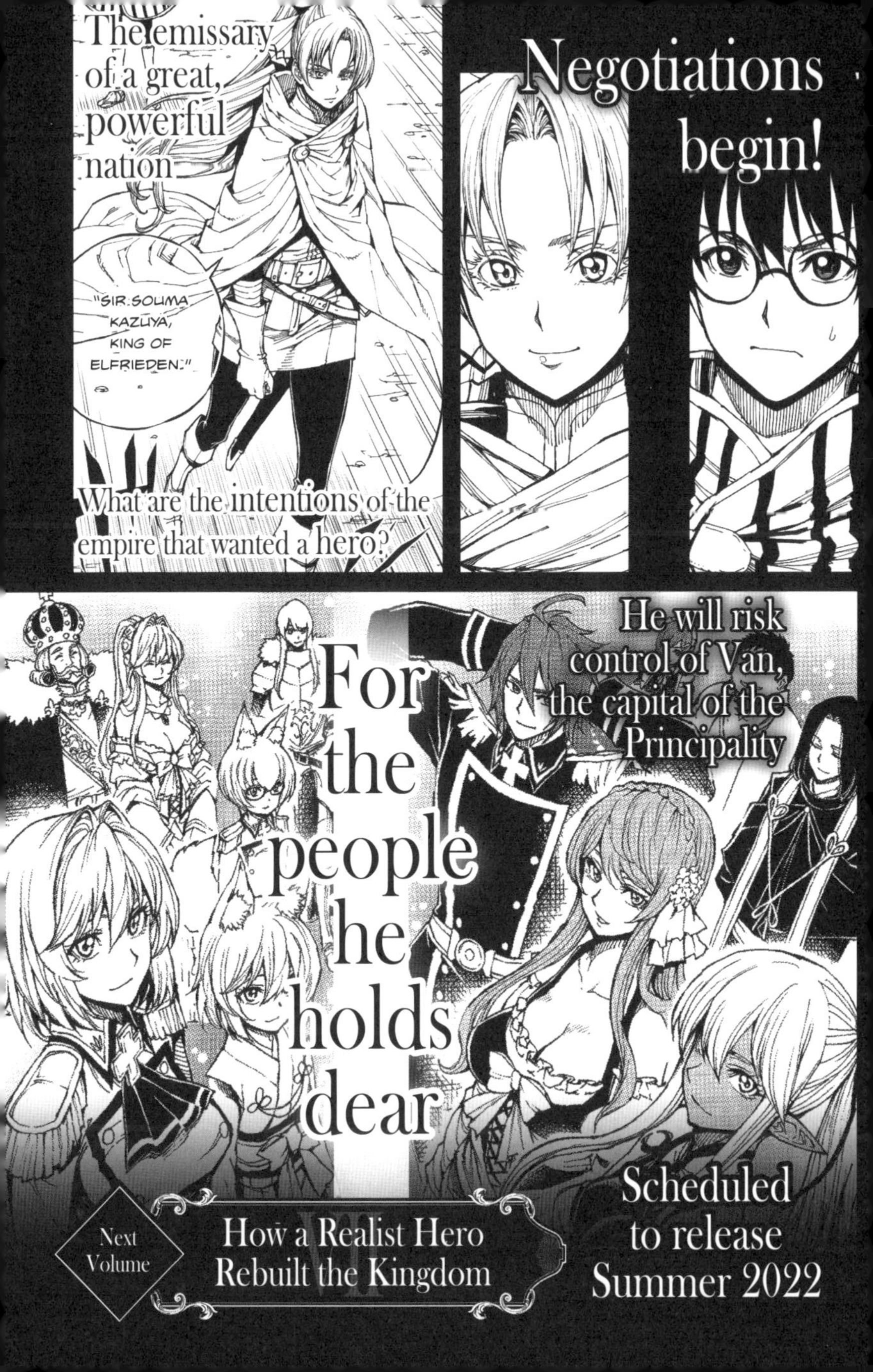

Negotiations begin!
The emissary of a great, powerful nation
"SIR SOUMA KAZUYA, KING OF ELFRIEDEN."
What are the intentions of the empire that wanted a hero?
He will risk control of Van, the capital of the Principality
For the people he holds dear
Scheduled to release Summer 2022
Next Volume
How a Realist Hero Rebuilt the Kingdom

HOW A REALIST HERO REBUILT THE KINGDOM (MANGA) OMNIBUS 3
by Dojyomaru (story) and Satoshi Ueda (artwork)
Original character designs by Fuyuyuki

Translated by Sean McCann
Edited by Meiru
Lettered & English Cover Design by Kelsey Denton

Originally Released as HOW A REALIST HERO REBUILT THE KINGDOM (MANGA)
VOLUMES 5 & 6
Copyright © 2020 Satoshi Ueda © Dojyomaru/OVERLAP

First published in Japan in 2020 by OVERLAP Inc., Tokyo.
Publication rights for this English edition arranged through OVERLAP Inc., Tokyo.

Find more books like this one at www.j-novel.club!

Managing Director: Samuel Pinansky
Manga Line Manager: J. Collis
Managing Editor: Jan Mitsuko Cash
Managing Translator: Kristi Fernandez
QA Manager: Hannah N. Carter
Marketing Manager: Stephanie Hii

ISBN: 978-1-7183-4105-0
Printed in Korea
First Printing: December 2021
10 9 8 7 6 5 4 3 2 1

How a
Realist
Hero

Omnibus 4
On Sale
Summer 2022

Rebuilt
the
Kingdom

Manga ✛ Satoshi Ueda
Original Work ✛ Dojyomaru
Original Character Design ✛ Fuyuyuki

j-novel
club

In Another World With My Smartphone, Illustration © Eiji Usatsuka

Arifureta: From Commonplace to World's Strongest, Illustration © Takayaki

J-Novel Club Lineup

Ebook Releases Series List

A Lily Blooms in Another World
A Very Fairy Apartment**
A Wild Last Boss Appeared!
Altina the Sword Princess
Amagi Brilliant Park
An Archdemon's Dilemma: How to Love Your Elf Bride*
Animeta!**
The Apothecary Diaries
Are You Okay With a Slightly Older Girlfriend?
Arifureta: From Commonplace to World's Strongest
Arifureta Zero
Ascendance of a Bookworm*
Banner of the Stars
Bibliophile Princess*
Black Summoner*
The Bloodline
By the Grace of the Gods
Campfire Cooking in Another World with My Absurd Skill*
Can Someone Please Explain What's Going On?!
The Combat Baker and Automaton Waitress
Cooking with Wild Game*
Culinary Chronicles of the Court Flower
Deathbound Duke's Daughter
Demon Lord, Retry!*
Der Werwolf: The Annals of Veight*
Discommunication**
Dungeon Busters
The Emperor's Lady-in-Waiting is Wanted as a Bride*
The Economics of Prophecy
The Epic Tale of the Reincarnated Prince Herscherik
The Extraordinary, the Ordinary, and SOAP!
The Faraway Paladin*
Full Metal Panic!
Fushi no Kami: Rebuilding Civilization Starts With a Village
The Great Cleric
The Greatest Magicmaster's Retirement Plan
Girls Kingdom
Grimgar of Fantasy and Ash
Guide to the Perfect Otaku Girlfriend: Roomies & Romance

Her Majesty's Swarm
Holmes of Kyoto
The Holy Knight's Dark Road
How a Realist Hero Rebuilt the Kingdom*
How NOT to Summon a Demon Lord
I Love Yuri and I Got Bodyswapped with a Fujoshi!**
I Refuse to Be Your Enemy!
I Saved Too Many Girls and Caused the Apocalypse
I Shall Survive Using Potions!*
I'll Never Set Foot in That House Again!
The Ideal Sponger Life
If It's for My Daughter, I'd Even Defeat a Demon Lord
In Another World With My Smartphone
Infinite Dendrogram*
Infinite Stratos
Invaders of the Rokujouma!?
Jessica Bannister
JK Haru is a Sex Worker in Another World
John Sinclair: Demon Hunter
Kobold King
Kokoro Connect
Lazy Dungeon Master
The Magic in this Other World is Too Far Behind!*
The Magician Who Rose From Failure
Mapping: The Trash-Tier Skill That Got Me Into a Top-Tier Party*
Marginal Operation**
The Master of Ragnarok & Blesser of Einherjar*
Middle-Aged Businessman, Arise in Another World!
Monster Tamer
My Big Sister Lives in a Fantasy World
My Friend's Little Sister Has It In for Me!
My Instant Death Ability is So Overpowered, No One in This Other World Stands a Chance Against Me!
My Next Life as a Villainess: All Routes Lead to Doom!

Our Crappy Social Game Club Is Gonna Make the Most Epic Game
Otherside Picnic
Outbreak Company
Perry Rhodan NEO
Reborn to Master the Blade: From Hero-King to Extraordinary Squire ♀
Record of Wortenia War*
Reincarnated as the Piggy Duke: This Time I'm Gonna Tell Her How I Feel!
Seirei Gensouki: Spirit Chronicles*
Sexiled: My Sexist Party Leader Kicked Me Out, So I Teamed Up With a Mythical Sorceress!
She's the Cutest... But We're Just Friends!
The Sidekick Never Gets the Girl, Let Alone the Protag's Sister!
Slayers
The Sorcerer's Receptionist
Sorcerous Stabber Orphen*
Sweet Reincarnation**
The Tales of Marielle Clarac*
Tearmoon Empire
Teogonia
The Underdog of the Eight Greater Tribes
The Unwanted Undead Adventurer*
Villainess: Reloaded! Blowing Away Bad Ends with Modern Weapons*
Welcome to Japan, Ms. Elf!*
When the Clock Strikes Z
The White Cat's Revenge as Plotted from the Dragon King's Lap
Wild Times with a Fake Fake Princess
The World's Least Interesting Master Swordsman

* Novel and Manga Editions
** Manga Only
Keep an eye out at j-novel.club for further new title announcements!